Diginaka

Diginaka

Subaltern Politics and Digital Media in Post-Capitalist India

Edited by

Anjali Monteiro
K. P. Jayasankar
Amit S. Rai

Orient BlackSwan

DIGINAKA: SUBALTERN POLITICS AND DIGITAL MEDIA IN
POST-CAPITALIST INDIA

ORIENT BLACKSWAN PRIVATE LIMITED

Registered Office
3-6-752 Himayatnagar, Hyderabad 500 029, Telangana, India
e-mail: centraloffice@orientblackswan.com

Other Offices
Bengaluru, Bhopal, Chennai, Guwahati,
Hyderabad, Jaipur, Kolkata, Lucknow, Mumbai,
New Delhi, Noida, Patna, Visakhapatnam

© Orient Blackswan Private Limited 2020
First published by Orient Blackswan Private Limited 2020

ISBN 978-93-5287-906-9

Typeset in
Minion Pro 10.5/12.6
by Le Studio Graphique, Gurgaon 122 007

031067

Printed in India at
Akash Press, Delhi

Published by
Orient Blackswan Private Limited
3-6-752 Himayatnagar, Hyderabad 500 029, Telangana, India
e-mail: info@orientblackswan.com

Contents

Images

Abbreviations

AAP	Aam Aadmi Party
AIMIM	All India Majlis-e-Ittehadul Muslimeen
ASI	Archaeological Survey of India
BACSA	British Association for Cemeteries in South Asia
BJP	Bharatiya Janata Party
BMC	Brihanmumbai Municipal Corporation
BSP	Bahujan Samaj Party
CBFC	Censor Board of Film Certification
CEE	Centre for Environment Education
CIO	Cry It Out
CIS	Centre for Internet and Society
CSDS	Centre for the Study of Developing Societies
DH	Digital Humanities
DIY	Do-It-Yourself
DVC	Damodar Valley Corporation
ECDA	Early Caribbean Digital Archive
FO	Finished Objects
GPS	Global Positioning System
GSP	Generalised System of Preferences
IBI	International Bureau of Informatics
IBM	International Business Machines
ICT	Information and Communication Technology
ICT4D	ICT for Development
IEEE	Institute of Electrical and Electronics Engineers
IITs	Indian Institute of Technologies
INR	Indian Rupee
IP	Internet Protocol

IT	Information Technology
JNU	Jawaharlal Nehru University
KRVIA	Kamla Raheja Vidyanidhi Institute for Architecture and Environmental Studies
KVSS	KacharaVahatuk Shramik Sangh
LOCKSS	Lots of Copies Keep Stuff Safe
MHADA	Maharashtra Housing and Area Development Authority
MLA	Member of the Legislative Assembly
NCP	Nationalist Congress Party
NDA	National Democratic Alliance
NDMC	New Delhi Municipal Council
NGOs	Non-Governmental Organisations
NRI	Non-Resident Indian
NWIO	New World Information Order
OBC	Other Backward Classes
RPI	Republican Party of India
RSS	Rashtriya Swayamsevak Sangh
SAADA	South Asia Digital Archive
SCLR	Santacruz-Chembur Link Road
SVJ Boyzz	Shivaji Nagar Boys' Group
TISS	Tata Institute of Social Sciences
UID	Unique Identification Authority of India
UKIP	UK Independence Party
UN	United Nations
VIP	Very Important Person
VR	Virtual Reality
WIP	Works-In-Progress

Acknowledgements

This edited volume emerged out of an eponymous international seminar organised in January 2016 by the School of Media and Cultural Studies, Tata Institute of Social Sciences (TISS). We would like to thank the Jamsetji Tata Trust and TISS for lending their support towards organising the seminar. We gratefully acknowledge early discussions on the theme of the seminar with Nishant Shah, who also suggested the names of several participants. Our colleagues at the School, some of whom have contributed to this volume, as well as others, all participated actively in making the seminar a thought-provoking space. We would like to thank Shilpa Phadke, Faiz Ullah, Nikhil Titus, K. V. Nagesh and P. Niranjana for their support throughout the process. We would also like to thank the staff members from the School who helped to organise the seminar: Barsha Dey, Vrushali Mohite, Sonal Gajaria, Debanita Biswas, M. D. Sawant, Bharat Ahire, Mangesh Gudekar, Darshana Buddhiwant, Vijay Kale and Chandu Parmar. Several students of the MA in Media and Cultural Studies, from the classes of 2016 and 2017, helped in putting together the seminar, and we are grateful for their enthusiasm and support; we would especially like to acknowledge the contribution of Aparna Srivastava.

Aditi Maddali provided editorial assistance in compiling the first draft of this volume and we would like to thank her for this. We gratefully acknowledge our fellow contributors for their patience and quick response time, which made our work a pleasure. Proteeti Banerjee of Orient BlackSwan guided us through the commissioning process, and Pooja Sanyal, through the editing and production of the manuscript; we express our gratitude to them. We also thank the anonymous reviewer for their valuable suggestions.

The cover image of this book is from a painting by Sudhir Patwardhan, who has generously shared it with us. Our sincere thanks to him. We are indebted to the late Marathi poet, Narayan Surve, with whose poem, *Bigari Naka*, we start our book. We gratefully acknowledge Popular Prakashan for permitting us to reproduce the poem, and thank Jatin Desai for his excellent translation from the Marathi original.

Anjali Monteiro
K.P. Jayasankar
Amit S. Rai

Glossary

Aaple Sarkar: Our Government

aa rahi thi: was simmering

adda: a place where people gather for conversation

andar se: from the heart

Bamanaghariliwan, Kunbyaghari daana, Mahar-Manga gharigaana: The Brahmin (priestly caste) households have their writings, the Kunbi (peasant caste) households have their grains, and the Mahar-Mang (Untouchable caste) households have their songs

bazar: market

bhagidari: partnership

Bharatavarsha: the Hindu *rashtra*

Bharatiya: Indian

Bigari Naka: a street corner where casual labour, skilled and unskilled workers assemble in search of work

chawls: a particular kind of apartment block, which has single tenements, opening out to a common corridor and with common sanitation facilities, which were built for working-class populations, especially mill workers, from the 1900s onwards

darsana: wherein the spectator is a mute witness to the spectacle of the Hindi film and identification is symbolic, not imaginary

darsanic: the mode of spectation premised on *darsana*

'*Degree, Income aur Wi-fi, Aam Aadmi Party Laayi*': 'Degree, Income and Wi-Fi, Aam Aadmi Party has brought you these'

dishoom dishoom: Literally, it signifies the sound which is heard when two actors are fighting in a popular Hindi film. Colloquially, it used to signify the bombast and style with which action films in India are made and loved.

dispositif: often rendered as 'apparatus'

Fakir: a religious mendicant

fiscaal: Finance Minister

gai: cow

Gandu Bagicha: *Gandu* Garden

gaumata: cow mother

gauseva: service of cows as a religious duty

gaushalas: literally, cow centres

Ghar Bachao Ghar Banao: Protect Homes Build Homes

Gurdwaras: place of worship for Sikhs

gurus: spiritual leaders

havans: a ritual burning of offerings in Hinduism

jevha mi jaat choral: 'When I had Concealed my Caste'

jhuggis: informal settlements

joona picture: older films

jugaad: cost-effective fix; hack; practical workaround

Kalasangini: companion of the arts

Kirtan: a practice of musical narration or storytelling, with religious or spiritual connotations

kulhad: a clay vessel; the Hindi word for cup

'*Kya dialogue maara!*': 'What a dialogue indeed!'

Lakshman Rekha: a prescriptive limiting boundary

la politique: politics

le politique: emancipated political subjects

manga: Japanese comic books

masala films: not just popular mass films, but also films that employ specific tropes that acknowledge not just the concerns of the audiences, but also recognise the presence of the audience members within the theatre space and the city

mayat yatra: death ceremony

mazaa: joy or pleasure

mazza: the point of pleasure

mohalla: neighbourhood

mohalla sabhas: neighbourhood assemblies

nāk/nakka/nas: nose

naka or *nākā*: crossroads; a meeting point or a junction, the eye of a needle, defile, gap, checkpoint

pavitra: pure or holy

Pishimoni: paternal aunt

praja: people

Ranibaugh: the city zoo in Mumbai

rashtra: State

sabhas: assemblies

safai karamcharis: manual scavenging workers

salt-*chowkies*: check post

Sant: literally, a saint

tehsils: a district or area that serves as an administrative division

varnashrama dharma: a modern name given to a set of scriptures and practices collectively termed 'Hinduism'; often used as a more accurate substitute for the term, 'Hinduism'

vellas: people with nothing else to do

yagnas: a ritual sacrifice in Hinduism

'Bigari Naka'

Right in the morning,
They get together
From no one knows where
At the street corner.

Men, women, a little child
Waiting for odd jobs—
Painting, masonry or simply cleaning.
Women huddled together,
Villagers—their dark glistening bodies
In clusters
Awaiting work,
On tenterhooks.

Like cattle herded,
Immigrants from several lands
Move towards the city
Towards the Bigari Naka
Agents bring jobs with their commissions
Or comes along a needy householder.
Women don't go alone;
They work together
And look after themselves.

They set up shacks
Anywhere ...
Raising brick on brick

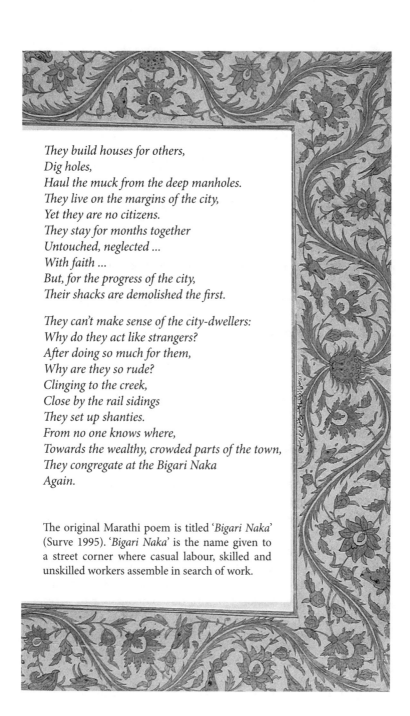

They build houses for others,
Dig holes,
Haul the muck from the deep manholes.
They live on the margins of the city,
Yet they are no citizens.
They stay for months together
Untouched, neglected ...
With faith ...
But, for the progress of the city,
Their shacks are demolished the first.

They can't make sense of the city-dwellers:
Why do they act like strangers?
After doing so much for them,
Why are they so rude?
Clinging to the creek,
Close by the rail sidings
They set up shanties.
From no one knows where,
Towards the wealthy, crowded parts of the town,
They congregate at the Bigari Naka
Again.

The original Marathi poem is titled 'Bigari Naka' (Surve 1995). 'Bigari Naka' is the name given to a street corner where casual labour, skilled and unskilled workers assemble in search of work.

A Test of Time

Digital Commoning against Neoliberal Precarity

AMIT S. RAI, ANJALI MONTEIRO AND K. P. JAYASANKAR

India's neoliberal authoritarianism is facing several crises at once, and digital ecologies play a role in all of them. How to register, exclude, and so control differently digitalised, mobile populations, whose own pirate media and informal economic practices rupture and put into question the values so quickly enshrined as postcolonial development after the malltiplex? In different ways, the chapters collected in this volume address this central problematic.

What are the values of postcolonial precarity? So many figures of Man have emerged in a zombie-like fashion since Foucault declared him dead back in the 1960s: all of them necropolitical subjects, each, in its singularity, marking the current and constant state of emergency as the lived crisis of different kinds of violence—capitalist, misogynist, patriarchal, postcolonial, monopolisation, life-as-debilitation (Puar 2017). Over the past two decades, India has seen the rise of a new postcolonial figuration of the masculinist, charismatic, religious leader. Prime Minister Narendra Modi's particular brand of authoritarian and Hindu neoliberalism has sought strategic synergies with digitally networked ecologies. From the insistence of Unique Identity linkages[1] with various State, quasi-State and corporate entities to the banning of currency notes and destroying of informal enterprises under a fancy new coinage, demonetisation, this biopolitics has pervaded all aspects of contemporary life.[2] Digital transactions and plastic money, ostensibly aimed at stopping the flows of unaccounted wealth, are offered up as the proud symbols of a new, corruption-free and aspirational India.

'*Fakir*' (a religious mendicant) Modi's form of biopolitical control—the Ayurvedic Man (Kandalgaonkar 2017)³—is parasitic on (poorly) managing the digital. While this domain is vast, here it is enough to note that digital saffron publics are part and parcel of Modi's successes. The practice of forwarding ominous astrological readings on WhatsApp in a series of communiques with blatantly chauvinist, casteist or misogynist messages will happen in the same thread; these have real ontological significance.

One Hindutva strategy has been to pursue and capture the intensive implantation of Internet habits throughout a newly biopoliticised, precarised postcolonial population. There are ontological and epistemological conditions of both this bodily implantation and the politico-material ecologies it captures form different terrains and histories of struggles, for example, Dalit, feminist and class struggles. At stake are the values, senses, and forces of work, identity and communication in India today. At stake as well, and as ever, is the question of an untimely militancy of solidarity, creating resonances queerly distributed throughout patterned but unpredictable ecologies—immense and immeasurable, but susceptible to change, self-organisation and control.

As editors also involved in our collective and singular discoveries through this process, we understood the contexts in which this volume would be published, as a mixed postcolonial political ecology and regime of capture-control that indeed willy-nilly combines with elements of High Theory (subaltern studies, postcolonial criticism, radical Dalit and Black studies, feminist and queer theory, and post-structuralisms of various sorts) the potential of the empirical examples. We were composing with our interlocutors a set of thoughts in the process of various discoveries; some on the connections between populism and digital ecologies, some on feminist geographies of the city, others on the digital capture of Dalit aesthetics. The collection of chapters here helps us to rethink the politics of India's *diginaka*s as reflections on the 'perverse' implantation of the technologies of neoliberalism. The term *Naka*, in Marathi, signifies crossroads, a meeting point or a junction. In the South Asian and Indian context, it is: 'a toll point or customs station on a road, especially at a state or national border; a checkpoint. Also (occasionally): a border patrol or customs officer.'⁴ Thus, *Naka*, as an emblematic metaphor, helps at once to complicate and render clear the nature of these subaltern negotiations in post-capitalist India. As a signifier, it also allows one to understand the complex transactions and intersectionalities of markers such as gender, caste, class and the urban–rural dividing practices in these digital mediations. The *Naka* is a space marked by spoken and unspoken regimes, with its own rituals of opening and closing, of access and control. Narayan Surve's poem, 'Bigari Naka', offers a resounding preamble, from which this volume aspires to derive its critical energies.

In each chapter, from considerations of participatory media practices against communalism, to the curatorial politics of digital colonial archives, to the embodied, gendered intimacies of the interface and of Facebook, the question of what the digital can do for agency in techno-perceptual assemblages[5] of neoliberal value comes to the fore. Through researches conducted in very different parts of India, these chapters further the critical assessment of digital or smart city discourses, policy and practices in India through the framework of perception, the documentary form, collective media practices, digital piracy, and work arounds in urban media ecologies. Prior research has pointed out the limitations of frameworks that assume a universal neoliberal gentrification of cities in which private property is 'developed' for more profitable ('higher and more productive') ends. In postcolonial cities such as Mumbai, Bengaluru and Delhi, enclosures of common lands imbricate with specific strategies of (monopoly) rent, regeneration, segregation, reclamation, intellectual property, and accumulation by dispossession of mostly Dalit, poor or religious minority communities. These molar shifts in contemporary capitalism in Indian cities are parasitic on the digitisation of urban life under neoliberal biopolitical production and its attendant transformations in perception, ecology, privatisation and politics. As the chapters in this volume show, a new digital archive is coming into being, and contemporary urban politics is responding and contributing to it, and at times, mobilising with it. Many of the chapters touch upon the practices of commoning in ecologies of social reproduction; linking social reproduction to questions of mobile technologies, these chapters pursue methodological and political experiments to establish a critical connection between forms of privatisation of common lands and communication, between the communalisation of politics and resources and managerial urban policy focused on creativity, innovation and digital networks, and feedbacked to the struggles around intellectual property and commoning know-how in India's cities today.

A key element of the transformation in perception brought on by the historical conjuncture of post-dynastic politics and neoliberalism in India is explored through the attention to the digital image in documentary practice in Chapter 1 by Paolo Favero and the considerations of the ethics of digital documentary or media practice in Chapter 2 by Anjali Monteiro and K. P. Jayasankar. The acceleration of information suggests a new aesthetic politics in Favero's view. The changing politics of images, characterised by the dissolution of the regimes of visuality in (post)colonial modernity, is an important methodological consideration in both chapters. In Chapter 1, Favero considers the advent of digital technologies as marking the emergence of a new visual discourse, a new 'model of vision', as Mitchell (1994) put it. Many of the chapters point to the perceptual conditions of possibility for the diverse implantation of neoliberalism in India. Favero points the way to a new diagram of this emergent ontology. Drawing on Crary (1990), he posits that the

> ... invention of Google glasses, the spread of life-logging cameras (that is, the wearable cameras taking a picture every 30 seconds, hence holding a visual diary of the users' life), the growing centrality of visual communication in social networking sites such as Facebook, all testify to how images (and, in particular, digital images) have penetrated the texture of our everyday life practices.

This is a point explored in Chapter 12 by Shilpa Phadke, a methodologically provocative memoir on Facebook's policing of breast-feeding activism. Both Phadke and Favero show how such technologies of expression and capture have become part of our 'being in the world' (Deleuze 1992; Merleau-Ponty 2012). Today, we have undoubtedly entered a new stage in the development of these apparatuses of biopowers, necropowers, geontopowers and ontopowers. As Favero puts it,

> The myriad of small gestures of voluntary self-monitoring, engendered by the sharing online of geolocated photos, the use of wearable technologies capable of taking pictures on our behalf

(see the life-logging camera phenomenon) or of grabbing our biometrical data in combinations with our movements in space and our payment habits (see, for instance, the market of smart watches) do, when combined, force us to rethinking our assumptions regarding the functioning of 'biopower' (Foucault 2008).

According to Favero, biopolitical technologies of image production and consumption confront the ethics and politics of our engagement with them. His attention is on 'that thin line that separates an enthusiasm for the possibilities that new images open up for us from a blind adherence to the politics that underpin them'. His argument touches on contemporary debates between those who affirm a naïve technophilic vitalism, and those who practice the slow learning necessary for the creation of common notions (common to two or more multiplicities). Favero's salutary focus on the politics of image-making reactivates a consistent theme in another context: shifts in techno-perceptual assemblages in a globalised, corporatised, neoliberal context entail continually reinvented organisations of feedbacks of massive aggregates of newly mobile perception with digital flows of information.

In Chapter 2, Monteiro and Jayasankar show how the deployment of the digital video by grassroots activists in Mumbai can allow for a more ethical and critical reflection on the possibilities of documentary practice. Developing from action research conducted since the early 2000s, when the digital video and CDs were first becoming accessible to new subaltern filmmakers, Monteiro and Jayasankar experiment with the affective capacities of informal digital ecologies, co-created with activists fighting communalism. Exploring the work of Waqar Khan and Bhau Korde, who were involved in the production of media materials, including video, for use within the Mohalla Committee movement in Dharavi, as a part of peace initiatives that were started in the wake of the 1992–93 ethnic violence in Mumbai, Monteiro and Jayasankar link their work to the deployment of the digital video by the residents of Sion-Koliwada in their struggles against eviction by big builders. Carefully focusing on the process of local content[6] production, the frames employed, the symbols and imagery used, and the affective dimensions of the material produced, they diagram 'how the digital narratives of resistance emerging from these spaces draw on both the large cultural repertoire of Bollywood as well as local performance traditions, not limiting themselves to evidentiary modes of storytelling'.

Their ethical documentary practice thus draws out the implications of this emergent diagram of action and thought for documentary filmmaking praxis. Specifically, with Monteiro and Jayasankar's practice, the focus on image-making politics is taken up in the participatory action research documentary project addressing the legacies and realities of communalism in Mumbai. Their work with Waqar Khan and Bhau Korde is exemplary for its ethical self-reflexivity, and it expresses the methodological experimentation in forms of solidarity and research or practice running throughout this volume. Both Chapter 1 and Chaper 2 make key interventions into the ethics of interactivity in the age of the digital. This enfolds both a consideration of the ethics of discourse (the popular and the realist, in Chapter 2) and the embodiment of perception (the forms of visuality in the digital in the case of Favero's analysis of the documentary). There is thus an affirmation of the necessity of thinking ontology and doing epistemology in ways that actively grapple with questions of justice and equality in and beyond digital ecologies in India.

A continued interest throughout the chapters is the transformation of the notion and practice of the public under neoliberalism, and Chapter 4 specifically discusses these different forms of populisms. Crucial to such transformations are shifts in collective and individual, pre-individual and habitual perceptions. Chapter 6 begins with Benjamin's famous analysis of perception in imperialist modernity: 'But now the reflected image has become separable, transportable. And where is it transported? Before the public' (Benjamin 2008 [1936]). Perhaps, given this relatively autonomous force of new media habituations, we would be better off following Whitehead (2008) and Shaviro (2014) in thinking of perception as prehension, or the co-evolving capacity for reciprocal causality in and through these ecologies. In the light of this, Maanvi asks in Chapter 6, 'How do people watch films in India?' Her work points to the 'atomisation of audiences' through the emergence of 'earphone publics', involving the shrinking and privatisation of the screen experience, from the single theatre screen to the multiplex, and further to the mobile interface. This movement also opens up possibilities for women to watch and engage with cinematic texts in new, and at times, subversive ways. Her explorations of the legacy of active film audiences after the digital turn suggest that these audiences are continuing to proliferate in digital processes and emergent forms that we are only now coming to appreciate.

As Abir Dasgupta argues in Chapter 3, India's post-liberalisation era has seen swift structural change, influencing, in turn, the modes of engagement of populations with institutions such as political parties, religious organisations and corporations. Dasgupta traces the effects of this structural change to the intersections of a complex interplay of religion, technology, politics and business. He shows that in the interstices of these domains, an emergent pirate modernity is affecting India's entry into the project of globalisation. Along with many of the other chapters, his work also explores how the discursive terrain of digital publicness in quotidian India is pervaded by the ideologies of gender and sexuality, caste, religion, nation and economic development that form the Hindutva nationalist project. This points to the understanding that the arrival of the Internet in India and the perceptual and practical forms it has begun to take is part of a general social phase transition in India's neoliberal and chauvinist democracy.

A new social synthesis (Sohn-Rethel 1978) rooted in a minority, Dalit, and Adivasi dissensus emerges within and against the crises of the entrepreneurial Hindutva State. Clearly, the rapid proliferation of Internet-capable mobile phones has been central to this emergence. The chapters, each in its own way, develop methodological propositions concerning action research on this emergence. From the notion of the specific publics assumed in the free Wi-Fi-based populism in Delhi (Chapter 4), to the curation of the digital archive of colonial power (Chapter 9), these chapters show the terrain of struggle in both the epistemic and ontological shifts afoot in Indian cities today. Through diagramming assemblages in dynamic and non-linear processes of actualisation and subject formation, forces of territorialisation of affect, habit and political practice have created volatile conditions for the Indian democracy. The affective turn influencing these researches situates the question of the aesthetic as a question of politics in techno-perceptual assemblages of the digital. A recurrent trope in this volume is the call for not only more democratic, but also more autonomous forms of political mobilisation that foreground the promised, but still potential politics of a radical digital commons.

This is brought clearly to the fore in Chapter 4, where Khan and Ullah argue that universal access to Internet connectivity and public Wi-Fi hotspots is a key modality of digital, 'smart' cities and Delhi's urban populism. Linked to the somewhat vague digital India/ smart cities programme, the protocols of registration and tracking infrastructures in free Wi-Fi create definite utility for the government at the expense of the 'governed'. Khan and Ullah note: 'Tax collection/ compliance, biometric-based identification of citizens/beneficiaries, and increased surveillance are some of the ends towards which the network infrastructure has already begun to be mobilised. More information will flow from the end of the citizens to the State than the other way around.' Their strategic focus on the intersections of digital access policies, populism and working class, and subaltern/Dalit mobilisation for social and economic justice brings together several key areas of radical and participatory research on smart city agendas.

In both Chapter 5 and Chapter 11, the authors develop experimental research methods to better understand the intersections of control or management and digital gadget use. Focusing on the domestic space-bound care-worker, Gajjala and Chattopadhyay show how women, in a distributed agency, produce an 'automated' subjectivity that allows the care-worker to be a simultaneous non-human and human actor. This distributed and networked agency is crucial to the efficient incorporation of healthcare technology within the domestic space. They suggest that the care-worker is a 'machinic subject' who facilitates the effective use of health-monitoring gadgets for the person cared for, while also functioning as a visual signifier of the 'human touch' in healthcare. Their work carries forward the feminist critique of primitive accumulation through the unpaid work of women in social reproduction by applying this to the question of affective care networks in and through digital media. They question work or labour through an exploration of informal spaces that are constructed as surplus and are extracted and ontologically managed for an emergent global economy 'through varying logics of commodification, informationalisation, financialisation and monetisation'. They show how 'women's work' and everyday practices of caregiving function in India today. Issues regarding layers of (digital and written) literacies, the biopolitics of differing temporalities, slow time or fast time or killing time, as well as space and place, emerge in nuanced ways.

In Chapter 5, Kumar, Rai and Thorat argue that Dalit history shows how a certain politicisation was effected through cultural, economic, organising, armed and parliamentary strategies, each of which had different relationships with specific histories of Dalit aesthetics. In this globally functional (if not total) neoliberal context, they ask, how do Dalit aesthetics express resistant forms of embodied ecologies of sensation and experiment with historically specific technologies? In what way does Dalit organising in the digital disrupt the historical role of the intellectual in Dalit emancipation, according to certain forms of Marxisms? Their chapter, which is a three-way conversation among authors from different social and intellectual locations, concludes

> Dalit aesthetics for a democratic dissensus and politics of emanci-
> patory solidarity is often forgotten, or sometimes appropriated.
> The invisibilisation of Dalit contributions to urban politics and
> aesthetics is the result. Today, social media movements have come
> to overshadow older strategies of oppressed people's movements,
> and this seems to be consistent with the depoliticising tendency of
> India's elite, upper caste consensus. Dalit organising in and through
> a digital and analogue aesthetics brings political movements into
> productive and antagonistic relation to art, cultural expression,
> subaltern identities and emancipatory justice.

This chapter touches upon the methodological wager running throughout this volume: how to think ontology and embodied practice in terms of collaborative research on subaltern conditions of injustice and inequality.

In Chapter 7, Kunal Ray develops a novel thesis. A new image of media praxis is emerging in India. Central to it are the sensorimotor circuits tied to the emergent aura and public bubble of the mobile phone. While his focus is on the 'depiction of technology in Indian cinema', he shows the forms of embodiment that have been folded into this transition. He critically assesses the role of technological devices through close analyses of Bengali films made after 2005. Drawing on the works of Giorgio Agamben, Annalee Newitz, Friedrich Nietzsche, Deborah Lupton, Tom Gunning and Sherry Turkle, among others, he shows how these devices have 'helped in creating new producers and users ready to experience new possibilities of film language and representation.'

Another ecology is explored by Nikhil Thomas Titus in Chapter 8. His analysis draws on current research on piracy ecologies and the work on modernity and media in India. His exploration of subaltern publics is incisive: neoliberalism is pushing out poor, working-class and Dalit social spaces. He considers Mumbai's video parlours and low-cost, single-screen theatres, their films and promotional strategies as part of a 'unique and alternate curatorial practice employed to attract and keep audiences entertained while also interrogating the intersection of technology and infrastructure that influence the functioning of the space and the larger perceptions that emerge through media reports surrounding them'. His work poses several key problems in terms of method and politics. The question of the affective environments of subaltern publics comes to the fore. What are the capacities to affect and be affected in these debilitated time-spaces (Puar 2017)? What kind of human and non-human agencies are creating frictions in contemporary publics? What is the relative importance of these assemblages of human and non-human agencies in a radical politics of emancipation? Here neoliberal policy affects and is affected by an always recalcitrant and habituated and strictly unknowable biopoliticised body:

> Current and former video parlour owners mention that the government has stopped renewing video parlour licenses in Mumbai, which means people usually rent licenses or may be forced to run their institution without adequate permissions in place. It may be difficult to fathom that in a time of immersive 24/7 connectivity, a considerable number of people still make provisional arrangements for their dose of recreation.

Titus shows that if 'a critique of cinema is a critique of society', then the study of Mumbai's video parlours and its diverse, low cost, 'B-film' viewing culture is strategic because 'these sites are institutions of resistance to established power structures controlling the distribution and flow of media content.' He points to a certain crisis in contemporary urban politics throughout India, in which intellectual rights, patenting, legislative structures, media content and infrastructures converge to capture the creative energies of the marginalised and underrepresented in society and create a forum through which diverse populations forge solidarities in the spatial and textual *diginakas* of cinema.

In Chapter 9, Souvik Mukherjee looks at how digital cemetery archives contain features such as comparative timelines and geotagged maps showing the locations of tombs. How does this extended 24/7 perception come to grapple with colonial ghosts? Critical here is the perceptual framework embodied in the design of the interface. As Namita Aavriti evocatively writes in Chapter 10 about her exploration of this new technology of interactivity and capture:

> The interface is a screen or a surface that allows two realms to interact, for instance, the real and the virtual, human and machine, or perhaps, even the past and the present. Our growing intimacy with the interface makes it invisible for us until it doesn't work or doesn't respond as quickly or burn as brightly as it usually does. Much seems to happen at the surface of the interface itself, and yet, it produces a sense of absorption, spatiality, depth and movement around and in it.

Aavriti's characterisation of the emergent digitised city resonates with many other chapters in this volume:

> Cities are primarily spaces of intense visuality. Here we examine how one aspect of the digital and technological is intertwined and part of the experience of the city that is, the interface, which, in a mediatised city like several in Asia, is part of a scaffolding of technologies, affective flows, networks, circuits of consumption and circulation, etc. .... Living in the mediatised city surrounded by forms of technology and ubiquitous availability of interfaces forms a sensory universe that is digital, to some extent artificial, occasionally cinematic but also pornographic, and often watching itself as a form of self-surveillance.

In Phadke's exploration of women nursing infants and different expressions of these practices on Facebook in Chapter 12, the interface of Facebook takes on another charge, in yet another method:

> Facebook becomes both the space where I escape from the constraints of motherhood as well as the space where I perform 'pleasurable motherhood', a narrative often missing from my phone calls to friends where I moan about the lack of time, space and

privacy. This chapter is in the form of an autoethnography and not only involves reflections on my own practices of social networking, but also comments on how others present themselves, specifically on Facebook.

While for Phadke, as the mother of an infant, 'Facebook became the metaphorical courtyard that facilitated a playful space that one could enter and leave at will', her chapter shows an acute awareness of the regimes of discipline and performance that underpin social media on an interface like Facebook.

For his part, Mukherjee suggests that such interfaces, when designed into digital archives, allow for a fresh approach towards the study of colonial cities and communities by bringing together different toolsets to record and sometimes recreate the stories of the people buried in these cemeteries:

> Starting with the cemeteries as a point of departure allows for a deeper engagement with local history and that of those people whose stories were not otherwise accessible .... The cemetery archive takes the study of colonial history a step beyond the understanding of colonial legacies through a 'Great Men' approach; rather, through a web 2.0 notion of an open-archive .... it attempts to open itself up to a larger community of researchers and other stakeholders who can add to the archive via a curated interface.

These new practices are finally, perhaps, one of the most important themes running through this volume. If archive fever is a form of power uniquely suited to neoliberal tables of value and their modes of capture, then Mukherjee shows that democratic potentials can neither be completely submerged nor fully captured. And it is precisely experimentation in the curating of emergent ecologies of sensation that traverses the digital and the analogue, feedbacked with new forms of political struggle. This is the complex terrain of struggle that this volume seeks to address, through different entry points that articulate the rhizomatic wormholes connecting the local with the digital.

NOTES

1. The Unique Identification Authority of India (UID) or the *Aadhar* project, initiated by the Congress-led government in 2009, is being

aggressively pursued by Modi's Bharatiya Janata Party (BJP) government, with compulsory linking to bank accounts, tax returns, cell phone numbers and financial assets being mandated, as well as access to welfare services and schemes based on the possession of the Aadhar card. In September 2018, the Supreme Court of India ruled that the Aadhaar Act, 2016, was constitutionally valid. While it upheld the linking of Aadhar with the PAN number for filing tax returns and for the grant of subsidies and welfare benefits, it rejected the proposal to link Aadhaar to bank accounts and mobile phone numbers on grounds of protection of privacy of citizens.

2. In November 2016, the Modi government withdrew from the circulation of currency notes of Rs 500 and Rs 1,000, which constituted almost 80 per cent of the total currency in circulation. This move caused immense hardship to the rural economy and the informal sector, both of which operated outside the formal banking systems.

3. Kandalgaonkar draws from the 1986 Bombay Plague as his pointed contribution to the Ayurvedic Man Welcome Trust Exhibition.

4. This term originates in the 1980s, from the Hindi word, *nākā*, or the eye of a needle, defile, gap, checkpoint, from *nāk* or nose, which could be traced back to the Prakrit word, *nakka*, probably related to the Sanskrit word, *nas* (Lexico, Oxford Dictionary Online).

5. The concept of a techno-perceptual assemblage links together the overall embodiment of media technologies, the specifically perceptual infrastructures of contemporary digital media, and the movement, vectors, and tendencies of a changing, co-evolving whole articulated (within the discourse) and encountered (in the practice) of assemblage theory.

6. Part of the aim of each of these chapters is to problematise the fetish for the local in both Left and Right public spheres in India. It is the notion of the local that needs displacement and reversal, now more than ever. Behind it lurks a pretentious anti-intellectualism that provincialises Europe by provincialising itself first and last—that is, as the authentic India. The local is *immediately* global, and the global is *immediately* local. What does this truism actually mean? It is indeed a methodological polemic, and in it is pursued a materialist and embodied regrounding of what is habitually referred to as reality. There are therefore no claims to authenticity in these chapters, no appeal to nativist chauvinisms that appear to attach themselves more and more to the art world, for instance, and its would-be academics-turned-curators. With different inflexions and histories, the conversations around secular democracy in India at the Tata Institute of Social Sciences (TISS), Kamla Raheja Vidyanidhi Institute for Architecture and Environmental Studies (KRVIA), Centre for Environment Education (CEE), Jawaharlal Nehru University (JNU), Srishti Institute of Art, Design and Technology, Jamia Millia Islamia, and

other universities today proceed in the face of a military-like cordon, a veritable *Lakshman Rekha* (a prescriptive limiting boundary) around non-nativist, internationalist, secular and critical thinking, and political creative practice. Thus, the local is merely one more mystified signifier for this authentic India that never has and never will exist. Who can speak for, to, with the Indian nation today? Is it the local? Rather, the gambit of this volume is that it is only a method of critical discovery that at times and at certain places resonates with a heterogeneous people's revolutionary becoming.

REFERENCES

Benjamin, W. 2008 [1936]. Micheal W. Jennings, Brigid Doherty and Thomas Y. Levin (trans.). *The Work of Art in the Age of its Technological Reproducibility, and Other Writings on Media.* Cambridge, MA: Harvard University Press.

Crary, Jonathan. 1990. *Techniques of the Observer: On Vision and Modernity in the Nineteenth Century.* Cambridge, Massachusetts: MIT Press.

Deleuze, G. 1992. 'Postscript on the Societies of Control', *October* 59 (Winter), pp. 3–7.

Foucault, M. 2008. *The Birth of Biopolitics: Lectures at the Collège de France, 1978–1979.* New York: Picador.

Kandalgaonkar, Ranjit. 'Ayurvedic Man: Encounters with Indian Medicine', 16 November 2017–8 April 2018. Available at https://wellcomecollection.org/exhibitions/WduTricAAN7Mt8yY (accessed 16 November 2017).

Lexico, Oxford Dictionary Online. 'Definition of Naka in English'. Available at https://en.oxforddictionaries.com/definition/naka (accessed 27 May 2018).

Merleau-Ponty, M. 2012. *Phenomenology of Perception.* London: Routledge.

Mitchell, W. J. T. 1994. 'Ekphrasis and the Other'. In *Picture Theory: Essays on Verbal and Visual Representation*, pp. 151–81. Chicago: University of Chicago Press.

Puar, J. 2017. *The Right to Maim: Debility, Capacity, Disability.* Durham: Duke University Press.

Shaviro, S. 2014. *The Universe of Things: On Speculative Realism.* Minneapolis: University of Minnesota Press.

Sohn-Rethel, A. 1978. *Intellectual and Manual Labour: Critique of Epistemology.* London: MacMillan Publishers.

Surve, Narayan. 1995. Jatin Wagle (trans.). *'Bigari Naka'*. Unpublished (Commissioned by Amit S. Rai, Anjali Monteiro, and K. P. Jayasankar for a film on Surve.)

Whitehead, A. N. 2008. [Corrected Edition]. David Ray Griffin and Donald W. Sherburne (eds), *Process and Reality: Corrected Edition*. New York: The Free Press.

PART I

Digital Politics

one

Interactive Documentaries

The Politics of an Emerging Genre

PAOLO S. H. FAVERO

INTRODUCTION

In the 1990s, several scholars suggested that the advent of digital technologies marked the emergence of a new visual discourse, a new 'model of vision', as Mitchell (1994) put it. This transformation, Crary announced, was 'probably more profound than the break that separates medieval imagery from Renaissance perspective' (1990: 1). A long way into the digital era, we can today easily observe how images have taken a new place in our lives. Owing in particular to their entanglements with new electronic tools (such as cheaper cameras, mobile phones, etc.) and with the Web 2.0's 'implicit architecture of participation' (O'Reilly 2005: 6), today images have become really ubiquitous. They have moved from the drawers of our desks and the archives of professional studios to the most interstitial spaces of our lives, literally creeping into our pockets and our bodies. The invention of Google glasses, the spread of life-logging cameras (that is, the wearable cameras taking a picture every 30 seconds, hence holding a visual diary of the users' life), the growing centrality of visual communication in social networking sites such as Facebook, all testify to how images (and, in particular, digital images) have penetrated the texture of our everyday life practices. They have become, for those of us living in parts of the world touched upon by such technologies, part of our 'being in the world' (Merleau-Ponty 2012).

The figures regarding these changes are indeed quite impressive. To mention but a few, it is estimated that every day 6.7 billion people view the world, in one or the other way, through their own lens. Facebook, a medium originally based on textual exchanges, grows today by one to two billion images per week. On a daily basis, five million pictures are uploaded on Flickr and two billion videos are screened on YouTube. YouTube alone has produced, in the past six months, that is, from the moment this chapter was written, more than what the first three main national channels in the US have been able to do in their entire 60 years of history. These figures are indeed interesting; but to what extent do they testify to the birth of a new 'model of vision', a new revolution in our visual culture? And also, what kind of aesthetics is emerging? And what are the politics of this aesthetics?

In this chapter, I want to attempt at offering some insights into these questions by entering into the topic from the vantage point of interactive documentaries, a visual language that I, alongside many other practitioners in and experts of this field, consider as one of the most avant-garde terrains of contemporary filmmaking.[1] An emerging terrain of scholarly attention, too (Aston and Gaudenzi 2012; Blassnigg 2005; Favero 2013; Galloway et al. 2007; Nash 2012), i-docs threaten conventional categorisations, hence offering a privileged platform from which to reflect further upon the changing politics of images in a digital environment. Starting with a brief introduction to this particular visual form,[2] I will then proceed to offer a typology for approaching the variety of different practices that can be found within this space. My next step will be to offer some (theoretical) insights into how i-docs can provide us with a window for exploring the changing meaning of images in a digital habitat. Finally, I shall discuss the politics of such image-making practices.

WHAT IS AN I-DOC?

A fairly new visual language that merges, broadly speaking, the tradition of the documentary film with the possibilities offered by Net 2.0 to produce a generative, complex, non-linear viewing experience, i-docs are difficult to define. At the core of this resistance indeed lies a paradox generated by the merger of two terms (interactive and documentary), around which there is little agreement. Regarding the documentary, its creator John Grierson suggested that 'documentary is a clumsy description, but let it stand' (1966: 145). Practitioners and scholars of this visual language have ever since been divided regarding what this term stands for. From critical readings such as Bruzzi (2000), who suggests that the documentary ought better be understood as a performance, to Minh-Ha's (1993) notion that the documentary is, in the end, nothing but a style, to more conventional perspectives claiming the documentary's *a priori* tightest proximity to truth, a long debate has bloomed, which seemingly sees no end. However, there is overall a certain agreement that the documentary film is a distinctive form of moving image language that aims at conveying a fairly unfiltered, unmediated and experience-near vision of the actual.

Conventionally, documentary films are considered to have kept alive the 'myth of photographic truth' (Sturken and Cartwright 2001), and to maintain a strong adherence to what is conventionally referred to as pro-filmic reality, that is, the reality that exists beyond and before the camera (Beattie 2008; Nichols 2001). To combine such a notion of the 'documentary' with 'interactivity' becomes, evidently, quite a tricky affair. A 'two way flow of information', interactivity can be seen to consist of, as Meadows (2003) suggested, primarily four stages: observation, exploration, modification and reciprocal change. While the first two terms may still perfectly fit within a broad definition of the documentary film, the third and fourth ones are indeed more problematic. To allow modification and reciprocal change (by the hands of the viewer or user) does seem to invalidate the mission of the documentary itself. If a documentary is somehow connected to the 'objective' portrayal of facts, how can it then include a process of eventual modification?

Typologies of I-docs

Despite inhabiting such an evident contradiction, i-docs could be defined as a 'documentary which uses interactivity as a core part of its delivery mechanism' (Galloway et al. 2007: 330), and that offers a variety of modalities for engaging the viewers and the world that surrounds them. Such different modalities of use have upheld the attention of many scholars, also giving birth to a few typologies. Nash (2012) divides the field into three formats: the 'narrative', the 'categorical' and the 'collaborative'. The former allows the viewer to connect events in a linear sequence (similar to what linear documentaries do); the categorical does something similar, yet on the basis of particular topics that exist for the viewer simultaneously; and the third directly engages the viewer as a producer of contents to be inserted in the work. Aston and Gaudenzi (2012) propose a similar model. They distinguish between 'conversational' films (which trigger a dialogue between the viewer and the machine used for viewing the documentary); 'experiential' films (which, with the support of specific interfaces, bring digital contents in touch with physical reality); 'hypertext' (which introduces the space of the explorable database); and finally, the 'participative' (which actually actively engages the viewers, asking them to take on an active role in the making of the documentary by sending out their own material).[3]

Pushing these categories a bit further, I believe that we can create another typology, based on a division among 'active', 'participative' and 'immersive' documentaries. When using 'active', I refer to those documentaries that offer the viewers a variety of angles from which to explore the materials that make up the documentary. Conventionally using different media (such as video clips, photographs, sound-files, maps, etc.), such i-docs primarily constitute a kind of creative archive that does not, however, allow viewers to actively change the materials on display (unless minimally, by inserting comments, etc.). Making up the vast majority of i-docs present in the market, such products can be exemplified by works such as *Prison Valley*, *High Rise*, *I Love Your Work* (see Image 1.1), and so on.

'Participatory' documentaries instead seem to focus primarily on the creation of new materials. Sharing the very process of production, these i-docs are probably at best exemplified by Al-Jazeera's *Palestine Remix* (see Image 1.2). Here, viewers are asked to actively re-edit snippets of materials taken from the company's archives, hence generating new interpretations of major events happening around the world.

Another example of this type of i-doc could be Blast Theory's *Rider Spoke*, a live, emplaced experience that invites cyclists to narrate stories about their city as they move in it and listen to the stories generated by other users, too. Along the same lines, we could possibly also mention *A Journal of Insomnia* by the NFB, where the participatory element takes over to the extent that the materials uploaded can only be visited upon a nightly appointment.

IMAGE 1.1: Screenshot of *I Love Your Work*

Source: Screenshot taken by the author on his computer of the 'Tapestry' interface of *I Love Your Work*, IDFA Doc Lab.

IMAGE 1.2: Screenshot of *Palestine Remix*

Source: Screenshot taken by the author on his computer of *Palestine Remix*, Al-Jazeera.

The last type of i-doc, the immersive, is in my view, the one aiming more explicitly at closing the gap between the image (the platform) and the everyday life of the viewer. Potentially experiential, haptic and/or emphatic in character, such documentaries move along a continuum that goes from expanded emplaced participatory forms (bordering on augmented reality) to Virtual Reality (VR) documentaries (the latest promise in the market of i-docs). Examples of this form can, hence, be found in *Karen* (another Blast Theory product). A smartphone application bringing a life coach (a kind of therapist) into the life of the user, *Karen* builds upon the principle of provocation and disturbance. Unexpectedly popping up on the user's phone, in the midst of their everyday life, in the shape of an SMS-looking message, *Karen* grabs information about the users' views and habits through a series of basic questions. On the basis of such information, *Karen* progressively makes the users rethink their views and habits about themselves and their own lives.

Indeed, we must, as I have already mentioned, insert within the category of immersive i-docs the booming field of VR and 360-degree documentaries that are today in the limelight in many international documentary film festivals. Ranging from online documentaries to those designed for VR goggles or smartphones, such products indeed offer an intensely interactive experience, allowing for what I have elsewhere defined as a form of disembodied embodiment (see Favero 2017). Among such projects, mention can be made, with regard to computer screen-based films, of Google's 360-degree series and films such as *Beyond the Map* (on Rio's favelas) or the *The Hidden World of the National Parks*. And with respect to VR-driven documentaries, we can look, among many others, into the works of Francesca Panetta.

Indeed, a number of projects are born today that blend virtual and augmented reality. One of these projects, which is worth mentioning, is the India–US collaboration *Priya's Shakti*. Born in the aftermath of the rape of a young woman in New Delhi in December 2012, this project gathers inspiration from the mythological figure of Priya, a devotee of Goddess Parvati, who survived a brutal rape. Ideated by Indian-American filmmaker Ram Devineni, it plays with Hindu mythology for the construction of a narrative in which Priya and Parvati join hands in struggling against gender-based violence. Aiming at reinserting into public consciousness 'ancient matriarchal traditions that have been displaced in modern representations of Hindu culture', the project results in a mixture of comic books, augmented reality and exhibitions. The main characteristic of *Priya's Shakti* is that it engages with the world offline. One of the strands of the project is, in fact, the use of the augmented reality app, Blippar, which allows viewers to get extra content while exploring images in the physical space. Exploring or scanning these images with the help of this app, viewers get access to special animation and movies that pop out of the walls (see Image 1.3).

IMAGE 1.3: Screenshot of the Trailer of *Priya's Shakti*

Source: Screenshot taken by the author on his computer of the trailer of *Priya's Shakti*, Ram Devineni, Lina Srivastava, and Dan Goldman (authors).

Let me conclude this section by suggesting that the formats that I have presented so far can also be (and already, to some extent, are) embraced by scholars in a variety of fields in the social sciences, and in particular, by ethnographers. The three typologies described in this section do indeed allow the image-maker or researcher to pursue different types of goals that range from the communication of research conducted on certain topics, to the production of new original material, and to proper instances of advocacy and activism (it is very important, in my view, for the researcher to be aware of the purpose of the engagement with such practices). They also require from the image-makers the capacity to establish a new set of reflections regarding the contentious relationship between content and form, or to quote Chris Wright (1998), between 'anthropological relevance' (the content) and 'aesthetic composition' (the form), where the meaning of the latter must, however, be stretched so as to include not only a general sense of the visual aesthetics, but also that of algorithmic aesthetics, and of the possibilities of the interface and the infrastructure adopted.

I-DOCS: IMAGES IN TRANSFORMATION

In their refashioning of the relationship between the viewer and the image (which incorporates a pretty radical refashioning of the very idea of visual communication), i-docs seem to materialise a number of changes that belong to the realm of digital images, at large. I identify four main critical areas in this regard.

The first characteristic of i-docs is that they bring still and moving images, sound, text and graphics within the same space, hence offering a viewing experience that transcends conventional media boundaries. A typical example of multimodality (Jenkins 2006), i-docs ask viewers to suspend the conventional media distinctions on which their habitual visual culture builds upon, marking out a shift that, as I have suggested elsewhere (see Favero 2013, 2014), can probably be approached with the help of what Ranciere (2008) has labelled 'imageness', a quality which goes beyond the strictly visual and that articulates a relation between 'the sayable and the visible .... the before and the after, cause and effect' (2008: 6). This collapse of media distinctions and the ontological instability of contemporary images can also be observed in many of the experiences that characterise today's contemporary art and popular culture. With respect to the former, mention could be made of David Szauder, the photographer who, in his series *Failed Memory*, created an algorithm capable of transforming images without intervening into them at the level of the visible. This exhibition built upon a series of morphed portraits that were the result of a hacking of the algorithm, which guided the act of recomposition of the image in the processor. And with regard to popular culture, the most evident example is indeed represented by the images produced with the smartphones of the last generation. Filled with metadata (of geolocative and relational nature), these photos evidently transcend the visible; their meaning is constituted in a dialogue between the visual, textual, audible and locative data.

A second aspect worth mentioning for understanding i-docs is the changing role of the spectator. Rather than passive users or viewers of the messages provided to them, here the spectators are increasingly identified as co-authors or producers of the works they engage with. Designed within the logic of hypertext, i-docs ask, in fact, as I hinted at above, viewers to construct the narrative by themselves, and hence, to actively produce meaning as they go along in the exploration of the materials contained in the platform. Here, authorship is a collaborative endeavour generated in a dialectic between an image-maker and what we must consider, borrowing again from Ranciere, an 'emancipated' spectator (Ranciere 2009).

It is important to point out, and here I come to the third key characteristic of i-docs, that this act of dialogic or shared narrative construction translates conventionally also into an act of community-making. Addressing the hybrid space between life 'offline' and 'online' (De Sousa e Silva 2006; Kabisch 2008), i-docs, as other platforms of creative image-making or image-sharing, have the potential to connect social actors in different locations with each other, turning, through the shared used of digital images, scattered individuals into a community. This is exemplified by *18 Days in Egypt*, an interactive crowd-sourced documentary created by documentary filmmaker and journalist Jigar Mehta and interaction designer Yasmin Elayat. Aiming at creating a new form of shared documentary that enables participants to chronicle the Egyptian Revolution through their own footage, photos, tweets and Facebook status updates, *18 Days in Egypt* deploys a variety of media and languages. Among them, I want to mention Popcornjs, an HTML5 media framework designed for integrating the web into video production. It is of fundamental relevance to the nature of this project that Popcornjs allows the participants to connect specific pieces of information available on the Internet to a specific video clip. Watching the clip, the viewer may choose to stop and deepen her/his understanding of the specific issues that pop up on the side menu and then proceed to watch the rest of the clip.

The fourth fundamental trait of i-docs is, as I have anticipated, that it threatens the certainties of authorship. With the transformation of the viewer into a co-creator of meaning, the role of the authors/ makers gets decentralised, transformed into something new. No longer 'directors', image-makers must now envision their mission as that of orchestrators, facilitators and curators. Their duty is to create and curate a space in which viewers can share their own experiences and reflections rather than safely guiding them through the linear path of the narrative. As I have discussed in this chapter, the responsibility of authorship is here shared by the image-maker and the spectator. This change is indeed part of a much larger scenario of transformations and it runs in parallel with similar changes happening in other (allied) fields of practice. With regard to documentary filmmaking, for instance, Shuddhabrata Sengupta, one of the members of the Delhi-based Raqs Media Collective, suggested to me during an interview,

> the scope of the image-maker, documentarist or artist today is no longer that of showing what was previously unseen given that today this, with the present spread of new imaging technologies, can be done by anyone. Rather her duty is to create a space in which viewers can share their own experiences and reflections around topics characterising their everyday life (Favero 2013).

This, I suggest, is a very important dimension when considering the possible dialogue between interactive documentaries and the ethnographic practice.

THE POLITICS OF I-DOCS

The political implications of the scenarios that I have delineated so far are indeed manifold. On one level, the practices that I have described imply a different politics of knowledge communication and production. Facing a creative archive made up of a variety of multi-layered, and perhaps, even contradictory materials, and immersed in direct contact with the images that make up such archives, the viewers are instigated to engage in a fairly open-ended, personalised exploration centred on their own 'knowledge-seeking strategies' (Färber 2007). Indeed, it is not my intention here to celebrate i-docs or similar platforms either as realms of total freedom for the viewer or as 'the' future of filmmaking. The limits imposed by software, interface and infrastructure, combined with the choices that lead to the selection of the materials presented and of the links generated between them, are indeed of remarkable importance. Nevertheless, it is also evident that such practices and technologies may represent tools that, compared with conventional ethnographic films or photo essays, offer a step in the direction of a more participatory and inclusive ethnography, one more attentive to the establishment of a dialogue with the viewers.

Materialising the modes of active spectatorship implied in Ranciere's (2009) notion of the 'emancipated spectator' as well as in Bourriaud's (1998) 'relational aesthetics', such practices also constitute a unique opportunity for the ethnographer—to close the gap between the ethnographic material they put on display and their viewers. While not representing a proper revolution in our ways of communicating ethnography, this change may indeed help us bring to the fore the nature of knowledge as a 'processual aspect of human social relations' (Banks 2001: 112), rather than as a static thing 'out there' waiting to be discovered and 'documented'.

We must also acknowledge that a dialectic with the viewers includes another possibility, too, that is, that of generating, with the help of this very same platform used for communicating, new ethnographic materials. Viewers can today, as we have seen, actively interact with online materials, generating not only interpretations, but also adding new materials capable of opening up new interpretations. Transforming a space of display into a space of ongoing production of ethnographic evidence, this practice may indeed not be an easy one to handle in the context of research; yet, it carries the potential of ongoing production of new insights and materials.

On a second level, the platforms and projects that I have explored in this chapter also indicate another kind of politics, a much more concrete one, leading to the formation or consolidation of communities of interest. This is exemplified at best by i-docs such as *18 days in Egypt* that I have discussed, which have become a living archive of the Arab Spring, and allow people from different countries to share information and agendas.

Similar examples can be found in *Everyday Rebellion*, a documentary and cross-media project that focuses on 'the creativity of non-violent resistance and modern forms of civil disobedience' or, in India, in *Bell Bajao* (*Ring the Bell*), the campaign targeting men to intervene against domestic violence. Made up of a series of video clips (not only uploaded by amateur filmmakers, but also by some well-known filmmakers), this project aims at telling true stories of men and boys stopping violence with one ring of a bell. Another example could be *The Ugly Indian*, a campaign aimed at creating awareness about filth in Indian public spaces. Parallel examples can also be found in the world of journalism. Self-reporting has today become a common practice for many bottom-up sites as well as for major news-reporting agencies. On such spaces, users can upload and share personal images; also, commenting on public events has become of fundamental importance for mainstream media.

Political parties, too, have joined the trend and engage with sharing the platform's fast tools for consensus-making and as arenas for campaigning. The examples are many, and range from India's Aam Admi Party (AAP), to UK's UK Independence Party (UKIP), to Italy's Five Star Movement. Running in parallel with the participatory experiments taking place in the contemporary global arts scene, these practices seem to speak about the emergence of new notions of citizenship. They echo Hardt and Negri's (2004) notion of the 'multitude' as an inherently antagonistic and political subject made up of singularities. A departure from conventional notions of community and political identity, the multitude is pure potentiality, a singularity that tends towards shared, common projects.

CONCLUSIONS

Much more work ought to be conducted in order to better explore the extent to which new media practices are not only signifiers of wider social and political transformations, but possibly also agents of such change. Behind the temptation of celebrating such new practices as signs of our entry into a new era dominated by active forms of spectatorship, by collaboration, co-curation, participation, and hence, by a new democratic spirit (Jenkins 2006), hides, in fact, the spectre of new forms of control and 'soft' capitalist exploitation (see Thrift 1997). As Boltanski and Chiapello (2007) have suggested, participation is the favourite form of expression of the contemporary 'spirit of capitalism'.[4]

Today's spontaneous forms of sharing information with the help of smartphone applications, smart watches, social media, etc., correspond, in fact, also to just as many acts of voluntary subjugation to the market. Hence, rather than active participants and co-creators, we could consider ourselves to be 'unpaid labourers' (Gehl 2009)[5], enthusiastic collaborators eager to be monitored, controlled and swallowed by the contemporary capitalist system. Read from a different angle, this situation also remands us back to Foucault's observations in *Discipline and Punish* (1977), where he showed us how, in the passage from Renaissance to modernity, the relation between vision and power had changed significantly. In pre-modern times, the fact of 'being looked at, observed, described in detail.... was a privilege' (Foucault 1977: 191). This is nicely embodied by the Hall of Mirrors of Versailles or by the royal parades, that is, those moments in which the King would give the people the right to look at him, exercising simultaneously his right to be looked at. In modernity, however, the hierarchy of this relationship got reversed. The act of looking became synonymous with control, monitoring, and hence, discipline. This is what Bentham's Panopticon was about. An innovative, more functional and humane way of building a jail, this was a model for disciplining society through vision. In this context, the King no longer had to be looked at, but was rather the looking subject. Metaphorically seated at the centre of the Panopticon, he progressively transfigured himself into a kind of Big Brother, seen by no one but able to see everyone.

Today we have undoubtedly entered a new stage in this development of power. The myriad of small gestures of voluntary self-monitoring, engendered by the online sharing of geo-located photographs, the use of wearable technologies capable of taking pictures on our behalf (see the life-logging camera phenomenon) or of grabbing our biometric data in combinations with our movements in space and our payment habits (see, for instance, the market of smart watches) do, when combined, force us to rethink our assumptions regarding the functioning of 'biopower' (Foucault 2008). As a set of techniques and mechanisms for population control that have the body at their centre, 'biopower' is today evidently acting also by means of the technologies of image production and consumption. As ethnographers engaging with images, we must today carefully consider the ethics and politics of our engagement with them, walking that thin line that separates an enthusiasm for the possibilities that new images open up for us from a blind adherence to the politics that underpin them. So, even though digital images have perhaps not started a revolution in our visual culture, they have lifted up a set of broader questions regarding the politics of image-making.

Notes

1. The avant-garde character of i-docs can be identified in the lack of a clear set of formal conventions defining it and also in the absence of a concrete market regulating it.

2. In a forthcoming publication (Favero 2017), I suggest that i-docs should be regarded as a visual form rather than a specific technology (see also Aston 2016). Rather than approaching i-docs as a set of specific formats and technologies, we should, therefore, perhaps look upon them as a direction, an inspiration for creating more inclusive participatory and multi-modal experiences capable of responding to the changing world that surrounds us. Hence, they function as a window into a much broader scenario concerning digital visual practices.

3. My student Suze van Boehemn has carried out an excellent discussion of these different forms in her thesis on 'Interactive Activism' (2014).

4. I would like to thank Giuliana Ciancio for sharing her views on co-curation and the 'spirit of new capitalism' with me.

5. Gehl suggests this with relation to YouTube users. I am grateful to Eva Theunissen for suggesting this text.

References

18 Days in Egypt. Available at http://beta.18daysinegypt.com/ (accessed 4 September 2019).

A. De Souza e Silva. 2006. 'From Cyber to Hybrid Mobile Technologies as Interfaces of Hybrid Spaces', *Space and Culture* 9(3): 261–78.

Aston, Judith. 2016. 'Interactive Documentary—What Does It Mean and Why Does It Matter?'. Available at http://i-docs.org/2016/03/27/interac:ve-documentary-what-does-itmean-and-why-does-itma?er/ (accessed 4 September 2019).

Aston, Judith and Sandra Gaudenzi. 2012. 'Interactive Documentary: Setting the Field', *Studies in Documentary Film* 6(2): 125–39.

Banks, Marcus. 2001. *Visual Methods in Social Research*. London: Sage Publications.

Beattie, K. 2008. *Documentary Display: Re-Viewing Nonfiction Film and Video*. London: Wallflower Press.

Bell Bajao (Ring the Bell), United Nations in India. Available at https://in.one.un.org/page/bell-bajao/ (accessed 4 September 2019).

Beyond the Map. Available at https://beyondthemap.withgoogle.com/en-us/ (accessed 4 September 2019).

Blassnigg, M. 2005. 'Feature Report: Documentary Film at the Junction between Art and Digital Media Technologies', *Convergence: The International Journal of Research into New Media Technologies* 11(3): 104–10.

Boltanski, L. and E. Chiapello. 2007. *The New Spirit of Capitalism*. London: Verso.

Bourriaud, N. 1998. *Relational Aesthetics*. Dijon: Les Presses du Reel.

Bruzzi, Stella. 2000. *New Documentary*. London: Routledge.

Crary, Jonathan. 1990. *Techniques of the Observer: On Vision and Modernity in the Nineteenth Century*. Cambridge, Massachusetts: MIT Press.

Everyday Rebellion. Available at http://www.everydayrebellion.net/ (accessed 4 September 2019).

———, facebook page. Available at https://www.facebook.com/EverydayRebellion/ (accessed 4 September 2019).

Färber, A. 2007. 'Exposing Expo: Exhibition Entrepreneurship and Experimental Reflexivity in Late Modernity'. In S. Macdonald and P. Basu (eds), *Exhibition Experiments*, pp. 219–39. London: Wiley-Blackwell.

Favero, Paolo. 2013. 'Getting our Hands Dirty (Again): Interactive Documentaries and the Meaning of Images in the Digital Age', *Journal of Material Culture* 18(3): 259–77.

———, Interview with Suddhabrata Sengupta, April 2013.

———. 2014. 'Learning to Look Beyond the Frame: Reflections on the Changing Meaning of Images in the Age of Digital Media Practices', *Visual Studies* 26(2): 166–79.

———. 2017. 'The Travelling I-Doc: Reflections on the Meaning of Interactive Documentary-based Image-making Practices in Contemporary India'. In Judith Aston, Sandra Gaudenzi and Mandy Rose (eds), *I-Docs: The Evolving Practices of Interactive Documentary*. New York: Wallflower Press.

———. 2018. 'To Swallow or to Get Swallowed, this is the Question: On Viewing, Viewers and Frames in the Context of "New" Images'. In T. Fillitz (ed.), *An Anthropology of Contemporary Art*. London: Bloomsbury Publishing.

Foucault, Michel. 1977. *Discipline and Punish: The Birth of the Prison*. New York: Random House.

_____. 2008. *The Birth of Biopolitics: Lectures at the College de France 1978–1979*. Hampshire and New York: Palgrave Macmillan.

Galloway, Dayna, Kenneth B. McAlpine and Paul Harris. 2007. 'From Michael Moore to JFK Reloaded: Towards a Working Model of Interactive Documentary', *Journal of Media Practice* 8(3): 325–39.

Gehl, R. 2009. 'YouTube as Archive', *International Journal of Cultural Studies* 12(1): 43–60.

Grierson, John. 1966. 'First Principles of Documentary'. In F. Hardy (ed.), *Grierson on Documentary*. London: Faber and Faber.

Hardt, M. and A. Negri. 2004. *Multitude: War and Democracy in the Age of Empire*. London: Penguin Books.

Kabisch, Eric. 2008. 'Datascape: A Synthesis of Digital and Embodied Worlds', *Space and Culture* 11(3): 222–38.

Jenkins, Henry. 2006. *Convergence Culture: Where Old and New Media Collide*. New York: New York University Press.

Meadows, Mark Stephen. 2003. *Pause and Effect: The Art of Interactive Narrative*. Indianapolis: New Riders.

Merleau-Ponty, Michel. 2012 [1962]. *Phenomenology of Perception*. New York: Routledge.

Min-ha, Trinh T. 1993. 'The Totalizing Quest of Meaning'. In Michael Renov (ed.), *Theorising Documentary*, pp. 90–107. New York: Routledge.

Mitchell, W. J. T. 1992. *The Reconfigured Eye: Visual Truth in the Post-photographic Era*. Cambridge, Massachusetts: MIT Press.

Nash, Katie. 2012. 'Modes of Interactivity: analysing the Webdoc', *Media, Culture and Society* 34(2): 195–210.

Nichols, Bill. 2001. *Introduction to Documentary*. Bloomington, Indianapolis: Indiana University Press.

O'Reilly, T. 2005. 'What is Web 2.0? Design Patterns and Business Models for the Next Generation of Software'. Available at http://oreilly.com/web2/archive/what-is-web-20.html (accessed 22 Nov 2016).

Popcorn-js.org. Available at https://github.com/mozilla/popcorn-js/ (accessed 4 September 2019).

Ranciere, Jacques. 2008. *The Future of the Image*. London: Verso.

_____. 2009. *The Emancipated Spectator*. London: Verso.

Sturken, Marita and Lisa Cartwright. 2001. *Practices of Looking: An Introduction to Visual Culture*. Oxford: Oxford University Press.

Szauder, David. *Failed Memory*. Available at https://www.ignant.com/2013/10/28/failed-memories-by-david-szauder/(accessed 4 September 2019).

The Hidden Worlds of the National Parks. Available at https://artsandculture.withgoogle.com/en-us/national-parks-service/ (accessed 4 September 2019).

The Ugly Indian. Available at http://www.theuglyindian.com/ (accessed 4 September 2019).
——, facebook page. Available at https://www.facebook.com/theugl. yindian/ (accessed 4 September 2019).
Thrift, N. 1997. 'The Rise of Soft Capitalism', *Cultural Values* 1(1): 29–57.
van Bohemen, S. 2014. *Interactive Activism*, Master's Dissertation, University of Antwerp, Belgium.
Wright, C. 1998. 'The Third Subject: Perspectives on Visual Anthropology', *Anthropology Today* 14(4): 16–22.

LIST OF I-DOCS CITED

A Journal of Insomnia. NFB. Available at https://www.nfb.ca/ interactive/a_journal_of_insomnia/.
High Rise. Katerina Cizek (dir.). Gerry Flahive (prod.).
I Love Your Work. IDFA Doc Lab. Available at https://www.doclab. org/2013/i-love-your-work-2/.
Karen. Blast Theory. https://www.blasttheory.co.uk/projects/karen/.
Palestine Remix. Al-Jazeera. Available at https://interactive.aljazeera.com/ aje/palestineremix/.
Prison Valley. David Dufresne and Philippe Brault. Available at http:// prisonvalley.arte.tv/?lang=en.
Priya's Shakti. Ram Devineni, Lina Srivastava, and Dan Goldman (authors). Available at https://www.priyashakti.com/about-us.
Rider Spoke. Blast Theory. Available at https://www.blasttheory.co.uk/ projects/rider-spoke/.

ꙮ two

Mumbai Sub-versions

The Place of Affect in Digital Video Activism*

Anjali Monteiro and K. P. Jayasankar

Introduction

This chapter attempts to look at two very different examples of the deployment of the digital video by grassroots activists within the space of Mumbai, in order to critically reflect on the possibilities of this work for documentary practice. These two instances are located at different historical junctures as far as the emergence of the digital is concerned—the first example is from the early 2000s, when the digital video and CDs were first becoming accessible to new, local filmmakers, and the next, in contemporary times, when the Internet and mobile telephony have a much larger reach and presence. We shall explore the works of Waqar Khan and Bhau Korde, who were involved in the production of media materials, including video, for use within the Mohalla Committee movement in Dharavi, as a part of peace initiatives that were started in the wake of the 1992–93 ethnic violence in Mumbai. Our second example is from the present decade, and looks at the deployment of the digital video by the residents of Sion Koliwada in their struggles against eviction by big builders.

The chapter seeks to understand the process of local content production, the frames employed, the symbols and imagery used,

*We would like to thank Bhau Korde, Faiza Khan and Prathamesh Shivkar for their illuminating conversations, which made this chapter possible. We also gratefully acknowledge our interactions over the years with the late Waqar Khan, from whom we have learnt much, as human beings and filmmakers.

and the affective dimensions of the materials produced. It focuses specifically on the texts created in the process of two very different struggles and seeks to understand both the concerns of their makers and the dynamics of their engagement with audiences. It will look at how the digital narratives of resistance emerging from these spaces draw on both the large cultural repertoire of Bollywood as well as local performance traditions, not limiting themselves to evidentiary modes of storytelling. It will also draw out the implications this might have for documentary filmmaking praxis and the transgressive potential of subjugated knowledges.

Peace Initiatives and Popular Media: *Hum Sab Ek Hain*

It was in 2001 that we first met Waqar Pyare Khan. He was a tailor who grew into a small garment manufacturer in Dharavi.[1] Waqar had survived the experience of the ethnic violence that rocked Mumbai in 1992. He lived in Dharavi and came to see us with Bhau Korde, a retired clerk in a school, who lived on the edge of Dharavi. They wanted to share with us a script for a short video on communal harmony that they were planning to make. Waqar and Bhau had done inspiring work on communal amity and conflict resolution after the 1992–93 ethnic violence,[2] building bridges between communities through *mohalla* (neighbourhood) peace committees.[3]

The violence impelled Waqar and Bhau to use various means to create dialogue and rebuild trust between communities; this included the use of popular media to reach the message of amity, within Dharavi and across the city:

> I felt that I needed to do my bit to bring people together again and restore peace and mutual trust. Aside from involvement in grassroots activities, such as meetings and cultural events, I felt that the media could be an influential way of reaching people and getting them to think of peace and amity. I thought of the idea of making a poster with four children of different religions, to bring out the essential oneness of all of us, however different we may be in terms of culture or religion (Jayasankar and Monteiro 2003).[4]

IMAGE 2.1: Poster Made by Waqar Khan after the 1992–93 Communal Violence

Source: Photograph of the poster by one of the authors, K. P. Jayasankar, in 2003.

The Dharavi *Mohalla* Committee disseminated this poster (Image 2.1) widely in public places and police stations across Mumbai; it became an iconic and popular image that received public acclaim. In 2001, Waqar and Bhau decided to follow this up with a television public service spot, thinking that they could reach a national audience. When they approached us to discuss their script, we decided to document the process of making the spot, thinking that it might be an interesting peg to hang a film on Dharavi, which we had been discussing with local groups since the mid-1990s. Our film, *Naata*, is woven around this story of the making of their film.[5]

Their film was truly an exercise in community participation, with people from the various neighbourhoods in Dharavi pitching in to make it possible. Transporters offered their vehicles to ferry actors, caterers looked after the food arrangements, and film industry technicians (camera crew, directors, makeup men) volunteered their services free of cost. There was no dearth of enthusiastic actors: doctors, nurses, children and parents, all playing themselves. These various people worked with miraculous and efficient coordination to complete the shooting of the spot in a single day at Essel Film Studios in Mumbai, in September 2001. Waqar bore the costs of hiring equipment and other production-related expenses from his earnings as a garment manufacturer.

IMAGE 2.2: The Shooting of the Spot, *Hum Sab Ek Hain*, in September 2001

Source: Photograph taken by one of the authors, K. P. Jayasankar.

The story of Waqar's spot is set in Gujarat and based on a real event: an earthquake that took place on 26 January 2001, in which many thousands of people lost their lives. The film starts with a Republic Day parade, with children participating in 'fancy dress', iconically representing the four major religions (Hindu, Muslim, Christian and Sikh). The earthquake that ensues creates death and chaos, in which parents are frantically searching for their children (Image 2.2). In a Bollywood-inspired series of coincidences, a Muslim father rescues a Hindu boy and this boy's father rescues the Muslim man's son. As both children need blood transfusions, the film shows Hindu blood being transfused into the Muslim child and vice versa. Casting aside all claims to medical authenticity, the spot shows the blood being directly transfused from Muslim to Hindu and from Hindu to Muslim, shattering atavistic notions of purity of bloodlines: 'The use of this melodramatic trope in Khan's spot, while at variance with all codes of realism,[6] is a popular and powerful metaphor that touches the hearts of audiences and gives the message that "We are all one"' (Jayasankar and Monteiro 2016: 173).

Our initial scepticism at the unrealistic and melodramatic scenario that Waqar's film presents has, over a period of time, with our involvement in his work and our experience of its production and reception, given way to a deep respect and understanding for what he is trying to achieve, and also a problematising of our own taken-for-granted notions of a desirable and effective text. Bharucha (1998) gestures towards several possibilities of textually deterministic critiques of the image, including putting forward the question, 'Why four boys and not four girls?' One could also critically interrogate the image through its connotation of caste hierarchies, as the Hindu boy is dressed as a Brahmin. We have had the opportunity to participate in many public screenings in Dharavi, where the audiences chose to ignore these layers and seized upon 'the opportunities offered by his film, perhaps transforming and opening themselves to the affective energy of his narrative practices, rooted in the idiom of the popular culture, obviating and making redundant the issues that such text-based critiques throw up' (Jayasankar and Monteiro 2016: 173). The exuberance of popular involvement and affective responses elicited by Waqar's film are, with all humility, somewhat different in nature from the responses elicited by our own documentary work, constrained as it is by both audience expectations from a documentary and our own insertion into a certain textual language (even as we try to escape it).

The telecast of Waqar's spot on Doordarshan's National Network in 2002 was an occasion for pride and celebration for all those who had participated in its production. Waqar and Bhau next ventured into the production of a feature-length film, which draws generously on clips from various Bollywood films, connected by an Amitabh Bachchan duplicate voice-over that seeks to provide a history of India from the colonial times to make a case for abandoning the divide-and-rule strategy employed by the British to create friction between religious communities. It exhorts people of all religions and communities to come together for the greater common good. This narrative is interspersed with interviews of eminent citizens that bolster this point of view. We helped with the shooting of some of the interviews for this film. Bhau, in a recent interview, reflects on why they chose this form:

> We brought some documentary films on communalism to show in Dharavi and when our boys saw these films, they said, 'We can't show these in Dharavi. All these shots of riots and all will create more problems among people.' Then we thought, why not use some good dialogues from films? People remember these dialogues and they love those scenes. So Waqar bhai started collecting scenes from films and we also used interviews of respected people. And we found that people liked the film and we had good discussions (Monteiro and Jayasankar 2015a).

Waqar's film, *Hum Sab Ek Hain* (*We Are All One*), 2002, with its uninhibited appropriation of language, idiom and images from popular cinema, and with its emphasis on the language of realism, logic and non-fictionalised truth, is perhaps able to reach audiences that tend to remain untouched by the modern, secular media.[7] In fact, it is this audience that is the target of Hindutva propaganda, which also tends to draw on the language of fiction, blurring the lines between myth and history (Rajagopal 2001). The question arises as to whether the disregard of this space of the mythic, the melodramatic and the popular by filmmakers like 'us', modern, secular and urban creators of non-fictional narratives, needs to be looked at critically and reflexively. The affective energy with which Bhau and Waqar could repurpose and redeploy the narratives of Bollywood to foreground their agenda of conflict resolution and peace, shuttling 'effortlessly between the melodramatic and the didactic, and the enthusiastic responses of audiences to these images brought us to question many of the patronising and simplified assumptions that are made about popular culture' (Jayasankar and Monteiro 2016: 176).

Waqar and Bhau's work in media was located within an entire ecosystem of initiatives to promote peace through meetings, inter-faith dialogue and joint celebration of festivals, defusing potential conflict through immediate, on-ground local interventions. Perhaps it was this location that also framed the reception and appropriation of the messages in their work by local communities. In many cases, the screenings were a part of the local celebration of festivals. For instance, the second feature-length film was first launched at the Ganesh festival celebrations at various locations across Dharavi, and received an enthusiastic response. It was later duplicated and disseminated to other groups and networks across the country. These were pre-Internet days, and hence, the mode of distribution was through CDs, which were cheap and which Waqar distributed free of cost to anyone who was interested.

What is also interesting in this context is the uncanny realisation that the strategy of repurposing of mainstream Bollywood images by Waqar is very similar to the massive recycling and repurposing that Dharavi and other such informal settlements do with the waste and refuse that the city produces. This poaching, facilitated by the advent of the digital, becomes an act of copy-Left resistance and gestures towards a subaltern media ecosystem, an alternative political economy of image production and consumption:

> Dharavi's ecological footprint is minuscule and its carbon credits worth a thousand green Oscars. It takes too little and gives back a lot. If places like Dharavi were destroyed, almost all the plumbers of the city would disappear, so would many policemen, taxi drivers, domestic helps, vendors, garbage recyclers .... The invisible political economy of the slum is a compassionate bulwark that shores up Mumbai. Without these vital spaces, Mumbai would collapse and rot in its waste (Jayasankar and Monteiro 2009: 15).

The deployment of the language of popular cinema by grassroots activists like Waqar brings into question many of the (elitist) assumptions that we tend to make about these narrative forms, with their appeal to melodrama and excess and their disregard for the codes of realism. As authors inserted within a different narrative paradigm, we began to realise the tremendous possibilities of the popular, with its tendency towards inclusiveness, and its ability to harness the affect of diverse audiences. Bhau makes an ironic comment on 'us' (and other filmmakers of our ilk) towards the end of *Naata*: 'There are many secular filmmakers who make good films. But it remains restricted to a small group only—secular filmmakers make secular films and have secular discussions on them! Ours was a different attempt. And to some extent, we feel we have been successful' (Jayasankar and Monteiro 2003).

Waqar adds to this by pointing towards the empowering role of local cultural production, which has its ear to the ground, and hence, a working understanding of the language of the popular. Pointing out that 'until now, we have been watching films on communal harmony and reading messages made by others', he argues:

> But today, the situation is such that it is imperative for all of us to stop watching passively and to speak out and make our own messages. Earlier, we felt that only big companies and rich people could make such messages. But now we feel that we too can speak. We think about what we should say and how we should say it. Their way of giving messages is different. But when people at the grassroots speak, it is practical. So now we have the confidence to do it our own way! (Jayasankar and Monteiro 2003)

This first encounter of subaltern communities with digital media in the early 2000s created the space for user-generated creativity, of which Waqar's work is one example. During this period and later, a number of video parlours came up in working-class neighbourhoods, providing accessible and cheap entertainment to local communities, mainly men and male youth. In the film *Videokaaran* (2009), Sagai, the owner of one such video parlour, speaks about how they would create their own versions of films by inserting pornographic or other melodramatic material into existing films, in order to cater to the tastes of their audiences. One sees a resonance with this aesthetics of excess, in a very different context, in Waqar's work. The emergence of the digital, which made Bollywood films both accessible and editable, made possible his acts of semiotic poaching, where he deployed this aesthetics of the popular in order to put across a message of communal amity. As Bhau mentions, the documentary films that showed the 'real' material of demolitions and riots, in the context of a rational argument against religious intolerance, were regarded by the local community as too close to everyday experience, and hence, likely to arouse strong antagonistic and polarising sentiments. The use of the more melodramatic language of Bollywood, removed from 'real' events, yet in many ways, connecting with the raw emotions of grief, anger, love and compassion, were seen as having a greater transformative potential, more able to engender conversation and dialogue between communities that had been torn apart by events beyond their control. This use of melodrama and more metaphorical imagery (for example, blood transfusion between religious communities) tends to be looked down upon by media-makers such as us, as non-rational, unreal, exaggerated and implausible. Perhaps it is time to rethink our prejudices.

SION KOLIWADA HOUSING STRUGGLES

The neighbourhood of Sion Koliwada, in Mumbai, not far from Dharavi, has been the site of a long-drawn struggle between the residents from the indigenous Koli fishing community and builders. The latter, in collusion with the Municipal Corporation and local politicians, have been attempting to use the slum rehabilitation scheme to forcibly evict the Kolis, who have been tenants of the Bombay Improvement Trust tenements since colonial times. This struggle, which has been supported by housing rights movements and activists, is symptomatic of the contestations over space in globalising Mumbai. The state, along with builder lobbies, has worked to gentrify working-class neighbourhoods and displace the poor, using a combination of market forces, government policies and coercive measures (Bhide 2014). This marginalisation of the poor is justified by a discourse of legality and productivity. According to the erstwhile Planning Commission of India, the 'development of slums drags down the productivity of the city and its potential contribution to economic growth' (Planning Commission 2011: 59). The housing rights movements, including the Sion Koliwada struggle, contest these discourses through various means.

The housing struggles of the Koli community in the Sion Koliwada chawls[8] date back to 2006, when Pilot Constructions, owned by builder Sudhakar Shetty, demolished a school and two chawls to construct a 13-storey building. The builder formed the Shiv Koliwada Cooperative Housing Society and fraudulently claimed that he had the support of 75 per cent of the residents, which is required for redevelopment. In early 2010, residents began to receive eviction notices from Brihanmumbai Municipal Corporation (BMC), stating that the corporation was requisitioning their homes on grounds of 'public interest' (Banerjee 2012). This was followed by an eviction order promising alternative accommodation. While some residents managed to get a legal stay, many others had their homes bulldozed the following January. Subsequent demolitions took place during the rainy season, when the evicted residents had no alternative but to take the tenement accommodation provided by the builder. Since 2010, the residents have been using all the means at their disposal, including legal cases, advocacy at the highest level, media coverage and agitation, in order to save their homes. At the present juncture, most of the *chawls* have been demolished and people forcibly resettled in adjoining buildings, where many are dissatisfied with their lot but see no alternative.

The access to digital technologies and the Internet has helped local communities produce, amplify and disseminate the stories of their struggle. A key figure in this work has been Prathmesh Shivkar, who began using his handycam to create evidence to support their struggles:

> I had a handycam and since 2010, I started recording the demolitions and other things happening as I thought it could be used as evidence in the cases we were filing against the builder. And it has proved really useful. When 25 of our women were arrested on false charges and the SI of the police station said that he was in the police station at that time filing the FIR against them, our footage showed him in our chawls arresting the women. That's how they were all set free (Monteiro and Jayasankar 2015b).

Shivkar and his friends from the Koli community, including people with backgrounds in animation and engineering, have collaborated with filmmaker Faiza Ahmed Khan, who has been working with the *Ghar Bachao Ghar Banao* (Protect Homes Build Homes) movement,[9] for the housing rights of citizens in informal settlements across the city. In 2011, when the struggle was at its height, and the group of young people in Koliwada had been both documenting the struggle as well as screening other films every night in Koliwada, the idea of making a short film was mooted. As Khan recalls:

> And someone from the basti said, '*Vaise hi footage mat dikhana* (don't just show footage like that), we are tired of looking at these kinds of images, *kuch doosra karo* (let's do something different).' So that's what sparked this idea of doing it in this humorous way which I feel is a very good way to get into these spaces. So that's when this friend who is also a Bollywood songwriter came on

board and worked with Prathamesh and some of these people on the script and shot it (Monteiro and Jayasankar 2015c).

Shivkar said that the group decided to use Koli cultural forms and make a satirical piece, as they felt that people were bored with watching reality footage of demolitions:

> If there is some entertainment then people will be interested and the message will go across. Of course, there should not be just entertainment, about 40% is okay to keep people's attention. We decided to make a documentary with our Koli style storytelling, with real footage and also animation. So we got the songwriter of *Tanu Weds Manu* and he helped us write a script in Hindi. Then we sat with our Koli women and made it in our own language (Monteiro and Jayasankar 2015b).

The resultant piece, which was 11 minutes long and took 10 days to make, using local actors and local talent, entitled *Chamatkari Builder Baba* (*The Miraculous Builder Baba*), 2011, combines song, narration and animation. A fictional Koli narrator, sitting with a group of other Kolis, tells a 'real' story, but in a satirical vein (Image 2.3). It has local Koli women acting, and the builders and the authorities are represented through animation figures, with the 'real' faces of the people involved in the demolitions. The video was put on YouTube and also screened

IMAGE 2.3: A Screenshot from the Film, *Chamatkari Builder Baba*

Source: Provided by one of the authors, K. P. Jayasankar.

in various informal settlements, with enthusiastic responses from audiences. It was the use of the actual faces of the builder and other stakeholders that created a legal problem, as Shivkar says:

> We eventually took it off YouTube, on the advice of our lawyers. Since there are cases in court regarding the matter, it can become a problem to us. We had some screenings initially and the film became very popular. We also made it in Hindi, with English subtitles, so that it could be shown in other communities. If we had used only caricatures, instead of real faces that would have been better. Then no one could have objected to it (Monteiro and Jayasankar 2015b).

DIALOGUING WITH AUDIENCES

It is the emergence of digital media, with its relatively easy access and low dissemination costs, which has created the space for these and other instances of grassroots media activism. Waqar's first film, made in 2001, was produced on a relatively high budget medium (Digibeta) in a commercial studio and involved costs that were borne by him and others in Dharavi. His later work, which involved mainly re-editing clips sourced from Hindi cinema, was made possible by the easy availability of these films in the digital format. As mentioned earlier, his work was widely distributed as low cost, mass-duplicated CDs, free of cost, through existing networks of peace activists and others working on issues of secularism and amity. The Sion Koliwada film was made on a cheap handycam by people within the community, who had media experience collaborating with professionals from the film industry; and in addition to being distributed in the digital format in a non-broadcast context, it was also uploaded on the web, which made it easily accessible, until legal compunctions resulted in it being taken down.

Over the years, with growing access to digital media, there are many more examples of community filmmaking that have been made possible by the advent of digital and web-based distribution. On the one hand, there are networks like Video Volunteers, initiated by activists who train local reporters across the country to produce news-format shorts that are shared online, and also locally in non-broadcast mode. On the other, there are community-initiated attempts, such as the Shivaji Nagar Boys' Group (SVJ Boyzz), who have made the *Govandi CID* web series, which uses a popular genre to talk about local issues such as drug addiction and the water problem (Malu 2015).[10] Another interesting community-based filmmaking initiative in Malegaon,[11] which has produced local versions of Bollywood films, has been immortalised by Khan in her film, *Supermen of Malegaon* (2012). There does seem to be a difference between the idiom and language that communities might deploy to make films and the kinds of films made by activists who seek to highlight the issues of the communities they work with. While the former tends to draw upon imagination and affect, the latter appears to stick to a very direct news-inspired narrative style, devoid of humour, irony or pleasure.

In various ways, both the examples discussed above, which have emerged from grassroots struggles, begin to pose interesting questions to our conception of the political documentary, in the Indian context, and its relationship with the real world out there. As Khan points out, in a critique of the evidence-driven political documentary: 'I would earlier see these films [political documentaries] as giving voice to the voiceless. But now I feel we are thrusting one kind of narrative on them all the time, that victim story that you spoke of and I feel like exploring other facets tells a richer story' (Monteiro and Jayasankar 2015c).

She finds herself rethinking her own filmmaking practice, which has been closely tied to people's struggles around housing rights.

> To be honest, I have also been rethinking about how I want to tell stories, because I have been shooting with GBGB Andolan a lot and I have all these hard disks of footage. But just how I was telling these stories, from a very rights-based perspective, it wasn't interesting even to me, and the people from the *basti* said, '*Yeh hame dekhna hi nahi hai*' ['We just don't want to watch this']. And I've also had to think a step back about how I might want to do this (Monteiro and Jayasankar 2015c).

While the self-image of the Dharavi and Koliwada texts might not be that of a political documentary, both these sets of texts have intervened in political contestations and have questioned the notion that the most effective way of getting audiences to think about issues and struggles in their everyday lives is necessarily to use the image as evidence. In both cases, the makers of these texts consciously rejected the use of 'real images', in one case because they were seen as too provocative, and in the other because they were seen as too boring. The use of fictional elements to frame and interpret real events was regarded by both sets of filmmakers as important in creating dialogue, discussion and initiating a process of change.

Both initiatives foreground the idea of dialogue (and perhaps melodrama), which is the spine of many Bollywood films and a marker of their artistic merit. '*Kya dialogue maara!*' ('What a dialogue indeed!') is a phrase often used to invoke the profundity and affective power of conversations, both in films and everyday life. The dialogues of many films like *Sholay* are commonly rattled off and enjoyed even today. Both Khan and Shivkar speak about the mnemonic function of dialogues in shaping and invoking collective memories. Dialogue, within a structure that shuttles between melodrama and didactic speech, which is a characteristic of Waqar's work, has allowed for the expression of and engagement with ideas, which would otherwise have been difficult to discuss in a communally polarised context, marked by suspicion and mistrust of the other. As Vasudevan (2002) points out, in a different context, in his analysis of *Hey Ram*,

> Central here is the publicness of melodrama, where the mode of excess, an inflated mode of speech, demeanor and iconic figuration, displaces the realist, intimate communication between characters. It is as if such expressive functions are meant to be seen and heard publicly, beyond the delimited narrative world we see on screen (2002: 13).

Conversations between fictional characters in a pastiche of film excerpts become conversations between communities in Waqar's film essays. In the Koliwada video, this dialogue articulates, in a satirical mode, ongoing contestations with the state and big capital— conversations that facilitate and build local resistance and solidarities.

Both the media processes have involved agency at every stage. The making of the Dharavi and the Koliwada films were joyful community initiatives, involving the mobilisation of and collaborations between people with a whole range of skills and potentials, some of them with linkages with media industries, and others who were first-time actors, performers and authors. The texts themselves eschew any victim-centred discourse or any attempt to directly represent painful 'real' events. Instead they have focused on how those affected by these events resist, transcend and creatively respond in difficult situations. The use of melodrama in Waqar's texts and humour in the Koliwada film work towards making space for a dialogue with audiences that is potentially empowering rather than enervating, as is sometimes the case with the more evidence-based political films, which sometimes tend to elicit expressions of victimhood rather than agency. These activists talk about the discourse of the real as incapable of establishing dialogue. Documentary films in the Indian context, particularly those with overtly stated political aspirations, have long tended to rely on and position themselves within the discourse of Platonic sobriety (Nichols 1991), eschewing what they perceive as the frothiness of melodrama and the unreliable evidentiary potential of the fictive.[12]

Waqar and Shivkar's initiatives move away from this discourse of the real to the exuberance of affective fictional dialogues—both literally and metaphorically. They hold the promise of rethinking the language of the political. This rethinking also affords us an insight into the local wisdoms that are often negated by both academic intellectual traditions and mainstream entertainment narratives. It gestures towards the resistance and transgression implicit in these local, subjugated, knowledges (Foucault 1980), which speak truth to power, opening up pathways for more complex and layered relationships with the realm of the real.

NOTES

1. Once touted as Asia's largest 'slum', with a population of nearly one million, Dharavi in Mumbai has often been represented as an undesirable space, full of recently arrived migrants, whose right to live in the city is often questioned by vigilante citizens' groups and Right-wing politicians. Dharavi has a long history of migration from the late-nineteenth century. It is a productive space and plays an important role in the economy of the city, as it is one of the major hubs of the informal sector that produces commodities ranging from food products to leather goods that cater to a large export market. For a fascinating account of the changing space of Dharavi, see Weinstein (2014).

2. On 6 December 1992, Hindu fundamentalists demolished the centuries-old Babri Mosque, built by the Mughal emperor Babar, on the grounds that it was the birthplace of the Hindu god, Ram. In the aftermath

of this destruction, violence broke out all over the nation. Mumbai experienced ethnic violence and clashes between Muslims and Hindus, as well as systematic targeting of Muslim neighbourhoods by Hindu fundamentalist groups that led to over 900 deaths between December 1992 and January 1993. For a detailed analysis of this cataclysmic event, see Menon 2012.

3. The *mohalla* committees are neighbourhood peace communities established in collaboration with the police in Mumbai in the 1990s.

4. All quotes in this chapter, unless otherwise indicated, are from the film *Naata* (Jayasankar and Monteiro 2003).

5. The focus of this chapter is not the film, *Naata,* but the films made by Waqar Khan.

6. The narrative shows scant regard for minor details like blood groups or blood-transmitted infections like HIV/AIDS.

7. One can perhaps draw on Rajagopal's (2001) notion of 'split publics', constituted by the English language and vernacular media, which he connects to the rise and growth of Hindutva in the early 1990s.

8. A *chawl* is a particular kind of apartment block, which has single tenements, opening out to a common corridor and with common sanitation facilities, which were built for working-class populations, especially mill workers, from the 1900s onwards.

9. This is a movement that has been fighting slum eviction and raising issues of inequity and corruption in land deals in Mumbai.

10. A film on this group, entitled *Govandi, Crime Aur Camera* (Shekhar et al. 2015) has been made by the students of the School of Media and Cultural Studies, the Tata Institute of Social Sciences (TISS).

11. Malegaon is a small town in Maharashtra that has a history of communal strife and economic recession.

12. This is, however, not to short-change the considerable writing, both in the Indian context and internationally, which complicates the conflation of the political documentary with the evidentiary and explores the place of affect and the performative within documentary practice. See, for instance, Bruzzi (2006), Rutherford (2011), Jayasankar and Monteiro (2016), among others. In the Indian context, the work of feminist documentary filmmakers such as Madhusree Datta and Paromita Vohra have engaged with the registers of melodrama and the fictional. The work of filmmakers such as Amar Kanwar, Mani Kaul, Ruchir Joshi and others has also inflected the political in a direction away from the evidentiary (Jayasankar and Monteiro 2016). We are, however, discussing here the relative absence of these elements within political documentaries that have been directly tied up with movements of social change.

REFERENCES

Banerjee, Shoujomit. 2012. 'There's Something Rotten in the Locality of Sion Koliwada', *The Hindu*, 9 June 2012. Available at http://www.thehindu.com/todays-paper/tp-national/theres-something-rotten-in-the-locality-of-sion-koliwada/article3507134.ece (accessed 5 December 2015).

Bharucha, R. 1998. *In the Name of the Secular: Contemporary Cultural Activism in India*. New Delhi: Oxford University Press.

Bhide, Amita. 2014. *The City Produced: Urban Development, Violence and Spatial Justice in Mumbai*. Mumbai: Tata Institute of Social Sciences.

Bruzzi, Stella. 2006. *New Documentary: A Critical Introduction*. New York: Routledge.

Foucault, Michel. 1980. *Power/Knowledge: Selected Interviews and Other Writings, 1972–1977*. New York: Pantheon Books.

Jayasankar, K. P. and A. Monteiro. 2003. *Naata: The Bond*. Mumbai: Tata Institute of Social Sciences.

———. 2009. 'Jai Ho Shanghai: The Invisible Poor in *Slumdog Millionnaire*'. In Ashwani Kumar, Jan Aart Scholte, Mary Kaldor, et al. (eds), *Global Civil Society Yearbook*. London: London School of Economics and Sage.

———. 2016. *A Fly in the Curry: Independent Documentary Film in India*. New Delhi: Sage.

Khan, Faiza Ahmed. 2009. *The Supermen of Malegaon*. Seoul: Korean Broadcasting Corporation. Available at https://www.youtube.com/watch?v=dqRq7ZpjF0I (accessed 5 September 2019).

Khan, Waqar. 2002. *Hum Sab Ek Hain*. Mumbai: Waqar Khan.

Krishnan, Jaganathan. 2011. *Videokaaran*. Mumbai: Tata Institute of Social Sciences.

Malu, Preksha. 2015. 'Govandi ka Chokras Present CID', *DNA*, 22 March 2015. Available at http://www.dnaindia.com/mumbai/report-govandi-ka-chokras-present-cid-2071114 (accessed 30 August 2017).

Menon, Meena. 2012. *Riots and After in Mumbai: Chronicles of Truth and Reconciliation*. New Delhi: Sage.

Monteiro, A. and K. P. Jayasankar. 2015a. Interview with Bhau Korde, December 2015.

———. 2015b. Interview with Prathmesh Shivkar, December 2015.

———. 2015c. Interview with Faiza Ahmed Khan, December 2015.

Nichols, Bill. 1991. *Representing Reality: Issues and Concepts in Documentary*. Bloomington: Indiana University Press.

Planning Commission. 2011. *Report of the Working Group on Financing Urban Infrastructure*. New Delhi: Planning Commission.

Rajagopal, Arvind. 2001. *Politics after Television: Hindu Nationalism and the Reshaping of the Public in India*. Cambridge: Cambridge University Press.

Rutherford, Anne. 2011. *What Makes a Film Tick? Cinematic Affect, Materiality and Mimetic Innervation*. Bern: Peter Lang.

Shekhar, Prateek, et al. 2015. *Govandi, Crime Aur Camera*. Mumbai: TISS.

Shivkar, Prathmesh, et al. 2011. *Chamatkari Builder Baba*. Mumbai: Prathmesh Shivkar.

Vasudevan, Ravi. 2002. 'Another History Rises to the Surface: "Hey Ram": Melodrama in the Age of Digital Simulation', *Economic and Political Weekly* 37(28): 2917–25.

Weinstein, Lisa. 2014. *The Durable Slum: Dharavi and the Right to Stay Put in Globalizing Mumbai*. Minneapolis/London: University of Minnesota Press.

'Gauseva' by WhatsApp

Hindu Nationalism and Online Mobilisation*

ABIR DASGUPTA

INTRODUCTION

India's post-liberalisation era has been a period of swift structural change that has produced consequent changes in the modes of engagement of populations with institutions such as political parties, religious organisations and corporations, as well as changes in the functioning of the institutions themselves. In this chapter, I wish to trace the effects of this structural change in the arena that is constituted by the confluence of religion, politics and business. I shall argue that a complex interplay between these domains has emerged, following India's neoliberal turn and entry into the globalisation project, which has produced a discursive terrain marked by the ideologies of gender and sexuality, caste, religion, nation and economy that form the Hindu nationalist project. I shall also argue that the arrival of the Internet, the shape that it has begun to take, and the rapid proliferation of Internet-capable mobile phones has been central to this interplay. Further, I shall explore how the medium effects of this technology constitute an epistemic shift in the relationship of a text to its author, in the structuration of the relationship of the 'user' to the texts, and the socially and spatially situated mobile device itself within ethical

*I would like to thank the anonymous reviewer for their insightful comments. Prajakta Bhave helped with the Marathi translations for this study. The chapter benefited from discussions with Anjali Monteiro, K. P. Jayasankar and Probal Dasgupta. Any omissions and errors are solely mine.

economies of affect and desire. This reconstructed interface, I shall argue, when seen as an assemblage, is dynamic and non-linear in its actualisation and is subject to forces of territorialisation of economies of affect, desire and political vocabulary. This central conclusion, I believe, offers a glimpse into the shape of the terrain of aesthetic politics in today's digital age.

This chapter has evolved from the observation of an online group. I have been a member of this group on the Internet-based mobile messaging platform WhatsApp, for a few months, following the interactions with a group of 'cow protection' activists on the outskirts of Mumbai during a film project. The group was started and is run by a cow protection activist in Ulhasnagar (a satellite township in the northern outskirts of Mumbai), who was my contact during the film shoots and was the one who added me to the group. During conversations with him, I learned that most of the group's 256 members reside in Thane district in the Kalyan and Ulhasnagar *tehsil*s (a district or area that serves as an administrative division). The ostensible purpose of the group is to aid in the distribution and marketing of milk that is produced at several *gaushalas* (literally, cow centres) within the Ulhasnagar *tehsil* area. The activist who runs the WhatsApp group is also a daily manager at one of these *gaushalas*; he manages the distribution of milk, and the ostensible function of the group is to facilitate communication between him and his customers. This function, however, is generally overshadowed by all the other activities that go on in the group. The group serves as a bulletin board for a variety of messages—partisan political propaganda, advertising, religious messages and many others. In fact, overwhelmingly, this propaganda function seems to be the unstated purpose of the group.

For the purposes of my analysis, I have looked at messages posted in the group over a month (October 2016). My study will attempt to marry the methods of critical discourse analysis and media assemblage analysis; however, given the nature of my access and the primary material, it will remain inadequate on some fronts. On the discourse analysis front, I shall proceed along the schematic offered by Fairclough (1989) in seeking to locate the text in the social conditions of its production and its interpretation and consumption. He suggests that one proceed through stages of description of the formal properties of a text, to understanding it as a 'product of a process of production and a resource in a process of interpretation', to seeking to understand the 'social determination of the processes of production and interpretation and their social effects' (Fairclough 1989: 26). While I have a large corpus of texts to examine, my study is not ethnographic, and thus, in attempting to map out subject positions, and affective practices of engagement, consumption and interpretation, I can only remain tentative.

To begin with, I shall attempt an analysis of the text itself. In the period examined, across October 2016, a total of approximately 1,750 messages were posted on the group. That is an average of about 60 messages a day. Of these, nearly 300 were to do with the cow—some were scientific, drawing their legitimacy from discourses of nutrition and animal rearing. Some posts concern milk, some concern questions of breeding. Some others were presented as scientific but are in fact not accepted by the mainstream scientific doctrine, particularly those concerning the medicinal value of cow urine and its various uses. Others still were mythological in their provenance—the cow presented as a divine figure in the Hindu pantheon. And most ominous were those posts concerning incidents where cows were 'rescued', that is, forcibly taken from someone else, often involving considerable levels of violence.

Four hundred odd posts were about politics. Some were specifically about political parties, usually partisan to the Bharatiya Janata Party (BJP), especially vitriolic regarding the Bahujan Samaj Party (BSP), the All India Majlis-e-Ittehadul Muslimeen (AIMIM), and other rival parties. Others served to fill the discursive contours of Brahminical ideologies of the Hindu nation, masculinity, sexuality and caste, as codified by *Sangh Parivar* authors. I offer a few examples here:

IMAGE 3.1: Screengrab of a Hindi WhatsApp Message

हिन्दी के एक महान लेखक हमेशा मिट्टी के कुल्हड़ में चाय पीते थे। एक बार उनके मित्र ने पूछा कि, चीनी मिट्टी का कप इतना खुबसूरत, चिकना और चमकीला होता है। फिर भी तुम इसे छोड़ कर बेडोल, बदसूरत मिट्टी के कुल्हड़ में चाय पीते हो आखिर क्यों। लेखक ने बहुत सुन्दर उत्तर दिया - देखो भाई, कप जो है वह गोरी अंगरेजी मेम है, दिनभर पता नहीं कितनों के होंठों से लगती है, परन्तु कुल्हड़ शुद्ध भारतीय नारी है जो केवल एक की ही हो के रह जाती है।

Source: Anonymous text message to WhatsApp group गौअमृत परिवार, 9 October 2016.

This message,[1] through a short anecdote, neatly sutures together the notions of caste and racial purity that undergirds Brahminical ideology with several active political agendas. First, the Hindu *rashtra* (State)—*Bharatavarsha*—speaks through the voice of a Hindi author. It is quite immaterial to the 'plotline' of the anecdote that the person be identified as a 'Hindi author'. The identification paradigmatically constructs a voice of authority who is (a) an intellectual; and (b) a modern Indian. In Brahminical social ideology, this positions him as an upper-caste man, and in Brahminical national ideology, this positions him as a Hindu.[2] He can, then, in diegesis, speak for the Hindu nation.

His explanation for his preference of the clay mug over the ceramic cup is an articulation of Brahminical ideologies of gender, race, sexuality, power and ownership. The ceramic cup is the deviant other, the white woman who is promiscuous and 'foreign', and therefore, undesirable and an unacceptable model of femininity by simile. For it to touch his lips is a violation of caste purity, and by association, so is the woman with sexual agency. Discursively, his *body* is defiled by the existence of this woman. The clay mug is textually identified as *Bharatiya*—Indian. In translation, I have used the words 'mug' and 'cup' to denote what in the Hindi original is a linguistic difference; the clay vessel is identified by the Hindi word for cup, *kulhad*, whereas the ceramic vessel is identified by the English word 'cup' transliterated into Hindi. This is a nationalist discursive gesture by which the Brahmin's claim to power and ownership over the labour of non-Brahmin working castes in the Hindu *rashtra* is established. Then, by simile, his caste ownership is extended to female sexuality, where the clay *kulhad* is the 'pure *Bharatiya* woman' who belongs to her husband. Clay paradigmatically signifies the earth, and thus, land. Simultaneously, the nation is gendered female, under male ownership, and is rendered Hindu, under Brahminical ownership, and the caste Hindu woman's sexuality is constructed as the repository of its ritual purity.

This model of gendered caste purity under the sexual regime of Brahminism, as explicated by the anecdote, is identified by Chakraborty (1993) as a central ideological pillar essential for the maintenance of ritual purity; and the invocation of the English woman as 'foreign' effects the discursive suturing to the ideologies of nationalism and the modern nation-state, constructed under caste. Further, it is a direct echo of the model of desirable Hindu femininity, as propagated under the ideological framework of Hindu nationalism.

Caste identification also formed a standpoint for political articulation and contestation among the participants in the group. Reflecting the alliances of Maratha and Brahmin groups that form the BJP–Shiv Sena government that was then in power in Maharashtra, were frequent messages representing the group interests of Marathi-speaking Brahmins and Marathas (and other dominant castes). Both positioned the Dalit movement in Maharashtra as the competing interest.

One example was a blog post that accused Maratha leaders of continuously invoking Shivaji and never Savarkar or Tilak, attributed to a Marathi-Brahmin author who detects a conspiracy to marginalise the historically significant Maharashtrian Brahmins. It asks other Brahmins that when 'they' (Dalits are rarely named explicitly in such posts, and are usually referred to by euphemism or an indirect gesture) have gotten politicians to pay attention to their heroes, why can't Brahmins do the same?

IMAGE 3.2: Screengrab of a Marathi WhatsApp Message

मराठी आमदार वा खासदाराकडून वा पक्षाकडून आपल्या जवानाना एकाही पैशाची मदत नाही....असे हे देशभक्त मग कसा देश सुधारणार, आता लोकानीच संघटीत होऊन जवानाना मदत केली पाहिजे. सैराट पिक्चर एक आठवड्यात करोडो रूपये कमावतो पण जवानाना मदत करण्यास पैसे नाहीत.☺☺

Source: Anonymous text message to WhatsApp group गौअमृत परिवार, 20 September 2016.

This is a message,[3] which accuses Marathi leaders of failing to spend any money on the welfare of 'soldiers dying at the border', compared unfavourably to the film *Sairat*[4] making many crores in a week.

Such messages serve two significant ideological operations of the Hindu *rashtra* movement. First, the revision of history to construct a teleology of Brahmin nationhood and a 'Hindu' history for the modern Indian nation, in line with the Orientalist historiographical narrative of a subcontinent under historical siege by foreign invaders. Second, following the first, is the construction of the 'defence' of the nation in terms of protection of its caste purity and according it primacy through the construction of a 'national' politics. Offering *Sairat*, an anti-caste film, and Shivaji, a non-Brahmin ruler, as counter-examples in both cases serves to emphasise the apparent 'deviation' of public interest from the discourse about protection of national Hindu caste purity.

About 200 odd posts were religious. These consisted of a variety of different religious messages. Some were notifications of events— *yagna*s (a ritual sacrifice in Hinduism), *havan*s (a ritual burning of offerings in Hinduism) and various other local events that were being organised by religious bodies. Some were quotations from texts or utterances by various *guru*s (spiritual leaders). Many were of the nature of religious 'news' or information—that a certain festival was coming up, or that a certain astrological alignment was imminent and that specific actions needed to be taken—certain kinds of food not to be consumed, certain kinds of activities not to be indulged in. Several were akin to religious sermons—discourses on morality and ethics that were situated in the scriptural canon that is constructed as the *varnashrama dharma* (a modern name given to a set of scriptures and practices collectively termed 'Hinduism'; often used as a more accurate substitute for the term 'Hinduism'). Many were simply greetings on different festivals. Some were even greetings that said 'Good Morning' in imagery laced with religious iconography.

Many posts which I call 'religious' were about the cow, the '*gaumata*' ('cow mother'). In fact, *gai*, the literal translation of the word 'cow', was almost never used; the animal, when referred to, was necessarily in the gendered religious honorific form. Some extolled the virtues of the cow's manure and urine and their apparent medicinal and agricultural uses. Others were concerned with the cow's sacral position, a frequent reference being to the fact that the cow was equivalent to a Brahmin in ritual purity.

Another type of *gaumata*-related material was not explicatory, or dialectic; rather, these were messages concerning and often images of the *gaushala* economy from across the state and other regions. It is relevant here to attempt a brief sketch of the political economy of *gauseva* (service of cows as a religious duty) in Ulhasnagar. There are five major *gaushala*s in Ulhasnagar, each of which has a similar administrative structure. They are run by trusts, which are controlled and funded largely by religious bodies and private individuals. Of the five *gaushalas*, two are run by Sikh Gurdwaras, one by a Jain temple, and two by Hindu Vaishnavite temples. These trusts are eligible for government aid via several national and state-level schemes under grants for agricultural development and are granted significant tax breaks and various other forms of State patronage. The financial strength necessary to run such operations—two of the *gaushalas* house more than a 1,000 animals each—is made possible by a confluence of the spheres of economy and religion. Ulhasnagar is a major tourist spot precisely for these large religious organisations. During my visits there, I spent time at one of these *Gurdwaras* (place of worship for Sikhs), which has thousands of visitors every day, with images of the *Sant* (literally, a saint) occupying large portions of billboard real estate on the entire route from the railway station to the complex. The other draw for these religious tourists is the presence of a large religious market in the town, one that is financially linked back to the same temples. These religious trusts are also beneficiaries of largesse from the thriving local business community.

Given the large-scale organisational task that the management of such levels of human traffic is, this entire ecosystem solicits and enjoys active political patronage. It maintains links with the local units of the Bajrang Dal and the Rashtriya Swayamsevak Sangh (RSS), as well as the Shiv Sena, and political cadre offer their services to visitors to ease their traversal of the circuits of religious bureaucracy in order to meet the priest that they wish to meet. Political cadre are also involved actively in the practice of *gauseva*, quite literally, in that they maintain surveillance regimes over the local population, on the lookout for people who dare to transgress the laws of a cow-worshipping land.[5]

Specific positions taken by the BJP regarding issues that were in the news were prominent in many posts. A theme that is continuous is opposition to China. 'Good Indian nationalist citizens' are encouraged to not buy Chinese-made products or products from Chinese-owned companies. China was mentioned in nearly 100 posts. Another theme is the centrality of Pakistan as a metonym for all that is morally reprehensible and of a China–Pakistan anti-India conspiracy. A very common trope was the army, invoked in over 200 posts. At that time, these themes were frequently part of the daily news cycle and subjects of reference by prominent BJP leaders. Frequently, messages on such themes would appear shortly after they had been addressed by a major leader, on social media or on a national media platform, appearing to reinforce in real time the idea being propagated.

About 150 posts were advertisements. Significantly, 110 were advertisements for programmes conducted by Art of Living, and for products sold by Patanjali. I shall explain shortly the reason why I point out these two groups. Other kinds of advertisements included those for health services that populate the Hindu religious ecosystem, such as medicinal uses of cow urine. The group also hosted a lot of news, both local and national, much of it from unreliable sources, and often known to be fake. Nearly 200 news items were posted on the group in a month. Some obviously fake stories were often immediately pointed out to be fake by other users, and the person sharing it was chided for propagating false news. Further, there was a fair amount of discussion; I counted nearly 500 posts that were part of conversations and were not forwarded messages. These were people who were likely strangers, or at best, casual acquaintances engaging in frequent political conversation. What was missing, however, unlike typical political platforms, were efforts at organising or mobilising members of the group towards specific tasks or actions.

As I have described, the texts divide themselves into various categories. There are certain obvious observations that can be made. As heteronormative and Brahminical in their construction, and unapologetically so, they clearly stand for and offer a conservative and status-quo-ist generative subject position to the reader. In the obsession with cows, they represent discourses that are prevalent only among certain caste groups in India; Ambedkar has described cow worship as a typically symbolic marker for upper-casteness. Historically, mobilising cow worship has been a project associated with upper-caste nationalism; while connections to the Sangh Parivar are ever-present, cow nationalism has never been restricted to the 'Hindutva' voices, and has been frequently patronised by Brahmin nationalist parties of every political hue. These organisations and platforms devoted to 'cow protection' have served as conduits for expression of several other central Brahmin nationalist agendas—the promotion of Hindi as a 'national' language, for instance. A wonderfully detailed exploration of the historical trajectories of such movements, specifically through the use of the press and the production of political texts to be read alongside religious texts, is offered by Mukul (2015).

The Sangh association, in fact, has not always meant electoral votes for the Sangh's political outfits, whether the Jana Sangh or the BJP.

This is where, however, what is significant to me is not merely the obviously political nature of the text. What I wish to point to is the mode of its reception, and the mode of its address. WhatsApp is a social media application that is characteristic of a new mode of engagement with media, and indeed one that implies a restructuring of the field of discourse itself. This group presents both as a bulletin board and as an *adda* (a place where people gather for conversation), a platform and space for discussion. In the present social media form of the Internet, the modes of proliferation of the word and the image have given them a new epistemic position. These texts, thus, aside from their ideological operations, present as 'utterances', or speech acts, affective in nature and constituting a milieu. However, I contend, the position of the author or the speaker, and its affective significance, distinguish the social media form of the Internet from Habermas' public sphere. Previous hierarchies and economies of legitimacy are now being subverted, with the dissociation of an image or a text from its author. Where Benjamin (1968 [1936]) notes that the age of mechanical reproduction 'abstracts' the likeness of an object via its image, the digital age seems to abstract the contents of an image or text from its source. Davis (1995) writes, 'there is no longer a clear conceptual distinction between an original and a reproduction in the virtual medium. The notions of distinct pure/original and impure/imitative states are "fictions". Images, words and sounds are received, deconstructed, rearranged and restored wherever they are seen, heard and stored' (1995: 381–86). Further, as Dede (2008) notes, 'the implications of Web 2.0 go much deeper: the tacit epistemologies that underlie its activities differ dramatically from .... "Classical knowledge"' in which the legitimacy of knowledge is derived from its adherence to a 'scientific' process of determination and its position in a universally acknowledged store of the products of such 'scientific' process (2008: 80).

As he writes, 'in contrast, the Web 2.0 definition of "knowledge" is collective agreement about a description that may combine facts with other dimensions of human experience, such as opinions, values, and spiritual beliefs' (Dede 2008: 80). In this context, the material in the group arrives to its reader shorn of its authorship, and thus, of its relational agenda, and as a bearer of legitimacy granted by its presence in the consensus group.

The reader, meanwhile, as a user of WhatsApp and an individual with an online footprint, more generally, is the occupant of a historically unprecedented position. They are the recipient and audience of a sequence of texts, as is the radio or TV audience; however, the sequencing is unstructured and participatory. Thus, even when the texts resemble recognisable forms, such as advertisements or political propaganda, they arrive as messages from their immediate social relations through the intimacy of their cell phone from personal mobile numbers, which distinguish them from texts created by institutions like television studios or advertising firms, even if their origin lay in such a source.

As de Mul (2009) writes, the fundamental characteristic of the computer as a medium is the constitution of a 'database ontology' (2009: 95). He argues that with the proliferation of database technologies based on relational models into virtually every computing system and task, databases function as 'material and conceptual metaphors' structuring our understandings and making everything—nature and culture alike—objects for recombination and manipulation (ibid.). With the abstraction of one's tastes and interests into quantifiable data points that are assimilable into a database ontology, as a user of the Internet, one is subject to regimes of surveillance and governance previously unimagined.

I argue that this characteristic of social mediatised communication has facilitated a specific confluence of systems of religion, politics and business to produce the discursive formation evidenced in the group. Nanda (2011) traces the formation of what she calls a State–Temple–Corporate Complex, in which the neoliberal forms of the State and the economy facilitate a modernised free market form of religion. Her argument is that religion is now increasingly resembling corporate forms of business, and in neoliberal India, it is granted State patronage and hand-holding, much as all other business is. She notes how central to the State–Temple–Corporate Complex's messaging is the co-option of discourses of 'modernity' by religion—in presenting itself as 'scientific' and creating knowledge-producing systems—UGC certified deemed universities, in fact!—towards the production of such material. One post perfectly characterises this tendency. This post claims that French and American researchers have shown that there is medicinal value in the practice of *havan*, and offers a lengthy essay steeped in scientific-sounding jargon on the subject. Nanda also notes the co-option of corporate methods of business by religion, particularly among cults of faith surrounding new-age capitalist religious entrepreneurs like Art of Living's Sri Sri and Patanjali's Baba Ramdev.

Ullekh (2014) describes the construction of data-driven political technology for the BJP's 2014 general election campaign, a strategy that is unprecedented in India and constitutes a new way of doing politics. He describes the BJP's strategy of employing advertising and data analysis professionals to choose groups and target messaging and propaganda to those groups to produce favourable electoral outcomes. This task of analysis and targeting is made possible by the same abstracting process that produces the epistemologies of Web 2.0. While much of this is built on automated and algorithmic processes, it also has a large human component. Today's tech-enabled Hindutva cadre base maintains a nationwide continuous coordinated flood of online messaging—texts of all forms serving a variety of propaganda and marketing purposes. In the specific local interface of the State–Temple–Corporate, and I would add Politics–Complex, what is produced, is this WhatsApp group.

The origins of the messages in the group lie in various systems of textual production. Some, no doubt, originate in formations like the BJP campaign war room. Others originate in corporate advertising systems of organisations like Art of Living and Patanjali. Others originate in the adaptation of the temple–*gauseva* system, a pre-existing form of political and religious mobilisation and identity expression for multiple Indian groups—to digital modes of communication. Together they represent a combination of the State–Temple–Corporate Complex with a Web 2.0 version of political communication.

At this stage, I am conscious that this chapter is faithful to a long tradition of scholarly scaremongering with regard to the invention and proliferation of a new media technology. History and current scholarship lay bare the problems with Adorno associating the rise of Fascism in Europe with the rising popularity of film. It is thus necessary for me to add a qualifying disclaimer: the observations presented here are not to suggest a causal and deterministic relation between the increasing normalisation of our mobile phone-centric data-driven lives and the rise of the Sangh to political power; rather, it is to offer a snapshot of the systems that have produced this moment, and to note its formal characteristics.

Political propaganda is not a new phenomenon. A quite similar clustering of Hindutva messaging, religious material and advertising has been available for more than a century in a range of sources and continues to be so. What is new is the compression of time and space that the neoliberal order heralds and the solidification of the boundary between a text and its author. In the spaces that are produced by this new structural condition, the force of an argument is self-inscribed in its presence in the space, rather than by its association to a specific actor.

A structural condition may be generative of political reality; however, to suggest that it is determinative is to deny the originality of human action and ahistoricise the specificities of power relations in local contexts. The group that has been the focus of my study is run for and by a specific community with a documented history and position within the local power dynamic, which I shall attempt to trace here.

Originally built as the Kalyan Military Transit Camp during the Second World War, the Ulhasnagar area was deployed as a refugee resettlement colony for refugees from Sindh, following Partition. The descendants of these Sindhi refugees continue to lay a claim to ownership of the city. A standing demand has been, for example, that the town be renamed Sindhunagar. It is largely this Sindhi community that dominates the political economy of the area. The town is an established production and trading centre. It hosts a large garment industry that serves both internal and export markets and is seen as something of a 'counterfeiters' paradise' (Kuber 2007). It is also a significant trading point for furniture and electronics, and hosts a large 'wedding market', a term that encompasses not only an actual wedding market, but also a large all-purpose religious market.

From as early as the 1960s, Ulhasnagar has been witness to a thriving unplanned and largely unregulated construction and real estate market as a consequence of the general trend of outward migration from Bombay city to the greater metropolitan region (Bhide

2014). Its population has also grown and diversified considerably; while the Sindhi community is still the single largest group at close to 40 per cent, there are significant minority Maharashtrian and Gujarati sections. As per the 2011 Census data, the Scheduled Caste population is about 17 per cent of the total 5 lakh (Census of India 2011). Here, in the absence of better data, particularly of the information collected in the 2011 Census regarding caste identity that the Government of India has chosen not to release, I am forced to extrapolate from inadequate information, and rely on circumstantial evidence. The Sindhi community's dominance over the political economy is iconicised in the textual construction of the town. One of only 10 cities in India to have an active Sindhi newspaper market, Ulhasnagar is among the larger in population, counting alongside cities like Ahmedabad, Jaipur and Ajmer.

Most narratives of the city, whether in sources such as tourist guides or official government reports, refer to the Sindhi community as central to the city's identity. There exist multiple online portals and Facebook pages, which refer to the city as Ulhasnagar and Sindhunagar interchangeably. A common joke in Bombay—one that still proliferates—is the phrase 'Made in USA' where USA refers to the Ulhasnagar Sindhi Association—the implication being that the product being referred to originates in the premium brand counterfeiting operations run by the Sindhi business community in Ulhasnagar.

Another marker that comes to one's attention is the political history of the town. Ulhasnagar is a characteristic example of the dialectical interaction of the State and politics that produces localised political dynasties across similar peri-urban and suburban parts of India, as described by Chandra (2016). Chandra's argument is twofold. First, he argues that the State, in its role as a gatekeeper of access to land, credit and resources, offers incentives to State officials, who gain returns in the forms of corruption, preferential treatment in allotments of credit, speedy processing of regulatory clearances, political protection, favourable treatment by the law and order machinery, and in multiple other ways. He argues that this form of political privilege is highly sought after by those already well placed—frequently rich businesspersons who feel the need for this level of access and power simply to maintain their estates and operations, which they run as virtual fiefdoms. Second, he argues, that the structures of party organisation encourage the granting of seats to family members of local political leaders, going to the extent of creating posts for them. Local political dynasties, he argues, often substitute for a local party organisation, across parties of all organisational and ideological categories, serving as an instrument of stability in protecting against defections and as a predictable mechanism for governance of party work at the local level.

Ulhasnagar has been treated as a personal fiefdom by one such dynastic family for close to three decades now. Suresh Kalani, its former Member of the Legislative Assembly (MLA), was the nephew of a local Congress leader and businessman, who was first voted to power in 1986. Since that time, he joined the Nationalist Congress Party (NCP) when it split from the Congress; and when leaving it, his wife Jyoti Kalani took over in his place at the NCP. He himself has joined the Ramdas Athavale-led faction of the Republican Party of India (RPI), which is an alliance partner in the National Democratic Alliance (NDA) government. His son, Omi Kalani, is also a prominent leader in the city and is increasingly being reported as a significant power centre in future elections. Between husband and wife, they have held the Ulhasnagar MLA seat from 1990 onwards, interrupted only by one BJP term. That BJP term, however, is significant. It was in the 2009 election, and the seat swung narrowly back to the NCP by a mere 2000 votes in 2014, despite a state-wide swing towards the BJP and the Shiv Sena. One can fairly safely assume that it is likely that the state and local BJP and associated organisations see this as a seat that can be won, particularly given the trends across Maharashtra in the 2014 elections and in subsequent political developments in the state.

A post-election survey conducted by the Lokniti-Centre for the Study of Developing Societies (CSDS) found that there had been a considerable swing among Maratha, and Kunbi and some Other Backward Classes (OBC) voters away from the NCP and in favour of the Shiv Sena and the BJP, respectively (Lokniti-CSDS 2014). Interestingly, the same survey also found that 84.6 per cent of the respondents claimed to receive political messages and news through WhatsApp, although the figure for mobile Internet usage in Maharashtra stood at 33.67 per cent just the year before (Bhattacharya 2013).[6] The discrepancy can be attributed variously to biases in the construction of the survey sample; however, the network effects of socially embedded mobile users cannot be neglected.

As Rai (2012) writes in a detailed ethnographic study on mobile phone use in urban and suburban India, the relationship with the Internet-enabled mobile phone in families, classrooms, workplaces, and other social and peer networks must be understood in the terms of media assemblage analysis, which takes into account the 'historically variable and also dynamically open forces, senses, and values' that have produced a variety of new communicative and media technologies and practices (2012: n.p.). He continues,

> [t]his is a nonlinear process that diverges without resembling, because the divergences are qualitative shifts in intensity and capacities. Because of this variability and openness to change and territorialisation, we must situate mobile telephony within a framework that can account for the temporality, intensity, and virtuality of ecologies of sensation. In this ontology, concepts are defined not linguistically but as the structure of a space of possibilities. Multiplicious ecologies, then, are virtual, that is, real but not actual, and capable of divergent actualization (2012: n.p.).

According to the Lokniti-CSDS survey, close to half the respondents read or disseminated political messages on WhatsApp daily or several times a week. Much of this engagement would have been on groups such as the subject of this study—constituted within a specific context of community and political relations, representing socially determined clusters within networks. For the protagonists of this engagement, the act of 'WhatsApping' is simultaneously dialectical and ethical, as it straddles the interface of the social and individual frames of reference with the affective character of mobile phone technology in the ecological and pragmatic contexts of its use. Rai collectively names such practices *jugaad* and notes the need for an epistemological perspective that shifts from representation to 'a thorough-going pragmatism of knowledge or ethical know-how .... [which] demands embodied experimentation with perception, sensation, matter, value, and force .... overturn[ing] the domination of a rarefied and abstract rationality' (2012: n.p.).

Rai is channelling Felix Guattari in his arguments, developing his call for a 'reconstruction of social and individual practices' as a force against 'technologies of socio-machinic reification' (2012:

n.p.). However, it is to another strand in Guattari's work, specifically the discussion on fascism and micropolitics with Giles Deleuze in *Anti-Oedipus* (2004) that I find these arguments leading me. For our protagonists on the WhatsApp group, the mobile phone has 'potentialised media habituation itself', according to Rai (2012: n.p.). My claim is that through their political engagements on this and other groups, what is being developed is a vocabulary and ethics of politics that crosses the boundary of discourse to enter into the economies of desire and affect. My intention is to recall Deleuze and Guattari's characterisation of fascism as a confluence of a multiplicity of practices developed in varying assemblages being subjected to a movement of territorialisation of the economies of desire and affect. In the milieu of utterances that such a WhatsApp group forms, what is achieved is a discursive territorialisation of affect. In database ontology, the mobile phone 'notifies' the user upon the receipt of each message. This moment, marked visually and aurally by the device's interface, constitutes an affective demand, which is resolved by the reading of the text, the reception of the utterance. The frequency, and the consistency and range, constitute a territorialisation in normalising and habituating the recipient to the interpretive, paradigmatic and moral stances of the Hindu *rashtra* ideology.

It is my claim that in the taxonomies that are invoked in the kinds of messages posted on this group, there is a specific version of such a force of territorialisation at work.[7] Further, such a territorialisation is always implicit in the structuring of political dialectics into a form of media habituation via such WhatsApp groups, whether of a Hindutva character or of a competing political group. The ideological and discursive strands that constitute the contents of the territorialisation in specific contexts are socio-historically determined and subject to the structural and affective effects of the neoliberal economy and polity.

With this, I have all the pieces of my argument. Nanda's State–Temple–Corporate complex in Ulhasnagar is run by dominant groups, which, given the historic, political and caste composition of the region, are likely produced in the flows of interaction between the dominant Maratha and Sindhi upper-caste communities. These groups control large segments of the local economy, and as a result, most of the remaining population is feudally beholden to them, in the standard manner of assimilation of Indian caste society with neoliberal globalisation. While Ulhasnagar has not been a BJP seat generally, this ideological and material composition of the community that it presents is potentially ripe for cementing a permanent 'safe' seat in the Vidhan Sabha, and for reaping the benefits of control over a well-located and networked urban centre with a high literacy rate and nearly 40 per cent unemployment, from which to recruit cadre and conduct wider operations. Within the BJP's immediate political calculus in Maharashtra, particularly in its various recent confrontations with the Shiv Sena, such an operation to flip the seat makes imminent sense.

To me, this group is evidence that these processes have produced a multiplicity of overlapping virtual networks, which may potentially map significant sections of the area and its population. Within these networks, flows an hourly stream of propaganda and political discussion created and disseminated due to the professionalisation of politics, which normalises to the point of banality the vocabularies of Hindutva and reactionary upper-caste nationalist politics. The effectiveness—the 'stickiness' so to speak—of this mechanism is in its dynamic effects on the emerging modes of communicative and media technology and practices.

In conclusion, I turn to tentatively attempt to articulate how the implications of this condition on progressive politics may be imagined. Of particular note is the readily available analogy between this mechanism and the regimes that govern the interface of human agency and embodied subjectivity, with the socially produced assemblages of practices regarding food, marriage, worship, kinship, habitation and sex, which constitute the ideological, ethical and pragmatic contours of the caste-d self. Caste produces vocabularies of politics in much the same way.

At this moment, it is increasingly impossible to hold on to Habermas's rational public sphere. As politics is re-aestheticised, as another fold of the ethical self is opened up to regulation, as the position of the text shifts further from its author and it is mobilised in an act of instantaneous re-constitution, each strand seems to be an irreversible emergent current. Guattari and Deleuze saw in capitalism a refuge from fascism, a free market in the economies of desire, institutionally protected from conquest by the mechanics of competition. This is one of their conclusions that lends itself more readily to questioning. One cannot, first, easily discard the classic fascist threat already contained within the institutions of the neoliberal political economy of the rise of the singular bigot strongman, as the past few years have so amply demonstrated. More broadly, in the context of fascism, as I have sought to describe it, as the neoliberal simulacrum simultaneously atomises and segregates, it also constructs diffuse, decentralised and divergently unpredictable localised micro-political regimes of affect, desire and vocabulary.

What is left to be clarified is that the centring of the contents of the texts in this study leaves gaps in the understanding of the affective political potential of such groups and content. Ethnographic engagements would enrich such an understanding. Further, to place this study in its proper context would mean an analytic sociological and economic study of the population represented in the group and the co-located populations that are not represented in it. I have attempted this only descriptively through secondary sources and it calls for further research.

NOTES

1. A great Hindi author used to drink his tea out of clay mugs. Once he was asked by a friend, 'When ceramic cups are so smooth, shiny and beautiful, why do you choose to drink from cups made of ugly shapeless clay?' The author responded, 'The cup is like a fair English lady, it touches many different lips every day, but the clay mug is like the pure "*Bharatiya*" woman who remains her husband's throughout her life' (translation mine).

2. Mukul (2015) traces the historical association of the movement for Hindi as a 'national' language and the upper caste 'Hindu' nationalist movements of central and north India.

3. There is not a penny's help to the soldiers from Marathi MPs and MLAs and political parties. If the patriots/nationalists of the country are like this then how will the nation would improve? So, now only people should collectivise and help the soldiers. Sairat movie earns crores in a week and there is no money to help the soldiers (translation by Prajakta Bhave).

4. *Sairat* (2016) is a Marathi feature film directed by Nagraj Manjule, which depicted an inter-caste marriage against social sanction and the resulting caste violence. The film—directed by a Dalit director, and self-consciously located in the anti-caste Ambedkarite tradition—earned

critical acclaim and viewership across the country, a feat not frequently achieved by 'regional' (non-Hindi) language cinema in India.

5. These facts are taken from interviews I conducted with cow protection activists during the shooting of a film in September 2016.

6. The figure for mobile usage stood at much higher at around 85 per cent. In Ulhasnagar, specifically, it was 65 per cent, as per the Telecom Regulatory Authority of India data.

7. A clarificatory note on my use of the notion of 'territory' is warranted here. I mean by it a particular constellation of affect, networking and ethical action in virtual space with constitutive references to the body. The currents which produce such an actualisation range from the locally specific to the larger discursive terrains of the nation and operate across time and space. In the context of this group, these currents draw from specific religious, political and ideological canons, and are constructed by the localised political economy in which its members are embedded.

REFERENCES

Benjamin, Walter. 1968 [1936]. 'The Work of Art in the Age of Mechanical Reproduction'. In *Illuminations*. New York: Schocken Books.

Bhattacharya, Suparna Goswami, 'Karnataka Records Lowest Mobile Users', *DNA*, 24 September 2013.

Bhide, Amita. 2014. *The City Produced: Urban Development, Violence and Spatial Justice in Mumbai*. Mumbai: Tata Institute of Social Sciences.

Census of India. 2011. *District Census Handbook Thane: Village and Town Wise Primary Census Abstract*. Maharashtra: Directorate of Census Operations.

Chakraborty, Uma. 1993. 'Conceptualising Brahminical Patriarchy in Early India: Gender, Caste, Class and State', *Economic and Political Weekly* 28(14): 579–85.

Chandra, Kanchan (ed.). 2016. *Democratic Dynasties: State, Party and Family in Contemporary Indian Politics*. New Delhi: Cambridge University Press.

Davis, Douglas. 1995. 'The Work of Art in the Age of Digital Reproduction (An Evolving Thesis: 1991–1995)', *Leonardo* 28(5): 381–86.

Dede, Chris. 2008. 'A Seismic Shift in Epistemology', *EDUCAUSE* 43(3): 80.

Deleuze, Gilles. 2004. *Anti-Oedipus: Capitalism and Schizophrenia*. London: A & C Black.

De Mul, Jos. 2009. 'The Work of Art in the Age of Digital Recombination', *Digital Material*, p. 95. Amsterdam: Amsterdam University Press.

Fairclough, Norman. 1989. *Language and Power*. London: Longman.

Kuber, Girish, 'Pappu's Ulhasnagar Gambit May Backfire', *Economic Times*, 9 Jaunary 2007.

Lokniti-CSDS. 2014. 'Maharashtra Postpoll 2014 Assembly Election: Survey Findings'. Available at http://www.lokniti.org/pdf/ Maharashtra%20Postpoll%202014%20Assembly%20Election-Survey%20Findings.pdf (accessed 6 December 2017).

Mukul, Akshaya. 2015. *Gita Press and the Making of Hindu India*. New Delhi: HarperCollins Publishers.

Nanda, Meera. 2011. *The God Market: How Globalization is Making India More Hindu*. New York: NYU Press.

Ullekh, N. P. 2014. *War Room: The People, Tactics and Technology behind Narendra Modi's 2014 Win*. New Delhi: Roli Books.

Rai, Amit S. 2012. 'On the Jugaad Image: Embodying the Mobile Phone in India', *Postmodern Culture* 23(1): n.p.

Registrar of Newspapers for India. Available athttp://rni.nic.in/ registerdtitle_search/registeredtitle_ser.aspx (accessed 12 September 2019).

Film Cited

Sairat. 2016. Nagraj Manjule (dir.). Essel Vision Produtions; Aatpat Production.

four

Whose Free Wi-Fi is it Anyway?

Politics of Online Access and the Rise of Digital Populism in Urban India

Aasim Khan and Faiz Ullah

Introduction

In recent years, there have been consistent interactions between scholarship on democratic reforms and the nature of technological changes represented by the growth of Internet-based services cutting across theories and fields. Hacker and Van Dijk (2000) have shown that the concept of digital democracy is indicative of a range of issues, while scholars interested in labour politics as well as those interested in the sociology of Information and Communication Technology (ICT)-driven changes have brought together a mutually shared research and advocacy agenda (Hübler and Hartje 2015). There is also a growing recognition of access as being about more than just information technology, and theories of 'information society' (Castells 1999; Hamelink 2003; Sassen 2001) have underlined that the sociology of technological advance has implications for the enrichment of citizenship and communication rights, in particular.

However, there is also scope to combine these perspectives with critical theory, and in this chapter, we seek to review the emerging discourse on technology in urban India and explore the phenomenon we identify as 'digital populism', with the promise of 'free Wi-Fi' being a defining aspect that we scrutinise. We think of digital populism as a mode of *anti-politics*, which claims for itself a certain newness, direct access to people, and a moral purpose. Following from the debates about populism being a form of politics that focuses on 'the people' (Roberts 2006), one finds an interesting conundrum where we encounter 'free' access being used as a please-all agenda in largely metropolitan urban settings in a country like India. Free online access should not be an obvious reality; after all there are perhaps broader audiences who fit the image of 'the people' that populist leaders can engage with. And yet, urban Indian today is rife with political groups, both communal Right-wing as well as more post-modern stripes, advocating 'free Wi-Fi', and explicating Internet users as 'the people' for whom having access is paramount.

We think it is important to understand and situate this emerging trend within the wider rubric of contemporary populism, which increasingly relies on new media and online networks to bypass traditional institutions of governance, especially in countries witnessing rapid urbanisation and ascendant neoliberalism. For instance, in Turkey, 'digital populism' seems to capture this turn towards new media among those seeking to evade conventional institutions of governance and accountability (Bulut and Yoruk 2017). While the issue of online access itself is not always considered central—Bulut and Yoruk, for instance, highlight the use of 'trolls' online—we think that before the content of such media is evaluated, it is important to map the underlying political economy that has fuelled the surge in calls for promoting 'free' access, and unpack the political logics that make it so central to contemporary populism.

In India, online access has already drawn a high degree of political attention, particularly when we look at contentious debates—from Internet governance to network neutrality. Public provision of Internet access has also emerged as one such issue, with political leaders and policymakers debating the promise and impact of online connectivity (Rakesh 2016). However, besides the legal and economic aspects, in this chapter, we are primarily concerned with the slippery terrain of *ideas*, over which the populist projects of free access are constructed. While there is a significant relationship that 'neo-populism' has with mass media access (Mazzoleni 2003), such questions have remained largely under explored till now.

With our mutual interest in the emerging discussions on democratic participation, we have also been interested and, to a certain degree, sceptical of the ways in which the discourse on access is advanced aggressively as a please-all 'free Wi-Fi' solution for all the problems of 'the common people'. We wish to unpack the discourse on what many marketing campaigns like to call 'unlimited Internet', and conceptualise the ways in which it is reconfiguring notions of citizenship and communication rights in urban India.

We chose this particular technology not because of its technical uniqueness; Wi-Fi, or 'Wireless Fidelity', is, after all, just one set of emerging technology standards promoted by the Institute of Electrical and Electronics Engineers (IEEE) since the late 1990s (IEEE website). Rather, it is because we see it as part of a public discourse that has gained tremendous political significance. We are keen to explore why successive governments that are laying out grand blueprints for bringing public services online—the latest is looking to make Digital India a flagship scheme—are so keen to promote 'free' access as the principal basis for building a pervasive media infrastructure (Digital India Programme, Government of India). Somewhere, we suspect that 'free Wi-Fi' has become a metaphor of the rising current of media populism in our country too, and we want to analyse these discourse(s). This is because it can help us rethink the concept (populism) within a specific policy context of the rapid digitalisation of urban India's public sphere.

Hence, rather than struggle with contested and historical conceptions of populism, in this article, we map the recent origins and trajectory of a particular ideal, one that places 'free' access at the centre of the public agenda. We seek to conceptualise the range of claims around it to evaluate how such conceptions let down genuine engagement and politics, be it in the realm of urban governance, labour in the city or citizens' communication rights, instead promising 'the people' an idyllic zone of uninterrupted online connectivity.

FROM A GLOBAL VILLAGE TO WI-FI IN THE CITY: AN IDEATIONAL HISTORY OF ACCESS

Ideas about online access can increasingly be observed to be at the heart of contemporary urban politics. Universal access to Internet connectivity and public Internet hotspots in cities has emerged as a lively domain of politics around the world. To be sure, we do not think such ideas and debates are entirely new; such notions have been around for as long as there have been technologies making communication possible between individuals and communities. In a previous era, for instance, the rise of outer space-based telecommunication and direct satellite broadcasting was seen to be holding a similar promise of economic and social development, premised on the idea that new applications would amend the fault lines dividing societies. ICT for Development (popularly known as ICT4D) projects, in a similar vein, have also been routinely designed and employed in largely rural and semi-rural contexts to bring marginalised rural communities to participate in various governance processes as well as the marketplace (McNamara 2003; Parthasarathy et al. 2005).

Satellite television experiments in the 1970s were carried out with the stated aim of transforming the 'underdeveloped' rural societies, besieged by poverty and beholden to 'tradition', into a developed and modern nation through education, technical training and fostering a scientific attitude among the people or audience (Monteiro 1998). While the impulse of using ICT4D still lurks in the policy domains, in the more recent years, urban clusters rather than rural, and 'far-off' places, have appeared more frequently in the discourse of 'access', indicating that there is an active shift in the underlying logic of connectivity and access. The ideas and political logic behind using technology to solve structural problems have driven this change over the last few decades, and it is important to understand the ways in which these ideas have emerged and evolved over time.

In the previous era, it could be argued that 'the key policy instrument', as observed by Saith and Vijayabaskar, 'becomes how to link, say, poor rural people to ICTs, not directly to land, nor directly to employment; access to ICTs is implicitly assumed to enable access to sustainable livelihoods' (2008: 27). But gradually, we move to a particular strand of discourse, which returns to the promise of urban settlements as the site for economic and even civilisation renewal. In a previous era, the 1960s, when powerful radio transmitters emerged, and satellite-based technologies came to dominate broadcasting, professional futurists like Arthur C. Clark advised governments that the transcontinental flow of information would obviate the need to live in the cities altogether. Marshall McLuhan similarly argued that any place in the world will be equidistant from anywhere else, and all sense of distinct places will shrink into a single harmonious space of the 'global village'.[1]

Traditional social scientific analysis of the 'Internet in India' has also been framed often within the parameters of 'national development', where technological change is placed largely within the context of the development of the mediatic infrastructure rather than in alignment with the broader current of social and economic transformations marked by the country's rapid urbanisation (Bhatnagar and Shware 2000; Singhal and Rogers 2000). In contrast to these frames wherein technological change was seemingly making either the urban entirely irrelevant or emerging as an extension of media-based nation-building, we notice that in the more recent years, in the context of providing access to the Internet, it is the city that is often the centre of attention in policy statements.

In fact, the idea of 'smart' technologies building a 'smart planet', marketed heavily in the 2000s by the Information Technology (IT) consultancies like International Business Machines (IBM), has gradually given way to an alternative ideal of the 'smart city', which shows the significance of the urban in the political imagination that relates the Internet to society (Smart Cities Mission, Government of India). We consider the current discourse on online access as a lens to analyse the underlying politics of citizen rights in India and explore how competing visions and ideas have led to competitive populist framing in terms of free Wi-Fi rather than a constitutionally recognised 'right to communicate' framework.

Before we begin, it is important to clarify that while we see the city as a site of active contestation and discursive politics, by no means do we argue that this might be the only way to think about links between technology and democracy. Also, we very much hope that this line of thinking would enable the opening of the debate on the growing significance of 'place', rather than an imagined seamless and featureless 'global village', which has become so relevant, again. We look forward to taking our analytical frame to, say, a state like Bihar, which remains largely rural, but has recently seen attempts to introduce online networks in its main cities (Indo-Asian News Service, *Hindustan Times* 2017). In order to consider how populist frames of free Wi-Fi provide a lens to understand the tectonic shifts in its politics, we shall briefly discuss the theoretical framework, which, we think, can be used to unpack the discourse on access in urban India.

Reframing Access: Three Iterations of Citizens' Rights to the Internet

How can the theories of citizens' communication rights engage with the ongoing discourse on democratic reforms as well as transformation, which define India's experience with urbanisation? In this section, we consider the three iterations drawn from critical theory that are useful to conceptualise the idea of citizens' communication rights and develop a theoretical framework relevant in the context of online access. In the three sub-sections, we shall first discuss these iterations evident in the literature on democratisation of Indian cities, and then consider how each perspective can also be used to evaluate the discourse on 'Free Wi-Fi' in contemporary Indian cities.

IA

The literature on urban democratic reform reflects on the trends towards 'localisation' and 'decentralisation' as virtues in good governance. In practice, however, like all processes of political reform, decentralisation has become deeply enmeshed in the political economy of urban service delivery (Harriss 2007). Indian cities, particularly Delhi, remain a crucible for a range of activities and for the discourse on reform, with parties like the Aam Aadmi Party (AAP) as well as leading nationalist forces experimenting with 'new' politics that challenges mainstream governance while demanding political decentralisation.

AAP's proposal to create *mohalla sabhas* (neighbourhood assemblies) is one such experiment in democratising governance.[2] This follows the older *bhagidari* (partnership) system instituted by AAP's predecessor, the Congress-run state government, which ruled the city for three consecutive five-year terms. Under this system, which was popularised across the metropolitan centres of the country in the 1990s, neighbourhood and market associations and non-governmental organisations (NGOs), interfaced with various civic departments to improve public infrastructure and services. While *sabha*s (assemblies) were to send elected representatives to the ward committees, *bhagidari* turned out to be dominated and driven overwhelmingly by the middle-class formations, which appeared to regard inclusive democratic processes as inefficient and corrupt.[3]

Such contestations are pivoted clearly along various intersections of class, caste and gender lines, and span urban and rural areas alike (Srivastava 2014). They also highlight, in quite concrete ways, the distrust of mainstream politics among the elite and the middle class, falling in line with the view that governance is a professional technocratic domain, and only those with demonstrable vision, political will, knowledge and administrative capabilities may be admitted into it. For far too long, it has been articulated frequently in popular media that the development of the country has remained beholden to the compulsions of clientele politics and must now be expedited through initiatives driven by conviction politics, leaving little room for participation, dialogue and deliberation on what are essentially issues that need to be seen through a broader lens of unequal citizenship in urban India (Jamil 2017).

The literature on experiments, which groups and parties like the AAP promote, shows that there is tremendous potential in terms of realising a city where different people desire to live in. If and how this potential will be realised is another matter. Although it is a framework through which various constituencies could come together and voice their ideas and opinions, much will depend on the political imagination that will animate it. *Mohalla sabha*s, like many formations based around the ties of caste and community—organising the forces of most Indian neighbourhoods—could easily slip into becoming entities that resist change, difference and complexity, if not cultivated with significant political content. Given the rise of the Hindu Right-wing to power in many parts of the country, Hansen (2017) warns of such pitfalls; he terms it as the 'weaponisation of the civil society'. In thinking about online access, we need to consider such trends if these are to be resisted.

Beyond Delhi, India's urbanisation experience has seen numerous such efforts towards democratic reforms. In cities like Bengaluru, and other emerging IT economy hubs, experiments in decentralised planning and service delivery have become the subject of intense public deliberations. In each instance, the ideals of a more democratised governance are pronounced, but quite often, the paths taken and the results vary from one instance to another. Public participation agenda in Delhi, as illustrated earlier, is very different from Bengaluru, where citizenship is associated with patterns of (elite) migration to the city, as it emerged as a hub for India's IT industry. This, in turn, is quite distinct from the politics of urban governance in Mumbai, where the agenda lurches fitfully between facilitating civic participation on one end and brute commercialisation on the other, both aimed at accommodating the politics of identity that has become the benchmark for citizenship in the city.

Digital access projects could be understood in the light of such variations, and it is important to explore how the discourse on 'free Wi-Fi' in Delhi can be compared to projects elsewhere, and what each particular variety of populist discourse reveals about the politics of citizenship and communication rights in urban India.

IB

A second dimension of citizenship and communication rights relevant to our analysis is the discourse on online access that relates to the digitalisation process of economic hybridisation in urban India. We have been seeing in different cities, including Delhi and its peripheries, changes in the way commodities are being produced and distributed. Production processes have been fragmented across territories, key operations have been outsourced, and precariousness has been built into the system strategically. Logistics and communication have become of central importance: pulling all the resources together while maximising value and minimising risk.

Alongside, there is an unprecedented growth in the service sector. In cities like Delhi, Mumbai and Bengaluru, and highly urbanised states like Kerala, there are millions of people working in restaurants, malls, e-commerce and delivery sectors, etc., for whom the ideas of a defined and stable workplace or a career trajectory do not exist; a worker employed with a call centre today could be a taxi driver or a security guard tomorrow. If the large numbers of migrant workers—Delhi, Mumbai, Bengaluru and Kerala are top draws for such a population—are added to this kind of mobility necessitated by informalisation and technological disruptions, the situation gets much more complex.

Such a workforce is extremely mobile and not amenable to be organised or unionised in the way workers in large automobile, steel or fertiliser plants, or larger or concentrated industrial areas or belts could be. Even in big manufacturing, there have been sustained efforts to fragment the labour organisations through a range of managerial practices. The Left, a force that has traditionally organised or represented workers in their political struggles, has evidently not been able to keep pace with these developments and still considers the workplace as the locus of politics. Many labour activists have now begun to look at neighbourhoods, or more broadly, the hybrid workspaces in urban areas, as sites of class organisation, as opposed to shop floors and factory gates.

This, labour scholars argue, could allow for a better understanding and appreciation of issues concerning class as a whole, across sectors (Surendran 2016). Conceived in this way, while keeping the articulation and struggles for better working conditions and wages alive, people could also be mobilised around the issues of housing, health, education and recreation (Harvey n.d.). While some scholars of labour have called this change in focus—from trade unions to other forms of cultural, community-based, voluntary organisations— the vernacularisation of politics (Bhattacharya 2016), we remain wary of such a term as it suggests a novel, transformational shift, whereas what seems to have happened is that it is perhaps after a long time that mainstream scholars of labour, particularly historians, have come to grapple with modes of politics outside its conventional class-based conceptions (van der Linden 2016).

It would also allow non-working members of the family to be included in the struggle, especially women, who are often engaged in unpaid or reproductive labour. Although neighbourhoods have always been important ways in which workers have accessed work, credit, networks necessary for survival in the labour market, and organisation, as pointed out by labour historians like Chandavarkar (2009), a broader approach could grant them a central position in working-class politics in the contemporary context. This possibility also allows for concerns of the working class to be aligned with the larger issues of the urban, where the workers raise their voices not only as workers but also as citizens (Agarwala 2013).

The current concerns and debates around the alarming levels of pollution in Delhi, for example, could be one issue around which various constituencies can come together and deepen the debate about progressive environmental policies and investments in more public-oriented solutions. Endemic violence against women is another issue, which already has and could further be invigorated to create the space for discussions on patriarchy, gender-based discrimination, violence in both public and private realms, and reforms in law and law enforcement. Again, access to online services, and in particular, Internet-based communications need to be considered in relation to this dispersion of work across the cityscape as well as a means to develop new networks and solidarity groups. As Castells (1999) has argued, the informationalisation of the economy accelerated since the arrival of the Internet and other communication technologies, and this only strengthened the trend away from the Fordist era of work and labour.

Towards this end, we ask how the discourse of 'new economy', which is so central to the new forms of labour and employment, also reflects a wider concern regarding the welfare of the workers as well as offers a new framework where Internet users can build their capacity to engage in labour activism and greater democratic participation.

IC

The third, and related, iteration of citizenship and communication rights *vis a vis* the Internet relates to the ways in which users of technology now navigate and make use of online media to exercise their voice in the city, as well as to organise political action, which often spills offline. Online spaces, without doubt, provide a crucial public arena for contentious politics, given that they are, as yet, relatively immune to the regimes of control of both the State and the market. In 'millennial India' (Udupa et al. 2019), online activism has brought nuance, diversity, and visibility to discourses that have historically been marginalised, while at the same time giving rise to new and often violent forms of exclusions in the public sphere.

But these changes are often interlinked with the citizens-as-consumers and their capacity to use or pay for and share data with the services providers. The workers, employed both in the rapidly shrinking organised sector as well as the unorganised sector, in the last few years, have begun to use the Internet as not only one of the key tools of organising, as pointed out earlier, but they also use Internet-based services, such as social media. The latter is accessed largely through their smartphones, which function as potent tools to resist the apathy and wilful misrepresentation of the mainstream or legacy media of their concerns or struggles. They particularly use images and recorded and live videos to document and disseminate testimonies, evidence and reports through chatting and networking apps, not only among themselves, but also to sympathetic activists, journalists and the public, at large (*The Quint* n.d.).

Urban landscapes today are markers of a global data infrastructure, which not only carries data about citizens but also crunches and reorganises it as per the algorithmic logic of transnational capital. According to Castells (1989), understanding the local context of the city requires thinking about the larger international system, where cognitive infrastructure becomes more prepotent than physical space, and drive development and growth. In Sassen's (2001) formulation, such urban spaces help put the focus on the 'specificity of the global as it gets structured in the contemporary period' (2001: xix); dispersed spatially but integrated as far as economic activities are concerned.

Online access thus involves processes that socialise the citizens within the emerging logic of global capitalism, and in this chapter, we also seek to understand the political imagination behind free Wi-Fi and the way it commodifies information about the individual user. As Jamil (2017), in her analysis of the trend of *museumisation* of contemporary Delhi, argues, quite often such practices involve marginalising the inhabitants within the ambit of chaos rather than seeing them as decision-makers responsible for making their own destiny. Online access, alongside the affordances of new maps and apps for the city, now actively mediates the life of the user and their claims to the urban space as citizens. Towards this end, we propose that it is important to recognise these complexities while thinking of questions of access and to bring into the discussion the themes of privacy and communication rights online.

Along with the theme of democratising governance, the recognition of changing modes of production, and the way in which we experience and correspond with our urban environment through social media, these iterations help us to frame the question of online access as an enabler of citizenship, and more broadly, of the politics of rights in contemporary India.

PART II

Free Wi-Fi: Varieties of Digital Populism

Considering these three iterations, the case of Indian cities' experiment in creating online public infrastructure for access offers a unique vantage point to understand how populist politics conceptualises citizenship in contemporary India. In recent years, online access has featured routinely in the official discourses on development. For instance, public connectivity in cities with population of more than 10 lakh is a key plank of the Digital India programme. With time, other aspects of the programme, those related to Internet access, are slowly coming to the fore. Tax collection or compliance, biometric-based identification of citizens or beneficiaries, and increased surveillance are some of the ends towards which network infrastructure has already begun to be mobilised. While a lot of interest has been generated in the 'peer-to-peer' modes of networking (De Filippi 2014)[4] enabled by the Internet, in reality, online access is also a means for governments to collect information from the citizens rather than the other way around, enabling what Ferguson and Gupta (2002) have recognised as a 'vertical encompassment'—a top-down, pervasive spread of the image of the state.

However, in spite of the broad national thrust, most flagship 'free Wi-Fi' schemes originated and have evolved along diverse roadmaps, with state-level agencies coining different discourses to justify the goal of increasing access to citizens in their respective regions. In Delhi, we have AAP's flagship 'Aam Aadmi Wi-fi' that constituted a popular plank in the elections held in 2013 and 2015. Although the initiative has been projected as a priority—given that the AAP-led government envisages deploying it to improve government service delivery, democratic participation, education, trade and entrepreneurship, tourism, and safety for women citizens (Government of NCT of Delhi Portal)—it has not, as we write, taken off in a significant manner.

The project, however, diverges from programmes elsewhere that seek to promote access through more market-oriented ways. Even within Delhi, for instance, the more autonomous bodies such as the New Delhi Municipal Council (NDMC), which maintains one of the 11 districts of Delhi, has taken the conventional route and got itself recognised as the only district in the 'smart city' project of the Digital India agenda. A few months later, NDMC declared Khan Market, one of the most exclusive markets in the city, as a free Wi-Fi zone. This was in sharp contrast to AAP's stated goal of allocating Wi-Fi spots on the basis of local participation and greater decentralisation.

In contrast, Karnataka's capital, Bengaluru, has seen state governments setting up projects promising free online access to citizens, with the flagship 'Namma Wi-Fi' project drawing direct and indirect contributions from the city's IT sector. This is in line with the nature and thrust of the neoliberal planning of the city's urban expansion, where the technocratic elite, along with what could be called the elite civil society formations, play a major role in shaping civic policies (Benjamin 2010). In comparing the discourse on free access in Delhi with the ideas promoted by the state governments in Mumbai and Bengaluru, and most recently in Kerala, we can see the diversity of populisms that mark this moment.

Bengaluru also holds a special place in India's digital transformation because the city became the first major IT hub to launch a 'free Wi-Fi' zone as part of a project aimed at developing the city's appeal to become India's IT capital in the early 2000s. The project itself was overseen by the founders of the prominent IT firms of the city, and unsurprisingly, the focus remained on the city's shopping district, which primarily draws the high-end clientele from the markets nearby. The applications most conveniently available are those that guide the user to consume or assist the elite citizens to find nearby public utilities, for instance, ensuring that private vehicle owners are able find a parking spot without having to go through the trouble of entering any public queue (Telecom Services, *Telecomlead* 2014).

More recently, Mumbai, the financial capital of the country, and a 'smart city' in the making, also launched a similar Wi-Fi scheme, which was developed and implemented with little public consultation. Instead, the government of the day emphasised a surprise element while inaugurating the scheme. Moreover, the state's discourse of a promised revolution in access has a resonance with the identity politics in the city. The allusion to '*Aaple Sarkar*' ('Our Government') is indicative that the project is government-managed, and that it is primarily aimed at linking the citizen to the State. If we contrast it with the Aam Aadmi Wi-Fi discourse in Delhi, where the technological affordance is given prominence, we can see that in Mumbai, the idea is to provide online access within the ambit of state's welfare and public service provision rather than enabling new modalities of public participation.

At the time it was first announced, in 2015, *Aaple Sarkar* Wi-Fi was flagged as the largest free Wi-Fi infrastructure in the world. More than 1,200 hotspots have since been created in the city, through which people could access the Internet free of charge till August 2017, although the quality remains deeply unsatisfactory as per most of its users (Madanapalle 2017). Moreover, the state government, rather than projecting it as a decentralised agenda, seems determined to monetise the service *en masse*, although the precise plan (such as price points) is yet to be finalised. Moreover, the populist agenda remains intact, as the dominant parties, including the various ethnic and sectarian groups, seek to utilise the opportunity to strengthen, quite literally, their patronage networks. In one recent instance, the issue of deciding the location for public Wi-Fi turned into a 'war zone' with violent assertions by rival groups that sought to dominate the politics of access and mark their desired ethnic group as the primary beneficiary of the scheme (Singh 2014).

The kind of *ethnicisation* of Wi-Fi in Mumbai is quite different from the technocratic approach in Bengaluru, where the projects were often executed with the city's IT sector as the primary stakeholder. If, in Mumbai, the spatial governance of these networks split along partisan and patronage political lines, in Bengaluru, the projects are drawn to represent the value of its IT sector and new middle classes, with most online access projects designed alongside the city's iconic arterial roads and shopping quarters. In both cases, however, the promise of free access makes no reference to partnering with the citizens, let alone allowing them to decide either on the location or the management of the systems (Kulkarni 2016).

In contrast to these models, albeit one more neoliberal than the other, Delhi's AAP has a lot more ambitious paradigm for developing access, whereby the promise of affordable connectivity has been brought within the ambit of its programme to decentralise the governance of public services. In its election campaign posters in 2015, headlines promising free Wi-Fi competed with other populist measures, including the slashing of the electricity bill by half and radically bringing down the cost of drinking water supply to the citizens (Kaushika 2015).

In its campaign promises of providing Wi-Fi, AAP's unconventional approach to promote more participation in decision-making was also made an essential component. Not only was the idea of established hierarchies inherent in the 'smart city' left out, but instead, the populist approach of giving power to the people was also emphasised by its leadership. When they took power in 2013, the AAP leadership publicly mocked the idea of a 'smart city', highlighting that such ideas cannot bear fruition until 'people live smart lives' (Express News Service, *The Indian Express* 2015).

The state of Kerala by far emerges as the only place where the government seems to have committed to the idea of providing Internet access to its citizens in a holistic manner. Neither does it conceive of Internet access as an election plank or perk, nor has it hived the Internet off to the private sector. Terming or recognising the Internet as a basic right, where two million poor citizens will get the access for free and the rest at a reduced rate, the state has committed Rs 10 billion as the budget for the project, which is expected to take 18 months to roll out (Think Change India, YourStory 2017).

Considering the different approaches and implementation aspects of Wi-Fi projects in Bengaluru, Mumbai and Delhi, we can see that the logic of digital populism is more than just a clash between a neoliberal market-driven model and a more democratic participatory version. Even in Delhi, it is not entirely clear whether the participation includes an agenda that places the needs of the citizens over the interests of the political agents implementing the scheme. Since its election, AAP had not made it clear what its own strategy is and whether it would push for greater access in ways that are radically different from the business as usual of declaring some urban habitats as 'smart cities'. This lack of clarity is becoming obvious in the way AAP has slowly ceded the online space, which it cultivated and used aggressively initially, in favour of strengthening the party 'on the ground' and overcoming governance challenges in Delhi after a series of electoral setbacks. It is telling that the party chose to celebrate its fifth anniversary at the Ramlila Maidan, the very ground from where it had emerged and mounted a challenge to mainstream political parties, instead of conventional media and online campaigns (Pillai 2017).

In their effort to engage more directly with technologists and bring them within the fold of public activism, AAP has been quite successful in building alliances with the corporate leadership of firms, including Facebook, which, the IT advisor argued, had shown great interest in developing Delhi's Free Wi-Fi scheme (Express News Service, *The Indian Express* 2015). But on the ground, the projects have run into the political divides and contested economies of distribution and infrastructure development. In April 2015, the party ordered one of the city's largest cable operators to pay an amount generally unheard of in India and settle the bills. It did so in the name of collecting entertainment tax on the content being delivered by these networks, but there seems to be no real political mobilisation in the name of access, which is of primary significance for the citizens (*Deccan Herald* 2015).

There is consensus among policy and political elites that Delhi needs better access to the Internet, but there is not enough discussion on the underlying logic that can be justified for providing 'free' access to its citizens. The absence of substantive political debates is clearly evident in the fact that even though a majority of the citizens living in Delhi use mobile networks rather than wired or Wi-Fi access, this fact is hardly ever discussed. To draw an analogy with drinking water, it is as if the 'supply' of water is being offered free by the dispensation (which is indeed true in the case of Delhi under the AAP government); however, most citizens rely on bottled water for their essential needs while being on the move. Populism seems embedded in each of the three politics models, the neoliberal Bengaluru model, the top-down clientele-based model of Mumbai's Wi-Fi programme, and the more grounds-up model developed in Delhi.

As a result, tensions have persisted and services remain abrupt. In Delhi, for instance, the AAP-led initiative, 'Delhi Dialogue', failed to reconcile the differences that cropped up regarding the allocation of various resources to run the Wi-Fi projects. While their hiring of a global technology expert from Apple certainly made headlines for the party, AAP's advisor Adarsh Shastri, who has been appointed key advisor for the city's Wi-Fi project, complained of non-cooperation from other stakeholders in the city's cable industry (Akram 2016). On their part, the major fibre network providers are arguing that offering free Wi-Fi across plans was being announced without proper consultation. In replacing politics with populism, the free Wi-Fi projects have resulted in a logjam, and efforts at publicity (through public questionnaires distributed in the media) are hardly adequate to either gather feedback or find the best route forward.[5]

Access and the Elusive Politics of Internet-enabled Labour

A second crucial dimension to be considered, as highlighted in our theoretical framework, relates to the distance between the easy access to Internet and the promise of a progressive turn in terms of the enhancement of labour rights in urban India. As discussed earlier, there has been a growing concern among scholars that urban neighbourhoods could potentially reinvigorate activism for greater social and economic justice and meaningful participation in governance processes. How does the discourse on access relate to these concerns? Are those promising the improving of connectivity also able to comprehend and challenge the sources of socio-economic inequality and fulfil greater participation of labour in society?

These concerns can be read in the public pronouncements as well as policy statements released by state governments and urban development authorities, which have often referred to free Wi-Fi as being a panacea for the growing discontent and disillusionment among the youth in the country. Even in states like Bihar and Uttar Pradesh, political leaders have consistently promised free Wi-Fi, aimed especially at the youth in the state. In Bihar, Nitish Kumar promised that free Wi-Fi would be made available in all the colleges of the state, while in the neighbouring Uttar Pradesh, 'youth icon' Akhilesh Yadav bundled the promise with another digital populist agenda of distributing 'free laptops' to students in the state (Kumar 2015).

The case of the more metropolitan areas, in particular Delhi, again opens up the possibility of drawing comparisons as far as this particular aspect of access is concerned. In Delhi, for instance, the ideal of Aam Aadmi Wi-Fi offers a new imagination of social impact that is more radical than any other case. Even beyond Delhi, for instance, in its campaign in neighbouring Punjab, the party leadership promised free Wi-Fi as a core component of its 'Youth Manifesto'. Extending the promise of access to all parts of the state, the party argued that this would help to generate millions of new jobs in the state and greater connectivity would turn the youth into 'job creators, instead of job seekers' (Press Trust of India, NDTV 2016). In the case of Delhi, too, the discourse mostly focuses on the youth, with free access often presented as a panacea for unemployment and addressing the challenges facing the city's growing labour force.

However, if anything, the somewhat radical discourse of easing access to underprivileged youth in urbanising constituencies pales in comparison to a more disingenuous discourse around labour that is advanced by the Hindu Right in India. While parties such as AAP still promise a college education and minimum income alongside access, best captured in its catchy slogan, 'Degree, Income aur Wi-fi, Aam Aadmi Party Laayi' ('Degree, Income and Wi-Fi, Aam Aadmi Party has brought you these'), the conservative cultural nationalist discourse endorses the disruption more blandly. Recently, at the World Economic Forum's India Economic Summit, a high-profile event aimed at laying out the future roadmap for India's burgeoning employment crisis, BJP's Union Minister of Railways, Piyush Goyal, remarked that job losses in the organised sector are not a cause of worry for the government, as young people are not so interested in seeking employment as they are in becoming entrepreneurs (ET Online, The Economic Times 2017).

Success stories in the digital economy are often linked to not just greater access to Internet, but are also based primarily on enduring hierarchies of knowledge production and social capital that have remained largely unmoved in today's India. Studies of the new economy consistently showcase that disparities in the new economy are marked by the traditional cleavages that exist in Indian society. There are very few, highly rated elite institutions like the Indian Institute of Technologies (IITs) (which coincidentally also provide AAP with its political leadership), while the basic educational structures, including primary education, are in a crisis for years. Internet-related entrepreneurs have, in almost every major success story, all come with privileged backgrounds, with most, if not all of the firms that survive having been founded by those with degrees from the elite management schools.

Citizenship, Data and a Possible Politics of Access in the City

It is obvious that there is politics driving the rise of Wi-Fi projects across India's cities. In Bengaluru, for instance, the government has already announced that as part of its 'smart city' project, such pilots will be inaugurated in 90 per cent of the city's most important public spaces. In Mumbai, the discourse of costless connectivity, which include increasing the current 500 spots to over 1,200, is also in the works. In each instance, the promise is one of 'democracy'; in the case of Mumbai, the login page hails it as an effort to build 'digital democracy'. As we have seen, there is little clarity on which institutions are likely to drive the deliberations on such projects. It is also not clear as to what might be the rights of the citizens once they are *online?*

Up until now, we have tried to explore how the two significant modalities of political participation, the discourse of governance and labour, have been largely left out in the vision for improved provision of access to online media and services. However, we can also see ways in which the discourse and politics of access can be an opportunity to move away from populist short cuts. As we see, the infrastructure of access is where the politics is really falling short; any discussion on digital democracy should also include the user side of the debate, that is, around the issue of data and the cost that citizens pay for accessing welfare services.

And it is in this third context of users' communication rights and their rights to work and live in the city, that we think the real change in terms of democratising governance might occur. We live in cities today that are mobile and highly networked, with Delhi, for instance, having over 10 million mobile devices for its residents to talk and communicate. Many of these smart devices are now used by labour on the move in the city, which are plugged into multiple communications networks at any given time. Thus, instead of trying (and failing) to give everyone free Wi-Fi, cities around the world are witnessing a new politics of infrastructure that focuses more on managing the costs and challenges of the current data-fuelled phase of global capitalism.

Even in global hubs of finance and capital, efforts to set up 'free Wi-Fi' have largely failed to move, with smaller, and perhaps more closely-knit communities faring better in building public networks. The reasons are obvious; with the globalisation of economies, there is now greater recognition that there are costs that the citizens pay whenever their communication data is collected in return for access, to the extent that there are arguments being made now that users should actually be able to monetise their data, especially when used by profit-making as well as state-sponsored agencies, which are routinely siphoning off their personal data through communication surveillance (Guildimann 2013). In New York, for instance, efforts to build a citywide network of 'links' has come up against questions regarding data security and privacy of online communication over such networks (Orf 2016).

The fact is that as mobile phone and cellular networks replace transcontinental satellites in the globalised economy, the debate about privacy and communication rights is becoming more and more significant. Today the Internet has emerged as the primary communication network at the global level, and norms set for communication rights in the previous era dominated by satellite technologies need to be renegotiated now. But so far, much of the literature has focused primarily on the role of powerful Western countries and their struggles to dominate and define communication rights since the 1970s. The spread of free Wi-Fi in India, and more broadly, the politics of access, makes India a crucible for communication rights, and the question of the Indian citizen's data is central to these debates.

In the European context, there is already a lot of scholarly discussion on how the current debates about the rights of citizens online relate to an earlier era when satellite networks led to the development of mass media around the world (Hamelink 2003; Padovani and Nordenstreng 2005). Given the rapid expansion of ICTs in the Indian media, we need a similar account that draws a comparison between the politics of media autonomy in the previous era's satellite and the more recent debates around online communication networks. In the context of Europe, Hamelink (2003) places the recent debates around the Internet-based new media within a deeper history of the 'right to communicate', which had taken place with the arrival of satellite networks several decades ago. This, he argues, requires the formal recognition of 'a right of everyone to take part in communication and design policies and laws accordingly' (Hamelink 2003: 121–63).

Various firms that provide information services in urban areas, including those collecting customised Global Positioning System (GPS) data of their customers, have to be brought within the framework, which had earlier required satellite operators to ensure that the rights of citizens, particularly from those marginalised by global information capitalism, be secured through the law and norms of the international civil society. How does the GPS data, which will get generated from various Wi-Fi projects around Indian cities, be governed internationally? The current discourses that emphasise free access, but make no qualms about the citizens' communication rights, portend an uncertain future. Since citizens' data is now a part and parcel of their existence, given the growing connectivity, commodifying it must be addressed within the rubric of social justice.

Besides collecting data from public Wi-Fi logins, increasingly, online public services are being made a part of the wider discourse on being an equal citizen of the city. For instance, public transport has emerged as a popular site for Wi-Fi services. In Delhi, under the 'Aam Aadmi Wi-fi' scheme, Wi-Fi provision on buses now also aim to assist women's safety, and provisions for access are bundled together with smart CCTV cameras on-board public transport (Press Trust of India, *The Indian Express* 2019). In contrast, in Mumbai, the discourse on free access reflects and aligns itself with the ethnic and cultural identity politics of public service provision, with political leaders vying for Wi-Fi for particular commuter routes that serve their constituencies. Unsurprisingly, entertainment on-board, rather than gender or other concerns, takes centre-stage. Meanwhile, in cities whose economy is driven by service sectors, like Pune and Bengaluru, the rationale behind such programmes prioritises the *needs* of their elite professional classes, with access provision made along strategic routes that serve the city's IT sector (Sen 2013).

The promise of public access should be to overcome precisely such populist practices; but rather than deliberate on how data and communication rights could be welded together, politics across regions relies on the populist promise of 'free' availability, thus avoiding genuine political deliberations among citizens. There are several instances before us now, which amply demonstrate that behind such freedom lies a model of digital commodification, since almost all free access projects are built around 'hyper local' strategies that reduce citizens' data into relevant consumer insights. Even as populist strategies serve the elite class of professionals, in turn, these very same Wi-Fi with GPS networks become a source for firms to gather personal details of their elite customers. And it is just not location information, but free access also helps companies collect fine-grained data about the individual 'footfalls', 'frequency', 'dwell time' and 'bounce rates' of the users (Dutta 2016).

There's a temptation to look at these as entirely new phenomena, but we only need to refer to a previous era, when satellite networks combined with GPS and electronic surveillance technologies similarly enabled to locate and mark people around the world. However, in the 1970s, the development of India's satellite programme led scientists, IT specialists, technocrats as well as the political leadership to play a more active role in the international debates about citizens' rights. Rather than reject the emerging inter-networked computer technologies and communication networks, India's leaders, along with many other Third World countries, turned communication into a pivot of the non-aligned agenda. While their quest for a New World Information Order (NWIO) contributed to an increasing degree of state intervention, even though often limited to cultural conceptions such as an 'Asian Telecommunity', public activism around communication rights set new norms and limits guarding individual liberties and rights.[6]

Today, as Wi-Fi and other access technology again sweep throughout the urban landscape, the debate on Indian citizens' rights, within what Jamil (2017) has called the 'global urban', has been overwhelmed by technospeak and a managerial approaches. While experts have warned that there are grave implications for both the privacy and security of the data being collected and shared by public Wi-Fi projects, in most instances, it has been found that not only is private data being collected by service providers illegally, but there is also a high chance that a hack could leak this information across the web (Rakesh 2016).

The scenario is not merely of significance from technical perspectives; increasingly, the fact that Indian citizens' communication has been left at the mercy of insecure online networks has started to draw worldwide attention. A recent study, conducted by a major cyber-security firm (Special Correspondent, *The Hindu* 2017), has shown that 96 per cent of Indians are unable to think about the risks involved in accessing online Wi-Fi. In a startling claim, the report also added as many as 73 per cent of the 'consumers' who they surveyed were willing to share their personal details as long as they could access strong Wi-Fi for free. These trends, which consistently take the view of citizens as consumers, indicate the extent to which free Wi-Fi populism has weakened the civil society; rather than deliberate as rights-bearing individuals and communities, the political discourse has misled citizens into a situation that has failed to generate any crucial public debate thus far.

However, beyond these occasional headlines, from our perspective, the real challenge is to address the digital populism inherent in the trend of promising 'free Wi-Fi' as a panacea for social justice reform. To us, it seems to be counterproductive both from the technical security perspective as well as, and more crucially, from the communication rights view. The 'take my data, give me Wi-Fi', which is how the report on India's privacy challenge summed up the findings, is a grave scenario that is indicative of a wider trend in urban India, where populism has replaced institutional checks and balances on private interests in urban governance. Besides potentially weakening the debate around citizenship in urban India, the discourse on free access has also evaded the deeper history of communication rights, in which India had played a crucial role in developing norms, not just for its own citizens, but also for satellite users worldwide.

CONCLUSION

In this chapter, we discussed the various aspects of what we called digital populism, that is, the politics of online access in India as it seeks to make things 'free' of cost, or so at least in its claims. We identified strands of various literature around urban India, which allow us to conceptualise the ideas that constitute the promises of free Wi-Fi. And we discussed three key iterations, which relate generally to the theme of communications and citizenship in urban India, and then discussed the case of free Wi-Fi projects in various cities in India to see how these concepts can explain the rise of digital populism.

While we have merely been able to signpost some of these concepts and frames in this chapter, we believe there is scope for substantial empirical work to substantiate the framework. In the context of the democratisation of urban governance, for instance, we found that there are actually a variety of political logics at work in different contexts; that is, digital populism is often laced with local variants, which dominate the public culture of the region or the city. In Bengaluru, we found the claims to be more in tune with the neoliberal logic that seeks to prioritise consumer citizens, while in Mumbai's more centralised version of 'sarkari' Wi-Fi, we found an identity-driven aggressive populism where rival ethnic parties are vying to secure Wi-Fi to build 'patronage networks'. Technology is quite literally a metaphor for local politics, and yet, the wider discourse on 'free' access indicates the ways in which these variations get aligned with the rise of a wider political current, which seeks to reduce politics to digital populism that only serves those in power.

In the national capital region of Delhi, we see a more complex story. The local 'Aam Aadmi-centred' Wi-Fi (alongside other populist welfare measures) reflects a post-modern governance aspiration to hand over governance to 'the common man'. However, this discourse completely dissociated online access from the challenge of employment or the concerns regarding communication rights. In fact, nowhere in the discourse of free access do we see any genuine recognition of rights such as privacy or media literacy, which are essential for any inhabitant of the rapidly digitalising city. Instead, the populist conception of free access exposes the residents to an unprecedented theft of their personal data, which flows from public to private interests. Thus, if the physical infrastructure is being determined by the populism of mainstream politics, we also point towards the imagination that can be brought into these deliberations. We think it is time to imagine another information order, along the lines once demanded in the satellite and Generalised System of Preferences (GSP) era, where the Indian citizen's rights get precedence over her/his capacity as a mere consumer or a client of a disingenuous political system.

NOTES

1. These discussions were often hosted by conferences led by the International Telecommunications Union, the United Nation's (UN's) telecommunication-related wing. Arthur C. Clarke was invited to one such conference held to discuss the potential for satellite radio in 1968 to give his views (Clarke 1968).

2. Although eventually, all the 272 wards of Delhi will have several *sabha*s, depending on their size, with considerable power at their disposal, some have already started functioning on a pilot basis. Earlier this year, a few *sabha*s were also roped into the process of planning the state budget.

3. To illustrate this, a confederation of 1,463 Resident Welfare Associations in Delhi expressed their opposition to AAP's Swaraj Bill and described it as an attempt to 'hijack the equitable, apolitical and democratic process of decentralised decision making via the RWAs and resident ward committees (RWC) by packing the Mohalla Sabha by its cadre who will run amok and vitiate the process of sensible decision making as per rule of law' (Polanki 2014).

4. While peer-to-peer networking has been a subject of interest for several interest groups, the activism around it has largely remained confined to specialist groups or public information campaigns. It has rarely spilled into the realm of people tinkering with technology itself. An illustrative case would be discontents around the setting up of mesh networks.

5. The Delhi government released a list of 10 questions to collect feedback from the public on the question.

6. Set up in light of large-scale commercial data transfers through satellite-linked computer networks, the International Bureau of

Informatics (IBI) aimed at the 'socialization of informatics' worldwide. While India did not formally endorse it, the alternative political agenda gained widespread popularity with over 45 Asian and African nations adopting its mandate by the late 1980s (Pohle 2012).

REFERENCES

Agarwala, Rina. 2013. *Informal Labour, Formal Politics, and Dignified Discontent in India*. New Delhi: Cambridge University Press.

Akram, Maria, 'Month On, Free Wi-Fi Project Still in Limbo', *The Hindu*, 3 May 2016.

Benjamin, Solomon. 2010. 'Manufacturing Neoliberalism: Lifestyling Indian Urbanity'. In Swapna Banerjee Guha (ed.), *Accumulation by Dispossession: Transformative Cities in the New Global Order*, pp. 92–124. New Delhi: Sage Publications.

Bhatnagar, S. and R. Schware. 2000. *Information and Communication Technology in Development: Cases from India*. Delhi: Sage Publications.

Bhattacharya, Sabyasachi. 2016. 'The Vernacularization of Labour Politics: Introduction'. In Sabyasachi Bhattacharya and Rana P. Behal (eds), *The Vernacularization of Labour Politics*, pp. 1–21. New Delhi: Tulika Books.

Bulut, E. and E. Yoruk. 2017. 'Digital Populism: Trolls and Political Polarization of Twitter in Turkey', *International Journal of Communication* 11: 4093–17.

Castells, Manuel. 1989. *The Informational City: Information Technology, Economic Restructuring, and the Urban-Regional Process*. Oxford: Basil Blackwell.

———. 1999. 'Information Technology, Globalization and Social Development', UNRISD Discussion Paper No. 114. Available at http://www.unrisd.org/unrisd/website/document.nsf/70870613ae 33162380256b5a004d932e/f270e0c066f3de7780256b67005b728c/ $FILE/dp114.pdf (accessed 19 September 2019).

Chandavarkar, Rajnarayan. 2009. *History, Culture and the Indian City*. Cambridge, UK: Cambridge University Press.

Clarke, Arthur, C. 1968. Conference on the Potential for Satellite Radio, International Telecommunications Union, UN.

Deccan Herald, 'Siti Cable Asked to Clear Tax Dues, Gets Rs 33-Cr Bill', 8 April 2015. Available at https://web.archive.org/web/ 20150710135001/http://www.deccanherald.com/content/470430/ siti-cable-asked-clear-tax.html (accessed 19 September 2019).

De Filippi, Primavera, 'It's Time to Take Mesh Networks Seriously (And Not Just for the Reasons You Think)', *Wired*, 1 February 2014.

Digital India Programme, Ministry of Electronics and Information Technology, Government of India. Available at http://www.digitalindia.gov.in/ (accessed 27 April 2017).

Dutta, Vishal, 'Startups are Using Hyperlocal Tech Like WiFi to Build their Businesses', *The Economic Times*, 4 May 2016.

ET Online, 'Piyush Goyal Says Job Losses is a Good Sign for Economy, Here's a Reality Check', *The Economic Times*, 7 October 2017.

Express News Service, '"Smart City" is NDMC Budget's Main Focus', *The Indian Express*, 26 March 2015.

———, 'Cities Cannot Get Smart Unless People Live Smart Lives: CM Arvind Kejriwal', *The Indian Express*, 19 October 2015.

Ferguson, J. and A. Gupta. 2002. 'Spatializing States: Toward an Ethnography of Neoliberal Governmentality', *American Ethnologist* 29(4): 981–1002.

Government of NCT of Delhi, Online Portal, 'Citizen Consultation on Wi-Fi Project', Available at https://web.archive.org/web/20160328194742/http://delhi.gov.in/wps/wcm/connect/f998068047a9643fb0eef5bdc775c0fb/DDC+wifi.pdf?MOD=AJPERES&lmod=-902999290 (accessed 27 April 2017).

Guildimann, Marc, 'The Free Market Can Actually Help Us Control Our Privacy', *Quartz*, 16 June 2013.

Hacker, Kenneth L. and Jan van Dijk. 2000. *Digital Democracy: Issues of Theory and Practice*. London: Sage Publications.

Hamelink, C. 2003. 'Human Rights for the Information Society'. In Bruce Gerard and Sean O. Siochru (eds), *Communicating in an Information Society*, pp. 121–64. United Nations Research Institute for Social Development.

Hansen, Tomas Blom, 'BJP has Weaponised Civil Society by Making Faceless Vigilante Hindu Anger an Ever-present Threat', *India Today*, 26 May 2017.

Harriss, J. 2007. 'Antinomies of Empowerment: Observations on Civil Society, Politics and Urban Governance in India', *Economic and Political Weekly* 42(26): 2716–24.

Harvey, David, 'Interview: David Harvey: Consolidating Power', *Roar*, n.d.

'Honda 2 Wheeler Workers Are on a Digital Dharna', *The Quint*, n.d.

Hübler, Michael and Rebecca Hartje. 2015. 'Smart Phones Support Smart Labour', Hannover Economic Papers (HEP) no. 559.

IEEE Website. Available at https://web.archive.org/web/20140123022741/https://www.ieee.org/about/technologies/emerging/wifi.pdf (accessed 19 September 2019).

Indo-Asian News Service, 'Bihar Launches Free WiFi for Students', *Hindustan Times*, 22 March 2017.

Jamil, Ghazala. 2017. *Accumulation by Segregation: Muslim Localities in Delhi*. Delhi: Oxford University Press.

Kaushika, Pragya, 'Aam Aadmi Party Delivers on Bijli-Paani Promise', *The Indian Express*, 26 February 2015.

Kulkarni, Tanu, 'Namma Wi-Fi: A Tale of Glitches', *The Hindu*, 8 May 2016.

Kumar, Anil, 'Wi-Fi, Credit Cards, Job Quota: Nitish Lures Youth and Women Voters', *Hindustan Times*, 17 September 2015.

Madanapalle, Aditya, 'Mumbai WiFi: We Could Only Connect to One in Four Aaple Sarkar Mumbai WiFi Hotspot Locations', *Firstpost*, 11 January 2017.

Mazzoleni, G. 2003. 'The Media and the Growth of Neo-populism in Contemporary Democracies'. In G. Mazzoleni, J. Stewart and B. Horsfield (eds), *The Media and Neo-populism: A Comparative Analysis*, pp. 1–21. Westport, CT: Praeger.

McNamara, Kerry. 2003. 'Information and Communication Technologies, Poverty and Development: Learning from Experience', World Bank. Available at http://documents.worldbank.org/curated/en/741291468779079516/pdf/300760PAPER0ICT0Learning0from0Experience.pdf (accessed 27 April 2017).

Monteiro, Anjali. 1998. 'Official Television and Unofficial Fabrications of the Self: The Spectator as Subject'. In Ashis Nandy (ed.), *The Secret Politics of Our Desires*, pp. 157–207. New Delhi: Oxford University Press.

Orf, Darren, 'NYC's Free WiFi Service is Turning into a Privacy Nightmare', Gizmodo, 17 March 2016.

Padovani, Claudia and Kaarle Nordenstreng. 2005. 'From NWICO to WSIS: Another World Information and Communication Order?', *Global Media and Communication* 1(3): 264–72.

Parthasarathy, Balaji, Kenneth Keniston, Solomon Benjamin and G. Dileep Kumar. 2005. 'Information and Communication Technologies for Development: A Comparative Analysis of Impacts and Costs from India', Department of Information Technology, Government of India and Infosys Technologies. Available at https://www.researchgate.net/publication/261472115_Information_and_Communications_Technologies_for_Development_A_Comparative_Analysis_of_Impacts_and_Costs_from_India?enrichId=rgreq-f78b809d4955b74b27aa9659f9034efd-XXX&enrichSource=Y292ZXJQYWdlOzI2MTQ3MjExNTtBUzoxMDI5Mzc0Njg2MDQ0MzBAMTQwMTU1MzYxMzc2Mw%3D%3D&el=1_x_2&_esc=publicationCoverPdf (accessed 27 April 2017).

Pillai, Soumya, 'AAP to Return to Ramlila Maidan for a "High Five"', *The Hindu*, 25 November 2017.

Pohle, J. 2012. 'Going Digital: A Historical Perspective on International Cooperation in Informatics'. In D. Frau-Meigs (ed.), *From NWICO to WSIS: 30 Years of Communications Geopolitics*, pp. 107–122. Bristol: Intellect Books.

Polanki, Pallavi, 'Citizens Group Opposes AAP's Mohalla Sabhas, Fears Hijacking of RWAs', *Firstpost*, 13 February 2014.

Press Trust of India, 'Six Wi-Fi, CCTV-enabled Buses Roll Out on Delhi Roads', *The Indian Express*, 23 December 2015.

_____, All-India, 'Punjab Polls: AAP Promises 25 Lakh Jobs, Free Wi-Fi Hotspots in Villages', NDTV, 4 July 2016.

Rakesh, Vanya, 'Privacy and Security Implications of Public Wi-Fi—A Case Study', The Centre for Internet and Society, 9 December 2016.

Roberts, Kenneth M. 2006. 'Populism, Political Conflict, and Grassroots Organization in Latin America', *Comparative Politics* 38(2): 127–48.

Saith, Ashwini and M. Vijayabaskar. 2008. 'Introduction: ICTs and Indian Social Change: An Agenda of Concerns'. In Ashwini Saith, M. Vijayabaskar and V. Gayathri (eds), *ICTs and Indian Social Change: Diffusion, Poverty, Governance*, pp. 13–32. New Delhi: Sage Publications.

Sassen, Saskia. 2001 [Revised Edition]. *The Global City*. Princeton: Princeton University Press.

Sen, Somit, 'Soon, Free Wi-Fi on State Mumbai–Pune Volvo Buses', *The Times of India*, 13 May 2013.

Singh, Varun, 'Shivaji Park Becomes Wi-Fi War Zone for Shiv Sena and MNS', midday.com, 18 July 2014.

Singhal, Arvind and Everett M. Rogers. 2000. *India's Communication Revolution: From Bullock Carts to Cyber Marts*. New Delhi: Sage Publications.

Smart Cities Mission, Government of India. 'What is a Smart City?'. Available at http://smartcities.gov.in/content/innerpage/what-is-smart-city.php (accessed 27 April 2017).

Special Correspondent, 'Take My Date, Give Me Wi-Fi', *The Hindu*, 19 July 2017.

Srivastava, Sanjay. 2014. *Entangled Urbanism: Slum, Gated Community, and Shopping Mall in Delhi and Gurgaon*. New Delhi: Oxford University Press.

Surendran, Aardra. 2016. 'Voluntary Associations in Public Sector Industrial Undertaking: Civic or Political Action'. In Bhattacharya and Behal (eds), *The Vernacularisation of Labour Politics*, pp. 25–45. New Delhi: Tulika Books.

Telecom Services, 'Bangalore Launches Free WiFi Hotspots in the Heart of the City, More Coming Soon', *Telecomlead*, 27 January 2014.

Think Change India, 'Kerala Becomes 1st State to Declare Internet as Basic Right; Announces Free WiFi for 20 Lakh Citizens', YourStory, 14 March 2017.

Udupa, S., S. Venkatraman and A. Khan. 2019. '"Millennial India": Global Digital Politics in Context', *Television & New Media*. Available at https://doi.org/10.1177/1527476419870516 (accessed 19 September 2019).

van der Linden, M. 2016. 'Global Labour: A Not-so-grand Finale and Perhaps a New Beginning', *Global Labour Journal* 7(2): 201.

꧁ **five**

Dalit Aesthetics in Digital Mumbai

Amit S. Rai, Rachna Ramesh Kumar and Shiva Thorat

Introduction

How do Dalit politics and culture engage with digital practices? This chapter presents different answers to the question. The conversation is ongoing; it is in process. In what follows, we explore different conceptions of politics, throughout developing a practice of posing the problem of the political in contexts of struggle. No synthesis has been attempted as yet, since it would do violence to the process at this point. This lack of synthesis bears some relation to what Shiva Thorat and Rachna Kumar have articulated as the 'mixed' nature of Indian Dalit politics: mixed modernities, mixed technologies, mixed subjectivities, mixed politics. We are thus avoiding answering the question of what is Dalit politics, by posing an epistemological and ontological question of the digital forms of Dalit practice. We also wish to signpost here, at the outset, that these mixed, non-synthesised formations attempt through experimental practices, to find a resonance, rather than a pre-given unity.

Since well before the founding of the Dalit Panthers in 1972, different modernist and postmodernist media technologies figured in Dalit struggles for emancipation from the Varna system. It bears some genetic relation to the practice of democratic dissensus (Ranciere 1999) and the emancipatory politics of solidarity (Omvedt 2010). Even before Ambedkar's socialist refashioning of Dalit dissensus, its necessarily profane, necessarily exceptional[1] dynamics have been expressed in different forms. Drawing on interviews conducted in Mumbai's Dalit communities, this chapter develops a critical assessment of digital practices in India through the framework of Dalit aesthetics of emancipation.

Before we begin this chapter, let us define the term 'Dalit aesthetic'. Patil (1988) noted that aesthetics has no choice but to depend upon the mainstream ideology of aesthetic, to assert its political philosophy; on the other end of the spectrum, Dalit aesthetics rejects this standpoint, choosing humanity over the artificial. Limbale (2004) asserts that Dalits may attain educational, economic, social and political success, but their unique Dalitness remains, due to their common experiences of subjugation, oppression and exclusion.

> There is one conception of doing 'political culture' which is clearly questionable. Artists, writers and performers would be naturally concerned with political problems and agendas of the time. Indeed they should be. When Picasso paints Guernica he is responding to a political reality. But to react to a political culturally. There is a danger in reducing the political in art to mere 'reacting and responding'. At the hands of a lesser artist the exercise might end up in producing manifestoes and posters or calendar art. There ought to be the political within art (Deshpande 2009: 42).

We are, at this point, forced to ask: what is the political in arts? In this chapter, we attempt to provide visual examples of the politics in art as the expression of Dalit aesthetics in digital Mumbai.

NEOLIBERALISM, DIGITAL PRACTICES AND DALIT LIFE

As was noted in the 'Introduction' to this volume, prior research has pointed out the limitations of frameworks that assume a universal neoliberal gentrificiation of cities, in which private property is 'developed' for more profitable ('higher and more productive') ends (Hesmondhalgh 2010; Pratt 2009). Therefore, in the perspective of one of the authors of this mixed analysis (Rai), in postcolonial cities such as Mumbai, the limited forms of commons that had been enshrined in socialist planning policy have now been more or less drawn under the neoliberal umbrella of urban policy (Chatterjee 2011; De Angelis 2017; Meiksins Woods 2007). One aim of this policy is the depoliticisation of urban communities and social relations more generally: riots, strikes, insurgencies and uncontrollable populations have been the targets of these urban strategies. India's nearly 100-year-old Dalit movement has a long and complex history in politicising precisely what Brahminical hegemony had secured as timeless and *pavitra* (pure or holy). This politicisation was effected through cultural, economic, organising, armed and parliamentary strategies, each of which had different relationships to specific histories of Dalit aesthetics. From this perspective, the embodiment of Dalit practice is as, if not more, important than its epistemology. Thus, in this globally functional (if not total) neoliberal context, how do Dalit aesthetics express resistant forms of embodied ecologies of sensation and experiment with historically specific technologies? In what way does Dalit organising in the digital disrupt the historical role of the intellectual in Dalit emancipation, according to certain forms of Marxisms? Drawing on Balibar, Hewlett (2012) has noted:

> It is through the proletariat that the Marxist critique of political economy can be articulated with the Marxist political project of changing the world. Once reduced by the capitalist economy to a mere labouring body, that is, the essentially negative product of capitalist society's disintegration of traditional sociabilities, the proletarian stands re-evaluated by Marxism as the ultimate historical subject. The proletariat thus constitutes an 'ontologically dissociated subject' (Balibar 1997: 248), whose empirical lives and ideologies differ from the abstract Marxist formulation as the embodiment of revolution (2012: 883).

He further states:

> Balibar hence notes the Marxist temptation, which is grounded in the double illusion of mastering the course of history and of the unity between the revolutionary organisation and the working class, of 'blindly forging ahead in the imagined "proletariat"' (ibid.: 249) (translation mine). In fact, however, the degree of conformity and the shapes taken by the proletariat in relation to this revolutionary project result from a sociological and cultural encounter with revolutionary intellectuals and activists (ibid.).

As we shall see, the question of the role of the intellectual in contemporary Dalit aesthetics is precisely a renewed site of struggle, and an emergent mixture in Mumbai today. In this chapter, we pursue this dialectic through other, non-dialectical questions: What is the gradient of Dalit agency imbricated with specific strategies of (monopoly) rent, sustainability, de- and re-politicisation, competitiveness, commoning, regeneration and reclamation, intellectual property, and accumulation by dispossession of mostly Dalit or ethnic minority communities? How do these forces directly, ontologically and epistemologically affect Dalit practice? These molar shifts in contemporary capitalism in Indian cities are parasitic on the digitisation of urban life under neoliberal biopolitical production and transformations in perception, ecology, 'frugal innovation', privatisation and smart city politics. What forms of Dalit organising and aesthetics effectively intervene in this new, 'creative' ecology? Focusing on cultural practices that unevenly integrate forms of mobile media and digital social networks, this chapter traces emergent and residual forms of caste and class domination in relation to new forms of cultural expression in Dalit communities and resistance movements.

We should say right away, however, that what follows is merely indicative of what is intended to become a multivolume/platform study of Dalit aesthetics. This study would include an encyclopedia of Dalit cultural expression and it would also be an ongoing digital archive and evolving toolkit of digital media activism for Dalit emancipation. Sambhaji Bhagat, a renowned singer, musician, writer, poet and activist, works through digital cultural expression. In an interview to the Scroll, he announced, 'We are here to disturb you, not to entertain you' (Shone 2017). In a conversation with one of the authors of this chapter (Thorat), he also observed that the dominance of digital practices has become crucial to Dalit cultural expression and this phenomenon could be the only challenge against fascist forces and the mobilisation of Right-wing politics. Sambhaji's songs circulate across various platforms. A Dalit from Panchgani, in Satara district, Sambhaji has been a member of his family's singing troupe since he was 10 years old. His family practices *Kirtan* (a practice of musical narration or storytelling, with religious or spiritual connotations). Sambhaji said:

> It was at Ambedkar College, Wadala, that I was influenced, affected and disturbed by the situation. I decided to stay because I got a bed, fan, table and books, luxuries which I cannot even think of in my house, and over and above the access to knowledge of movements and the people, through Babasaheb. He began engaging with the politics and writings of Ambedkar. 'Same cultural expression in 2017, transforming and evolving digital media activism through

YouTube channel (private) and broader discipline movement of Kalasangini'[2] (Shone 2017).

By situating Dalit aesthetics at the intersections of forces of privatisation of common lands and resources, managerial urban policy involving creativity, innovation, digital networks, and struggles around intellectual property and commoning workaround know-how to hack India's elitist smart cities, we aim in this chapter to relate a conversation around politics in the neoliberal city to the submerged histories and potential futures of Dalit aesthetics of organising, cultural expression and social reproduction in Mumbai.

These processes of social reproduction are increasingly entwined with a broad array of digital practices. These are unevenly integrated into macroeconomic dynamics of neoliberal measure and digital control. Thus, recently, in Mumbai, plans have been floated to transform Kurla and Oshiwara into business hubs:

> In smart cities, data collected through sensors enable real time monitoring by authorities and is used to enhance efficiency in utilities and citizens' services such as electricity, water, drainage, gas, traffic, parking, etc. Effective eco-friendly transportation systems, transparent processes for commercial activities and online approval systems are other hallmarks of a smart city. Madan said introducing smart city components in Oshiwara would be difficult because much development had already taken place there and the authority would have to resort to retro-fitting (Smart Cities Projects 2014).

In the meantime, 'the development authority is re-tendering the contract for the development of Bandra Kurla Complex as a smart city, despite good response from companies' (Smart Cities Projects 2014). Other developments are also on board, as the state information technology department asks the MMRDA to reduce manpower requirements for smart city initiatives:

> MMRDA will first cover the 175-hectare area with a public wi-fi network having a high Internet speed of 5 Mbps. Ninety surveillance cameras will be set up in the E-block and G-block of the complex with direct co-ordination between security agencies. A smart parking facility will be introduced for vehicles to know the nearest available parking slots of the 3,000 in the complex. Citizen-centric

mobile applications will be launched for emergency services and to provide details of nearest restaurants (Smart Cities Projects 2014).

What are the key modes of urban and social plasticity and police in this smart city vision? Expert authority (a form of police) attempts to ground itself in real time data streams generating ecologies of sense and matter that are folded into everyday life. The proper subject (the subject of propriety, property, consumption, commodity and competition), the always connected digital subject, will be an effect of algorithmic logistics (transportation systems, transparent processes for commercial activities and online approval systems). Paradoxically, this will be a retro-fitted digital subject: harkening back to forms of national identity before digital, mobile communication became a widely accessible experience, functioning within the built space before smart retro-fitting, the citizen produces her own value in an always complexifying social network, in the correlations of datasets, of their digital registrations (WhatsApp, Facebook, E-mail, ATM withdrawal, direct debits, etc.). This is one perspective on the framework of Dalit digital practices; in this critical perspective, there is no outside, only a kind of correlation between power and the Dalit subject through the variable mesh of algorithmic control systems.

A GLANCE AT DALIT HISTORY IN MUMBAI

However, Dalit history speaks to the resistance-within-debility of all oppressed lives. Thus, Dalit history as forms of resistance and refusal of domination within the agricultural and industrial working classes in India is a history that must be understood today through an interdisciplinary prism of the intersections of caste-class-gender-ability-labour-ecology (Hegde 2010). This is a difficult method to follow through on. It requires a certain strategic essentialism, but in that very strategy, transmuting essence into power (Deleuze 1992; Spinoza 1992; Spivak 1984, 1988). These histories, linked as they have been to a radical Black tradition in the African diaspora, are narrated and created in literature, music and various arts in very different parts of India. We should also keep in mind that for generations, non-European, anti-modern forms of non-elite rural–urban ecology have been integrated into a political vision of emancipation without domination in Dalit social reproduction; today's business and management fetish of sustainability and eco-friendly production actively erases, while appropriating this active dimension of Dalit struggle. Literature, music and art celebrated and guided socio-political movements in Maharashtra, such as the role of cultural production in the 1960s Samyukta Maharashtra Movement (Dandvate 2005: 36–39).

Dalit aesthetics suffuses and co-evolves with the informally hacked smart city. One way is by claiming urban space for dance. In Mumbai's Dalit communities, dancing is an important part of surviving caste oppression. At times, this culture comes into public representation and the informalised marketplace of culture (and hence, entrepreneurial capture), for instance, in Mumbai, 'The Culture 2016' dance competition was organised in Phoenix Market city, Kurla by Spykar, a sports brand. One of the crew members, Sadanand More, said, 'The mainstream society and their dance culture is seemingly ignoring the fact of urban poor talent. We are trying to showcase through the programme that such groups in the hundreds of millions have not only created expanding empires, but thriving global industries with their feet.'

Dance and Mumbai have a very strong connection; it has its own character in Dalit Mumbai. All the depiction of dance starts from the slums-eye perspective (Nandy 1998), and anyone looking for underground dance talents knows this. Programmes that have free entries have become popular attractions. Mohammad Hussain, a 24-year old from Surat, Gujarat came to 'The Culture 2016' to pursue his dancing talent. Bollywood movies like *Any Body Can Dance* (2013) and *Any Body Can Dance 2* (2015) are said to be the representation of the dance culture in India. But are they? Hussain is a precarious cognitariat working in a garment company as a supervisor while pursuing a degree in Commerce. His dream is to become a dance master. Prasanna is a 20-year old who came from Nepal to try his luck in 'locking and popping', which is a hip hop dance form: 'This event is one of the good dance platforms that people like me can use to show off their talents. TV shows and movies don't really give us chances. Still, "The Culture" has its own biased sentiments.' He also said, 'Only thing is here that I can meet [a] lot of people like me who have not been given any chances, be it family, school or society.'

Women who come to 'The Culture 2016' say they are not able to find their own space because everything is male-dominated. Priya Jha said, 'Even a miracle won't see the men give us enough space. You can see all the movies, even in mainstream shows .... women's roles are secondary' (Thorat 2016b).

Digital practices are part of this subaltern dance culture, enabling the fashioning of lives both within (competitive positioning) and against (infrastructures of commoning) postcolonial capital (Hewlett 2010; Mandarini 2006; Tronti 2010). Shifts in technology, style, organisation, mobilisation, agency and value are differently correlated within and across dance performances; women contest male control, different communities encounter and more or less compete with each other, and infrastructures are improvised through a cash economy. In this digitised aesthetic culture for forms of identity, dance, image, technology, music and movement combine to affirm new possibilities of assemblages, while marking the reality of subaltern everyday precarity, subordination, securitisation, gender domination and elitist subjectivation. For these dancers, neither is the fact of Dalit oppression remarked on, nor does it become a fixed symbol of the event or culture, but rather, becomes differently scaled and vectored, and also becomes enduring occasions of a counter-actualisation of the powers, forms and practices of domination circumscribing caste in Mumbai today.

CASTE, MIGRATION, ENTERTAINMENT

In Mumbai, migration has an important caste dimension; one can speak today of Dalit ecologies of social reproduction that diagram the symbiotic associations of its various structures (regimes of blockage, flow, strata and value). The financial and entertainment capital of India, Mumbai, is known for the Hindutva–Maratha–Savarna caste politics as well as for being the seat of different industrial and financial powers (see Gidwani and Sivaramakrishnan 2003; Hansen 1996). It is in this context that we must contextualise the various interfaces that have formed between Dalit culture and digital technologies in India. The agenda of Internet-enabled and digital urban spaces has affected cultural production in Dalit communities. In the Indian context, where caste has horizontally and vertically divided groups, internal conflicts have forced the lower castes and Dalits to migrate, in an attempt to leave the problem of caste behind them in their villages. But in Mumbai, Dalits have encountered neoliberal entwined urbanism and caste domination, and are increasingly constituted by subalterns 'who reside in cities and feel "at home" there, but, at the same time, continue also to be involved in the politics and culture of their villages of origin' (Gidwani and Sivaramakrishnan 2003: 341).

Seemingly far from mainstream Bollywood, intellectuals and activists such as Annabhau Sathe (Maitreya 2017a), Amar Sheikh,[3] Namdeo Dhasal (Ketkar 2016), and Saadat Hasan Manto (Manzoor 2016) participate in the Dalit cultural sphere of Mumbai, a sphere which is now also partly digitised. This is not only a space of representation cutting across urban and rural space, but also a representational or symbolic space. Dalit digital aesthetics pushes us to rethink the matter of materialism in critical geographies involved in the radical transformations of the social space after the digital.:

> ... in Lefebvre's (1991: Ch. 2) sense where social space is understood as a (historic) 'production' of the following triad: (a) routinised social relations of production and reproduction ('spatial practices'); (b) enacted conceptions of spatial environments and orders ('representations of space'); and (c) the lived spaces of everyday life with their (often tacit) symbolic associations and codings ('representational spaces') (Gidwani and Sivaramakrishnan 2003: 341).

To delve further into Lefebvre's conception:

> For Lefebvre, the category 'spatial practices' includes, as part and parcel of the organisation of production and reproduction, the particular locations and built environments that give material context to these relations. Indeed, if there is one lesson to be taken away from Lefebvre's work, it is his insistence on the materiality of space (and, correspondingly, his disdain for purely ideographic invocations of space) (ibid.: 341).

New media geographies of Mumbai are emerging. These critical practices and discourses help us to understand better the ongoing organisation of resistance and refusal of Dalit and working-class political movements in relationship to digital ecologies. But perhaps there is a reason for this?

For instance, during the Samyukta Maharashtra Movement, according to official records, 105 people died and many were displaced (see Omvedt 2004). This history of struggle folds into ongoing cultural practices. What are the forms of material and signifying expression, subjectivity and creative resistance that have emerged in and through these Dalit movements? Performers such as Sathe have affirmed a Dalit politics that is rooted in solidarity and democratic equality (what Ranciere calls 'dissensus'). In these subaltern cultural spheres, partially neoliberal and partially autonomous subjectivities engage and accommodate 'religious ethnicity', as well as express heterogeneous discourses in and organisational forms of digital ecologies, enabling the medium to digitally materialise Dalit action. To say this, we realise, does not amount to very much in terms of rigorous claims to better understand the relationship between technology and Dalit emancipation. Perhaps we can mutate our question at this point: what digital practices further a politics of solidarity for Dalit emancipation? If Dalit subjectivity forms from the affective flows of exploitation and oppression, as well as the resistant powers of capacities emergent and residual throughout Dalit ecologies of social reproduction, what practice can compose new assemblages of resistance in this re-stratified, changing but ossified, domain?

'Mumbai is not for Maharashtrians, it is for everyone else', *'Mumbai tumchi, bhandi ghasa amchi'* ('Mumbai is yours, but utensils are ours, wash those'), are upper-caste jibes against Dalits. Brutal and violent, these comments are a part of the contexts of everyday Dalit practice in the psycho-geographies of caste-stratified Mumbai. Music and literature have their pan-Maharashtrian refrains, such as, *'Bamanaghariliwan, Kunbyaghari daana, Mahar-Manga gharigaana'* (The Brahmin (priestly caste) households have their writings, the Kunbi (peasant caste) households have their grains, and the Mahar-Mang (Untouchable caste) households have their songs). This refrain divides people according to caste households, as in a Brahmin household, you will find writing, in a Kunbi household (land-owning peasant caste), you will find food (grains), and in a Mahar-Mang (Dalit) household, you will find songs. The Dalit oral tradition of singing has now been folded into neoliberal aesthetics and Bollywoodised rebrandings; their entertainment value is repeated, extracted, abstracted and financialised. The Dalit is also appropriated at the level of culture: Dalit aesthetics as social media fetish.

DALIT ART, INDIAN ART

Art in India has Dalit origins. This is a startling fact to anyone who has not understood that the Varna system, as it proliferated its mechanisms and divisions, produced an image of pleasure-in-entertainment that oriented the flow of labour and pleasure from the Dalit to the Brahmin (see, for instance, the Natyasashtra). What happens when these communities undergo the phenomenon of migration, politicisation and digitisation? They carry this now-transformed and transplanted culture into contexts in which its hybridity and mixed practices develop new ecologies. Mumbai's Dalit communities are deeply imbricated in the social reproduction of upper-caste homes, as if Dalits were a kind of 'standing reserve' in the performance of chronically underpaid and non-unionised caste-based work in the domestic sphere. In this context, Dalit art affirms an emancipatory search for (sometimes religious, sometimes secular, often an affective mixture of the two) wisdom and emancipation. This search is deeply circumscribed by neoliberal caste structures constructed so as to ensure their own reproduction.

Newly digitalised Dalit expressive practices directly challenge these institutionalised structures. For example, the Mumbai-based 'Yalgaar Cultural Troupe', which has connections with leading Ambedkarite movements, gives live performances, and communicates, brands and markets its music through WhatsApp and other digital social networks and platforms. Dhammarakshit, lead singer of the troupe, said, 'It is important to change our performances just like people are changing. We should create a platform, which will be convenient for people to access. The reason for this is that people are victims of the phone and Internet nowadays. If we reach them, it will be great ...' In these Dalit cultural space-times, the push of capitalist social network media and the pull of Dalit organising for emancipation exist side by side. This is the condition of all art: captured freedom, virtuosity in a straitjacket. Dalit aesthetics makes this ontological and epistemological condition explicit.

Between the 1960s and 1980s, the Dalit author Baburao Bagul, through his empassioned prose, for example, *Jevha Mi Jaat Choral* (*When I had Concealed my Caste*) (Maitreya 2017b), 1963, showed how deep-rooted the caste system continues to be, even as a source of pain, which is horrible and lingering in Mumbai. He observed that by developing an epistemological aptitude, the poorest of the poor were struggling to live a life of dignity and survive the violence of caste. Bagul was one of the first people who took a look at how different kinds of forced transmutation of the migrant lower castes can function in the interests of the upper castes in Mumbai.

Embedded in a political philosophy of emancipation from all forms of domination, Dalit aesthetics breaks with the norms of dominant culture as and for entertainment. The agenda of authors like Bagul and Dhasal in Mumbai was not to achieve the apotheosis of the academic adornment of words, but rather, it was a straightforward ideological project. Their shared agenda was emancipation from the reality of caste domination. For instance, Dhasal's poem *Gandu Bagicha* (*Gandu* Garden):

> ... *it has already torn*
> *The condom of delusion*
> *To tatters* ...

> (Dhasal 1986)[4]

And the words that were necessary for this literature subverted the fetish of expressions and modes of discourse in dominant Indian aesthetics. The agenda of Dalit aesthetic is to open the question of what is particular and universal in Dalit consciousness-for-emancipation. The revolutionary writings that sprung out of this aesthetic made readers think and change the very form of the art. The works of people like Sathe and Sheikh follow this form of aesthetic.

ORGANISING AESTHETICS

In this chapter, we aim at bringing smart cities discourses and policy in India as an elite and corporate-driven agenda, rooted in critical relation with what human geographers have called the idea of the 'post-political' city. Guided by 'experts' whose knowledge has been legitimated through a capitalist-oriented scientism, the smart city policy aims to maximise the monopoly rents extractable from any city, given its specific combination of exploitable human, material, locational and infrastructural resources (clustering of hubs, etc.). In the contexts of Mumbai (in our examples), where the processes of urbanisation without (formal) industrialisation have transformed the city in the past three decades, how is cultural production caste-stratified (in terms of India's caste history)? And how has this historically caste-stratified cultural practice changed through digital social networks? How has mobile communication changed cultural production in Dalit cultures of struggle? How does this fold into and/or escape from, and point towards emancipation from the smart city's capitalist command and control—lines of flight with non-capitalist landing, as De Angelis (2017) urges? In the global North, creative industries (closely related to the smart cities agendas) increase a city or region's competitiveness through what Florida (2019) called the 'three T's' of the creative economy: tolerance (a universal, and hence, provincial notion of urban cosmopolitanism), technology (overwhelmingly oriented towards the value-generating sector in Internet protocol [IP]-generating software and services), and talent (that is, human resources, or following Marx, the commodity creative labour). How does the smart city affect the city's politics, specifically Dalit politics, in and through a distinctive collective aesthetic?

This chapter comes out of the contexts of a conversation among the three of us. Through it, we have begun to formulate a participatory research agenda with different practitioners of digital workarounds. In this work, we have put our findings in relation to other studies of social media in South Asia. The chapter allows a renewed consideration of the relations of power, the performances of identity, and the material ontologies within Dalit aesthetics. Much of the most provocative work in this field follows Clough (2018), Shaviro (2014) and Harman (2005) in considering aesthetics as, first, philosophy, and affirming its multiplicious embodiments. Here, we consider Dalit aesthetics as a concerted and consistent set of practices aimed at creating what Davidson and Iveson (2015), following Ranciere (1999, 2006), have called a dissensus for equality, rooted in sometimes oppositional, sometimes social reproductive (and often both) modes of collective organising and community leadership. In specific ways, these forms of Dalit agency are mediated, remediated and intensified through artistic methodologies, mobile media, social networks and digital technologies, more generally. While these technologies are thoroughly rooted in what Foucault (1983) and Ranciere (2006) note as being the historical connections between policy, police and politics, in postcolonial India, the specific conditions of urbanisation without industrialisation oblige us to consider relations of power and capital accumulation in a predominantly informal economy.

Now, through several decades of socialist planning and non-aligned geopolitics, what has been built up are differential, distributed, probabilistic, Big Data generating, and biopolitical, that is popula-tional habits (Clough 2018; Grosz 2017; Malabou 2005; Ravaisson 2008). In the pirate kingdoms (Sundaram 2009) of Mumbai, informal workarounds enfold practices of cash-and-barter economies in what business and management scholars have pre-critically termed 'frugal innovation' (Rajdou et al. 2012) but are better understood through the framework of ecological practices of commoning (De Angelis 2017). In this postcolonial and post-probabilistic context of an increasingly dominant 'India Shining' aesthetics (rooted in neoliberal forms of measure and 'quality control,' and upper-caste domination) and Dalit aesthetics of resistance (rooted in the collective and democratic demand for equality, justice and emancipation), the 'smart city' creeps forward through the material and cultural dispossession of Dalits in the name of formalising the economy. One sees the proliferation of enclosures, not only of forms of monopoly rents (Harvey 2002) but also in the spatial and violent forms of social apartheid enclosing Dalit communities, and securitising elite, largely upper-caste Hindu and resource-intensive gated 'communities'.

Consider the organising practice of Dadarao Patekar, who helped wage a struggle for the rights of Mumbai's *safai karamcharis* (manual scavenging workers) (Thorat 2016a; see also Balasubramaniam 2011; Guru 1998; Omvedt 2004). Thorat writes,

> It would not be an exaggeration to say that manual scavenging remains one of the worst forms of caste atrocities in the country. For the upper castes and the middle class, such a job is an abomination to a point where let alone doing the work, they even cover their

faces when people involved in manual scavenging cross their paths. The long rail tracks, the lifeline of Mumbai, are littered with human waste, and cleaning it remains a job that is almost exclusively reserved for Dalits (2016a).

Thorat (2016a) spoke with Dadarao Patekar, who has been a contract *safai karamchari* (a person employed in sanitation-related work) for the past 18 years:

> For Dadarao Patekar, 43, covering his face is not an option .... Beyond the job itself, the issues that his fellow workers face highlight the structures of caste domination in Mumbai. Patekar is a contract safaikarmachari in the Brihanmumbai Municipal (BMC) and deputy president of Kachara Vahatuk Shramik Sangh (KVSS) .... He rubbishes the ideology of upward social mobility, and believes that such terms are hypocritical .... How is access and knowledge of new technologies of scavenging—especially those touching on the health and safety of the workers themselves—denied or obstructed in the reproduction of caste hierarchies? (2016a).

Patekar says that most people engaged in this profession belong to the Dalit community, and he condemns such practices that are rooted in caste domination (Thorat 2016a). His early life perhaps expresses such condemnation:

> Patekar's father had to migrate from the drought-prone area of Marathwada; he could never complete his education due to caste-based poverty. Patekar says, 'Caste-based profession can only be demolished when the deprived class will get education. Mahatma Phule fought in his era; still it is the same. We have to fight like Mahatma Phule, to destroy the evil society of caste system. We need to organise and educate ourselves' (Thorat 2016a).

Concerned about the way in which workers are treated, with permanent workers getting more respect than temporary ones, he further states,

> ... the struggle for their rights is a long and tough road. 'There are a lot of ongoing rallies and assertions against this. Every month we organise two or three morchas or produce statements in front of the regime to show that we are asserting more than we can', he says .... Contract workers are not paid allowances by the BMC, and are not even provided with basic equipment like hand gloves, raincoat

and shoes. These basic technologies touching upon the very health and safety of the workers are an important means of reinforcing caste domination (Thorat 2016a).

Thorat also goes on to say that

Recently, in an incident that highlights the health dangers of the job, a safai karmachari from Thane was injured; the Thane Municipality Corporation did not pay any heed. To protest against this incident KVSS protested and organised a symbolic *mayat yatra* (death ceremony) in the name of Thane Municipal Corporation. Patekar in his political life has organised more than a thousand rallies (Thorat 2016a).

It is important to consider the media ecology of these Dalit rallies, as in them is bound up both a question of aesthetics and a practice of politicisation. As Ranciere puts it:

The police says that there is nothing to see on a road, that there is nothing to do but move along. It asserts that the space of circulating is nothing other than the space of circulation. Politics, in contrast, consists in transforming this space of 'moving-along' into a space for the appearance of a subject: i.e. the people, the workers, the citizens. It consists in refiguring the space, of what there is to do there, what is to be seen or named therein (quoted in Davidson and Iveson 2015: 553; see also Ranciere 1999: 29–30, 2001: 22).

The formal digital practices in India are said to optimise automation and mechanisation through an algorithmically architected infrastructure, which changes in real time by organising its code in resonance and tension with the tendencies of the big data generated through urban interaction. Yet, in Mumbai, which also purports to be, to an extent, a smart city, the manual labour of caste-enforced scavenging remains absolutely crucial to the social reproduction of both the formal and informal economies (Thorat 2016). In some way, all forms of scavenging work directly and precisely because of their caste basis are located outside the formal economy, yet are central to social reproduction as such (ibid.). Is there a specific Dalit economy, one in which Dalits both resist and institute forms of police, policy and politics, cutting across formal and informal economies? What is at stake between, for instance, a solidary feminist practice and Dalit organising, in terms of the logistics of this Dalit economy? These logistics are also forms of subjectivation, and therefore, have an affective structure or aesthetic. How do Dalit and non-Dalit participants and observers differently experience these rallies? In Patekar's practices of organising rallies, practices of politicising caste atrocities that touch on the very ontological conditions of social reproduction for Dalits— access to water, for instance—create speculative emancipatory spaces and at times halting traffic, disrupting stratified urban space, de-naturalising social antagonisms, and refusing economies of casteist austerity. Postcolonial dissensus, a space-time of revolutionary materialism, is created in this process, and a redemocratisation of the city through Dalit politics becomes sensibly and increasingly urgent.

Thorat (2016a) delves further into this dissensus:

> Recently, in the Kurla *jhuggis* (informal settlements), KVSS called a meeting on the privatisation of education in India. Neeta Salve, a resident of the Kurla said, 'I really embraced what Dadarao said because I never had this kind of knowledge of education. I assumed that education is expensive so no need to educate my child. Dadarao make me believe that there are good people who really work for the society and that education remains the strongest way to fight casteism' (2016).

Patekar says:

> '... We did not do much in our career but I will work for future. I don't want to see my children do this work'. Patekar goes at 8 AM for work and finishes by 2 PM everyday; after that he works for KVSS all the time .... In Mumbai there are 24 wards and every ward has more than 1,000 safaikaramcharis. To organise them it is important to talk to them personally and mobilise them .... This fight is likely to continue and it is unlikely that Patekar will give up ... (Thorat 2016a).

Thorat (2016a) continues:

> ... In Dalit practice, and highlighted in Patekar's own, pedagogy out of caste and class oppression necessarily is a collective, and commoning experience of what Moten and Harney (year) call 'fugitive study'; moving beyond that demand for commoning knowledge, Patekar insists on the importance of access to formalised, state sanctioned education, thereby repoliticising a social institution—education—that is increasingly withdrawn

from dissensual debate and rigorous contestation, enclosed within the private property regime of the upper caste/class.

As Iveson and Davidson recently argued:

The city and its constitutive peoples become an emancipatory space when it is viewed as a community of equals. But Ranciere's equality presupposition is not naïve to expertise. He demonstrates this most clearly in his exposition of Joseph Jacotot, the 17th-century French schoolteacher who documented his radical pedagogy. This approach proceeded with the premise that students have an ability to learn in the absence of any master or authority ... (2015: 555).

They further state:

What Ranciere seeks to show using Jacotot is not an equality of knowing, but rather the political implications of egalitarian contingency. It is not that anyone can do anything (i.e. some kind of ethical and political relativism), but rather that we must presume the equal ability of all to learn and, by extension, the equal ability to govern, adjudicate and mediate (Davidson and Iveson 2015: 555).

For Ranciere, *la politique* (politics) is the encounter of two hetero-geneous processes: the government's 'police' and the emancipating 'political' game of equality through the formation of *le politique* (emancipated political subjects) (Jaoul 2011; Ranciere 1999). How does the smart city design shape the terrain of play for this politics in Dalit lifeworlds? Today's postcolonial India is developing the smart city as an extension and mutation of both the police and the market. Egalitarian contingency is an important dimension to Dalit aesthetics, one increasingly interfaced in and through digital ecologies and bodily capacities. Such emancipatory impulses play a significant part in the life and work of Satish Rajguru, a 35-year-old Wi-Fi service provider, living and working out of one of the many Maharashtra Housing and Area Development Authority (MHADA) building societies, a low-income and mostly Dalit government housing scheme (Thorat and Kumar 2015). Well-known in the society for his social work rooted in Dalit solidarity and emancipation, Rajguru and his family work for the welfare of their communities. The Dalit aesthetic has been adapted by Rajguru as a pedagogical ritual of commemoration. Every year, between April and June, along with the other residents of the MHADA society, he helps to organise a programme to commemorate

Ambedkar Jayanti (the festival held on B. R. Ambedkar's birthday on 14 April). He and his team help to arrange the logistical infrastructure for the event, with some residents documenting the event on various types of cameras, some other residents helping to set up chairs, some others organising the stage. This yearly programme performs Dalit community (ibid.).

Rajguru is also looked upon as a kind of ideal family man, his wife Deepa is well-educated and an Ambedkarite; as she says of Ambedkar and water supply on the Jayanti, *'Jinke wajah se hummein paani mila hai, uss din toh pani milna hi chahiye'*('*It was because of Babasaheb Ambedkar we got water, especially on his birth anniversary, we will surely get water (supply)*') (Thorat and Kumar 2015). Satish's mother is a socially and politically important figure when it comes to water shortage issues in the society. On days that there is shortage in the daily water supply, she is the first one to go door-to-door to call people downstairs to question and demand why there is no water (ibid.). Satish is an autodidact of Internet technology and now uses that knowledge to provide his community with Internet connectivity. This work is also a training for organic intellectuals; his rounds from home-to-home allow him to gather not only his equipment and service rents, but also a way to understand the digital and material needs of his community better. Indeed, he aims to create a consensus of all Dalits in Mumbai. Rajguru, as a Dalit digital entrepreneur, has nurtured deep links to social change and emancipatory education programmes within the Dalit community. It bridges both the formal and informal economies, the home and the world, the analogue and the digital, and in a variety of ways, it is involved in forms of social reproduction of Dalit life and culture. Rajguru is both an agent of and actant in Mumbai's smart cities (ibid.).

CONCLUSION

This chapter, raising more questions than it has answered, has evolved through the collaboration of the three of us, by sharpening the questions of media ecologies in the cultural practices of subaltern and Dalit struggle. What has become clear throughout our conversation is that the methods of engaging with these practices have to evolve *in situ*, and that what remains relevant continually shifts while forms of power nonetheless produce (ideological and habituated) experiences of overall stasis.

Dalit dissensus challenges this stasis on several registers at once. At the level of ecology, Dalit communities have invented autonomous forms of social reproduction having partly-capitalist, partly-commoning ecologies. These ecologies are non-linear and volatile; solidary research must also consider the ethics of representation within such fluxes through virtual and materialist questions at once. What has been the tendency and capacities of these questions when put in the context of ongoing social apartheid, economic exclusion, and enforced 'informalisation' as caste austerity? Modi's Bharatiya Janata Party (BJP) government has pursued a fiscal approach with the aim of creating one mammoth Indian market; while demonetisation and tax reform have taken aim at macro-economic imbroglios in the circulation of national and household wealth, the lives of Dalit women and men have overwhelmingly been adversely affected precisely because of their precarious, cash-based infrastructures of social reproduction. Paradoxically, it is also precisely these everyday infrastructures of social reproduction that, as we have seen, are creatively assembled in diverse practices expressing potential and actual ecologies of struggle that proliferate in differently scaled forms. How can these struggles transform the practice of research and the politics of knowledge in contemporary postcolonial feminist media ecologies of research? And how, in turn, do (and can) the solidarities and complicities across research and organising enliven or block an emancipatory politics commensurate with our present conjuncture of masculinist and Hindutva capitalist security?

Digital technologies have wrought changes in mainstream aesthetics. Dalit aesthetics for a democratic dissensus and politics of emancipatory solidarity is often forgotten, or sometimes appropriated. The invisibilisation of Dalit contributions in urban politics and aesthetics is the result. Today, social media movements have come to overshadow older strategies of oppressed people's movements (Thorat and Bannerjee 2017), and this seems to be consistent with the depoliticising tendency of India's elite, upper-caste consensus. Dalit organising in and through a digital and analogue aesthetics brings political movements into productive and antagonistic relation to art, cultural expression, subaltern identities and emancipatory justice. In keeping with the commoning dynamics of Dalit aesthetics, the digital is adapted and repurposed to be accessible to all, and thus, repoliticising the very form of smart city digital technologies. In the examples we have provided, Satish's mother participates in water struggles, and her resilience is her aesthetic; Satish develops entrepreneurial and commoning strategies with newer forms of technology, rejecting the status quoist 'accepting what everybody else got' by accessing and commoning resources; and his wife is adapting technology to change the educational opportunities for her children and other young Dalit people, sharing the thought of Babasaheb Ambedkar through social media and public pedagogy. Through Dalit rallies for manual scavengers, dancing in malls, creating music and painting portraits to continue the fight for water in spaces like the MHADA, the Dalit aesthetic activates the democratic dissensus of Mumbai, the city where Dalits continue to seek rights to space and identity, long after the Samyukta Maharashtra Movement.

One future avenue of this ongoing research concerns emergent habits and Dalit aesthetics: Jio, a new telecom venture by Reliance Corporation, featured free Internet for a couple of months, and many poor people were drawn into their marketing campaign. Ads like 'India's hooked on Idea 4G' (Idea 2017) make the viewer wonder whether the idea is to sell the product or warn users of the consequences of its use. Dhammarakshit, a Yalgaar troupe member, who performs mostly in Mumbai and has cinema industry experience, said, 'To people like me who can earn but not spend money on Internet, Jio is helpful but it is like sweet poison' (Thorat 2016b).

This attempt at a theoretical and political resonance across London and Mumbai is from the prehensions of a mid-career academic raised in upper-caste settings, and now teaching critical media theory in a business school whose mission affirms solidarity for justice and equality, and from the perspective of two organic Dalit-Bahujan intellectuals, one a poet/filmmaker, and the other a social psychologist, both independent researchers, and acute participant observers in contemporary digital practices. From these perspectives, we offer the chapter as indications and first approximations of future conversations and collective study on the subject.

Notes

1. Here, we mean exception in Agamben (2005) and Benjamin's (2008) sense, linking its necropolitical logic to caste and exploitation in India— the Dalit lives as the debilitated exception in a perpetual state of exception. We do not mean exception in the sense of American 'exceptionalism'!

2. The term *Kalasangini* translates to 'companion of the arts'.

3. Amar Shaikh (Meheboob Shaikh) was born at Barsi, Solapur district, Maharashtra. He was known as a revolutionary poet. He also played a major role in the Samyukta Maharashtra Movement.

4. This poem became an example for showing anger through verse (Ketkar 2017).

References

Agamben, Giorgio. 2005. 'State of Exception', Kevin Attell (trans.). Chicago, Illinois: The University of Chicago Press.

Balasubramaniam, J. 2011. 'Dalits and a Lack of Diversity in the Newsroom', *Economic and Political Weekly* 46(11): 21–23.

Bagul, B. 1963. *Jevva Mi Jaat Chorli (When I have Cancelled My Caste)*. Mumbai: Akshar Prakashan.

Benjamin, W. 2008. *The Work of Art in the Age of its Technological Reproducibility, and Other Writings on Media*. Cambridge, Massachusetts: Harvard University Press.

Chatterjee, P. 2011. *Lineages of Political Society: Studies in Postcolonial Democracy*. New York: Columbia University Press.

Chopra, R. 2006. 'Global Primordialities: Virtual Identity Politics in Online Hindutva and Online Dalit Discourse', *New Media and Society* 8(2): 187–206.

Clough, P. 2018. *The User Unconscious on Affect, Media, and Measure*. Minneapolis: University of Minnesota Press.

Dandvate, M. 2005. *Dialogue with Life*. New Delhi: Allied Publishers.

Davidson, M. and K. Iveson. 2015. 'Recovering the Politics of the City: From the "Post-political City" to a "Method of Equality" for Critical Urban Geography', *Progress in Human Geography* 39(5): 543–59.

De Angelis, D. M. 2017. *Omnia Sunt Communia: On the Commons and the Transformation to Postcapitalism*. London: Zed Books.

Deleuze, G. 1992. 'Postscript on the Societies of Control', *October* 59: 3–7.

Deshpande, S. 2009. 'The Practice of Social Theory and the Politics of Location', *Economic and Political Weekly* 44(10): 40–46.

Dhasal, N. 1986. *Gandu Bagicha*. Mumbai: Shabd Publications.

Florida, R. 2019. *The Rise of the Creative Class*. New York: Basic Books.

Foucault, M. 1983. 'The Subject of Power'. In H. Dreyfus and P. Rabinow (eds), *Michel Foucault: Beyond Structuralism and Hermeneutics*, pp. 16–48. Brighton: Harvester.

Gidwani, V. and K. Sivaramakrishnan. 2003. 'Circular Migration and Rural Cosmopolitanism in India', *Contributions to Indian Sociology* 37(1–2): 339–67.

Grosz, E. 2017. *The Incorporeal: Ontology, Ethics, and the Limits of Materialism*. New York: Columbia University Press.

Guru, G. 1998. 'Understanding Ambedkar's Construction of National Movement', *Economic and Political Weekly* 33(4): 156–57.

Hansen, T. B. 1996. 'The Vernacularisation of Hindutva: the BJP and Shiv Sena in Rural Maharashtra', *Contributions to Indian Sociology* 30(2): 177–214.

Harman, G. 2005. *Guerrilla Metaphysics. Phenomenology and the Carpentry of Things*. Chicago: Open Court.

Harvey, D. 2002. 'The Art of Rent: Globalization, Monopoly and Cultural Production', *Socialist Register* 38: 93–110.

Hegde, S. 2010. 'The Call of Difference: Agency, Subalternity and Beyond', *Economic and Political Weekly* 45(33): 82–84.

Hesmondhalgh, D. 2010. 'Normativity and Social Justice in the Analysis of Creative Labour', *Journal for Cultural Research* 14(3): 231–49.

Hewlett, N. 2010. *Badiou, Balibar, Ranciere: Re-thinking Emancipation*. London: A&C Black.

———. 2012. 'Marx, Engels, and the Ethics of Violence in Revolt', *The European Legacy* 17(7): 882–98.

Idea, 'India's Hooked on Idea 4G. #LookLook (60)', YouTube, 31 May 2017. Available at https://www.youtube.com/watch?v=2W_9oUwDAcI (accessed 20 October 2019).

Jaoul, N. 2011. 'Manju Devi's Martyrdom: Marxist-Leninist Politics and the Rural Poor in Bihar', *Contributions to Indian Sociology* 45(3): 347–71.

Ketkar, Sachin, 'A Language of Heterogeneity: The Poetry of Namdeo Dhasal', Sahapedia, 21 June 2016. Available at https://www.sahapedia.org/language-of-heterogeneity-the-poetry-of-namdeo-dhasal (accessed 17 November 2017).

Limbale, S. 2004. *Towards an Aesthetic of Dalit Literature: Histories, Controversies, and Considerations*. New Delhi: Orient BlackSwan; Ann Arbor: University of Michigan.

Maitreya, Yogesh, 'The Sound and Fury of Anna Bhau Sathe's Words: An Icon of Maharashtra's Dalit Literature', Firstpost, 15 October 2017a. Available at http://www.firstpost.com/living/the-sound-and-fury-of-anna-bhau-sathes-words-an-icon-of-maharashtras-dalit-literature-4140067.html (accessed 17 November 2017).

_____, 'Maharashtra's Dalit Literature Visionary: How Baburao Bagul's Words Exposed a Casteist Society', Firstpost, 21 October 2017b. Available at https://www.firstpost.com/living/maharashtras-dalit-literature-visionary-how-baburao-baguls-words-exposed-a-casteist-society-4159491.html (accessed 22 November 2017).

Malabou, C. 2005. *The Future of Hegel: Plasticity, Temporality, and Dialectic*. London: Psychology Press.

Mandarini, M. 2006. 'Marx and Deleuze: Money, Time, and Crisis', *Polygraph* 18, Article 3, 73–98.

Manzoor, Sarfraz, 'Sadat Hasan Manto: He Anticipated Where Pakistan Would Go', *The Guardian*, 11 June 2016.

Meiksins Wood, E. 2007. *Democracy Against Capitalism; Renewing Historical Materialism*. Chicago: Aakar Books.

Nandy, A. (ed.). 1998. *The Secret Politics of our Desires: Innocence, Culpability and Indian Popular Cinema*. London: Palgrave Macmillan.

Omvedt, G. 1991. 'The Anti-caste Movement and the Discourse of Power', *Race and Class* 33(2): 15–27.

_____. 2004. 'Untouchables in the World of IT', *Contemporary Review* 284(1660): 286–88.

_____. 2010. 'Caste in the Census', *Social Change* 40(4): 405–14.

_____. 2012. 'Understanding Caste: From Buddha to Ambedkar and Beyond'. New Delhi: Orient BlackSwan.

Oommen, T. K. 1984. 'Sources of Deprivation and Styles of Protest: The Case of the Dalits in India', *Contributions to Indian Sociology* 18(1): 45–61.

Patil, S. 1988. *Abrahmani Sahityache Saundaryashastra*. Pune: Sugava Publications.

Pratt, A. C. 2009. 'Policy Transfer and the Field of the Cultural and Creative Industries: What Can be Learned from Europe?' In L. Cong and J. O'Connor (eds), *Creative Economies, Creative Cities*, The GeoJournal Library, Springer, 98: 9–23.

Rai, Amit, Rachna Ramesh Kumar and Shiva Thorat, Interview with Sadanand More.

_____. Interview with Prasanna.

_____. Interview with Dhammarakshit.

Radjou, Navi, Jaideep Prabhu and Simone Ahuja. 2012. *Jugaad Innovation: Think Frugal, Be Flexible, Generate Breakthrough Growth*. New York: John Wiley and Sons.

Ranciere, J. 1999. *Disagreement: Politics and Philosophy*. Minneapolis: University of Minnesota Press.

_____. 2006. 'Thinking between Disciplines: An Aesthetics of Knowledge', *Parrhesia* 1(1): 1–12.

Ravaisson, F. 2008. *Of Habit*. London: Bloomsbury Publishing.

Shaviro, S. 2014. *The Universe of Things: On Speculative Realism*, Vol. 30. Minneapolis, Minnesota: University of Minnesota Press.

Shone, Satheesh, 'Watch: How Sambhaji Bhagat is Helping Dalit Musicians in Maharashtra Go Digital', Scroll.in, 16 November 2017. Available at https://video.scroll.in/858107/watch-how-sambhaji-bhagat-is-helping-dalit-musicians-in-maharashtra-go-digital (accessed 17 November 2017).

Smartadmincp, 'Mumbai Metropolitan Region to Develop 5 Smart Cities', Smart Cities Projects, 20 December 2014. Available at http://www.smartcitiesprojects.com/tag/mumbai-smart-city-plan/ (accessed 12 November 2017).

Spinoza, B. 1992. *Ethics: With the Treatise on the Emendation of the Intellect and Selected Letters*. Indianapolis: Hackett Publishing.

Sundaram, R. 2009. *Pirate Modernity: Delhi's Media Urbanism*. London: Routledge.

Velaskar, P. 2012. 'Education for Liberation: Ambedkar's Thought and Dalit Women's Perspectives', *Contemporary Education Dialogue* 9(2): 245–71.

Thorat, Shiva, 'Dadarao Patekar: Fighting for the Rights of Mumbai's Safai Karamcharis', TwoCircles.net, 19 August 2016a. Available at http://twocircles.net/2016aug19/1471584474.html (accessed 17 November 2017).

——, 'In Mumbai, Dancers Shake a Leg in the Hope for a Better Future', TwoCircles.net, 21 December 2016b. Available at http://twocircles.net/2016dec21/1482330513.html (accessed 12 November 2017).

Thorat, Shiva and Rachna Ramesh Kumar, Interview with Satish Rajguru, 2 November 2015.

Thorat, S. and A. Bannerjee, '#solidarity; hyprocrisy of activism', Presentation at the Aesthetics and the Political in Contemporary India: Deleuzian Explorations, Tata Institute of Social Sciences (TISS), Mumbai, 17 February 2017.

Tronti, M. 2010. 'Workerism and Politics', *Historical Materialism* 18(3): 186–89.

Films Cited

Any Body Can Dance. 2013. Remo D'Souza (dir.). Siddharth Roy Kapur and Ronny Screwvala.

Any Body Can Dance 2. 2015. Remo D'Souza (dir.). Siddharth Roy Kapur.

PART II

Digital Negotiations

perturb six

Cinema, in Your Pocket

Theorising Film-watching on a Mobile Screen

MAANVI

INTRODUCTION

> *'But now the reflected image has become separable, transportable. And where is it transported? Before the public.'*
>
> —*The Work of Art in the Age of Mechanical Reproduction*
> (Benjamin 1936)

How do people watch films in India? Common sense and academic literature have an easy answer to the question—in a theatre. Despite the brief interruption caused by the coming in of television in the mid-1980s and 1990s, the supremacy of the theatre as the cornerstone of analysing film-watching in India remains unquestioned. But then, why was I grappling with this question? In a pilot research I had conducted to study representations of love in popular Hindi films, I had assumed that the space where the viewer would first encounter and actively view the film would be in a theatre. An assumption, which I found much to my surprise, to be incorrect, and as one respondent informed me, 'woefully behind the times'. Most of my respondents admitted that out of the five latest Hindi films they had seen, almost two had been on screens other than the theatre— on mobile phones, laptops and tablets. Unlike the almost ritualised activity of going to a theatre to watch a film, people I spoke to said that they usually watch films while travelling to work. Respondents said that instead of watching the whole film at one go, with the interval for gossip and washroom breaks, they watch a film in parts; pausing it when they want, selecting only songs or funny scenes to watch, and fast forwarding the 'boring' bits.

There is a subtle shift away from the theatre to other screens—like laptops, mobile phones and tablets—as spaces to watch films in India. This shift is accompanied by a change in the profile of the Hindi film viewer. As Ganti (2012) argues, 'the urban middle-class film-viewer represents the ideal audience member for an industry concerned with the issues of prestige, respect and global circulation' (2012: 17). For this 'gentrified' viewer, the multiplex is often the preferred space to watch a film, with the space becoming a symbol for middle-class aspirations to comfort, luxury and exclusivity (Athique 2011). While the theatre's dominance is not under threat, it no longer retains the pole position as the preferred choice to watch films for a majority of people in India.

But why young women? The possibility of subversion and the threat of 'moral corruption' means that for a large section of women in India, owning a mobile phone does not necessarily mean that they have complete control over it. Most respondents in the study spoke about their first mobile phone in terms like 'allow' and 'permission', implying that even when the mobile phone may be economically affordable to the woman, it may not be as accessible to her within the patriarchal family structure for a variety of other reasons—usually moral connotations attached with the consequences of owning a mobile phone. This interplay of morality, ownership and technology, when looking at women using mobile phones, is the reason why this chapter chooses to focus on the woman viewer.

Who is a woman viewer? On the mobile phone, a woman can choose which film to watch. For a woman, this film could be one she may not be allowed to watch in theatres ('adult films', as a majority of the respondents in the study asserted) or one which might be dated, but still shape her ideas of the world around her (belonging to the 'favourite films that are always on my phone' category). Thus, this chapter looks at the consequences of 'owning' a screen where the woman is free to choose and customise media content, and analyse these choices through the prism of safety, mobility and morality. In this context, what does it mean to watch a film outside the theatre?

METHODOLOGY

In India, watching films on mobile phones is a relatively new trend, aided by the emergence of smartphones and digital piracy. But despite its popularity, there is not a lot of conversation around this activity, whether in academic circles or among people who actually use their phones to watch films. One of the reasons for this seeming lack of information is the understanding that the way in which a film is seen is not nearly as important as the actual text of the film being watched. This apparent normalisation of the fact that mobile phones can be used to watch films, and the general indifference to the screening device when studying film-watching, led me to use a mix of methodologies to conduct my research: in-depth, semi-structured interviews; focus group discussions; and a virtual discussion thread located on Quora, a question-and-answer social networking website.

The sample for this study (for the semi-structured interviews and focus group discussions) was selected through non-probable sampling, specifically, snowball sampling. Thirteen semi-structured interviews and one focus group discussion were conducted over a period of three months with male and female respondents belonging in the age group of 18–25 years. Despite the study focusing on women watching films on mobile phones, men were also interviewed to obtain a perspective on the gendered aspects of film-watching. The respondents mainly belonged to the urban middle class and included students enrolled in undergraduate and graduate programmes and working professionals, most of whom migrated to Delhi and were not 'native' residents. Ten out of 16 respondents have come to Delhi from neighbouring states like Uttar Pradesh, Haryana and Bihar.

LOOKING AT THE SCREEN: HOW FILM-WATCHING TRANSFORMS WHEN THE SCREEN SHRINKS

The short answer to why women watch films on the mobile phone is convenience. But unpacking this term reveals various connotations. In this case, convenience is located in the context of spatial accessibility to a woman in the public space; the aspirational, exclusivist location of the multiplex in a mall and the stereotypes associated with a woman going to the theatre alone. Apart from economic unaffordability, access also becomes framed in the context of 'comfort'/'discomfort'. For a woman, the mobile phone is invested with anxieties of safety, and also, of morality. The debates around these issues are inextricably intertwined with the use of the mobile phone as a screen. Since gender, screen and audience are intertwined in a complex way, it is helpful to think of the three as being in a triangular relationship, with convenience at the centre of this framework.

This chapter analyses traditional approaches to film-watching in India. It takes into account three approaches—Madhav Prasad's 'darshanic' spectator, audience ethnographies, and Bourdieu's taste and distinction to explain the choice and experience of watching a film in a theatre. Drawing on these approaches, the chapter formulates an amalgamated theory of film-watching in India.

The popular Hindi film is the generic text that the chapter focuses on while analysing watching films on the mobile phone, and thus, the transformations of film-watching experience is influenced by the text of the film. Therefore, before we proceed further into analysis, it is essential to locate the Hindi film and define the 'popular' Hindi film and popular Hindi film audiences in the context of this study.

BEING 'POPULAR': THE HINDI FILM AND ITS AUDIENCES

For the purpose of this chapter, I would like to define the popular Hindi film as an assimilation of various genres, and its characteristic feature is what Vasudevan (2010) argues to be its heterogeneous popular format. However, the study is also cognisant of the capitalist industry, which 'produces and markets these films' and is 'determined by a variety of factors, including the political structure and the hegemonic project of the modern state' (Prasad 1998: 16).

As far as defining the popular Hindi film audience is concerned, their heterogeneity is an essential factor, especially in the way different audiences receive a single popular film text. However, these 'dispersed, anonymous audiences' (Prasad 1998: 16) are created by the industry itself, who base production on their imagination of the desires of these audiences. Interestingly, this construction of the Hindi film audience is often premised on box office success. As Ganti (2012) argues,

Box office success or failure either reinforces or revises filmmakers' assumptions about audiences—from their composition and tastes, to intellectual abilities and codes of morality; therefore, I argue that for Hindi filmmakers the box-office serves as a metonym for the practice of film consumption and operates as a technology of 'social envisioning' ... (2012: 282).

Since film-watching on mobile phones leads to the creation of an isolated audience, this chapter will align itself with looking at audiences as dispersed and autonomous. However, a caveat must be introduced. Among the many changes that have been brought about by the coming in of the multiplex, one of the most important has been the emergence of the 'multiplex film'. When the single screen theatre became multi-screen multiplex, it introduced the space for Hindi films which were not all-encompassing in their outlook. The 'genre' film became a saleable commodity, because there were audiences who were interested in a niche film, and more importantly, there was a screen to exhibit them. As Vishwanath (2007) argues, 'the multiplex reinforces, and legitimates, the dominance of the consumable middle class family film, whilst at the same time offering, through its excess capacity, a toehold to film-makers producing small offbeat films' (2007: 3293).

THE WAYS WE WATCH CINEMA

Keeping these definitions of the popular Hindi film and Hindi film audiences in mind, the subsequent section draws on three approaches to theorise film-watching on mobile devices.

The 'Darsanic' Spectator

Basing his analysis on the feudal family romance,[1] Prasad (1998) posits the 'darsanic' spectator in opposition to the spectator in traditional Hollywood cinema. In Hollywood, the spectator is 'an isolated, individualised position of voyeurism coupled with an anchoring identification with a figure in the narrative' (Prasad 1998: 74). However, in Hindi cinema, the structure of spectation is premised on 'darsana', wherein the spectator is a mute witness to the spectacle of the Hindi film and identification is symbolic, not imaginary.

The darsanic mode of spectation derives from the 'darsana' tradition in Hindu worship. Darsana implies a mode of being seen, where the devotee is seen to be included in a divine order simply by being seen (or in the field of view) of the deity. Extrapolating these ideas into the Hindi film, the spectator does not 'see' the Hindi film hero, but goes to the theatre to be seen—to be in the presence of divinity, in a way. The screen becomes the point of mediation, and the theatre, the temple. This is not to say that the hero in a popular Hindi film can be un-problematically treated as a demi-god, but rather, that the structure of spectation that guides film-watching in India is based on such a construction.[2] As Prasad argues,

> ... Contrary to the voyeuristic relation, in the darsanic relation the object gives itself to be seen and in so doing confers privilege upon the spectator. The object of the darsanic gaze is superior, a divine figure or a king who presents himself as a spectacle of dazzling splendour to his subjects—the 'praja' or people (1998: 76).

The darsanic gaze embodies symbolic identification as opposed to imaginary identification. Symbolic identification implies that the viewer identifies with 'the other precisely at a point at which he is inimitable, at the point which eludes resemblance' (Prasad 1998: 76).[3] Imaginary identification, on the other hand, is when the viewer identifies with the other as a personal identity. The hero is not a superhero (symbolic identification, as in the Hindi film) who can fight, romance and solve mysteries. He is, instead, an everyman, *just like me* (emphasis mine). A significant example of the darsanic gaze and the symbolic identification inherent in such a structure is looking at the audience reaction to MGR. Pandian (1989) argues that MGR was a subaltern hero, not only in terms of the values he embodied on-screen, but also in terms of his persona off-screen. Describing the way audiences reacted to an MGR film, he says that in Tamil Nadu,

> ... It is a thin line that divides entertainment from ritual and various kind of social festivities. In fact, watching MGR films has become almost a ritual in itself. One can witness crowds gathered to watch MGR films, burning camphor before huge cut-outs of him, distributing water to the populace—as one would before a deity during temple festivals (Pandian 1989: 65).

The *darsanic* mode of spectation is an important paradigm to understand film-watching in India, with an emphasis on the screen and the spectator. And it becomes even more significant when one is looking at watching a film on the mobile phone, because it brings to fore attendant issues of the shrinking screen, a new form of symbolic identification, and the effect that the small screen has on the 'larger-than-life' perception of the Hindi film.

For film-watching on mobile phones, the '*darsanic*' theory cannot be used in isolation since it still confines itself to a psychoanalytic approach to film-watching. The '*darsanic*' structure of spectation locates the film-goer in isolation and does not take into account the effect that the audience has on the spectator while watching a film and the spatiality of the film-watching space.

Audience Ethnographies

Meaning-making in a theatre does not take place in isolation. The Indian audience is as much a producer of meaning as a consumer of the intended meaning inherent in the text of the film. They are not a passive audience, but one who actively and continually make meaning while viewing the film. Continued engagement of the viewers with the film may manifest in ways that include singing along to the songs, selective viewing, and transforming the viewing experience for fellow viewers in the theatre through commentary. All these strategies not only alter the meaning of the film being viewed, but also ensure that the memory of watching the film is associated with other meanings that are dependent on the environment in which the film was consumed or received. Keeping this in mind, the second approach which the study draws its arguments from consists of audience ethnographies conducted in a theatre, and subsequently, on a television screen to determine the ways in which audiences interact with, make meaning of, and contribute to the text of the film. Srinivas (1998) unpacks active audiences by focusing on popular Hindi film audiences. She posits three kinds of viewing that the audiences partake in: selective viewing, collective viewing and passive viewing (ibid.).

Focusing on 'habituated viewers' (viewers who regularly go to the theatre and are habitually familiar with the form of the popular Hindi film), Srinivas (1998) identifies selective viewing as the activity when viewers select scenes to watch *in the theatre*, instead of watching the whole film. It is interesting to note that she is arguing that viewers in a theatre practice selective viewing, when this is seen as a characteristic feature of film-watching on mobile phones. Just as viewers watching a film on the phone break up the film form into chunks to selectively watch favourite scenes, songs or the 'entry sequence' of the hero, audiences in the theatre also walk in and walk out of the theatre. This leads to the audiences 'selecting fragments with which to construct a collage-like whole' (ibid.: 329).

Audience ethnographies focusing on the viewing of a specific text of a film also throw up interesting insights, which can be extrapolated into film-watching on mobile phones. For instance, in her ethnography of audiences of *Hum Aapke Hain Koun?*, Uberoi (2001) juxtaposes the pleasure obtained by audiences from watching the film with a critical analysis of the image of the 'ideal Indian family' that the film constructs. She analyses audience's responses to the 'Indian values' embodied in the 'clean, family film'[4] (Uberoi 2001: 312). But throughout her analysis, she emphasises the varying responses (sometimes even contradictory) to the same event in the film.

Although audience ethnographies are a useful way of analysing the way in which an audience interacts with the screen, and they bring to the fore the potentially fragmentary nature of 'collective viewing' (selective viewing, heterogeneous meaning-making practices), they still do not foreground the choice of the viewer in relation to the screen. They assume that the first encounter between the audience and the text of the film will take place inside a theatre. They do not explain the motivations behind the choice of a viewer to watch a film in a theatre, as opposed to other screens like the television, laptop or the mobile phone.

Bourdieu's Taste and Distinction

It is in the context of the viewer's choice that this study draws on Pierre Bourdieu's study of taste and distinction among classes in a specific cultural context. Bourdieu (1984) argues that our perception of what constitutes aesthetic enjoyment is constituted by a system of social classification. Aesthetic enjoyment implies within it the question of 'taste'. Taste, then, is not an inherent value associated with certain forms of entertainment, but becomes a construction by consumers who are locating themselves in a specific class position. He argues that in the 'economy of cultural goods', there is an overall logic which governs the ways of consuming cultural goods that 'are regarded, at particular moments as art' (Bourdieu 1984: 1).

Taking the popular Hindi film as a 'cultural good', and extrapolating Bourdieu's arguments, there are certain forms of consumption of the Hindi film text that are considered legitimate, like the theatre. Watching a film anywhere else is understood to take away from the 'aura' (Benjamin 1936) of the text. However, even within this institute of legitimation (in this case, the theatre), there is a choice made by the consumer, pertaining to which film to watch. As has been argued, 'The apparently neutral decision of which film to see is conditional upon where we recognize ourselves in profiles of magazines, newspapers, reviews, 'titles' like rom-coms etc.' (Harbord 2002: 3).

Thus, film exhibition spaces are invested with diverse symbolic statuses; for instance, the multiplex, with exclusivity and middle-class aspiration, and the mobile phone, with privacy and comfort. Bourdieu's theory of institutes of legitimation (1984) becomes particularly significant when we look at mobile phones because they are perceived to be 'alternative' devices for film viewing, and therefore, become inscribed in the 'popular art/high art' binary, wherein the multiplex becomes the preferred choice for film-watching for the well-off, middle class, while the mobile phone is seen as the preferred choice for the working classes.

A 'Mobile' Theory of Film-watching

Drawing on all the above three approaches, I would like to propose a film-watching experience which includes the following three elements. It takes into account the class position of the viewer, reflected in the 'choice' that the viewer makes when deciding where to watch a popular Hindi film. Once inside the theatre, the film-watching experience is influenced by a collective, 'active' (Srinivas 1998) viewing constituted in part by the interaction of the 'crowd' with the screen. But, simultaneously, meaning-making in the theatre is fragmented, heterogeneous in nature, and influenced by the socio-political context of the individual viewer. And finally, at the level of the spectator, the viewer engages in symbolic identification through the '*darsanic*' mode of spectation, which may or may not be problematised by the existence of the individuated audience in a multiplex. Simply put, the film-watching experience gradually isolates the viewer, starting from her/his class position in a stratified society, to a member of the audience in the theatre, and finally, as an isolated, individual spectator practising '*darsana*'.

Extending this theory to film-watching on mobile phones, the three elements are distorted and transformed in various ways. One, the '*darsanic*' spectator becomes redundant, because with the mobile phone, the spectator does not have to go to the theatre to be 'seen by divinity'; the divine comes to her. And at her beck and call. When watching a film on the mobile phone, the viewer can play a film any time she wants, pause it as she feels like it and can skip chunks of the film if she wishes. When the screen on which a film is seen becomes small, the viewer feels more 'connected' to the film; as a respondent emphatically stated, while watching films on mobile phones, she feels more 'connected' to the film. This connection can be understood as a relation of equivalence, as opposed to the devotee–divine relation in the '*darsana*' structure theorised by Prasad (1998: 75).

Two, with the collective audience in a theatre, the film-viewing experience of the cinema crowd becomes even more fragmented. However, as the subsequent section will argue, it does not lead to a completely isolated viewer, but to the emergence of what I propose to call 'earphone publics'.

And finally, the social values invested in film exhibition spaces become more classified, in congruence with the increasing stratification of classes. As the final section in this chapter discusses, this leads to the construction of a hierarchy of screens for the Hindi film viewer. The dynamics of the 'choice' for a certain screen become even more complex when the film moves from the theatre to the mobile screen, and as interviews conducted for the study exemplify, 'taste' becomes further invested with middle-class anxieties and a desire to identify with an elite cultural class in a society.

Defining Earphone 'Publics'

Ria,[5] a 21-year-old student, said, 'It is only when I am watching with more people that I feel going to the theatre is easier. Sharing your one tiny little screen with multiple people is hard, so I guess that is the major disadvantage.'

The desire to watch a film in a clean, safe space with a 'decent' crowd is one of the major attractions of visiting the multiplex. This differentiation between the 'decent' crowd and the general 'cinema' crowd is a major premise on which the space of the multiplex is built. In her ethnography of the Indian film audience, Srinivas (1998) argues that the audience inside a theatre in India is an 'active audience'. They interact with the film playing on the screen and participate in meaning-making collectively. When an audience whistles, hoots loudly or laughs at unintended places, it changes the intended meaning of the film.

Thus, traditionally, film viewing in the Indian context has been seen as a 'collective experience'—one that draws on the life experiences of its heterogeneous audience to produce meaning, which may or may not coincide with the intended meaning of the film. But when we move to the multiplex, the construction of the space is such that it encourages a more private film-watching experience. The social expectation of the multiplex is that it comprises an audience who are made up of separate individuals, as opposed to a cinema 'public'—who receive the text of the film in its entirety and collectively participates in meaning-making of this text. The plush seats of the multiplex, the spaces between the seats, and more importantly, its location in a mall, which is a clear symbol of class and material aspiration, means that the audience in the multiplex theatre is more individual than in a single screen theatre. Talking about the switch between single screen theatres and multiplex, which many viewers unconsciously make, Vishwanath says,

> The appearance on screen of their favourite stars like Raj Kumar, Chiranjeevi or Upendra would be cause not merely for hooting, whistling, etc., but at times extreme adulatory forms of fan behaviour such as throwing coins on the screen or performing an 'aarti' when the hero appears. As against this, the appearance of a

Brad Pitt on a multiplex screen is received in a passive, suave and sophisticated manner (2007: 3290).

This individual experience of film-watching becomes even more individual when the screen shrinks from that of the theatre to the smartphone. This 'atomisation of audiences', as I would like to call it, reaches its logical extreme when the viewer is watching a film on his or her phone. Compared to a multiplex, wherein the film-watching experience is still framed in the context of the fellow viewers (even if it is not 'collective viewing'), when watching a film on the mobile phone, there is no one between the screen and the audience. Extending the continuum of increasing individualisation of the audience, from Srinivas's collective audience to Athique's 'steady flow of consumers moving effortlessly and individually in a private, commercial space' (Athique 2011: 155), I would like to propose the emergence of 'earphone publics'.

The reasoning behind calling mobile audiences 'earphone' is that the earphone is symbolic of various strategies used by a woman to negotiate the public space. Yet, even when she is at home, it becomes a tool for her to create a personal space. As Ria told me,

> When I am outside and someone sees me engrossed in my phone, they know not to disturb me. Like even when I am at home and sitting with other people, if both of us start to look at our phone that means our conversation is over .... It's literally giving a signal that I don't want to talk right now, and yes that is how I identify my private space. Like even when my parents are at home and I am usually hanging out with them, but the moment I catch hold of my phone even they know that there is no way to get through to me. That's basically my private space.

Thus, even in the space of a home, where she is 'safe', the phone is used to define a private space. The use of the word 'earphone', then, not only indicates an individuated viewer, but also a strategy to create a private space. Yet, I choose to locate this individualised viewer as a part of the 'public', much in the same vein as the cinema 'crowd' in a theatre. This is because, despite the individual experience of watching a film on the mobile phone, most respondents spoke about how they discussed the film together. They asserted that they would watch the film individually, but that the film would be discussed in detail with their friends and acquaintances. Moreover, films on mobile phones are usually transmitted through networks of friends, implying an almost recommendation-based system where one film travels through various social networks (both virtual and otherwise).

Another interesting transformation that takes place when the screen shifts from the theatre to the mobile phone is with regard to the control that the viewer has on the film-viewing experience. When watching a film on the phone, a viewer can pause whenever she wants, or skip the parts she does not like, or return to some scenes or songs in the film, which she likes. Varsha, a 21-year-old student, says,

> If I go to the theatre then I have to watch the film for three hours and then there is the whole problem of going alone. The point is when you go to the theatre you have to watch until the whole film ends, you may sleep but you have to wait. On the phone, even if I have sat down without cooking dinner, then I can watch the film, pause it, make dinner and then watch it again. But in the theatres you can't do anything, you have to watch the whole thing even if *dimaag kharaab bhi ho raha ho* [you're going crazy]. On phones, you can take a break and then go back to watching it.

Thus, the viewer is no longer just participating in the meaning-making process (by receiving certain film texts in a way not intended by the filmmaker). She is almost constructing her film-viewing experience, and in that, is closely aligned with the production of the text of the film. For instance, when a viewer chooses to fast forward certain portions of the film, or pause it at a moment when the text has no space for that intermittent pause, then she is circumnavigating the syntagmatic text. Or simply put, she is altering the film's inner logic, which is manifested in the edits, the script and the sequences of the film. Here, I would like to argue, that watching a film on the mobile phone transforms the position of the viewer, and inscribes her as a producer—of meanings and of the film text itself.

For a woman viewer, her inscribed position as a producer of meaning becomes even more significant when looking at the issue of access to mobile phones and film-viewing spaces. As discussed earlier, owning a mobile phone is associated with 'moral corruption' for women in India. Even with the rise of the 'multiplex culture', theatres are not always accessible for women—economically and socially. Thus, when a woman watches a film on the mobile phone and asserts herself as a 'producer', she constructs her film-viewing experience in a way that negates the barriers of access. She does so with her comfort and convenience in mind.

STORY VERSUS ACTION: THE HIERARCHY OF THE SCREENS

Why does anyone watch films? While the size of the screen, pixels, sound effects and visuals are important factors which determine the viewing experience, the pleasure gained from the text of the film is the main objective of watching a film. For instance, even if a viewer has unfettered access to the multiplex, or the mobile phone, the nature of the films she chooses to watch not only determines which screen she will watch the film on, but also how she will watch the film. This section looks at film-watching on mobile phones from the point of view of the film text. Lata, a 24-year-old student, says,

> English movies, or 3D movies, I prefer watching it in the hall. Or even a horror movie, I want to watch it in the hall. For phone, I watch only 'normal' movies. Like *Mary Kom*.[6] In that, the movie was okay, there weren't too many fighting scenes like there is in *Singham*. Where there is good 'action', like in the English movies, so when you see it in the hall, the joy, and the *mazaa* [joy or pleasure] you get from there is different.

A 'normal' film may easily be seen on the mobile phone, since apparently, the small screen does not interfere with the enjoyment of the film. On the other hand, a film belonging to the action genre with the usual staples of car chases, explosions and sound effects might not have the same impact on a small screen, as it might on a 60 mm theatre. This distinction between 'normal' films and action films as the main criteria to determine which film to watch on the phone was a constant refrain in all interviews. There were variations in the binary, with 'normal' being replaced by terms like 'story-driven' and action being replaced by terms like 'picturisation', but the implication was the same.

To critically look at this binary[7] between 'story' and action, it becomes important to do three things. One, to deconstruct the terms 'normal', 'story-driven' and action; two, to locate this deconstruction in the context of the age-old debate between 'melodrama' and 'realism' in popular Hindi film studies; and three, to problematise this binary between 'story' and action by introducing two notable exceptions—trailer as a filtering tool and 'comfort'.

Let us look at the term, 'normal' films. When asked what exactly 'normal' means, Lata went on to explain,

> Like 'normal' movies are small budget, looking at particular issues. Even in *Piku*, the disease of constipation was the central focus and such a good movie came out of the issue. Like in *Dum Laga ke Haisha*, the good thing shown is that no one wants to marry a fat girl. The realities of the society are shown in these films. So these movies if you are seeing it in phone, story driven, educational films, even if you are seeing it in the phone, you will get the same message that you will get in the hall or TV. Action or horror is better in the TV or hall, because the quality is better there.

There are two significant implications to be noted here: one, the argument that 'normal' movies show reality (and are realistic, in that sense) and often carry a 'message' in them; and two, that the realism of 'normal' movies is unaffected by the size of the screen because the story is so dominant to the grammar of the film that visuals, cinematography and sound do not matter as much.[8] In 'normal' movies, the story is the king, as Hindi film stars are fond of saying. Following this logic, these two characteristics put the 'normal' film firmly in the domain of realist cinema.

But what is realist cinema? For the purposes of analysis, the study will borrow from Prasad's (1998) conception of realist cinema[9] and then extrapolate this distinction to apply to popular Hindi films produced in the era of 'corporatisation' of the film industry (Ganti 2012: 5). According to Prasad, the difference between melodrama and realism can be understood in terms of 'representation that gives itself to be seen' (Prasad 1998: 73), that is, melodrama, and representation that is seen without it giving itself to be seen. Drawing on Rossellini's story about how he trains non-actors, Prasad argues that the man who is conscious of the camera and assumes a pose to represent his 'real' self is not an example of realism.

On the other hand, realism 'wishes to retain the task of representation for itself' (Prasad 1998: 73). Thus, even though Lata believes that the film, *Piku*, for instance, to be a realistic depiction of a father–daughter relationship, she is unmindful of the fact that what she perceives to be 'real' is instead a representational strategy performed by the director, writer and the actor. The notion of the 'normal', thus, initially, becomes problematised at this level. In the context of the Hindi film, the main difference between melodrama and realistic cinema is in the role of the spectator.

In the melodramatic film, there is 'a message/meaning that derives from a transcendent source and is transmitted to the spectator by the performance' of the film (Prasad 1998: 21). On the other hand, according to Prasad, in the realist mode of cinema, there is no transcendental message that is derived. The meaning or the 'message' of the film is what the spectator makes of it. Simply put, in realist cinema, there is no inherent meaning that pre-exists performance. Meaning is produced 'through the combined activity of the artist producer and the spectator on the text as raw material' (Prasad 1998: 21).

Again, going back Lata and her example, she perceived *Dum Laga ke Haisha* to be a film which speaks out against discrimination of women in society on the basis of their body type, by showing a confident, intelligent, overweight girl who is not concerned about what society thinks of her. The film had a one-point 'message'—a powerful story of an overweight girl.

While the 'message' is dominant in the film (like it was marketed in posters and interviews), it is not the only takeaway from the film. For instance, the film could also be a critical comment on the way the digitalisation of music through the coming in of CDs led to the breakdown of cassette shops and had an adverse impact on cassette shop owners.[10]

Therefore, once the message becomes multiple, instead of a single, absolute 'takeaway', the realism of the film also starts coming into question. Surabhi, a 24-year-old student, said,

> When you watch a film on mobile, you can only watch those films which you can feel *andarse* [from the heart]. For me, the image and the sound of the film don't matter that much. I don't want it particularly. It is the whole story that touches me, and gives me happiness. And it is those films I like watching on the phone. Because I think the phone removes these other things—the image and size—and the story starts to matter more.

The quote above almost locates the story-driven film in isolation and argues that the mobile phone is an important (and maybe even desirable) tool which enables this isolation. Interestingly enough, resonance of this argument can be inferred from Prasad (1998). He argues that the realist film 'achieves an internal articulation that guarantees its identity as a separate, individual product' (Prasad 1998: 21). In effect, he is saying that realist cinema (analogous to story-driven films, with the aforementioned caveats) is a film text which can be looked at as an individual product. Watching a film on the mobile phone allows the elements within the text like sound effects and visuals to recede in importance, and hence, the mobile phone screen emerges as more suited for story-driven films.

Action films, on the other hand, are not considered suitable to be seen on the phone. Most respondents said that they would watch films like *Singham* or 'English films with VFX and special effect' in a theatre, rather than on the phone. The small size of the screen, which might seem like an advantage when watching a story-driven film, is a nuisance when one is watching a film where the main attractions are large sets, scenery and opulent visuals. The point of pleasure, then, (*'mazza'*, as has been so effectively pointed out), is the grandness of the film—the scale on which it is mounted. The *'dishoom dishoom'*,[11] which reverberates in a dark theatre, is not the same when it is heard on earphones. Action, here, is used as an umbrella term for all genres of films which require a spectacle—a performance. Going back to Prasad's theorisation of the melodrama and the realist cinema, a melodramatic film is defined as a film where the meaning of the film is 'transmitted to the spectator by the *performance*' (emphasis mine) (Prasad 1998: 21). And thus, if in a melodramatic film, the performance is hindered by externalities like the lack of a suitable screen, then the film fails to have an 'impact'. This can be seen to correspond with the 'joy' that the Surabhi speaks about.

The binary between 'action' and 'story' is not rigid, by any estimation. There are complications, and most significantly, exceptions where the content of the film (story/action) does not play a role in determining the choice of the screen. The exceptions, interestingly enough, are based on the 'social life' of the film. The following is an excerpt from a focus group discussion:

When I heard about 'PK', I decided I wanted to watch it in the theatre, because it looked 'different' ...

By seeing the trailer also we can judge whether, whether this film will be OK or not ...

Like *Bombay Velvet*, the trailer was not very attractive. Negative feeling *aa rahi thi* (was simmering) ...

Dil Dhadakne Do I want to watch in the theatre. It looks very lively, and fun!

In the era of corporatisation of the popular Hindi film industry, each production house puts aside a large amount of money for the publicity and promotion of the film. Trailers, thus, have become a significant part of the 'social life' of a film, especially because the trailer is the first glimpse that the viewer gets into the film. In some cases, like with *Bombay Velvet*, a badly edited trailer fails to live up to the hype, and leads to the film being unsuccessful (as has been widely speculated since most viewers seemed to have taken out a verdict on the film even before watching it). Significantly, the trailer acts as *a filter* for the viewer—a tool which determines whether the film is worthy of being seen in a multiplex'; and I would like to argue that the 'trailer-as-a-filter' is even more significant for the woman viewer.

This is because the multiplex is not a very accessible space for the woman. First, economically, she may or may not be in a position to afford the exorbitant rates. Second, she is unable to 'inhabit' the class position that is expected of her in a mall. In a mall, 'women are expected to demonstrate their class position through their dress and demeanour' (Phadke et al. 2011), and their inability to do so marks them as outsiders. This makes the theatre socially inaccessible to them. Third, there exists the barrier of spatial inaccessibility. Even if one is able to afford the multiplex, belongs to the class position familiar with the exclusivist space of the mall (where most multiplexes are located), if there is no one accompanying the woman viewer, then chances are that she will not go. Watching a film in India in a theatre, alone, is an activity that is seen as the sole domain of 'spoilt women'[12] or worse, 'weirdos'. It is in this context that the trailer as a filtering device becomes significant enough to bypass the story-versus-action binary.

Dil Dhadakne Do, for instance, is a film solely based on witty repartee and anguished dialogues of a dysfunctional, upper-class

Delhi family on a cruise. There is very little in the syntagmatic text of the film that would make it suitable to be seen only on a big screen. But *Dil Dhadakne Do* is a glossy, big-budget production with scenic views of Turkey and a glimpse into the privileged lives of the upper-middle class Delhi. And thus, as a respondent in the focus group discussion respondent mentioned, she would watch it in a theatre.

Another exception to the story-versus-action binary has to do with the nature of the mobile phone as a storage device. Most of my respondents spoke about 'comfort' films that they have stored on their phones, which they see whenever they need a 'pick-me-up'. For instance, Harshita, a 21-year-old student, says, 'I have *Mughal-e-Azam* on my phone at all times, they're just there inside my phone. It's my go-to film. *Mughal-e-Azam* and *Dilwale Dulhaniya Le Jaayenge* are just my comfort films.'

In the context of this study, I would like to call these films 'comfort films'. Differing in genre, most of these films are not new releases. They are older, sometimes from the 1990s, and sometimes, as in the case of Harshita, from the 1960s. Significantly enough, some of these films are not 'blockbusters' or successful when they released. For instance, as a respondent, Preeti, a 23-year-old student, passionately told me, 'I always have *Anjaana Anjaani* on my phone. I just love it, the songs, everything. I have seen it around 20 to 30 times!'

Released in 2010, *Anjaana Anjaani* starred Ranbir Kapoor and Priyanka Chopra and was marketed as an unlikely romance. The film was widely panned by critics and audiences alike, with one reviewer calling it a 'daft' (Verma 2010) film. Financially, it was declared a 'hit' with opening weekend collections of Rs 257.50 million (Adesara 2010). However, despite good collections, the film was not something one would call a Hindi film classic.

Not only do 'comfort' films circumnavigate generic binaries (like the story-versus-action binary), but they also pass the test of time, the vagaries of box office success, and the brickbats handed by the critics. Thus, the mobile phone becomes a storage device for women, and in the kind of media content on the phone, an extension of her personality. The woman viewer exerts an ownership ('my') on the content they most like to watch. But simultaneously, in the case of 'comfort' films, they also become film critics, film archivists, and when they recommend and distribute these films to others, film distributors.

CONCLUSION

Watching a film in India is an exciting activity, but the contours of
film-watching are undergoing a subtle transformation. When it comes
to the mobile phone, the paper proposes a film-watching experience
which slowly individualises the viewer—starting from her class
position in a stratified society where she makes the choice to watch a
film either on the phone or the screen, to her location as a member of
the audience in the theatre, and then finally, as an individual spectator
interacting with the screen through the structure of 'darsana'. When
the screen shifts to the mobile phone, it marks the emergence of
'earphone publics'; viewers who are individualised when they are
watching a film, creating a private space through earphones, an almost
solitary way to watch a film.

This chapter also develops two ways to construct a hierarchy of
screens, based on the concept of 'choice'. One, based on accessibility
and comfort wherein the theatre still reigns supreme; but its position
is challenged by the mobile phone, which removes some of the
disadvantages associated with watching a film in the theatre.

Two, when the criteria are constructed on the basis of the text
of the film. In this classification, a binary exists between 'story' and
'action'. While story-driven films, aligning themselves with the realist
mode of cinema, are deemed suitable enough to be viewed on a screen,
action or melodramatic films with grand visuals and sound effects are
preferred to be seen in a theatre. However, as has been noted, there
are two notable exceptions to this binary. One, when the trailer of
the film acts as a 'filtering' tool, building up a hype for films that do
not conform to this binary, and yet are perceived to be films that can
be only seen in a theatre. Two, the category of 'comfort' films, which
are stored in the mobile phone, and viewed repeatedly, regardless of
the binary; these are often dated and old, and adhere to a 'popularity'
index that has nothing to do with success at the box office.

NOTES

1. Prasad uses the category, 'feudal family romance', to define the
dominant structure of symbolic authority retailed by the mainstream

Mumbai film and mirrored in the work of the major film industries of the south.

2. Similar to the fandom inspired by Rajnikant, NTR, MGR, and now, Salman Khan in popular Hindi films.

3. In this case, embarks on particularly heroic stunts which are removed from reality.

4. Uberoi critically analyses the term 'clean, family film', looking at the construction of Indian values and morality.

5. Names have been changed to protect the identity of the interviewees. The aliases are arbitrary names used by me, and have no significance beyond the scope of this study.

6. Refer to Appendix I for the summaries of films cited.

7. A fluid binary, as subsequent discussions will prove.

8. Film is an audio-visual medium. And to attempt to say that the visuals and the sound effects do not matter at all, only story is relevant is foolish, and frankly, impossible. What the analysis means when it refers to terms like 'sound' and 'visuals' is cinematography and sound design, which are mounted to dominate the story, and which often become the attraction of a film for many viewers.

9. The study is cognisant of other definitions of realist cinema in the context of Hindi films. Refer to Vasudevan (2010), Das Gupta, (1991) and Pinney and Dwyer (2001).

10. Ibid.

11. Literally, it signifies the sound which is heard when two actors are fighting in a popular Hindi film. Colloquially, it used to signify the bombast and style with which action films in India are made and loved.

12. Refer to Phadke, Khan and Ranade (2011) for a discussion on the 'loitering' woman and her subsequent construction as a 'bad girl'.

References

Adesara, H., 'Box Office: *Anjaana Anjaani* Nets Rs 250 Million in Opening Weekend', Business of Cinema, 5 October 2010. Available at http://businessofcinema.com/boxoffice/box-office-anjaana-anjaani-nets-rs-250-millionin-opening-weekend/32069 (accessed 27 September 2019).

Athique, A. 2011. 'From Cinema Hall to Multiplex: A Public History', *South Asian Popular Culture* IX (02): 147–60.

Benjamin, W. 1936. 'The Work of Art in the Age of Mechanical Reproduction'. In H. Arendt (ed.), *Illuminations: Essays and Reflections*. New York: Schocken Books.

Bourdieu, P. 1984. *Distinction: A Social Critique of the Judgement of Taste.* Cambridge, Massachusetts: Harvard University Press.

Ganti, T. 2012. *Producing Bollywood: Inside the Contemporary Hindi Film Industry.* Durham; London: Duke University Press.

Harbord, J. 2002. *Film Cultures.* London: Sage Publications.

Pandian, M. 1989. 'Culture and Subaltern Consciousness: An Aspect of MGR Phenomenon', *Economic and Political Weekly* 24(30): 62–68.

Phadke, S., S. Khan, and S. Ranade. 2011. *Why Loiter? Women and Risk on Mumbai Streets.* New Delhi: Penguin Books.

Prasad, M. 1998. *Ideology of the Hindi Film: A Historical Construction.* New Delhi: Oxford University Press.

Srinivas, L. 1998. 'Active Viewing: An Ethnography of the Hindi Film Audience', *Visual Anthropology* 11(4): 323–53.

Uberoi, P. 2001. 'Imagining the Family: An Ethnography of Viewing *Hum Aapke Hain Koun...!*'. In R. Dwyer and C. Pinney (eds), *Pleasure and the Nation: The History, Politics and Consumption of Public Culture in India.* New Delhi: Oxford University Press.

Vasudevan, R. 2010. *The Melodramatic Public: Film Form and Spectatorship in Indian Cinema.* New Delhi: Permanent Black.

Verma, S., 'Anjaana Anjaani is a Daft Film', Rediff.com, 1 October 2010. Available at http://www.rediff.com/movies/review/review-anjaana-anjaani/20101001.htm (accessed 27 September 2019).

Vishwanath, G. 2007. 'The Multiplex: Crowd, Audience and the Genre Film', *Economic and Political Weekly* 42(32): 3293.

Films Cited

Anjaana Anjaani. 2010. Siddharth Anand (dir.). Nadiadwala Grandson Entertainment.

Bombay Velvet. 2015. Anurag Kashyap (dir.). Phantom Films.

Dil Dhadakne Do. 2015. Zoya Akhtar (dir.). Excel Entertainment and Junglee Pictures.

Dilwale Dulhania Le Jaayenge. 1995. Aditya Chopra (dir.). Yash Raj Films.

Dum Laga ke Haisha. 2015. Sharat Katariya (dir.). Yash Raj Films.

Mary Kom. 2014. Omung Kumar (dir.). Bhansali Productions and Viacom 18 Motion Pictures.

Mughal-e-Azam. 1960. K. Asif (dir.). Sterling Investment Corporation.

Piku. 2015. Shoojit Sircar (dir.). Yash Raj Films.

Singham. 2011. Rohit Shetty (dir.). Reliance Entertainment.

seven

Digital Devices and New Narratives of Bengali Cinema

Kunal Ray

Introduction

The opening scene of Rituparno Ghosh-directed *Abohoman* (2010) features a conversation between an ailing father (Deepankar Dey as Aniket) and his son (Jisshu Sengupta as Apratim). Aniket is an internationally feted filmmaker and Apratim has recently made his directorial debut. In the conversation that follows, Aniket and Apratim discuss shifts in film technology. Aniket asks his son Apratim about the latter's experience of working on video. Apratim responds by cautioning his father that he may not enjoy working on video, having worked on film all his life. He further adds that the density, tone and longevity of film is greater than that of video. Aniket ruefully wonders what the purpose of this longevity is before stating that he finds his old work lacking in many ways. He then adds that video is perhaps better because you can shoot as much as you like, delete when you please, and even start anew at any moment. At this point, Apratim asks his father to rest for a while and not talk so much. Aniket then perplexingly asks his son, 'What is a film all about?'

Aniket's question perhaps captures the crux of this above-mentioned conversation. Although it may appear as a dialogue and a meandering exchange about film and video technology, a close viewing of the film would reveal that these opening remarks actually determine the central focus of the film. This conversation is essentially about their lives—the son, Apratim, the harbinger of hope and promise, and the father, Aniket, not resistant about embracing the new and volunteering to edit out many moments (unhappy, unproductive, unsatisfying) from the film reel of his life and start afresh. What is perhaps noteworthy is the employment of technological terminology, which brings about this discussion to the forefront of film narrative. This indicates a mutual permeation of science and culture, which has enabled new narratives in recent Bengali cinema made after 2005. The presence or dominance of digital devices in contemporary life cannot be ignored. Long gone are those days when our cinema portrayed science and technology as either detrimental to humankind or mere do-gooders during moments of national crisis. That narrative has changed. In a spate of recent Bengali films made after 2005, filmmakers are seen acknowledging the presence of digital technology or devices in our lives and new narratives, thoughts, discourse, insights solely enabled by these devices. Thus, the use and depiction of digital devices like cellular phones, laptops and cameras have transcended the mere function of smartness or communication and have entered our private spaces, almost playing a pivotal role in the larger narrative of life. This is precisely the sentiment that a cluster of new Bengali films seems to echo.

Abohoman is the story of a well-known filmmaker and his extramarital relationship with his protégé, Shrimati alias Shikha (Ananya Chatterjee), which leads to familial strife, almost embittering the father–son dynamics. When Shikha comes to audition for the role of Binodini Dashi, the iconic nineteenth-century Bengali theatre actor, Aniket is watching a projection of Guru Dutt's *Pyaasa* (1957). Shikha almost asserts herself in front of the projector, obstructing the projection partially, and faces a volley of questions, or rather, a kind of interrogation from a mildly irritated Aniket. This is a significant moment in the film. Aniket's leading lady is screen-tested or rather, introduced to the audience of the film partially through a device, the projector. The film camera looks at her unaffected, unwaveringly, and allows the audience to do the same. Thus, through the combination of two devices, the projector and the camera, we are introduced to Aniket's leading lady, who later becomes his muse.

Another instance from the film should be mentioned here. While editing the raw footage of the film that Aniket is directing with Shikha as the lead, he finds a shot where Shikha is found winking at the camera. While his colleagues find the gesture obscene and inappropriate, Aniket cannot help but admire Shikha's unabashed and uninhibited spontaneity. This almost marks the beginning of a relationship between the filmmaker and his muse, entirely enabled by the camera. Thus, at all critical points in the film's narrative, we are encountered with devices or machines that play a pivotal role by breaking free from their traditional designated function of being helpless, inanimate objects controlled by a human presence and introduce new possibilities of film language and expression. Benjamin (1936) considered the camera and the vision it produced to be the inception for a theory on cinema. In his kino-eye theory, Vertov (1924), and along with him, Epstein (2014), agree that the camera produces autonomous thinking independent from a human subject. Deleuze's advocacy of camera autonomy is also well-known (Huygens 2007: 18). In this chapter, I shall endeavour to identify contemporary Bengali films made after 2005 and argue that digital devices effectively essay a new role in the narrative of the film by shedding their traditional function of being mere mannequins.

Digital Devices Perform a Strategic Function

Foucault (1980: 195) defined the *dispositif* (often rendered as 'apparatus' in English translation) as a 'formation which has as its major function at a given historical moment that of responding to an urgent need. The apparatus thus has a dominant strategic function.' Italian philosopher Agamben published a critical reconstruction of Foucault's concept of the *dispositif* in a small volume of essays (2006) and later translated it into English, titled *What is an Apparatus?* (2009). Agamben remarks: 'Further expanding the already large class of Foucauldian apparatuses, I shall call an apparatus literally anything that has in some way the capacity to capture, orient, determine, intercept, model, control, or secure the gestures, behaviours, opinions, or discourses of living beings' (2009: 14).

The cellular phone in *Antaheen* (2009) is in concurrence with the idea and role of the apparatus, as outlined by Foucault (1980) and Agamben (2009). It appears at all the important junctures in the film, fulfils the urgency of communication and controls human conduct or rather, aids our comprehensive understanding of characters and their inner lives. *Antaheen* is a tale of urban emptiness, which also manifests in various relationships in the film. Abhik (Rahul Bose) is a tough cop who develops an online relationship with Brinda (Radhika Apte). They meet at social events but remain oblivious to their virtual identity until the end of the film. The prominence of the cellular phone is demonstrated right from the opening credits of the film. Invariably, all the important characters are seen conversing on the mobile phone during the exposition of the film. These conversations also reveal the nature of their relationships with the correspondents and the people around them. The mobile phone or the apparatus, so to speak, enables this understanding for the viewer. We realise that the inclusion of these digital devices is perhaps not accidental, but rather, well-intentioned. For instance, Brinda's first interaction with Abhik is actually a cell phone conversation. Brinda is a dynamic journalist and wants to interview Abhik about an arms haul. He declines saying the matter is subjudice. She concludes that he is snooty and officious. At another instance, Abhik receives a call from Ranju (Kalyan Roy) and their intimacy can be easily ascertained.

On the contrary, the strained relationship between Mrs Shalini Mehra (Mita Vashist) and her business magnate husband referred to as V. K. (Shauvik Kundagrami) is revealed during their first appearance in the film. They are engaged in making independent conversations on the mobile phone but remain oblivious to each other's presence in the same room. The tension is palpable and the device offers an escape route for both. It is later revealed that Mrs Mehra blames V. K. for the death of her daughter from her first marriage, which possibly explains the rift in their relationship. The audience is introduced to Ranju and Paaro (Aparna Sen), who are on the verge of a separation yet maintain an amicable relationship. They make frequent phone calls to each other, which is their only point of contact for a significant part of the film. The film identifies the cellular device as a marker of authority. It enables the audience to gauge the state of mind or the internal on-goings in the lives of these characters and controls their emotional being in a major way.

Even a thriller like *Buno Haansh* (2014) solely relies on mobile phones and iPads. Amal (Dev), the innocent victim of a devious plan, is hounded by hardened criminals. They track his movements, exchange information with their associates through instant messaging, FaceTime each other, and avail every technological possibility to trace him. Thus, digital devices facilitate this manhunt, and Amal narrowly escapes an attempt on his life. The characters in the film almost become synonymous with the devices they use. The gadgets seem like an extension of their selves.

Aniruddha Roy Chowdhury, the director of both *Antaheen* and *Buno Haansh*, further confirms:

> Those gadgets are an integral part of our lives and I have incorporated them intentionally in the film narrative. It was a conscious choice. It's habitual to check messages on WhatsApp and Facebook as soon as we wake up in the morning. Twitter and LinkedIn have become inseparable part of our lives. My phone is more important than my reading glass. I just cannot do without it. So how can one make contemporary films about contemporary issues without digital devices? These devices govern our lives. Relationships are created, nurtured and destroyed on the virtual medium on a regular basis (Ray 2015).

DIGITAL DEVICES AND INTIMACY

Turkle (2007) notes:

> Objects are able to catalyze self-creation .... Objects bring together thought and feeling. In particular, objects of science are objects of passion .... I have also touched on the idea that we often feel at one with our objects. The diabetic feels at one with his glucometer, as increasingly we feel at one with the glowing screens of our laptops, our iPods, and our BlackBerries. (2007: 9).

Turkle thinks through her objects. They function as a catalyst between intellect and emotion. They are companions to our emotional lives and they create intimacy. We also tend to humanise objects and treat the inanimate as animate. I shall elaborate on some of these observations with reference to objects such as cellular phones and laptops by citing examples from relevant Bengali films.

Dosar (2006) directed by Rituparno Ghosh revolves around a couple—Kaushik (Prosenjit Chatterjee) and Kaberi (Konkona Sen Sharma). Kaushik is bedridden after a near-fatal car crash, which leads to the death of Mita (Chandreyi Ghosh). Kaushik and Mita were involved in an extra-marital relationship. This causes great humiliation and pain to Kaberi. Towards the beginning of the film, Mita urges Kaushik to clandestinely plan a weekend far away from the city where his mobile phone would be out of network coverage area. This is how intrusive the device or the cellular object has become, almost endangering privacy.

Kaberi is completely ignorant of Mita's presence in Kaushik's life until the car accident reveals unsavoury details. Ghosh was a master creator of nuanced moments. The state police recover Kaushik's mobile phone from the accident site and hand it over to Kaberi. She brings the device home but cannot resist the temptation to pry into his message inbox. In the inbox, she finds a text message from Mita, comprising lines from a highly erotic Bengali poem. Kaberi holds the device, sits motionlessly for a while, and dials Mita's number on an impulse. Mita's recorded voice responds. That is the only instance of contact between the two women in the film. This interaction with the other woman, or at least, a moment of privacy/intimacy is afforded through the mobile phone. Thus, digital objects both impede and facilitate intimacy.

Newitz (2007) writes:

> My laptop computer is irreplaceable .... I carried it on my back all over England, Cuba, Canada, and the United States. When I use it in bed, I remember to keep the blankets from covering its vents so it doesn't overheat. I've taken it completely apart, upgraded its RAM, and replaced its original operating system with Linux. It doesn't just belong to me; I also belong to it (2007: 88).

This intimacy or emotional life that Newitz suggests is, perhaps, not foreign to many of us. To illustrate what a device might mean or the space it claims in interpersonal relationships, I would suggest a few instances from *Antaheen*. Abhik, the feisty young cop, yearns for a moment of intimacy with an absolute stranger (Brinda) through Internet chat sessions. Regardless of his busy schedule, he makes time to chat with this stranger in his virtual life. This is a private, interior world that Abhik has created for himself, and nobody, not even *Pishimoni* (paternal aunt; Sharmila Tagore), otherwise very dear to him, has access to this subterranean space. Abhik safeguards his 'online self'. This interior world is facilitated through his laptop, the object which allows him the luxury of intimacy on the virtual platform, something he perhaps lacks in his real relationships.

In the same film, Paaro (Aparna Sen) is quite declarative about her love for photography. She reminisces about her photo expedition to Tibet and regularly cleans her camera, although she may not use it too frequently now. It is an almost maternal relationship that Paaro seems to have acquired with the device. The camera reveals a self to which viewers do not have much access. The device almost constructs a narrative of life unseen and gone by. The camera has witnessed her personal upheaval, which is probably why several of the emotional scenes are choreographed around the presence of the device in the frame. This is how devices enable new narratives, or to put it in a different way, digital devices have found a new agency, a purpose they lacked in Bengali films before. *Antaheen* was also a musical hit. The word 'telephone' features in the lyric of a popular song from the film and it has a symbolic potential. 'Telephone' in the lyric alludes to memory. Thus, in all relationships in this film, technological devices reduce distance—physical, spatial as well as emotional.

The last scene in *Dosar* is a conversation between Kaberi and Kaushik while reclining in bed. Kaushik wonders: how would Kaberi react if Mita were still alive? In her response, Kaberi begins to recite the erotic poem she had found in Kaushik's mobile phone inbox, and the end credits soon take over the screen. Unknowingly, Kaberi has internalised the text, perhaps the verse penetrates deep to provide an insight into the relationship that has scarred them forever.

DIGITAL DEVICES ARE WRITING EQUIPMENTS

German philosopher Nietzsche was troubled by multiple physical ailments. He took to the typewriter in 1882 to combat his failing eyesight. He soon remarked to a music composer friend, 'Our writing equipment takes part in the forming of our thoughts' (Carr 2008). Mobile phones and laptops are akin to Nietzsche's writing instruments in films, and they essay a similar function in the construction of thoughts. In a thriller like *Buno Haansh*, the thoughts of Sohag (Shrabonti), nearly bedridden, perennially ill, and almost desperate to find out about the wellbeing of her friend Amal (Dev) are entirely conveyed through text messages. The tone, brevity and urgency of the messages depict Sohag's mental state. She endeavours to almost dialogue through the text messages that she writes. Even the news of her death is conveyed to Amal through a text message.

McLuhan (1964) claimed that 'the medium is the message' (1964: 19). He further stressed upon how the medium awakens and alters thoughts and senses. A proponent of technological determinism and the Medium Theory, McLuhan draws attention to the characteristics of the medium rather than the content of the message it conveys. The medium is the symbolic environment of a communicative act. Similarly, in *Dosar*, when Kaushik receives his mobile phone after being discharged from the hospital, he begins to delete all messages sent by Mita—an act of ritualistic cleansing of the device. The cellular device is a site of memory; it enabled the textual exchange of thoughts and privacy. Kaushik's act of deleting the messages is akin to editing out or delinking inglorious episodes from private memory.

Chitrangada: The Crowning Wish (2012) is a story of desire. Choreographer Rudra Chatterji (Rituparno Ghosh) feels trapped in a man's body and is preparing to undergo a gender change operation to embrace womanhood and adopt a child with his partner, Partho (Jisshu Sengupta). Rudra is admitted in the hospital during the process and meets Subho (Anjan Dutt), a counsellor. At each critical juncture in their conversations, Rudra receives a text message from an unknown number. These messages, in the form of baffling questions or witty quotes or even jokes, work as a distraction for Rudra, and the narrative changes from a sombre to a relatively cheerful mood. The text messages appear as a much-needed intervention in the film narrative, offering relief and respite in an otherwise mundane hospital setting. For example, Rudra at one point says that perhaps he does not understand *Chitrangada* (Rabindranath Tagore's dance drama) well enough, although he has staged it and received great reviews. At that critical point, he receives a text message saying, 'Why is it that everyone wants to go to heaven but nobody wants to die?', and the mood transforms, the dialogue changes. The text message works as a catalyst to alleviate tension. Towards the end of the film, in a dream sequence, Rudra receives a message, which reads, 'Why is a building called a building even after it is complete?' Rudra wonderingly sends a response asking 'Why?' Finally, Shubho, the counsellor, is identified as the receiver of the message, and he says, 'Because no transition is ever complete. It is an ongoing process.'

This response elicited by the text message is also a comment about Rudra's attempted transition to acquire a new identity, a new gender. It is also revealed to us, although not in concrete terms, that Shubho is a figment of Rudra's imagination. Rudra is perhaps delusional. Thus, this entire game of messages and the final revelation is anchored, scripted and orchestrated through the cellular device. The mobile phone is identified as the creator and originator of the plot.

The movie camera is no less a writing equipment in *Dosar*. Entirely shot in black-and-white, Ghosh scripts a narrative through his chosen palette (privileging black-and-white over colour), which lays bare a story of betrayal, despair, suffering and a wide array of fundamental human emotions. In an interview to Ziya Us Salam (2006), Ghosh comments:

> It was the requirement of the subject. If *Chokher Bali* was all bright and colourful, *Antar Mahal* was highly contrasted. And *Raincoat* quite muted except in flashback. The colour of the film is according to the subject. In *Dosar*, I talked the story of various couples resorting to extra marital relations. No other colour could have shown this angst, this feeling so beautifully but I have not been judgemental. The black and white medium gave me the umbrella to join all the incidents and disparate elements in the film, link up the characters without losing on the ethos (Us Salam 2006).

DIGITAL DEVICES AND THE SOCIOLOGICAL NARRATIVE

Sociologist Deborah Lupton (2013) remarks:

> In response to these new technologies and their impact on selfhood and society, a sub-discipline of sociology has emerged in recent years, now often referred to as "digital sociology". While this term is new, the focus of its research is not. Since the advent of personal computers and the internet, sociologists have researched many varied social issues relating to people's use of computerised and online technologies (2013: 2).

Kaushik Ganguly offers a sociological narrative of class and sexuality through his film, *Laptop* (2012), a hyperlink story which surveys different sections of society through the journey of a stolen laptop. The laptop is the protagonist of the story. In an interview to Meenakshi

Shedde (2011), Ganguly mentioned, 'I'm not techno-savvy, so the laptop is a mystery to me. But because it also has memory, I thought it could be a character. And as the memory travels (as the laptop changes hands), it can change people's lives' (Shedde 2011).

Social and other digital media are not only an inherent feature of everyday life for many people, but they also constitute and configure social life. Life itself has become technologised and mediated (Lash 2007). This mediation that Lash talks about is depicted in this film through the journey of the laptop. The narrative centres on the trajectory of the movement of the device.

We are introduced to almost all the characters in the film at a laptop store—the wealthy Banerjee couple (Churni Ganguly and Sawata Chatterjee), Indra (Rahul Bose) who is estranged from his wife and probably comes for a quick meeting with her at the store, and Jiyon (Gaurav Chakraborty) and his family who are enquiring about the price of a laptop. Three different sections of society and their aspirations coalesce at the same site—the laptop store—and this almost determines the narrative that is about to unfold.

A laptop is stolen from a fertility clinic by a taxi driver to pay for his wife's medical expenses. He sells the device to Jiyon's father (Pijush Ganguly) who cannot afford a new laptop for his son, a promising student of computer science. The laptop gives us an insight into their socio-economic condition and becomes the primary vehicle of taking the plot forward. From Jiyon, the laptop reaches Partho (Kaushik Ganguly) who is a blind writer. Partho is completely reliant on his typist, Subha (Ananya Chatterjee). While typing Partho's words, Subha feels like an equal participant in the process of creation. She therefore views the laptop, which newly arrives to take over writing manually, as a breach of their contract. She could not allow any transgression in her territory of writing. She sells it to Indra (Rahul Bose). The laptop introduces us to Indra's solitary existence and his affection for children. While fiddling with the device, he accidentally chances upon the medical history of Gourab and Durba Banerjee and finds out that their only son is born out of his sperm donation. Indra immediately leaves for Darjeeling to meet the child. Thus, the device not only enables a sociological comment about people, but also highlights the social practice like sperm donation. All the important actions or decisions in the film are mediated by the laptop, and it encompasses a wide trajectory of social relationships and behaviour. All conflicts in the narrative are borne out of the laptop. We are introduced to the best and the worst in human beings owing to the presence of the device. It works like a social signifier.

DIGITAL DEVICES AND OTHER TECHNOLOGIES

Art historian Gunning (2004) notes:

> I maintain that cinema teaches us about technology not only through an examination of its own mechanics, modes of production and means of expression, but through its representation of, and interaction with, other technologies. From its origins film has been drawn to other technologies through a powerful series of affinities ... In other words, a technology not only interacts with other technologies, it transforms social practice and human experience. This encounter between the interacting systems of technologies creates the complex terrain that I call modernity (2004: 19–20).

The modernity that Gunning alludes to is perhaps evinced in great measure in the film *Shabdo* (2013), a commendable cinematic feat achieved by director Kaushik Ganguly. A tribute to film technicians, who are often unrecognised for their contribution, *Shabdo* chronicles the story of Tarak (Ritwick Chakraborty), a Foley artist. Tarak is so consumed by sounds of objects that he ignores human sounds. He is almost a transformed man owing to his interaction with sound technology. He obsesses about his craft; demonstrates a sense of ownership about the devices/processes used to create sound. His personal life suffers a setback owing to these developments. Tarak begins to listen to fewer words and more effects. His occupation becomes a challenging obsession. His brain slowly refuses to register human speech. His psychiatrist (Churni Ganguly) suggests that the only way to cure him is to compulsorily make him listen to human voice.

Shabdo is the story of sound. The film is an exposition to the creation of Foley sound or the construction of background sound in film. It enables the understanding of another technology, the method of construction of sound. The sound recording studio is treated like a character in the film where Tarak discovers his true calling and craves for perfection in the minutest replication of sound. Such detailing aids our understanding of the central character and his impediments. We realise that the subject of the film is cinema itself. How is a film made? What is the process of film-making? We encounter a plethora of devices used in the creation of sound. Sound technology thereby empowers a narrative in cinema that was never heard or seen before.

CONCLUSION

Digital devices are our constant companions. It is unimaginable to live in denial of their all-encompassing presence in every sphere of private and public life. They facilitate intimacy, archive memory, and offer access to an alternative digital existence. How can cinema therefore not register its presence in human life and interactions?

Since the early days of cinema, film theorists have obsessed about the role of technology in film and its seminal contribution to the growth of a still nascent art form like cinema, but there is somewhat scanty attention paid to the significance of individual devices or objects in the film narrative. The cluster of recent Bengali films studied in this chapter perhaps indicates a change by reimagining the forms and functions of these devices. These narratives have appropriated digital devices as an integral presence in the film and will hopefully extend the possibilities of film language and representation.

REFERENCES

Agamben, Giorgio. 2009 [2006]. *What is an Apparatus?*, David Kishik and Stefan Pedatella (trans.). California: Standford University Press.
Benjamin, W. 2008 [1936]. Micheal W. Jennings, Brigid Doherty and Thomas Y. Levin (trans.). *The Work of Art in the Age of its Technological Reproducibility, and Other Writings on Media.* Cambridge, MA: Harvard University Press.
Carr, Nicholas, 'Is Google Making Us Stupid?', *The Atlantic*, July/August 2008. Available at http://www.theatlantic.com/magazine/archive/2008/07/is-google-making-us-stupid/306868/ (accessed 15 December 2015).
Epstein, John. 2014. *The Intelligence of a Machine.* Minneapolis: University of Minnesota Press.

Foucault, Michel. 1980. *Power/Knowledge: Selected Interviews and Other Writings*, Colin Gordon (ed.). New York: Pantheon Books.

Gunning, Tom. 2004. 'Fritz Lang Calling: The Telephone and the Circuits of Modernity'. In J. Fullerton and J. Olsson (eds), *Allegories of Communication: Intermedial Concerns from Cinema to the Digital*, 19–37. Bloomington: Indiana University Press.

Huygens, I. 2007. 'Deleuze and Cinema: Moving Images and Movements of Thought', *Image [&] Narrative* 18. Available at http://www.imageandnarrative.be/inarchive/thinking_pictures/huygens.htm (accessed 20 November 2015).

Lash, S. 2007. 'Power after Hegemony: Cultural Studies in Mutation?', *Theory, Culture & Society* 24 (3): 55–78.

Lupton, D. 2013. 'Digital Sociology: Beyond the Digital to the Sociological'. In N. Osbaldiston, C. Strong and H. Forbes-Mewett (eds), *The Australian Sociological 2013 Conference Proceedings: Reflections, Intersections and Aspirations, 50 Years of Australian Sociology*, p. 2. Melbourne: TASA

McLuhan, M. 1964. *Understanding Media: The Extensions of Man*. New York: McGraw-Hill.

Newitz, Annalee. 2007. 'My Laptop'. In Sherry Turkle (ed.), *Evocative Objects*, pp. 88–91. Cambridge, MA: MIT Press.

Ray, Kunal, Personal Communication with Aniruddha Roy Chowdhury, 15 November 2015.

Shedde, Meenakshi, 'Laptop's Memory Made it My Protagonist: Filmmaker Kaushik Ganguly', *DNA*, 11 December 2011.

Turkle, Sherry (ed.). 2007. *Evocative Objects: Things We Think With*. Cambridge, Massachusetts: MIT Press.

Us Salam, Ziya, 'Of Marital Blues', *The Hindu*, 27 November 2006.

Vertov, Dziga. 1985 [1924]. *Kino-Eye: The Writings of Dziga Vertov*. Berkeley: University of California Press.

Films Cited

Abohoman. 2010. Rituparno Ghosh (dir.). Big Pictures.

Antaheen. 2009. Aniruddha Roy Chowdhury (dir.). Mumbai Mantra.

Buno Haansh. 2014. Aniruddha Roy Chowdhury (dir.). Reliance Entertainment.

Chitrangada: The Crowning Wish. 2012. Rituparno Ghosh (dir.). Shree Venkatesh Films.

Dosar. 2006. Rituparno Ghosh (dir.). Planman Motion Pictures.

Laptop. 2012. Kaushik Ganguly (dir.). Rose Valley Films.

Shabdo. 2012. Kaushik Ganguly (dir.). Rose Valley Films.

eight

The Other Cinemas

Recycled Content, Vulnerable Bodies,
and the Gradual Dismantling of Publicness[*]

NIKHIL THOMAS TITUS

When a tiny establishment in a slum in Chembur, an eastern suburb in Mumbai, was demolished by the Municipal Corporation in 2006 to make way for a flyover to connect two congested suburbs, several men stood around to watch the crane take apart the walls of an institution they had patronised for years—a video parlour. These parlours cater to the demands of men who are first-generation migrants, daily-wage earners, or belong to other low-income groups. The establishments find favour with them either at the end of a day's

---

*I must acknowledge the support of the theatre and video parlour personnel and audience members who are mentioned in the chapter and who consented to being interviewed and filmed, especially Mr Jaktap, who facilitated our access to his video parlours in Chembur, Mumbai. I would also like to thank my senior colleagues and peers who have made this chapter possible: Anjali Monteiro, K. P. Jayasankar, Shilpa Phadke, K. V. Nagesh, Amit S. Rai, Neepa Majumdar, Laura Brown and David Pettersen, for their inputs and guidance; Barry John King and the IAMCR Popular Culture Working Group, 2015 and 2014; Faiz Ullah, with whom I did a period of field work in 2014 and we presented *Screening Out the Public: Cultural Rights of the Marginalised Citizens in Mumbai*, at Bazaar Cinema, Media Piracy: The Politics and Practices of Borrowing, Queen Mary University of London, 2014; Suhail M., with whom I did a period of field work in 2010, and Sanjay Pratap Singh, with whom I worked in 2008–09. Special thanks must be extended to the Tata Institute of Social Sciences (TISS) M-Ward Project Team, the School of Media and Cultural Studies, class of 2012, and Mangesh Gudekar.

labour or when they are unable to find work for extended periods. Low ticket prices enable the audiences to be entertained, and they also provide shelter during periods of unemployment. They are sites of leisure as well as an essential institution that harbours these men in a city where there are few other spaces that hold potential for 'time-pass',[1] thus forming a space where they may be able to enjoy comparatively affordable entertainment. Over the years, there have emerged media reports of instances where criminals were traced to a video parlour; thus, the police took to shutting down such institutions in the area.[2] Current and former video parlour owners mention that the government has stopped renewing video parlour licenses in Mumbai, which means people usually rent licenses or may be forced to conduct their trade without adequate permissions in place. It may be difficult to fathom that in a time of immersive 24/7 connectivity, a considerable number of people still make provisional arrangements for their dose of recreation.

Institutions such as video parlours, while being a critical node within low-cost leisure networks, also help us to interrogate taste hierarchies by providing a curatorial practice not based on the criterion of rejection; enabling an accommodative, alternate and unique canon of inclusivity. Sundaram (2010) has imagined this culture of interdependence as a form of democracy enabled by the piratical, bringing together in a synergetic manner, technologies and communities that might not otherwise have found a common ground. This volatile and fluctuating potential for collaboration and resilience is the function that minor cinema cultures can offer, through spaces that are well within the physical networks of the bourgeois, but not necessarily something that they would choose to bring into their everyday consciousness. Larkin (2016: 209), in his work on Nigerian cinema, observes that while video films have become a matter of intense focus in academia, they are rarely accorded the qualification of being worthy of textual analysis; instead, they are studied in terms of the environments of coloniality, piracy and economics, which are reflected in the broad narrative and production strategies.

The televisual turn that Nollywood has been compelled to adopt has incited what can be termed as an aesthetic anxiety over formal characteristics by drawing a parallel between the lack of production value and the lack of intellectual and ideological rigour in representations on screen. While Nigerian films and their exhibition sites are perceived as being able to produce an alternate public sphere—integrating realms of cinematic publics alongside the domesticity of television—the texts themselves are yet to be granted the agential status of cultural artefacts that can influence and interact with social and historical phenomena. This situation faced by Nollywood is similar to conditions experienced by B-grade and video films produced for exhibition sites like the video parlour in Mumbai. While the significance of local environments and the political and economic conditions surrounding such alternate cinema has been acknowledged, the texts are largely sidelined from other mainstream narratives such as those produced in Bollywood. But in the rare instance when awe and inspiration are accredited to such films, there is a conscious attempt to keep the texts out of conventional screening spaces. Safety nets, such as that of the 'cult', keep the work from permeating the larger consciousness of our culture through acts of 'exclusion by homage', a term drawn from Rancière that Liang (2009: 28) refers to in his work on media sharing.

This chapter proposes video parlours and low-cost single-screen theatres, their films and promotional strategies, as part of a unique and alternate curatorial practice employed to attract and keep audiences entertained, while also interrogating the intersection of technology and infrastructure that influence the functioning of these sites, and larger perceptions that emerge through media reports surrounding them. Low-cost film exhibition venues define a space, which is an alternative to the art house; while the art house functions on the idea of exclusivity of the audience and space, the video parlour is the space of the inclusive. This is not a 'paracinema', as interpreted by Sconce (1995), where patrons choose to associate with a category of cinema to oppose dominant tastes, but it is still a counter-movement that, by its very existence, proves to be a compelling reminder of the eclectic communities and styles that are suppressed in the neoliberal paradigm of development.

This is an exhibition arena that troubles predictable and conformist norms for curation, censorship and the accessibility of cinema. The discourse around video parlours and low-end single screen theatres pivot upon the publics that frequent the institutions, and the aesthetic and moral insinuations of the cinema exhibited there, usually citing concern over each of these issues. The reportage frequently comprises references to piracy and pornography, derived from posters stuck across key transport routes and locations in the city where rents are relatively low and migrant and working-class communities are settled in informal housing. Such impressions of these lower-class institutions betray the great middle-class cinema-going fear of the betel-chewing, poorly dressed, back bench masturbator—the pervert who lingers in the darkness of a cinema hall. Mumbai's fascination with making itself a world-class city means that there has emerged an unacceptable space, content, aesthetic and an audience which needs to be moved out for development to take place; overlooking the fact that these communities and institutions were the building blocks of the city and still comprise a vital labour force that maintains its fragile edifice.

Like elsewhere in the world, cinema in India is integrally linked to the working class; an affordable form of entertainment, cinema in the early decades of the twentieth century developed alongside the mills and ports and expanded with the ever-growing number of workers that poured into the city. As working-class institutions and housing colonies begin to wither away across Mumbai, the cinema space, too, has been transformed with the advent of multiplexes in the late 1990s. Multiplex theatres have caused a fundamental rearrangement in cinema at the level of screens and seats, which in turn begins to influence the ideology that surrounds cinema and its audience. In the past decade, there has been a spurt in the number of screens, but at the same time, a reduction in the number of seats per 1,000 population.[3] A change in the spatial experience of cinema through 'multiplexisation'[4] caused a blurring of classes; and at the same time, caused a much stronger reiteration of the same. Multiplexes generally have only one single floor per screen, which provides the illusion of classless seating, yet its very location and pricing exclude lower classes as potential audience members.

A higher per-seat pricing can effectively translate fewer audience members into a more profitable segment to be catered to, as opposed to larger volumes of low-cost ticket sales. The initial development proposal for multiplex theatres speculated that they would keep low-cost options open for the clientele; for instance, the first two rows of the theatre were reserved for low-cost seating. Over the years, these low-cost options have either been entirely done away with or are applicable only to select shows at certain times of the day. An industry that began with a strong association with the working class seems to have deserted that vast population and its problems in favour of narratives of a more elite class, whose problems can crudely be defined as existential. The era of the 'angry young man'[5] in the Indian socio-cultural context has morphed into the era of the Non-Resident Indian (NRI), an acronym that has turned into a status symbol paralleling that of the Very Important Person (VIP) in India. The working-class narratives and concerns that dominated the screens up to the 1990s have made way for the professional globetrotter, someone who has a home in London or San Francisco, but is at home in a hamlet in India. This manifestation has been aggravated by processes of globalisation leading to the opening of overseas media markets, such as North America and Europe, as a source of investment in films, a location for production, and a target market for the films produced.

By having currency exchange rates outstandingly higher than the Indian Rupee (INR), a single cinema-goer in these markets contributes approximately five to 15 times what an audience member in the Indian market does. In effect, serving significantly smaller numbers of diasporic populations in the developed markets of the world provides greater profit margins to the producers of such media content. This physical and global finance-based bias also takes the form of exclusion in the narratives of the cinema associated with that space. The surge of the Indian middle classes towards the multiplex in the late 1990s, and the production of cross-over[6] and new-wave narratives, intended for overseas markets, serve as *prima facie* validation of the connectedness of these occurrences.

Given the competitive market space and ever-increasing real estate prices in cities like Mumbai, it may be easy to imagine why people responsible for running institutions like single-screen theatres, which usually occupy a substantial area, may be desirous to sell or convert them into multiplexes. But the globalised market does not ensure this smooth transition; protracted dealings with investing parties, handling of government regulations, and consideration of the views of the loyal clientele are still part of the negotiation structure for 'redevelopment' projects across the city. One instance that highlights the potential for gentrification and elements of impedance inherent in the process is that of the Aurora Theatre, a popular site in Matunga, a predominantly South Indian suburb of Mumbai. Begun in the year 1942, this theatre, too, is on the verge of being redeveloped into a multiplex. Owner Nambi Rajan explains, 'We have no option but to explore the idea of a multiplex. The amount of technology required to screen films, plus other exhibition costs, are too much for a single-screen theatre to bear' (Titus 2010). Aurora, which currently seats about 700 people, will seat around 300 after its redevelopment. When interviewed in October 2010, Rajan said that the process should be underway in about 2 months' time. In 2016, Aurora was still negotiating the terms of redevelopment, and for now, it continues to show one Tamil, one Telugu, one Malayalam and one Hindi movie to cater to the different audiences in the area at the rate of approximately Rs 60–120 ($1–2) per ticket. As he also remarks,

> There's something about the discipline that you have to follow in the multiplex; you are just not able to express yourself. The stall (lower floor seating) is missing and that takes with it a lot of the atmosphere. When we turn Aurora into a multiplex, we'll try to keep the rates the same and the atmosphere may not be 100 per cent, but we'll try (Titus 2010).

It is this irregular pace of gentrification and development in the city that on the one hand, serves as a frustrating hurdle in imagining Mumbai as a first-world city, and on the other hand, a reassurance of the possibilities of subversion that abound in the political and cultural realm.

While processes of gentrification in the city appear to have taken hold over cinema production and narrative, alternate viewing practices have also emerged in the same decade, with technological migrations from the VHS Tape to the CD, the DVD, USB, and most significantly, with the Internet and technologies like peer-to-peer torrent networks, and video sharing facilities like YouTube. These apparatuses of sharing and viewing create the new-age audience member who is capable of instantly reviewing the minutest of details of the text or its author—producing meta-subjects, capable of reflecting on their own positions vis-a-vis the text, allowing for a grimy and blurred space in the otherwise overtly immaculate and crystalline forms that cinema assumes.[7]

Such fluctuations in the ephemeral realm of cinema, combined with unique exhibition strategies, keep the concerns and ideas of an otherwise vast, neglected, and often invisibilised segment of audiences mirrored on the screen. One site of research where these textured dimensions of cinema, audience and infrastructure make a pronounced appearance is the municipal 'M-Ward'[8] of Mumbai. The area has one of the lowest human development indexes in the city, and a population estimated by non-governmental organisations (NGOs) to be near one million people, with an area that is approximately 56 sq. km.[9] Due to various redevelopment and infrastructure projects, including the World Bank-funded Santacruz-Chembur Link Road (SCLR) project, it has become arguably the best-connected suburb of Mumbai. In the past, this area was used as a site to resettle low-income communities from other, more expensive real estate in the city.[10]

The allure of revamping infrastructure and establishments in the city encircles even the screening spaces; of the seven theatres in the area, only three are running in fully functional capacity (Titus 2016). The others are barely managing daily screenings, likely awaiting takeover and redevelopment rights. Multiple mass infrastructure projects in Mumbai, and what is generally articulated as increased spending power amongst middle-class residents, has resulted in such a rapid rise in the land value that the properties occupied by minor businesses, like video parlours, are valued at several times the revenue that they have generated over the years. The negative mind space occupied by these institutions and the lack of adequate support from the state also reflects a drive to modernise and sanitise the city. Converting Mumbai to Shanghai is the euphemism commonly used, where a great amount of focus is placed on either demolishing slums or low-class housing or institutions under various 'rehabilitation/ urban renewal' schemes, or keeping them out of sight by constructing high walls around these settlements in the major business areas of the city. The ambition is to create uniform flows of vision throughout the city, directing it through infrastructure, where unhindered vision acts as a precursor to the smooth flow of capital across urban space. A modern cityscape is one that is unified, organised and devoid of interferences in its network.[11]

The films screened in low-cost theatres are often 'recycled', and incidentally, several patrons are involved in the recycling industry, employed as solid waste management personnel or as contract labourers who are helping to 'redevelop' various parts of the city.[12] The act of denying rights of existence to such institutions is not just an expression of anxiety over cultural forms and aesthetics, but also the manifestation of a strong bio-political sentiment against the enculturation of certain bodies within certain boundaries—based on consumerist notions of rights and privileges of citizens. When lower-class men congregate in the city for purposes other than work, it is deemed inappropriate; and while the unsuitability of the screening material is one worry, there is also the concern of 'able-bodied' men dedicating time to leisure when they should be offering their labour to the city.[13] As Shilling (2005) describes in his text on the body, in the individualised climate of the urban space, there lies little room for collective bodies, and especially those that cannot consume or be displayed as ideal to the model of the imagined city. The body becomes an object of management, with the degree of control varying with the class and consumption capacity of the collective. Often imagined as freeloaders by the middle class and treated so by state authorities, these peripheral communities spend higher-than-average percentages of their income on entertainment and other basic needs, precisely due to the discriminatory policy framework that is operational.[14]

The act of participating in the consumption of risqué content, in the presence of other men, is part of a larger and common practice of articulating hegemonic masculinities, something that for these particular classes of men has been confined to residual sites like low-cost theatres. Video parlours, single screen theatres—their exhibition spaces and curatorial practices—reflect the state of the communities they are situated in. Their audiences are heavily male-dominated and single-screen theatres do get the occasional female member in the audience, but always accompanied by a male companion. One of the reasons for the low number of women is that they are often left behind in native towns or villages to care for families. In successive generations of migrants, where sufficient finance has been arranged for families to live together, the woman is usually confined to the house and related chores. Even when the woman is a wage earner for the family, the possibility of 'public' leisure is denied, through a combination of designs based on patriarchal notions of honour and safety. The men who frequent video parlours usually begin their day by congregating at the *naka*s or junctions of the main streets of the suburbs, where contractors arrive with trucks and hire the required numbers of labourers for a daily wage. If any men are unable to gain employment for the day, they have to return to their bare tenements. But in some cases, houses are rented out on a shift basis; workers from the night shift occupy the rooms in the day time, leaving the day time unemployed labour force with no place to return to, other than spaces like the video parlour.

Bhimrao, a 25-year-old labourer from Nanded, Maharashtra, explains the living conditions in a 10ft x 20ft accommodation shared by ten men: 'Try staying in that room for more than an hour, it is absolutely bare, and there's little space to move about, you either fall asleep or step outside' (Titus 2017b). The video parlour owners and managers, being perceptive of the peculiar work-life circumstances among their audience, have catered their pricing and screening policy accordingly. They sell 'double tickets', which can mean double action— that the film has a lot of action sequences—but also that one ticket can buy two or even three films at a time. The duration of these two to three films is based on a work or sleep cycle of 6–8 hours. Sheikh, a former video parlour manager who now owns and operates video parlours, mentions in an interview, that if a patron walks in midway through a screening, they usually let him stay for the full length of the next two films. He also clarifies that unlike multiplexes, they do not have too many rules for the patrons to follow; people can bring in their food and eat or drink as they like, talk to their colleagues, or just relax (Titus 2008) (see Image 8.1).

The parlours utilise projectors or TV screens connected to DVD/USB players, and these pieces of equipment are very well invested in and maintained. The room has one fire extinguisher—for emergencies. The seating is basic, with no backrest on the benches; those who enter early can grab a part of the wall to lean on. Mohan Nandedkar, a 40-year-old *naka* labourer, initially suggests that there are several locations in the city where one could spend their time, listing the Gateway of India or *Ranibaugh* (the city zoo) as potential options. On being pressed about the distance and expense related to travelling to these locations in the city, he grants that 'Other than the street corners we can only go home or to a theatre, and the bigger theatres are expensive, and their shows don't change daily.' When

IMAGE 8.1: Waiting for Work: Bhimrao (centre) and his Friends at a *Naka* in Ghatkpar (E), Mumbai, on a Sunday Morning (July 2017)

Source: Photograph taken by the author.

asked if the formal businesses along the street would mind so many people congregated there after 10 am, he replies, 'There might be some issue if so many people wait here after the businesses open.' His cohort has rarely lingered around until then. The conditions of these transient working populations can be aggravated in extreme weather, like heavy rains or summer heat, which make finding shelter even more critical, or during periods when industries like construction experience slowdown and are not able to employ high numbers of individuals (Titus 2017c).[15]

Sagai, former video parlour owner and second-generation resident in the city, when asked about the entertainment options available to the multitudes of daily wagers and manual labourers, declares, 'It is true that these parlours are the only options for them, but nothing can stand in the way of development and eventually it will benefit them' (Titus 2014). The expectation and hope of benefits trickling down is often the basis on which some community members agree to redevelopment policies for low-cost neighbourhoods. Sagai's response is also reflective of the distinction between first-generation migrant labour and others in the city who may have managed to accumulate some capital through their years of struggle and now hope for a better life through political agendas imposed on them. In many ways, Sagai's musing about his community and livelihood is woefully realistic, and reminiscent of Bauman's (2000) reading that the community that has 'fallen' has to surmount great odds to rise up again through the modern infrastructure that has taken its place, which leaves the vulnerable even more insecure in the city.

Despite being targets of exclusionary notions of growth, the parlours have had an interesting history. Films from across the world are screened here. An example of the ingenuity of curation in these spaces is the screening of a film by Anthony M. Dawson, pseudonym for Antonio Margheriti, a prolific Italian filmmaker whose body of work includes *Cannibal Apocalypse*, a 1980 horror film and cult classic. His films are well past their prime in the mainstream distribution networks, most certainly in Mumbai. This film had been dubbed in Hindi and the title changed to suit the taste of the local audiences— *Adimanav Aur Sarprani* (*The Primitive Man and the Snake Queen*), 1982 (Image 8.2). It has also been contextualised with a reference to well-known filmmaker Steven Spielberg and his popular Indiana Jones franchise. Roman Polanski's *Bitter Moon*, 1992, was recently screened in one such theatre. The modified poster now portrayed a bikini-clad woman, the identity concealed by the typeface—most likely an image borrowed from outside the film—with a pair of disembodied legs in the foreground, and the titled changed to *Bewafai* (*Betrayal*), 1992 (Image 8.3).

Films playing at these locations are almost always issued censor certificates, and rarely, if ever, have pornographic material inserted into their reels; the incitement provided by the posters is what largely contributes to imaginations of illicit activity at such locations. As these exhibition sites often maintain a low profile, they function by their audience discovering the locations mostly by word of mouth, the only obvious signs of these theatres in the main streets of the city being either the printed posters or hand-written schedule charts for the day. The hand-written schedules often announce routine screenings of older films that are crowd favourites, or television shows and sporting events like cricket matches. It is not unusual for the posters to display multiple languages like Tamil, Hindi and English, based on the audience that they are expected to lure (Image 8.4). Depending on the time of day and the film being screened, these parlours can draw

IMAGE 8.2: Creative Captioning: *The Primitive Man and the Snake Queen* Being Screened at Video Parlours in the Chembur Govandi Area (May 2014)

Source: Photograph taken by the author.

audiences ranging from college students, to labourers and working-class men. These unique modes of advertisement, references to extra-diegetic elements, and hand-written schedules suggest a relationship to the early years of cinema and vaudeville. The posters are a site of complex mediation; while many migrants are unable or unwilling to

IMAGE 8.3: A Poster of *Bewafai* in Deonar, Mumbai (March 2014)

Source: Photograph taken by the author.

be expressive, it is these visible sites that can produce a faux sense of proximity and awareness about the population.[16] This 'attraction' aesthetic in the posters acts as a double-edged sword that not only draws the audiences to the cinema, but also attaches impressions of crudeness, naivete, and even deviance, to the institution and its

IMAGE 8.4: Screening Schedules for Video Parlours Pasted on Street Corners in Mumbai (March 2014)

Source: Photograph taken by the author.

audience; without adequate consideration of the richness of the cinematic content and tradition, or the socio-economic contexts that impose themselves upon such communities.[17]

It is unfortunate that the creativity and passion displayed by the video parlour curators go unappreciated by conservative quarters within the intellectual property rights and licensing regimes. Video parlour operators are compelled into perpetual innovation—from curating unique offerings, to introducing new stars to the audiences, redesigning posters, renaming films, and authoring DVDs with select scenes from films that 'click' with audience—these cinephiles are undeniably revitalising a cinema that many are happy to forget. They are, in a way, unlocking the value of the 'intellectual property' by putting back into circulation media artefacts that otherwise may not generate any value for either the audience or the distributors. Several patrons mentioned how they unambiguously preferred *joona picture*, or older films, of their screen idols like Amitabh Bachchan, Mithun Chakraborty, Akshay Kumar and Rajnikanth.[18] Such opinions suggest an inability to relate to, or even an unwillingness to participate in the narratives that have emerged in Mumbai cinema since the early 2000s. It is in connecting to this sentiment within the audiences that the video parlour owners and managers show tremendous resourcefulness in terms of finding an unending stream of content that will suit their tastes, as well as keep them out of the harsh glare of the authorities on the lookout for defaulters.

The perception among many upper-class filmgoers is that lower-class audiences are mindless in their pursuit of film stars, violent films or pornographic scenes. But the patrons interviewed were keen to emphasise that while they did enjoy watching steamy scenes, their focus was on a good story that provided exciting *twists*, and were not pleased with the association made with pornographic or B-Grade material.[19] Every year, there are several films released with so-called *twists* in their narratives; however, not all of them make it to such theatres. What many audiences and theatre owners refer to as *masala* films are not just popular mass films, but they are also films that employ specific tropes that acknowledge not just the concerns of the audiences, but also recognise the presence of the audience members within the theatre space and the city. These subjective experiences challenge long-standing perceptions of the text, dominated by discourses of absence, where relationships between films, stardoms and spectators have been imagined as distant and convoluted, usually routed through avenues like the box office or mass and social media coverage.[20]

Projects such as *Cinema City* (Dutta, Bhaumik and Shivkumar 2013) have looked at the historic and economic dimensions of screening spaces in Mumbai; but the intersection of infrastructure, precarity and the piratical in making significant contributions to the cultural and political sphere of the city and its cinema is a prospect that demands renewed focus. This creative repurposing of content breathes value into an artefact that has lived out its useful life in conventional circles. Liang (2009) argues that what is often framed within the purview of 'piracy' is potentially providing 'new' avenues and audiences. It is this potential that the state and its regimes of licensing, in tandem with bourgeois-aesthete perceptions of cinema, completely ignore. Video parlours are then left to their own devices to ensure their profitability and survival, unable to justify in the elegant terms of an art house or the legal parlance of the state, why they should be looked at as an essential service, which deserves attention akin to those institutions fulfilling housing or sanitation necessities in the city. Evident across the city are tropes of how such prejudiced regimes overlap with what is essentially a land-grab operation for the real-estate and corporate lobby with state backing. If the film is not pirated, the electricity is; if the electricity is not pirated, the building is; and if the building is not, then most probably, the land it stands on will be. Issues like piracy or consumption of pornography manifest here, not provoked by the inability of audiences to pay for the material they utilise, or their incompetence in comprehending a complex narrative, but through the unwillingness of the State and society to sanction leisure opportunities to a population that is deemed perpetually expendable, transferable and replaceable.

The category of 'trash' that often situates itself on low-cost and low-class exhibition is a relation imposed on these sites and populations through conservative cultural politics. But there are groups of film enthusiasts across the city, who have adopted the auteurs and films within this category, and emphatically display their affection through social networks and active film clubs. Some low-budget B-films such as *Gunda* (*Gangster*), 1998, and *Loha* (*Iron*), 1997, have managed to attain the status of cult films through networks in spaces like the esteemed Indian Institute of Technology (IIT), with blogs, books, newspaper articles, comparisons to the grind house or the paracinema culture in America, and academic writing contributing to this process of 'cultification' of the work. Such networks are also known to comprise young, predominantly male intellectuals whose academic rigour and vocabulary contribute to the legitimisation of such works, as articles of study and awe, rather than lowly pulp produced in dark alleys and screened in moribund arenas to a lumpen audience. These paracinema audiences differ from the audience found in video parlours, through the distinction of choice, the fact that they can decide and access any cinema or exhibition space of their own volition. The video parlour spectator is mostly confined to that space by precarious financial and cultural conditions, at times unable to access locations they are familiar with, which have been 'redeveloped' to make them accessible to the middle and upper classes in the city.

Deepak Cinema in Lower Parel, Mumbai recently underwent renovations and is now called the Matterden Center for Films. The renovated single screen theatre will now serve as an 'art house' location, screening classics from the genres of world cinema and Indie films. It is said that initially the theatre will screen one show in the evening at the rate of Rs 100 per ticket. It used to be a theatre that screened Hindi and Bhojpuri cinema, but now it is surrounded by a redeveloped office space that is occupied by some of India's biggest real estate developers and corporations. A newspaper article on this new development and the new art house space concludes by saying, 'Should these high-powered denizens choose to rub shoulders with the usually scruffy and sartorially challenged cineastes who lurk at such venues, they will be treated to screenings of international classics such as *Bicycle Thieves*, *Rashomon* and *The General* ...' (Ramnath 2014). Pinney, in ... *What Happens When Peasants 'Get Hold' of Images* (2002: 358), reports about the screening of Phalke's *Lanka Dahan (The Burning of Lanka)* at the West End Cinema at Girgaum, Bombay:

> Barnouw and Krishnaswamy record that when Rama appeared, the audience prostrated itself before the screen (Barnouw and Krishnaswamy 1963: 15). It has been claimed that when it was shown in Pune the crowds almost broke down the door and that in Madras the film's takings had to be transported in a bullock cart with police protection ... (Pinney 2002: 358).

At one level is the mythification of the medium itself and its processes; the idea that there is now a greater technology that has the ability to give shape to the complex ideas of storytellers, and in the process, it is creating a sophisticated cinema. But through an examination of the norms of censorship and control over exhibition spaces, it seems that the understanding of cinema, censorship, and most significantly, its audiences has not changed all that much in the 100 years of Indian cinema. Audiences may not break down the doors of the theatres, or that is not a serious concern, but there is a prevailing anxiety that they may collapse boundaries in society to fulfil the conflation of 'spectators and supplicants', which can slip towards conflating spectators with perpetrators. In instances where criminals were traced to video parlours in Mumbai, often, the relation drawn is between the content screened at the video parlour and crimes against women and children (Mustafa 2014).

Such cases receive prolific coverage in the 'breaking news' culture of today; combined with middle-class morality, this coverage seems to convey an image of widespread perverseness, which, if left unchecked, will infect the rest of the society. The social role of lower-class institutions and the people they serve are not mentioned; what is made obvious is the 'publicness' of the service that such institutions provide. As illustrated by Larkin (2008: 2), '... the experience of going there is greater than the films themselves. It is this excess, the immaterial experience of cinema emerging from the assemblage of built space, film and social practice, that became the target of regulation.' The attempt seems to be to simply wipe out low-cost entertainment options for the working-class populations of the city without even providing them with an opportunity to make a case for their space. Sagai makes a compelling argument about publicness when he recalls,

> People used to watch films together at a theatre or in a video parlour but now that they are shutting down, people are watching more content online with computers and on mobile phones, with probably much fewer people around the screen. The next step is the Google Glass where you watch alone and nobody interferes (Titus 2014).

Sheikh, the video parlour owner, feels that despite several efforts and rumours of demolitions, his video parlour has been able to run relatively hassle-free with help and support from patrons. He says, when asked about the possibility of shutting down, 'We'll worry about shifting or shutting down when we have to, I have been hearing such stories for ten years now' (Titus 2008). Jeffries attests in her work on fear and the city: 'In an increasingly punitive legal and built environment, a discourse of rampant criminality is deployed to support ever more elaborate modes of enclosure' (2014: 254). If such spaces for distribution of content help a vast section of society indulge in 'publicness', then fear is the tool of repression.

With the availability of cheap mobile hardware and affordable data plans, several regular and potential video parlour patrons have now shifted to watching films on their smartphones. Many small stalls that facilitate this mode of media consumption by downloading content from the Internet and transferring it to memory cards for a small fee, have come up in various localities across Mumbai (Image 8.5).

IMAGE 8.5: A Download Centre in Mumbai with a Collage of Films Available for Download at Approximately Rs 8 each (June 2017)

Source: Photograph taken by the author.

At a glance, it appears that these alternate media centres are in abundance and enjoying vibrant and healthy patronage. How does one begin to understand this system that thrives in the gaps left by mainstream media and legal networks? One consideration is the idea of *jugaad* (cost-effective fix; hack; practical workaround), which Rai (2013) refers to as a 'practical workaround'. But even this term, in its usage in lay parlance, never encapsulated the kind of legal implications now imposed in such a context. Rai quotes T. H. Choudary,

In the 1990s the Left, socialist, progressive members of the Planning Commission in India thought of the telephone as elitist .... It is rumoured that the then telecom minister said, while responding to complaints of poor quality phone calls and high bills, 'it is not compulsory to have a telephone, anyone can surrender it at any time' (2013: 1).

Today it is not uncommon to find a cell phone in the most deprived households in Mumbai, because it connects people to information, and hence, opportunities for employment, as several of these household members are part of the unorganised labour market. With the sale of the mobile phone spectrum to private firms, a new and more potent tool has been deployed to work at the behest of both the state and the pirates. Most people may consider this benign, but it is a connection to the authority structures that is far stronger and more pervasive than it has ever been. Despite persistent concerns of being traced, the download centres are an interesting display of how networked infrastructures end up having their (piratical) second lives, without which, in such congested environments, the recreational potential would be severely curtailed. It is facets such as this within networked infrastructure that lends a resilient edge to recreational environments. Parks and Schwoch (2012) work on more potent technologies like satellites and their transnational footprints, examine 'cultural' roles such as broadcasting, and more 'extractive' relationships such as use by corporates and government entities.

Along similar lines, it is important to interrogate the function of mobile phones and the increasing number of applications or apps in curating and influencing cultural life, as well as its more exploitative characteristics. Theatres not listed on ticketing apps, and where physical tickets must be purchased in person, have dropped out of the mind space of the most upwardly mobile class of theatre patrons. Conveniences such as credit card payment facilities or online ticketing are not just efficient and convenient tools that are meant to serve a 'targeted' segment of the audience, but they are also actively disassembling low-cost screening spaces and converting them into enclaves for the upper classes.[21] This is not to suggest that the theatres are in poor upkeep because of the apps serving other theatres, but rather, a lack of networking and association with new digital infrastructures only seems to push them further into the hands of such a design. A productive approach might be to frame the debate as one of *jugaad* against the tyranny of the algorithmic. In Stripas's words, 'What is at stake in "algorithmic culture" is the gradual abandonment of culture's publicness and the emergence of a strange new breed of elite culture purporting to be its opposite' (Stripas 2015: 395). There appears to be a lot more choice but very few decisions to be made. If a theatre is not listed on a popular booking app, is it worth going to? If a film is not listed there, is it worth watching? The seemingly 'public/crowd wisdom' is now 'increasingly becoming a private, exclusive and indeed profitable affair' (ibid.: 407). The idea of 'collaborative filtering' sometimes does not convey—perhaps because of the common connotation of the word collaboration, suggesting an involvement of all parties concerned—the picture of a coercive structure deeply rooted in political, social and economic power structures within society, which can force non-conforming cultural forms and artefacts into defunction.

The creativity of 'recycled' filmic content, alternate low-budget production or distribution centres, modified and piratical treatments of infrastructure, and collective bodies battling eviction from within class- and caste-based boundaries are treading the line between legitimacy and illegitimacy, visibility and invisibility, and forging potentials for strong networks of resilience across cityscapes. Given the ominous possibilities emerging through current technology, there are equally resilient workarounds feasible for those unable to get access to 'certified' spaces or infrastructures through which they may connect with media forms and socio-political discourse. If we are to accept the thought that 'a critique of cinema is a critique of society', then the shortcomings in a society are the shortcomings that cinema itself has been unable to overcome. The study of Mumbai's video parlours, single-screen theatres, and its diverse, low-cost, B-film-viewing culture is unique because these sites are institutions of resistance to established power structures controlling the distribution and flow of information in society. These are crossroads at which intellectual rights, patenting, legislative structures, media content and dominant networks seem to be converging, and going up against the creative energies of the marginalised and underrepresented in society, creating environments through which diverse populations forge solidarities through the spatial and textual sphere of cinema.

Notes

1. 'Time pass' is term commonly used in various Indian languages, especially in Hindi. It may suggest the availability of some time for leisure and indulgence in an activity, or even unemployment.

2. An article in the *Mumbai Mirror* reports the Police Commissioner of Mumbai associating the increase in crime in the area with the parlours and ordering the closure of these video parlours (Mustafa 2014).

3. Theatre owner Moin Agadhi informed me that there is no exit in the cinema space allotment policy. While a theatre space must always remain a theatre space, any redeveloped site is lawfully bound to retain only 33 per cent of its space for the purpose of film exhibition (Titus 2017a).

The tabloid *Mumbai Mirror*, reporting on the closure of the New Empire Cinema, one of the oldest single screen theatres in Mumbai, states that in 1908, when it was a space of live theatre, it had seating for a 1,000 people. The theatre underwent major renovations in 1996. The number of seats reported at that time is 581. Burge Cooper, the owner of the New Empire, claims that the current financial losses of the theatre are about Rs 2,58,00,000, and he also claims that the management even contemplated reducing the number of seats to ensure that the theatre became profitable. To conclude, Cooper states that '... maybe we are not that famous anymore. Or, no one bothers about single screen theatres in this age of multiplexes' (Singh 2014).

4. Multiplexisation is the term coined to describe single screen theatres being converted to more expensive, and arguably, more comfortable theatres with multiple screens, screening different films at the same time.

5. Other than its references to literature, the angry-young-man phase in Indian cinema refers to a series of working-class characters portrayed by Amitabh Bachchan in the 1970s and 1980s.

6. Crossover: cinema with Indian characters, often with transnational origins, and where a significant part of the narrative is in English.

7. Emerged through a presentation (Liang 2013).

8. Located in the eastern part of the Mumbai, it comprises parts of suburbs like Chembur, Mankhurd and Ghatkopar.

9. Often divided into M-East and M-West wards, their total size would be close to 56–60 sq. km (Ward-MW).

10. The Eastern Expressway, Santacruz-Chembur Link Road (SCLR), Eastern Express Highway, Monorail, Metro, and at least four major railway stations (Kurla, Chembur, Ghatkopar and Mankhurd) are in or adjoining the ward; some of these even serve long distance trains from across the country. It is also a ward that is an entry point into the island city of Mumbai.

11. Haussmanisation of urban space, gendered implications in the gaze of the flaneur, and unifying the organism known as the modern city (Graham and Marvin 2001; McQuire 2008).

12. The term 'recycled' is used in reference to films being played which are well past their sell-by date to mainstream theatres and multiplexes in the city.

13. '... the information needs of the poor has to be more than wanting to watch a film or even dreaming of becoming a film maker' (Liang 2009: 28).

14. Water can cost almost 50 to 100 times more in informal housing areas than it costs in other parts of the city. Several newspaper reports and research studies have shown that the cost of production of 10,000 litres of water is approximately Rs 24, and formal housing colonies are charged Rs 24 for 1,000 litres of water (Gupta 2005; TNN 2015).

15. His colleague Bhimrao, 25 years old, mentions that he has sown Rs 30,000 worth of cotton and is in Mumbai for two months to earn money as a labourer. He does not expect to make any significant income on the cotton. Various reports on the labour force in Mumbai have established the connectedness of unorganised contract labour to peasant, minority, and marginalised caste communities from surrounding regions, due to larger policy failures or neglect of the state and the resulting agrarian crisis (Titus 2017b).

16. Mediation and censorial proximity are mentioned in Köhn (2016).

17. A cinema that draws attention to its production technology and appearances rather than a dominant narrative. See Gunning (1990).

18. Amitabh Bachchan, Mithun Chakraborty and Rajnikanth are popular film stars who began their careers in the 1970s and early 1980s and rose to stardom in that period. Rajnikanth especially continues to be one superstar who dominates the box office in South India, and at times, in other parts of the country as well with most of his releases. Akshay Kumar has been on the rise steadily in the 2000s, and in 2015–16, he was considered one of the highest paid film stars in the world.

19. Karan Singh, a 25-year-old migrant worker from Uttar Pradesh, told me while waiting for a screening to begin at Amar Theatre, 'People think there is sex in these movies, but I come here to learn about the story. I like to watch films with sudden twists .... A lot of these posters are too explicit, they expose too much, that's not right.' Speaking about his love for cinema, he says, 'I have a passion for films and understanding how they are made, if you noticed, my name is the same as Bollywood director Karan Johar. He is the only film director who is thin and so am I .... My friends and I travel to Film City (in Goregaon, Mumbai) and we wait there for stars to arrive, I was there just yesterday, the police drove us away when the shooting began ...' (Titus 2017d).

20. Nakassis (2016: 313) conceptualises 'frayed threads radiating outwards'.

21. Of the seven theatres at the research sites, only two multiplexes had credit card payment and online ticketing facilities. These theatres attract the most crowds and the other five are in various stages of disrepair or redevelopment.

REFERENCES

Bauman, Zygmunt. 2000. [Reprint Edition]. *Community: Seeking Safety in an Insecure World*. Cambridge; Malden, MA: Polity Press.

Dutta, Madhusree, Kaushik Bhaumik and Rohan Shivkumar. 2013. *Project Cinema City*. New Delhi: Tulika Books.

Graham, Stephen and Simon Marvin. 2001. *Splintering Urbanism: Networked Infrastructures, Technological Mobilities and the Urban Condition*. London: New York: Routledge.

Gunning, Tom. 1990. 'Cinema of Attractions: Early Film, Its Spectator and the Avant-Garde'. In Tom Gunning, Thomas Elsaesser and Adam Barker (eds), *Early Cinema: Space-Frame-Narrative*, pp. 56–63. London: BFI Publishing.

Gupta, Sourendu. 1997. 'Water Supply: Mumbai/Bombay Pages'. Available at http://theory.tifr.res.in/bombay/amenities/water/ (accessed 21 June 2016).

Jeffries, Fiona. 2014. 'Reappropriating the City of Fear', *Space and Culture* 17(3): 251–65.

Köhn, Steffen. 2016. *Mediating Mobility: Visual Anthropology in the Age of Migration*. New York: Columbia University Press.

Larkin, Brian. 2008. *Signal and Noise: Media, Infrastructure, and Urban Culture in Nigeria*. Durham, NC: Duke University Press.

———. 2016. 'Hausa Dramas and the Rise of Video Culture in Nigeria'. In Jonathan Haynes (ed.), *Nigerian Video Films 2016*, pp. 209–57. Chicago: University of Chicago Press.

Liang, Lawrence. 2009. 'Piracy, Creativity and Infrastructure and Infrastructure: Rethinking Access to Culture', *The Global Flow of Information: Legal, Social, and Cultural Perspectives, Social Science Research Network*. Available at 10.2139/ssrn.1436229.

———. 2013. 'New Media and Film Culture', Lecture, School of Media and Cultural Studies, Tata Institute of Social Sciences (TISS), Mumbai. January 2013.

Nakassis, Constantine V. 2016. *Doing Style: Youth and Mass Mediation in South India*. Chicago: University of Chicago Press.

Parks, Lisa, and James Schwoch. 2012. *Down to Earth: Satellite Technologies, Industries and Cultures.* London; New Brunswick; New Jersey: Rutgers University Press.

Pinney, Christopher. 2002. 'The Indian Work of Art in the Age of Mechanical Reproduction Or, What Happens When Peasants "Get Hold" of Images'. In Faye D. Ginsburg, Lila Abu-Lughod and Brian Larkin (eds), *Media Worlds: Anthropology on New Terrain*, pp. 355–69. Berkeley; London; Los Angeles: University of California Press.

Rai, Amit S. 2013. 'On the Jugaad Image: Embodying the Mobile Phone in India', *Postmodern Culture* 23 (1). Available at https://doi.org/10.1353/pmc.2013.0022 (accessed 12 November 2017).

Ramnath, Nandini, 'Another House for Art Cinema', Livemint, 8 July 2014. Available at http://www.livemint.com/Leisure/TwSnLFPzYfUfEjdowBqwgP/Another-house-for-art-cinema.html (accessed 12 November 2017).

Sconce, J. 1995. '"Trashing" the Academy: Taste, Excess, and an Emerging Politics of Cinematic Style', *Screen* 36 (4): 371–93.

Shaikh, Mustafa, 'Maria Orders Outpost in Place of Old Shivaji Nagar Police Station', *Mumbai Mirror*, 6 November 2014. Available at https://mumbaimirror.indiatimes.com/mumbai/other/Maria-orders-outpost-in-place-of-old-Shivaji-Nagar-police-station/articleshow/45052332.cms (accessed 12 November 2017).

Shilling, Chris. 2005. *The Body in Culture, Technology and Society.* London: Sage Publications.

Singh, Virat, 'The End', *Mumbai Mirror*, 26 July 2014.

Stripas, Ted. 2015. 'Algorithmic Culture', *Ted European Journal of Cultural Studies* 18 (4–5): 395–412.

Sundaram, Ravi. 2010. *Pirate Modernity: Delhi's Media Urbanism.* Abingdon, Oxon: Routledge.

Titus, Nikhil Thomas, Interview with Rafique Sheikh, May 2008.

———, Interview with Nambi Rajan, Unpublished Video Recording with Suhail M., October 2010.

———, Interview with Faiz Ullah, Sagai, March 2014.

———, Field Observations in Chembur, Mumbai, August 2016.

———, Interview with MoinAgadhi, July 2017a.

———, Interview with Bhimrao at Ghatkopar East, on the Footpath Outside Waman Hari Pete Jewellers, July 2017b.

———, Interview with Mohan Nandedkar, July 2017c.

———, Interview with Karan Singh outside Amar Theatre, July 2017d.

TNN, 'BMC to Hike Water Charges from June 2016', *The Times of India*, 15 June 2015. Available at http://timesofindia.indiatimes.com/city/mumbai/BMC-to-hike-water-charges-from-June-16/articleshow/47680663.cms (accessed 21 June 2016).

Video Parlous (edited clip). Available at goo.gl/Hjh3N7.
'Ward MW—Welcome to The Municipal Corporation of Greater Mumbai'.
    Available   at   http://www.mcgm.gov.in/irj/portal/anonymous/
    qlwardmw?guest_user=english (accessed 6 November 2016).

FILMS CITED

Bitter Moon. 1992. Roman Polanski (dir.). France; UK; USA: Les Films
    Alain Sarde; Le Studio Canal+.
Bitter Moon. 1992. [Hindi Dub: *Bewafai (Betrayal)*]. Roman Polanski
    (dir.). France; UK; USA: Les Films Alain Sarde; Le Studio Canal+.
Cannibal Apocalypse. 1980. Anthony M. Dawson (Antonio Margheriti)
    (dir.). Italy; Spain: New Fida Organization; Jose Frade.
Gunda (Gangster). 1998. Kanti Shah (dir.). Maruti Films, India.
Hunters of the Golden Cobra. [Hindi Dub: *Adimanav Aur Sarprani
    (The Primitive Man and the Snake Queen)*]. Anthony M. Dawson
    (Antonio Margheriti) (dir.). Italy: Regal Film; GicoCinematografica.
Loha (Iron). 1997. Kanti Shah (dir.). Jockey Film, India.

nine

Digitising Memories

A *Digital Archive of Kolkata's Forgotten Colonial Cemeteries*

SOUVIK MUKHERJEE

INTRODUCTION

The colonial memories in India have witnessed an interesting and perhaps predictable fate. Unlike the rather violent removal of the imperialist magnate Cecil Rhodes's statue from Cape Town University in April 2015 (BBC 2015), in India, the fate of such memorials is to be forgotten or to be relocated to obscurity. In fact, quite often, reactions to our colonial past are just as R. K. Narayan describes in his short story 'Lawley Road', where the statue of a Sir Frederick Lawley is first pulled down in the mistaken thought that he was 'a combination of Attila .... and Nadir Shah with the craftiness of Machiavelli' (Narayan 1999: 391) and then reinstated when people realise that Sir Frederick had, in fact, been a great benefactor of the city, and none of the things that he was earlier thought to be. In the confusion that arises as to the colonial past and what to do with the Sir Frederick Lawley statues, much that needs to be remembered is often forgotten by historians.

As history is rewritten and monuments built over, a more recent medium of data curation could potentially come to the rescue. The digital 'archive', which is considered one of the main deliverables from the recently developed discipline called 'Digital Humanities' (DH), and has already been employed to create vast searchable repositories of the works of Blake, Shakespeare, Whitman and Tagore, could be used to record and curate information pertaining to the lives of people during colonial rule by the British and other European powers. Of course, despite the reactions to colonialism, Indian history is replete with references to certain prominent figures, while much less is known about the quotidian lives of those other Britishers and Europeans who settled in India and became part of its social and cultural fabric. In an attempt to explore the lives of these people, whom the history books miss out and the country has largely forgotten, the digital archives of some of the colonial cemeteries was mooted, and two projects, one on the then ruinous Scottish cemetery in Kolkata, and another on the almost forgotten Dutch cemetery in Chinsurah, were started. In researching these 'ordinary' lives, many important stories have been uncovered; whether it is the story of the man who stopped human sacrifice in Odisha, or that of the first ice-making industry in the country, these projects reconstruct the colonial settlements through the narratives of the people buried in the cemeteries. This chapter looks at the two cemetery archives within the DH paradigm.

The word 'archive', of course, has a specific meaning in DH that many traditional archivists disagree with. Theimer (2012), in her appraisal of the differences between the use of the word by archivists and by digital humanists, states:

> Archivists would not refer to online groupings of digital copies of non-digital original materials, often comprised of [sic] materials (including published materials) located in different physical repositories or collections, purposefully selected and arranged in order to support a scholarly goal, as an 'archives'—and so the confusion of an Archivist tourist in the land of Digital Humanities (2012: n.p.).

Her worry is that 'in the broadening of "archives" to extend to any digital collection of surrogates there is the potential for a loss of understanding and appreciation of the historical context that archives preserve in their collections, and the unique role that archives play as custodians of materials in this context' (Theimer 2012: n.p.). Price (2009), the creator of the *Walt Whitman Archives*, is clear on what he sees as the role of the digital archive:

> Archive has gradually come to mean a purposeful collection of surrogates. As we know, meanings change over time, and archive in a digital context has come to suggest something that blends features of editing and archiving. To meld features of both—to have the care

of treatment and annotation of an edition and the inclusiveness of an archive—is one of the tendencies of recent work in electronic editing (2009: n.p.).

Price calls for the creation of an inclusive and open-ended thematic collection that encompasses geo-spatial and temporal data that is trans-linguistic and cross-cultural. The notion of archiving surrogates, although paradoxical, is currently the major concern of DH. Kirschenbaum identified the contrast with the older notion of the 'archive' in the migration of the word from noun to verb. The verb usage is relatively more recent and 'has come to do the double duty with the act of copying, so archive is coterminous with duplication and redundancy' (Kirschenbaum 2013: n.p.). Kirschenbaum refers to the LOCKSS or Lots of Copies Keep Stuff Safe project and moving away from the artefact situated in its unique archival context, speaks of preservation via multiplicity. All of these three positions make valid arguments from their own perspectives, and it is within the rubric of all of these varied positions and its own unique problems that the digital archive of the colonial cemetery will be described.

Although it might not have been perceived as such, the colonial cemetery is in itself, undoubtedly, an archive, in Theimer's more traditional sense. Death, religious beliefs and economic prosperity have contributed to the elements that the archive consists of. The current custodians of the cemeteries, whether it is the Archaeological Survey of India (ASI) (for the Chinsurah Cemetery) or the Kolkata Scottish Heritage Trust (for the Scottish Cemetery) or the British Association for Cemeteries in South Asia (BACSA), are, to varying degrees, responsible archivists, as they maintain records of the tombs and are committed to their brick-and-mortar restoration. However, where they are limited is the wider connections that the tombs have to related information: such as obituaries, anecdotes, personal documents and locations, similar to Price's focus on the relations across planes of reference. Some of these, it must be remembered, need to be reconstructed from scattered pieces of recorded memory, and these are not even the digital surrogates and copies that Kirschenbaum speaks of. In some cases, they are recreations based on piecing together digital surrogates as well as speculative research to fill in the vacant spaces. For colonial architecture and built-environment, the challenges of destruction are substantial.

Let us take the seventeenth-century Dutch settlements in Bengal as an example. These Dutch colonies lasted almost over two centuries; yet, what little remains of them today is under threat of encroachment. The Dutch Kuthi in Baranagore, just outside Kolkata, has recently been pulled down by local realtors after having lasted out the Dutch (Asian Heritage Alert 2014), British and post-Independence regimes. Many of the original Dutch buildings in Chinsurah, such as the Dutch fort, Fort Gustavus, were built over by the British after they took over. The Dutch themselves destroyed some of their own heritage: the old Dutch Cemetery in Chinsurah was destroyed by a Dutch governor and moved to its present location in the same town in around 1753. Some of the buildings have survived, such as General Perron's palatial house, which now houses the Hooghly Mohsin College.[1] The boundaries of the fort have been marked by iron pillars by the British conquerors, and one or two old mansions still remain standing. A notable piece of surviving Dutch heritage is the 'New' Dutch Cemetery, with its grand obelisks, mausolea and pedestal tombs from the late-eighteenth and early-nineteenth centuries that are now under the care of the ASI. The protection by the ASI helps to a great extent because other major cemeteries have long given way to the need for land to build upon as well as to what might be called a postcolonial reaction. As Chadha comments,

> Today, the Park Street cemetery sporadically features in the imagination of the people of Calcutta as a space where the masters of a bygone era are buried. In a postcolonial nation, the colonial masters do not have any place; they are the dead who must be removed from the sight of the living. In the past few years, huge apartment complexes have mushroomed around the cemetery, along with a multi-storied parking lot (2006: 345).

Chadha points out how immediately after the Indian Independence, there was a call to raze the two major heritage cemeteries on either side of the posh locality of Park Street in Calcutta.[2] He identifies the dual colonial function of the memorials in the colonial cemeteries as being bereavement monuments as well as the material manifestation of the victory of an occupying power. However, unlike the negative heritage sites such as Nazi war memorials, 'this heritage can neither be appropriated in the nationalistic imagination nor can it be completely negated—it can at best be forgotten' (ibid.). The French Cemetery in Calcutta is now the Apeejay School, and the North Park Street Cemetery (where James Achilles Kirkpatrick, Dalrymple's 'White Mughal', and Richmond Thackeray, the father of the novelist, were buried) is now the site of the Assembly of God Church School and Hospital. Buettner (2006) rightly remarks,

> From their origins as commemorative sites for European dead, they were subsequently converted into makeshift accommodation for the homeless, settings for leisure activities, public toilets, or used as implements for cooking or washing; finally, they have witnessed more recent efforts to restore some of their original meanings and reassess the value of the Raj, and reflect the divergent interests of elite and plebeian Indian social sectors (2006: 30).

She also asks whether even people in post-Empire Britain are interested in any of the stories that these cemeteries have to tell. The postcolonial situation of these relics of colonial regimes runs the risk of being forgotten and dismissed both by the former colonisers and the colonised alike. With them, disappears the history that they carry.

Unlike other monuments, colonial tombstones have always been neglected—even in the 1900s, Busteed (1908) writes about how the old tombs are not being cared for; the concern is reflected in Cotton (1907) as well as in minutes by the Viceroy, Lord Curzon. Nevertheless, attempts to record the data on the tombstones were also an ongoing process. One of the most notable attempts at doing this was the *Bengal Obituary* published by Holmes & Co. in 1837. The Jesuit priest, Father Hosten, contributed many articles to *Bengal Past and Present*, where he wrote about various European cemeteries scattered across Bengal and other provinces. After the Indian Independence, the son of a former British businessman from Kanpur, Theon Wilkinson, formed BACSA, whose members still actively record inscriptions and photograph tombs across South Asia. This interest arises out of a range of factors. Chadha describes the colonial cemetery as the 'location where the abject interacts with memorial *fragments* to produce a narrative of the past. Here, inscriptions transform the cemetery into a metaphor of the past, which provides a rich history of the earliest colonial settlers of Calcutta—a kind of a material genealogy of the past' (2006: 357). The inscriptions, often very detailed (especially those dating back to the late-eighteenth and early-nineteenth centuries), are rich sources of information about the people buried in these tombs. See, for example, the epitaph of Gregorius Herklots, who was the *fiscaal* (Finance Minister) of the Dutch Government at Chinsurah, and later, a magistrate under British rule when the Dutch ceded Chinsurah to the British:

> Here lie buried the mortal remains of Gregorius Herklots Fiscal. Chinsurah. He was born at Bremen January 1768. Arrived at Chinsurah in 1789, resided there for a period of sixty three years and died May [ ] 1852 Aged 84 years .... Employed in responsible offices by both the Dutch and English governments, he discharged the duties of public life with unblemished integrity, fidelity and zeal (Mukherjee and Mitra 2014: n.p.).

It continues:

> He resided with the most child like faith upon the promises of the redeemer and made submission to his master's will law of his life. His religious principle was especially exhibited a Christian hospitality, in liberality to the missionary cause and in kindness to the poor. His Christian duties as a husband, a father and a citizen he sought to fulfil [sic] according to the law of Christ and through his spirits aid him with the warmest esteem (ibid.: n.p.).

His birthplace, career and character are described in detail, and the huge pyramid-topped tomb where he is buried is testimony to his position in society and his wealth. While it is important to consider the tomb in its location and in comparison to the other tombs around it, just as the traditional rationale of the archive requires, the copying of the inscription by the compilers of the *Bengal Obituary* (1851) or the companions of Father Hosten and the photography by BACSA show how the archiving of the cemetery was already an act of surrogacy and multiplication via copying well before the advent of DH.

With the techniques of DH, the aim is to effect a re-creation or revival of the memory of the colonial settlement as it existed in Chinsurah, and the fuller understanding of the legacy of a community such as the Scots through the Scottish Cemetery project. The DH project involves the following activities:

- Photographing gravestones and tombs (where necessary, and in as much detail as possible).
- Accessing and digitising burial registers.

- Transcribing headstone inscriptions and inserting architectural, biographical, geographical, demographic, literary and historical metadata.
- Recording such data in a digital database with facilities for framing flexible and comparative searches, the building of timelines and creating map locators.
- Connecting the information that is, at present, available only in scattered fragments across free information repositories, cemetery databases and genealogy websites.
- Building a website with open access to the database and search facilities.

There are distinct similarities here with what BACSA and earlier research has done. Father Hosten's comment on data collection is noteworthy: 'By this time my youthful coadjutors had become so thoroughly imbued with the spirit of antiquarian research that a picnic to Serampur without plenty of inscriptions to copy would have been the dullest thing imaginable' (Hosten 1915: 42). This is very similar to the gen-ed students in Presidency University doing DH, and a handful of trained postgraduates visiting the cemeteries in Chinsurah and Kareya Road and copying down epitaphs, taking GPS readings and photographing tombs, often before a post-work meet-up at the nearby restaurant. In this respect, the DH project is a *remediation* of what Hosten and BACSA have done earlier. There are distinct differences in that the data-collectors in the current project carry Android devices with geolocating software and cameras that can take high-resolution photos. The data is also stored in an Excel file on Google Docs and then in an SQL database that forms the back-end data for the digital cemetery archive. Bolter and Grusin (2000) define *remediation* as 'new media doing exactly what their predecessors have done: presenting themselves as refashioned and improved versions of other media' (2000: 14–15). They also point out the impossibility of any medium working in isolation and state that the novelty of recent media lies in the ways in which they refashion older media and also, the ways in which older media, too, refashion themselves as a response.

The database of the colonial cemetery is, therefore, an archive, but it is also a remediation of the archive, just as the earlier iterations of the DH project by Father Hosten or BACSA would have been.

Those still uncomfortable with calling it an archive may switch to the phrase 'themed digital collection' instead, but it would nevertheless be important to note that the archive and its remediated form have been constantly in interplay, ever since the first efforts at recording the stories that the cemeteries tell us.

The digital cemetery archive, given its distinct media-specific advantages over Father Hosten or BACSA's projects, does more in terms of what Price describes as the translinguistic and the cross-cultural; the collection and presentation of data is also trans-medial. Besides the data available from the headstones, researchers in the project search for further data in the burial registers, and often, a lot more emerges from following trails to parents, grandparents and children. Burial registers also reveal the place of death, and sometimes, the cause of death. Wills and probate documents, newspaper articles, private correspondence, obituaries, and in less common cases, biographies, reveal a great deal that helps in (re)constructing the story of many of the people buried in these cemeteries. Massive amounts of data on colonial India have been digitised and are now available either on public or private databases. Some of these are notoriously overpriced, such as the South Asia Archive, now owned by Taylor and Francis, but the most comprehensive repositories, such the Digital Library of India,[3] archive.org, Hathi Trust[4] and the West Bengal Digital Library are available for free access. Besides the data available online, there is, predictably, a vast amount that has not been digitised. These range from basic offline compilations, such as Hodson's *Officers of the Bengal Army 1758–1834* (2001), to more obscure biographies of native catechists. The other major source of information, offline, would be the newspapers; and again, here, there is much painstaking reading to be done, as very few Indian newspapers from this time have been digitised. Often, research on an individual leads to links with others in the database, and it is necessary to hyperlink between entries.

Finally, a metadata system has been devised by the team, both before and after reviewing the full dataset. As such, it is easier to search and filter based on categories or combinations of categories set by the metadata selection. The website for the project has been designed in Drupal, and the platform allows for a full-text search within the entire archive. A more nuanced search based on selected parameters is also enabled within the archive. The stories that emerge are therefore assemblages of digital copies of a rather mixed set of data obtained from and through various media. To return to the story of Herklots now, would be to enter such a mesh of stories.

Herklots's family, hailing from Bremen, Germany, has deep roots in the Dutch East India Company and his father is buried in Cossim *Bazar* (market), not far from Murshidabad. He also served as Interim Governor of Chinsurah, and would have been quite wealthy, as he was in charge of all the import and export from the colony. He is also found in British scientific records as recording early-morning temperatures outside Chinsurah to aid the preparation for the 'Chinsurah slush' or the local substitute for ice. He also appears as a witness in the Pertaubchand case, where an impostor had claimed the throne of Burdwan, and as Herklots had met the person being impersonated, his testimony was of major importance in settling the claims of the kingdom. His son trained as a doctor in England and translated the *Qanuni Islam,* a book written by a Muslim colleague from Madras that lists the Islamic laws in India. Of his daughters, one married the Swiss preacher, Alphonse Lacroix, who was one of the first missionaries to preach in Bengali and who was very close to William Carey and the Baptist missionaries. Another daughter, Hannah Mullens, is supposedly the author of the first Bengali novel, *Phulmani o Karunar Bibaran (A Narrative of Phulmani and Karuna)* (1852). Herklots, in his distinctive tall pyramid-topped pedestal tomb, is a classic example of a forgotten story of early colonial India, its easily-missed cosmopolitanism, and the European influence on Indian culture. This is a story that would never have been told other than by his now-forgotten tomb in Chinsurah and the DH project that explored the links.

There are many more stories in the archive of the Dutch cemetery. They fit into a larger archive–narrative framework, and there are many archival projects out there that also work on similar principles. For example, the South Asia Digital Archive (SAADA) aims to 'enable people who have been marginalized to have the power and authority to establish and enact their presence in ways that are complex, meaningful, substantive, and positive to them in a variety of symbolic contexts'. SAADA digitises 'historic materials and collect[s] born-digital sources located in private and family collections' (SAADA

2015). A similar archive is the Early Caribbean Digital Archive (ECDA), which presents the

> narratives of the lives of enslaved Caribbean peoples [that] appeared in a great variety of venues, particularly at the high point of the abolitionist movement in England during the late eighteenth and early nineteenth centuries. Many forums, such as newspapers, novels, poems, and essays, were specifically created in order to highlight slave voices (ECDA 2015).

The curators see the Caribbean slave narratives as being distinct in form, theme and content, and state that the purpose of the exhibit is to 'highlight these distinctions and connections by considering the genre's emergence and development in the multilingual and multicultural contexts of the Caribbean' (ECDA 2015). Similar to these repositories, the Jewish Calcutta Archive also reconstructs the history of the Jewish community in Calcutta through a rich and rare collection of digital surrogates of photos and other artefacts, and the now shrinking community is once again, as it were, appreciable in its former prominence. The cemetery archive, too, collects and records stories 'from below', or the stories of those people in colonial India whose stories have never been told.

From the salt-*chowkies* (check post) clerk, the police constable, to soldiers and servants, the archive reflects a vast demographic range. The community of Eurasians, later called Anglo-Indians, is also one whose stories emerge more clearly in the cemetery archives. Besides, the individual stories, the digital medium, allows for certain collective conclusions to be drawn from the dataset. One such example is the geographic distribution of the places from where the people who are buried have come or the places that they have worked in. Image 9.1, based on the data from the Scottish Cemetery, shows a clear concentration around Scotland and East Asia. Many of the Scots who arrived in Bengal ended up in government employment or as plantation owners in Bengal and East of Bengal. However, we also see people in the US, Europe and Australia, and these links need to be studied further by historians.

Another such study from the dataset reveals the common cause of death during these times. Cholera and childbirth are by far the most common reasons for mortality, and the general picture is grim

IMAGE 9.1: A Word-Cloud Created from the Cemetery Database Showing the Common Causes of Death in the Period

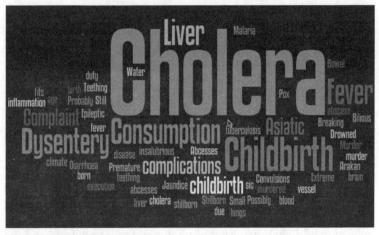

Source: Provided by the author.

and reveals the insalubrious conditions in which survival rates were rather low. The cemetery archive, in some cases, also goes beyond its purported remit of recording the stories of the people who are buried in the cemetery and provides details of others whose stories are connected to the place. One such example is the story of Isaac Titsingh, the Dutch Governor of Chinsurah, a scholar who could speak Chinese and Japanese and was a regular contributor to the Asiatic Society. Titsingh had secured trade rights from China before any other European had done, and in Japan, he was so popular that he is remembered even today as a *manga* (Japanese comic books) character. The Chinsurah Cemetery website also attempts to reconstruct the town as it would have looked like during Dutch times, and forms a part of a larger project on colonial Chinsurah, commissioned by the Dutch Embassy in India that uses interviews, oral history and geotagging to reconstruct the history of the town (see Image 9.2).

Both the cemetery archives, of the Scottish Cemetery, Kolkata, and the Dutch Cemetery, Chinsurah, contain other features such as comparative timelines and a geotagged map showing the locations of the tombs; the Scottish Cemetery project, for example, is not yet complete and more developments are on the way. As a DH project,

IMAGE 9.2: Isaac Titsingh, the Dutch Governor of Chinsurah, a Popular Character in Japanese *Manga*

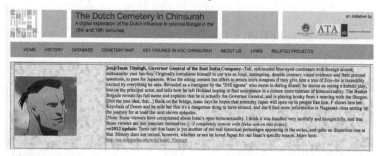

Source: Provided by the author.

the archive allows for a fresh approach towards the study of colonial cities and communities by bringing the toolset of the DH archive to record and sometimes recreate the stories of the people buried in these cemeteries. Starting with the cemeteries as a point of departure allows for a deeper engagement with local history and that of those people whose stories were not otherwise accessible and where the zones of contact between the different communities, whether British, Dutch, Portuguese or Bengali are better studied. The cemetery archive takes the study of colonial history a step beyond the understanding of colonial legacies through a 'Great Men' approach; rather, through a Web 2.0 notion of an open archive, just like some of the similar archives described here, it attempts to open itself up to a larger community of researchers and other stakeholders who can add to the archive via a curated interface. As such, within the Indian context of DH, the cemetery archive projects point at possibilities beyond the traditional DH archives, directing towards a rethinking of the corpus of literary texts and authors, to give way in turn to a rethinking of the very notion of archives for the study of colonial history, and arguably, the notions of colonial history itself.

Notes

1. Perron, incidentally, served the Scindias and amassed great wealth, which he brought to Chinsurah after his forces were routed in battle against Lord Lake and Arthur Wellesley.

2. Park Street was formerly called Burial Ground Road in the early days of the city's history.

3. The Digital Library of India collection is now available on archive. org.

4. Much of Hathi Trust is free in the US.

REFERENCES

Asian Heritage Alert. 2014. Dutch Kuthi of Baranagore, Kolkata, Heritage in Peril.

BBC News. 2015. 'Rhodes Statue Removed in Cape Town as Crowd Celebrates'. Available at http://www.bbc.co.uk/news/world-africa-32236922 (accessed 28 December 2015).

Bolter, J. D., and Richard Grusin. 2000. *Remediation: Understanding New Media*. Cambridge, Massachussetts: The MIT Press.

Buettner, E. 2006. 'Cemeteries, Public Memory and Raj Nostalgia in Postcolonial Britain and India', *History and Memory* 18(1): 5–42.

Busteed, H. E. 1908. *Echoes from Old Calcutta: Being Chiefly Reminiscences of the Days of Warren Hastings, Francis and Impey*. Calcutta: W. Thacker and Co.

Chadha, A. 2006. 'Ambivalent Heritage: Between Affect and Ideology in a Colonial Cemetery', *Journal of Material Culture* 11(3): 339–63.

Cotton, H. E. 1907. *Calcutta, Old and New: A Historical and Descriptive Handbook to the City*. Calcutta: W. Newman.

ECDA. 2015. Available at https://ecda.northeastern.edu/.

Hodson, V. C. P. 2001 [1927]. *Officers of the Bengal Army 1758–1834*. Uckfield, East Sussex: Naval and Military Press Ltd.

Holmes and Co. 1851. *The Bengal Obituary: Or, A Record to Perpetuate the Memory of Departed Worth*. Calcutta: W. Thacker and Co.

Hosten, Rev. H. 1915. 'Christian Inscriptions from Serampur', *Bengal Past and Present*. Vol 23, p. 42.

Kirschenbaum, M. 2013. 'The .txtual Condition: Digital Humanities, Born-Digital Archives, and the Future Literary', *Digital Humanities Quarterly* 7(1): n.p. Available at http://www.digitalhumanities.org/dhq/vol/7/1/000151/000151.html.

Mukherjee, S., and A. Mitra. 2014. 'Gregorius Herklots', The Dutch Cemetery in Chinsurah, Presidency University, Kolkata; Embassy of the Netherlands, India.

Mullens, H. 1852. *Phulmani O Karunar Bibaran (A Narrative of Phulmani and Karuna)*. Calcutta: The Calcutta Christian Tract And Book Society.

Narayan, R. K. 1999. *A Town Called Malgudi*. New York: Penguin Classics.

Price, K. M. 2009. 'Edition, Project, Database, Archive, Thematic Research Collection: What's in a Name?', *Digital Humanities Quarterly* 3(3): n.p.

SAADA (South Asia Digital Archive). 2015.

Sharif, Jafar. 1972. *Islam in India or Qanuni Islam*. London: Curzon Press.

Theimer, K. 2012. Archives in Context and as Context, *Journal of Digital Humanities* 1(2): n.p. Available at http://journalofdigitalhumanities. org/1-2/archives-in-context-and-as-context-by-kate-theimer/.

PART III

Digital Affect

ten

Interface Intimacies*

Namita Aavriti

Tactile Surfaces

The interface is multiplied over multiple devices in the present moment of globalisation and late capitalism—from the mobile phone, tablet, laptop, desktop, multiplex screen, cinema screen, advertising billboards, announcements, screens in buses and planes, and so on. Lives in the mediatised Asian city are crowded with an array of screens and surfaces that are tactile and even interactive. The promise is simultaneously that of being plugged into a network and of intimacy, of the munificence of neoliberalism and capitalism, but also of capitalising on private pleasures. In the overarching structure of how technology was harnessed by the State for its projects of development (television), growth (dams) and wealth (information technology), what is of interest to me is how the uses of technology by people have often exceeded and escaped the amount of technology that was granted to them by the State, and the regulation and control that the State attempts to have over its use in everyday life.

The interface is a screen or a surface that allows two realms to interact, for instance, the real and the virtual, the human and the machine, or perhaps, even the past and the present. The purpose of the interface is to simplify, guide and translate our actions through visual icons and gestures. It simultaneously conceals (code, labour, infrastructure, circuitry, wires, etc.) and reveals (graphic user

---

*The title of this chapter is borrowed from a workshop jointly conducted with the Centre for Internet and Society (CIS) in 2012. Although the chapter has been reworked a number of times since then, for the lack of imagination, the title remains the same.

interface, result or product, etc.). Our growing intimacy with the interface makes it invisible for us until it does not work or does not respond as quickly or burn as brightly as it usually does. Much seems to happen at the surface of the interface itself, and yet, it produces a sense of absorption, spatiality, depth and movement around and in it. In this chapter, I examine some of these aspects of how we relate to the interface.

A caveat to be placed at the outset is that I am aware that most of the interfaces that we use are dependent on cheap, and often, gendered labour in electronics and manufacturing companies in China, Malaysia and other countries in East and South East Asia (Ong 1987; Verite 2014). It is not possible in this chapter to address these disparities and the exploitation of labour that are gendered or otherwise, depending on existing hierarchies of exclusion and gross inequality (Nakamura 2015).

ABSORPTION AND SENSATION (OR SEX AND PLEASURE)

Image-making via easily available digital devices (phone, cheap cameras, etc.) is considered a leisure activity or part of the consumerist culture, and is not regarded as akin to image-making by the film industry. Home movies or amateur filmmaking from earlier periods are perceived largely as having documentary or archival, but not aesthetic value (Zimmerman 1995). Neither does amateur film produce startling images, nor does it seem to have ambitions in this regard, nor does it have philosophical or filmic value (ibid.). Contemporary, amateur image-making (from the early 2000s onwards), whether on phones, cameras or other devices, is understood as an aspect of image and information-based late-capitalist culture, and without political or social value or content. My contention here is that these images are not necessarily only to be viewed as primary material or artefact for research, ready samples for remix filmmaking, or only as records of historical note. These films are also about aesthetic choices and values, notions around sexuality, gender, and practices of making new, real and surreal images, and are often an insidious challenge to dominant modes of image-making emanating from the film and advertising industry.

Amateur pornography, for instance, is one kind of image generated by the surplus of digital and cheap media that is now easily available. Such videos are often raw, and lack the glossy and technical sheen of cinema that is produced via an organised film industry. Unlike pornography that was previously available, such as soft pornography films from Kerala or other parts of India, these videos are produced by individuals in the act of having sex, who are either openly or secretly recording these acts. It rarely captures a completed sexual act, and the act of recording is often discarded in the throes of sex, or ceased out of the fear of being caught or recognised. The videos are stained by an aura of realness that paradoxically lends itself to imaginative realms, and urban legends of suicide, murder, forced marriage, fleeing the country or the small town, and so on. There are often scandals around well-known figures such as politicians, godmen, actresses, actors and others, but most amateur pornography consists of videos of ordinary people, and mostly, women are captured in the videos.

Such pornography is often watched on the tiny mobile phone interface, laptops, computers in cyber cafes, but rarely on any kind of large screen. The large screen or the cinema screen in India remains the most highly regulated interface of consumption of media, on which strictures of pre-censorship (K. A. Abbas Vs. Union of India 1971) and the *diktat* of the Censor Board of Film Certification (CBFC) still apply (CBFC Website). Under the new cyber law regime, even cyber cafes are controlled by rules that demand identity proofs of all users, spatial arrangement of computers in the cafe, and so on.[1] Mobile phones and bluetooth exchanges, and phones pre-loaded with porngraphy are the relatively new and untraceable networks via which a lot of exchange of pornographic material takes place (Holla 2013).

The pornographic clip, in spite of its short length and hazy resolution, absorbs the viewer into its own universe, which is probably not too far from the ordinary world and sexual habits of the viewer himself or herself. These clips are surrounded by the buzz of stories of how they were made; and on other occasions, they evoke a sense of familiarity because of how the actors look (unlike stars), what their bodies are like, the details of the spaces and rooms that they occupy, and their habits and gestures that uncannily reflect one's own.

In the early 2000s, a pornographic film which was allegedly a couple's private video from a holiday was leaked when it was given to a video store for conversion. An edited version of this video footage was titled *Mysore Mallige* and circulated via the Internet and offline. In 2007, a documentary filmmaker, Bharath Murthy, released a film with the same title as the pornographic film; this film explores how we consume pornography, what is its relation to love and sex in India, and the filmmaker speculates about the context and making of the original pornographic film. Through his documentary film, Murthy, along with his partner, Alka Singh, explore what it feels like to place yourself in the cross hairs of a video that could be pornographic—an insulting, inquisitive or invasive gaze, even if it was their own.

I interviewed Murthy about his film (Aavriti 2009), where he talks about what he found compelling about the pornographic film, *Mysore Mallige*, and also points to a certain separation from cinema: 'I was immediately struck by the *directness of the images*. For the first time, I saw an Indian couple having sex in that kind of detail and reality. A new image appeared that had not been there' (ibid.; emphasis mine). For Murthy, this directness was relatively superior in terms of seeing a reflection of oneself in the world of images, especially in contrast to what cinema does in providing a glossy, unrealistic image. His response, perhaps, is not entirely about representation, simplistically understood, but in terms of the affect of intimacy and the tactility of such images.

The affective force of these images is experienced in how they absorb the viewer in spite of not having the technical prowess of cinema, and their affective trace lingers in the sense of ghostly eeriness, especially in the urban legends and tales of duplicity that surround the making of these videos. Here, I look particularly at one aspect of some of these videos—the use of the night shot.

Night Shot

Deleuze speaks of how sensation is felt in the body—like it is a body without organs, but with levels, and sensation passes from one level to another, one order to another, or one area to another. This idea of 'sensation' is different from 'sensational'. Sensation acts directly on the nervous system; and this refers to the ways in which the body moves, whether it is the twist of arousal in the stomach, the fine movement of fear along the skin that raises goosebumps, or the unending tear of pain along all the nerves of the body. The unstructured sensations that are likewise set in motion in the film-viewing experience cannot be only understood in terms of a framework of representation and correlation of ourselves with the characters on the screen. Something infinitely more takes place while watching; sensations and meanings are shared between the film as an entity or body and the viewer; the body of the film entwines with the body of the viewer (Barker 2009).

Watching pornography is different from the immersive experience of watching a film. The objective of pornography is fulfilled when the viewer is conscious not only of her or his inter-relationship with the pornographic video or clip, but also, can eventually separate and attend to her or his own corporeality (by being aroused or masturbating). Indeed, the purpose of pornography is to gratify these immediate bodily needs. Thus, rather than a completely immersive experience like watching a film, it can be said that pornography is in the liminal space between the body of the viewer and the film.

Pornography is similar to other body genres such as horror, suspense and comedy, where the aim is to elicit bodily reactions (Williams 1989) or to absorb the body of the viewer entirely into the filmic space. However, there is also a tug of corporeality that makes it different because it has to allow for the existence of the viewer in two spaces simultaneously, that of their body and of the film. Nevertheless, there are aspects of film and cinema studies that are especially relevant for understanding the affective force and trace of pornography, and especially, the absorption and sensation into the material.

A particular aspect of what marks the absorption into material such as amateur porn is the hazy nature of the low-resolution shots, and in some instances, the use of the night shot or the low-lux shot, as it is sometimes called. This particular shot is not a technological innovation, and in fact, is possible with any ordinary camera and even old cameras since it uses the infrared part of the spectrum. It is only because cameras attempt to imitate human sight that particular ways in which the digital or mechanical eye of the camera can actually see the world are 'extra features' that have to be turned on. The night shot[2] or the low-lux shot gives the image a greenish tint that is often ghostly. This greenish, blurry tinge obliterates individual characteristics like specific skin tone or hair colour, making people caught in such a video seem like anybody.

The pornographic film, *Mysore Mallige*, is almost entirely shot in the night-shot mode. The camera often moves close into the face and body of the girl—the surface is that of a blur, but the implicit invitation is to touch. In Murthy's documentary film series based on unravelling the responses to this film, there is a particular conversation about the meaning of the night shot, specifically as it is used in the porn film. One of the viewers says that he saw the same film with the night shot corrected and the colours restored to normal. In his rather vehemently stated opinion in the documentary, the corrected film was not the same experience. As he said, 'It didn't have the same impact.'

Murthy's documentary film tracks down a particular moment in the original pornographic film—the moment when not only is a curtain moved to reveal an old fort in Mysore nearby, but also, light falls on the girl, revealing that it is daylight outside, and also the colour of her skin, clothes and hair, slightly more than in the greenish tinge of that night shot. The night shot does not effectively correct images if there is sufficient light, and thus, the fort outside is bathed in the natural light of the day; the building outside the window of the couple's room is like an intrusion of society and drearily coloured normalcy into their private space of sex and romance. This brief revelation carries a certain charge, also because an important detail about their likely whereabouts is suddenly and abruptly revealed.

The aura of erotic intimacy produced by the night shot is undercut by a constant sense of distrust—why does the man want to record these most intimate acts, after all? What do we know about this woman that the camera (and our gaze) chases incessantly? What about her subjectivity is assumed, cloaked, revealed and lost forever? This unease in *Mysore Mallige* is paradoxically felt most in the single shot that is not in the tonalities of a night shot—when the outside world sheds its bright sunlight into the private world of the couple. Lovers always betray each other; this perhaps is no revelation; it is the porosity, fragility and reproducibility of the videos within which they love and betray each other that then allows images from these videos to slip into the circuits of public circulation and discourse.

The night shot, with its qualities of unease and intimacy, is also evocative of horror films, and the same technique is used quite effectively in Bollywood films like *Ragini MMS* (2011). In *Ragini MMS*, a boy wants to make a sex video without the girl knowing it, and thus, takes her along to a desolate cottage at the outskirts of the city. The film combines the bodily thrills of horror and pornography; the pretty girl in the greenish tint of the night shot is instantly evocative of *Mysore Mallige*. She is simultaneously sexually thrilling, frightened, and an unlikely ghostly apparition. There could be no thicker plot of motivations, both ancient and new, as the haunted house is not only ridden with ghosts, but also rigged with surveillance cameras. What becomes evident upon viewing *Ragini MMS*, and has effectively been used as a ruse throughout the film, is that the affective relationship to small amateur porngraphic videos is not necessarily only a flood of immediate responses (of desire or disgust) that suffuses the body, but also a haunting of the circuitries of being, a sensation of unease, arousal and misgivings that stays with you for a long time.

A close zoom into the body gives an experience of intimacy, and additionally the night shot suggests a different register of intimacy— of being in low-lit rooms or at the night time. The night-shot mode is also largely found only in amateur cameras. Barker (2009) theorises relations of the film and the body—at the level of skin (fleeting contact) and musculature (with the apparatus). The muscular relationship and connection with an elongated chase scene in a film is about the movement of the apparatus (the screen, the camera) and its visceral relation to the body, while the momentary tactile contact is about 'a fleeting, incomplete kind of access to the other, which is pleasurable in its impermanence and incompletion' (Barker 2009: 30). Barker's contention is that the film is also a being, not necessarily to be understood only as the filmmaker (or whose vision it is), nor as an anthropomorphic understanding of the film as the body. Barker relies largely on Merleau-Ponty's work on phenomenology and Vivian Sobchack's work in film studies. She says, 'In so far as the embodied structures and modes of a film are like those of a filmmaker and spectator, *the film has the capacity .... to not only have sense but also to make sense ...*' (Sobchack quoted in Barker [2009: 55–56]; emphasis mine).

The analogy she uses is that of a fleeting interaction between the film and the body at the level of skin—skin which denotes a border, but also, concomitantly, leakage. The affect of disgust, pleasure, revulsion and tactility are mostly felt, and sometimes, revealed or exposed on the skin. Watching a short porn clip that is barely three-minutes long momentarily suffuses the senses with arousal and disgust; and then, other sensations replace it, that of one's own corporeality, and gratification or revulsion, and *sometimes*, a lingering sense of unease.

The particular use of the night shot as an aesthetic in cinema allows for an insight into the tactile, porous image that it produces and the sensations that surround it. The interface, in this instance, is one that allows for an absorption into itself—a mutual relationship of submergence rather than the separation of the viewer from the interface or media. This relationship is very similar to the relation with the cinematic screen, which, albeit larger, works with the logic of bodily responses and relationship with the viewer. Unlike cinema, however, this interface has certain almost acrobatic skills to change its size, to move across spaces, and to occupy different, both domestic and exterior worlds. How does one begin to form concepts and theories about these relations with varied interfaces? A beginning is suggested here in the concept of the mutual engorgement. We are taken in, and then taken in again. Barker refers to the relation of the film and the body as a mutual feeding off each other's energy and suggests that we are drawn to films because they are like us, but not quite; they are faster, more mobile, more 'intimate and immense' than we are. She says, 'The connection between viewer's body and the film's, and between our human and cinematic bodies and the world at large, is at once intimate and immense, involving surface and depth. It is a mutual inspiration in and of the world' (2009: 154).

In the post-2000s period, facets such as the night shot, blurry or low-resolution image, hand-held, and certain kinds of point-of-view images (such as the viewpoint of a man holding a mobile camera) have, in themselves (in combinations and separately), become the markers of the pornographic. This is not just suggested by descriptions of pornographic clips on popular amateur pornographic websites, but also in how these clips are referred to and shot in mainstream cinema, in films such as *Dev D* (2009), *Love, Sex aur Dhoka* (2010), *Shor in the City* (2011), *Ragini MMS*, and many others. The pixelated quality of a mobile phone video, the static far away shots from a CCTV camera, the absence of an audio track, or the popular songs attached *post facto* to the video, the video on loop, or otherwise edited by anonymous people—are all now recognisably part of amateur or ordinary practices of making videos.

SPACE AND SCAFFOLDING

Cities are primarily spaces of intense visuality. Here, we examine how an aspect of the digital and technological is intertwined and part of the experience of the city, that is the interface which in a mediatised city, like several cities in Asia, is part of a scaffolding of technologies, affective flows, networks, circuits of consumption and circulation, etc. In a manner similar to how ethnomusicologists believe that sonic flows create spaces around them and sonic environments, interfaces create a space around themselves, but this space is not limited only to itself; rather, it expands to include the experience of the city. Living in the mediatised city, surrounded by forms of technology and ubiquitous availability of interfaces, forms a sensory universe that is digital, and to some extent, artificial, occasionally cinematic, but also pornographic, and often, watching itself as a form of self-surveillance.

Some examples of this particular sensory experience evoked by the small and big interfaces in the mediatised city can be found in the popularly circulated images of the 25 January 2011 revolutionary uprisings in Egypt, whether that of several mobile phones raised to capture a moment of fevered sloganeering, or that of the laser lights that marked out a military helicopter. Several cities across Asia, depending on levels of prosperity, have large and interactive screens similar to the one at Times Square in New York, which record the average person on the street or tourist into a large screen and project it back to them. But there are more prosaic examples as well, like the countless shops and ATMs that have boards with warnings of surveillance cameras, or large monitors that show through various split screens the different sites of the shop or the hotel, screens through which especially its exterior and entrance are watched. Large malls pipe sounds of the ocean to people walking through and blow fumes of cookie-smelling air towards people to convince them to be consumers of the latest cookie shops.

Ahmed (2014) explores the possibility of affects being sticky or contagious, and says that exploring affects in this manner disrupts the idea that they travel only from the 'inside out'. But still, the contagion does not spread just anywhere; it is contingent often on *who we are*. For instance, a woman who has been assaulted but has not spoken about it for years, or even decades, is moved to share her story on social media along with many others in the #MeToo movement that happened after actors started talking about their experience of assault, sexism and harassment by Harvey Weinstein and others in Hollywood (Fangzhou and Knowles 2017; Farrow 2017). There is a link, or perhaps, a series of interconnected links between the inside and the out. In fact, as Ahmed says, it is the existence of emotions that suggests the existence of an inside and an outside: 'I suggest that emotions are crucial to the very constitution of the psychic and the social as objects, a process which suggests that the "objectivity" of the psychic and social is an effect rather than a cause' (Ahmed 2014: 10).

Ahmed describes atmosphere (of a room, a context or a place) as simultaneously made by our own affect as well as by others: 'If bodies do not arrive in neutral, if we are always in some way or another moody, then what we will receive as an impression will depend on our affective situation' (2010: 36). She says, 'the atmosphere is already angled, it is always felt from a specific point' (ibid.: 37). To use Ahmed's lexicon, a device with an interface, for instance, a smartphone, could be described as a 'happy object'. We are oriented towards it with largely positive imagery produced by the advertising industry, and mean to see it as something that connects us to family, friends, and largely, to potentially promising relations within heteronormativity and patriarchy.[3]

Charles Hirschkind's work (2006) on music and tape cultures in the Middle East provides some insights into understanding how technological devices or effects (sound, image, etc.) can impact the experience of a space, or how surrounding technologies can produce a sense of spatiality. Hirschkind evocatively describes how cassette sermons are part of the sensorium of everyday life in the Middle East, and how they form a kind of technological scaffolding. This notion of scaffolding is particularly useful, as it refers not so much to a concrete or established structure within which there are affective flows (for instance, the legal system would be one such structure). But instead, it suggests a slight or skeletal framework or structure, whether of illegal circulation, market-based exchanges, affective flows, or of interactions between informal networks and nodes of power. *It allows for the exploration of technology not as a singular force or phenomenon that impacts people's lives, but in terms of how it relates and connects to other things, people, moments and events in the world.*

Scaffolding also suggests the notion of folding, or how affects, behaviours and habits are folded into this structure of circulation and consumption. Latour (2002), too, speaks of technology as being a fold or detour rather than a tool that takes a person from point A to point B; he argues that it has never been functional or neutral, but has always introduced enfoldings, detours, drifts, openings and translations. Deleuze speaks of fold in relation to the folding or doubling of one's own thought in relation to another, or thought itself as a folding against the 'forces of the outside' (2006). Another related idea would be that of assemblage explored by Deleuze and Guattari when they talk about 'a thousand plateaus', which refers to the intersecting nature of institutions and processes that are at work in any phenomenon.

What Hirschkind brings to these existing concepts is an attempt to understand the sensorium, that is, the affects, sensibilities and perceptual habits produced by the constant aural soundscape of cassette sermons in the Middle East, whether it is listened to devoutly or merely heard tangentially. This notion of the sensorium does not necessarily locate experience in a silent interior, but towards one where the body is practically engaged in the world. Such a description is not just about sensations and subjectivity, but is also *inclusive of the space in which the body is*.[4] We are therefore not constantly talking of embodiment and sensation in terms of what is *in the body*. But rather, we are talking about what is around, above the body, pressed close to it, or has a fragile link; not just what surrounds it, (almost suffocating it) but also that which has in loose, tight and tenuous relations with it, what it has fleeting and real contact with, and what it merely sees or hears slightly. The sensorium emerges not as a tight box of immediate surroundings, but as how the world is experienced, involving all that enters, exits, leaves a trace, and is part of the 'affects, sensibilities and perceptual habits' (Hirschkind 2006: 22).

Depth, Movement or Change, Time

The interface can also offer an experience of time, and this has been explored especially in relation to cinema. When we are stressed or under pressure, time is immediate, visceral and actual, but time can also be languid, allowing for the swirling in of the past (memory) and the future (desire). This is taken from Deleuze's (1989) work on cinema that draws on the concepts developed by Henri Bergson on time; there is a difference drawn between our lived world or experience and what is available to us in the present, the actual, and what intervenes from the past or the future, or the virtual. I list below three instances of interfaces post-2005 and explore in detail a fourth one that seem to inspire a falling into the virtual:

- In the last few years (approximately 2009 onwards), one of the most popular genres of games on mobile phones and tablets is the endless runner games that allow for an interminable road or path or train track to open up through the interface. Whether it is a hooded boy or the punk girl on a Tokyo track in 'Subway Surfer', an explorer running away from natives in 'Temple Run' or an 'Angry Granny' escaping from the asylum, the game allows for the player to run faster and deeper into the interface that seems to open up infinitely, providing a sensation of falling into the interface, of a perceived depth and movement, an absorption into another space or time.

- Narendra Modi, the Prime Minister of India, had transmitted speeches simultaneously to 52 villages via a three-dimensional hologram during his election campaign (Prime Minister Narendra Modi's website). The three-dimensional representation of Modi has some glitches and stalls, or perhaps, it buffers; it is a faintly coloured-in outline of a yellow kurta-clad man against a dark background with slightly more depth than a regular projection.

- Sometime before, in 2012, when Modi was still only a contender in the race for power, the Bengaluru traffic police experimented with the minds of the people by placing several rather odd cut-outs of traffic policemen around the city. A rather short policeman stood at the forks in the roads, sharp curves and dangerous intersections, and he seemed to be looking at you as you sped by. These 'policemen' are designed to function slightly like reflector lights, so that if approached from a speeding car, the cut-outs seem quite realistic. But if you are walking, these cut-outs are flat and two-dimensional, obviously not a real policeman, although, perhaps, still mildly scary.[5]

The fourth instance that I choose to focus on here is an archival photograph of the first Prime Minister of India[6] that is often considered emblematic of the history of science and technology in the Indian territory, of the thrall of modernity, and specifically, scientific development in the early years of independent India. It is a photograph in which Prime Minister Jawaharlal Nehru is pointing towards a dam and standing with a woman named Budhni Mehjan. A photograph, too, is an interface providing a surface that is tactile and engrossing—that allows for passing through like in a digital interface. A photograph necessarily is a snapshot of an instance and invisibilises what comes before and after the specific instance of the photograph itself (Benjamin 2007) (see Image 10.1).

IMAGE 10.1: Photograph of Budhni Mehjan and Jawaharlal Nehru

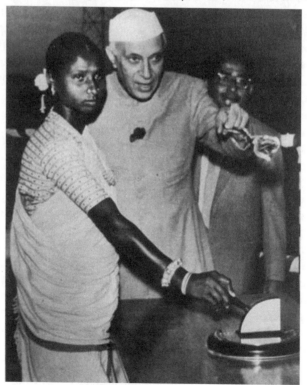

Source: Padmanabhan (2012).

The story of Budhni Mehjan was partially uncovered in an article by Padmanabhan (2012), and very few traces of this story can be found, except its recent mention in ambedkar.org. (ambedkar.org 2001). Budhni Mehjan's life was changed by this one interaction, a gesture that has been captured in the photograph. She pulled the lever to inaugurate the dam with Nehru and garlanded him, and it was the latter act that led to them being considered married by the Santhali community to which Budhni belonged. For the rest of her life, she was shunned by her community. Later, she was dismissed from her job at the Damodar Valley Corporation (DVC), at the very same dam she had inaugurated, as captured in the famous photograph.

Padmanabhan, in this far-too-short piece on Budhni, gives a glimpse of how her life was changed by the act of inaugurating the dam, as were the lives of countless others, mostly tribal communities, whose temples, houses and livelihoods were submerged in the dams or destroyed by massive power projects. The legacy of this moment is apparent in the resistance to development in Odisha, Bastar, the Narmada valley, and in countless other places across the country.

To return to the photograph that concealed as many stories as it told, Benjamin (2007) says that a photograph is not only of an act not yet completed but it is also of a moment that is already over; and thus, we always arrive too late or too early. A photograph seems saturated with melancholy at its own irrelevance to history; yet, it gives a moment 'a posthumous shock' (2007: 175). This is definitely true of the photograph of the seemingly humdrum encounter between the most important ruler of the nation and a 16-year-old tribal girl. Benjamin (2009) poetically denies a photograph finality: 'It is the product of an apparatus that substitutes light for shade, shade for light' (2009: 739). I would grant photographs their insistent power, their ability to turn up as themselves over and over again, even when perspectives change over time or the depth of our engagement alters. The surface of the photograph provides a place to pause. A historical photograph provides an interface to look back into time, past its surface, to something that was, to fall through all that it summons, an often-told story, memories and fragments of being from another time.

If one stares at it too long, the photograph seems to emanate time, and a falling-through that the modern interface aspires to as well. Several of our most important life experiences now occur through or via interfaces, whether learning of important news developments, like watching the two planes crash into the World Trade Center in September 2011; a personal email or a sexual chat; a revelation through an ordinary piece of information shared by someone else anonymously on a medical or health bulletin board online; a sexuality-related query on Yahoo answers that makes a person feel less alone; meeting one's future lover through a role-playing game; watching a sexual clip that one's boyfriend made without permission and uploaded on a pornographic website; learning about a grandparent's death on the phone—the list is endless. Affective engagements that surround interfaces are not special or intrinsic only to the interface, but are also slanted through its two-dimensional surface, which expands to offer sensations of spatiality, absorption and depth. These are the three aspects that have been tentatively explored here—both in terms of the sensation itself and the link to tactile surfaces like the interface.

Philosopher and feminist Beatriz Preciado (2008) describes the contemporary that we live in as pharmoco-pornographic capitalism, especially in the global North or the West. Preciado speaks of gelatinous technologies that we inhale and imbibe, and that are part of our bloodstream, and that change moods and habits, whether through hormones, medical or psychiatric drugs, recreational drugs, and they relate these to parallel historical developments, such as the global diffusion of pornographic and sexual images (2008). Preciado explains that pharmoco-pornographic capitalism is the new regime of the production of sex and sexual subjectivity, saying, 'This is the age of soft, feather-weight, viscous, gelatinous technologies that can be injected, inhaled—incorporated. The testosterone that I use belongs to these new gelatinous biopolitical technologies' (Preciado 2013).

Preciado's description of gelatinous technologies that are inhaled and are part of the body proposes a different kind of interface— between a molecule and another, something that is also suggested in the writings of Donna Haraway. This leaves us with the question of what our relation would be to these futuristic interfaces that relate to us from within the body.

There are already other far more ubiquitous instances when technology is melded within the body, such as the pacemaker and the ordinary ultrasound machine that peers into the organs, into what the ordinary eye cannot see, or the night shot and the extra zoom of the camera that extends our vision. Instances of detecting cancer via an examination of our genetic makeup gestures to the possibility of the genetic code being an interface into our understanding of our body's health and risks.[7] Bio-art and a few strands of performance art, prosthetic limbs, eyes replaced by cameras, etc. open up other ways of thinking through the communion between the body and technology, such as our link to animality, to distortion and expansion of the body's facilities, or to changing experiential encounters with the universe. Many of these ways offer tantalising ways of rethinking and theorising our relationship with technology.

DATA AND THE INTERFACE

Larger processes of datafication (including national identity cards, biometric voter ids, etc.) are beginning to be put into place by governments across the world, often even in the face of vociferous opposition from people. In a few countries, largely in the global North, like the UK, these schemes have been pushed back successfully; but in most middle- and low-income countries across Asia and Africa, there is a rising number of data-based government projects, avowedly for welfare, but also for surveillance, and these projects are often in active collaborations with corporate entities. Many government and civil society projects will be measured in terms of their impact through the use of data, and this is officially a part of the United Nations 2030 Agenda for Sustainable Development Goals that were concretised in September 2015 (Shephard 2016). Data-based studies, however, do have the benefits of providing a perspective that allows for seeing patterns, though still provide only 'partial knowledge' (Haraway 1988).

Websites such as 0xdb.org, powered by the software Pan.do/ra, provide an array of tools to analyse the filmic object, through the number of cuts, the duration of scenes, the general hue and the saturation index of a film. It offers the film up as a lateral slice, giving only a sense of its content, and this is different from what is offered by an absorption into its narrative arc or a falling into its affective realm. I have worked to build the digital documentary archives of Pad.ma, and it has been interesting to often pose the question of the image, and particularly, of cinema to theoreticians, as to what challenges digital tools and programmes offer to various disciplines. Blithely stated that the film, whether documentary or cinema, its images, whether of dreams or of the anxious present are 'reduced' to data, which can then be calculated, tabulated and re-represented in different ways.

0xdb.org is able to show the film as a timeline, as a map, as indexed by colour and by shot length rather than by the narrative. What do these new viewing methods do? While this might seem limited to a few people, for instance, traditionally, obviously the editor, the filmmaker would always see the film as made of bits that were pulled together to form a contingent whole or story. Here, the digital archivist is added to this list as well. But this is not necessarily true, as ordinary practices around video cultures, such as remixing, fan videos and other forms have allowed countless others to also see the film as a breakable object, or as data; and arguably, this has been possible, or at least, practically conceivable since the advent of the video, and not just the digital video or the Internet.

Another instance of data analysis is Porngram (Mazières et al.) that maps the evolution of words frequencies in the titles and tags of almost 8,00,000 pornographic videos. The mapping from 2008–12 reveals a sharp increase in revenge as a pornograpgic tag, indicating the growing interest in non-consensually made or shared images. It shows a steady interest in love and sex as tags, and a decline in use of hardcore. Porngram, or other similar kinds of dataset experiments, could be used to map shifts in user tastes, the proliferation of kinds or genres, the emergence of alternative sexuality pornography, or the scattering of human sexuality into a manic array of niches.

Another element of data studies is network analysis, which is not new, and was proposed in Latour's work on the actor-network theory, in particular (Latour 2005). Latour's reading of networks is interesting, as the actants here are not limited to humans, but also include technology. Latour says about the theory that 'It does not wish to add social networks to social theory but to rebuild social theory out of networks' (Latour 1996: 369). However, Latour clearly suggests that all such networks are mapped from within, and not from a distant position, that is, the person mapping the network is always in it. This ensures that we continue to table the question around the production of knowledge—*who gets to study what (and whom)*—which must be asked again and again in the Indian context.

One such example of network analysis is the Radiagram (Ambapardiwala et al. 2011), where a group of coders and researchers unpacked the scam around the allocation of spectrum by the Indian government through the interface of a diagram. This pictorial representation of the network includes journalists, judges, 'fixers', politicians, CEOs, corporates; it is not the presence of a particular criminal mind or person (in this instance, Nira Radia, a corporate lobbyist) that ostensibly connects the network, and hence, engineers the corruption of a system. But rather, it is the incessant buzz of networked conversations, which, in themselves, cannot singularly be called out as illegal, but they are actually how appointments to the government are made, and how judicial decisions on resource allocation for spectrum or coal are taken. In other words, it shows the sordidness in the assemblage of intersecting institutions and processes at work (see Image 10.2).

IMAGE 10.2: Radiagram

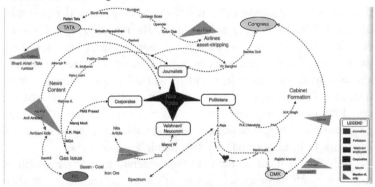

Source: Provided by the author, screenshot from Pad.ma.

CONCLUSION

When a device is switched off, or growing dim with low battery, that is perhaps when we become most aware of the surface of the interface itself; there is a thin film of dust particles and scratches that are usually lost in the shine of what we are absorbed in, as well as finger marks and other often unexplainable translucent and opaque marks that cover the surface.[8] Hughes traces a history of the cinematic experience, especially in theatres in Chennai, and speaks of possible sensual and affective elements of film-watching that are historical now—of the large dark space of the cinema that surrounds the body, dust and insects dancing in the light of the projector, of the largely mobile trajectories of early cinema that were assumed to be stationary. In this tracing of the social and cultural history of cinema, are hints of possible sensual and affective elements of film-watching in a cinema hall in the 1900s. That description of dust and stillness can be brought to the flat surface of the inactive interface as well. The moment when the interface is off is one of those odd moments when one realises how this blank, inanimate surface usually allows us to be partially or fully immersed or to fall through, rather than stay at its surface.

The popular understanding of technology is that it alienates us from humanity and from 'nature', and also perhaps how it changes our experience of culture and sociality. The understanding that technology alienates us from bodily and visceral encounters, from what labour it exacts from us or others, is also part of most academic thinking, and this is a condition that has been commented upon by various scholars, especially those critiquing the thrall of capitalism and neoliberalism. Some scholars comment upon it as an alienation that we must find ways to oppose, such as the Marxist auteur Franco Berardi or the feminist scholar and historian Lata Mani, and those who work in digital humanities, like the later work of Sherry Turkle. Others, while conceding that a change is wrought in how we relate to each other, the use of technology by the government, and so on, they also suggest that technology produces folds and detours, and sometimes, ways of enriching life in different ways from what we knew earlier, for instance; such suggestions have been made by Bruno Latour, Giorgio Agamben, and an array of new media scholars such as Matteo Pasquinelli, Beatriz Preciado, and others.

My contention here is that if the interface slants our interactions to take place via its surface, but this surface offers sensations of absorption, spatiality and depth, are we then merely looking at a new ground for understanding our affective condition? I am aware that my attempt at capturing the different aspects and phases of how the interface is/was experienced is not in any way exhaustive. For a relatively new form of technology, the expanse is enormous, from the early stages of sharing pornography, social media, online dating and hook-ups, Fintech, online movements (feminist, transgender, Dalit, 'Black Lives Matter') and online discourse, to the increasing use of national identity cards and biometric voter ids, and so much more. What is so unique about where we are now? The interface has been granted the power of administrative, and sometimes, almost adjudicative functions, the algorithms working silently to determine credit scores, employability, political futures (Tufecki 2014), and personal or romantic possibilities; and on social media, lists of potential women contributors and speakers are collaboratively created and crowd sourced, and on the other hand, are lists of harassers, assaulters or 'shitty men' (Donegan 2018). Fingerprints are used to verify who we are in relation to the interface, and more often than not, they do fail (Yadav 2016) (personally, my middle index finger is the only one out of the 10 impressions taken that is verifiable across my Aadhar card and my bank account). Will the interface also judge, perhaps more effectively bridging the gap between general and abstract processes of law and our needs for particular and singular justice (Derrida 1992)? Here, although I seem to separate the technological from the human sharply, as if the interface is technology, even if increasingly imbued with artificial intelligence, this is not my intention. There is a chaotic mutation that takes place at the surface of and through the interface that mirrors us, and even exceeds humanity; it is immersive and even fantastical; and how we fall through it endlessly without quite reaching a place of stop or closure seem to be exactly those profound qualities that we desire and want to experience.

NOTES

1. Information Technology (Guidelines for Cyber Cafe) Rules, 2011: Section 4 deals with the identification of users; Section 5 deals with the log register that must be maintained by every cyber cafe; Section 6 deals with the physical layout in a cyber cafe.

2. Night shot or night mode (low-lux) is an option now available on most digital cheap cameras, which allow for recording in low light and night conditions. It renders the visual slightly green and best used for close-ups. As a visual technique, it has been used in horror films like *The Blair Witch Project* (1999) and *Ragini MMS* (2011).

3. Ahmed's theorising focuses particularly on those who fall outside the conventional expectations of heteronormativity and patriarchy, and are melancholic subjects or affect aliens, for example, the figure of the feminist killjoy.

4. Another similar study is ethnomusicology of loudspeaker music in parts of South India. It points to the ways in which affective flows are engineered into the structure of the sonic environment, for instance, the morning prayers that can be heard on loudspeakers through neighbourhoods in Karnataka, Tamil Nadu, Kerala, and other parts (Kirchner Long Karel 2003).

5. Policemen are often the first direct and bodily contact that any person in a situation of a crime, accident or other crisis has with the State, either as an accused, a victim or a bystander; and this encounter with State power, even in its quotidian avatar, is necessarily fraught and anxious for many people. In encountering the fake unsmiling policeman on the roads of Bengaluru, who is meant to control the traffic behaviour of people, one can see glimmers of deception, intimacy and violence—the interface that conceals as much as it reveals.

6. My fascination with this photograph has its roots in a personal story that led me to realise that an image that I had seen shared within my family is actually both similar to that of Budhni Mehjan and Jawarharlal Nehru, and miles apart. In this photograph found in a family album, Jawarharlal Nehru is congratulating my father, a young engineer who will fulfill the scientific dreams of the nation. Nehru, in this photograph, does not look as confident as he does with Budhni Mehjan, but my father's wide smile and his obvious pride more than make up for it. The story, of course, is more than the photograph and my father, too, is cloaking his own insecurities and doubts (Aavriti 2013).

7. Angelina Jolie's controversial decision to have a mastectomy prior to the diagnosis of her breast cancer, but when her genetic code suggested that there is a tendency or inclination in her to develop breast cancer. The decision provoked a furore of conversations about the possible motivations behind her disclosure, the act of mastectomy itself, the role of the pharmaceutical industry, the patenting of synthetic and real genes, and so on.

8. A game called Cracked Screen, available on Android phones, particularly captures this sudden moment of becoming aware of the surface of the interface. Once installed, this app allows one to simulate a cracked screen by a simple touch on the surface of the interface that then shatters the screen at that point, and this is accompanied with a sound of the screen breaking.

REFERENCES

Aavriti, Namita, Personal Interview with Bharath Murthy, August 2009.

———. 2013. 'The Father Piece', *Peaking Duck* (2): 5–13.

Ahmed, S. 2010. 'Happy Objects'. In M. Gregg and G. J. Seigworth (eds), *The Affect Theory Reader*, pp. 29–51. Durham; London: Duke University Press.

———. 2014. *The Cultural Politics of Emotions*. Edinburgh: Edinburgh University Press.

Ambapardiwala, Z., S. Bhangar and N. Vasudevan. *Radiagram*, June 2011. Available at https://files.pad.ma/Radia/gram/ (accessed 10 October 2013).

Ambedkar.org, 'Tribal "Wife" of Nehru is Outcast, Driven to Poverty', 30 March 2001. Available at http://www.ambedkar.org/News/Tribalwife.htm (accessed 10 September 2012).

Barker, J. M. 2009. *The Tactile Eye: Touch and the Cinematic Experience*. Berkeley; Los Angeles: University of California Press.

Benjamin, W. 2007. *Illuminations*. Gurgaon: Penguin Random House India.

———. 2009. Gesammelte Schriften, Vol. 1, Pt. 3. Ann Arbor, Michigan, University of Michigan: Belknap Press.

CBFC website. Available at http://cbfcindia.gov.in/ (accessed 8 October 2013).

Craggs, R., 'Egyptian Protesters Bombard Helicopter with Lasers', *Huffington Post*, 1 July 2013. Available at http://www.huffingtonpost.com/2013/07/01/helicopter-laser-photos-egypt-protesters_n_3528371.html (accessed 10 September 2013).

Deleuze, G. 1989. *Cinema II: The Time-image*. Minneapolis: University of Minnesota Press.

———. 2006. *The Fold: Leibniz and the Baroque*. London: Bloomsbury Publishing.

Derrida, J. 1992. 'Force of law: The Mystical Foundation of Authority'. In D. Cornell., M. Rosenfield, and D. Carlson (eds), *Deconstruction and the Possibility of Justice*, pp. 3–67. New York: Routledge.

Donegan, M., 'I Started the Media Men List My name is Moira Donegan', *The Cut*, 12 January 2018. Available at https://www.thecut.com/2018/01/moira-donegan-i-started-the-media-men-list.html

Fangzhou, L. and H. Knowles, 'Harassment, Assault Allegations Against Moretti Span Three Campuses', *The Stanford Daily*, 16 November 2017.

Farrow, R., 'From Aggressive Overtures to Sexual Assault: Harvey Weinstein's Accusers Tell Their Stories', *The New Yorker*, 23 October 2017.

Haraway, D. 1988. 'Situated Knowledges: The Science Question in Feminism and the Privilege of Partial Perspective', *Feminist Studies* 14(3): 575–99.

Hirschkind. C. 2006. *The Ethical Soundscape: Cassette Sermons and Islamic Counterpublics.* New York: Columbia University Press.

Holla, A., 'Sex on the Go: Demand for Mobile Porn', *The Times of India*, 17 May 2013.

Hughes, S. 2010. 'When Film Came to Madras', *BioScope: South Asian Screen Studies* 1(2): 147–68.

————. 2012, Paper presented at ASA 2012, Jawaharlal Nehru University.

K. A. Abbas Vs. Union of India 1971, AIR 481.

Kirchner Long Karel, E. 2003. 'Kerala Sound Electricals: Amplified Sound and Cultural Meaning in South India', Thesis Dissertation, University of Chicago, Chicago.

Latour, B. 1996. 'On Actor-network Theory: A Few Clarifications', *Soziale Welt* 47(4): 369–81.

————. 2002. C. Venn (trans.), 'Morality and Technology: The End of the Means', *Theory, Culture and Society* 19(5–6): 247–60.

————. 2005. *Reassembling the Social: An Introduction to Actor-network Theory.* Oxford: Oxford University Press.

Mazières, A., Mathieu Trachman, Jean-Philippe Cointet, et al., 'Data Love; Porn Data', Sexualitics. Available at http://sexualitics.org/ (accessed 1 August 2013).

Nakamura, L. 2015. 'The Unwanted Labour of Social Media: Women of Color Call Out Culture as Venture Community Management', *New Formations: A Journal of Culture, Theory, Politics*, pp. 106–12.

Ong, A. 1987. *Spirits of Resistance and Capitalist Discipline: Factory Women in Malaysia.* New York: SUNY Press.

Padmanabhan, C., 'Recovering Budhni Mejhan from the Silted Landscape of Modern India', *The Hindu*, 2 June 2012.

Preciado, B. 2008. 'Pharmaco-pornographic Politics: Towards a New Gender Ecology', *Parallax* 14(1): 105–17.

————. 2013. 'Testo Junkie: Sex, Drugs and Biopolitics', *Eflux Journal#*44. Available at http://www.e-flux.com/journal/testo-junkie-sex-drugs-and-biopolitics/ (accessed 25 June 2013).

Prime Minister Narendra Modi's Website, 'Shri Modi's 3D Interaction Enters Guinness World Records', 14 March 2013. Available at http://www.narendramodi.in/shri-modis-3d-interaction-enters-guinness-world-records/ (accessed 30 June 2013).

Randhawa, S. 2017. 'Ten Facts About Your Computer: Health, Hardware and the Toll on Women', Gender IT: Femtalk. Available at www.genderit.org/node/4900/ (accessed 22 February 2017).

Shephard, N., 'Big Data and Sexual Surveillance', *Association for Progressive Communication: Issue papers*, December 2016. Available at https://www.apc.org/en/pubs/big-data-and-sexual-surveillance (accessed 6 January 2016).

Tufecki, Z. July 2014. 'Engineering the Public: Big Data, Surveillance and Computational Politics', *The First Monday: Peer-reviewed Journal on the Internet*, 19(7). Available at http://firstmonday.org/article/view/4901/4097 (accessed 10 February 2017).

Verite. 2014. *Forced Labour in the Production of Electronic Goods in Malaysia: A Comprehensive Study of Scope and Characteristics*, Verite. Available at www.verite.org/wp-content/uploads/2016/11/VeriteForcedLaborMalaysianElectronics2014.pdf (accessed 15 February 2017).

Yadav, A., 'Rajasthan Presses on with Aadhaar after Fingerprint Readers Fail: We'll Buy Iris Scanners', *Scroll.in*, 10 April 2016. Available at https://scroll.in/article/806243/rajasthan-presses-on-with-aadhaar-after-fingerprint-readers-fail-well-buy-iris-scanners (accessed 10 February 2017).

Zimmermann, P. 1995. *Reel Families: A Social History of Amateur Film* (*Arts and Politics of the Everyday*). Indiana: Indiana University Press.

Films Cited

Dev D. 2009. Anurag Kashyap (dir.). UTV Spotboy.

Love, Sex aur Dhoka. 2010. Dibakar Banerjee (dir.). ALT Entertainment.

Ragini MMS. 2011. Pawan Kripalani (dir.). ALT Entertainment.

Shor in the City. 2011. D. K. Krishna (dir.). ALT Entertainment.

The Blair Witch Project. 1999. Daniel Myrick and Eduardo Sánchez (dirs). Robin Crowie and Gregg Hale.

The Jasmine of Mysore. 2007. Bharat Murthy (dir.). India; Japan.

What Are You Looking At? 2007. Bharat Murthy (dir.). Public Service Broadcasting Trust, India.

Circuits of Affect, Care and Materiality*

RADHIKA GAJJALA AND SRIYA CHATTOPADHYAY

INTRODUCTION

Pivotal to this chapter are questions about work or labour through informal spaces that gets constructed as surplus, and extracted and managed into a (transitioning/emerging) global economy through varying logics of commodification, informationalisation, financialisation and monetisation. Particularly, a significant common theme binding together our four main intersecting research projects is a focus on how 'women's work' and tacit practices or contributions are made visible/invisible in transitioning economic times. Issues regarding layers of literacies, biopolitics of differing temporalities, slow time/fast time, as well as space and place emerge in nuanced ways.

We would like to introduce the concept of 'critical research as practice' as we proceed with our analyses and findings. Critical research, using the various qualitative research method tools based on Humanistic/heuristic investigations—the way we carry it out—unpacks processes and reveals various actors engaged in this process, as well as the subject positions formed through the engagement of these actors in various contexts, circuits and networks. It also reveals the hierarchies that form around these processes, as well as the ways in which individuals work within these hierarchies. The larger goal is to unravel in order to advocate and work for better and more equitable organisational cultures overall. The research can speak to policy,

*Two earlier versions of this chapter were presented at the Diginaka Symposium at the Tata Institute of Social Sciences (TISS) in January 2016, and at the Grazier Lecture at the University of Southern Florida, USA in April 2016.

programme development in educational institutions, technology startups, health care institutions and society in general.

In what follows, we will describe how we came to build the theory around (women's) agency, labour and affective circuits of care through digital materiality by examining two very different contexts of use of technologies for work and leisure in the domestic space. Our entry into each of these research themes began with questions about digital/mobile technology use through the domestic space, women's labour in both the home space and as prosumers, and the ways in which women negotiate agency in their use of time for leisure and work through the domestic space as well as in becoming public in the digital space (Gajjala et al. 2016). These themes are explored in relation to (health) care workers and Do-It-Yourself (DIY) hand fibre-crafters, with a focus on noting how each of these groups uses digital technology in building affective circuits. However, health gadgets, spindles, looms, knitting needles, crochet needles and mobile phones are all technologies featured in this investigation.

This chapter thus draws on two parallel investigations. One has to do with women of the global North and urban global South, who assert their agency—negotiating and redefining boundaries of the digital and the material—through the use of digital tools, as they use these tools to form networks and communities for fibre-handicrafting-related exchanges. The other has to do with female careworkers in global South contexts and the use or control of smartphones. Such control is actually an extension of the more tangible and tactical everyday lines of control drawn by the families of the patients to ensure that the careworkers do not overstep perceived social class, gender and caste boundaries that pre-exist as societal norms or hierarchies. This forms part of the overall socio-cultural management of familial boundaries and privacies—inclusions and exclusions based on pre-existing social hierarchies of gender, caste and class. Take the example of AP, a 52-year-old careworker in India looking after a 75-year-old lady. Her smartphone usage is controlled by the patient's family in the US, who do not encourage her to share her daily schedule with her own family members, who also live in India. Her prepaid phone bill is paid for by the employers, who use this to assert their dominance on her gadget use. She is not allowed to access any entertainment apps, because these will detract her from discharging her duties—almost as if her work hours constitute 24 hours of the day. LM is yet another careworker entrusted with looking after a seven-year-old girl. Her employers have bought her a cell phone, with only incoming calls facility, thereby ensuring that she cannot make any calls herself. The parents of the girl call LM every hour, and she has to give updates of the work done. There is no option to use the gadget for leisure.

We use these points of investigation and online and offline ethnographic encounters to raise questions about digital boundaries and differing contexts in which digital circuits of affect, care and materiality are mobilised. This chapter problematises the idea that connectivity in itself leads to the assertion of agency on the part of users. We reveal some assumptions generally made about the use of technology as liberating, and those of mobile phones as somehow automatically allowing the female user to reach outwards and into freedom from social constraints. In order to do so, we discuss two groups of women who use digital/mobile technologies from the domestic to the 'outside' space, and note how, in each of these groups, the use of the same sorts of digital gadgets leads to different kinds of results in terms of negotiated agency.

The projects juxtaposed in this chapter thus reveal a tension between agency and digitality—in one instance, groups of women invested in non-machine-made fibre-crafting engage in a particular kind of 'digital materiality' to reclaim agency in the domestic and Internet-mediated public space, thus, in effect, reshaping both the private and the public space through their intervention. In the other instance, the careworker herself becomes a technology that facilitates the use of DIY health gadgets, while her use of mobile communication tools is highly monitored and controlled.

In Image 11.1, the image of the hospital room, spindle and smartphone tells a story of connections or affective circuits between a 92-year-old woman patient on the hospital bed, her youngest daughter watching over her, and a woman who came in to change sheets and clean the patient. It was literally just a moment of recognition, a quick flash of mutual joy and sadness, and of possible shared knowledge of skill, tactility and process—where the spindle was the connector among the three women in a moment of affective and aesthetic nostalgia.

IMAGE 11.1: Affective Circuits

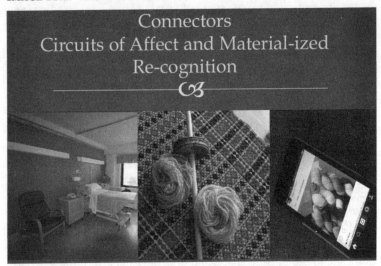

Connectors
Circuits of Affect and Material-ized
Re-cognition

Source: Provided by one of the authors, Radhika Gajjala.

The two groups of (mostly) women we write about may be seen as engaged in competing and in unrelated struggles where one set of women may be thought of as either from the global North, or seemingly, from more privileged global class locations, and another set of women as 'subaltern' women from the global South. Even so, we need to be aware that this binarising is a function of policy. We must remember that terms like the global North and global South 'are not natural scales, but formed precisely out of the struggles that seemingly they only contain' (Pile 2009: 13).

We arrived at an understanding and conceptualisation of digital material agency through research in the contexts of DIY hand-fibre-crafting networks that interweave digital and tactile production, while also using digital technologies to connect the domestic space to the public space. In addition to several years of offline ethnographic work carried out by travelling to handcrafting communities in India, Indonesia, Northwest Ohio and Norway, one of us has interviewed over 65 women who use digital tools in sharing their handcrafting process and handcrafted products, while connecting with each other in online communities and the online public space. In this context, then, we look at how outward flows of information and affective women's work from the domestic space produces public and/or interactive relational digital networks through mobile technologies. Using this understanding of negotiated agency—where women balance handcrafting work that traditionally gets associated with and contained within the domestic/household space—with being individual, self-defining agents in control of their product, process and aesthetics, we look at the Indian context of home-bound care-giving workers.

A Word on Method

Feminist grounded theory (Wuest 1995) and constructivist grounded theory (Charmaz 1983) are used to parse out themes of similarity and dissimilarity. We examine themes along a spectrum of agency and control through technology use in domestic space. For instance, when does access through technology lead to safe public space interactions? We know that women's ability to speak out in digital public space is impacted by hierarchies that emerge in discursive communities, and by offline socio-cultural events and biases that are replayed online. Thus, in some of her recent research, one of us (Gajjala) has found that women gamers and game developers who have not experienced as much of toxic environment locally (as in Norway) are beginning to be fearful of digital public exposure in a post-Gamergate global gaming environment.

Tangibility and Affective Materiality in DIY Fibre Cultures

DIY fibre-handcrafting communities have been forming across the geography over the past 20 years or more through the use of the Internet, but these comprised mostly women from the global North (or from urban regions in the global South). Primarily, their interest lies in sharing their passion for fibre-crafting and finding other people with a similar enthusiasm for all things yarn- and fibre-related. Digital sharing and community-building practices that include everyday rituals of sharing allow these crafters to connect with each other, and connect across distance. However, to be part of these digital formations, the participant must have or be in the process of acquiring the skills (in varying degrees) of producing tangible fibre-handcrafted items. The tacit types of knowledge associated with these forms of crafting are implicit in this sharing of the touch, feel and skill of crafting. Detailed descriptions of the process are mostly only recognisable by others who also engage in this sort of handcrafting practice. The tangibility of the offline artefact or creation invokes a sensory understanding of the digital images and text-based descriptions shared. It is this constant harking back to the tangible objects and the ritual of making that keeps it 'real' as circuits of (self) care and affect are formed.

These women are actually using traditional women's labour space and tools to create resourceful spaces of invention and aesthetic experiences for themselves. These tools would not have been considered technologies of leisure in a community that relies on handcrafted fibre-work for the supply of textiles. As a non-profit worker working to economically empower crafters in a developing world context, noted in discussions about these communities (Tummuru et al., pers. comm. 2016)—why would someone take on such labour-intensive work for leisure? These women are not engaged in parlour embroidery or leisure-knitting. Neither are these women fulltime homemakers— most of them have salaried jobs across a range of jobs and careers, from working at a checkout counter in a store to being a professor at a university. Yet, for their 'me' time, they take up complex fibre-crafting projects and spend social time either in physical knitting and spinning circles, or sharing online their works-in-progress (WIP) and finished objects (FO) with fellow fibre-crafters through Instagram, ravelry.com, Facebook groups, Tumblr, YouTube, and even twitch.tv. They are deeply and affectively invested in their (alter) identities of the 'spinner', 'weaver', 'knitter', 'crocheter', and so on. Spindles, knitting needles, spinning wheels and weaving looms, in these particular DIY settings, become associated with leisure, even as these are tools for work in other settings in contemporary times. As they become tools of leisure, their value to the user lies in their affective materiality and the tangible products that are created through their use. Thus, affective materiality becomes manifest in perceptual acts in digital networks; and in acts of sharing by the users of leisure mobile technologies as they share their craft-making processes and encounter the crafted items in the digital form.

SUBALTERN CAREWORKERS AND MACHINIC SUBJECTIVITIES

In her work on call centre workers in India, Vora notes how management and quality control technologies impact call centre workers. 'Machinic subjectivities' are produced, resulting from workers' reorientation of themselves 'to protect their personalities from their communication work' (2015: 38). They not only organise and discipline themselves in relation to control mechanisms and networked flows of affect and information, but they also organise and discipline the customer or client so that the communication stays on the task concerned. Drawing on this conceptualisation of machinic subjectivity, we extend it to the context of (mostly female) healthcare workers in the domestic space in the Indian context.

The intersection of control/management and digital gadget use by a domestic space-bound subaltern careworker produces an 'automated' subjectivity that allows the careworker to be simultaneously a non-human and human actor, which is crucial to the efficient incorporation of healthcare technology within the domestic space. The careworker is the machinic subject that facilitates the effective use of the DIY and other health-monitoring gadgets for the person cared for (patient, child or senior citizen), while also functioning as a visual signifier for the 'human touch' in healthcare. The context we discuss here draws on continuing ethnographies, interviews and visual analysis looking at female healthcare workers in India.

In the case of these women, their use of DIY healthcare technologies, as well as leisure-oriented gadgets such as smartphones, turn them into 'automated' human connectors in a care-circuit that transmits affect and information. Levina (2012) notes with regard to Health 2.0 websites, and Gardner (2013) notes with regard to DIY healthcare technologies that digital technologies partake in the extreme privatisation of healthcare by placing the responsibility for health management on the individual, requiring both technical and medical literacies for reading the body through medical technology gadgets. What both Levina and Gardner describe are particular urban, global North contexts. In the case of the global South healthcare, however, the very same technologies allow for the formation of healthcare worker training centres focused on comparatively low-skilled technology and healthcare training. This allows for a subaltern labour force to be recruited and trained in performing tasks that would otherwise have to be performed by the individual who is ill, old or disabled, or by direct members of her family.

The necessity for a mediating layer of health technology labour force that receives very specific deskilled training in the use of particular health-monitoring gadgets comes about through a re-organisation of the healthcare system around new technologies that require technicians to work closely with medical doctors. Yet, the hierarchy of healthcare must be maintained, where the medical doctor is an expert, and the careworker is unskilled. Affect must be produced and circulated in order for the system to be effective. Thus, affective work as well as the discipline or management of careworkers occur in and around communication technologies, and through the domestic to the digitally networked space.

Communication technologies are critical for maintaining the human connection, not only for the person being cared for, but also for allaying fears of family members. Careworkers give updates to family members living far away (often the ones paying the care worker) via email and mobile phones. For instance, MI, one of the women interviewed, lives in Princeton, New Jersey, US, and has to rely on a hired domestic careworker to look after an elderly family member in India (who suffers from Alzheimer's Disease). The cell phone and Skype calls have become ways in which the careworker connects with the family members in the US. In-phone instructions (commands such as 'Go Back', 'Delete', 'Upload', etc.) are in English, or in some vernacular script. Often, the careworkers are illiterate; they may not even know how to sign their name. For example, AP cannot read or write either English or the script of her mother tongue. So, she is unable to comprehend any of the phone guiding commands and depends on her employers' help to navigate the working of a mobile phone. Yet, she still manages to get videos recorded and sent. These same communication technologies are also critical for connecting careworkers with their own families. This personal use of such technologies, however, is highly monitored and controlled.

For example, AP activated her WhatsApp account, but was forced by her employers to discontinue using the app because they felt that she could use it to share images of her patient and possibly family heirlooms with her own family, thereby risking the safety of both her patient and the priceless material possessions of the family. This fear was only perceived to be possibly true, there being no instance of cheating or thievery on the part of either AP or her family. Again, control was asserted through the threat of sacking without reference.

AP always resisted control through the threat of walking out on her job. This happened thrice during the first eight years of her employment with the family. In one instance, she went back to her own family for three months. She then successfully negotiated a much higher salary and increased perks before returning to her work. This was repeated twice, and each time the increment percentage went up by bigger margins. However, such was the quality of her carework, that her assertion of control was accepted, and her demands met by the employer family.

The resistance to control exerted by AP's employers resulted in a tug of war of power. This was governed by whose need was greater at any given time. Thus, although the carework provided was critical to the employers' family, if they found a substitute, then the onus to re-seek employment fell on AP. And when suitable substitutes were not available, the bargaining power rested more with her.

Also, careworkers may be compared to the governesses of yore in countries like England in the early 1900s, for instance, as evidenced in literary works such as *Jane Eyre* by Charlotte Bronte (2000 [1847]). Neither were these women servants to be kept below the stairs, nor were they treated as family equals. The big distinction between them and servants was that they were educated, trained to be well-mannered, and spent much time with employers' children. However, they were still not considered equal in status to the family members, or were deliberately kept so to maintain social distinctions; and this dichotomy they faced placed them almost in a no man's land. Neither the servants nor the family treated them as friends.

It was the same for AP. The other domestic help did not befriend her. In fact, she herself established superiority over them by giving orders about what to do; yet, the family did not place her at par either.

Smartphone-Wielding Florence Nightingales in India

'Florence Nightingale could not have imagined this: nurses in India wielding tablet computers or smartphones, moving from one patient's home to another, providing care and a range of services that would otherwise be available only in a hospital' (Das 2015). Such reports about very elite healthcare providers are currently more aspirational than actual. Yet, they reveal a future vision for how to extract affective labour through the spread of such gadgets amongst healthcare workers. They follow a pattern of selling technologies that is rooted in ideas of labour-saving and extended leisure time. As Wacjman (2013) has noted, so-called labour-saving devices are repeatedly sold to women in the name of leisure and empowerment, but in actuality, they increase the work and responsibility, for this sort of work shifts into the informal private space that these technologies now inhabit. Carework, similar to housework, is located in the domestic and private space, and lends itself to further privatising through the use of DIY technologies.

The elder careworkers in India are mostly women trained to provide a certain level of deskilled medical care by assisting the aged patients with the use of medical DIY technologies such as kits for checking diabetes sugar level, blood pressure, and so on. They also ensure that the person in their care is following the prescribed routines and taking the medication given by the physician. Thus, they are able to make sense of rudimentary medical jargons, how the health insurance system works (paperwork is of critical importance at the point of hospital admission in India), and they even know how to set up doctors' appointments—all part of the new set of duties that careworkers perform today, with more and more younger family members living far away from elderly patients that the careworkers are hired to look after. They not only come trained in the use of healthcare technologies, but they are also trained in the use of tablets and smartphones. In this instance, the use of these gadgets is part of their labour.

KB, a careworker in India, for example, has to report to her employers in the US at every step of her carework, every day. If she takes her patient out for a walk, she has to call and let the family members know the moment she returns home. Yet, her own personal use of gadgets is strongly controlled. Since these workers are doing intimate work, there is a risk that they might share private details of the work with their own family members. The particular careworker must be police-verified. If she is not, then the employers keep strict control and watch over her data use, since the employers fear identity theft and record theft, as seen in the case of AP. Thus, the availability and use of leisure gadgets by careworkers—whether in the context of their work or for their personal use—is closely monitored to avoid the possibility of important and private information being shared with outsiders, which would put the elderly who are being cared for at risk. This monitoring is based on panics generated around concerns for the security of the person being cared for. As noted by SC, who has hired one such caregiver, there have indeed been instances where the careworker's out-of-work partner has stolen from, or even killed, the elderly patients. These fears have further caused employers to heighten security measures, especially with such instances being reported across media.

In terms of future visions, the security of the elderly family members (for whom the careworkers are hired) is further complicated by the affordability of smartphones. It makes social media access affordable for the careworker's personal and leisure use as well, and it remains to be seen how this pans out, as multiple relational, affective and gendered work circuits are activated in various directions through this phenomenon. About two years ago, the use of smartphones would have been considered a luxury, and most working-class Indian populations used a mobile phone with minimal fancy features. Now, in 2016, we see that the use of smartphone apps associated with leisure, such as Facebook and WhatsApp, is widespread (Arora and Rangaswamy 2015), even amidst low-income and informal settlements.

Based on interviews with those who hire these careworkers and with the careworkers themselves, it is possible to observe that there is strict control over careworkers' use of mobile phones. This is so even when they bring in their own gadgets. Yet, being so equipped with leisure tools makes them potentially available for fragmented affective, and even beck-and-call labour. There are instances when they use their email, phone and Skype to connect their elderly patients with the outside world and family members elsewhere. It remains to be seen what protocols will be established legally and socially to redraw the boundaries of control and/or protection in these situations. In AP's case, she is called to give the update during Skype calls; but once that is done, she is expected to wait in the next room while the family members chat with her patient. The line drawn here is a social one, where she is to speak only on her duties; after that, it is family Skype time, and she is excluded in a pointed manner to highlight the fact that she is, in fact, not part of the family, but just the hired help.

Comparing various local contexts of the gendered healthcare worker and changing technologies, it is possible to see machinic subjectivities interacting, producing standardised services through rhetorics of change. For instance, in Norway, Dyb and Corneliussen (2017) have found that when the implementation of technology in welfare or healthcare settings carried with it the rhetoric that welfare technology is about the people and not about the technology, the incorporation of technology was more effective. However, it was more effective because the human service worker herself was trained well into a 'machinic subject' that made the technical instruments seem natural to the care environment.

As we continue to think through these connections, we also draw on an ethnographic understanding of the ways in which technology is incorporated and adopted into medical care, and how this produces positive or negative affects for the patient (specifically through personal encounters with two different intensive care unit contexts—one in Hyderabad, India, and the other in Voss, Norway). The understandings from this research can be taken forward into policy work and recommendations around issues of organisational culture and healthcare services.

Conclusion

This chapter is based on ethnographies and interviews conducted in contexts where we examine affective flows and circuits of information around gendered care work. In this process of circulation of care and information, the careworker herself turns into a controlled, monitored transmitter of affect and information. We note that the materialisation of circuits of affect and care occurs through an automating of subaltern labour (Gajjala 2013). The careworker, we argue, merges with the very technology that she routinely operates as she facilitates circuits of care and affect, while her subaltern body remains socially invisible even as she is a key actor. Thus, her automated, machinic and cyborg subjectivities are both human and non-human. Her presence allows healthcare programmes to claim that their care systems are human and personal—while the control and management of the careworker allows her to become an efficient healthcare technology. In some instances, therefore, her automated presence makes the technology invisible, and in other instances, it makes her invisibility as a human being surface the sanitised, modern and technical efficiency of the healthcare organisation.

Therefore, in one context, these women display an active insistence on intentionality and de-alienation, while in the other context, the potential for de-alienation through a transmission of affects using gadgets and distance communication is actively mediated by the employers and the community within which the gendered careworker resides. In the latter context, the careworker herself simultaneously becomes invisible as a human body and visible as transmitting technology. In one scenario, it is the gendered (or feminised) body that intervenes to produce circuits of care and affect, and in the other, even while the gendered carework produces and circulates affects, there is social and managerial control on the use of the mobile technology.

Further, digital boundaries are mediated, and even produced, through offline social and policy control. Take, for instance, the case of social panics around the use of mobile phones by young women in parts of rural and semi-rural India, which resulted in the banning of the use of mobile technologies by young girls and women in the name of protection (*The Quint* 2016). Thus, the control of the gendered body and its relationship to technology is re-asserted in the name of productivity, social protection and effective use of technology.

Although this chapter delves into the seemingly divergent worlds of handcrafters from the global North, on the one hand, and careworkers from the global South, on the other, these binaries are brought together through the circuits of affect and digitality that binds them. When technology gives both power and voice, but such effects are controlled or channelised into various circuits, the challenges effectively become manifold, and continue to unfold in myriad ways as digital progress continues.

REFERENCES

Arora, P. and N. Rangaswamy. 2015. 'Digital Romance in the Indian City', City and South Asia, Harvard South Asia Institute.

Bronte, C. 2000 [1847]. *Jane Eyre*. Oxford: Oxford University Press.

Charmaz, K. 1983. 'The Grounded Theory Method: An Explication and Interpretation'. In R. Emerson (ed.), *Contemporary Field Research: A Collection of Readings*, pp. 109–28. Boston, Massachusetts: Little, Brown and Company.

Das, S., 'Homecare Nursing Goes Hi-Tech with Latest Smartphones and Tablets to Nurses', *The Economic Times*, 21 February 2015.

Dyb, K. and H. G. Corneliussen. 2017. Kapittel 9: Om teknologiensomikkefikkværeteknologi–diskurser om velferdsteknologi.

Gajjala, R. 2013. 'Automating Subaltern Labour: Circuits of Care in Developing World Health Care Support Systems', 2013 NEH Lecture Series by Dr Radhika Gajjala. Available at https://www.youtube.com/watch?v=r9cq1TcgBS0 (accessed 9 October 2019).

_____. 2016a. 'DigiNaka Located: Materializing Circuits of Affect and Care through Domestic Space', Plenary Talk at 'DigiNaka: Where the Local Meets the Digital', January 2016. Biennial International Seminar organised by the School of Media and Cultural Studies, TISS, Mumbai.

_____. 2016b. 'Circuits of Affect, Care and Materiality', Grazier Lecture at University of Southern Florida, US, April 2016.

_____, Interview with AP, Kolkata.

_____, Interview with LM, Mumbai.

_____, Interview with MI, Princeton, New Jersey.

_____, Interview with KB, India.

_____, Interview with SC, India.

Gajjala, R., et al. Personal Communication with Members of DIY Fibre-Handicrafting Communities, 14 September 2016.

Gajjala, R., J. M. Dillon and S. Anarbaeva. 2017. 'Prosumption'. In P. Rössler, C. A. Hoffner and L. Zoonen (eds), *The International Encyclopedia of Media Effects*. Available at 10.1002/9781118783764.wbieme0178.

Gardner, P. 2013. 'Making a Normal Hyperproductive Ethos: The Gendered Labor of Making and Using Fitbits, Nike Bands, and Jawbone Ups', Presented at International Communication Association Conference, San Juan, Puerto Rico.

Levina, M. 2012. 'Our Data, Ourselves: Feminist Narratives of Empowerment in Health 2.0 Discourse'. In R. Gajjala and Yeon Ju Oh (eds), *Cyberfeminisn 2.0*, pp. 13–30. New York: Peter Lang Publishing.

Pile, S. 2009. *Geographies of Resistance*. New Jersey: Taylor and Francis.

The Quint, 'Women Don't Need Mobile Phones: UP, Gujarat Village Heads', 20 February 2016.

Vora, K. 2015. *Life Support: Biocapital and the New History of Outsourced Labor*. University of Minnesota Press. Kindle Edition.

Wuest, J. 1995. *Feminist Grounded Theory: An Exploration of the Congruency and Tensions between Two Traditions in Knowledge Discovery in Qualitative Health Research* 5 (1): 125–37.

Wajcman, J. 2013. *Feminism Confronts Technology*. Wiley. Kindle Edition.

Isolated Bubbles

*Reflections on Performing
New Motherhood on Facebook*

SHILPA PHADKE

INTRODUCTION

The phone intrudes—it rings when I am trying to latch my baby, or when I am turning on the pump.[1] It rings when I am trying to take good advice and sleep with my baby. It rings when I am just on the verge of tears for no reason at all, and sometimes, the very ring makes me cry for I know a real conversation is impossible, either because I have baby demands or because my brain is mush and I cannot think coherently, much less carry out a conversation. Facebook, on the other hand, is in my control. I go there when I wish, and present myself as I wish. I lurk. I perform. I read. I pretend I am footloose again. I carefully read the posts of other mothers with children belonging to the same age as mine. Facebook becomes the social lifeline that links our 'isolated bubbles' together.

This chapter reflects on new motherhood, that is, mothers of infants under the age of six months, who are often tied to their babies by the biological and social processes of breastfeeding and mothering. Here, I think through the idea of living in an isolated bubble controlled by the rhythms of one's own body and that of an infant, which allows for a particular kind of intimacy to develop between people on a social networking site, because it becomes one's primary means of socialising. Further, because this space is virtual, it does not demand that you look presentable, or have at least half an hour available in order to socialise. It provides, in a strange way, the possibility of conversations without the need to 'have time' to have them. In this chapter, I engage with the idea that the space of social networking becomes a space where one can become, for short stretches of time, the person one was before becoming isolated in the mother–baby dyad, and pretend (in between feeds) that one is living *that* life again.

Paradoxically, the site also becomes a space to 'demonstrate' the joys of motherhood, which often conceal the sense of isolation that it also often entails. This performance is both real and unreal—and works both as a form of reassurance as well as connecting one to a world that includes more than just you and your baby. I use my own experiences of writing and reading on Facebook to suggest that the performance of motherhood and mothering on social networking sites offers us complicated narratives, not just about representation, but also about the act of mothering itself.

Facebook becomes both the space where I escape from the constraints of motherhood, and also the space where I perform 'pleasurable motherhood', a narrative often missing from my phone calls to friends, where I moan about the lack of time, space and privacy. This chapter is in the form of an auto-ethnography and involves reflections on my own practices around and performances in social media; however, it also comments on how others present themselves, specifically on Facebook. I think through contradictions in relation to these performances that often conceal as much as they reveal. Examining what they might reveal, I reflect on how parenting is performed for a wider audience than ever before.

Contextually, both my narrative and the reflections therefrom are located in upper middle-class urban contexts that take access to certain kinds of technology for granted. The reflections on both representation as well as the materiality of, say, breastfeeding are located in this context, and I do not claim any kind of representativeness, even of this class. My intention is to use the personal pronoun and my observations to gesture towards ways of seeing social media today. Methodologically, auto-ethnography, as a form, is reflexive, subjective and locates the body of the researcher at the centre of the research, even as it seeks to make observations that gesture towards larger cultural phenomena; and this has been my effort here.

CONTEXT: AUTO-ETHNOGRAPHY AND PERFORMANCE

I embark on the journey of writing an auto-ethnography with no little trepidation. As Denshire has pointed out, 'auto-ethnography is a relatively young and contested field', where 'the introspective and subjective performances' in the act of writing are questioned in regard to their value as ethnographic accounts, and their veracity as research that is publishable is challenged (2014: 2).

Some auto-ethnographic accounts also run the risk of being seen as self-indulgent, or worse, illegitimate. Writing erotic auto-ethnograpy, Blinne (2012) suggests that she was afraid that it would not be seen as scholarship at all. She writes, 'talking about masturbation might mean that I will be passed over for employment opportunities or denied avenues to present or publish my writing. Perhaps my research will be declared as "not research", "illegitimate", "self-indulgent", or maybe even "masturbatory"' (Blinne 2012: 955).

Similarly, where narratives of motherhood are often located in what have come to be called 'mommy blogs', auto-ethnographic accounts of motherhood run the risk of being seen as extensions of these blogs, as somehow less than scholarship. Further, how might one understand reflections on performance that take place via the medium of an auto-ethnographic performance? How do I engage with performance, not only that of others, but also my own? What are the choices I make, in choosing to reveal or hide? And no less relevantly, there is auto-ethnography itself as academic performance. How does one begin to decode these performances within performances?

One is used to using the personal pronoun as a way to mark one's location, as a way to articulate disclaimers, and to be open about one's subjective location. But when one's subjective location is, in fact, the object of study, there is a peculiar discomfort in writing in the personal pronoun. The politics of location we are taught do not include writing about the self in the personal pronoun 'I' to mean actually writing about the self. In this short piece, I struggle with these concerns without necessarily arriving at any answers.

SOCIAL NETWORKING AS SOCIALITY

It is 2 am, and although I am not quite wide awake, I cannot sleep either. I sit on my bed and log into Facebook. I post a comment on a friend's status update. She responds instantly. Within minutes, I am in the middle of not one, but three separate conversations. And suddenly, trying to get back to sleep is not a priority anymore. Some of these are with people in my time zone, and some are with people in other time zones, where they are 'expected' to be awake at this hour. Some of them ask, 'What are you doing up?' Some others do not. They are mothers of other infants and know exactly why and how I am on Facebook at *this hour.*

I began two life-changing conversations with friends on email chat while discussing why breastfeeding was so hard. In those hours in the middle of the night, I cried my anxiety, my fear, and my guilt, and found not only echoes of it all in my friends' virtual voices, but also, more reassuringly, a sense of hope and comradeship. Online, with others, I am not just looking to transcend my suddenly very immanent body, but also looking for reassurance that this body that was threatening to take over my entire self was 'transient'.

Facebook also becomes an alternate community for others like me, mothers of babies, who are awake at odd hours of the night, and with whom I can sometimes discuss in a flurry of messages the various sagas of early mothering. On days that were so unstructured so as to be completely chaotic, where there was not a minute to call my own, the night became my friend. I found I was not the only new mother logged into Facebook late at night or very early in the morning. So many others friends, colleagues and acquaintances were there. We were virtual friends, but we became 'friends' in another sense by 'virtue' of sharing a location, that of having infants at the same time, of finding ourselves hooked to Facebook at the same time. Well after midnight on one such night, a 'new(er)' mother, whose daughter is about a year younger than mine, called me to ask, 'Does one ever sleep again?'

I could read articles my friends posted and comment on them, reminding myself that my brain was still functioning about things other than counting wet nappies to figure out if my baby was getting enough milk. I could revel in the sense of community and the intimacy of those dark hours, when one is alone or apparently alone, but now, because of this virtual space, never really alone unless one wants to be.

Bauman (2011) expresses not a small dismay over the loss of privacy, intimacy, secrecy, and what he perceives to be real friendships. He expresses concern about their lack of durability, and their perpetual state of transience, and the lack of commitment or strict discipline. However, for some of us, the fact that social media spaces did not require a commitment to be there at specific times, to indeed to be there at all was liberating. In some ways, Facebook also approximates a virtual 'public space' in that one is free to come and go as one wishes to. One could also have conversations on Skype or other chat applications with friends, but these are dependent on one's more intimate friends being online. These intimate conversations spaces also often come to a standstill with an expectation of being there consistently for your friend for some interaction or the other. Facebook, on the other hand, allows for greater latitude in 'arrivals' and 'departures' from the space.

For me, Facebook became the metaphorical courtyard that facilitated a playful space that one could enter and leave at will. I do not generalise this to all users' experiences, and I am aware that this kind of an online platform may also contain expressions of antagonism and hostility. I am also aware of studies that demonstrate that Facebook is geared towards 'happy' updates and does not organically allow for expressions of discontent, which may further mean that reading such updates makes the user still unhappier in the face of the 'happiness' surrounding her. Paradoxically, it was this performative element, combined with factors described earlier, that was liberatory for me.

In one update, a friend whose daughter was then a few weeks old, wondered how people had parented before the Internet, before one could google or update in one's Facebook status one's fears and anxious queries. And in so many ways, my experiences of both pregnancy and the early weeks of motherhood have been framed by intimate connections with and obsessive searches on the Internet. What is this intimacy that the Internet facilitates, even as it allows the supreme selfishness of choosing when you want this intimacy, and ending it with a click of the laptop cover?

Talking to a friend on the phone, one of the few whose phone calls I take, I sigh and say how other mothers seem so much better adjusted than me: 'Look at everything they manage to do. Look at how their kids eat/ drink/ sleep.' 'Right', she said, 'Think about how you look to other mothers. Who knows what lurks under the FB exteriors?' I laughed, but I knew what she meant. On Facebook, I, too, looked like a really well-adjusted mother.

In many ways, I was a lucky mother. I was far from being alone. I had a supportive partner, an amazing mother who was holding it all together, and friends who empathised; and yet, there was a sense of loss of control. Facebook and my posts were among the few things I felt I could control.

PHOTOGRAPHS AS PERFORMANCE

One night, with our days-old daughter asleep next to us, my significant other and I spend over an hour deciding on which of her pictures to upload. As we uploaded them, we were gratified by a barrage of 'likes' and comments exclaiming in superlatives, which seemed to justify, at that moment in our sleep-deprived state, our inexplicable choice to become parents. We smirked about the other *vella*s (people with nothing else to do) awake at 2 am. We moaned about the precious hour we spent on Facebook, when we could have slept instead. A month later, my significant other went back to work. I had *six months* of maternity leave.

Photographs are especially performance;[2] they are carefully curated so that as little as possible of the sleeplessness and exhaustion shows. Sometimes you do not look at yourself in the mirror anymore. You simply look at photographs, mostly photographs of the infant so that you can justify the hours you spend in catering to her needs, by convincing yourself of how beautiful and wonderful she is. In any case, one would prefer to not see photographs of oneself because who wants to see the result of those sleepless days and nights.

For reasons of privacy, and yes, I admit it, superstition, I did not post about my pregnancy on Facebook. But many of my Facebook friends did, and do, and for them, before there can be the photograph of the child, there is often the ultrasound of the foetus; the (usually)

indistinguishable mass that people coo and exclaim over. This is
the in-utero photograph, the tool through which people are now
supposedly able to bond with their child before it is born. The three-
dimensional images allow one to exclaim over the 'shape of the nose'
or the 'perfection of a foot', or even the 'determination of a closed fist'.

Petechsky (1987) pointed out fairly early on, decades before the
advent of social media that the ultrasound 'photograph' of the foetus
begins to stand in for pictures of the child. She engaged with the
ways in which this image has been used by the anti-abortion lobby.
However, she acknowledges that for those women who are pregnant
with babies they want, the ultrasound image often creates a sense of
bonding. The need for an image to make things more real invokes
Sontag's assertion that 'Needing to have reality confirmed and
experience enhanced by photographs is an aesthetic consumerism to
which everyone is now addicted' (Sontag 1977: 18). Sanger suggests
that the ultrasound approximates just such a moment and practice
and is, in fact, the moment when the modern mother meets her baby
(2008: 366–67).

Of course, the ultrasound photograph is not the end. Then comes
the clamour from the Facebook world for the photo of the baby
bump—images which, when produced, allow the person's virtual
community to participate in the performance of the pregnancy. Not
just bellies, but also images of belly art begin to proliferate.

The pictures invite one to play voyeur, and yet, the very image
of the pregnant belly defies judgement. Talking about intimacy and
performance, I once came across photographs of not just a naked
pregnant woman, but also her equally naked husband, which were in
someone else's newsfeed, on which they had commented, and which,
in turn, turned up in my newsfeed. It was fascinating for me to think
of this space as a complex performative space in which ideas of the
private and public are breached with impunity. It seems that once again
the idea of the sacred 'pregnant' space allows for the presentation of
the body as sacred.

Soysal writes, 'With Facebook, I enter an extended arena of
sociality where the reigning (traditional) conventions of disclosure
are breached, all friends are trusted with private, inner worlds, and
intimacies are exhibited in public without much ado' (2010: 376).
Is it then that ideas of privacy (and here, I am referring to privacy

from one's friends, not Facebook itself, which is a different although equally relevant question) are transformed by social networking sites? I would argue that while this may be partly true, it is also true that these revelations and images are curated to achieve a desired effect. People may be reckless in the photographs they post (or, at least, I think they are reckless), but they are not doing so without thought.

Further, displays of intimate photographs of ultrasounds and pregnant bellies do not elicit the disparagement that overly intimate romantic photographs might. Rather, these images are subject to a flood of likes and congratulatory comments.

Women (and men) frequently use photographs of their children as their profile photographs on Facebook. Roiphe (2012), pointing an accusing finger at the many such 30-something women who are 'guilty' of this, argues that these photographs 'signal a larger and more ominous self-effacement, a narrowing of worlds'. 'Where have all of these women gone?', asks Roiphe, and wonders what these pictures of babies on women's Facebook pages say about the '"the construction of women's identity" at this particular moment in time?' (ibid.). It may well be that using photographs of one's children might free women of the burden of looking 'halfway decent', or of being themselves, as Roiphe suggests (ibid.). I would, however, like to suggest another possibility, that women use these photographs not as an act of self-effacement, but as an act of constructing a very particular identity. Roiphe asks why women who work, have varied interests and support causes would choose to erase themselves in this way. I would argue that for many women, the photographs of their children are about not just performing motherhood in a particular way (although that is there, too), but also in a world that is increasingly about 'happy families', a way of demonstrating that they have it all.

When my daughter was one-week-old, I wrote, 'Time telescoped and time extended. It feels like yesterday. It feels like forever ...' Friends quoted me with this and I felt duly gratified. I made no mention of the fact that I was dazed and really had no idea, no real idea what to do with this baby.

At 12-days-old, my status update read: Shilpa Phadke 'finds herself simultaneously lessor, supplier, waitress and cleaning lady in the newly opened Aradhana Milk Bar run under the sole proprietorship of a six point something pound dictator.' This was accessible only to some of my friends and had a carefully cultivated, slightly complaining, but secretly delighted edge to it. What I did not say, what I could not say, even to that small (small for Facebook) group of 50 (or maybe it is 80) friends is that breastfeeding was driving me crazy; that at every feed (ranging in number from 10–15 times in a 24-hour period), both my daughter and I cried.

Sometimes I was honest, but I used other people's words to express my own feelings; when my daughter was nearly two-months-old, I quoted Rebecca West, who wrote, 'Motherhood is the strangest thing, it can be like being one's own Trojan horse.'

At little over three months, I wrote: Shilpa Phadke 'caught up with a friend post midnight on chat and is reminded that sometimes you need that connection more than you need sleep!!' At eight months, I wrote: Shilpa Phadke 'is sitting in the garden writing while Aradhana has a post walk nap in her pram. Ohh the combined joys of motherhood and academia!' What I did not say was that this bliss lasted all of 20 minutes, three of which I spent updating my Facebook status.

Was I lying? Perhaps not. My posts on Facebook indicated one side of my mothering experience; the one I felt less vulnerable sharing; the one that seemed to be desirable; the one that a variety of people could easily smile at and click the 'Like' button, thus affirming my own current location as a new mother, and in some measure, actually assuaging the sense of isolation I felt, providing me with a sense of (perhaps not completely false) connection to a larger world. There I felt confident of communicating. On Facebook, my breasts did not leak at the wrong moment. If my baby pee-ed on me, nobody had to know. If my back ached every time I got in and out of bed and I felt I had aged 10 years, I could carefully curate pictures so that none of this was visible.

Our parenting is now subject to a level of scrutiny and surveillance previously unimagined, oddly invited by ourselves. We must look perfect, obsessively photograph our children, and have children who say delightful things in ways that can be conveyed in photographs or status updates to others. Facebook then is, perhaps, parenting's most public site of performance.

Some Inconclusive Thoughts in
Lieu of a Conclusion

The maternal body, especially the lactating body, is central to the act of early mothering. With or without breastfeeding, women are expected to demonstrate both intimacy and competence in the way we deal with our infants. A *Time Magazine* cover in 2012 showed a mother breastfeeding her three-year-old while he stands on a stool to reach her breast. This cover unleashed a storm of both supporters of breastfeeding after infancy and detractors who saw it as bordering on obscene. On Facebook, too, there was a barrage of posts in support of and against it. These posts became a way of demonstrating a politics as well—one that was pro-breastfeeding or against it, for attachment parenting or against it, for Cry It Out (CIO) or against it.[3] Both groups are vociferous in support of their own positions and post various articles to buttress their positions. Another set of conversations, particularly focusing on how photographs of breastfeeding are often taken down by Facebook as inappropriate, while photographs that stereotype and stigmatise women or perpetuate a rape culture are not deemed inappropriate.[4]

If breastfeeding was among the 'unseeable' things of Facebook, there are other less obvious ways of disciplining as well. There are some things that you simply cannot say publicly as a new mother. Motherhood is, across cultures, eulogised and placed on a pedestal, and so when one undermines the myth of motherhood gloriousness, one is at an acute risk of then falling off the unasked for pedestal. Further, and much worse, it makes you sound like you do not love your child. And this would never do because it is not enough to love your child, but you must also demonstrate it, not just to the child, but also to your whole social media world.

Notes

1. Breastfeeding is an art and a science. In the parlance of breastfeeding, the phrase, 'to latch on', means (for the baby) to get its mouth into the correct position around the nipple (to feed). The pump is a contraption, manual or electric that allows lactating women to pump breastmilk, which can be stored and fed later.

2. 'Photographs play an important role for any Facebook user with over 300 million images being updated daily and that can be swapped between users. Much of the research conducted on Facebook and SNSs in general has focused on impression management, friendship performance, networking, online/offline communication and privacy issues' (Mod 2010).

3. Attachment parenting is a phrase coined by pediatrician William Sears. This parenting theory argues that sensitive and emotionally available parenting helps the child to feel secure and fosters socio-emotional development and well-being (2001).

CIO is a phrase used to refer to many methods of sleep-training a child. This theory suggests that it is alright to let a baby cry for a specified period of time (often a short period, or slowly increasing the periods) before offering comfort. It is most famously associated with pediatrician Richard Ferber, although he himself did not use the phrase. Ferber argued that crying is, for some children, an unavoidable part of sleep-training (2006).

4. A Facebook policy change made in May 2014 has now lifted the ban on showing the female nipple for breastfeeding mothers (Chemaly 2014).

REFERENCES

Bauman, Zygmunt. 2011. 'Privacy, Secrecy, Intimacy, Human Bonds—and Other Collateral Casualties of Liquid Modernity', *The Hedgehog Review* 13(1): n.p. Available at https://hedgehogreview.com/issues/the-shifting-experience-of-self/articles/privacy-secrecy-intimacy-human-bondsand-other-collateral-casualties-of-liquid-modernity.

Blinne, Kristen C. 2012. 'Auto (Erotic) ethnography', *Sexualities* 15(8): 953–77.

Chemaly, Soraya, '#FreeTheNipple: Facebook Changes Breastfeeding Mothers Photo Policy', *HuffPost*, 6 September 2014. Available at https://www.huffpost.com/entry/freethenipple-facebook-changes_b_5473467 (accessed 18 October 2016).

Denshire, Sally. 2014. 'On Auto-ethnography', *Current Sociology Review* 62(6): 831–50.

Ferber, Richard. 2006. *Solve Your Child's Sleep Problems*. New York: Touchstone Books.

Mod, Greg Bowe B. A. 2010. 'Reading Romance: The Impact Facebook Rituals Can Have on a Romantic Relationship', *Journal Of Comparative Research In Anthropology And Sociology* 1(2): 61–77.

Petchesky, R. 1987. 'Fetal Images: The Power of Visual Culture in the Politics of Reproduction', *Feminist Studies* 13(2): 263–92.

Roiphe, Katie, 'Disappearing Mothers', *Financial Times Magazine*, 31 August 2012. Available at http://www.ft.com/cms/s/2/0bf95f3c-f234-11e1-bba3-00144feabdc0.html#axzz2bmTibm4h (accessed 18 October 2016).

Sanger, Carol. 2008. 'Seeing and Believing: Mandatory Ultrasound and the Path to a Protected Choice', *UCLA Law Review* 56: 351–408.

Sears, William and Martha Sears. 2001. *The Attachment Parenting Book: A Commonsense Guide to Understanding and Nurturing Your Baby*. Boston, Massachusetts: Little, Brown and Company.

Sontag, Susan. 1977. *On Photography*. New York: Farrar, Straus and Giroux.

Soysal, Levent. 2010. 'Critical Engagements with Cultural Intimacy: Intimate Engagements of the Public Kind', *Anthropological Quarterly* 83(2): 373–400.

Notes on the Editors and Contributors

Namita Aavriti is a writer, lawyer, and researcher.

Sriya Chattopadhyay is faculty at the Department of Communication and Journalism, Shippensburg University, Shippensburg, Pennsylvania.

Abir Dasgupta is an independent journalist based in Mumbai and former graduate student from the School of Media and Cultural Studies, Tata Institute of Social Sciences, Mumbai.

Paolo S. H. Favero is Associate Professor of Film Studies and Visual Culture, the University of Antwerp, Antwerp, Belgium.

Radhika Gajjala is Professor of Media and Communication (joint appointed faculty in American Culture Studies), Bowling Green State University, Bowling Green, Ohio.

K. P. Jayasankar is Professor and Chair, Centre for Critical Media Praxis, School of Media and Cultural Studies, Tata Institute of Social Sciences, Mumbai.

Aasim Khan is Assistant Professor in Social Sciences, Department of Humanities and Social Sciences, IIT Delhi.

Rachna Ramesh Kumar is a media researcher based out of Mumbai. She is trained in Applied Psychology.

Anjali Monteiro is Professor and Dean, School of Media and Cultural Studies, Tata Institute of Social Sciences, Mumbai.

Souvik Mukherjee is Assistant Professor and Head, Department of English, Presidency University, Kolkata.

Shilpa Phadke is Associate Professor, School of Media and Cultural Studies, Tata Institute of Social Sciences, Mumbai.

Amit S. Rai is Reader in and Convener of the MA course in Creative Industries and Arts Organisation, Queen Mary, University of London, London.

Kunal Ray teaches literary and cultural studies at FLAME University, Pune.

Shiva Thorat is a media producer at the Centre for Education, Innovation and Action Research (CEIAR), Tata Institute of Social Sciences, Mumbai.

Nikhil Thomas Titus is a PhD student in Film and Media Studies, the University of Pittsburgh, Pittsburgh, Pennsylvania.

Faiz Ullah is Assistant Professor, School of Media and Cultural Studies, Tata Institute of Social Sciences, Mumbai.

Maanvi is a journalist and researcher based in Delhi.

Index

CW0554433

The Military in
British India

The Military in British India

The development of British
land forces in South Asia,
1600–1947

T.A. Heathcote

The Praetorian Press History of the British Army
Series Editor
Ian F.W. Beckett

First published in Great Britain in 1995 by
Manchester University Press
Reprinted in this format in 2013 by
THE PRAETORIAN PRESS
An imprint of
Pen & Sword Books Ltd
47 Church Street
Barnsley
South Yorkshire
S70 2AS

ISBN 978-1-78159-075-1

A CIP catalogue record for this book is available from the British Library.

Typeset by Concept, Huddersfield, West Yorkshire.
Printed and bound in England by CPI Group (UK) Ltd, Croydon, CR0 4YY.

Pen & Sword Books Ltd incorporates the imprints of Pen & Sword Aviation,
Pen & Sword Family History, Pen & Sword Maritime, Pen & Sword Military,
Pen & Sword Discovery, Wharncliffe Local History, Wharncliffe True Crime,
Wharncliffe Transport, Pen & Sword Select, Pen & Sword Military Classics,
Leo Cooper, The Praetorian Press, Remember When, Seaforth Publishing and
Frontline Publishing.

For a complete list of Pen & Sword titles please contact
PEN & SWORD BOOKS LIMITED
47 Church Street, Barnsley, South Yorkshire, S70 2AS, England
E-mail: enquiries@pen-and-sword.co.uk
Website: www.pen-and-sword.co.uk

Contents

Dedication
To 459 (Essex) Heavy Anti-Aircraft Regiment,
Royal Artillery, Territorial Army, 1955–1961,
this work is affectionately dedicated.

Acknowledgements

I acknowledge with gratitude all those friends and colleagues who have helped and encouraged me to complete this work, but especially: Andrew Orgill and Pam Bendall, librarians of the Royal Military Academy Sandhurst and the Staff College, Camberley, respectively; Gary Sheffield, Christopher Duffy, Ian Beckett, Martine de Lee and other members of the academic departments at RMAS; June Mallaband and Chris Bridger, as well as Tricia Lotherington of PA Services, Fleet, who typed the manuscript; and my wife who forwent two summer holidays *en famille* while I undertook research and writing.

Notes on the Transliteration of Indian Words and Names

Ideally a system of transliteration should enable the reader not only to know how a word is pronounced, but also how it is written in its original script. A character or group of characters used in one language should have an equivalent character or group in the other. This is not easy to achieve in the transliteration of South Asian languages into English, for a number of reasons. The Devanagari script, used for all the major Indian languages except Urdu or 'Hindustani', is logical and consistent and, with the addition of a few extra letters, fits not only the Indo-European languages of the north but also the Dravidian ones of the south. Urdu, originally a military *lingua franca*, as indicated by its name, the language of the 'ordu', the horde or camp, but later developing a literature of its own, poses some problems as except for the aberration 'Roman Urdu' (i.e. written in the Latin script for the benefit of those whose first language is English) it is written in the Persi-Arabic script, the characters of which were devised for a Semitic not an Indo-European tongue.

The real difficulty, however, arises from the capricious nature of English orthography. A script in which the letter 'c', for example, can give two quite different sounds in a single word such as '*cycle*' or in which the letter 'y' can be either a vowel or a consonant, defies any attempt at consistency. Likewise, for want of a character such as is used in Cyrillic or Indian scripts, English uses two letters ('ch') for a single sound, as in '*itch*' but has to use the same combinations of letters for a different sound in words not of English origin (e.g. *loch*). This sound, in words derived from Indian languages, is usually indicated by *kh* (as in *khaki* or dust-coloured) but, unless the group is underlined, it can be taken for an aspirated 'k' (as in the English work-house). Yet 'h' in early attempts at transliteration was often used to indicate either dental consonants (i.e. those pronounced with the tip of the tongue against the back of the teeth), or retroflex ones (pronounced with the tip of the tongue turned back to touch the top of the hard palate) which are a distinctive feature of South Asian languages. The English sound *ch* is generally indicated in modern transliteration by the letter 'c'.

The middle two letters of an Indian word such as Pathan, however, are not pronounced 'th' as in either 'the' or 'thing', but as in 'hothouse'. To this source of confusion may be added the circumstance that the pronunciation of English vowels has changed over the years, and there is no easy way of distinguishing, in writing, between long and short vowels. 'Oo' gives a long 'u' when in 'boo' or 'coot', but a short one, at least in standard English, in 'book' or 'foot'. A short 'a' is denoted by 'u' in cup. A long 'a' needs two letters, as in 'laugh', except that 'au' has generally come to be read as indistinguishable from 'aw'. Thus the place name most logically rendered into English as Panjab was in the early days written down as 'Punjaub'.

In this book the writer has attempted to use the forms most familiar to western non-specialists at the present day, and has thus used, in this instance, Punjab. This is necessarily a subjective approach and results in inconsistencies, such as the preference for the forms Kanpur and Awadh rather than Cawnpore and Oude, but the retention of Calcutta and Bengal, etc. Likewise the writer has preferred *lakh* (100,000 or, in Indian notation, 1,00,000) to *lac*, but has retained *crore* (10,000,000 or, in Indian notation, 1,00,00,000, i.e. 100 lakhs) to *karor*, and has followed a similarly unsystematic system in the case of other Indian terms, ranks and titles.

Probably most non-specialist English readers will, like the writer, find the 'Hunterian' system, used by the Government of India in the last seventy years of British rule, the easiest. Its rules can be found in any of the language textbooks used by British officers in preparation for the Hindustani examinations which it was necessary for them to pass prior to permanent appointment. A particularly useful example is *The Munshi* by Mohamed Akbar Khan Haydari (Delhi, 1922, 6th edn) which begins with the proverb: 'To have other than the best, when the best is to be had, is the wisdom of unwise people.'

Preface to the Second Edition

The two decades since this work was first published have seen a steady revival of interest in the history of British military activities in South Asia. Shortly after the original publication, the National Army Museum mounted a major exhibition on the Indian Army in 1999 supported by a fine catalogue with supporting essays, including one by the author of this book, Alan Guy and Peter Boyden (eds), *Soldiers of the Raj: The Indian Army* (1999). A more recent exhibition at the National Army Museum has been of the early artistic legacy of the British and East India Company Armies, as demonstrated again in a catalogue, *Indian Armies, Indian Art: Soldiers, Collectors and Artists, 1780–1880* (2010). The artistic legacy of the early challenge for the Company in expanding British influence over the state of Mysore was the focus of Anne Buddle (ed.), *The Tiger and the Thistle: Tipu Sultan and the Scots in India, 1760–1800* (1999), accompanying an exhibition at the National Gallery of Scotland.

More recently, there have been two major conferences on the subject of the British Indian Army, one at the Imperial War Museum, London, in May 2009, and another held by the British Commission for Military History at Oxford in the summer of 2012. The subjects covered by their proceedings indicate the way in which the history of events and policies, formerly seen as merely a product of post-imperial nostalgia, has been given a new relevance by the challenges of the early twenty-first century. Among these themes are the re-examination of the 'martial class' theory that loomed so large in the British recruitment of Indian soldiers, the problems of low-intensity operations on the North-West Frontier, the two world wars of the last century, and the consequent transformation of what had become an imperial gendarmerie into a modern conventional army, such as it had once been.

The British military in India has also been recast in the wider context of more contemporary concerns with the previously Eurocentric nature of military history. Stephen Peter Rose, *Societies and Military Power: India and Its Armies* (1996) puts the British experience in the much longer context of Indian history from antiquity to the post-independence era. Indian historians have also advanced new interpretations as in the essay collections, Partha Sarath Gupta and Anirudh Deshpande (eds), *The British Raj and its Indian Armed Forces, 1857–1939* (2002) and Kaushik Roy (ed.), *War and Society in Colonial India, 1807–1945* (2006). The latter has a useful introduction on the impact of 'agrarian', 'subaltern' and 'cultural' studies on the specific histori-ography of the Indian Army. Roy is also responsible for *The Oxford Companion to Modern Warfare in India* (2009).

It has become increasingly clear that, in expanding their empires, Europeans adapted to local conditions, including existing patterns of warfare. There are two useful introductions. Douglas Peers (ed.), *Warfare and Empires: Contact and Conflict between European and Non-European Military and Maritime Forces and Cultures* (1997), covers aspects of European military interaction with Africa, Asia and the Americas from 1415 onwards. The equally wide-ranging Wayne Lee (ed.), *Empires and Indigenes: Intercultural Alliance, Imperial Expansion, and Warfare in the Early Modern World* (2011) concentrates on evidence of European adaptation of indigenous military and diplomatic norms. In India in particular, the East India Company conformed to traditional means of raising armed forces within the existing military labour market, as described in the first edition, with more recent studies by Stewart Gordon, 'The Limited Adoption of European-style Military Forces by Eighteenth Century Rulers in India', *Indian Economic and Social History Review* 35 (1998), 229–45; G.J. Bryant, 'Asymmetric Warfare: The British Experience in Eighteenth Century India', *Journal of Military History* 68 (2004), 431–69; and Kaushik Roy, 'Military Synthesis in South Asia: Armies, Warfare and Indian Society, 1740–1849', *Journal of Military History* 69 (2005), 651–90. The application to India of the concept of the fiscal-military state now familiar to students of the English and British armies in the early modern period is considered by C.A. Bayly, 'The British-Military-Fiscal State and Indigenous Resistance in India, 1750–1820', in C.A. Bayly (ed.), *Origins of Nationality in South Asia: Patriotism and Ethical Government in the Making of Modern India* (1998), 238–75.

The developing relationship between the East India Company and native sepoys is examined in Seema Alavi, *The Sepoys and the Company: Tradition and Transition in Northern India, 1770–1830* (1995); G.J. Bryant, 'Indigenous Mercenaries in the Service of European Imperialists: The Case of the Sepoys in the Early British Indian Army, 1750–1800', *War in History* 7 (2000), 2–28; and Channa Wickremesekera, *Best Black Troops in the World: British Percep-tions and the Making of the Sepoy, 1746–1805* (2002). Douglas Peers, 'Colonial Knowledge and the Military in India, 1780–1860', *Journal of Imperial and Commonwealth History* 33 (2005), 157–80, posits the need for British officers to study local cultures. Indications of potential disciplinary problems with native armies were already evident with the mutiny at Vellore in 1806, for which the most recent source is James Hoover, *Men Without Hats: Dialogue, Discipline and Discontent in the Madras Army, 1806–7* (2007). Indiscipline was partially a reflection of different military cultures, as explored by Douglas Peers, 'Army Discipline, Military Cultures and State-Formation in Colonial India, c.1780–1860', in Huw Bowen, Elizabeth Mancke and John Reid (eds),

Britain's Oceanic Empire: Atlantic and Indian Ocean Worlds, c.1550–1850 (2012), 282–307.

If Mysore was one early challenge for the Company, another was that posed by the Marathas, against whom three wars were fought between 1778 and 1819, for which the most recent study is Randolf G.S. Cooper, *The Anglo-Maratha Campaigns and the Contest for India: The Struggle for Control of the South Asian Military Economy* (2005). Cooper has also considered Arthur Wellesley's logistics during the Second Maratha War in 'Beyond Beasts and Bullion: Economic Considerations in Bombay's Military Logistics, 1803', *Modern Asian Studies* 33 (1999), 159–83. Recent general studies of Wellesley in India are to be found in Anthony Bennell, *The Making of Arthur Wellesley* (1997), and Bennell's Army Records Society edition of *The Maratha War Papers of Arthur Wellesley, 1803* (1998).

Inevitably, perhaps, the coming of the Mutiny or Revolt of 1857 looms large in studies of the early nineteenth century. Two works by Douglas Peers appeared just too late to be considered for the first edition of this volume, namely 'Sepoys, Soldiers and the Lash: Race, Caste and Army Discipline in India, 1820–50', *Journal of Imperial and Commonwealth History* 23 (1995), 211–47, and *Between Mars and Mammon: Colonial Armies and the Garrison State in Early Nineteenth Century India* (1995), the latter especially emphasising the relative precariousness of Company and British rule. Military concerns thus fuelled the First Burma War (1824–26) and the seizure of Bharatpur (1825–26). The theme of a garrison state has also been followed by Tan Tai Yong, *The Garrison State: The Military, Government and Society in Colonial Punjab, 1849–1947* (2005).

Continuing unrest was illustrated by the mutiny at Barrackpore in 1824, covered by Premansu Kumar Bandyopadhyay, *Tulsi Leaves and the Ganges Water* (2003). Recent work on the Mutiny or Revolt of 1857 itself includes T.A. Heathcote, *Mutiny and Insurgency in India, 1857–58* (2007); *The Mutiny Letters of Colonel H.P. Pearson, August 1856–March 1859* (2008); Rosie Llewellyn-Jones, *The Great Uprising in India, 1857–58: Untold Stories, Indian and British* (2007); Saul David, *The Bengal Army and the Outbreak of the Indian Mutiny* (2009); Sabyasadhi Bhattacharya (ed.), *Rethinking 1857* (2007); Kim Wagner, *The Great Fear of 1857: Rumours, Conspiracies and the Making of the Indian Uprising* (2010); and Biswamoy Pati (ed.), *The Great Rebellion of 1857: Exploring Transgressions, Contexts and Diversities* (2010).

One lesser known aspect of the aftermath addressed in this book is covered in more detail in Peter Stanley, *White Mutiny: British Military Culture in India, 1825–75* (1998), dealing with the experience of the European regiments of the East India Company and the 'white mutiny' of 1859 when they were incorporated into the British Army. So far as the new Indian Army is concerned, as suggested earlier, the issue of the martial races has drawn attention as in David Omissi, *The Sepoy and the Raj: The Indian Army, 1860–1940* (1994); Lionel Caplan, *Warrior Gentleman: Gurkhas in Western Imagination* (1995); Mary Des Chene, 'Military Ethnology in British India', *South Asia Research* 19 (1999), 122–35; Kaushik Roy, 'The Construction of Regiments in the Indian Army, 1859–1913', *War in History* 8 (2001), 127–48; Thomas Metcalf, 'Sikh Recruitment for Colonial Military and Police Forces, 1874–1914', in Thomas Metcalf, *Forging the Raj: Essays on British India in the Heyday of Empire* (2005), 250–81; and Heather Streets, *Martial Races: The Military, Race and Masculinity in British Imperial Culture, 1857–1914* (2004), which encompasses Scottish Highlanders as well as Sikhs and Gurkhas. The literature as a whole is summarised in Kaushik Roy, 'Beyond the Martial Race Theory: A Historiographical Assessment of Recruitment in the British-Indian Army', *Calcutta Historical Review* 21–22 (1999–2000), 139–54.

Aspects of discipline are covered in Kaushik Roy, 'Coercion through Leniency: British Manipulation of the Courts Martial System in the Post-Mutiny Indian Army, 1859–1913', *Journal of Military History* 65 (2001), 937–64'; and idem, 'Spare the Rod, and Spoil the Soldier? Crime and Punishment in the Army of India, 1860–1913', *Journal of the Society for Army Historical Research* 84 (2006), 9–23. A different perspective is that of Nile Green, *Islam and the Army of Colonial India: Sepoy Religion in the Service of Empire* (2009).

Curiously, since the publication of the first edition of this book, the British soldier in India has been almost entirely neglected beyond the popular survey by the late Richard Holmes, *Sahib: The British Soldier in India, 1750–1914* (2005), and Douglas Peers, 'Imperial Vice: Sex, Drink and the Health of British Troops in North Indian Cantonments, 1800–58', in David Killingray and David Omissi (eds), *Guardians of Empire: The Armed Forces of the Colonial Powers, 1700–1964* (1999), 25–52. European volunteers in India, however, have been covered in Kaushik Roy, 'India', in Ian Beckett (ed.), *Citizen Soldiers and the British Empire, 1837–1902* (2012), 101–20; and Chris Kempton, *The Regiments and Corps of the HIEC and Indian Army Volunteer Forces* (2012). Logistics and its contribution to both sepoy welfare and military strength has also been discussed by Kaushik Roy, 'Feeding the Leviathan: Supplying the British-Indian Army, 1859–1913', *Journal of the Society for Army Historical Research* 80 (2002), 144–61; and idem, 'Equipping Leviathan: Ordnance Factories of British India, 1859–1913', *War in History* 10 (2003), 398–423.

Military campaigns in India have continued to see the publication of popular accounts but Indian military performance has also been subjected to more rigorous academic scrutiny. Tim Moreman, *The Army in India and the Development of Frontier Warfare, 1849–1947* is an important study of the Indian Army's 'way of war'. Moreman has also contributed 'Watch and Ward: The Army in India and the North West Frontier, 1920–39', in Killingray and Omissi (eds), *Guardians of Empire*, 137–56. Imperial policy has been discussed by R.A. Johnson, 'Russians at the Gates of India? Planning the Defence of India, 1885–1900', *Journal of Military History* 67 (2003), 697–743. Later frontier warfare has also been illustrated in Brian Robson, *Crisis on the Frontier: The Third Afghan War and the Campaign in Waziristan, 1919–20* (2004); and Alan Warren, *Waziristan: The Faqir of Ipi and the Indian Army: The North West Frontier Revolt of 1936–37* (2000). A recent interest has been in political officers on the frontiers as in Christian Tripodi, 'Peacemaking through Bribes or Cultural Empathy? The Political Officer and Britain's Strategy towards the North West Frontier, 1901–45', *Journal of Strategic Studies* 31 (2008), 123–51; and idem, *Edge of Empire: The British Political Officer and Tribal Administration on the North West Frontier, 1877–1947* (2011)

Aspects of Kitchener's pre-war reforms are covered in Tim Moreman, 'Lord Kitchener, the General Staff and the Army in India, 1902–14', in David French and Brian Holden Reid (eds), *The British General Staff: Reform and Innovation, c.1890–1939* (2002), 57–74. The problematic performance of the Indian army on the Western Front is the subject of a popular account, Gordon Corrigan, *Sepoys in the Trenches: The Indian Corps on the Western Front, 1914–15* (1999), which can be supplemented by Mark Harrison, 'Disease, Discipline and Dissent: The Indian Army in France and England, 1914–15', in Mark Harrison, Roger Cooter, and Steve Sturdy (eds), *Medicine and Modern Warfare* (1999), 185–203; David Omissi, *Indian Voices of the Great War: Soldiers' Letters, 1914–18* (1999); and George Morton Jack, 'The Indian Army on the Western Front, 1914–15: A Portrait of Collaboration', *War in History* 13 (2006), 329–62. Equally difficult experiences in Mesopotamia are covered in Nikolas Gardner, 'Sepoys and the Siege of Kut-al-Amara, 1915–16', *War in History* 11 (2004), 307–26; Kaushik Roy, 'The Army in India in Mesopotamia from1916 to 1918: Tactics, Technology and Logistics Reconsidered', in Ian Beckett (ed.), *1917: Beyond the Western Front* (2009), 131–58; and Andrew Syk's Army Records Society edition of *The Military Papers of Lieutenant General Frederick Stanley Maude, 1914–17* (2012). The problem of post-1918 'Indianisation' is touched upon in Mark Jacobsen's edition for the Army Records Society of *Rawlinson in India* (2002), Rawlinson's tenure as Commander-in-Chief in India extending from 1920 to 1925.

The wider context is covered in Anirudh Deshpande, *British Military Policy in India, 1900–45* (2005); Kaushik Roy, 'Military Loyalty in the Colonial Context: A Case Study of the Indian Army during World War Two', *Journal of Military History* 73 (2009), 497–530; idem, (ed.), *The Indian Army in the Two World Wars* (2011); and Alan Jeffreys and Patrick Rose (eds), *The Indian Army, 1939–47: Experience and Development* (2012). The fall of Singapore in February 1942 was a particularly low point, as discussed by Alan Warren, 'The Indian Army and the Fall of Singapore', in B. Farrell and S. Hunter (eds), *Sixty Years On: The Fall of Singapore Revisited* (2003), 207–89. It contributed to the creation of the Indian National Army, which is among the subjects dealt with in Christopher Bayly and Tim Harper, *Forgotten Armies: The Fall of British Asia, 1941–45* (2006). In Burma, however, the fortunes of Indian Army were transformed, as discussed by Daniel Marston, *Phoenix from the Ashes: The Indian Army in the Burma Campaign* (2003); and Tim Moreman, *The Jungle, the Japanese and the British Commonwealth Armies at War, 1943–45: Fighting Methods, Doctrine and Training for Jungle Warfare* (2005). An aspect of the demise of the Indian Army is illuminated in Daniel Marston, 'The Indian Army, Partition and the Punjab Boundary Force, 1945–47', *War in History* 16 (2009), 469–505.

For students of the British Army, which for almost a hundred years formed a third of the forces at the disposal of the Government of India, themes of transformation have again become important. As it withdraws from its cantonments on the North German plain, where it found for fifty years a comfortable exile mirroring its time in India, it is changing back from being a continental force to an expeditionary one. Its recent expeditions to Iraq and Afghanistan, though undertaken as part of USA-led multi-national forces, illustrate the unchanging problems of such operations. Among these are those of asymmetrical warfare, set amid a hostile terrain of deserts and mountains, and of recruiting local troops capable of being efficient without becoming a threat, all of which were experienced by the armies of British India. Away from the battlefield, the British Army in association with its international allies is currently helping to build new nations and new armies to succeed those left behind in the retreat from Empire. A particular contribution takes the form of training and educating local officers, a subject of major controversy in the later years of the British Raj, as shown in this book. Although the proper task of the historian, in Ranke's words, is 'to say what really happened', it is allowable to speculate on what, in the light of history, might happen next. Many commentators envisage the emergence of new failed states in regions formerly within the British Indian Army's area of responsibility, where the British Army might once again find itself deployed on peacekeeping or nation-building operations.

This book is essentially a constitutional history rather than a work of War Studies, but its themes of the importance of civil-military relations, inter-service and inter-personal rivalries, and unceasing conflict between the rival demands of finance and defence remain equally important in both fields. Though recent wars in the Gulf and Afghanistan have seen the publication of numerous histories and memoirs, aimed at widely different levels of readership, the constitutional history of the armies involved there has received but little attention. It is hoped that, as a new generation of politicians and soldiers finds itself facing old problems, the re-issue of this work will prove timely in filling a gap in knowledge. History does not repeat itself, but it does resemble itself.

T.A. Heathcote
January 2013

Preface to the First Edition

This book, coming from the pen of one trained at the School of Oriental and African Studies in the University of London, is unavoidably a work of oriental history rather than imperial history. Why then is there a volume in a series on the history of the British Army which treats its subject as a British episode in the history of the Indian military rather than as an Indian episode in the history of the British military? The writer has set out to make two points. The first is that in India, as elsewhere, *vixere fortes ante Agatnemnona* ('There were heroes (lit. strong men) before Agamemnon'), quite literally so in the Indian case, where there are heroes with an antiquity as great as those of Homer. Despite the fact that British orientalists have for over two centuries studied the history of South Asia, including the campaigns of its great Muslim and Hindu rulers, many popular works published in the United Kingdom during the British period of Indian history (and some published since its end) give the impression that before the coming of the British all forms of higher military knowledge were beyond not merely the experience but even the competence of Indian fighting men. The existence of Indian generals and soldiers who proved doughty opponents to even an Alexander the Great or a future Duke of Wellington was glossed over. The achievements of armies involved in the creation or destruction of empires as rich and populous as any of their contemporaries in the West were ignored. European victories over Indian troops, largely the result of temporary advantages in military technology or political organisation, were ascribed to cultural or racial superiority, despite the fact that the British conquered India largely by the use of Indian manpower. Nevertheless, Indian officers and Indian soldiers displayed their ability to master new Western techniques as soon as these appeared to advantage in Indian battles, with such success that the British ensured Indian access to modern weapons and military education was kept to an absolute minimum. For the Indian military, as for Indian society as a whole, the British represented merely a temporary change in the composition of the country's dominant minority. This is not to say that the Indian military was unaffected by its association with the British. Indeed, it is tempting to say that those who seek examples of the culture and traditions of the old British Army should look for them among the officers and soldiers of the armies of India and Pakistan.

The second point made in this book is that India was by no means the source of military strength to the British that it seems at first sight. It is true that troops of the British Army stationed in India were paid for by Indian rather than British revenues. It is also true, however, that both the East India Company and the India Office were always concerned to keep the number of these troops as small as possible, and to ensure that they were employed for the purposes of British India rather than the British empire as a whole. The British Parliament too kept a scrutiny on the size of the British forces maintained by Indian funds, lest they be used by a British Government to implement policies for which supplies would not be voted by the House of Commons. The most that can be said is that troops in India, whether of the British or Indian armies, formed a reserve of trained manpower which the British Government could, in emergency, hire from the Indian Government. Such a purpose, however, was not that for which they were maintained, and might have been achieved more effectively by other means. In some respects India was a source of weakness rather than strength. Service there for the British Army amounted to a kind of exile and was said by the recruiters to have an adverse effect on their efforts. The Government of India, anxious to minimise expenditure, provided the military with equipment which lagged behind contemporary European standards, so that service in India did little to fit troops for service outside India except in the most basic aspects of soldiering. When ultimately re-equipment became necessary (as much for political as military reasons), it could only be achieved at the expense of other British needs, outside India. By the end of the Second World War, the costs incurred by the British Government in employing Indian troops outside India, and in maintaining additional British troops inside India, were so great as to wipe out all India's financial debts to London and so remove one of the greatest obstacles to the ending of British dominion in South Asia.

It is now over sixty years since the British Army left India. During that time the British Empire has become, as its poet Rudyard Kipling forecast, 'one with Nineveh and Tyre'. Although the population of post-imperial Britain includes two million of all classes whose origins lie in the Indian sub-continent, no more to them than to their English fellow-citizens does a recollection of the achievements of Anglo-Indian arms loom large. Yet a general interest lingers, encouraged by adventure films of the 1980s, or even by televised repeats of those of the 1930s, whose welcome suggests that each new generation continues to re-act against the conventional attitudes of its predecessors. Thus as 'revisionist' history has become 'mainstream', the writer claims to be 'post-revisionist'. It is his hope that this work will encourage the renewed interest in Indian history and give a greater understanding of those khaki-clad figures who, for a few rupees a month, held the garrisons and outposts of one of the greatest empires the world has ever seen.

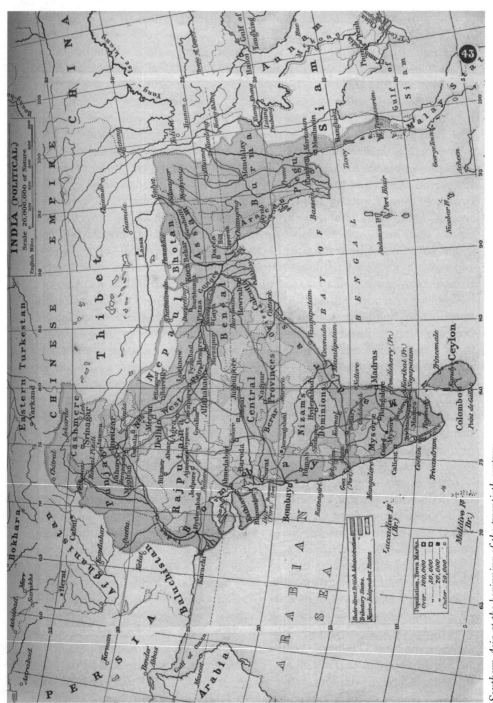

Southern Asia at the beginning of the twentieth century.

Chapter 1

India's Military Heritage

The thread of military events has been woven into the robe of Indian history from the earliest recorded times. The most ancient literary source, the Rig-Veda, alludes to the conquest of the north west by the Aryans, an Indo-European people who used their superior military technology, the war chariot, to achieve the overthrow of the civilisation of the first Indus Valley cities. The Aryans themselves were followed by other Indo-Europeans, spoken of with disapproval by the early texts as unorthodox in their beliefs and ritual. The little kingdoms set up by the Aryan tribesmen became the components of larger states. By the mid-fourth century BC, when Indian events first came to be recorded by Western historians, the early Hindu empire of Magadha controlled all the Ganges basin, while that of the northern Indus was part of the Persian empire. In 326 BC Alexander the Great, having become ruler of Persia, arrived to assert his claim to its twentieth satrapy or province. After a great battle on the banks of what is now known as the Jhelum, called by the Greeks the Hydaspes, King Porus (or Paurava) of the Punjab was defeated, but the nobility of this ruler and the bravery of his men led Alexander to leave him as a vassal and march down the Indus, eventually to return home through the desolate wastes of Makran.[1] A new emperor arose in Magadha, Candragupta Maurya, who drove out the garrisons left by Alexander. This emperor's son, Asoka, one of the greatest rulers of Indian, or indeed world, history, extended his dominions southwards to the edge of the Tamil plain and north-westwards, far beyond the passes to cover the whole of modern Afghanistan by the time of his death (*c.* 232 BC).[2] The lions which surmount the columns he put up to mark the boundaries of his empire now appear on the badges of the Republic of India, replacing the crown used during the time of British rule.

A hundred years after Asoka, invaders came again. First there were Hellenic rulers from Bactria, who first took the Kabul valley and then set up dynasties in the Punjab. Next came the Sakas or Scyths. These were replaced by an Iranian dynasty, the Pahlavas, which briefly ruled North West India around the time of Christ. Then came a Turkish people, known to the Chinese as the Yueh-chih, one of whose tribes, the Kusanas, controlled much of Central Asia and Northern India until the middle of the third century AD before losing all beyond the Indus to the Persians.[3]

Then, with the successors of these various invading hosts absorbed into Hindu ways, a new empire arose, that of the Guptas. Samudra Gupta, the Napoleon of India, established his authority over most of the Ganges basin, and his son Candra Gupta II extended it westwards over the Punjab and southwards over the Deccan. At the end of the fifth century AD, however, the Hunas, referred to in contemporary Byzantine chronicles as the Hephthalites or White Huns, who a century earlier had occupied Bactria, followed the customary invasion routes through the mountains into Western India and settled in Rajasthan. The power of the Gupta empire gradually weakened, though its glory was partially restored by the great King Harsa, who came to the throne in AD 606 and ruled for forty-one years until his death at the age of fifty-seven.[4] The history of India in the four centuries that followed is not unlike that of Europe at the same time, with a once-powerful empire breaking up into successor-states, ruled over by warlike monarchs who set up their own dynasties and indulged in warfare as the true sport of kings. Although these wars maintained the martial skills of Indian commanders and soldiers at the same high level as those who had opposed Alexander the Great a thousand years previously, they ultimately proved disastrous for the political and economic strength of the Hindu kingdoms. Most disruptive of all was the practice of the ancient ritual of the *asvamedha* or horse sacrifice. A consecrated horse was released to wander for a year, followed by a picked band of warriors, who would demand that all kings on whose territory the horse went must acknowledge the overlordship of their own king, or give battle and capture the horse. If the horse remained free at the end of the year, it was returned to the king who had released it and was sacrificed with great re-joicing. Every king with the power to do so sought to perform this ceremony, which in effect meant that every state was always liable to invasion by its neighbour.[5]

Hindu armies were all-embracing in their composition, and assemblies of 500,000 or more strong were frequently recorded. Nevertheless, only a small proportion of the manpower so embodied actually bore arms. The caste system meant that each occupational group carried out its own special tasks – grooms, grass cutters, sweepers or sanitary orderlies, metal workers for the sharpening and repair of weapons, leather workers who provided and repaired saddlery and equipment, tent pitchers, water carriers, medical staff, veterin-arians, bearers or porters, domestic servants of all kinds, merchants to supply food for men and beasts, and a whole host of the official and unofficial fol-lowers whose presence is an essential adjunct to any army at any time, but whose specialisms were developed in Indian society to such a marked extent.

For those whose specialism was actually to do the fighting, the warriors themselves, battle was a great religious rite, a high sacrifice in itself.[6] Astrol-ogers were consulted as to the most propitious time for the commencement of operations. Purification ceremonies were performed on the eve of battle and troops going into combat were addressed by their priests, just as is the case in even the most sophisticated of modern armies at the present day. Another practice, still common everywhere, was the delivery of inspiring messages from the king or ruler, although the promises of booty, if not of glory, which accompanied such messages in former times are nowadays discouraged. Battle was considered to be merely a series of individual combats, with the courage and morale of the mass depending upon the visible performance of their leaders. As in most other armies of ancient and medieval times, if a leader fell, only the noblest or the bodyguard continued to fight on, while the rest made their escape as best they could.

Most orthodox Hindu texts argued that fighting was part of the warrior's *dharma*, the duty appointed for his class. Rules of conduct, similar to those of Christian chivalry, were laid down, which had the effect of minimising the adverse consequences of warfare upon those who took part in it. Ideally, a mounted man should not strike a dismounted one; soldiers fleeing, wounded, disarmed, or asking for quarter, should not be slain; poisoned weapons were forbidden; the proper reward for victory was the homage rather than the dispossession of the conquered.[7] Women, children, priests and other non-combatants should be spared. Conversely defeat was a disgrace, the stain of which might only be wiped out by suicide. Cowardice in the face of the enemy was the greatest of shames, incurring not only disgrace in the present life, but suffering in the hereafter. The Hindu belief in *samsara* or the transmigration of souls, and the general assumption that the innumerable changes through which the life force passed were governed by its conduct in each preceding stage, did something to mitigate the harshness of war and to lessen the fear of death (if not of the process of dying), just as do all higher forms of religion. Thus, although a man might be born into a high position in society as a reward for good deeds in some previous existence, if he behaved badly he might be abased in some future one, perhaps being reborn as a snake or a worm, or even a woman. A king who slew the sacrosanct person of an envoy for example, could expect to be reborn in torment, along with all his advisers.[8] This particular law no doubt expressed the strong personal interests of the *brahmans*, the priestly class, who were the most likely to be used as envoys, as well as those of the rulers who needed the free passage of heralds and ambassadors for the making of war and peace alike. Most civilised societies protect the persons of envoys for much the same reason. There was thus a disposition on the part of Hindu kings and of Hindu soldiers to make war in as humanitarian a way as the business of killing and being killed allows.

It must be admitted that in and after the stress of battle, when men's baser passions are aroused, the rules were not always observed, any more than were those of medieval chivalry. Indeed, in modern times, the broadly similar provisions of the Geneva conventions are not invariably observed by all parties. Campaigns were commonly associated with massacre, pillage, and rape, especially if the forces involved were those of petty warlords rather than enlightened and powerful emperors certain of victory. The Dravidian south always displayed a greater degree of ruthlessness towards defeated enemies and non-combatants alike, but even in the Aryan north military necessity was accepted as a justification for departure from the ideals of behaviour. The *Arthasastra* or *Treatise on Statecraft*, attributed to Candragupta Maurya's great minister Kautilya (also known as Canakya and Visnugupta), predated by a thousand years the unscrupulous (or realistic) views of Niccolo Machiavelli in its recommendation that a king should do everything necessary to win a war, including the destruction of crops, assassination and treachery.[9] The *Arthasastra* also taught that a live dog was better than a dead lion, advice that many Hindu rulers would remember when faced with the necessity of reaching an accommodation with an overwhelming invader and which permitted Hindu soldiers to surrender when further resistance was hopeless, in the same manner as is allowed by Western convention.

Hindu armies drew their troops from a variety of sources. The six categories usually listed were the hereditary troops, who rendered military service to their ruler by virtue of their belonging to the *ksatriya* or hereditary military class of the divinely ordained four-fold division of Hindu society; mercenaries, who had no stake in the country, but were efficient and would fight for whoever paid the best wages; corporation troops, in effect private armies normally employed by merchant guilds for the defence of caravans and centres of trade in unsettled areas; contingents sent by subsidiary allies; defectors from the enemy; and wild tribesmen from the hills and jungles, suitable for unconventional or localised campaigns. Traces of all these categories continued to be found in forces maintained by the British when they ruled India, and medieval Hindu armies also included units with a corporate and continuous existence like that of British regiments. Such armies and such endemic warfare required great resources. The standard texts recommended that, after putting one-sixth of his revenues into his treasury in jewels and precious metals, a ruler should spend 50 per cent of what remained on what modern governments call 'defence' expenditure. Most of the revenue came in the form of the government's share of the crop, a tax from which some villages were exempted in return for providing troops. The vast deposits in the royal treasury, however, did little to assist the economy of the kingdoms or to create the wealth to pay armies. Frequently they had a negative effect, in that displays of opulence, intended to demonstrate the greatness and prestige of their owner, served only to attract the envy of his neighbours and invite aggression from beyond his borders.

Thus it came about that between 1001 and 1027 Mahmud the Iconoclast, Sultan of Ghazni, in Afghanistan, raided the rich and divided kingdoms of Western India seventeen times, returning to his hill kingdom with great caravans of slaves and booty and leaving behind him a trail of defeated Hindu armies, desecrated temples, and ruined cities as far south as Kathiawar and as far west as Bundelkhand. He annexed the Punjab and the Arab kingdoms of Sind but then left the rest of India to its own devices.[10] It was not until 1191 that a Muslim army again pressed into India. The first invasion, over-confident and for once faced with a united opposition, was thrown back, but in 1192 Muhammad of Ghor returned with a larger force, whose mounted archers routed the traditionally organised army of Hindu rulers, who put their faith in elephants as the decisive arm of warfare. During the next ten years, all the northern plains of India fell to the Muslims. In 1206 Muhammad of Ghor was assassinated and his general and former slave, Qutb-al-Din Aibak, became Sultan of Delhi.[11]

Qutb-al-Din, 'the Pole-Star of the Faith', was followed by other sultans, mostly of Turkish descent, ruling from Delhi under whom Muslim rule in India was consolidated and extended until, by AD 1340, only the southern-most tip of the peninsula remained unconquered by the hated *Turuskas*. Muslim historians give numerous accounts of fortresses stormed, treasuries seized, cities sacked, temples burnt, garrisons slaughtered, priests massacred, and the surviving men, women and children enslaved in such numbers as to bring about a collapse in the price of slaves all over Central Asia. Never-theless, the rule of the Muslim sultans was far from being a continuous holy war. Many rulers were men of piety and learning, whose respect for scholar-ship (as evidenced by the employment and respect they gave to historians) was better than that of some modern governments. Strictly speaking, Hindus were, as polytheists, guilty of giving God a partner, and so were not entitled to the concession offered to Christians and Jews, of paying the *jizya* or poll tax as an alternative to the choice of conversion or death. In practice, the suc-cessful generals who conquered India were more concerned with dividing up the spoils of victory God had given them, than with depopulating it of those whose labours created the spoils. Many of those enslaved were indeed con-verted to Islam, either by force or in despair at ever being received again in their own society. Others, outcasts in Hindu society, saw in the egalitarian faith of the Prophet some improvement in their lot, and those of little conviction had no objection to a religion which promised salvation and lower taxes. Thus a substantial Muslim population grew up from these sources, as well as from settlers and their descendants.

At the same time, however, no prudent Muslim ruler, whether sultan or local garrison commander, could ignore the still powerful, warlike and proud Hindu chieftains whose ancestral holdings lay around them. Even Mahmud of

Ghazni himself, the man who refused to accept ransom for the Siva-lingam of Somnath, one of the holiest shrines in India, because he would not answer on Judgement Day as one who had taken money to spare an idol,[12] maintained a strong force of Hindu troopers. His son Mahsud ordered his Muslim officers to respect the religious scruples of their Hindu comrades, and almost every Sultan of Delhi confirmed Hindu rulers in their positions of authority in return for a tribute of money, men or military support. Subordinate rulers, Hindu and Muslim alike, paid as little tribute as they could when the Sultan was weak, and as much as they were forced to when he was strong, and all might take up arms in rebellion if extortion, oppression or ambition drove them so to do.

The people who led Hindu resistance, first to the Muslim invasions and subsequently to the establishment of Muslim dominion over India, called themselves the Rajputs, the Sons of Kings. Their ancestors are generally believed to have been those who invaded and colonised India during the middle centuries of the first millennium AD and who, like other invaders before them, were absorbed by the culturally superior society of the Hindus. The myth was created that the original ksatriyas had grown impious and were destroyed, in response to the prayers of the brahmans, by the gods who then created the Rajputs as the new ksatriyas. This was a rationalisation of the defeat of the country's previous defenders and the incorporation of their successors into the Hindu system literally with the blessings of the brahmans.

The new masters held sway over all northern and central India, and some long retained their earlier possessions in Afghanistan. At their courts learning was cultivated as a matter of pride and credit to the government, while the figure of the *Charan* or Bard rose to great importance, as the curator of the kingdom's unwritten records, the historian of the dynasty, the producer of precedents, and the expounder of epics. Rajput noblemen and their clan followers accepted in their entirety the Hindu philosophy of war as the proper activity of kings. Their society was not unlike that of England and Scotland in the medieval period, or even the popular conception of the American West, where men were used to bearing arms and using them at their own discretion; where an insult could be wiped out only in blood; where the kidnapping of heiresses and the theft of cattle were freely practised by those with the power to do so; and where the retainers of local magnates considered themselves bound in honour to serve them to the death.[13] Although, by their continued internecine warfare and obsession with a quixotic code of chivalry, they fatally weakened their ability to repel the advance of the Muslim invaders, the Rajputs' power to make war remained significant until well into the British period, despite their insistence on clinging to long-outdated systems of military organisation, tactics, and technology laid down in the ancient Hindu treatises.

Foremost among such weapons systems were the war elephants, India's distinctive contribution to the art of warfare. They were first recorded by Western historians at the battle of Gaugamela (330 BC), when a squadron of fifteen was included with the Indian contingent in the army of Darius III. They seem, like the British tanks at Cambrai in 1916, to have been either too unfamiliar to the generals or too few in number for decisive use. It was not until Alexander's men reached the Hydaspes that they were faced by a whole corps of fighting elephants which, though eventually defeated, inflicted heavy casualties. The report that King Bimbisara of Magadha, the next monarch to the east, commanded several hundred of these sagacious pachyderms was an important factor in the decision of Alexander's army to go no farther.[14] The elephants subsequently became a major arm in Western classical armies, some even being included with the Roman troops that conquered Britain.

In India they were considered to be royal beasts, whose ownership was reserved to the government. Their primary role was in the charge, for which the strongest and largest bulls were specially trained, their tusks tipped with sharpened steel, and their flanks protected by bamboo or leather armour. They were also used to smash palisades or push down gates, or for other combat engineering tasks, such as forming a bridge over shallow rivers or ditches.[15] Smaller bulls and cows were used as baggage animals, giving an excellent cross-country performance in a country which until modern times had few made roads. With the invention of the gun, they were taken into the artillery service as draught animals. British as well as Indian commanders found them excellent mobile command posts, and elephants continued in use by the artillery in India until the early twentieth century.

Indian generals were fascinated by the elephant arm for over 2,000 years, despite repeated evidence of its weaknesses. Disciplined armies, admittedly not always readily available in Indian conditions, could usually avoid the worst impact of the elephant charge by opening lanes in their battle line, just as the Romans did against the elephants of Pyrrhus or Hannibal. Even the best trained elephant was liable to be panicked by the sights, smells and sounds of battle, especially by incendiary devices, and might, joined by its companions, turn into a common enemy, trampling friend and foe alike. Several decisive battles were lost when a Hindu king's elephant rushed in the wrong direction, leading his soldiers to draw the conclusion that he was deserting them, so that the whole host collapsed like a ruined building. Although the Muslim invaders themselves had come to power by defeating Hindu armies that relied on elephants, they in the course of time became dependent upon elephants themselves and were defeated by subsequent invaders in much the same way.[16]

During the thirteenth century, these invaders were the Mongols. The first inroad was led by Chingiz Khan himself. His riders reached the upper part of the Indus valley, but the climate of the Punjab plains was sufficient to out-weigh the prospect of plunder and the old warrior turned back to his native steppes. Other Mongols entered Northern India after him, some as invading armies which were eventually thrown back by the armies of Delhi in which Hindu contingents fought alongside their Muslim overlords. Others came as peaceful traders and adopted the faith of Islam, though liable to be attacked on suspicion of being potential 'fifth columnists' when they grew numerous enough to cause resentment and rich enough to be worth plundering.[17]

A far more terrible invasion was that of the Amir Timur of Samarkand, more familiar to students of English literature as Tamberlane the Great. Despite the zeal with which various Sultans of Delhi had persecuted those guilty of unbelief, or of believing the wrong thing, the vast majority of their subjects continued to practise the Hindu religion. This was felt by Timur to be as pitch upon the faces of all true believers. Moreover, India contained great riches, notwithstanding the depredations of earlier invaders, and its defences, because of a civil war between two rival contenders for the *masnad* or throne of Delhi, were weak. As he wrote in his autobiography, his purpose in entering Hindustan was, therefore, twofold: 'The first thing was to war with infidels, the enemies of the Islamic faith, and by this holy war to acquire some claim to reward in the life to come. The other was a worldly object, that the army of Islam might gain something from plundering the wealth of infidels.'[18] In the autumn of 1398, with a force of 90,000 Central Asian horsemen, he crossed the Indus and advanced on Delhi. On the ancient battlefield of Panipat he was met by an army (mostly of Muslim soldiers under Muslim commanders) which included 120 war elephants. Once again, however, the elephant threat proved to have been overrated. Timur gained an easy victory and captured Delhi, which was subsequently sacked with most of its citizens being killed or enslaved.

The Delhi Sultanate had already lost its control over the Deccan and the Peninsula. Hindu power revived in the far south with the establishment of the state of Vijayanagar in 1336. Ten years later Zafar Khan, viceroy of the Deccan, unilaterally declared himself independent of Delhi and set up his own state. This lasted until the closing decades of the fifteenth century, during which the governors of the five provinces into which it was divided each in turn declared themselves independent Sultans. These rulers fought among themselves, and against Vijayanagar, in a series of campaigns ending with the destruction of the latter in 1565. Some of these sultans were men of humanity. Others were brutal tyrants, details of whose capriciousness and cruelty are best left in the decent obscurity of the learned language in which they were chronicled. In military terms the major consequence of this period of Indian history was the establishment of a Muslim population in the Peninsula, the descendants of the first expeditionary forces sent from Delhi, and of other adventurers coming down from the north as mercenaries seeking employment in armies of the contending monarchs. This population, whose original existence and subsequent survival in power depended on its supremacy in arms, preserved its own martial traditions, and remained a reservoir of military manpower. Yet again the pattern was repeated of warlike invaders arriving from the north to become a dominant minority holding sway over a passive subject population.[19]

In the year 1524 Zahir al-Din Muhammad, surnamed Babur, the Tiger, ruler of Kabul, previously of Samarkand, a descendant of Sultan Timur, 'placed my foot in the stirrup of resolution and my hand on the reins of confidence in God' (as he put it, in the graceful Persian idiom)[20] and invaded India following the example of his famous and awe-inspiring ancestor. He was also related, rather distantly, to Chingiz Khan, though, like Timur, he was in fact a Turk by ethnic origin, and utterly hated the Mongols. Nevertheless, it had become the custom for the inhabitants of Hindostan to refer to any set of invaders from Central Asia as Mongols and so it was that Babur, after some initial setbacks, became the founder of the great Mughal empire that eventually ruled over almost all India. His decisive victory over the Sultan of Delhi on 21 April 1526, on the old battlefield of Panipat, proved yet again how a relatively small force of desperate but well-led horsemen from Central Asia could almost literally ride rings round the much larger but unwieldy hosts of the Indian plains. Sultan Ibrahim put a lakh of men into the field with a hundred war elephants. He was, however, inexperienced in war, in Babur's words, a general 'who marched without order, halted or retired without method, and engaged without foresight'.[2] Babur, on the other hand, was not only a practised commander but had at his disposal the latest military technology, a battery of wheeled artillery, that would become the great gun park which was the pride of the imperial Mughal armies. After the death in this battle of Sultan Ibrahim and 15,000 of his Muslim and Hindu soldiers, all the chivalry of the Rajputs took the field, seeing a chance to regain Hindustan for themselves. At Khanua (Kanwaha) on 16 March 1527 their army, including now 500 war elephants and 80,000 cavalry, tried the same tactic of a frontal attack on Babur's field works as had the late Sultan of Delhi, with similarly disastrous results.[22] Babur's heirs and successors, ruling first from Delhi, then Agra, then Delhi again, followed the familiar pattern of conducting campaigns, whether against each other or in the conquest of the remaining Muslim and Hindu princes of India, in the traditional Indian way of warfare.

The military system of the Mughals likewise soon came to resemble in many ways those of their predecessors. Essentially these systems were dictated by the problems of governing a large area with no faster system of communication than that which could be achieved by dispatch riders travelling by post horses over unmade roads. 'Dihli dur ast' (Delhi is far away) was the saying of many a Mughal official, reluctant to comply with unwelcome instructions such as those requiring the transmission of revenue. Most rulers worked on the sponge principle, allowing their subordinates to soak up the revenue and then squeezing them to obtain the proceeds.

The military and revenue systems in fact were interdependent. Although at times the major officers of the state were paid a regular stipend, the usual method adopted was one of *jagir*, the assignment of the revenue of a given area, in return for which the *jagirdar* or holder of the assignment was required to perform his civil duties and to maintain a stated number of cavalry troopers or *sawars* (literally, 'riders').[23] This arrangement allowed a ruler to divide up the proceeds of conquest among his followers, while at the same time producing the military garrisons by which the conquest was subsequently maintained. The disadvantages included a reluctance of assignees to give up (or of rulers to resume from their old supporters) their assignments when the holders became too old to perform military service in person, and the tendency of the more ambitious assignees to use the armed men whom they retained under this system for purposes other than those approved by their ruler. Indeed for a ruler to assign too much of the revenue invited disaster, since, without forces of his own, he was dependent on the reliability of the magnates of whose contingents his army was composed.

A further problem was that assignees who actually lived in the areas whose revenues were assigned to them and who, in most cases, were actually involved in collecting the revenues (normally the government's share of the annual crops) tended to become local chiefs. Indeed, often they originally had been local chiefs, Hindu rajas whose lands were not worth the trouble of absolute conquest, or whose military resources made them too hard a nut to be worth cracking as long as they passed on the proper share of the revenue and acknowledged a nominal subjection. At the other extreme, assignees tended not so much to misuse the military contingents they were expected to keep up, as not to keep them up at all and pocket that element of the revenue intended for their upkeep, with the result that when the army was called out, the expected numbers of trained, properly equipped, and well mounted men failed to materialise. When, in an attempt to enforce assignees to meet their obligations, periodic musters were ordered, the same men and horses moved round from assignee to assignee ahead of the muster-masters, to be counted over and over again, hired by each assignee in turn for the duration of the muster. The abuses were countered to a certain extent by systems such as branding the horses and describing the troopers, but all depended upon the honesty, efficiency, and energy of those operating the system, just as it did in Europe at the same time.

The highest officers of the Mughal empire, the *Subadars*, holders of a Suba or province, were at first called *Sipahsalars*, 'commanders of the troops', and the senior officials of the Mughal state were known as *mansabdars*, 'holders of commands'. There were thirty-three levels of *mansab*, each grade distinguished not by a title but by a number, from 10,000 down to ten, according to the number of troopers the *mansabdar* was expected to maintain.[24] The later Mughal emperors recognised that many who were granted high rank would not in fact produce the appropriate number of men, and introduced a system of parallel ranks, with the higher figure being honorary (*zat*) and the lower being that of the actual number of troops (*sawar*) to be maintained. The proportion of permanently employed soldiers in Mughal armies was small and comprised the household troops, artillerymen and other specialists, including the elephant drivers. All could be used for the many ceremonial functions inseparable from Indian court life. Otherwise the army was composed of the contingents produced, with varying degrees of enthusiasm, by assignees who tended to become hereditary local governors, where sons were allowed to succeed fathers in office if central authority was too weak to enforce the appointment of another nominee.

The relationship between the revenue and the military systems in India was, until well after the Mughal era and well into that of the British, virtually one of symbiosis. The main purpose of collecting the revenue was to ensure payment for the military on whom the power of the government was based, while the main purpose of the military was to ensure the collection of the revenue from which it was paid. Even inter-state campaigns can be considered as having been undertaken with a view to increasing the base of the revenue, which in turn paid for the army which made the conquests, and the still larger army required to hold them. The expansion of the British Indian forces which took place in step with the expansion of British territorial possessions in India simply maintained a pattern set by the Mughals. Troops not involved in campaigning were required to accompany the agents of government whose task it was actually to collect the revenue, in cash or in kind. It is not without significance that the official title of the British district magistrates in the first provinces to be acquired by the British in India was 'Collector'. The method of gathering the land revenue from the cultivators varied from region to region, but the conventional method in Hindustan was essentially one of tax farming. Wealthy individuals contracted with the government, or its assignees, to hand over an agreed sum and retain the remainder of what they had raised. Generally these tax-farmers (*zamindars* or land-holders) had a hereditary interest in the villages whose revenue they levied, and through custom and practice all sides knew what could reasonably be yielded, with reductions allowed in times of drought or other natural disaster. Where an area was the subject of disputed control, however, cultivators might be subjected to demands from rival rulers. Distress was also caused when, as in the early British period, market forces were left to determine what could be raised. Rival contractors tried to outbid each other in promises of what they could raise, in order to secure or retain their holdings, regardless of the productive capacity of the land and its cultivators. Troops were required to accompany the collectors, in order to ensure that zamindars actually disgorged all that they had contracted to hand over. Sometimes even artillery was included in such expeditions. As British rule became fully established, the military presence became a guard of honour rather than a threat to reluctant payers. Nevertheless it long continued, partly as a customary way of recognising the social status of those involved, and partly in acknowledgement of their martial spirit. While local chiefs expected to pay what was due, it was thought something of an insult to imply that they would have done so except under compulsion. In most societies taxpayers tend to pay their dues only in response to the threat of *force majeure*. In Indian society the threat took the colourful and visible form of a body of troops. When the revenue was collected, the troops were required to act as escorts against what was, in unsettled areas, a very real threat of raids by armed gangs or bandits (sometimes, the same people who had just paid it over) as it was taken back to the local seat of government.

It was with a military system based on these principles that the Mughal empire and its rivals conducted their campaigns during the course of more than 300 years. These included struggles against those Muslim states in Bengal and in the Deccan, which had previously been subject to the Sultanate of Delhi; wars of rebellion and succession among the Mughal princes themselves; invasions by Iranians and Afghans from those Central Asian territories where the Mughals themselves had originated; and, within India, risings by new or reviving Hindu powers. Akbar, the greatest of the Mughal emperors, came to power after a victory at Panipat in 1556 over a Hindu army which, in defiance of the lessons of military history, had relied on its 1,500 elephants.[25] Later his policy was to conciliate the still powerful Rajput princes, employing them in positions of trust and making them pillars of his state, with their troops becoming contingents in, rather than opponents of, the imperial armies. He even, to the dismay of good Muslims, enacted ordinances tolerating Hindu religious practices, and experimented with his own composite faith, the Din Akbari, shocking the orthodox by issue of coins with his own image and the superscription 'Allah-o-Akbar' which, while it declared 'God is great', could also be read as 'God is Akbar'.[26] Unfortunately for the empire, after his death in 1605 his successors, especially the puritanical Aurangzeb who reigned from 1659 to 1707, believed that spiritual was to be preferred to material gain and, by re-imposing the hated *jizya* or poll tax on non-believers and destroying temples and shrines, forfeited the loyalty of the principal Rajput chieftains. The Rajput war (1679–1709) drained the empire of troops and treasure needed to deal with the rising power of the Marathas in the south.[27]

Maharastra, the country of the Marathas, is a region of rocky hills and jungle-covered valleys lying on the western side of the Deccan. It was liberated from Muslim rule after an armed struggle led over a period of some twenty-five years by the great Hindu national leader Sivaji. Like Ho Chi Minh in twentieth-century Viet Nam, he succeeded in defeating first one imperial power and then its even stronger successor, with Bijapur and the Mughals corresponding to France and the USA. Sivaji's methods could be taken as a perfect model by any revolutionary war leader. Operating from bases in difficult country where superior conventional forces could not easily deploy, he and his men, dubbed by a frustrated Aurangzeb 'mountain rats', moved among his own people as the fish swim in the sea. He followed the standard technique of the guerrilla, retreating when the enemy advanced, harassing him when he halted, following him when he retreated, and attacking him when he weakened. Mughal armies moved ponderously from place to place, hampered by their elephants, their heavy artillery, and by the presence for years on end of the Emperor's entire court, including the imperial *zanana* or harem. Sivaji's men, mounted upon their hardy hill ponies and forbidden on pain of death to bring women into camp, moved across the country at will, hanging upon the Mughal flanks, picking off dispatch riders and isolated detachments, capturing horses and weapons which were then used to equip more men to fight against their former owners, and destroying the crops needed to feed the imperial armies or to provide the revenues from which they were paid. It is significant that one of Aurangzeb's last letters, written at the age of eighty-eight as he fell back to Ahmadnagar, whence a quarter of a century earlier he had begun his campaign to crush the Maratha rebels, includes the phrase 'The complaints of the unpaid troops are as before.'[28] As the Mughal strength waned, that of the Marathas grew, until finally they took to the field as a conventional army, capturing town after town and establishing garrisons from coast to coast across the whole peninsula.

Sivaji himself died in 1680, aged fifty-three, having ruled as monarch of an independent Maratha kingdom for fifteen years. During this period he turned his guerrillas into a regular army, complete with artillery and logistic support and composed of men from all classes, each assigned to an appropriate position. In his military as in his civil administration he deliberately adopted the nomenclature and systems advocated by the classical Hindu authorities. He preferred to employ his troops directly, paying them from the revenue of crown land, rather than the *jagir* system, which always tended to degenerate into one of hereditary fiefs. Revenue was assessed at the rate of 40 per cent of the crops, and collected with the aid of the army in accordance with the custom of the country.[29]

When the Mughals and their successors were too weak to oppose them, the Maratha army undertook the collection of revenue from neighbouring states. Basically this was nothing more than a large-scale protection racket by which, in return for the right to levy the *chauth* or quarter of the land revenue of a given area (sometimes supplemented by a further tenth, the *sardesmukhi*), Maratha troops assumed the burden of its defence. In practice there was no one else against whom this defence was needed. The deliberate division of the revenue collection of single district among several Maratha chiefs, together with the details of what was due being known only to the government accountants, meant that much hardship was endured by the cultivators in these districts, or indeed in any district through which Maratha troops passed. Eventually all pretence of legitimate assessment was abandoned and the soldiery became mere plunderers.[30]

While Maratha power was growing in the Deccan, a new force emerged in the plains of the Punjab, made up of those who called themselves the Sikhs or 'disciples'. These were followers of the *guru*, or teacher, Nanak (1469–1539) who stressed the unity of God, the importance of good works in achieving ultimate salvation through successive rebirths, and vanity of idols and caste. On Nanak's death one of his disciples succeeded him as *guru* and so on until the tenth and last of the *gurus* of the Sikhs, Govind Singh, who led them from 1675 until he was put to death by the Mughals in 1708. The first four *gurus* were men of peace, teachers of a simple sect which drew its members mostly from the humble elements of society in the Punjab where Nanak had taught. The eclectic Emperor Akbar granted to the fourth *guru*, Ram Das, a piece of land by a water tank with healing properties called the Pool of Everlasting Life (Amritsar) which became the holy city of the Sikhs. Later *gurus* fell foul of the Mughal authorities, as much for political as religious reasons. The Sikhs increased in militancy until they were finally organised by Govind Singh into an order known as the *Khalsa* or chosen ones. Each male Sikh adopted the name of *Singh* (lion), shared a sacramental meal forsaking caste, renounced wine and tobacco, and adopted the five 'Ks' of a warrior ready to fight in defence of his people and religion (*kes, kaccha, kankan, kirpan* and *kangha*, or unshaven hair, short drawers, comb, dagger, and discus).[31] The wearing of the *pagri* or turban, judged in modern times to be an item so distinctive and necessary a feature of the Sikh community as to override all other dress codes, or even the dictates of safety in combat or other hazardous occupations, was not prescribed by Govind as essential. Being a Sikh was, and is, not a matter of race, but of creed, just as is being a Christian or a Muslim, though undeniably most Sikhs are Punjabis or of Punjabi descent.

On Govind's death, a false *guru* embarked upon a campaign of merciless revenge against the local Mughal authorities, provoking an equally merciless response, with a resultant legacy of ill-feeling between Muslim and Sikh which endured in the Punjab through successive generations. This was the last real military success of the Mughal empire amid wars of succession, court intrigues, and the rebellion of its own officials, who turned the provinces over which they had been appointed into independent states. In 1737 a Maratha army reached the outskirts of Delhi itself and then vanished as quickly as it had appeared. In 1739, as so often in the past, the weakness of the defences of the rich plains of Hindustan attracted invaders from the North West. Nadir Shah of Iran defeated the Mughal army at Karnal, not far from Panipat, and from the subsequent massacre of the hapless citizens of Delhi gave a new word to the Hindustani language, *nadirshahi*, a holocaust. The captain of Nadir Shah's bodyguard, Ahmad Shah of Afghanistan, having carved out a kingdom for himself in his native country in the 1740s, followed his late master's example and raided into Hindustan on his own account.[32]

The last great battle between non-European powers in India before the departure of the British nearly two centuries later took place between Afghans and Marathas at Panipat on 13 January 1761. Far removed from Sivaji's original mountain rats, the armies of the Maratha states which had succeeded his kingdom took the field with all the bad old ways of the Hindu armies that for 700 years had gone down before hardy adventurers from Muslim Central Asia. They marched with all the luxury and heavy baggage trains, including families and non-combatants, that had hampered the Mughals whom they had themselves defeated.

The result, despite a desperate and hard-fought struggle, was the same old one. The last battle of Panipat in 1761 was to the Maratha Confederacy what Gettysburg would be to the Southern Confederacy a century later. Hardly a family on the defeated side, from the lowest to the highest in the land, did not lose a friend or relative. 'Two pearls have been dissolved', ran the casualty list, 'twenty seven gold mohurs have been lost, and of the silver and copper the total cannot be cast up.'[33]

Four years earlier, at Plassey (Palasi) in Bengal, a small force of British red-coats, supported by Indian soldiers trained and equipped in the European fashion, had won a major victory over their Indian opponents in the open field and a new military power had arisen in the land.

Notes
 1. E.J. Rapson, *Cambridge History of India, Vol. 1. Ancient India*, Cambridge, 1935, Ch. 15.
 2. *Ibid.*, Ch. 18.
 3. *Ibid.*, Ch. 23.
 4. A.L. Basham, *The Wonder That Was India. A Survey of the Culture of the Indian Subcontinent before the Coming of the Muslims*, London, 1954, pp. 63–4.
 5. *Ibid.*, p. 42.
 6. *Ibid.*, p. 126.
 7. *Ibid.*, p. 126.
 8. *Ibid.*, p. 127.

9. *Ibid.*, p. 125.
10. W. Haig, *Cambridge History of India, Vol. III. Turks & Afghans*, Cambridge, 1928, Ch. 2.
11. *Ibid.*, Ch. 3.
12. *Cit.* in H.M. Elliot and J. Dowson, *The History of India as Told by Its Own Historians*, London, 1867–77, Vol. 4, p. 181.
13. H.G. Rawlinson, *India. A Short Cultural History*, London, 1937, Ch. 12.
14. V.A. Smith, *The Oxford History of India*, Oxford, 1923, pp. 64–5.
15. Basham, *op. cit.*, pp. 129–30.
16. *Ibid.*, p. 130.
17. V.A. Smith, *op. cit.*, pp. 226–7.
18. *Cit.* in Elliot and Dowson, *op. cit.*, Vol. 3, p. 389.
19. Haig, *op. cit.*, Ch. 5.
20. *Babur Nama (Memoirs of Babur) cit.* in Rawlinson, *op. cit.*, p. 285.
21. *Ibid.*
22. Percival Spear, *India: A Modern History*, Ann Arbor, 1961, p. 122.
23. Denison Ross, *Cambridge History of India, Vol. IV. The Mughal Period*, Cambridge, 1937, pp. 455–6.
24. *Ibid.*, p. 316.
25. V.A. Smith, *op. cit.*, p. 344.
26. Rawlinson, *op. cit.*, pp. 309–14.
27. *Ibid.*, pp. 346–7.
28. *Cit.* in Rawlinson, *op. cit.*, p. 351.
29. V.A. Smith, *op. cit.*, pp. 427–35.
30. *Ibid.*
31. Rawlinson, *op. cit.*, pp. 377–83.
32. V.A. Smith, *op. cit.*, pp. 358–9.
33. *Ibid.*, p. 464.

Chapter 2

The Origins of British Military Power in India, 1600–1764

The constitutional basis of a British military presence in India lay with the grant in 1600 by Queen Elizabeth I of a Charter to the Company of Merchants of London trading to the East Indies. This Company was granted the monopoly of all trade between England and all lands from the Cape of Good Hope as far east as Cape Horn, except for any place in the possession of a Christian prince, whose own subjects might trade with England as he wished. The monopoly was not, however, intended to be in restraint of trade, but to promote and regulate it and to provide for its protection by arms if necessary. The purpose of arrangements which placed trade in the hands of a particular group was to ensure the exclusion of individuals who, in search of a quick profit, might alienate local authorities on whose goodwill a regular prosperous trading system depended. A company which held the monopoly could be relied upon to govern the activities of its members and servants with a view to the long-term interests of itself and the nation of which it became, in its chartered area, the representative. It was hoped that a body of merchants, who generally speaking find peace more profitable than war, would be particularly anxious to avoid occasions of dispute. On the other hand, as the East Indies were a vast area, a year away from orders or help from home, the East India Company was empowered to arm its ships and servants for their own protection and to make laws, not repugnant to the laws of England, for their regulation.[1]

The constitutional right to establish trading stations or 'factories', where their local factors would do any necessary business between the arrival of one annual voyage and the next, and to fortify or garrison them, was also dependent upon individual charters granted by the rulers in whose domains these lay. The first such station on the subcontinent of South Asia was established on the west coast, at Surat, by authority of a grant from the Mughal Governor of Gujerat. On the east coast a factory was set up at Masulipatam around 1620 and the Company's first fortifications were built at Armagaon in 1625. The first grant of land with the right to construct defence works and collect revenue was made in August 1639, when the Company's factor on the Coromandel coast obtained a grant from the local representative of the Raja of Chandragiri. This monarch, the vestigial successor of the Hindu empire of Vijayanagar (destroyed by the Sultanates of southern India after the battle of Talikota in 1565), thus played his part in the foundation of a new empire that would become paramount in India. The fort, named in honour of England's patron saint, and built – despite the objections of the East India Company's home authorities to the financial implications – was Fort St George, the official title of what subsequently became the Presidency of Madras.[2]

In 1661 the Portuguese settlement at Bombay was ceded to the English Crown as part of the dowry of Charles II's queen, Catherine of Braganza. A battalion of 400 troops, the first element of the British Army to serve in India, was sent to take possession but, as a result of opposition by the local Portuguese officials and a refusal by the Mughal authorities to allow it to disembark at Surat, it did not succeed in doing so until 1665, having lost seventy-five per cent of its numbers to tropical or other illnesses. Reinforcements were subsequently sent and the whole garrison, together with the rest of the Bombay establishment, was handed over by Charles II to the East India Company in 1669.[3]

The charter granted to the Company by Charles II on his restoration in 1661 took account of the existence of permanent British possessions in India. It empowered the Company to maintain warships as well as the armed East Indiamen which it chartered and to recruit men as regular soldiers, with whom it could lawfully make war against any non-Christian prince. When the charter was renewed in 1683, the Company's right to maintain local fleets and armies, subject to ultimate Royal authority over their employment, was further confirmed.[4] It was with forces raised under the provisions of this charter that the Company began its first war against an Indian power, a campaign in 1688–90 against the government of the Mughal Emperor Aurangzeb.[5]

The charter of 1661 established the London East India Company as a permanent joint stock corporation. Major stockholders could summon and vote in a General Court, which determined Company policy and appointed an executive body made up of twenty-four committee men, headed by an elected Governor and Deputy Governor. The same charter empowered the Company to appoint governors and councils to rule over its major settlements and execute the directions they received from their masters in London. Their right to exercise martial law was specified in the charter of 1669 handing over Bombay to the Company, and extended in that of 1683, which authorised the Company's governors and factors to 'execute and use within the said Plantations, Forts and Places, the Law called the Martial Law, for the defence of the said Forts, Places, and Plantations, against any foreign Invasion, or domestic Insurrection or Rebellion'.[6] By granting this right to the Company, the Crown recognised that the Company's holdings in India had become rich enough and large enough to attract military threat and merit military defence.

The East India Company's first regular troops were those taken over, with Bombay itself, from the Crown in 1669. Most of the original contingent of royal troops which had landed four years previously had succumbed to the effects of the climate, drink and disease, but replacement drafts from England and locally recruited mercenaries of European descent (mostly Portuguese with a few Frenchmen) gave the East India Company a Bombay Regiment of two companies and a total strength of five officers, 139 European other ranks, and fifty-four Indian Christians or 'topasses' so-named from the Persian word 'top' or gun. An additional company under command of Captain Shaxton arrived in 1671 and Shaxton was appointed by Governor Aungier to be a member of the Bombay Council and Deputy Governor.[7] It was to this company that three years later fell the unenviable distinction of committing the first of the numerous acts of mutiny that disfigure the record of British arms in India. As with so many mutinies, the grievance was a financial one, the troops objecting to the losses they suffered when their notional pay was exchanged into local currency, and to what they did receive being further diminished by stoppages to pay for their uniforms. One mutineer was hanged, Shaxton was sent back to England and Aungier was ordered that in future his Council should be drawn only from the Company's factors, not its military servants. The Council of the Company's settlement at Surat, to which Bombay was subordinate, recorded its view that soldiers were a 'querulous ungrateful people, and never satisfied'.[8]

After the Glorious Revolution of 1688 the East India Company, which had been patronised by James II, received little sympathy from William III or the Whig majority in Parliament and the latter resolved in 1691 that a new East India Company should be founded. Lavish bribes by its own directors secured a fresh charter for the original or London Company in 1693 but the new Company of Merchants of England trading to the East Indies was itself granted a charter in 1698.[9] These disputes in England led to difficulties in India, where the Mughal authorities found it difficult to distinguish between two sets of English merchants, each traducing the other as thieves and pirates. In November 1701 Aurangzeb placed an embargo on trade with both of them and on all other European companies, pending the payment of compensation for losses inflicted by pirates and the provision of anti-piracy patrols.[10] In a compromise effected in 1702 by Lord Godolphin, the two rival East India Companies were combined into a single body, known from 1709 until 1833 as The United Company of Merchants of England trading to the East Indies. This company inherited the powers of both its predecessors in England and India. Its government was vested in a Court of twenty-four Directors, including a Chairman and Deputy Chairman, generally referred to as 'The Chairs',

to be elected by the General Court composed of major holders or 'proprietors' of the Company's stock. The Directors were also empowered, according to the English Company's charter of 1698, to appoint and remove
governors and officers and to 'raise, train, and muster such military forces
as shall or may be necessary' for the defence of their forts and factories.[11]
In India, the Company legitimised its position by obtaining a charter or
farman in 1716 from the Mughal Emperor Farrukhsiyar, a great-grandson of
Aurangzeb, and the third emperor to come to the throne since the latter's
death nine years earlier.[12]

At the time of the War of the Austrian Succession in Europe, the 'country
powers' (the various South Asian states) certainly seemed strong enough. The
Mughal empire was the mere shadow of a great name, but its successor states
had large and well-practised armies at their disposal. In the south, the *suba* of
the Deccan was ruled by Asaf Jan, once the Wazir (or finance minister) of
the whole empire, who had since his resignation from this post in 1724
established himself as a virtually independent ruler. Although still technically *Subadar* or Governor, he adopted the honorific title Nizam-ul-Mulk
(Sovereign of the Land) and, from the name of his capital city, became known
to the British as the Nizam of Hyderabad. Though defeated by the Marathas
in 1738, he and his generals had twenty years of active campaigning to their
credit. Much the same could be said of Anwar al-Din, appointed by the
Nizam in 1744 to be Nawab of Arcot, from which city the territory of the
Carnatic was governed.[13] This included the Coromandel coast, in which
were situated the English factories of Fort St George, at Madras, and Fort
St David, at Cuddalore, a few miles from the factory established in 1683 by
the French East India Company at Pondicherry.[14]

Anwar al-Din, in response to a request from the French, warned both
European Companies not to make war within his dominions. Governor
Morse of Madras replied that he had neither the means nor desire to make
war, but pointed out that he had no power over the Royal Navy, which had
begun to make valuable prizes of French East Indiamen off the Coromandel
coast. When in 1746 the British naval squadron moved to the Bay of Bengal, a
group of French ships appeared off Madras, with a regiment of regular
infantry from the French Army, supported by locally raised Indian troops led
by Joseph Dupleix, Governor of Pondicherry. The garrison of Fort St George
put up only a token resistance, and Governor Morse and his council surrendered in anticipation of being able to pay a ransom, a proceeding then as
common in European as in Indian conduct of war. It then became clear,
however, that Dupleix had no intention of conforming to this agreeable
convention but planned to hold the place indefinitely.[15]

This episode had profound military and political consequences. Fort
St David was left as the only British trading station on the coast. The

Company's authorities there hastened to strengthen its fortifications and raise 2,000 watchmen, while the Bombay government hurried a force of European and Indian soldiers round from the west coast and recruited additional local levies for their own defence. When the news of the fall of Madras reached London, the Directors appointed the first regular soldier to be Commander-in-Chief of all their forces in India. This was Major Stringer Lawrence, the father of the Indian Army, an experienced infantry officer who had been a captain in the British Army before accepting this appointment from the East India Company.[16] In addition to his position as C-in-C, he was appointed a member of the Madras Council, third in seniority, but was not to rise above that position. The British government, alarmed at the sudden prospect of losing the trade of southern India to the French, sent twelve independent companies of infantry which reached Fort St David in July 1748. The question of a Company's officer having command over these royal troops was avoided by the appointment of Admiral Boscawen as C-in-C of all British naval and military forces in the East Indies.[17]

Anwar al-Din's reaction to the French seizure of Madras was that, as the town lay within his dominions, it should revert to him. When Dupleix refused to hand it over, a conventionally organised Mughal army, commanded by Anwar al-Din's son, Mahfuz Khan, laid seige to it. A sally by French infantry and field guns demonstrated that Mughal cavalry could be defeated by the rapid artillery and musketry fire of a well-drilled Western army. Further encounters between French and Mahfuz Khan's troops had a similar result. Although the style of fighting practised by European armies in the mid-eighteenth century was not unknown to Indian generals, it had not previously carried all before it. English attacks, often in conjunction with the forces of Indian states, against pirate strongholds on the west coast had had limited success. As recently as 1739 the Portuguese had been defeated by the Marathas, losing Bassein, their last remaining major fortress in India.[18] Anwar al-Din himself, surprising the French when they first reached Fort St David, proved that European troops were not invincible. The ease with which the French defeated Mahfuz Khan owed at least as much to the indiscipline of the Mughal troopers as to the discipline of the French infantry, and to the faulty tactics of the former as to the superior technology of the latter. The French victories nevertheless had a psychological effect on the great princes of southern India, out of all proportion to the number of men involved, and created the impression that European troops, or Indian troops drilled, armed, and disciplined in the European style (raised first by the French and then by the English) could have a decisive effect.

The War of the Austrian Succession ended in 1748. In India Dupleix had failed to take Fort St David and the English, despite Stringer Lawrence's men, the twelve British companies and Admiral Boscawen's battle fleet, had failed to take Pondicherry. Madras was restored to the East India Company at the peace treaty of Aix-la Chapelle but, despite this treaty, English and French soldiers continued to find themselves on opposing sides in Indian campaigns. The rival Companies made alliances with Indian rulers or with those who wished to become Indian rulers, since there were by this time disputed claims to the thrones of Hyderabad (following Asaf Jan's death in 1748) and Arcot (following Anwar al-Din's death in battle in 1749). The rival European Companies had at their disposal what was, in Indian warfare, a new weapons system, well-drilled flintlock musketmen and field artillery. Their local representatives were happy to put them to work as mercenaries in the service of any Indian prince who could pay for them with cash and, in the long term, promises of trade concessions.[19] Although the ability of European infantry to defeat much larger bodies of Indian cavalry (once the initial surprise factor of their novel tactics had worn off) could not be taken for granted, their presence on one side or the other might be enough to tip the balance. Thus if one army had a European contingent, its opponent needed to have one as a counter to it. The Directors of the English East India Company, as their military changed from being a local defence force into a field army, had to give up their old policy of having no 'gentlemen' in their employment and replaced the superannuated subalterns and volunteer civil servants on whom they had previously relied with experienced officers, available from British regiments reduced at the end of the War of the Austrian Succession.[20]

This different class of officer turned out to be spirited not only in the field, but in their attitude to their civil superiors, especially over financial questions. The rates of pay of the Company's troops were fixed on the assumption that they would serve only in the Company's fixed defences on the coast. Once they were required to go into the field, they incurred additional expenses, including the cost of transport, hire of tentage, and the purchase of all kinds of personal supplies which they would not have otherwise needed, and therefore they were compensated by the issue of *batta* or field service allowance. Officers in garrison at Fort St George and Fort St David were given free rations until Lawrence arranged for this to be replaced by a messing allowance which continued to be paid in addition to the service *batta*. In 1749 Anwar al-Din's illegitimate son, Muhammad Ali, whose claim to the throne of Arcot was supported by English troops, paid an additional allowance to the officers in recognition of the expense and attendant risks of carriage of articles of European origin from the coast to the theatre of operations inland. He subsequently discontinued this payment, as he had granted *jagirs* to the Madras government which provided the funds to pay the military contingents provided for him by the English. The Madras government, however, chose to regard this allowance as an act of personal generosity by the Nawab which, it told the aggrieved officers, they could expect to see renewed when he was again in full possession of his dominions. The officers' further remonstrances were greeted with accusations of mutiny. Officers were recalled to the coast in ones and twos on the pretext of relief, to prevent the whole corps refusing to do duty, and three were arrested as ringleaders.[21]

Every officer was needed at this period as British military power in India was built up. Companies of German and Swiss mercenaries were sent out by the Directors, though the latter caused difficulties by insisting on maintaining their own separate codes of discipline and were moreover inclined to desert to the French or any country power which might offer better wages.[22] The passage of the Mutiny Act in 1754 replaced the old Articles of War as the basis of military discipline in British India, though strongly opposed in Parliament because it had the effect of allowing regiments of the British Army to be sent to India. The French government, however, had sent its own troops to India in support of the interests of the Compagnie des Indes. These troops were therefore, within months of the passage of this Act, matched by the arrival at Madras of the 39th Foot. Their commanding officer, Colonel Adlercron, outranked Stringer Lawrence (though the latter was simultaneously granted a royal commission as Lieutenant Colonel), and so assumed command over all land forces in Madras. Supreme command was taken by Admiral Charles Watson, whose squadron had escorted the East Indiamen which brought the troops. The Mutiny Act also provided that officers of the British Army were to have seniority over officers of the Company's service in the same rank, much as was the relative position of regular officers to militia or colonial forces. This arrangement, though in itself reasonable enough, was later to become a source of grievance in India, just as it was already becoming in the American colonies, since it took no account of seniority within each rank.[23]

The major innovation of the period was the gradual replacement of the watchmen by a new kind of Indian soldier, the sepoy. The name, derived from the Persian *sipahi*, a regular soldier as distinct from a quasi-feudal retainer, was applied to Indians who were armed, trained, and, to a large extent dressed, in the European style. Equally importantly, at least when it came to raising recruits, they were promised pay in the European style, in cash at the end of each month. No great skill was required to load and fire a flintlock musket, while the battlefield drill of eighteenth-century armies could, under efficient officers and sergeants, be learnt in a matter of weeks, as its greatest exponent, Frederick the Great, freely asserted. Not only were sepoys easier to recruit than Europeans, but they were also cheaper to maintain and less likely to succumb to the tropical diseases and intemperance which carried off the European soldiers with such regularity. Sepoys were formed into companies on the European model, each commanded by its own subedar. As the success of this innovation, first introduced by the French and then adopted by the

British, became apparent, it was taken up by the country powers and by 1760 a sepoy contingent formed part of the standard order of battle of all major Indian armies.

The great majority of these sepoys came from the plains of Hindustan, particularly from the eastern (*purabi*) region between Bihar and Agra. This gave them the name 'easterners' (*purabiya*) or, as the British called them, 'poorbeahs'. They were also known as Baksaris or 'buxerries' from the name of the city, Baksar (Buxar) which was their most prominent recruiting centre. Centuries of warfare in northern India had encouraged the development of a society in which everyone of the slightest consequence carried weapons. Swords and spears were readily available and even muskets were to be found in private hands. During the Mughal period, the most influential Rajput groups, desirous of maintaining their own status, had introduced new forms of genealogical orthodoxy and created a more narrow Rajput identity, virtually confined to their states in Western India, or Rajasthan. The Rajputs of the east, mostly living in peasant agricultural groups, were excluded from this group and thus were denied the opportunity of serving as troopers in the contingents supplied to the imperial armies by the great Rajput princes. They were still, however, inspired by the Rajput ideal of *naukari* or service. Their culture was still one in which young men sought honourable and profitable employment as soldiers for a few years before returning to their villages to set up as respected and prosperous peasant proprietors.[24] A new outlet for this spirit opened with the arrival in the military environment of the matchlock musket, which was most effective in the hands of practised infantrymen. From the middle of the seventeenth century, therefore, the great majority of the matchlockmen serving with the Mughal forces in the Deccan campaigns were Purabiyas recruited at Baksar. They were organised into permanent companies and provided an element of stability in the predominantly cavalry armies of the time. In the best-managed Mughal armies, regular shooting tests had been conducted, with the musketeers classified, according to the results, into one of three grades, and their pay adjusted accordingly. Just like the gentlemen troopers, the matchlockmen were described in detail on the muster rolls, to prevent impersonation. One Ganga Ram, for example, was listed on 24 September 1646 as 30 years of age, the son of Khanna, a Rajput, with blue eyes, several scars and three moles on his face, a resident of Baksar, and due to be paid five rupees *per mensem*.[25] No Indian army maintained any central recruiting system. Instead, reliance was placed upon intermediary agents. In the sixteenth century this function had been performed mostly by zamindars, who not only collected the revenue, but raised warbands from among those who lived in their district. By the late Mughal period, zamindars, although they continued to employ armed retainers, no longer acted as either recruiters or leaders of fighting men, and had been replaced in these roles by jemadars (*jama'dar*, the holder of a group or collection), the military embodiment of the labour contractor or jobber, a figure long established in Indian custom. 'Jemadar' was for long a rather nebulous term in respect of the size of the 'gang' or company which such officers produced and led, and corresponded to the early use of the English word 'captain' to mean a military commander rather than the holder of a particular rank. Some commanded as few as fifty, others a thousand or more. Jemadars selected recruits on the basis of their past and future good character and their general acceptability. As the main purpose of military service was to enhance the prestige and the income of the individual and his family, such patronage was a valuable asset, the future possession of which was not to be risked by introducing anyone likely to be a bad soldier. The system therefore was geared to producing the kind of recruit who would be acceptable in terms of physique, spirit and social background to the other members of the war-band and who would, in short, 'fit in', an ability which has an undeniable military value in maintaining the cohesion of small groups during the stresses of active service.

When the British first began to raise Indian troops for the defence of their trading stations, it was to the jemadari system that they turned, as the normal local way of finding soldiers. The first such men were a company of Rajputs, commanded by their own officers and armed with their own weapons, raised at Madras in 1664. Similar Rajput companies were raised in Bengal in 1682 and at Bombay in 1684.[26] The precise areas from which these men were recruited is not easy to determine, but all three presidencies were employing Purabiyas by the middle of the following century. The duties, drills, and conditions of service of musketeers in the new European-style sepoy battalions were not so different from those in the companies of Mughal matchlockmen as to inhibit Purabiya recruitment, and the East India Company found no difficulty in raising its Indian infantry. Although two-thirds of the sepoys who fought in Clive's army at Plassey in 1757 had been raised in Madras, and only one-third in Bengal, the Madras troops were of Purabiya descent, if not of actual birth. Their commander, Keshar Singh, was a well-known Baksari *jemadar*, and their agent at Madras, Parbat Singh, himself had a Purabiya name.[27] Indian officers when recruiting naturally gave preference to members of their own families and would have been thought by members of their own society to have behaved disgracefully had they acted otherwise. Thus it was that Purabiya soldiers continued to be employed in the expanding British Indian armies, especially that of Bengal which was stationed nearest to their home area. Although Rajputs or even Brahmans formed the majority of recruits so raised, Muslim peasant-warrior communities also contributed their share.

In 1756, after fifty years, war came to Bengal. A new young Nawab, styled Siraj-al-Daulat ('Sir Roger Dowler' to the British) was alarmed at the dominance which the European Companies had achieved by their military intervention in the affairs of the Deccan and the Carnatic. He was, moreover, aggrieved by the loss to his revenues resulting from the English claims to exemption from transit tolls. Although his predecessors had authorised the construction of fortifications at Calcutta against Afghan raiders in 1697 and against Marathas in 1742, a British proposal in 1756 to improve these defences (in case the French might take Calcutta as they had Madras) was answered by the Nawab marching upon first the East India Company's factory at Kasimbazar, which fell without a struggle, and then Calcutta itself, which put up only a brief resistance. The senior officials escaped in the Company's ships. Their juniors were taken prisoner and put in the fort's detention cell or 'black hole' where most died of heatstroke. This incident was caused mostly by negligence on the part of the captors but subsequently passed into British folklore as an example of deliberate cruelty.[28]

The reinforcements that Pitt had sent from England to counter the French arrived to find that they were needed against the Nawab of Bengal. Joined by five companies of Europeans and 1,200 sepoys from Madras, they picked up the surviving two companies of Bengal European Infantry and seventy volunteers from those of the Company's civil servants who had escaped from Calcutta and its outstations. Calcutta was recaptured by a *coup de main* six months after it had fallen. The constitutional position was a complicated one and a dispute arose between on the one hand Admiral Watson, who appointed Captain Eyre Coote of the British Army to be commandant of Fort William and, on the other hand, Lieutenant Colonel Clive, who, as well as holding a rank senior to Coote in the British Army, was the senior military officer present of the Company's service. Against this could be argued that he was under the orders of the President and Council of Madras, not those of Bengal, and that the two Presidencies were quite independent of each other. Watson threatened to bombard the Fort, with Clive in it, if Coote's authority was not recognised. Clive defied him and only yielded when Watson landed in person and, acting as supreme commander, handed over control to President Drake of the Bengal Council.[29]

News of the outbreak of the Seven Years War spread the conflict in Bengal. Siraj-al-Daulat at first offered his protection to the French factories in his territories, but then withdrew it, with a view to settling his differences with the British and obtaining their aid against Ahmad Shah, the victor of Panipat, the master of Delhi, and the possible next invader of Bengal. At the end of March 1757 Chandarnagar, the base of French trade in Bengal, was captured by the British. Clive then marched against Siraj-al-Daulat, reaching Plassey (Palasi) on 23 June. Against 1,000 European and 2,000 sepoys, Siraj-al-Daulat had an army of 50,000 but, as many of these were led by Mir Jafar, a nobleman whose own aspirations to become Nawab Clive had secretly agreed to support, only about 12,000 came into action. Once again, European-style discipline, musketry and field guns were able to defeat a largely cavalry army in what came to be recognised as being – although a mere cannonade by comparison with other engagements fought upon Indian soil – one of the decisive battles of South Asian history. A grateful Mir Jafar, on becoming Nawab of Bengal, not only paid over vast sums, which his treasury could ill afford, to Clive and the members of the Bengal Council but granted to the East India Company the right to collect the revenue of twenty-four parganas or districts around Calcutta, the first major British territorial holdings in Bengal.[30]

With Bengal secure, the British were able to restore their position in Madras. The French were defeated by Eyre Coote at the Battle of Wandewash on 22 January 1760 and his subsequent capture of Pondicherry, after a siege lasting from 16 November 1760 to 16 January 1761, brought the French Indian empire to an end. The last involvement of Indian troops in the Seven Years War was the successful expedition sent from Madras in 1762 to capture Manila in the Spanish Philippine Islands, the earliest demonstration that troops from British India might have a part to play in imperial as well as local power politics.[31]

In Bengal, Nawab Mir Jafar found himself unable to cope with the problems of government. His western districts were raided by Marathas claiming to collect a share of the revenue on behalf of the Mughal Emperor, and by the army of the new Mughal Emperor, Shah Alam II, collecting on his own behalf. His eastern districts failed to produce the revenue on which his British friends counted for the payment of their troops and indeed for all their other expenses in India. The British authorities at Calcutta persuaded him, in August 1760, to retire in favour of his son-in-law, Mir Kasim, who assigned the revenues of further districts to the British in return for troops for the defence of what remained of his state. When he tried to restore his depleted treasury by challenging the Company's claim to exemption from inland trading tolls, the British sent these troops to arrest him in July 1763. This attempted coup failed and several hundred men, Europeans as well as sepoys, were taken prisoner. The British then declared war on Mir Kasim though their initial movements against him were hampered by a mutiny, first of their European troops and then of their sepoys, over arrears of pay and prospects of prize money. Order was restored by a mixture of cajolery and threats, but the commander of the Bengal forces, Major Carnac, was replaced by Major Hector Munro, a stern disciplinarian. Another incident, considered by him to be mutiny and desertion with intent to join the enemy, was according to the conventions of the Baksaris nothing more than the attempted renegotiation of their contract in favour of another employer. An entire battalion decamped but was pursued and captured. Twenty-four men were put to death by the conventional Mughal punishment for mutineers, being blown away from the muzzles of guns.[32] Mir Kasim fell back with his army into Awadh (Oude) the heart of Hindustan. There the Nawab of Awadh, and Wazir of the empire, Suja-al-Daulat, then in company with the Emperor Shah Alam II, had mustered a combined force to exact tribute due from the neighbouring region of Bundelkhand. Mir Kasim joined them in this expedition, and they in turn marched to restore him to his place in Bengal, still constitutionally a province of the Mughal empire.

They were met by Munro, at Baksar, on the Awadh-Bengal border, on 23 October 1764. Against the allies' 50,000 men, including a sepoy brigade in Mir Kasim's service (led by a German mercenary, known locally as 'Samru', who had murdered Mir Kasim's 200 European prisoners of war at Patna), the British mustered 900 Europeans and 7,000 sepoys with twenty field guns. In their hardest fought battle in India thus far, the British lost over 800 men before the allied army gave way, leaving 2,000 dead on the field. Mir Kasim fled, to die in poverty. Samru and his sepoys found employment with the Nawab of Awadh, who made peace with the British. In return for an under-taking that he would receive his long unpaid share of it, Shah Alam granted to the East India Company the land revenue of Bengal, Bihar and Orissa. In practice this placed the government of that province under British control and the last Nawab of Bengal, Mir Jafar's son Najm-al-Daulat, retired on a handsome allowance.

In 1764, recognising that they now had a standing army that had increased in size ten-fold in ten years, the Directors changed their method of appointing officers. Those in the British regiments then being recalled from India were still permitted to transfer to the Company's service when their units returned to Europe. They thus, except in the artillery where this system did not apply, realised a substantial sum by the sale of their commissions, though accepting permanent service in India. All other appointments to commissions were to be made from candidates sent out to India as cadets.[33] Cadets did duty as private soldiers in European units, occasionally in combat, forming elite sections for special tasks. Promotion for all was by seniority in each Army, unlike the British Line, where the senior in each rank could in normal circumstances succeed to a vacancy only in his own regiment, and only by payment of a substantial sum for his new commission, so that those who could afford it might purchase promotion over the heads of those who could not. The seniority principle, intended to avoid the probability of corruption, was also applied to all ranks in the sepoy companies, with the seniority being that within each company. Any exceptions to this rule, if the next in line for promotion were considered unfit to hold higher rank, required the approval of the local government. The first subedars and jemadars, men of independent means who had produced their own companies in the traditional Indian way were, in the course of time, succeeded by those who had come up through the ranks. The military disadvantage of this was compensated for by the political benefit of phasing out a body of independent contractors who, in the un-settled conditions of eighteenth-century India, might use their troops, paid and armed by the British, for their own purposes. A notable case was that of Subedar Yusuf Muhammad Khan who, for his distinguished services in the Carnatic was appointed commandant of all the Company's sepoys in the Madras Army and granted an extensive *jagir* by the Nawab Muhammad Ali ('Subedar' by now meant 'Indian captain'). He subsequently attempted to use his own troops to establish an independent state in alliance with Haydar Ali (who had come to power in neighbouring Mysore by just such a means) but was eventually hanged by the Nawab as a rebel.[34]

In the space of a single decade the position of the military in British India had changed, more radically than it had in the first century and a half of the East India Company's entire existence. A few companies of ill-led Europeans, retained for the local defence of a few coastal trading stations and supple-mented in emergency by war-bands obtained from Indian military contrac-tors, had been replaced by a standing army of European and Indian regulars. Instead of being financed out of the profits of the Company's trade, they were funded by the revenues of the territories which they had conquered. The infantry sepoy had emerged as the most effective type of South Asian soldier.

Nevertheless, the institutions and authorities under which the military operated remained in essence the same. The Company's very existence as a body depended upon the grant (and periodic renewal), of its charter from the British Crown, voted by a majority in Parliament. The Company's Governors and councils in India were subject to the Court of Directors, and the Com-pany's military was subordinate to the local Governors. A new element had emerged in the arrival of British Army troops, but the Mutiny Act of 1754 had ensured that all came under the same operational command locally. In South Asia the position of the Company continued to derive from Mughal imperial grants. Like the other South Asian powers, the Company had the authority to collect revenues and apply them to the maintenance of troops on which in theory the Mughal government could call when required. In practice, the British, like any other South Asian powers who could do so with impunity (by 1764, all of them) provided the troops for whose maintenance the revenues had been alienated only when it suited them and ultimately used them to overthrow the power of their nominal overlords or that of rivals. For the time being, however, the British government was content to exert its power over British India through the East India Company, and the Company was happy to leave the task of ruling the provinces whose revenues were in its hands to the princes who were themselves nominally agents of the Mughal Emperor, but whose possession of their thrones was actually dependent upon British military support.

Notes

1. W.A.J. Archbold, *Outlines of Indian Constitutional History*, London, 1926, pp. 10–12.
2. H.H. Dodwell, *The Cambridge History of India, Vol. V. British India 1497–1858*, Cambridge, 1929, pp. 88–9.
3. J. Keay, *Honorable Company*, London, 1991, pp. 132–4.
4. Archbold, *op. cit.*, p. 15.
5. V.A. Smith, *The Oxford History of India*, Oxford, 1958, pp. 426–7.
6. *Cit.* in Archbold, *op. cit.*, p. 33.
7. P. Cadell, *History of the Bombay Army*, London, 1938, pp. 23–4.
8. *Cit.* in Cadell, *op. cit.*, p. 24.
9. Dodwell, *op. cit.*, p. 98.
10. Keay, *op. cit.*, p. 187.
11. *Cit.* in Archbold, *op. cit.*, p. 23.
12. V.A. Smith, *op. cit.*, p. 33.
13. Dodwell, *op. cit.*, p. 119.
14. V.A. Smith, *op. cit.*, p. 456.
15. *Ibid.*, p. 459.
16. W.J. Wilson, *History of the Madras Army*, Vol. 1, Madras, 1882, p. 25.
17. *Ibid.*
18. Dodwell, *op. cit.*, p. 14.
19. P.J. Marshall, 'The Seventeenth and Eighteenth Centuries', Ch. 1, *The Raj*, ed. C.A. Bayly, London, 1990, p. 21.
20. Cadell, *op. cit.*, p. 51.
21. W.J. Wilson, *op. cit.*, pp. 34–5.
22. *Ibid.*, p. 64.
23. R. Callahan, *The East India Company and Army Reform 1783–1798*, Cambridge, Mass, 1972, pp. 35–6.
24. D.H.A. Kolff, *Naukar, Rajput and Sepoy. The Ethno-history of the Military Labour Market in Hindustan 1450–1850*, Cambridge, 1990, *passim*.
25. *Cit.* in Kolff, *op. cit.*
26. *The Army in India and Its Evolution*, Calcutta, 1924.
27. Kolff, *op. cit.*
28. Smith, *op. cit.*, p. 479.
29. Keay, *op. cit.*, p. 308.
30. Archbold, *op. cit.*, p. 44.
31. Wilson, *op. cit.*, p. 161.
32. A. Broome, *History of the Rise and Progress of the Bengal Army*, Calcutta, 1850, p. 458.
33. Wilson, *op. cit.*, p. 217.
34. *Ibid.*, p. 386.

Chapter 3

The British Conquest of India, 1764–1822

Although the East India Company had become by 1765 an Indian power itself, its future as such was by no means safe. In particular, the economic base upon which its military, and hence political, strength was built was endangered by the rapacity of its own servants. In Madras this became known, from the nomination of the local currency, as the age of 'shaking the pagoda-tree' while the cry of 'Nizzy will pay' was used to justify all kinds of expenditure incurred by government in the name of the Nizam of Hyderabad. The position was most serious in Bengal in that, while revenues of this province were expected to be so profitable as to finance all British activities in India, they were actually being syphoned off, following the Mughal precedent, by the officers expected to collect them. Many of such officers, military and civil alike, were relatively new to Bengal, having been hastily appointed, or transferred from Madras or Bombay, to replace the experienced men lost in the Patna massacre. All hoped to make their fortune by private trade and the munificence of Indian princes or their courtiers, while the Directors continued to pay them low salaries on the assumption that the opportunities for local profit made anything more than what amounted to a retaining fee superfluous. The new opportunities for peculation enabled fortunes to be made in a far shorter time than previously. This reduced the time that the Company's servants were exposed to the hazards of the climate and diseases of India and so enabled larger numbers to return to the United Kingdom with enough money to buy country estates, seats in the House of Commons, and stock in the East India Company. By the first of these activities, the returning 'Nabobs' (as they were known, from the English corruption of the title *nawab*) aroused the envy of the landed gentry who formed the dominant class of Georgian England.[1] By the second, they threatened the political control by that class of the ruling ministry. By the third, they effectively became the masters of their own former employers. In 1764, disturbed by reports from Bengal that the activities of their servants there were so extreme as to be likely to kill the goose that laid the golden eggs, the Court of Proprietors (the stockholders) proposed that Robert Clive, who had left India in 1760 and been ennobled and promoted to major general in recognition of his services, should return as Governor and Commander-in-Chief of Bengal and impose some kind of financial probity, or at least economy.

In the military sphere, the major economy to be effected was the reduction of *batta*. Mir Jafar, in 1757, had followed the example of Nawab Muhammad Ali in Madras by undertaking to pay to the Europeans employed in his support *batta* at the same rate as they received from the Company. When the revenues from which this was paid were assigned to the Company, the Directors saw no reason to pay the same allowance twice and instructed Clive to reduce expenditure under this head. Accordingly (after having taken about a year to sail from London to Calcutta), he ordered in December 1765 that troops in and around Calcutta, who were by definition not in the field, should receive no further *batta*. Those in cantonments farther inland were to be allowed half-*batta*, to compensate for the cost of obtaining essential supplies (including necessities such as, for a captain, thirty bottles of Madeira, thirty of beer, and fifteen of spirits *per mensem*) and those in the field, full *batta*. In August 1765 Clive had re-organised the Bengal Army into three brigades, each under a colonel, and each composed of a company of artillery and one battalion of infantry (all Europeans), with seven battalions of sepoys. He had also increased the established number of British officers in the Bengal sepoy battalions to a captain, two lieutenants and two ensigns, all of whom benefited from the existing *batta* regulations. The 1st Brigade, at Monghyr on the Ganges (some 250 miles inland from Calcutta) and the 3rd Brigade, another 100 miles up-river at Bankipur, near Patna, were now reduced from rates of double to half *batta*. The 2nd Brigade, at Allahabad, 200 miles farther up-stream on the River Jamna, continued to receive full *batta* in cantonments and double *batta* in the field, as Allahabad (resumed by the Mughal Emperor from the Nawab of Awadh, with British military support) was technically a foreign country, where the Company was bound to pay *batta* once on account of distance and once more for the extra expense of field service.[2]

The consequence of these reductions was much the same as it had been in Madras fifteen years earlier, but on a larger scale. Although the field officers (i.e. majors and above), most of whom had obtained their promotion to field rank through Clive's recent re-organisation, were thereby sufficiently well paid to accept the loss of *batta* without complaint, the captains and subalterns were not. When their initial letters of remonstrance were rejected, they made, in all three brigades, agreements to resign their commissions simultaneously unless the old rates of *batta* were restored. Those who refused were threatened with permanent ostracism by their fellows. Articles were drawn up, with the subscribing officers undertaking to contribute funds to buy commissions in the British Army for any Company's officer whose resignation was accepted, or who was otherwise victimised for joining the combination. A large number of civil servants agreed to support this fund, as they had a grudge against Clive for his insistence that they should, as ordered by the Directors, sign a covenant not to accept presents from any person in India, so putting an end to the lavish subventions from Indian princes and their agents by which many a 'nabob's' fortune had been made.

Just as had been the case in Madras, the combination collapsed in the face of government determination. Few officers were prepared to press matters to extremes. Those in the 3rd Brigade at Bankipur never actually sent in their commissions and those in the other two continued doing duty as volunteers while they waited for a government response to their action. At Monghyr, where the rank and file of the European battalion fell in ready to support their officers, the officers declined to join them, and the authorities paraded sepoy battalions under Indian officers with every intention of firing on the Europeans if need be. The idea of a fund to compensate anyone victimised collapsed when Clive threatened to give the Secretary at War the names of any officers dismissed for insubordination, so ensuring that they would not be permitted to buy a commission in the British Army, where, as he pointed out, they would in any case suffer a net loss of income.

Meanwhile he asked the Madras and Bombay Councils to send him every officer and cadet they could spare (to replace Bengal officers who might resign), and European troops to counter any disaffection among the Bengal European soldiers. Private letters from Bengal officers to their colleagues in Madras were censored. Emergency commissions were offered to civil servants (only two accepted), and consideration was given to promoting sergeants and corporals. In the end a few scapegoats were court-martialled and cashiered, though nearly all of these were eventually reinstated, among them Colonel Sir Robert Fletcher, commander of the 1st Brigade at Monghyr, whose previous distinguished services did not save him from the charge of complicity because he had not reported all he knew of his officers' intentions. Those who had resigned their commissions had them restored, but as new appointments, thus placing them in seniority below those who had not resigned or who had come from Madras in response to Clive's appeal. The Company's officers thereafter were required to give an undertaking to serve for a minimum of three years and not to resign without giving a year's notice. This enabled the authorities to counter any future revival of the officers' claim that immediately upon resigning they ceased to be under military law, and could not be charged with failure to obey orders.[3]

In Southern India, the Madras Presidency embarked upon a war against Haydar Ali of Mysore. At first regarded by the English and the country rulers as something of an upstart, Haydar had risen in eleven years from the position of Commander-in-Chief of the army of the Raja of Mysore to being by 1766 the *de facto* ruler of the entire state. The Madras Council was at first disposed to a policy of appeasement, on the principle that he might prove a useful counterpoise to the power of the Marathas, then beginning to recover from their defeat at Panipat. Then, fearing that his growing strength and ambition would lead him to threaten the Company's protegé Muhammad Ali, Nawab of Arcot, the Madras Council in November 1766 formed an alliance with the Nizam, who had, for his part, formed an alliance with the Marathas to secure Haydar Ali's downfall. All three allies then marched against Mysore early in 1767, but Haydar Ali delayed the progress of the Marathas by a scorched earth policy and then bought them off with 35 lakhs of rupees. The Nizam then quite literally transferred his army from the British camp to that of Haydar Ali, in the anticipation that if the British were defeated in the field he could recover the Northern Sarkars which the Mughal Emperor Shah Alam had granted to the Company. The Madras Army, commanded by Colonel Joseph Smith, defeated the combined forces of Haydar Ali and the Nizam at the battle of Trinamalai (26 September 1767). This had the effect of returning the Nizam to his alliance with the British and obtaining from Haydar an offer to make peace. His offer was rejected by the Madras Council, to which the Nizam had offered the *diwani* or civil government of all Mysore (which was not in his power to give). Haydar renewed the war and, displaying all the able generalship which had made him such a feared opponent, made short work of the scattered British garrisons and other detachments. Smith, with the main force, was hampered by the presence of Nawab Muhammad Ali, whose troops were merely an added drain on the resources of the devastated countryside of which he was the nominal ruler, and by two members of Council (appointed by their colleagues as 'field-deputies'), who constantly interfered with his dispositions and questioned his orders. By February 1768, however, Smith had forced Haydar's army to retreat, but Haydar himself, with 6,000 horsemen, slipped away to re-appear outside the walls of Fort St George. The Madras government, seeing no end to a war which had ruined the revenues and incurred military expenditure while destroying the means of paying for it, was happy to accept Haydar's proposals for peace, a mutual restitution of conquests and prisoners, and an agreement that each party would, in return for payment at fixed rates, send troops to support the other if it were the subject of aggression.[4]

The Madras government's conduct of this campaign drew much criticism. The Directors disapproved of the appointment of field-deputies: 'Our opinion is, that when the Company has made choice of a proper person to be a Commander-in-Chief, all trust and confidence should be reposed in him to direct the plans and operations of the campaign.'[5] Many of Smith's problems had arisen from lack of supplies and rations for his men. The Madras Council blamed the Nawab for failing to supply them, but it emerged that the councillors had since 1761 given themselves the contracts for army supply as a means of supplementing their income, and that no other tenders had been invited. 'We were yet much more astonished,' continued the Directors, 'that of all the Members of our Council not one had honour or virtue enough to reject a proposal which was as wholly incompatible with their duty as it was unworthy their character and station to accept.'

While the Company's servants and shareholders grew rich, the Company grew poor. By becoming a territorial power it had incurred the burden of all the defence and other public expenditure inseparable from the business of a state. The war against Mysore had ruined Madras and in 1770 a terrible famine along the lower Ganges plain had the same effect on Bengal. The Directors were obliged to ask financial aid from the British government. This was granted, but only on terms giving the Cabinet more effective power over the Company's revenue, civil, and military affairs. This power was expressed in Lord North's 'Regulating Act' of 1773.[6] The Act replaced the Company's Governor of Fort William and his large council of ten or more, by a Governor-General and four councillors, initially nominated by the Crown, but still controlled by the Court of Directors. This Court was itself reformed by the same Act to give it a greater element of continuity, with a quarter of its members in future to be elected each year, and holding office for four years instead of all being elected for one year only. The Governor-General in Council was also given control over the power of the Madras and Bombay Governments to engage in hostilities with country powers, except where grave danger would result from waiting for instructions.

In 1774, acting before the new restrictions upon their powers to wage war could come into force, the Government of Bombay became involved in the struggle over the disputed succession to the Peshwa, Narayan Rao, the fore-most of the Maratha princes. Anticipating benefits similar to those which had been gained by their colleagues in Bengal and Madras from similar inter-ventions in Indian politics, the Bombay government agreed to support Raghunath Rao, uncle of the late (murdered) Peshwa, against a Regency ruling in the name of Narayan Rao's posthumous infant son. A force of some 2,500 men, consisting of four European companies and four sepoy battalions from the Bombay Army, and two companies of European grenadiers and a sepoy battalion lent by Madras, marched towards Poona (Pune), the Peshwa's capital. A hard-fought battle at Aras on 18 May 1775, in which Raghunath Rao's contingent proved a useless rabble while the Maratha cavalry and elephants destroyed the Madras grenadiers, was eventually won by the Com-pany's troops. Raghunath thereupon assigned control of several valuable areas to the British, including the former Portuguese holdings at Bassein and Salsette. At this point orders came from the new Governor-General in Bengal disavowing the alliance with Raghunath and ordering a suspension of hostilities.[7]

The new Governor-General was the former Governor of Bengal, Warren Hastings, whose anxiety to guard against the renascent power of the Marathas had involved the Company in the Rohilla War of February-April 1774. Hastings had a distinguished record as a Bengal civil servant, having fought at Plassey as a volunteer and gained, in the subsequent decade, a reputation for incorruptibility. In 1773 he discontinued the payment of revenues from Bengal to the Emperor Shah Alam, on the grounds that the latter was passing the money on to the Marathas in return for their military support. While this was true enough, Shah Alam was entitled to his share of the revenue and to do with it as he chose. In this instance he used it to secure the ejection from Delhi of a Rohilla chieftain who had been installed there by Ahmad Shah after the battle of Panipat in 1761. The Rohillas, descendants of earlier Afghan military adventurers, had given their name to the neighbouring region, Rohilkhand, where they had obtained extensive grants from the Mughals. The Marathas, after recovering Delhi for Shah Alam, prepared to march into Rohilkhand. The Rohillas asked the Nawab of Awadh for aid, which he agreed to provide at a price but when the Marathas, distracted by the succession to the Peshwaship, did not invade, the Rohillas refused to pay. The Nawab, long desirous of adding Rohilkhand to his own territories, made this a *casus belli*. In August 1773 he met Hastings at Benares and concluded a treaty of friendship which placed one of the Bengal Army's three brigades at his disposal in return for Rs 210,000 monthly. In consequence of this arrangement, which transferred some 30 per cent of Bengal's defence budget to that of Awadh, the brigade marched with the Nawab's army into Rohilkhand and secured a quick victory over their ill-organised opponents. Awadh, strengthened by the expropriation of the Rohillas and safeguarded by its contingent of the Bengal Army, became a strong buffer state against the Marathas and remained a loyal ally of the Company. The only protest in the Bengal Council came from the Commander-in-Chief, Brigadier General Sir Robert Barker, who had a number of personal grudges against Hastings. What, he asked, if the Emperor, slighted by these proceedings, withdrew the *sanads* by which the Company held its rights in India? Hastings, speaking more like a soldier than a civilian, replied that it was not *sanads* but the sword which had given the British the dominion of Bengal, and which alone would maintain it.[8]

Most members of the new Governor-General's Council then being set up by the Regulating Act took a different view of the episode. The new Commander-in-Chief of Bengal, and thus of all the Company's forces in India, Lieutenant General Sir John Clavering, a British Army officer, was named in the Act as successor to the Governor-Generalship if Hastings died or resigned. The other three Councillors were Philip Francis, an English politician with his own designs on the Governor-Generalship, Colonel the Honourable George Monson, who had been Coote's second-in-command at

Pondicherry, and Richard Barwell, one of the Company's civil servants. The three newcomers saw their duty as the extirpation of misgovernment and oppression by the Company's servants, and formed the view, later to be shared by the Directors, that the campaign against the Rohillas, with whom the Company had no quarrel, was an example of both. They regularly out-voted Hastings in Council until Monson's death in September 1776, after which Hastings was able to use his casting vote. Prior to this Hastings had, in frustration, declared he would resign if the position remained unchanged. The Directors took this as a resignation and when the news reached Calcutta in June 1777, Clavering claimed the Governor-Generalship. Hastings denied he had resigned, and was supported by the Judges of the Supreme Court which the Regulating Act had set up at Calcutta. He and Barwell then voted Clavering's positions as C-in-C and Second in Council to be null and void but were, in their turn, over-ruled by the Supreme Court. Clavering's death on 30 August 1777 brought this particular battle to an end and he was replaced by General Sir Eyre Coote, the victor of Wandewash.[9]

In August 1773 the Madras Government sent its troops, led by Major General Joseph Smith, against the Raja of Tanjore, who was in dispute with its ally, the Nawab Muhammad Ali. Tanjore was stormed on 17 September 1773, the raja was made prisoner, and his territories were appropriated by the Nawab. In March 1774 news of this reached the Directors, who did not discuss the question until after the last ships of the season sailed for India three weeks later. Thus it was not until December 1775 that Lord Pigot (who had last been Governor of Madras twelve years earlier) arrived with orders to take over from the existing Governor, reprimand his Council, and restore the raja. He found that his Commander-in-Chief was Sir Robert Fletcher, who had appealed successfully against dismissal following the mutiny of the Bengal officers in 1766 and had been appointed C-in-C Madras in 1772. There he had challenged the authority of the Governor as the Commander-in-Chief of Fort St George, and returned home to resume his seat as a Member of Parliament before again being sent to Madras in succession to Major General Joseph Smith.

Pigot's action in restoring the raja gained him the enmity of most of the Madras Council. He nominated one of his own supporters to be Resident at Tanjore, but Fletcher considered that his own second in command, Colonel Stuart, would be a better choice. Moreover, the appointment could then be combined with that of commander of the large garrison there, which the raja had agreed to accept and pay for, as the price of his restoration. The majority voted against Pigot, who then refused to sign the orders requiring the exist-ing commandant at Tanjore, Colonel Harper, to hand over to Stuart. The majority ordered the Council's secretary to sign them in the Governor's name. Pigot then charged two of the majority with subversion, thus preventing them from voting until their case was heard, and thereby gaining control of the Council by his own party. The original majority called upon the civil and military officers of the Presidency to obey the Council as previously constituted. Pigot ordered Fletcher's arrest for failing to obey him, as the Governor. Stuart, acting as C-in-C after Fletcher had developed a fever, then ordered his Adjutant General to arrest Pigot. Pigot appealed to Admiral Sir Edward Hughes, commanding a Royal Naval squadron then off Madras, but the majority refused Hughes's orders to give him safe conduct to the flagship. Pigot declined the compromise offer of a passage on board an East Indiaman and remained under house arrest.[10]

Although Hastings and his Council, in a rare unanimity, supported the Madras majority, the Court of Directors insisted that the office of the Governor must be respected. They ordered the release and restoration of Pigot, to be followed by his immediate recall, and that of his entire Council, to London for an investigation, and by the court martial of the military officers involved. By the time the orders reached Madras both Pigot and Fletcher had died. Those who had formed the majority of the Council were eventually convicted and fined heavily, but Stuart (by then a brigadier general) and the remaining officers successfully pleaded that they had been obeying the orders of the civil government of the day. The Madras command meanwhile devolved first upon Colonel Ross Lang of the Company's service, and then, in February 1778, Major General Hector Munro, the victor of Baksar. At the same time, Sir Thomas Rumbold, a Madras civil servant who had begun his career as an officer in the Madras Army and had fought as a captain at Plassey, arrived from England to replace Pigot.

A few months later the outbreak of a new war between the British and French governments put the armies of all three Presidencies in India into the field. Pondicherry, restored to France after the Seven Years War, fell to the Madras Army on 8 October 1778 after a month's siege. In June 1780 Haydar Ali of Mysore invaded the Carnatic with 70,000 men, including sepoy battalions led by French officers. Within a month he was raiding the suburbs of Madras and had gained possession of almost every fort in the country. Those garrisoned by the British had been so ill provisioned by the civil authorities as to be incapable of resistance, and the gates of those held by the Nawab's own officers were in the Mughal tradition 'opened with a golden key', i.e. by bribing the commandant. The space of twenty-one days during August and September 1780 saw a reduction of British military prestige in India to a level lower than it had been since before Plassey. The war continued for another four years. In October 1780 Hastings sent Sir Eyre Coote, with every rupee and soldier he could spare, to take over operations in Madras. Hampered by lack of transport and supplies, Coote relieved the few garrisons still holding out but undertook no major operations until the summer of 1781, when he gained a victory over Haydar at Porto Novo. Haydar, supported by a French brigade which disembarked in the Carnatic in March 1782, was able to keep the field with a large army, which included sepoys captured or deserted from the armies of Nawab Muhammad Ali and his British allies. Coote, quarrelling with the new Governor of Madras, Lord Macartney, returned to Bengal in September 1782 to reassert his position as C-in-C there. Haydar, despairing of eventual success in a war where, despite his continued victories on land, the power of the British at sea enabled them to continue the struggle, fell back from the Carnatic to consolidate his hold on the west coast. Five naval engagements fought between the squadrons of Sir Edward Hughes and the French Admiral de Suffren during 1782, had, in fact, left British control of Indian seas in the balance, and the arrival of reinforcements for the French army continued to distract the Madras Government. Haydar died of blood poisoning in December 1782. Coote died in April 1783, suffering a stroke while his ship was pursued by two French men-of-war as he sailed back to resume command in Madras.[11]

On the British side, the war had been conducted in an atmosphere of continual constitutional crises. Lord Macartney, an ambitious Irish peer with a creditable record in British public life, was the first Governor of an Indian Presidency not to have risen from the Company's service. He took full advantage of the provisions of the Regulating Act which allowed the minor presidencies to make war independently of the Governor-General in Bengal in response to urgent local dangers. Coote, as C-in-C, India, took a seat in the Madras Council when he was actually in the presidency but, while Macartney argued that he should be bound by the views of the majority in Council, Coote took the view that, in the conduct of the war, he spoke as a member of the Supreme Government in Bengal.[12] Coote also claimed that the Madras Government's failure to provide him with the pack oxen and supplies he considered necessary prevented him from making any decisive moves against Haydar Ali.[13] Macartney replied that Coote seemed to consider that the Governor had no other part to play in the conduct of the war than to be a 'bullock agent' and openly expressed his disappointment that an army so expensively appointed had achieved so little.[14] He also mounted minor expeditions (including one led by the displaced Sir Hector Munro) without consulting Coote, while the latter was absent in the field with his main force. Coote, on his final visit to Calcutta, obtained from Hastings powers to act virtually as the military dictator of Madras, but died before the issue could be tested.

With Coote dead and Munro having returned to Europe, command in Madras passed to Major General Stuart, the same officer who had arrested Lord Pigot. He had, since then, resumed his military duties and had lost a leg in the war against Haydar Ali. Like Coote, he maintained that the C-in-C was, in all military matters, the sole competent authority. He went even further, by arguing that, as his commission was in the British Army rather than the Company's Army, he was, at least in his command of the British troops in Madras, not obliged to comply with the directions of the Company's civil authorities.[15]

Stuart continued to exasperate Macartney, who on 17 September 1783 used his own powers as Governor to dismiss him from the Company's service on the grounds of disobedience. This had the effect of reducing him to his substantive position as an officer on the British half-pay list, since he held the rank of major general only by virtue of his employment as C-in-C of the Company's Madras Army. He was thus disqualified from exercising authority over either British or Company's troops and Major General Sir John Burgoyne, the next senior officer of the British Army then in Madras, was ordered by Macartney to take over command of the British troops. Burgoyne, however, stated that he considered himself still under Stuart's orders, whereupon Macartney sent a Company's officer with a party of sepoys to arrest Stuart and so physically prevent him from giving any orders at all.[16] At the same time he promoted Colonel Ross Lang of the Madras Army to be lieutenant general and commander of the Company's forces. Burgoyne assumed command of the British troops but, after countermanding orders issued by Macartney, was himself arrested on 31 December 1783, and replaced by Major General Campbell, the next senior British officer. There matters rested until May 1785, when a British Army officer, Lieutenant General Sir John Dalling, arrived with authority to command all the troops in Madras. Lang retired with a special pension and Burgoyne, acquitted by court martial, was recalled to Europe.[17] Macartney resigned in June 1785 and, on returning to London, was provoked into a duel and wounded by Stuart.[18] Hastings, who had earlier seriously considered suspending Macartney, a move which Stuart would have been only too happy to execute, himself resigned in February 1785.

The British had not only to deal with questions of civil-military relations, but with relations between the British and the Company's Armies. After Stuart's arrest, the officers of British regiments in Madras refused to admit that Lang had authority over them in law and declared that, though they would follow his operational orders, they would do so as volunteers. The Company's officers, on their part, protested at the lavish grant to British Army officers of brevet ranks (i.e. ranks higher than those permitted by the established strength of the Army, to permit the holder to exercise higher powers of command). This had taken place during the Seven Years War, but the number of British troops in India, and the duration and scale of operations, had been much smaller than they were in the 1780s and the grievance was not so greatly felt. In 1784 a petition by Madras officers to the Court of Directors pointed out that four British Army colonels had become brevet major generals, seven lieutenant colonels had become brevet colonels, six majors and three captains had become brevet lieutenant colonels and one captain a brevet major, whereas the Company's Madras establishment was only one major general, two colonels, four lieutenant colonels, and four majors of infantry (there was also one major of artillery).[19] This meant that, whether in the field or garrison, almost all the commands were taken, by virtue of their military seniority, by British Army officers who had limited knowledge of Indian conditions. Their regimental duties were left to be performed by their junior officers, but even the most junior British army officer had seniority over the longest-serving Company's officer of the same rank. Colonel Fullerton of the 98th, who commanded in 1783–84 what was probably the most successful expedition in the war against Tipu, and who stood as Macartney's second in his duel with Stuart, recorded that the Madras officers had far more experience of independent command than their British equivalents, and were 'habituated to act in emergency with a facility that few subordinate officers in Europe ever have a prospect of acquiring'.[20]

The Company's officers, promoted in turn according to their seniority within the Army, gained wide experience as they moved from post to post, so that when, usually after many years, they reached the rank of captain, they were fully competent in their profession. Lang, in his support for their petition, quoted the case of a well-qualified captain with seventeen years' service in the Company's Army being obliged to serve under the orders of a newly arrived British captain of twenty-six months' service. An even more extreme case was that of a British Army lieutenant aged fourteen, who took command of a picquet consisting mostly of sepoys whose own officer had been a subaltern for fourteen years.[21] A similar petition, signed by 132 Bengal Army officers, and endorsed by Hastings in October 1783 protested that, notwithstanding the extent to which their service had grown into a large, regular, standing army, they were still obliged to defer to those of the same rank in the British service. They asked the Directors not to allow officers who had spent their lives in the Company's service to be subordinated to young British Army officers 'many of whom have not been so long in Existence as the Dates of our Commissions'.[22] It was not until 1788, however, that some action was taken to remedy this grievance and, even then, only in connection with a quite separate constitutional issue.

Ten years of war had revealed the weaknesses of North's Regulating Act. It had required the Court of Directors to lay before the British government all correspondence with India dealing with foreign affairs, but provided no formal machinery whereby the government could control the orders which the Directors sent to their servants in India. It left the Governor-General, and the Governors of the minor presidencies at the mercy of the majorities in their own Councils, and left the British military, sent to India in support of British foreign policy, unclear of their exact constitutional position. The expansion of European power meant that British foreign policy in India could no longer be separated from that in the rest of the world. Moreover, in an age when patriotic Englishmen in America and patriotic Irishmen nearer home had defied in arms the authority of the British Government, there was some anxiety that yet another body of British citizens should be maintaining regular armies, fortifications and warships, not under the Crown's control. Charles James Fox, Lord North's ally in the House of Commons, introduced a bill in 1783 to remedy this situation by giving to the government of the day the right to appoint all civil and military officers in British India. The prospect of any government having the patronage of India at its disposal, so that it could thereby secure so much support in the House of Commons as to maintain itself in power indefinitely, provoked the wrath of George III, who announced that anyone who voted for it would no longer be considered the King's friend. The Fox-North coalition fell and William Pitt the Younger came to power, with the Indian question in urgent need of a solution.[23]

Pitt's India Act, carried in 1784, established the constitutional framework by which British India would be governed for the next seventy-four years.[24] The most important feature was the establishment of a Board of Commissioners for the Control of India, presided over by a Secretary of State, who soon became for all practical purposes its sole member. The three senior members of the Court of Directors were formed into a Committee of Secrecy, which alone dealt with the Board and relayed its orders in all matters of civil and military government of India. The patronage of India, including even the right to appoint and recall a Governor-General, remained with the Court of all twenty-four Directors, although in practice, because the Act gave it a veto over these offices, the Board nominated the Governor-General, Governors and C-in-Cs. The number of members of the three Presidential Councils in India was reduced to four, composed of the Governor-General or Governor, the local C-in-C, and two others. The C-in-C, India, when in Madras or Bombay was to take the local C-in-C's place in Council with the local C-in-C then allowed to sit but not vote. C-in-Cs were not to succeed a Governor-General or Governor without express orders from the Court of Directors. At the other extreme, the Act provided that no cadets should be appointed to the Company's Army under the age of fifteen or over that of twenty-two (or twenty-five if they had previously served at least a year in the British Army).

While the civil servant who had saved British India returned home to face impeachment, the general who had lost America was sent to govern British India. Finding a successor for Warren Hastings was not easy for the Directors. The appointment was eventually accepted by Lieutenant General

Lord Cornwallis who needed neither a title nor a fortune and whose surrender at Yorktown was blamed upon his superiors. At his insistence, amend-
ing acts were passed enabling him to overrule his Council in emergency, and
to hold the office of C-in-C India as well as that of Governor-General.
Cornwallis thus took over these two posts in September 1786.

The same principle of combining the posts of Governor and C-in-C was
applied at Bombay, where Major General William Medows was appointed in
1787, and at Madras, where he went on to hold the same two offices between
1790 and 1792. His replacement at Bombay by Major General Sir Robert
Abercromby placed all three presidencies for a time in the hands of military
men.

The new Board of Control made the reorganisation of the military in India
one of its first concerns. Henry Dundas, Pitt's tireless ally throughout his
long ministry, was the architect of the Cabinet's Indian policy and headed the
Board from its inception. He decided that in future there would be a
contingent of the British Army stationed in India at all times, not only for the
duration of hostilities with a rival European power. They therefore pressed
for the transfer of the Company's European troops to the British Army and
the grant of royal commissions to officers who remained with the sepoys.
Cornwallis felt that fair consideration should be given to the officers.[25]
Indeed he objected throughout his entire Indian career to the Directors'
policy of paying low salaries to their civil and military servants alike on the
principle that they would make a good living out of the many opportunities,
honest or otherwise, of profiting from their service in India, at least if they
survived the effects of the climate and tropical disease. Probably the greatest
achievement of his Indian administration was to secure an honest civil service
by paying its officials so well that they did not need to be dishonest. Concerning the military officers, he wrote to the Duke of York on 10 November 1786:
'they have no head to look up to; the promotion of rank has always gone by
seniority; and the lucrative commands have been given to those who have had
interest' (i.e. influence). 'Consequently there has been no spur to merit. The
Company's officers have no regiments or governments to look forward to . . .
If they cannot save some money, they must go home without rank or pay,
condemned to disease or beggary. Under these circumstances, the most rigid
general must relax a little and suffer practices that are in some degree
repugnant to the nice feelings of a soldier.'[26] He recommended to Dundas
that the Company's officers should take rank with those of the British Army
according to the date of their respective commissions within each rank. Their
transfer to the British Army would, he felt, weaken the control over them of
the Company's local governments in India.

Dundas continued to advocate the replacement of the Company's Europeans by British regiments.[27] In October 1787 he used the renewed tension

between Britain and France as the occasion for informing the Directors that four new British regiments were to be raised and sent to India. Their officers were to be drawn equally from the British half-pay and the Company's redundant officers who would thus regain employment in their profession and cease to be an unprofitable charge on official funds. Only one of the four new lieutenant colonels, however, was to be a former Company's officer, and even that would be in a regiment whose colonel, unlike most regimental colonels, would go with it in command. The Directors protested that this would adversely affect the interests of their own officers, of whom 600 were at the time surplus to establishment while the 1,800 in post stood to find themselves junior to officers of the new British regiments, eighty-six of them their own former comrades. The grievances sent home in the officers' petitions of 1783 were alluded to, and a delegation of the Company's officers then on leave in England waited upon the Court of Directors to press their case.

As the international crisis waned, the Directors urged Dundas to cancel the orders for the new regiments, and allow the Company to recruit its own Europeans instead. When the Board of Control refused to bargain, the Directors voted against accepting the troops on their ships or paying them from Indian revenues.[28] Prior to 1781 the expenses of maintaining British troops in India had been borne by the British government, as they were sent there in furtherance of British foreign policy rather than the Company's interests. In 1781 it had been enacted that the Company would pay two lakhs of rupees per regiment per annum, but only for troops sent at the Company's request. The ministers responded with the Declaratory Act of February 1788[29] which gave authority to the Board of Control to order troops to India at the Company's expense irrespective of the wishes of the Court of Directors. Great opposition was encountered, however, even among the government's supporters, for fear partly of an extension of ministerial patronage and partly of a tyrannical government raising troops from Indian revenues who could be used against the hard-won rights and liberties of Englishmen. Accordingly, provisions were added limiting the number of European troops that could be maintained in India to 8,045 from the British Army and 12,200 from the Company's Army. This had the effect of negating all the previous proposals of replacing the latter by the former.

The government went some way to redressing the grievance over relative seniority in 1788. Thereafter, all the Company's officers were granted commissions by their Commanders-in-Chief giving them powers of command over British troops, in the East Indies only, and solely while in the service of the Company, with seniority according to the date of their commission from the Governor-General or Governors of Bengal, Madras and Bombay respectively, which gave them their power of command over the Company's troops. All brevets held by British Army officers in India were cancelled, and no more granted, though British officers who had attained their substantive rank before the end of hostilities in 1783 were allowed to retain their seniority over all Company's officers of the same rank. These concessions did little, however, to address the problems caused by the rapidity of promotion in the British Army permitted by the purchase system (and indeed thought to be one of its advantages, both for the officers and the Army) compared with the slowness of that in any service where it depended upon seniority. Moreover, there were relatively few posts of field rank in the Company's service, as far the greater part of its 112,000-strong Army consisted of sepoy battalions, which were commanded by captains. A newly promoted captain in command of a sepoy battalion was still junior to an equally newly promoted captain in command of a British company, irrespective of their individual length of service. Nevertheless, few wished to give up the actuality, or hope, of commanding a sepoy battalion, with all the military prestige and financial allowances that went with it, in order to become a junior captain in a junior British regiment and, when the four new regiments were eventually formed, they were officered mostly from the British half-pay (as Cornwallis had forecast would be the case).

Consideration of Indian army reform was postponed until Cornwallis returned to England in February 1794. He had sailed from Calcutta six months earlier, and was succeeded as Governor-General by Sir John Shore, a Company's civil servant, and as C-in-C by Major General Sir Robert Abercromby, a British Army officer previously C-in-C at Bombay. In September 1794 Cornwallis was formally requested by Dundas to produce a plan for re-organising the army in India such as would improve the security of the British possessions there, and would also bring to an end the friction between the King's and the Company's troops, and between the Company's own three presidential armies. His plan, submitted to the Board of Control in November 1794, recommended that all the Company's troops, native as well as European, should be transferred to the King's service, but the native troops should form a separate Indian Army. European troops and their officers would simply become part of the British Army and, on doing so, conform to its existing rules for commissions and promotion. Officers of the Indian Army would hold the King's commission and rise by seniority within their regiment to the rank of major and thereafter, within their arm and presidency, by seniority as before. The ninety-five battalions of sepoys were to be reduced to eighty. The remaining units were to be formed into forty regiments each of two battalions. Each regiment would be commanded by a colonel and each battalion by a lieutenant colonel, as in the British Army. The Company's officers were to opt to join either the British or Indian Armies and thereafter no exchanges would be permitted. Those who wished subsequently to sell their commission would be allowed to do so. Furloughs of up to three years would be granted without loss of pay and officers could retire on full pay of their rank after six years' service as an ensign and on a scale proportionate to rank up to twenty-six years for lieutenant-colonels. Any brevet promotion which had been granted to all officers of the King's Army would be matched by similar grants to officers of the Company's Armies. To balance this, the double *batta* paid in Bengal would be abolished, as would be various other lucrative emoluments. Allowances for field service were to be standardised throughout the three Presidencies.

Although this plan remedied many long-standing grievances, the time taken to prepare it, and the time it took for correspondence to pass between London and India, had an unsettling effect. Before leaving India, Cornwallis had circulated many of his ideas among the officers of the Madras Army.[30] When the officers of the Bengal Army, on whom they bore most hardly, learned of them from their Madras comrades, there was an immediate outcry. Committees were formed, petitions drawn up, and agents were sent to lay their case before the Directors. The officers of all three Presidencies were opposed to promotion by regimental instead of Army seniority, and to the introduction of British Army officers into the European regiments (which would have been the consequence of absorbing these units into the British Army). They insisted on the same rank being attached to the same level of command in the Indian as in the British service before any transfer from the Company to the Crown, and on the Indian Army, including its European element, remaining separate from the British Army.[31]

A pamphlet published by the Bengal officers early in 1794 condemned Cornwallis's proposals and explained that, because of the pay of the low rank to which they were restricted, the Company's officers were dependent upon the various allowances he proposed to abolish. They argued that whereas in the eighty regular infantry battalions of the British Army (36,540 bayonets), there was one officer for every fourteen soldiers and a general for every 430, in the Company's ninety-five battalions of infantry (59,280 bayonets) there were no generals, and only one officer (at least in Bengal) for every forty-eight sepoys. The weakness of this particular argument was that the Company's units also had a full complement of Indian officers in each company, but this was not remarked upon by either side in the dispute at the time. Unauthorised meetings and assemblies of officers continued in the Bengal Army with increasing indignation on both sides throughout 1794 and 1795, and the wilder spirits even talked of arresting Shore and Abercromby and ordering their own men to oppose movements by British troops. Shore was sufficiently concerned to order the admiral commanding the East Indies squadron to stand by to bring troops from Madras, and even contemplated the use of sepoys, and European mercenaries from the armies of friendly country powers. In January 1795, however, moderate opinion re-asserted itself, partly in response to Abercromby's assurances that something would be done to meet any legitimate grievances.[32]

Protracted discussions in London had resulted in significant changes to Cornwallis's original scheme. The Directors were initially cool towards their officers' complaints. Dundas was sufficiently concerned at reports of disaffection and agitation to meet a committee of officers and to receive their formal objections to Cornwallis's plan, much to the latter's disgust. In January 1795 the Directors formally notified the Board of Control that they would on no account consent to the transfer of their Army to the King's service.[33] The ministers, distracted by the spread of revolutionary ideas at home and abroad, and by the familiar tale of a British army being defeated in the Low Countries, felt the time was inopportune to force the issue. In April it became clear that they could not, in any case, command a majority in Parliament for the addition of 60,000 regular soldiers to those at the disposal of the Crown, for the very same reason that had brought them to power twelve years earlier. The patronage of India could not be entrusted to party politicians. Accordingly, when in January 1796 orders for army reform were eventually sent to India, they contained nothing about amalgamating the European units with the British Army, or transferring the sepoy units to the Crown. The main reform was the re-organisation of the infantry into forty regiments, each of two battalions, together with new provisions for paid furlough, pensions and promotion to general officer rank.[34]

The accompanying orders reducing *batta* and other allowances and introducing promotion by seniority within the new regiments provoked a storm of protest in Bengal, even from the former moderates. Once again petitions and protests were drawn up. The reduction in officers' allowances without fully compensating increases in the level of their rank was compared unfavourably with the lavish increases by which Cornwallis had bought out the corrupt practices of the Indian civil service. The introduction of promotion to field rank by regimental seniority, and to subsequent command by selection, was condemned on the grounds that this would allow promotion to be affected by chance (if casualties occurred more frequently in one regiment or another) or favouritism (if officers were selected on the subjective grounds of supposed merit rather than the objective ones of length of service, for which all had contracted on accepting their commissions).

Shore and Abercromby together formed the view that there was nothing to be gained by driving the Bengal officers into a refusal to obey orders. While any insurrection would have easily been put down, for the officers of Madras and Bombay, while content to benefit from any concession secured by those of Bengal, were not willing to join them in a mutiny, the very possibility was enough to weaken the efficiency and loyalty of the Bengal sepoys and, in turn, the security of British possessions in India. Moreover, with the war against

France continuing to go ill for the British, an efficient Bengal Army led by well-motivated officers was infinitely more useful than one reduced to inefficiency by the mass resignation of its officers, or even their departure to a rival Indian employer. Accordingly in May 1796 Shore and Abercromby decided to hold up the introduction of regimental promotion and, while complying with the letter of their orders to end the specified allowances, followed the precedent set by the Madras Government in paying separate new allowances equal to those which were discontinued.

Once again the ministers turned to Cornwallis. After being appointed Governor-General for a second tour in February 1797, he again put forward his old proposals for bringing the Company's European units into the British Army, for regimental promotion, and for filling commands by nomination rather than seniority. With Dundas's approval, he demanded that his instructions from the Directors who were, constitutionally, his employers, should give him absolute power to re-organise their Army as he saw fit.[35] When the Board of Control formally supported him, the Directors responded by calling a meeting of the Court of Proprietors on 5 May 1797. This voted against giving Cornwallis the instructions he wanted. Once again disasters nearer home, including mutinies in the Navy, distracted the Cabinet from taking issue with the Company and in August Cornwallis resigned, going to Ireland in 1798 to deal with the rebellion which had broken out there.[36]

The only part of his Indian Army reforms to be implemented against the wishes of the local officers was the creation of the new regiments and the introduction of regimental promotion. This meant the separation of the European from the Native line in the infantry, though not in the other arms, as there was no European cavalry in the Company's service, and all gunners, European or Native, continued to belong to their respective single regiments of artillery at each Presidency. Infantry officers permanently posted to a native regiment feared a loss of prestige, while those remaining in a European regiment feared a loss of command opportunities, with their chances of extra income and greater distinction. The introduction of retirement pensions, and the prospect of promotion offered by the increased number and rank of the officers authorised for the new regiments, made this reform the easier to accept. For every regiment of two battalions, each of ten companies, there was a colonel, two lieutenant colonels, two majors, seven captains and a captain-lieutenant, twenty-two lieutenants and ten ensigns. This meant that each battalion had two field officers, four captains and sixteen subalterns, in place of the one captain and eight subalterns previously allowed.

The extra British officers were also expected to make the sepoy battalions more combat-worthy as, in the campaigns against Mysore and the Marathas, sepoys were thought to have performed better when led by British rather than native company officers. Insofar as there was an average qualitative superiority, the British derived it partly from at least a notional study of their profession (easier for those with a Western education than for those without), partly from their identification with the regime for which they were fighting (whereas the native officer had no vested interest other than his pay and its arrears) and partly because promotion by seniority, although it prevented corruption, meant that promotion was just as slow for the native as for the British officer. In a society where men grew, and felt, old more quickly than in Europe, a sepoy was likely to be a grandfather sooner than becoming a subedar. Those who still retained their physical and mental energy were often regarded with suspicion. The native commandants of battalions had been abolished in 1781 on the grounds that, if feeble they were useless, and if influential they might exert their influence against their British paymasters. The addition of so many more British company officers left the native officers (one subedar and one jemadar per company) with nothing to command. Although in battle they remained as courageous as anybody else, in barracks they became more like welfare officers or trade union officials, mediating between the troops and British officers who became, paradoxically, the more remote as they became more numerous.

A series of wars between 1799 and 1805 left the British masters of Mysore, where Haydar's son Tipu Sultan fell fighting to the last, and victorious over the Marathas. Cornwallis was again sent out as Governor-General and C-in-C, but died soon after arrival in India. His successor, Sir George Barlow, the last civil servant to become Governor-General under the Company's rule, faithfully implemented the Court's instructions to make peace and reduce defence expenditure.

In Madras the new local C-in-C, Sir John Cradock, decided that, with the coming of peace, it was time to smarten up his Army. Regulations were published banning the personal ornaments and coloured marks upon their foreheads which sepoys had customarily worn in military as in civil life, banning the beards which to many was an outward sign of their virility, and ordering moustaches to be trimmed to a specified pattern. Worse still, with the enthusiasm which peace-time commanders so often display for military tailoring, Cradock devised a new pattern of head-dress, designed like the other changes to make his men look more like British soldiers. This had an unsettling effect on the troops. The displacement of so many princes in so short a period had revealed to everyone the true extent of British power in South Asia. Although the presence of Christian missionaries (the 'padres' as they were called by Indians, irrespective of sect) in British India was always discouraged by the East India Company, everyone knew that Christianity was a missionary religion and also that Indian rulers (such as Tipu Sultan), zealous in their own faith, had been known to order the forcible conversion of their subjects. Making men look like Christians through the adoption of the uniform of Christian soldiers was feared to be a step to making them become Christians, so facing men with a choice between pollution and ostracism on the one hand, or the loss of the economic and social benefits of military service on the other.

At Vellore (Vellur) where the survivors of Tipu's family had their residence, there was a combination of irreconcilables who saw no reason why the dynasty so recently displaced should not rise again, and of sepoys suspicious of the intentions of their British employers. In May 1806 nineteen grenadiers of the 2nd Battalion, 4th Madras Native Infantry, refused to wear the new head-dress and only submitted after two of their number received 900 lashes each. Statements obtained by the British from local spiritual leaders that the new head-dress infringed neither Muslim nor Hindu codes went unheeded. Other holy men preached resistance and it was rumoured in the bazaar that after fifty years the end of British dominion was at hand. Discipline, which Cradock's regulations had been intended to tighten, in fact began to crack. In June 1806 a sepoy, Mustafa Beg, warned his colonel that a mutiny was being planned but, as his story was referred for investigation by a board of native officers who were involved in the plot, he found himself thrown in the cells as a troublemaker. He was still there on 10 July 1806 when the mutiny broke out.

The Vellore incident differed markedly from all previous sepoy mutinies. These had all been concerned with purely military grievances, connected with arrears of pay or conditions of service. Indeed, only eight years earlier the European artillery at Madras itself had mutinied over these very questions, settled only after the authorities had hung three of the ringleaders and blown away one from a gun in the old Mughal custom. Previous action had taken the form of desertion, or seizure of government property. At Vellore, for the first time, the issue raised was one of religion. For the first time too, the return to power of an Indian regime was envisaged. Led by native officers, sepoys of the garrison opened fire with musketry and artillery on barracks where 370 men of the 67th Foot were asleep, killing or wounding nearly 200 of them. The British rushed the magazine but, finding it empty, took refuge over the main gateway, suffering more casualties, including all the surviving officers, in the process. Inside the fort, Tipu's old flag was hoisted in place of the British colours.

Sixteen miles away at Arcot news reached the commander, Colonel Rollo Gillespie, some three hours after firing started. At the head of a troop of his regiment, the 19th Light Dragoons, he reached Vellore within two hours, and climbed up a rope of buckled belts to take command of the gateway until his horse artillery arrived. Like most South Asian fortresses, Vellore had no defences to protect its gates against cannon fire. The usual procedure when a siege was anticipated, that of bricking them up, had been pre-empted by

Gillespie's rapid response. His guns shot the gates away and the cavalry rode in, trapping the mutineers who, lacking any clear leadership of their own, made little resistance. Some 400 were killed in the fort and, of the remainder who fled or surrendered, seventeen were executed after a drumhead court-martial. About 600 men who had not been taken in arms, but who had at best remained as bystanders, were dismissed. Tipu's family was removed to Calcutta. The rest of the Madras native army remained obedient to orders. Sir John Cradock and the Governor of Madras, Lord William Bentinck, were recalled. The new Governor, Sir George Barlow (whom the Board of Control had refused to confirm as Governor-General), blamed missionaries for disturbing the Army and continued to discourage their activities.[37]

In response to demands for military economies ordered by Barlow while acting Governor-General, both Bentinck and Cradock had agreed that the Madras Army's tent contract system could be abolished. This system was merely an additional allowance to commanding officers, in peace and war, for providing their regiments with tentage which was only needed, and therefore only provided, in war. Colonel John Monro, Quartermaster General of the Madras Army, on being ordered by Cradock to investigate the system, reported that it gave officers a strong personal inducement to neglect their duty and that, from his six years' experience of it, the disadvantages of this were obvious. This brought a storm of protest from officers who accused Monro of impugning their honour. Monro denied such an intention, but the officers called for him to be court-martialled. On Cradock's recall, the post of C-in-C, Madras, had been given to Major General Hay Macdowall, but without the seat in Council that normally went with it. In the spring of 1809 he had resigned over this issue and was awaiting passage home, while his relations with Barlow, whom he blamed for his exclusion from the Council and for excessive military retrenchment, sank to ever lower levels. The judge advocate general of the Madras Army, to whom the question of Monro's conduct was referred, ruled that there was no case to answer.[38]

The officers thereupon withdrew their demand for a court-martial and prepared a memorial to the Court of Directors, asking for an investigation to clear their name of any suggestion of misconduct. Barlow, however, refused to forward it. Macdowell ordered Monro's arrest, and refused to forward his subsequent appeal to the Governor. Barlow, nevertheless, learned of the arrest and ordered Monro's release. Macdowell then published a General Order, reprimanding Monro for appealing to the Governor, and accusing him of insubordination and disrespect to military authority. Barlow then suspended from their position in the Company's service both Major Bowles, the over-zealous Deputy Adjutant General who issued the General Order in Macdowell's name, and Colonel Capper, the Adjutant General, who, though absent when the order was published, insisted on being held responsible for his deputy's actions. A group of officers then presented Bowles with an address commending his conduct, subscribed to a compensation fund for him and prepared a memorial to be sent to Governor-General, Lord Minto.

Three months later Barlow responded by suspending, without trial or warning, several senior officers for encouraging the address to Bowles and for signing the memorial to the Governor-General, of which Barlow had obtained a copy, although in fact it had not actually been sent. He also congratulated the officers stationed at Hyderabad for their good conduct in refusing to be associated with these protests. This provoked these officers into threatening to march on Madras unless Capper and Bowles were reinstated and their replacements dismissed. The European regiment at Masulipatam, on being ordered to sea as marines, refused to go. Its officers arrested their colonel and made common cause with those at Hyderabad. Barlow ordered all officers to sign a document asserting their loyalty. Only 150 of the 1,300 officers in the Madras Army signed, as even loyal officers objected on the grounds that a signature implied their own loyalty had been in doubt.[39]

Even more serious incidents occurred before discipline was restored. British regiments were moved to where they could overawe the Company's Europeans. Proclamations were issued to the native officers and sepoys pointing out that their British officers' quarrel was a private one with the government which controlled the pay and pensions of all ranks. Nevertheless, at Seringapatam, the European officers, on being informed by Barlow that as punishment for failing to sign the document of loyalty they would be removed from their regiments, drove a British detachment out of the fort, seized the treasury and prepared for a siege. Two sepoy battalions marching to join the mutiny were attacked by government reinforcements and lost about 200 before a sally from the fort allowed them to join the garrison, which then turned its guns on the loyal troops. Then, despite troops from Jalna and the Northern Sarkars being on their way to join them, the officers of the Hyderabad committee decided that matters had gone too far. They all signed the document and sent messages to officers of the other stations encouraging them to do likewise. Seringapatam surrendered and, by the time that Minto arrived at Madras on 11 September 1809, intending to quell the mutiny in person, he found that all was quiet. Twenty-one officers who had been the most active in the mutiny were tried by court-martial or summarily dismissed. Papers were called for in the House of Commons. The Directors approved all Barlow's actions except for the suspension of Bowles and the removal of the other officers without proper evidence or trial.[40] The affair ended Barlow's prospects of succeeding Minto as Governor-General, which he had been promised, and he was recalled in 1812. Macdowell was blamed for encouraging the officers in their resistance to Barlow's economies but, as the East Indiaman on which he had sailed for England was lost without trace, he never received this censure. Never again, however, was a Commander-in-Chief appointed without a seat in the Governor's Council.

Far away, at Badajoz, Lord Wellington, the sepoy general who had learnt in India many of the campaigning skills that would bring him victory in Spain, wrote to his old Indian comrade Sir John Malcolm that nothing could have been more absurd than the pretext for the officers' action. Monro, he said, should not have been court-martialled for giving his opinion, harsh though it was towards his brother officers but, rather, court-martialled had he *not* given it when ordered. As to whether the governor had the right to protect Monro from his C-in-C, this was a question upon which:

> no man can have a doubt who has any knowledge of the constitution of Great Britain, and particularly that of the Indian governments. I who have arrived pretty nearly at the top of the tree should be the last man to give up any point of right or military etiquette. But I have no doubt whatever, not only that it was the right, but that it was the duty of the governor in council to interfere to save Colonel Monro.[41]

The emergence of the British as the paramount power in South Asia came with the campaigns of the Marquess of Hastings. Governor-General and Commander-in-Chief from October 1813 to January 1823, he held the latter appointment longer than any other officer, and the former longer than anyone except Warren Hastings, its first holder. Lord Hastings, unlike his predecessor Minto, who had been previously President of the Board of Control, had no knowledge of India and little of public office. His military career had been unremarkable, and his appointment, at the age of fifty-eight, was thought to owe more to the influence of his friend the Prince Regent than to his perceived merits. He soon had the chance to show his ability as a strategist when the revival in 1814 of a long-standing dispute over the old northern borders of Awadh led to war with Nepal. After initial disasters including the defeat and death of Major General Gillespie, the hero of Vellore, the superior resources of the British brought them success in 1816. Nepal ceded territory and accepted British protection, but without the requirement for a subsidy. Nepali Gurkha soldiers, who had, man for man, proved themselves a match for British soldiers and Bengal sepoys, were enlisted into the Bengal Army.[42]

At the end of 1817 the Maratha princes, determined to resist further British expansion, gathered their men for their last great battles. At Poona the Peshwa Baji Rao II attacked and burnt the British Residency, only to see his army defeated by the Bombay troops at Kirkee (Khadki) on 5 November 1817. The Bhonsla Raja of Nagpur attacked the British Residency there before going down to defeat at Sitabaldi on 27 November 1817 and outside Nagpur itself on 16 December. Holkar's army, despite the effectiveness of its seventy well-served guns, was smashed at Mahidpur on 20 December. At Koregaon, on 1 January 1818, a thousand Bombay sepoys and twenty-four Madras European gunners held off the Peshwa's last army, 20,000 strong. At the end of hostilities the British were unchallenged.[43] The Peshwa and Bhonsla were deposed and their dominions annexed by the Company. Holkar, Sindia, and the Gaekwar of Baroda accepted British protection, and control of their foreign and defence policies. Hastings, conscious of the consequences of his campaigns, ordered that the Mughal Emperor should no longer be presented with the formal gifts of honour rendered by a subject to a sovereign. Although until 1835 the Company would continue to strike currency bearing his cipher, India was now subject to a new empire and a new military system.

Notes

1. L.S. Sutherland, *The English East India Company and Eighteenth Century Politics*, Oxford, 1952, *passim*.
2. F.G. Cardew, *A Sketch of the Services of the Bengal Native Army*, Calcutta, 1903, pp. 30–4; A. Broome, *History of the Rise and Progress of the Bengal Army*, Calcutta, 1850, pp. 550–9; V.A. Smith, *The Oxford History of India*, Oxford, 1923, p. 478; H.H. Dodwell, *The Cambridge History of India, Vol. V. British India 1497–1858*, Cambridge, 1929, p. 179.
3. A. Broome, *op. cit.*
4. H. Beveridge, *A Comprehensive History of India*, London, 1865, Vol. 2, pp. 272–82.
5. Court of Directors to Governor and Council of Madras, 15 September 1769, *cit.* in W.J. Wilson, *History of the Madras Army*, Vol. 1, Madras, 1882, p. 278.
6. 13 Geo. III, c. 63.
7. P. Cadell, *History of the Bombay Army*, London, 1938, pp. 86–90.
8. Beveridge, *op. cit.*, p. 325.
9. Dodwell, *op. cit.*, Vol. V, pp. 228–9; Beveridge, *op. cit.*, pp. 421–8.
10. Wilson, *op. cit.*, Vol. 1, pp. 340–1; Beveridge, *op. cit.*, pp. 396–7.
11. E.W. Sheppard, *Coote Bahadur: A Life of Lieutenant General Sir Eyre Coote KB*, London, 1956, p. 178; H.C. Wylly, *A Life of Lieutenant General Sir Eyre Coote*, Oxford, 1922, p. 361.
12. Beveridge, *op. cit.*, pp. 501–2.
13. Governor-General in Council, Bengal to Governor in Council, Madras 11 March 1782, *cit.* in Wylly, *op. cit.*, pp. 272–3.
14. Keay, *Honourable Company*, London, 1991, p. 417.
15. Beveridge, *op. cit.*, p. 509.
16. Wilson, *op. cit.*, Vol. II, pp. 82–4 and Wilson, *op. cit.*, Appendix O.
17. Wilson, *op. cit.*, Vol. II, p. 136.
18. Keay, *op. at.*, p. 418.
19. Wilson, *op. cit.*, Vol. II, pp. 117–19.
20. *Cit.* in Wilson, *op. cit.*, p. 120.
21. *Cit.* in Wilson, *op. cit.*, p. 121.
22. *Cit.* in R. Callahan, *The East India Company and Army Reform 1783–1798*, Cambridge, Mass, 1972, p. 87.
23. J. Steven Watson, *The Reign of George III*, Oxford, 1960, pp. 263–7.
24. 24 Geo. III c. 8.
25. Callahan, *op. cit.*, pp. 43, 104.
26. Cornwallis to Duke of York, 10 November 1786, *cit.* in Callahan, *op. cit.*, p. 24.
27. Callahan, *op. cit.*, p. 79.
28. *Ibid.*, pp. 92–3; Archbold, *op. at.*, p. 92.

29. 28 Geo. III, c. 8.
30. Callahan, *op. cit.*, p. 120.
31. *Ibid.*, pp. 132–3.
32. Beveridge, *op. cit.*, p. 675; Wilson, *op. cit.*, pp. 280–3; Callahan, *op. cit.*, Ch. 7.
33. Callahan, *op. cit.*, pp. 144–5.
34. Wilson, *op. cit.*, Vol. 2, pp. 280–8; Cardew, *op. cit.*, pp. 66–9; Cadell, *op. cit.*, pp. 123–4.
35. Beveridge, *op. cit.*, p. 676; Callahan, *op. cit.*, pp. 201–5; J. Steven Watson, *op. cit.*, p. 382.
36. *Ibid.*
37. 'Report of a Commission on the Vellore Mutiny, assembled 9th August 1806'. Return to an address of the House of Commons 15 May 1861. (Parliamentary Papers 1861, Vol. XLII). A.D. Cameron, 'The Vellore Mutiny', unpub. Ph.D. thesis, Edinburgh, 1984, *passim;* Beveridge, *op. cit.*, pp. 811–16; Wilson, *op. cit.*, Vol. 3, Ch. XVIII.
38. Beveridge, *op. cit.*, pp. 840–5; A. Cardew, *The White Mutiny*, London, 1929, *passim;* Wilson, *op. cit.*, Vol. 3, Ch. 20.
39. *Ibid.*
40. *Ibtd.*
41. Wellington to Malcolm (pte) 3 December 1806, *cit.* in Beveridge, *op. cit.*, p. 846.
42. F.G. Cardew, *op. cit.*, pp. 117–27; V.A. Smith, *op. cit.*, pp. 565–7; P.J. Marshall, *New Cambridge History of India*, Cambridge, 1987, p. 44; Dodwell, *op. cit.*, pp. 378–9.
43. Cardew, *op. cit.*, pp. 128 ff; V.A. Smith, *op. cit.*, pp. 567–71; Cadell, *op. cit.*, Ch. VIII; Dodwell, *op. cit.*, pp. 379–83.

Chapter 4

The Culmination of the Company's Raj, 1822–1858

During the second quarter of the nineteenth century, British India became not merely the strongest but the paramount power in South Asia. Through a combination of military victories over the remaining country powers that offered opposition, and military protection to those that offered submission, the East India Company succeeded the Mughals as the next Indian empire. Paradoxically, the greater its power in India grew, the more its freedom of action was constrained by the authority of the British Government in London, while the same Indian soldiers who had conquered their own sub-continent in its service became alarmed at the consequence of their own achievements. The Company's regime would eventually be brought down by a combination of these two processes but, like a falling star, blazed most fiercely as it approached its end.

The administrative institutions to support the establishment of the new empire were already in place by the beginning of this period. As early as 1763 the business of the Bengal authorities was divided between a Secret Department, which dealt with military plans, operations, and the conduct of relations with the country powers, and a Public Department, which dealt with all other matters, including military appointments and fortifications. The Select Committee, which had been set up by Clive to conduct secret business, disappeared in 1774 and its function was taken over by the Secret Department. Although the records of the two departments were separate, both were headed by the same permanent secretary until 1783 when a separate official was appointed to each. A Military Department was created out of the Public Department at the end of 1776 to deal with all matters of military expenditure, returns of casualties, recruits, lists of officers, and any other question of pay, pensions, and promotion.[1]

Another Military Department was set up in 1786, as part of the Secret Department, and took over control of matters affecting officers' promotions and appointments. This was abolished in 1790 and the original Military Department, which had in the interim been known as the Military Department of Inspection, resumed its original title, which it would retain until 1906. Various other changes culminated in Wellesley's reorganisation of

1798, by which time the three Secret, Political, and Foreign Departments had become separate though all were still headed by the same permanent secretary. The first to hold this combined office was a military man, Lieutenant Colonel William Kirkpatrick, and most of the Residents at Indian courts with whom these departments dealt were also soldiers. Kirkpatrick's successors, however, were civil servants, as were the secretaries of all the other departments except the Military Department, where the secretaries continued to be military officers.[2]

The East India Company's home establishment in London developed along broadly similar lines. Until the beginning of the nineteenth century all reports from their servants in India reached the Court of Directors through their Committee of Correspondence, which had its own permanent secretary. Secret matters, including operations of war, were dealt with by the Court's Secret Committee in consultation with the Board of Control which also had its own permanent officials. In 1804 a separate Military Department was established at the Company's offices in East India House to handle all business with the military departments of the three Indian presidencies. A permanent secretary was appointed to this department in 1809. The first incumbent was a former captain in the Bengal Army. He was restored to his military position and remained as secretary of the Military Department until he retired with the rank of major general in 1837. His successor, Philip Melvill, a civil servant, held the post until it was abolished in 1858. In 1834 the Committee of Correspondence (composed of the Chairman and Deputy Chairman of the court and the next nine senior of the twenty-four Directors) disappeared. The number of non-secret committees was reduced to three, of which one, the Political and Military Committee, dealt both with the conduct of diplomacy with Indian states, and the administration of the Army.[3]

The Company continued to depend upon the Charter Acts for its legal existence, and each renewal made changes to take account of the shifting political position in the United Kingdom and in India. The Act of 1793,[4] passed at a time when the attention of most British statesmen was turned to the threat of invasion from Revolutionary France, gave the Board of Control the power to divert the whole of the Company's revenue to defence if it thought necessary, without leaving a single rupee for other purposes of government, still less of dividend. In the negotiations, which lasted from 1808 to 1812, leading to the Act of 1813,[5] Dundas made his last, unsuccessful, attempt to combine the Company's Army with that of the Crown in India. Under the provisions of this act, the patronage of Indian appointments remained with the Company and training colleges were set up for its future civil and military officers, at Haileybury and Addiscombe respectively. The number of British troops that the Board of Control could order the Company to pay for (unless the Directors actually asked for more, which was generally considered to be an improbable contingency), was raised to 20,000 officers and men. Any others would have to be paid by the British taxpayer, if voted for by a watchful Parliament.

The Charter Act of 1833[6] brought further changes. The Company lost the right to carry on commercial activities in India or anywhere else. Thus it ceased to be legally known as 'the United Company of Merchants of England trading to the East Indies' and became officially, as it long had been in ordinary usage, merely 'The East India Company'. Its Indian administration was to be headed by a Governor-General in Council, replacing the Governor-General in Council of Bengal, heading a new Government of India, in which 'the superintendence, direction, and control of the whole civil and military government of all the said territories and revenues in India' was vested. Below this government were to be four presidencies, each with a governor and council of three members. The four presidencies were the existing ones of Madras and Bombay, and two new ones, Bengal and Agra, formed by the division of the existing Bengal presidency. Notionally this might have led to the creation of a fourth Army and C-in-C for Agra. Certainly it was envisaged that the C-in-C, India would henceforth be separate from the C-in-C, Bengal, as the Act provided that when there was no C-in-C, India, or when the office was combined with that of the Governor-General, the C-in-C, Bengal, should take the place of the C-in-C, India, as an extra-ordinary member of the Governor-General's Council. Local Cs-in-C were likewise extra-ordinary members of their respective Governor's Councils so that, without its own C-in-C, Agra would not have enjoyed the equality of position with the other presidencies that the Act envisaged.

When these orders reached India, Bentinck, the Governor-General and C-in-C, India, was at Ootacamund (Utakamand) in the Nilgheri hills of the Madras Presidency. He delayed the implementation of those setting up the new Agra Presidency long enough for there to be a change of view in London, and in 1835 a new Act[7] allowed the Directors to appoint a Lieutenant-Governor for Bengal and Agra respectively, selected from any of their servants who had been ten years in India, instead of Governors and Council. As this was a cheaper alternative, it was readily adopted, and the first Lieutenant-Governor of the North West Provinces (Agra) was appointed in 1836. The Governor-General of India continued to act as Governor of Bengal until a Lieutenant-Governor was appointed there in 1854, and all the military and political business which in Madras and Bombay was devolved to these local governments was, for Bengal, exercised by the Government of India. The 1833 Charter Act also added a fourth member of the Governor-General's Council, to provide expert advice on drafting Indian legislation, a power which was by the same Act taken away from the local governments. The remaining three members were all to be servants of the Company, and the practice began of including among them an army officer who could provide expert advice from the point of view of the Indian military, as the C-in-C India was always at this period a British Army officer, usually with limited local experience, and in any case often absent from the seat of government on campaign or tours of inspection.

The expansion of the Company's territorial possessions in South Asia had been matched by the increase in the size of its Armies. By 1823 Bengal and Madras each had eight regiments of sepoy cavalry and Bombay had two.[8] These regiments were paired to form brigades, which were administrative rather than tactical formations, each under a Colonel conforming to the system in the infantry, where Colonels commanded regiments each of two battalions. Each of the three Armies retained its European artillery and infantry regiments, but the sepoy element in both these arms steadily expanded. In 1803 the totals of sepoy infantry battalions were thirty-eight, in the Bengal and Madras Armies, and nine (including one of marines) in the Bombay Army. In 1813 the totals were fifty-four, fifty and eighteen respectively and, by 1823, sixty, fifty and twenty-four.[9]

In 1824 each of these units became a separate corps.[10] The cavalry regiments retained their existing numbers and names, while each infantry battalion became a regiment. Those which had existed prior to re-organisation by Cornwallis in 1796 were renumbered in their original sequence and the remainder in order according to the date of their being raised. The military justification for this step was that, under the Cornwallis system, the authority of the lieutenant colonels commanding units was weakened by the powers of administrative control held by the colonels of cavalry brigades or infantry regiments. The units were rarely co-located either in peace or war, just as was the case in the British Army, and the need for a battalion commander to refer matters such as recruiting, leave, or promotion to his distant regimental colonel caused exasperation to the officers and puzzlement to their sepoys. A further unsettling effect was the movement of officers between units for, as their promotion took place by regimental seniority, a vacancy in one battalion might be filled by an officer from another. Cross-postings, to take account of consequential promotion in the subaltern ranks, brought officers to command men who were strangers to them, although the turbulence caused by promotion according to Army seniority, in the system abolished by Cornwallis, had been even greater, especially with a smaller number of British officers in each battalion. The most potent reason for re-organising the Armies into single-unit corps was to ease the blockage of promotion which arose from officers staying in the service as long as possible in the hope of promotion to senior rank, and of eventually retiring with a higher pension. Doubling the number of corps doubled the number of colonels, and gave immediate promotion to one lieutenant colonel, one major, one captain, one lieutenant and one cornet or ensign in every unit, while all the others moved up one place in the seniority lists.

In addition to these troops, the Company raised numerous irregular corps. These performed a variety of auxiliary roles, and were particularly useful in supporting the administration of newly acquired territories, assisting in the collection of revenue, the suppression of disorder, escorting officials, guarding public buildings, and the like. The mounted units provided an alternative to the native light cavalry. By 1857 there were eighteen regiments of Irregular Cavalry in the Bengal Army and seven of Irregular Horse in that of Bombay. Although the dress and side arms of the men conformed to Indian rather than European pattern, the significance of the term *irregular* lay in the way in which these units were officered and organised. They had no permanent cadre of British officers and could therefore be raised without the administrative problems that occurred when regular units were affected. Irregular regiments had only four appointments for Europeans. These were the commandant, second-in-command, adjutant and surgeon. As the combatant officers belonged to regular corps, which, with an establishment of twenty-four officers each in the cavalry and twenty-six in the infantry could easily spare them, no financial outlay was involved apart from the extra allowances which they received for filling these staff posts. The officers benefited not only from the extra pay, but from a higher status and more professionally satisfying duties than were available for them as junior officers in their regular regiments.

Irregular regiments of cavalry adopted the Mughal *silladari* system. A *silladar* or 'man-at-arms' was paid higher wages than a regular sepoy, in return for providing and maintaining his own horse, weapons, clothing and equipment. The state thus in effect contracted out these functions to the silladar regiments as, for the sake of uniformity, the men were required to obtain them through regimental sources. To cover the cost of initial outlay, the soldier lodged a deposit or *asami* (literally a 'place' or 'billet') with the regiment, refundable on death or retirement but forfeited in case of desertion or dismissal, so ensuring a high quality of recruit and discipline. If a horse was killed or hurt on duty, a replacement was provided from regimental funds. If it went lame or sick from neglect, the soldier's pay was reduced to infantry rates until it recovered or he supplied another. Wealthy troopers were, subject to numerical limitations, allowed to provide *asamis* for men who could not afford their own. These men, known as *bargirs*, were often younger members of their own family, or others who gave part of their pay to their sponsors, in effect as interest on the loan of their deposit.

The sea long remained, to the majority of South Asians, an alien and unknown element. Most of the great Indian empires were land powers and few, even those with extensive coastlines, maintained navies or exercised control over the sea lanes of the Indian Ocean. In the classical Hindu period, ships sailed from South Asia east and west to Indonesia and the Red Sea[11] but, by the time of the early Muslim invasions, advances in ship design by Arab and Chinese naval architects had made Indian vessels unprofitable. Moreover, with increasing stress being laid upon the importance of performing every detail of prescribed ritual, religious authorities had come to teach that sea voyages, if only because conditions on board ship did not allow food to be prepared and consumed with the proper observances, would result in irretrievable pollution for members of the *brahman* and *ksatriya* classes. This religious objection to sea travel was the more readily accepted by those to whom the sea was an object of fear and suspicion. South Asian seamen, drawn from the lower two classes, continued to display their courage and resourcefulness but, to the law-givers, sailing the ocean sea was an activity perilous to body and soul alike. 'The Muslim invasions encouraged xenophobia, and the people who had planted their colonies from Socotra to Borneo became, with religious sanction, a nation of land-lubbers.'[12]

So it was that when the East India Company began to recruit sepoys from the men of high religious class whose homes lay in what had become the centre of Hindu culture, it found them reluctant to embark upon its ships. With Muslim and lower-class Hindus there were no religious scruples to overcome, but sailing in the late eighteenth century was like flying in the late twentieth, statistically safe, but with occasional disasters whose dramatic effect outweighed that of more familiar accidents. It was therefore particularly unfortunate that, although in 1767 three battalions of sepoys had sailed from Bengal to the Northern Sarkars to support the Madras troops engaged with Haydar Ali, two companies of grenadiers were lost without trace on their way back in 1770.[13]

Thereafter, whenever Bengal troops were needed outside their own Presidency, they generally marched overland, despite the delays, desertions and expense involved. If men were required to travel by sea to a theatre of war in India or elsewhere, the usual practice was to raise new units, made up of volunteers from existing battalions. The move by sea to Madras in 1790 of the 1st Bengal Cavalry was made easier by most of the men in this arm being Muslims. Men who volunteered for these new units received substantial bounties, so that this system was more costly than that which obtained in Madras and Bombay, where existing units were simply ordered to embark, though only after their formal consent was obtained in each case. The Bengal Army raised a battalion of marines in 1795 (converted to the line in 1803), who had no objection to seaborne duty, but in the same year the 15th Battalion of Bengal sepoys stationed at Midnapur, after volunteering to sail with the expedition to Malacca, mutinied when ordered to march to its embarkation point.[14] It was dispersed by the 29th Battalion with its accompanying light guns. The 29th became very unpopular with other battalions for its part in suppressing this mutiny (resulting in the disbandment and disgrace of the 15th) and, in an unsuccessful attempt to force the government to disband it, four units subsequently refused orders to march to the Northern Sarkars.[15] The grudge may have arisen from the perception that the 15th had been punished for refusing to embark and that the 29th were men who would force others to do so.

A generation later, the objection by Bengal sepoys to go on board ship was as strong as ever. On the outbreak of the 1st Anglo-Burmese war in 1824, the British, appreciating the difficulties of the country where Bengal and Burma meet, decided to make use of their naval power and so sent a force which landed at Rangoon. Only one battalion of sepoys (the former marine regiment), together with two British regiments, came from Bengal, while Madras sent seven battalions of sepoys and three of Europeans.[16] The war did not at first go well for the British, despite their superior technology, including the Company's new paddle-steamer *Diana* which it was hoped would overawe the superstitious by moving up the Irrawaddy without sails or oars. It was therefore decided to open a second front in the Arakan. Reports of the terrible climate, of disease, of Burmese skill in jungle warfare, and of the superhuman powers of the Burmese General, Maha Bandula, depressed morale among the troops assembling for the new campaign, and a higher than usual number of desertions were reported among sepoy battalions en route from Hindustan to lower Bengal. At Barrackpur, the large military station fifteen miles from Calcutta, the newly renumbered 26th, 47th and 62nd Bengal Native Infantry, were told that, to avoid going to Arakan by sea, they would march there overland. In India, sepoys customarily provided their own carriage for their personal effects, including the heavy brass cooking and drinking vessels which each man used to avoid the risk of ritual pollution. In this instance, as the road to Burma lay through strange and dangerous country, the normal operation of market forces meant that the contractors who supplied pack bullocks would only do so at high prices. The troops therefore asked for the provision of carriage by the government, or for additional pay and allowances to cover the extra cost of providing their own in the usual way. When these requests were refused, gatherings took place at which men agreed not to march until their demands were met. Subsequently, some bullocks were found for them, and advances of pay were offered. The Indian officers of the 47th, the first regiment warned for duty, reported it ready to march, and told their men that when the Company went to war they ought not to shrink. According to the sepoys, they added that the regiment was going to Rangoon by ship.

The subsequent refusal by the 47th to parade for inspection in marching order brought the Commander-in-Chief, General Sir Edward Paget, up from

Calcutta with a squadron of Indian cavalry (the Governor-General's Body-guard), two British battalions, and a troop of the Bengal Horse Artillery. The 47th presented him with a petition to the effect that they would not go on board ship nor march anywhere for that purpose.[17] They asked only to be allowed to take their discharge. Paget, a one-armed veteran of the Peninsular War, replied that there was no intention of sending them to sea but he would have no negotiations with them until they returned to duty. The 47th, joined by groups from the 26th and 62nd fell in, without the Indian officers, at dawn on 2 November. Paget addressed them through an interpreter but was met with further protests.[18] He then ordered them to ground arms and, when only one man obeyed, the gunners suddenly revealed their presence and opened fire. The leaderless sepoys fled without resistance. Eleven were killed in the cannonade and pursuit, many were arrested, some were later hanged and others sentenced to the chain gang. The native officers were dismissed and the 47th's name was deleted from the Bengal Army List.

Paget's action was not well received by the Bengal Army. There was a feeling that, left to themselves, Bengal officers could have persuaded the men to obey orders and that Paget's approach, based upon British notions of discipline, disregarded the local ways of settling disagreements. A court of enquiry's findings hinted that Paget, by concealing his guns behind his other troops, had not given the sepoys a fair chance of appreciating his intentions and that they would have surrendered in the end. They also pointed to the fact that the sepoys, though each had the full regulation sixty rounds in their pouches, had not loaded their muskets and did not return fire. Their action, said the court, was 'an ebulliation of despair at being compelled to march without the means of doing so', and if proper carriage had been provided at the right time, none of the other complaints would have been made 'and the late 47th Regiment would now have been contending against the enemies of the state'.[19]

Paget had little sympathy with this attitude. The sepoys, he said, were not less mutinous for not having loaded their muskets and he had had no intention of giving them the chance to do so. He returned to England to become Governor of the Royal Military College at Sandhurst and later gave evidence to a House of Commons committee on Indian Army discipline.

> There is a great spirit of insubordination in the army, at least in that which I had the opportunity of more particularly seeing, which is the Bengal Army. A sort of spirit of independance prevails among the officers, which is totally inconsistent with our ideas of military discipline. I had abundant opportunities of seeing it myself and had the proofs before me of that spirit; and I have reason to think, from what I have subsequently heard, that it is by no means subsiding.[20]

Wellington at much the same time was equally suspicious of the Indian Army's officers and sepoys alike. In 1826, commenting upon proposals by Sir John Malcolm's recently published proposals advocating the amalgamation of the three presidential armies, he wrote, 'My opinion is not altered by perusal of Malcolm's. He is a very clever fellow, and has considered these subjects more than I have', but, he added, the sepoys and their officers had a record of mutiny, 'and seeing what armies have done in different countries of Europe, and are capable of attempting, and knowing them as I do, and knowing moreover the sort of men whom you must employ to manage them, I cannot but think it fortunate that they are three separate and distinct armies.'[21]

Only two years later, the officers of the Bengal Army were again at odds with their employers over the *batta* question. In 1801 Shore had averted the threat of a mutiny of officers, whose *batta* the Court had ordered him to reduce, by continuing to pay it, whether they were in the field or cantonments, in the guise of an accommodation allowance. In return the officers were required to provide their own accommodation at all times. Officers' quarters were sold by the government to their occupants, who in turn sold them on to their successors. The Court of Directors repeatedly ordered that in the stations nearest to Calcutta, this allowance was to be at half the normal rate, but both Hastings, and his successor, Amherst, returned the orders to London for reconsideration, so delaying implementation by at least a year every time this was done. The cost of the eventual British victory in Burma led the Court of Directors to look for economies and *batta* again became an issue.

In 1828 a new Governor-General, Lord William Bentinck, arrived. Some twenty years earlier he had been recalled from Madras after the Vellore mutiny and now military discontent again threatened to blight his administration. His orders were to effect retrenchment in government expenditure, starting with the reduction of officers' *batta*. The Commander-in-Chief, Lord Combermere (who, as Sir Stapleton Cotton, had commanded Wellington's cavalry in the Peninsula) resigned in protest, and the two remaining members of the Governor-General's Council signed the order only because, as its civil servants, they felt obliged to carry out the Company's policy. One of them, Sir Charles Metcalfe, nevertheless minuted his view that the allowances of officers even on full *batta* were barely sufficient, and that any reduction would cause suffering to the individuals affected and injury to the public good. This view was held, and expressed, even more strongly by the officers themselves. The usual protests were drawn up and memorials presented to the C-in-C for submission to government. Bentinck himself let it be known that he would be glad to rescind the order if the Court of Directors agreed (though this did not save him from ostracism by Calcutta society, or the nickname 'The clipping

Dutchman').[22] The Court, however, would not hear of it, and denounced the tone of the memorials as contrary to military discipline. The officers, together with the civil servants who suffered similar reductions in income, had no choice but to accept, and wait with increasing impatience for promotion or transfer to posts which carried other allowances.

Increasing attention was paid at this period to retirement on pension as promotion prospects worsened. There was still the chance of an occasional campaign, such as that against Bharatpur which Combermere had stormed in 1826, where Lake had failed. In general, however, most operations were against local rulers or peasants resisting the collection of the revenue, and these did not result in either the glory or the consequential promotion through battle casualties that large-scale conventional wars provided.

As the British came to replace the Mughals as holders of the empire of India, their attention turned towards the north-west, from which invaders had come to overthrow so many earlier Indian empires. Even the Mughals themselves had been brought down not so much by the British as by Nadir Shah of Iran and Ahmad Shah of Afghanistan. To the long-established fear of invading hordes from Iran and Central Asia was added a new anxiety that, arising from the extension of European power into Asia, these hordes would have the benefit of European military assistance. By the 1820s, just as they would in the late 1940s, the Russians had changed, in the perception of British public opinion, from being the brave allies, the endurance of whose people and the skill of whose armies had delivered Europe from a dictator, into the evil empire which practised tyranny at home and encouraged it abroad. Moreover, an army which in the space of two years had pursued the forces of Napoleon back from Moscow all the way to Paris, just as its successors would those of Hitler from Stalingrad to Berlin, was one to be taken seriously, even if the assistance it gave was limited to military advice and training.

In 1839, therefore, to counter a threat (which had actually disappeared) that Iran, under Russian influence, would occupy Herat and from there re-assert Iranian control of Afghanistan, a British Indian army marched through Sind to Kandahar and Kabul. Shah Shuja-ul-Mulk, the last of Ahmad Shah's dynasty, was restored to his throne with British support, and the Amir Dost Muhammad, who had replaced him, was deposed. The Amir had offered the British an alliance but only at the price of their support in recovering the province of Peshawur, which he had lost to Ranjit Singh, Maharaja of Lahore. As the British wanted the alliance of this powerful neighbour even more than that of the more distant Amir of Kabul, Shah Shuja (who had already conceded Peshawur to Ranjit Singh in return for his promise of support) was their preferred choice. He was not, however, that of the Afghans, and a widespread rebellion in 1841 led to the notorious 'retreat from Kabul', an episode as potent in the folk memory of British soldiers as that of the retreat from Moscow a generation earlier had become in that of the French. The fact that most British garrisons in Afghanistan held out, that it was the cold of the Afghan winter rather than the weapons of the Afghan tribesmen which destroyed the Kabul troops (scarcely a brigade strong) and that in 1842 two British divisions marched from opposite ends of the country to meet in Kabul itself, cannot destroy the image of an entire British army destroyed, and all its military and diplomatic staff killed or held hostage.[23]

As the British would find again in 1879–81, and the Soviets would a century later, the brilliance of victory was dimmed by the dust of the cost of occupation, while any ruler installed in Afghanistan with the aid of foreign troops was instantly seen by his subjects as the puppet of a foreign ruler. In October 1842 (much as in 1881) a change of government in London resulted in a change of policy in India, and the army was recalled, leaving Dost Muhammad to resume his throne.

Lord Ellenborough, who replaced the discredited Lord Auckland as Governor-General in February 1842, was more successful in his wars. Sind, occupied by the British in 1839 on the grounds that it had once been part of the empire which they were restoring to Shah Shuja, was annexed after a brief campaign culminating in the battle of Miani (February 1843). General Sir Charles Napier, the conqueror of Sind, remained there for four years as its governor, holding both civil and military authority. Though subsequently both the government and garrison of Sind were made subordinate to Bombay, this unification of civil and military command long remained a feature of the administration of Sind. Until 1877 the political superintendent of the Upper Sind Frontier commanded the (predominantly cavalry) Sind Frontier Force, conducted British foreign policy with the neighbouring independent ruler of Baluchistan, and was also the chief magistrate of the district.

The annexation of Sind brought two military problems to the British. The first was that they now had a permanent border with the independently minded and warlike tribal communities of the wild country between South and Central Asia. The inhabitants of this country, long accustomed to raiding their more settled neighbours, continued to do so when these became British subjects. In 1844–45 Napier waged a successful campaign, in which, by the employment of novel devices such as mountain artillery and a camel corps for operations respectively in the hills and deserts of this frontier, he demonstrated that well-led regular troops could secure victories over ill-armed tribesmen regardless of terrain.[24]

The second problem was that of finding regular troops willing to serve there. To the Bengal Army, Sind was a foreign country, with an objectionable climate. The reduction in *batta* that followed the annexation of Sind (which thereby ceased to be a 'foreign' station, though still just as expensive to live in) made service there even less popular. In 1844, when Bengal troops were ordered to go there, 190 sepoys in the 4th Native Infantry, and ninety in the 69th applied for their discharge and were granted it even though hostilities were in progress. The 7th Light Cavalry and 34th Native Infantry refused to march, and the former changed its mind only when the latter was disbanded and its men dismissed for mutiny. The 64th agreed to march only when its commanding officer promised them that full field *batta* would be paid. When they reached Sind and found that he was in error, they refused to accept their pay, the conventional method of protest among troops with a grievance, but no intent to mutiny. Subsequently, however, men stoned their brigade commander, with the result that about seventy were dismissed and the regiment deprived of its colours, while its colonel was cashiered for misrepresentation and inefficiency.[25]

The last independent Indian power was the kingdom of Lahore. Neither the geographical term 'the Punjab', nor the religious one 'the Sikhs' are accurate synonyms for this state, as not all its dominions lay within the Punjab – the Five Rivers Land – nor did all the Punjab come under its sway. Likewise, not all its subjects were Sikhs, nor did it rule over all Sikhs, nor even over all territories under Sikh princes. After the execution by the Mughal authorities in 1715 of Banda Singh ('the false *guru*'), his surviving followers fled to the Himalayan foothills. 'The Sikhs, it was thought, had been hammered out of existence. But the hammering did not in fact reduce them to a pulp, but hardened a remnant to tempered steel.'[26] After the invasions of Nadir Shah and Ahmad Shah weakened Mughal control of the Punjab, Sikh war bands reappeared in the plains, gaining recruits and converts, and forming political entities which spread from the Indus almost to Delhi itself. In 1799 Ranjit Singh, the teenage head of one of these groups, obtained from the Mughal Shah Zaman a *sanad* recognising him as ruler of Lahore. From here he went on to capture Amritsar in 1802, Ludhiana in 1806, Multan and Kashmir in 1818–19, Ladakh in 1833, and Peshawar in 1834, so establishing a kingdom whose population, though largely Sikh, comprised a high proportion of Hindus and Muslims, both Punjabis and Afghans. Sikh states on the east side of the Satlej managed to avoid absorption by accepting British protection.

This state was built up and defended by an army which, by the time of Maharaja Ranjit Singh's death in 1839, amounted to some 75,000 men. About half of these were contingents furnished by eminent landholders in accordance with the traditional system of military tenure. Others were Akalis or Sikh zealots. The true strength, however, lay in the 35,000 regular soldiers, organised in the European manner and trained by European officers, including a number of Napoleon's veterans. The infantry and artillery, dressed in imitation of the Company's sepoys, were at least their equal in terms of drill, equipment and morale.

In the struggle for power at Lahore which followed Ranjit Singh's death, the regular army assumed the role of a Praetorian Guard, giving its support to whichever of the contending parties offered the best terms. While observing the existing chain of command for discipline and training, each regiment had a soldiers' committee or 'panch' (literally, a 'five'), based on the pattern of the councils by which Indian villagers had managed their own local affairs, independent of kings and governments, since classical Hindu times. The committees decided whom to support, and officers led the regiments accordingly. In 1845 the ruling party at Lahore, headed by the Rani Jindan (acting as regent for her infant son Dhalip Singh), Lal Singh (the Wazir or Finance Minister), and Tej Singh (the Commander-in-Chief) decided that their best hope of survival lay in a war with the British. If the army won, its attention would be distracted from politics and its appetite would be met by the proceeds of new conquests. If it lost, the British would ensure it was reduced to a manageable size, a step which no ruler at Lahore dare take and expect to live. At any event, the Rani and her advisers were sure that if they crossed the river they would destroy a great army.

On 11 December 1845 the Lahore troops crossed the Satlej river into British-protected territory. The invasion was not unexpected. Ellenborough had in 1843 waged a campaign against the Maharaja Sindia of Gwalior to ensure that he would not be a threat if war came with the Sikhs and the British had 40,000 men stationed between the Satlej and Delhi. It was, nevertheless, a tactical surprise and a brief but bloody campaign ensued. Both sides were handicapped by civil-military problems in their respective commands. On the Sikh side, the army, with good reason, had doubts about its leaders' desire to win. Neither Lal Singh nor Tej Singh trusted each other's whole-hearted devotion to securing a victory. On the British side, Sir Hugh Gough, the C-in-C, was hampered by the Governor-General, Lieutenant General Sir Henry Hardinge, a veteran of 'The Hundred Days'. Hardinge, as a serving officer, volunteered to serve under Gough, an offer which could scarcely be refused but which made for difficulties when, as Governor-General, he was able to overrule the C-in-C's strategic plans on political grounds. Gough's standard tactic, a frontal attack by infantry against an unshaken enemy, cost his own army dear at Ferozeshah on 19–20 December 1845, but a victory by Sir Harry Smith at Aliwal on 28 January 1846 and another by Gough at Sobraon on 10 February 1846 finally drove their enemies back to Lahore.

After the first shock of defeat, a mood of resistance to British control developed in the kingdom of Lahore. When Sir Henry Lawrence, the British Resident, became President of the Regency Council, and it was announced that British garrisons would remain by its invitation for a further eight years, he appeared as the representative of an occupying power and the chiefs who supported him were stigmatised as collaborators. Reforms aimed at benefiting the cultivators alienated the great landholders. Above all, the army, like the German Army after the First World War, felt that it had not been defeated but stabbed in the back. Unemployed and disbanded soldiers blamed the British for their plight and those still in the service made common cause with their old comrades. When, in April 1848, two British officers were murdered by dissidents at Multan, a local act of defiance became the first clash in a new war. Troops loyal to the government, led by British officers, failed to capture Multan and in September a much larger body sent as reinforcements went over to the other side.

The course of what then became the Second Sikh War in many ways resembled that of the war which was to come in the plains of Hindustan nine years later. There was the same discontent among the leading classes in society at the assumption of rule by the British, the same anger among men thrown out of work, despite previous honourable service, by a government policy of reducing the number of those employed by the state, the same unease among the population as a whole at reforms which seemed to threaten long-established religious and cultural practices and the same kind of enemy, a well-armed regular soldier trained in the most up-to-date Western tactics.

There was the same hard level of fighting too. Hardinge had returned to the United Kingdom at the end of 1847 to succeed Wellington as C-in-C of the British Army. His successor, Earl Dalhousie, at the age of thirty-five the youngest Governor-General ever, combined great personal energy with a firm belief in the superiority of Western over Indian values. He readily accepted the challenge of a new war and Gough marched to re-establish British supremacy. At Ramnagar on 22 November 1848, he was nearly defeated. Chilianwala (13 January 1849), was another Ferozshah in the scale of its casualties and the doubtful nature of its outcome. At Gujerat, 'the battle of the guns', on 21 February 1849, Gough at last used his superiority in artillery and secured a decisive victory. Dalhousie, on his own initiative, annexed the kingdom of Lahore to British India as a new province, the Punjab.

Although the Second Sikh War was fought by the British without the civil-military difficulties of its predecessor, the immediate aftermath contained a full measure of them. The news of Chilianwala was greeted in London with a general outcry at Gough's poor generalship. Yielding to popular opinion, the Court of Directors appointed Sir Charles Napier to succeed him. In the ten weeks between Napier leaving England in late February and reaching India in early May (travelling by steamship through the Mediterranean and the Red Sea, and overland through Suez) Gough had triumphed at Gujerat and the war was over. Dalhousie was as jealous of his own position and prerogatives as Napier was of his. The sixty-eight-year-old veteran, the conqueror and former governor of Sind, whose officials freely contrasted their own achievements favourably with those of the Punjab which Dalhousie had made his own, was warned by the imperious young nobleman at their first meeting to keep his place. Both were individuals of determined character and each soon developed a strong dislike of the other's personality and proceedings.

Their final clash arose from the ever-vexed question of *batta*. When the Punjab was annexed it ceased to be a foreign country and therefore the allowances paid to troops serving outside British territory were discontinued, just as they had been in the case of Sind, and with just the same result. The sepoys perceived that the consequence of their victory in battle was a diminution in their pay. Only those stationed on the border with Afghan territory, the new North West Frontier of British India, were exempt, being virtually on permanent field service against the continual risk of Pathan (Pashtun) tribesmen raiding from the hills. In several units, including the 13th, 22nd and 32nd Bengal Native Infantry, sepoys made the conventional protest of refusing to accept pay they considered to be below the proper rate. At Amritsar, the 66th Bengal NI refused to perform duty. Napier, who had experienced much the same problem in the midst of his hill campaign in Sind, acted with his characteristic decisiveness. The regiment was marched to Amballa where all its non-European personnel were discharged and its colours and number in the Bengal Army List were handed over to the Nasiri Gurkha Battalion, which had fought well in the recent wars.[27] Napier's aim, apart from showing how he would deal with insubordination, was to demonstrate to the Hindustani Purabiyas that he could easily find other troops to replace them if they did not wish to serve on the offered terms. There were already six regiments of Sikh infantry (raised in 1846) and twelve Punjabi regiments, cavalry and infantry, in the British order of battle. To Napier's chagrin, those belonging to the Punjab Frontier Force came under the Government of India in the Foreign Department (i.e. the local political authorities), not under him as C-in-C, India. His actions, changing the composition of the 66th from Purabiya to Gurkha, and recruiting the Nasiri Gurkha Battalion to full strength to replace the men remustered in the 66th, were carried out without reference to the Government of India. Although within his legal powers, it had political implications, and Dalhousie expressed his disapproval at not being informed of these orders before they were given.

While firm in his response to the insubordination which it provoked, Napier had no sympathy with the order to withdraw *batta* and, by taking an opportunity of countermanding it, brought about his own downfall. While Dalhousie was at sea, and without the agreement of the other members of the Governor-General's Council, Napier suspended the orders reducing the Punjab *batta*. Dalhousie responded with a formal letter from the Government of India in the Military Department to the Adjutant General of the Bengal

Army stating that the Governor-General in Council (one of whose members was the C-in-C), viewed the C-in-C's orders on the Punjab *batta* with regret and dissatisfaction, and that the Governor-General in Council would not again permit the C-in-C to usurp its proper authority by issuing orders changing the pay of the troops. Napier responded to this public rebuke by submitting his resignation and returned to England in March 1851. He subsequently published a book, *The Defects, Civil and Military, of the Government of India*, in which he paid off old scores against the East India Company, its policies and employees. His criticisms of the Bengal Army in particular were to be proved only too well founded, by the disaster which overtook it in 1857, four years after Napier's death.

With the Punjab secured, Dalhousie went on to take every opportunity of annexing other Indian states, which were too weak to offer military resistance. Satara (created by Lord Hastings in 1819 as a principality to be held by the last descendant of Sivaji), Nagpur, Jhansi, Sambalpur, and a number of others were annexed on the failure of natural heirs to their respective thrones. Awadh, whose rulers had long been faithful and generous allies of the British, had been an independent Muslim Shi'a kingdom since 1819 when, with British encouragement, it had ceased to acknowledge Mughal sovereignty. Protected by British troops against the consequence of misgovernment, but refusing to accept the advice of British Residents to improve their administration, successive Kings of Awadh had been criticised for tyranny, oppression or neglect. Nevertheless, as in 1809 half of Awadh had been ceded to the Company in return for a guarantee of protection of the other half against internal and external enemies alike, the British had no claim on Awadh.

Its annexation in February 1856 on the grounds that the British government, if it did not stop maladministration, would be seen as party to it, was generally regarded as an invasion. The monarch, Wajid Ali Shah, had been a patron of learning and his court at Lucknow (Lakhnao) had become a centre of Urdu culture. His subjects had not invited the British to liberate them. Many of those who had loyally served the state as soldiers, scholars or administrators, or in humbler capacities, lost their livelihood, as the new rulers introduced a ruthless and short-sighted policy of reducing public expenditure in order to reduce taxes. The cultivators saw no improvement in their lot, and the many Purabiyas recruited from Awadh lost the privileged position which they had enjoyed locally through their connection with the British. Indeed, they, like all Awadhis, also lost their independence.

The Bengal sepoys soon had a more personal grievance. In the spring of 1852 a second Burmese War had begun. One division from the Bengal Army, including some of the recently raised Punjabi units, and another from Madras, supported by nineteen steamers mounting 159 guns between them, waged a campaign in the jungles and paddy-fields of lower Burma. Pegu was annexed to British India, and the entire Burmese coastline came under British rule. The 38th Bengal Native Infantry refused to embark for the war but the new C-in-C, General Sir William Gomm, was no Napier, still less a Paget, and no disciplinary action followed. The subject was one of those covered by Dalhousie in the series of nine memoranda on Army organisation which he submitted to the Court of Directors, and the question was one of the first to be resolved by his successor, Lord Canning, who assumed office on 1 March 1856.

Later that year Canning directed that all new recruits for the Bengal Army should be enlisted for general service only (as was already the case for those of the Madras and Bombay Armies). Even Muslim sepoys, who had no religious scruples about going to sea, were adversely affected by this, as they had benefited equally with their Hindu comrades from the bounties offered to those who would embark for overseas duty. To those Hindus whom no amount of money would induce to sail, the new regulation meant that their sons would be cut off from a form of honourable and lucrative employment that men of their communities had followed for generations. There were no other large armies in South Asia in which the Purabiyas could enlist as an alternative to the East India Company's service. Even those who were already serving, on whom the new conditions were not binding, feared that they would be subject to moral pressure to embark, and find themselves at sea, unable to perform their ritual ablutions, or prepare their food properly, or becalmed and obliged to eat salt beef. Some even feared that there was a scheme to pollute men through sea travel, and oblige them to become Christians: people who ate and drank all kinds of impure things without discrimination and who had few rules of religious hygiene.[28]

It was a conflict between old religion and new technology that led to the outbreak of mutiny in the Bengal Army in 1857. Soldiers had known since classical times that to impart spin to a projectile would improve its range and accuracy. In the design of firearms this is best achieved by cutting a spiral groove (rifling) in the bore of the piece, through which the projectile is driven by rapidly expanding gasses when the weapon is fired. Experience in the Crimean War of 1854–56 had shown the British that the Minie rifle, issued to selected regiments, was superior to the old smooth-bore musket and, accordingly, the new small-arms factory at Enfield Lock, in the countryside ten miles north of London, went into full production with an improved version. The East India Company, so that its Army should have the same modern equipment as the British Army for which it was a local substitute, ordered large quantities of the new Enfield rifles and despatched them to India. The Enfields were muzzle-loaders, like the smooth-bores which they replaced. Their ammunition came in the form of paper tubes (cartridges), each containing the standard charge of gunpowder and lead bullet. The cartridge was opened by soldiers using their teeth, since one hand was required to hold the weapon while the other held the cartridge. The cartridges of the new Enfields were greased, using tallow or lard, to lubricate the rifling. The composition of the grease was a matter of importance to men who would be defiled by putting into their mouths either beef, sacred to Hindus, or pork, unclean to Muslims. The rapidly spreading belief that fats from these animals were indeed used in the manufacture of the new cartridges, either deliberately to destroy men's religion, or at best indiscriminately by defence contractors using the cheapest material in their usual greed for profits, caused deeply felt alarm.[29]

At first it seemed that a simple solution could be found. In January, 1857, Major Bontein, commanding the Arsenal of Dum Dum, near Calcutta, where details from each regiment were being sent to learn the new drill, heard of the discontent. He paraded the men and asked those who wished to complain to step forward. About two-thirds did so. In a disciplined manner, they stated their religious objections and suggested that beeswax or coconut oil would be an equally effective, but acceptable, substitute. These alternatives indeed later were authorised, while in Madras the cartridges would be issued ungreased, and the sepoys bought *ghi* (clarified butter) from the bazaar to use as the lubricant. In Bengal, however, even the new shiny paper of the cartridges was feared to be manufactured from forbidden animals, while a new rumour spread that the English were grinding up cow and pig bones to mix with the flour sold in military bazaars.

The 34th Bengal Native Infantry was at this time due to march from Barrackpur, near Calcutta, to relieve the 19th at Berhampur, a hundred miles to the north. An advance party reached there on 24 February and enjoyed the hospitality usual on such occasions. On 26 February, men of the 19th Bengal Native Infantry refused to accept the issue of even the old pattern cartridges. In the evening they seized their arms and refused all orders. The garrison commander, with only native artillery and cavalry left at his disposal, neither of which were useful in the dark, decided not to force the issue, and the regiment returned to duty on condition of not being ordered to take suspect cartridges.

Canning determined to make an example of the 19th, on the grounds that whatever the sepoys' fears, nothing could excuse mutiny under arms and open defiance of their officers. The 84th Foot was recalled from Burma and sent with the 53rd Foot and two troops of Bengal Horse Artillery to Barrackpur. The 19th Bengal Native Infantry was marched there from Berhampur. Two days before its arrival Sepoy Mangal Pande called on his comrades of the 34th, still at Barrackpur, to rise and assist him in killing their European officers. He succeeded in wounding his Adjutant and Serjeant Major before being arrested by a Muslim sepoy of the same regiment. The guard, led by

Jemadar Iswari Pande, turned out but made no attempt to assist. The two Pandes (a common name among Purabiyas, and one subsequently used by the British as a synonym for Hindustani mutineers) were tried by a court-martial of native officers and sent to the gallows, but as every sepoy knew that native officers only brought in the verdict they thought that their British officers expected, it was widely felt that they were martyrs. Much the same was felt when the 19th Native Infantry was disbanded after arrival at Barrackpur, as was the 34th on 4 May 1857.[30]

At Meerut, near Delhi, the skirmishers of the 3rd Bengal Light Cavalry were ordered to parade on 24 April to demonstrate to the rest of their regiment the new drill for breaking instead of biting the cartridges. Only five out of the ninety accepted the cartridges. A court of inquiry found that the action of the remainder stemmed from fear of public opinion only. A native court-martial, with one member dissenting, convicted them to ten years' hard labour. On Sunday 9 May the eighty-five troopers, the elite of their regiment, many of them old soldiers, some with medals from the First Sikh War, were put into chains in the presence of the whole garrison and led off to prison, while some of their comrades began to consider plans for an appeal.[31] That evening, while the European troops fell in, without arms, for church parade, there began an appeal to the sword. Some of the cavalry broke open the city gaol to release the skirmishers, letting out every other prisoner as well. Sepoys of cavalry and infantry alike, joined by the city mob, attacked European officers, civilians, women, children, Indian shopkeepers, servants, and anyone who got in their way. Others did what they could to protect their own officers. Some decided to remain with their regiments, right or wrong. Some just made themselves scarce.[32]

During the night, the mutineers marched to Delhi, where the three sepoy battalions there, among them the same 38th which had refused to go to Burma, joined them, as did every criminal who hoped to profit from a breakdown of order and every patriot who desired a restoration of Mughal power. All Europeans, and many Indian Christians, were attacked, regardless of age or sex. Some escaped, helped by local people, some were robbed, some were murdered, with little effort made to protect them by Bahadur Shah, the old and irresolute Mughal monarch. Nine British members of the Bengal Ordnance Department defended the great magazine before blowing it up, five surviving to win the recently instituted Victoria Cross for valour. Bahadur Shah sent a camel rider to Agra to notify the Lieutenant-Governor of Bengal's North-Western Provinces that mutineers had taken Delhi. Then he waited for the British to come and restore order. When they did not come, he endeavoured to rule despite the indiscipline of the sepoys, the ambition of his sons, and the uncertain loyalty of his subjects.[33]

North-west of Delhi lay the recently conquered province of the Punjab. There, the Chief Commissioner, Sir John Lawrence, and a band of fifty-six officers selected from the best volunteers of the Bengal Civil Service and Army, governed a population that had no special reason to support the con-tinuation of British rule. It was for this reason that it had a garrison of 60,000 men, of whom 36,000 were Purabiyas with the rest either Europeans or Punjabis. News of the events at Meerut and Delhi reached Lahore by telegraph on the morning of 12 May. It was decided that the risk of a new Punjabi rising was less than that of a spreading sepoy mutiny and action was at once taken to disarm the Hindustani regiments. On 13 May the three battalions and one cavalry regiment at Mian Mir piled arms without incident.

The Punjab proved to be an unlooked-for source of strength to the British cause. Punjabis had little cause to support the British who had defeated them barely a decade earlier, but even less to sympathise with the Purabiya sepoys who had contributed so conspicuously to that defeat and made up so large a part of the army of occupation. Sikhs especially had only ill feelings towards the Mughal dynasty whose rulers had persecuted the later *gurus* and their followers. Young men, whether Sikh, Punjabi Muslims, or Pashtuns from the hills, saw glittering prospects of looting Delhi and the other great cities of Hindustan if they joined the British side. Punjabi princes also threw in their lot with the British, or at least refrained from any movement against them. The British had the weapons and officers of disarmed units with which to arm and lead the new ones they raised from Punjabi recruits (including old soldiers of the Lahore army). Hindustanis who mutinied, far from home, found every man's hand against them and only made their escape if well-armed and moving in regimental groups.

Delhi remained the critical point of the whole campaign. When days went by with no sign of the British, Bahadur Shah accepted with some reluctance the reins of authority pressed into his hands by the sepoys and attempted to set up some kind of government, to which those holding *jagirs* in his kingdom rallied with their military contingents. The British troops at Meerut had been unable to pursue the mutineers to Delhi without leaving their own civilians at the mercy of the city mob, which had committed the worst of the attacks on Europeans and which normally would have been suppressed by the very troops that had mutinied. General Anson, the C-in-C, India, was 150 miles away with most of his European troops in the Himalayan foothills, where they were stationed for the hot weather. Before he could take the field he had to organise transport and supplies. When he did march, it could only be at night, as movement by European troops by day in the plains during the hot weather was liable to put most of them out of action long before they encountered the enemy. Anson himself died of cholera en route to Delhi.[34]

His successor, Sir Harry Barnard, a Crimean veteran, joined forces with the troops from Meerut, encountering opposition from mutineers along their line of march, and winning the first major engagement of the war at Badli-ki-Serai, five miles from Delhi, on 8 June. They then encamped on the ridge overlooking Delhi, so denying the opposition any chance of establishing a secure seat of government. The first group of reinforcements, the Corps of Guides, arrived on 9 June, after a march of 580 miles from Peshawur, but the British were too few to invest the city, still less to attack fortifications they had themselves modernised. Barnard died of cholera on 5 July. His successor, Major General Reed, was invalided to the hills eleven days later and command passed to Brigadier General Wilson. Large-scale reinforcements fought their way down from the Punjab to arrive by mid-August but not until the arrival on 3 September of the siege train from Ferozepur, despite desperate attempts by their enemies to intercept it, were the British able to take the offensive.[35]

The fate of Delhi had the greatest consequences. The final attack included a week's continuous bombardment before the city walls were stormed on 14 September. Six more days of street fighting followed before resistance was ended. The four months' fighting cost the British side 3,537 dead and wounded, out of a total of 11,200 soldiers (3,300 Europeans, 7,900 Indians). A total of 1,170 casualties, over 20 per cent of those involved in the assault, were suffered on 14 September alone. The defenders, who included large numbers of religious warriors and armed retainers of chiefs loyal to Bahadur Shah, as well as mutineers of the Bengal Army, suffered even heavier losses, as did the unfortunate inhabitants of Delhi in the subsequent sack of their city. The Mughal princes surrendered. Three were shot to forestall any rescue, twenty-three were later hanged as rebels and Bahadur Shah, who had been given a promise that his life would be spared, was put on trial for rebellion.[36]

If Delhi was the head of the insurgency, Hindustan was its heart. After three weeks of rising mistrust and tension between the British (whose intelligence officers warned that the example of the Meerut and Delhi mutineers might be followed anywhere) and the Bengal sepoys (who feared that British precautionary measures would lead to their own immediate or eventual destruction), both sides were proved right. During the night of 30 May a mutiny broke out at Lucknow. Loyal men of the 13th and 71st Bengal Native Infantry, fighting alongside the 32nd Foot, defeated the mutineers, who then marched to Delhi. Those of their number who had been taken prisoner were tried by court-martial and hanged. Elsewhere in Awadh, however, the newly installed British administration collapsed, as the garrisons of the various district headquarters joined the mutiny. As had been the case at Meerut, in some cases, the soldiers ensured that no harm came to their officers. In others, Europeans including women and children were murdered, with civilian rioters joining in the attacks. In yet others, local landholders protected European refugees and helped them escape before going themselves, with their retainers, to fight against the British who had, the year before, taken their country. At Benares, on 5 June, the 37th Bengal Native Infantry was in the process of being disarmed when shooting started, and the sepoys were dispersed by Colonel Neill and his Madras European Fusiliers, rushed up by steamer and the first few hundred miles of railway in India. The Allahabad garrison mutinied the next day and many Christians, and Hindu pilgrims too, died at the hands of local criminals. Neill reached Allahabad and relieved the fort there on 11 June. The many acts of reprisal which he and other British officers authorised began to have a counter-productive effect for, as they were imposed with little regard for guilt or innocence, most of the local population fled on his approach, making it difficult to obtain the local labour, transport and supplies on which his troops depended.[37]

The next garrison up the Ganges was at Kanpur (Cawnpore). The commander, Major General Sir Hugh Wheeler, an ageing but able veteran of the Maratha wars, believed that if his sepoys mutinied, they would desert and march to Delhi. He therefore built field works outside the city into which, when the mutiny did occur on 4 June, the European community and loyal elements moved. The mutineers (2nd Bengal Irregular Cavalry, 1st, 53rd, and 55th Native Infantry) were, however, joined by the forces of Nana Sahib, adopted son of Baji Rao II, the last of the Peshwas, deposed by the British in 1818, and holder of a *jagir* near Kanpur until his death in 1851. Nana Sahib, to whom the British had declined to grant either the Peshwa's titles or his allowances, then led the combined force against Wheeler's entrenchments.[38] After three weeks' desperate resistance, and influenced by the plight of his non-combatants, Wheeler accepted Nana Sahib's promise of safe conduct by river-boat to Allahabad and surrendered on 27 June. After reaching the boats, he and the remnants of his command were attacked. Of those who survived, the men were shot and the women and children taken back into Kanpur.[39] On 30 June, Major General Havelock, a sixty-five–year-old veteran of campaigns against the Afghans, Punjabis and, most recently, Iranians, with forty-two years' commissioned service to his credit, arrived to take over command from Neill at Allahabad. He marched for Kanpur on 10 July, hoping to rescue the European women and children, but fought his way into the city a week later only to find that all had been murdered just before his arrival.[40]

He pushed on through the mid-summer heat to Lucknow. There the British community, increased by refugees from elsewhere in Awadh, had been under siege since the beginning of July, following the defeat of an ill-starred effort to counter the mutineers approaching from Kanpur. The Residency, the seat of British government, was well-fortified and stoutly defended by a mixed force of British regulars and volunteers, strengthened by loyal sepoys and military pensioners. Nevertheless, casualties steadily rose. Women and children suffered, like the men, from disease, the heat and enemy artillery. Supplies of food, munitions and medical supplies steadily dwindled. Havelock's own force, reduced by fighting and sickness to 1,364 rank and file and ten guns, fell back towards Kanpur on 30 July to await reinforcements. Neill, holding Kanpur with the aid of a policy of frightfulness, told Havelock he should have pressed on and that this retreat was a blow to British prestige. Havelock answered that he stood in no need of such advice from an officer under his command and that, but for the military emergency, he would have placed Neill under arrest.[41] On 3 August, after receiving a few reinforcements, he resumed the offensive, only to be forced back to Kanpur where Neill needed support against another large force of insurgents. This was defeated at Bithur on 16 August but, with his own force reduced to barely 700 effectives, and further disturbances lower down the Ganges, Havelock, despite his unbroken record of victory whenever he had actually encountered his opponents, could do no more until reinforcements arrived.

They arrived at Kanpur on 15 September, led by Sir James Outram. He, though the senior ranking of the two generals, lived up to his reputation as 'the Bayard of India' by ceding command to Havelock and accompanying the troops only in his capacity as civil Commissioner.[42] Nevertheless, but for the long-standing personal friendship between the two men, civil-military relations would have proved just as difficult as when a military Governor-General and a C-in-C, India, were in the field together during the first Sikh War, for Havelock was bound to move his army in accordance with Outram's political directions. Nevertheless, Outram's decision gained the concurrence of both the Governor-General and of the newly arrived C-in-C, India. This was Sir Colin Campbell, a Highland officer who had served in the Peninsular War, the West Indies and the Punjab. Re-employed on the outbreak of the Crimean War, he commanded the 'thin red line' at Balaclava, a battle from which he was one of the few British generals to emerge with his reputation enhanced.[43] On 19 September, as the weather became cooler, and reinforcements arrived at Calcutta, the British again advanced from Kanpur. They fought their way into Lucknow a week later, losing thirty-one officers and 504 men killed and wounded out of 3,197, with Brigadier General Neill among the fallen, but the Residency was reached. It was however, reinforced rather than relieved and the siege continued, with the besiegers defiantly proclaiming the restoration of the former dynasty. It was not until 17 November that a relieving force led by Campbell himself, and including a brigade of heavy guns manned from HMS *Shannon*, finally reached Lucknow. The fighting was still by no means over. An army composed of Nana Sahib's men and mutineers of the Gwalior Contingent, led by Ramchandra Panduranga, better known as Tatya Tope, an officer of the late Peshwa's service, was still in the field and succeeded in recapturing Kanpur on 27 November.[44] Campbell abandoned Lucknow and after sending his non-combatants to safety turned to face this new threat. Tatya Tope was defeated on 6–7 December and Kanpur was re-occupied by the British. A column of British troops from Delhi then fought its way eastwards to join forces with Campbell on 4 January 1858.

Lucknow was now as politically significant as Delhi had been in the first phase of the war. It was a focus of loyalty for the mutineers of whose country it was the capital, as of the Awadhi landholders *(taluqdars)* whose king had ruled there until the previous year. They had proclaimed the restoration of his dynasty, they still had a formidable power in the field, and they still challenged the legitimacy of British dominion over Hindustan. It was not, however, until the campaigning season was almost over that Campbell was able to begin his offensive. He marched from Kanpur on 27 February 1858 and, after a carefully conducted ten days' siege, took Lucknow by storm on 21 March. As retribution for the sympathy which so many of them had displayed for the insurgents, Canning proclaimed to the landholders of Awadh that, with the exception of only six named individuals, all were deemed to have forfeited their grants and would have to rely upon the mercy and justice of the British Government for the retention of life and liberty. On the evidence of British policy during the previous decade, most landholders assumed this meant general confiscation and, rather than tamely lose their place in the world, many who had previously remained neutral now rose in arms against the British. It was not until February 1859 that Awadh was reconquered, and even then a few desperate bands held out in the jungle-clad hill areas on the borders of Nepal.

The third major campaign of the war was in Central India.[45] Jhansi, a small state in Bundelkhand, had been ruled by a Maratha prince, Maharaja Gangadhar Rao, a friend of the British until his death in November 1853. In March 1854 Dalhousie had set aside Gangadhar Rao's dying request that the state be ruled by his widow, Rani Laksmi Bai, in the minority of his adopted son, and annexed Jhansi under the doctrine of lapse. The troops maintained by the late Maharaja were disbanded and their place taken by the 12th Bengal Native Infantry, which was still stationed at the city of Jhansi three years later, and which mutinied on 5 June 1857. The British officials and clerks held out for four days in the fort but, having neither provisions nor any hope of relief, came out hoping for safe conduct, only to be killed with their women and children. Some fifty-five people were murdered, the worst massacre in the whole Indian Mutiny, except for those at Kanpur.

Some sixty miles north west of Jhansi, the Gwalior Contingent, a subsidiary force of Company sepoys imposed upon Sindia after his defeat in the campaign of 1843, mutinied on 14 June 1857. Europeans who escaped the massacre there found refuge with the maharaja, and were subsequently escorted to Agra, sixty miles to the north. Sindia temporised with the troops of the Contingent until September 1857, when Tatya Tope arrived in person and persuaded them to join the operations against Kanpur that caused Campbell to abandon Lucknow at the end of the month.

The column of troops from the Bombay Army, led by Major General Sir Hugh Rose, reached Jhansi on 21 March 1858. By this time all in the British camp were convinced of the Rani's treachery, while she and her people were determined to resist the return of British rule by force of arms. On 31 March an attempt by Tatya Tope to relieve the city was defeated and Jhansi was stormed on 3 April, with much slaughter. The Rani escaped, through the self-sacrifice of her Afghan bodyguard, and joined Tatya's army. This force crossed into Gwalior, hoping that Sindia would at last make common cause with Nana Sahib, who, having taken the title of Peshwa, claimed the leadership of all the Maratha princes. Sindia's army went over to the invaders but he himself refused to join them and fled to the British at Agra. Rose, pursuing Tatya, captured Gwalior on 20 June. The Rani of Jhansi was killed in a skirmish with the advancing British forces on 17 June. On 29 June Rose handed over command to his chief of staff, Robert Napier, who pursued Tatya Tope and what was left of his army across the Chambal into Rajasthan. Tatya Tope, betrayed and captured in April 1859, was hanged as a rebel, though this was something of a technicality as he was a subject of the last acknowledged Peshwa, Baji Rao II, until his death in 1851, and had sworn no oath to the Company. His master, Nana Sahib, escaped to the Nepal jungles with a lakh of rupees on his head. His fate remains unknown to historians. Jung Bahadur, ruler of Nepal, told the British that his officers believed the Nana Sahib died of fever on 24 September 1859. Other witnesses claimed to have seen him alive after that date, in Nepal or even, as late as 1895, in India itself, in the shape of a wandering mendicant.[46]

Notes

1. A. Harrington, *Guide to the Records of the India Office Military Department*, London, 1982.
2. *Ibid.*
3. *Ibid.*
4. 33 Geo. III, c. 52.
5. 53 Geo. III, c. 155.
6. 3 & 4 Will. IV, c. 85.
7. 5 & 6 Will. IV, c. 52.
8. *East India Registers*, London, annually 1804–1858.
9. *Ibid.*
10. F.G. Cardew, *A Sketch of the Services of the Bengal Native Infantry*, Calcutta, 1903, pp. 142–3; P. Cadell, *History of the Bombay Army*, London, 1938, pp. 165–6.
11. A.L. Basham, 'Notes on Seafaring in Ancient India', *Art and Letters (Journal of the Royal India, Pakistan and Ceylon Society)*, London Vol. 23, 1949, p. 60; R.K. Mookerji, *History of Indian Shipping*, London, 1918.

12. A.L. Basham, *The Wonder That Was India*, London, 1954, p. 231.
13. Cardew, *op. cit.*, p. 36.
14. Cardew, *op. cit.*, p. 66.
15. R. Callahan, *The East India Company and Army Reform 1783–1798*, Cambridge, Mass, 1972, pp. 174–5.
16. Cardew, *op. cit.*, p. 146.
17. H. Beveridge, *A Comprehensive History of India*, London, 1865, Vol. 2, p. 159.
18. *Ibid.*, p. 160.
19. *Ibid.*, p. 161.
20. *Ibid.*, p. 162.
21. Wellington to the Rt Hon. Sir Charles Wynne (pte) 7 August 1826, *Despatches, Correspondence and Memorials of Arthur, Duke of Wellington*, London, 1856.
22. V.A. Smith, *The Oxford History of India*, Oxford, 1958, p. 587.
23. T.A. Heathcote, *The Afghan Wars 1839–1919*, London, 1980, pp. 32–67.
24. H.T. Lambrick, *Sir Charles Napier and Sind*, Oxford, 1952.
25. Cardew, *op. cit.*, p. 202.
26. V.A. Smith, *op. cit.*, p. 610.
27. Cardew, *op. cit.*, pp. 241–2.
28. 'A few words relative to the late Mutiny of the Bengal Army and the rebellion in the Bengal Presidency. By Shailc Hedayut Ali, Soobahdar and Sirdar Bahadoor, Bengal Seikh Police Battalion commanded by Captain T. Rattray', *cit.* in M.R. Gubbins, *An Account of the Mutinies in Oudh*, 3rd edn, London, 1859, pp. 533, 560; J.W. Kaye, *A History of the Sepoy War in India*, 3 Vols, London, 1877, Vol. 1, pp. 466–9.
29. G.W. Forrest, ed. *Selections from the Letters, Despatches, and other State Papers preserved in the Military Department of the Government of India 1857–1858*, 3 Vols, Calcutta, 1893–1902, Vol. 1, pp. 1–5, pp. 227–11.
30. S.N. Sen, *Eighteen Fifty Seven*, Delhi, 1957, pp. 50–4; Trial of Jemadar Issuree Pandy, 10 April 1857, *cit.* in Forrest, pp. 177–207.
31. Sen, *op. cit.*, pp. 57–8.
32. Sen, *op. cit.*, pp. 60–2.
33. *Ibid.*, pp. 70–3.
34. Kaye, *op. cit.*, Vol. II, pp. 168–71.
35. Cardew, *op. cit.*, pp. 271–2.
36. *Ibid.*, pp. 272–5; Sen, *op. cit.*, pp. 79–118.
37. Sen, *op. cit.*, pp. 154–6.
38. P.C. Gupta, *Nana Sahib and the Rising at Lucknow*, Oxford, 1963, pp. 68–9.
39. Sen, *op. cit.*, p. 157.
40. Sen, *op. cit.*, p. 158.
41. *Ibid.*, p. 206.
42. *Ibid.*, p. 218; J.C. Pollock, *Way to Glory: The Life of Havelock of Lucknow*, London, 1957, p. 219; Divisional Order by Maj.-Gen. Sir James Outram dated 16 Sept 1857, *cit.* in W. Brock, *A Biographical Sketch of Sir Henry Havelock, KCB*, London, 1858, pp. 219–20, and in A. Forbes, *Havelock*, London, 1890, p. 179.
43. A. Forbes, *Colin Campbell, Lord Clyde*, London, 1895.
44. Sen, *op. cit.*, Ch. 4; P.C. Gupta, *op. cit.*, Ch. 5; Kaye, *op. cit.*, Vol. II, Book V, Chs 1–4; Forrest, *op. cit.*, Vol. 2, Chs 1–7.
45. R.G. Burton, *The Revolt in Central India 1857–58*, compiled in the Intelligence Branch, Army HQ India, from the dispatches of the campaign, Simla 1908; Sen, *op. cit.*, Chs, 7–8; G.W. Forrest, *A History of the Indian Mutiny Reviewed and Illustrated from Original Documents*, 3 Vols, Edinburgh and London, 1904–1912, Vol. 3, Chs 1–7, 19.
46. Gupta, *op. cit.*, pp. 200–203.

Chapter 5

The Reconstruction, 1858–1864

The Indian Mutiny was the last and most terrible of the British wars in India, and the most far-reaching in its consequences. It was both more and less than a mutiny. It could not have begun if so many sepoys of the Bengal Army had not collectively refused to obey orders, the very definition of mutiny. The use of their weapons against their officers, non-combatants, and those who chose to remain under orders was not mutiny but murder or attempted murder. Remaining in a formal body under arms, and declaring allegiance to rulers other than the East India Company to whom a soldier's oath of loyalty had been freely given was rebellion. Not every sepoy mutinied, even among the Purabiyas. Many were disarmed, irrespective of their intentions, and spent the war under surveillance in their barracks. Many were deserters rather than mutineers, committing a serious military crime but following a not unreasonable course of action in the summer of 1857 when it seemed to many that, in accordance with the widely believed prophecy and the evidence of their own eyes, the rule of the East India Company had ended the century after it began at the Battle of Plassey. Nevertheless, the revolt could not have spread as far as it did, had it not been more than a mutiny.

The areas in which British rule most comprehensively collapsed, and where resistance to its re-imposition was most bitterly prolonged, were among those where it had been most recently imposed and where it was most strongly resented. They were also those nearest to the Purabiya homeland, so that the combination of military indiscipline and political opposition which elsewhere, where they existed, could be contained separately, here turned into a potent insurrection. It was not a war of national independence. Most of India was not involved, and more Indian soldiers and non-combatant followers served in the British ranks than opposed them. Many princes saw themselves as no more dependent on the British than they had been on the Mughals, and no more needful of rising against the former than of rallying to restore the latter. It was, however, in Awadh, Jhansi, and the nominally independent kingdom of Delhi, a war of liberation, in which local elites, with the support of the politically conscious, fought as robustly against the forces of the British occupation as did the mutinous sepoys.[1]

What distinguished the Indian Mutiny from all the other British wars in South Asia was the element of racial hatred and the consequent involvement of non-combatants. Many other wars in India, as in Europe, had seen massacres of innocent women and children. No other war in India, however, had seen British families slaughtered. Even the Afghans, despised by the civilised Hindustanis as uncouth barbarians, had treated the English ladies who fell into their hands during the retreat from Kabul with respect, and had eventually returned them unharmed.[2] The worst crimes in the mutiny of 1857 appears to have been committed by civilian mobs or individual psychopaths rather than mutineers, though as they formed a common enemy, the British made no distinction between them and took revenge on anyone they could find.[3] British fury was intensified by the many lurid stories published in the Anglo-Indian press, by comparison with which modern tabloid journals are models of accuracy and understatement.

Atrocity stories were as readily accepted by the British as pollution stories had been believed by the sepoys, on as little evidence in both instances. Men on both sides seemed to believe most easily the stories of what they most feared. For the sepoys of the time, this was the loss of their soul's immortality. For the British, it was their women and children falling into the hands of sadists and killers, especially those of a different, and subject, race. The effect of this was to madden both sides into reprisals and atrocities such as so often occur in slave rebellions or in wars of race and religion. Acts of revenge by the British were in full swing even before the Kanpur massacres. When the details of that episode became known, with accounts of the discovery of blood-stained tresses, children's shoes, and all the pathetic detritus of cruelty such as would, late in the following century, become too familiar from television news broadcasts, the rage of the soldiers grew even stronger. Revenge was sought irrespective of involvement. Guilty and innocent alike, men and women, even loyal sepoys fighting for the British, were all liable to be murdered, as 'no quarter' became the general cry. Men were hanged or blown away from guns (the old Mughal punishment for mutiny) with little or no trial.[4]

Decent men of all ranks on both sides condemned the excesses of those in their own forces. Shahzada Firuz Shah, a young and pious member of the imperial house who escaped from Delhi and built up an army with which he fought the British for two years, issued a proclamation on 17 February 1858, declaring that the delay in defeating the English was caused by people killing innocent children and women, contrary to all orders, and to the dictates of the Holy Law. Sir Colin Campbell countermanded orders given by Brigadier Neill to degrade condemned prisoners by ritual pollution. Canning, whose first declaration to the people of Awadh earned him an unprecedented public rebuke from Ellenborough at the Board of Control for its unjustifiable and impolitic severity, subsequently implemented a more merciful policy, on

Cabinet orders and with the personal approval of the Queen, only to be sneered at in both England and India as 'Clemency' Canning.[5]

Stories of atrocities by the British side as well as by the mutinous sepoys were reported in the English papers by correspondents such as William Russell who had made his name in the Crimea, but popular indignation at the latter proved greater than at the former. There were even calls for companies of 'gentlemen volunteers' to go to India to assist in punishing the mutineers. The Duke of Cambridge, C-in-C of the British Army, poured cold water on this idea. A professional soldier himself, he saw no value in these untrained and over-enthusiastic avengers. Instead, he authorised the first twenty-five regiments of the Infantry of the Line each to raise a second battalion to meet the emergency in India, so increasing the number of infantry units in the British Regular Army (including Foot Guards and the Rifle Brigade) to 124.[6]

For all the alarm and anger felt by the British, they were not faced with a general uprising of the whole population, nor even of the entire politically-conscious or military elements of it. Members of the intelligentsia, who rarely make common cause with soldiers except in times of genuine revolution, passed resolutions condemning those who mutinied.[7] In all the Madras Army only one regiment refused an order to march. The remainder, though already having come to be viewed by officers of the other Armies as lacking in martial spirit, remained at their duties and deterred any possible move by the Nizam of Hyderabad's forces to support the Mughal restoration. In fact, the Nizam regarded the activities north of his domain as an uprising that could only benefit his dynastic enemies, the Marathas. In Maharashtra, however, not a sword was drawn to support Nana Sahib's revival of the cause of the Peshwa.[8] The loyalty of the Bombay Army, despite its own claims to being better disciplined than that of Bengal, may have owed much to the Maratha origins of a third of its men as well as to its traditional rivalry with the Bengal Army. Six of the thirty-two Bombay infantry battalions and one of the eight Bombay cavalry regiments wavered in their reliability, although only elements of two battalions, and of two artillery companies actually mutinied.[9] One-third of the Bombay Army were Purabiyas, often recruited from the same villages as those in the Bengal Army who had mutinied. Like those in the Punjab, they would have found it difficult to get home if they had mutinied. Unlike those in the Punjab, for whatever good or bad reason, they did not try.

Many Indians joined the British. For every British soldier in the field there were twenty Indian 'followers', official or unofficial, providing all the logistic services without which an army could not function in India, among them sword-cutlers, grooms, grass-cutters, water-carriers, cooks, bullock-drivers, washermen, sweepers, bearers, sanitary men, barbers, traders and 'bazar-walas' of all sorts. Exactly the same could be said for the armies on the opposite side. Both sides too, had their lawbreakers, thieves and murderers, sometimes claiming to act from noble causes. Others were on neither side and robbed or killed both impartially, from custom as much as conviction, and for pleasure as much as profit.

The impact of these dramatic events in India upon public opinion in the United Kingdom was such that the Cabinet had to be seen to be taking some action. That action was the abolition of the East India Company's government, thus incidentally justifying all those who had prophesied it would end a hundred years after Plassey. The Charter Act of 1854 had already foreshadowed this.[10] The Company's charter had not been renewed for the customary twenty years, but only for so long as Parliament should provide, and its holdings were declared to be in trust for the British Crown. The number of Directors had been reduced from twenty-four to eighteen, of whom six were nominated by the British government, and at least twelve had to have served ten or more years in India. The C-in-C in each Presidency was given complete control over both the royal and the Company's troops stationed there. The appointment to military cadetships remained a matter for patronage but entry to the civil service was henceforth by open competitive examination, and the Company's civil service college at Haileybury was ordered to close by 1858. This act also removed any limit on the number of the Company's European troops and allowed these to be decided by the Board of Control. There was little left for the Company to do and it had, by 1857, become just as much a shadow of a great name as had the King of Delhi from whom it held its titles to power in India.[11]

On 12 February 1858 the Prime Minister, Lord Palmerston, tabled a bill in the House of Commons 'for the better government of India'. This proposed to abolish the East India Company as the vehicle through which British control of India was exercised, and to vest all its powers in a Cabinet minister or president, with a council of eight former Directors or others with Indian experience. Despite strong objection from the Company's supporters, who argued that the mutiny had not sprung from any deficiency in the machinery of government and that to abolish the Company while the war was still going on would only unsettle still further the inhabitants of India, the first reading was carried by 318 votes to 173.[12]

It would have undoubtedly become law but for the Orsini affair – an attempt by Italian assassins to murder Napoleon III, the emperor of a friendly, indeed an allied, state. As the assassination had been planned by terrorists who had been given political asylum in England, French opinion was outraged and French officers spoke of crossing the Channel to bring the offenders to justice. A conciliatory measure which would have made conspiracy to murder, even in another country, a felony under English law was condemned by British public opinion as truckling to foreign tyrants. Gentlemen volunteers, unwanted for service in India, began to think about defending their own hearths and homes. Palmerston's government was defeated on 19 February and was replaced by that of the Conservatives led by Lord Derby and Benjamin Disraeli.[13]

The new ministers then tabled their own India Bill, containing essentially the same provisions as those against which they had voted when in opposition. The main difference lay in the composition of the new Council, which Disraeli proposed to draw from a variety of interested groups. Four of its eighteen members were to be drawn from the military, including one from the British Army with a minimum of five years' service in India, and one from each of the three presidential Armies with a minimum of ten. During the Easter recess these complicated proposals were ridiculed as 'fancy franchises', typical of Disraeli's flamboyance and absurdities, so yet a third series of measures was introduced, and the India Act was finally passed in August 1858.[14] The delay was mostly caused by Lord Ellenborough, the former Governor-General, President of the Board of Control in this ministry, publicly censuring Canning for his first proclamation to Awadh, treating it as a defeated state rather than a rebellious province. When Ellenborough 'leaked' this rebuke, weeks before it could reach Canning in India, such indignation was expressed by Canning's political friends that Ellenborough himself had to resign to keep the (minority) government from being defeated.[15] His successor, Lord Stanley, became responsible for securing the passage of the India Bill and for the far-reaching changes in the Indian civil and military machine which stemmed from it.

The Act replaced the Board of Control and the East India Company with a new department of state, the India Office.[16] This was headed by the Secretary of State for India (replacing the former President of the Board of Control) and a Council of India, drawn from men with experience of civil or military service in India. These councillors, originally fifteen in number, later reduced to ten, were paid a pensionable salary and held office for a fixed period, thus providing advice which was independent of the party in power. To protect Indian revenues from raids by the British Treasury, all new expenditure had to be sanctioned by the Council. For the first fifty years of its existence the Council proved a stabilising influence though, in the twentieth century, as the pace of change in Indian politics quickened, its members tended to become out of date in their views, so leading to conflicts of opinion between the India Office in London and the Government of India itself.

The Act transferred all contracts and engagements of the Company to the Crown. All new appointments of civil servants and of cadets for the Indian artillery and engineers were to be by open competition. Other cadetships were to be by patronage divided among the Secretary of State and his Councillors, so that of every seventeen, the former could give two and the latter one each. One-tenth of all military cadetships were reserved for the sons of civil or military officers who had served the Crown or the Company in India. All the military and naval forces of the East India Company were deemed to be the Indian forces of the Crown, and their members were placed under the same obligations towards the Crown as they had undertaken towards the Company.[17]

A proclamation issued by Canning at Allahabad in the name of Queen Victoria on 1 November 1858 announced the change of Raj. All those now the Queen of England's subjects were called upon to bear true allegiance. Canning was declared Viceroy of India and his successors continued to enjoy that title, though it never had any parliamentary sanction and the legal title of chief executive of British India remained Governor-General. The princes of India were assured that no further territorial expansion would take place at their expense. Protection was promised to all from interference in their religion or customary rights of inheritance. Clemency was offered to all except convicted murderers, and amnesty to all those laying down their arms by January 1859.[18]

On the whole, the proclamation was honoured and had the desired result of allaying many of the fears and grievances which had fuelled the Mutiny. Some elements of it were derided by the irreconcilables, who refused to believe that the British would make so radical a change in their ways. In practice, the promise on which the British most blatantly reneged was that on which the Queen had said she set the greatest store:

> And it is our further will that, so far as may be, our subjects, of whatever race or creed, be freely and impartially admitted to office in our service, the duties of which they may be qualified by their education, ability, and integrity duly to discharge.[19]

This was, in fact, a weakening of the wording of the 1833 Charter Act.

> No native of the said territories, nor any natural-born subject of His Majesty resident therein, shall by reason only of his religion, place of birth, descent, colour, or any of them, be disabled from holding any place, office, or employment under the said Company.[20]

Indian gentlemen who had qualified at British medical schools for posts in the Company's medical service were excluded from Crown employment in India for a generation after 1858. Indian soldiers were denied commissions for even longer. Europeans were divided about their transfer from the Company's to the Crown's service. On 2 November 1858, men of the 4th Bengal Light Cavalry at Lucknow declared that they did not consider themselves bound to serve the Queen unless re-enlisted for that purpose and paid the usual bounty. Brigadier Chute, the garrison commander, asked for advice on how to respond. He was told by the Adjutant-General of the Bengal Army, whose department dealt with all personnel matters, to inform the men that they were mistaken but, as they were young soldiers in a new regiment, he should do so in 'a temperate and kindly' manner. He did so and reported on 6 November that all was well. On 9 November the C-in-C, Sir Colin Campbell, newly ennobled as Lord Clyde, reported that the 1st Madras Fusiliers, then in the field on active service with him in Awadh, had raised the same claim.[21] The fusiliers countered the government's claim that they had already sworn an oath to the Queen on attestation for the Company's service, by saying that this was only as subjects, not as soldiers joining her Army.

Clyde obviously sympathised with Neill's veterans against the penny-pinching politicians, for his Chief of Staff, Major General Mansfield, wrote to Major General Birch, Secretary to the Government of India in the Military Department:

> Lord Clyde would beg leave to call to the recollection of the Governor General, with the greatest deference to his Excellency ... that, in the old regiments of the Crown, a man cannot be transferred from one to another without his free consent, he having enlisted to serve in a particular regiment. Thus it happens that although the conditions of servitude are precisely the same in the various regiments of Her Majesty's service, wherever necessity requires that the complement of one regiment should be filled up at the expense of others, 'volunteers' are called for, who receive a bounty in consideration ... Perhaps there is no rule that the soldiers more clearly understand or to the principle of which they cling with greater tenacity ... Lord Clyde would request the closest attention to the manner in which the soldier would view any attempt to deprive him of what he considers a right. It would be difficult, if not impossible, to make him understand any legal argument by which the very principle of his military existence might, in his opinion, be set aside.

Clyde therefore suggested that the European soldiers should be discharged and enlisted with the usual bounty 'to prevent a feeling of irritation arising in the army of a very inconvenient and perhaps dangerous tendency', adding that he would not suggest this but for his 'intimate acquaintance with British soldiers and the manner in which they feel the rights they possess in common with other Englishmen'.[22]

Canning refused to accept this advice. Parliament had enacted the men's transfer and, irrespective of any previous oaths, it was, he said, supreme in such matters. The Government of India could not disregard the law, and had never had the power to discharge soldiers of the British Army, which was what all its European troops now were. He pointed out the 'imprudence' of giving 15,000 men (6,000 of them in the vitally important artillery), their discharge while the country was still unsettled. (The men, of course, would not re-engage once discharged unless the bounty was paid and not all could be counted on to re-engage in any case.) It would, he added, be dangerous if the native troops saw a disagreement between the Europeans and the government, and they might demand similar terms for themselves. Nevertheless, he agreed to forward the case to the government in London, though warning that he saw no prospect of a different answer.[23]

The matter was referred to the law officers of the Crown for consideration. On 31 December 1858 Lord Stanley, the Secretary of State for India, expressed both his agreement with the Governor-General and his hope that the men would cheerfully await the outcome of the investigation into their claim. On 24 February 1859 he notified the Government of India that the law officers considered Parliament to have acted within its powers, and therefore that the claim was invalid. Six weeks later, when the papers reached India, the men were so informed in a General Order. On 2 May at Meerut, where the sepoy mutiny had begun two years earlier, men of the Bengal Artillery and Light Cavalry gathered in unauthorised assemblies. Inflammatory slogans were written on latrine walls and various acts of indiscipline were reported from a number of other stations.[24]

Canning now found himself faced with the prospect of the mutiny which Clyde had warned him would happen if the men's feelings were disregarded. Three British regiments about to sail for England after serving in the recent campaign were ordered to remain in India: '... we have no choice but to do so', he reported 'for some days a collision between large bodies of our English soldiers has been imminent. Such a catastrophe would be painful and deplorable enough at any time and in any part of the Queen's dominions; but what its consequences would be in India in the still unsettled state of many classes of Her Majesty's native subjects, no man can predict.' He conceded that the men would have to be allowed to take their discharge. He thought that not many really wanted to go, but feared that others would be carried along out of comradeship, or anger at the government, or the influence of agitators, in which case 'the Government of India would be gravely embarrassed, not merely by the absolute diminution of the strength of the army, but by the moral effect which the departure of so many English soldiers, manifestly against the will of the Government, will be sure to produce on the native mind'.[25]

More evidence came in the discontent among the 'dumpies' (as wits had named the Company's Europeans from the relaxation of their height rules during the recent campaign). A court of enquiry held at Mian Mir on 12 May interviewed men of two troops of horse artillery, three companies of foot artillery, and the 3rd Bengal Light Cavalry. Of the junior ranks, 578 declared themselves dissatisfied, and only 117 satisfied. The NCOs, with more at stake, divided into 108 satisfied and thirty-four dissatisfied. On 17 May the GOC of the division at Meerut reported to Mansfield that several horse artillery units were implicated 'in the *strike*, as they call it'.[26] The views of the 1st Madras Fusiliers, now back in their own presidency at Bangalore, were expressed by their commanding officer:

> they feel themselves insulted as men, as Englishmen, they being transferred as cattle from one party to another: this idea is so forcibly and indelibly impressed upon their minds, their hearts, that they feel themselves degraded in their own estimation, and they believe they are so in the estimation of everyone. Their consent to be transferred to the Queen's service has never been asked, therefore they are no longer Englishmen, no longer men, but slaves, cattle, sheep.[27]

Artillerymen took the same approach. Were they, they asked, to be handed over, like their gun-bullocks and ordnance, from one set of masters to another? At Berhampur, on 17 June, the 5th Bengal Europeans refused orders, only 120 out of 550 remaining at their duty until a steamer from Calcutta arrived four days later with 500 British infantry and two field guns. When a change of policy was announced,[28] the crisis ended. At Mian Mir, of the 260 gunners, 136 decided to leave, 124 to stay, and of the 638 cavalry troopers, 606 left, and only thirty-two remained.

Canning was obliged to report that the men would not recede from their claim that they had sworn only to serve the Company, and that as the Company was no more, they were released from their oath. Moreover, Palmerston, in his place as Prime Minister, had told the House of Commons, when introducing his India Bill on 12 February 1858, that those who disliked changing their service from the Company to the Crown would be equitably entitled to their discharge: 'We have found that the knowledge of his Lordship's declared opinion is very general among the troops and that they place great reliance upon it ... It is certain also that the combination to persevere in these demands has been much more widespread than we had in the first instance reason to believe.'[29] Men who insisted on their discharge were therefore told they could have it with a free passage home, but those who re-enlisted in India were still refused the customary bounty.

Meanwhile, the future of the European, as of the Native, elements of the Indian Army had already been decided by the Peel Report of 1859.[30] This document comprised 252 pages of closely printed text, with evidence given to the Commission in person by fifty expert witnesses from all arms of the three Indian Armies and from the British Army, and other experts on Indian affairs, including Lord Ellenborough, together with eighty-one appendices of written submissions from a similar cross-section of those still serving in India, including Lord Canning.

The Commission, headed by Major General Peel (the Secretary of State for War), also included Stanley, the Duke of Cambridge, his Adjutant-General, Lieutenant General Sir George Wetherall, Lieutenant General Sir Harry Smith (hero of the Sikh and Kaffir Wars) and six other senior officers of the British and Indian Armies. They convened on 15 July 1858 and were asked to answer twelve questions. These were:

1. On what terms should those in the Company's army be transferred to the service of the Crown?
2. How many European troops should be permanently stationed in India once the Mutiny campaign was over?
3. What should be the proportion of European to native troops in the cavalry, artillery and infantry respectively?
4. Was the European element to be made up of troops from the British Army serving limited tours of duty in India, or should it be raised for permanent local service there?
5. What was the best means of regularly relieving the former, or maintaining the efficiency of the latter?
6. Would it be possible to consolidate the Company's European forces with the British Army and allow subsequent exchanges, with justice to all the Company's officers?
7. Should European and Indian troops be mixed at either regimental or brigade level?
8. Should troops for any local European forces be recruited directly in the United Kingdom, or by volunteers from British units in India?
9. Should colonial troops be raised for service in India?
10. Should the native Indian forces be organised on the regular or irregular system, and in what proportion to each other?
11. Should the native component include artillery?
12. Should cadets for the native Army be attached to European units?

After taking evidence between August and December 1858, the Commission submitted its findings to Parliament on 7 March 1859. A wealth of evidence had been collected either in initial statements or in response to its members' subsequent questioning of witnesses, and practically every aspect of the organisation, discipline and practices of the military in British India had been examined. The Commission's own answers to the questions it had been set were as follows.

Question 1 had already been decided by the India Act of August 1858, which provided that all members formerly of the East India Company's Armies were guaranteed 'the like Pay, Pensions, Allowances and Privileges, and like Advantages as regards Promotion and otherwise, as if they had continued in the Service of the said Company'.[31] Therefore there could be no change in the system of promoting officers by regimental seniority. The number of European troops was to be flexible, according to the needs arising at any time, but normally to be 50,000 in the Bengal Army, and 15,000 each in those of Madras and Bombay. The proportion of native to European cavalry and infantry was to be, at most, two to one in Bengal, and three to one elsewhere. Artillery was to be manned by British gunners except at stations unsuitable for European constitutions. It was noted that many 'military police' corps were not constabulary bodies at all, but really little different from sepoy units. These were in future not to be given training in battle tactics nor allowed to become an alternative to the Army.

The most bitterly contended argument was over the existence of a separate local European force. The minority, supported by the opinions of many, including Canning himself, gave its view that permanent residence in India was essential to allow officers to learn the language and customs of the theatre in which they would be serving, and to provide a pool of expertise from which the government could draw for all purposes. The minority view was that the anomaly of having a local European force in India was no greater than the anomaly of the British being in India at all, and that to separate the officers of the European from those of the native forces would damage the *esprit de corps* of the latter (an argument advanced at the time of Dundas's attempted reforms). They did not accept that there were problems in recruiting Europeans for local service, nor in regard to their health, as the mortality in newly arrived British regiments was worse than that of the troops permanently stationed in India. Finally, they argued that only by having its own local Europeans could the Government of India be sure that, in a sudden emergency, the British Government would not withdraw troops from the defence of India for employment elsewhere.

All these points were countered by the majority. They found no other case in history of the co-existence of two distinct armies supplied from the same sources both of officers and men, serving the same sovereign. The ancient ill feeling between the British and Indian Army officers would only be made worse if there were to be two sets of British troops in the service of the Crown. A local force deteriorated more quickly, in Indian conditions, than one regularly relieved. The military resources of the state, maintained for imperial purposes, would be crippled if a large percentage of them were assigned exclusively to the Indian Government. Local troops in the Crown's service would come to feel themselves inferior to those which fought the Crown's battles all over the world, while they would themselves deny to the British Line its share of experience and glory in Indian campaigns. The number of British troops must always be a matter for Parliament, and no British government would leave India with a force smaller than was needed there.

The difference in cost between troops of the British Line and local Europeans was considered insignificant. If the Line produced better troops, then the wisest policy was to employ them. Recruiting from the limited number of suitable young men willing to enlist as regular soldiers would lead to difficulties if two armies were bidding against each other for their services. As those in favour of retaining locals admitted that they gained from the presence and example of British Line regiments, a number of these would be needed to continue to serve in India in any case. Accordingly, the majority recommended that all should belong to the British Army.

The answers to the other questions were: that the systems of regular reliefs for the British Line should continue, with the maximum length of any unit's tour fixed at twelve years and if locals were to be continued, they should have their own depots in the United Kingdom, where their recruits would be available for home defence in case of emergency; that exchanges between officers of the British Line and the locals would be desirable if a means could be found of overcoming the difficulties, especially in respect of the pension funds, to which (if the government did not take them over) all new officers would have to subscribe in order to keep them solvent; European and native soldiers were not to be mixed below brigade level (only the artillery officers had supported the idea of mixing races within units, and only then with Indians in non-technical positions) though every brigade was to have at least one European unit. Locals, if retained, should continue to recruit both directly in the UK and by volunteers from the Line in India, as was the existing case; it was inadvisable to raise regiments of coloured men from the colonies for Indian service; the irregular system should be adopted for all Indian cavalry, except for the existing regular cavalry regiments of Madras and Bombay; Indian infantry should, for the most part, be regular; native artillery should be disbanded, to ensure that this decisive arm should never again be in the hands of any but Europeans, though the interests of all those in the three Armies who had served loyally were to be given every consideration; and all cadets for the native Army should be trained in England and attached to regiments of the British Line for practical experience before joining their own.

Additional recommendations were that: native regiments should be recruited from 'different nationalities and castes, mixed promiscuously through each regiment'[32]; all natives were to be recruited for general service; the uniform of the native troops was to be modified, and assimilated to the dress of the country so as to be more suited to its climate; the scientific branches of the Army were to be reserved to Europeans, but Indian pioneers were to be raised to relieve British sappers of arduous duties which exposed them to the effects of the climate; the powers of commanding officers in Indian units were to be increased, and they were to have the same powers of promotion of their men as those in the British Line, replacing promotion by seniority; pay and allowances (including *batta*) should be simplified; there should be one C-in-C in India (C-in-C of the Bengal Army), and the chiefs in Madras and Bombay should be 'general officers commanding' the forces there. The report ended by drawing attention to the adverse consequences of the small number of officers doing duty with their regiments, in consequence of their being withdrawn for staff or other employment. It offered three solutions. The first was the formation of staff corps from which officers would be drawn for any duties. The second was that all officers on extra-regimental duty should be 'seconded' (i.e. replaced in their absence by supernumaries with the consequent additional cost of paying for them). The third was to place all European officers on presidential, rather than regimental, lists for promotion. The staff corps system was that finally chosen.

The subsequent decision to implement the majority's view and abolish the local European force had profound consequences for the British Army. Before the Mutiny there had been four cavalry regiments and twenty-two battalions of the line (some 24,000 officers and men) in India. Even when the Company's Europeans (6,000 gunners and 8,000 infantry) were added to the British Army, this was still less than half the 80,000 men recommended by Peel as the future British garrison in India. The Royal Artillery, by absorbing the three Indian artillery regiments, doubled in size and therefore did not need to raise additional units to meet its new Indian commitment. The infantry, however, had to retain the twenty-five extra battalions it had raised for the Mutiny campaign, as well as the single-battalion European regiments, three from each presidency, which were re-mustered as the nine junior corps of the Infantry of the Line.

The British cavalry too needed extra units. These were found by raising three new regiments of Light Dragoons (numbered 19th, 20th and 21st) from the Bengal European Light Cavalry, with extra officers drawn from those surplus in the Bengal, Madras, and Bombay cavalry respectively, which were being remustered as irregulars, as the cheapest option. Officers in those twelve new Line regiments retained the Company's system of promotion by seniority and subscription. 'Purchase' was forbidden, though moves were later made to introduce it. It had never existed in the Royal Artillery and Engineers, and the officers of these arms continued to be promoted by seniority, with those who joined from the Indian corps remaining on separate rolls for this purpose.

The opportunity was taken to grant new commissions to all officers of the Indian Armies. Previously they had held two. One was from the Governor-General, in the case of Bengal, or the Governors of Madras or Bombay respectively, appointing the holder to a particular regiment in the Company's service. The other, granted since 1788 on behalf of the Crown by the C-in-C, India, gave powers of command over all troops in any part of the East Indies, for as long as the holder was in the Company's service. The Company's commissions had not been recognised as valid in the United Kingdom until 1855. The first Company's officer to become a C-in-C (at Madras) was Sir Patrick Grant in 1856, and he was only allowed to succeed Anson as C-in-C, India, as an 'officiating' appointment pending the arrival of Campbell, another British Army officer. From January 1861 new commissions were granted only in the Staff Corps, worded to give powers of command over all British troops anywhere, but not (unlike British Army commissions) in any specified regiment.

Several members of the Council of India expressed objections to this new modelling of the Indian military machine. Major General Sir Henry Durand had serious doubts about the irregular system.[33] It provided too few British officers in the units and, by increasing the command skills and habit of authority of native officers, heightened the risk to British security. During the Mutiny, he said, the inefficiency of native officers had been a benefit to the British (presumably referring only to those who fought on the other side). Another member of the Council, Colonel H.T. Prinsep, also argued that the establishment of officers in the irregular system was too low. In the siege of Delhi, he said, irregular units had replaced their entire officer strength three or four times over, which had only been possible because of the large number of officers present whose regiments had mutinied. Even so, could the forty-five regiments of the British Line henceforth to be in India, from whom the Staff Corps were to be recruited in the future, provide enough officers? 'Government will be at the mercy of any combination they may make to demand higher pay and better terms.' The Mutiny was caused not by too many officers present in each regiment, but too few, and to make the whole native Army irregular was insanity.

Major General Willoughby took the same view.[34] He pointed out the inconsistency of arguing that there had been too few officers in the regiments when the irregular system would produce exactly that result. He thought that only with officers of exceptional ability could irregular units do well, and that it was undesirable to increase the self-reliance and military knowledge of native officers. The seniority system, which produced native officers no better in this respect than their men, had worked to the advantage of the British during the Mutiny.

With officers no longer being recruited directly for the India service, the old East India Company's Military Seminary, recently renamed the Royal Indian Military College, at Addiscombe was closed. Willoughby noted that the effect of this was to transfer the 10 per cent of cadetships promised by the India Act to the sons of old Indian officers, from the patronage of the India Office to the War Office, as the only cadets in the British Army were at the Royal Military Academy, Woolwich, or the Royal Military College, Sandhurst. This complaint was later remedied by the introduction of Queen's

India Cadets, who were nominated by the India Office. Nevertheless, as Willoughby saw it, the increase in the British Army was at the expense of the cheaper Indian Army: 'Almost at every stage, up to the present time, new charges are imposed on India, and still the pledges of Parliament are not redeemed, and no wonder, because the only mode in which expenditure could be kept down, and those pledges redeemed, was by the maintenance of a considerable local army.'[35]

The Peel Report had, by implication, called for a reduction in the number of native troops. These, at the beginning of 1857, had totalled 226,000 men. Peel recommended 100,000 in Bengal and 45,000 each in Madras and Bombay, giving a total of 190,000. In the initial period of reconstruction, Madras escaped with the loss only of four of its eight light cavalry regiments and twelve of its fifty-two infantry battalions. Bombay lost seven regiments of irregular horse and seven of infantry, though only two of these in each category had existed in the pre-Mutiny order of battle. Bengal, however, had seen the disbandment of all ten of its light cavalry regiments, ten of its eighteen irregular cavalry regiments, and fifty-nine out of seventy-four regular infantry regiments. Only 8,000 of the old 120,000 Bengal sepoys remained with the Colours. On the other hand, large numbers of new regiments had been raised on the irregular system, to deal with the emergency, so that in August 1860 there were still twenty-nine regiments of cavalry and sixty-three of infantry in the Bengal native army. Many of the emergency units were made permanent in the re-organisation of 1861 and they, with the surviving regulars, were renumbered in a new sequence of nineteen cavalry and forty-eight infantry regiments, of which four were Gurkhas. Also counted in the Bengal total was the Punjab Frontier Force of five cavalry and twelve infantry units, though it remained under the command of the local government, not the C-in-C, India.

Consideration was given to the groups from which the regiments should be recruited, and especially if those of low castes, who had been enlisted during the Mutiny, should replace the fastidious high-class Purabiyas. Sir Hugh Rose, who succeeded Clyde as C-in-C, India, in June 1860, called for reports on their men's suitability from the commandants of levies made up of low-class men. There was a mixed response. Captain Hall, of the Alighur Levy, said they were unclean in their habits, polluted the contents of food storage bins by their touch, and ate rats and mice and other vermin.[36] On the other hand, Lieutenant Colonel Bruce of the Oudh Police Battalion wrote 'it is strange that without either order or rule of Government, the Bengal Army should have become a quasi-masonic body of Brahmins and that the lower caste men who fought with at any rate equal courage should have been entirely replaced'.[37] He described his own men as brave, muscular, desirous of military service and willing to eat and drink anything with anybody.

Rose took a strong line against racial and class prejudice and recommended a policy of equal opportunities for all men:

> The Commander in Chief thinks it impossible that Her Majesty's Government could, under the influence of the very liberal policy which they follow with respect to the Natives of India, exclude any race of the Queen's subjects from the ranks of Her Majesty's Army. If some of these races are ... deprived of that self-esteem which is the right of all men, certainly the Government ought not to deprive the members of those castes of just the very means that will raise them ... The Commander in Chief is surprised that some of the reports should urge that men of the low races are not fit for Soldiers because their habits are dirty. The writers forget that cleanliness, the antidote of this defect, is one of the first and commonest attributes of discipline. They cannot have seen the recruits of some of the nationalities of Europe who join the army in a state of remarkable filth but become clean and smart soldiers.[38]

These honourable sentiments, however, were not shared by the majority of Bengal officers who, despite the lessons of the Mutiny, still preferred the Purabiya Rajputs and Brahmans, as smarter soldiers with a tradition of military service. The Bengal Army however, was reduced by about a third, and about half of its men were now drawn from the Punjab, or other districts beyond the borders of Hindustan.

Rose suggested a three-way distribution of recruits in the new Bengal Army. Eighteen regiments were to consist entirely of men from the same class and area. Twelve were to have recruits from both the Punjab or Hindustan, and from different communities, but grouped into homogeneous troops or companies. Twelve were to be recruited from anywhere in the Presidency and the men mixed in their companies as was the case in Madras and Bombay, and as had been recommended by Peel, irrespective of caste, religion, or district of origin. There were various opinions as to the merits of each arrangement. Troops from the same background might have a higher *esprit de corps* and fight better, but they might fight the better against the British government if their home community were to rise against it. Against this was the need to find employment for the young men of traditionally warlike communities, and a safety valve allowing them to fight for the British instead of against them. The India Office recommended this approach and that regiments so recruited should not normally serve outside their home province, to keep the troops near their families (who, unlike those of Madras, generally remained in their home villages). Tables were drawn up, carefully detailing the class composition of each unit based on the principle that no single community should, overall, be preponderant. Initially these were distributed in confidence to commanding officers, in case the native or, for that matter, the European press commented on them, as it would have been impossible to disguise the fact that recruiting policy was based on a mistrust of those being recruited, and the consequent aim of neutralising the chances of any combination against the government by its own soldiers.[39] The orders were eventually published in 1864, but those in respect of low-class men were widely disregarded by commanding officers who recruited men of higher class instead. Rose's successor, Sir William Mansfield, decided that low-class men had not proved good soldiers, and that they should in future be excluded,[40] a course which was eventually followed in Madras and Bombay.

The same combination of continuity and change characterised the reconstruction of the higher levels of Indian military administration. The Indian Councils Act of 1861[41] gave the Governor-General an executive council of five ordinary members, of whom three were to be drawn from one of the Indian services and, of the remaining two, one was to be a lawyer and one a financier. All were to hold office for five years. The C-in-C, India, was to remain as an extra-ordinary member. The business of government was divided among the five ordinary members on a 'portfolio' system, rather than them considering every question together, though, rather like cabinet government, all remained jointly responsible for whatever policy was adopted. The Governor-General took personal charge of the Political Department and was thus his own foreign minister.[42]

The Military Member, appointed since 1834 to give the Indian Army's point of view (which the C-in-C, India, drawn from the British Army, could not provide) on the whole range of official business, now became the member in charge of the Military Department. This radically altered his role for, although he was not allowed to command troops while a member of the Council, he now had a clear responsibility for exclusively military matters, the personnel and logistic subjects with which the Military Department had long been concerned. The secretariat of that department continued to be staffed by serving military officers of the Bengal Army. Initially, the system worked satisfactorily, though in later years a spirit of rivalry developed between the Military Department and Army Headquarters, especially when membership of the former changed from being a permanent specialisation into a tour of duty from which promotion or posting back to the Army, in command or staff appointments, might occur.

A broadly similar arrangement was adopted in the India Office. The Council of India divided into committees, each with a chairman who dealt directly with the ministers (the Secretary and Under-Secretary of State, of whom normally one sat in the House of Commons and the other in the House of Lords). There was a Permanent Under-Secretary, who with his deputies and assistants, provided the framework of administrative support for each of the committees and for the ministers. The Military Committee was chaired by the longest-serving of those members of Council who had previously been Indian Army officers. Its secretary was not a civil servant, but a serving senior officer of the Indian Army, with his staff drawn from the same source. The arrangement persisted until the end of the British period. This 'Military Secretary' became the Secretary of State's principal adviser on Indian Army affairs, and was thus able to represent the views of the Indian military at the highest level, a matter of importance when the Commander-in-Chief was an officer of the British Army, and when the civil government of India made proposals with which the officers of its Army were not in sympathy.

Notes

1. E. Stokes, *The Peasant Armed: The Indian Revolt of 1857*, ed. C.A. Bayly, Oxford, 1986, pp. 226ff (editor's concluding note).
2. T.A. Heathcote, *The Afghan Wars 1839–1919*, London, 1980, p. 78.
3. G.W. Forrest, *A History of the Indian Mutiny*, Vol. 1, London, 1904, pp. 478–9.
4. J.W. Kaye, *A History of the Sepoy War in India*, Vol. II, London, 1878, pp. 236–7.
5. M. MacLagan, *'Clemency' Canning*, Oxford, 1962, p. 138.
6. W. Verner, *The Military Life of HRH George, Duke of Cambridge*, Vol. 1, London, 1905, p. 130.
7. S.N. Sen, *Eighteen Fifty Seven*, Delhi, 1957, pp. 407–8.
8. *Ibid.*
9. P. Cadell, *History of the Bombay Army*, London, 1938, pp. 200–2.
10. 16 & 17 Vic, c. 95.
11. W.A.J. Archbold, *Outlines of Indian Constitutional History*, London, 1926, pp. 111–13.
12. H.H. Dodwell, *The Cambridge History of India*, Vol. VI, 1932, pp. 206–7; H. Beveridge, *A Comprehensive History of India*, London, 1865, Vol. 3, pp. 688–91.
13. J. Ridley, *Lord Palmerston*, London, 1970, pp. 479–81.
14. 21 & 22 Vic, c. 106.
15. MacLagan, *op. cit.*, pp. 196–201.
16. Archbold, *op. cit.*, pp. 114–16.
17. *Ibid.*
18. *Cit.* in MacLagan, *op. cit.*, pp. 350–2; and in Archbold, *op. cit.*, pp. 117–19.
19. *Ibid.*
20. 3 & 4 William IV, c. 85, Sect. 88.
21. IOR L/MIL/7/5441.
22. COS Bengal to Government of India (Military Dept) 10 November 1858, IOR L/MIL/7/5441.
23. MacLagan, *op. cit.*, p. 243.
24. *Ibid.*, pp. 244–6.
25. Gov.-Gen. in Council to Secretary of State for India, 14 May 1859, IOR L/MIL/7/5441.
26. GOC Mirath (Meerut) to COS Bengal 17 May 1859, IOR L/MIL/7/5441.
27. CO 1st Madras Fus. to Mil. Sec, C-in-C Madras, 25 May 1859, L/MIL/7/5441.
28. Gen. Order of Gov.-Gen. No. 883 dated 20 June 1859; H.C. Wylly, *Neill's 'Blue Caps'*, Vol. 2, Aldershot, 1933, pp. 136–7.
29. Gov.-Gen. in Council to Secretary of State for India, 24 June 1859, IOR L/MIL/7/5441.
30. Report of the Commissioners appointed to inquire into the Organisation of the Indian Army, IOR L/MIL/7/5441.
31. 21 & 22 Vic, c. 106.
32. IOR L/MIL/7/5441.
33. *Ibid.*

34. Minute by Maj.-Gen. Willoughby dated 12 January 1861, IOR L/MIL/7/5441.
35. *Ibid.*
36. Enc. in Adj.-Gen. Bengal to Sec. to Government of India, Military Dept 29 September 1860, IOR L/MIL/7/156A.
37. *Ibid.*
38. *Ibid.*
39. Adj.-Gen., Bengal to Sec. to Government of India, Military Dept 15 August 1862, with reply dated 25 August 1862, IOR L/MIL/7/156A.
40. Adj.-Gen. Bengal, Letter No. 268 N dated 20 March 1868, IOR L/MIL/7/156A.
41. 24 & 25 Vic, c. 67.
42. W.W. Hunter, *The Indian Empire*, London, 1892, p. 508; Dodwell, *op. cit.*, p. 229.

Chapter 6

The Army of Occupation, 1862–1902

After 1858 a history of the military in British India must turn from the battlefield to the council chamber to find its most fruitful source of conflict. There were no more battles fought in India until the end of British rule there. All the wars involving troops from India were either on the frontiers, against ill-armed tribesmen, or across the borders, against weak neighbouring states (Afghanistan, Burma, Tibet) or overseas against Ethiopians, Sudanese, Arabs, or Chinese, all of whose military equipment tended to be behind that of their Western-armed opponents. Not until 1914, when sent to fight the Germans in France and in East Africa, and the Turks in Mesopotamia, did Indian soldiers again fight a conventional war against enemies at least as well armed as themselves. In 1941 they found themselves defending India against a Japanese enemy that was, at least in the short term, both better equipped and better led, but even then the fighting barely touched the South Asian sub-continent.

The new system preserved British control partly by an end to further annexation (though the British already held practically every area of economic or strategic importance) but mostly by using half the Indian Army to watch the other half, and using one-third of the British Army to watch them all.

It was indeed upon the British Army that the new system had the greatest impact. Previously, the number of British regiments serving in India had been a small proportion of the whole, sent there for long periods, and to a large extent composed of officers and men who volunteered to remain there, transferring to other units when their own eventually returned to the United Kingdom. With the increase in the British garrison, practically every regiment other than the Guards went in their turn to India and, with the adoption of the short-service system in 1870, far more men passed through the units in India than had done so in earlier times. Unlike those stationed in the United Kingdom, or even in the colonies, where (except when on campaign) regiments were mostly in a social environment which was a microcosm of the UK, troops in India were in an alien but ancient civilisation, whose all-pervasive power to absorb its conquerors could only be resisted by an intensification, on their part, of their own apart-ness. So each regiment became, to a far greater extent than was either possible or necessary in its home environment, a village community in exile. The colonel assumed the role of squire, his field officers that of local gentry, the subalterns that of their sons, the medical officer, chaplain, and paymaster stood in as village doctor, vicar and bank manager, the sergeants filled the roles of bailiffs and stewards, and so on. The steadily increasing connection between British infantry regiments and particular areas of the United Kingdom only increased this communal feeling. In 1871 the Secretary of State for War, Edward Cardwell, allotted to each regiment a district (in most cases a county or great city), in which it would permanently maintain its depot and from which it would, for preference, draw its recruits. A decade later, under another Liberal War Secretary, Hugh Childers, the Line regiments incorporated the names of these districts into their official titles, in place of their old numbers. Distinctive regimental marching tunes, often based on local folk songs, and new regimental badges, often incorporating heraldic devices with local associations, were taken into use, and accompanied the regiments to India as to the other stations.

All such sights and sounds served to emphasise the separation of regiments not merely one from another, but collectively from the South Asian society in which they were serving. Of the need and justification for that separation, the average British soldier had no doubt. The site of the Kanpur massacre remained a place of pilgrimage. At Lucknow, the British flag was never lowered, by day or night, until the end of British rule. On Sundays, after Meerut, every British soldier went on church parade with a firearm in his hand and ball ammunition in his pouches. Moreover, in a land of castes, the soldier belonged to that of the warrior, marked out from the subject population by race, religion and way of life. When the regiments returned home, even though it was to their own society, they brought these attitudes with them, and became more exclusive among themselves, and with regard to their fellow-citizens, than before. The 'regimental spirit', hailed by traditionalists as a distinctive feature of the British Army, was one of many cults which the numinous environment of South Asia helped shape and foster, and without its Indian experience the British Army's institutional development would have taken other directions. Many Indian words, such as 'khaki', 'puttees', and 'cummerbund' were adopted by the British Army. 'Padre', meaning a military chaplain, owes more to the Army's long experience of India, where since the Portuguese period this word was used for any Christian priest, than to the Peninsular War.

Since the days of Dundas, British ministers had seen India as what Lord Salisbury, in 1882, called 'an English barrack in the Oriental Seas,'[1] but the garrison there, British or Indian, was maintained at Indian expense for the defence of India. If any part of it could be sent elsewhere, other than for very short periods, it was clearly not needed for that purpose, and therefore could be dispensed with, at least as a charge to Indian funds. Of the nine British units sent from India to the China War in 1859, only one, an artillery battery, came back. One cavalry regiment and seven infantry battalions became permanent reductions, though the latter had only been lent to India for the duration of the Mutiny campaign, having been diverted in 1857 while en route to the China campaign. Two battalions sent to the Maori War in 1860 likewise were permanently struck off the Indian establishment. The British units sent to Ethiopia in 1867–68 were back within five months, as were the battery and battalion sent to Perak in 1875, the two batteries sent to Malta in 1878, and the two batteries and two battalions sent to Egypt in 1882.[2]

Of all those who played a part in re-shaping the armies in India, the officer whose influence lasted longest was Colonel (ultimately Field Marshal Sir) Henry Norman. He began his career in the 31st Bengal Native Infantry, seeing active service in the Second Sikh War and subsequently on the Punjab frontier. During the Indian Mutiny, still a regimental lieutenant, he was acting Adjutant General of the army before Delhi, where his circle of friends included Frederick Roberts, Donald Stewart, Edwin Johnson, and Peter Lumsden, all of whom would rise to high positions in the Indian military. He served on Campbell's staff during the Awadh campaign and was wounded in action. With that capacity for compiling statistics which so characterised his work in the field and subsequently, he calculated that he took part in nearly eighty actions, including skirmishes. He was made temporary Adjutant General of the Bengal Army in April 1859 and had to deal with the problems of the 'Dumpy Mutiny', in which his sympathies, like those of his C-in-C, were entirely with the troops.

He returned to England in 1860 and found that his experience of combat and staff duty made him much in demand. He was appointed a member of the Hotham committee on the amalgamation of the Company's Europeans with the British Army and in September was selected for the newly created post of Assistant Military Secretary at the Horse Guards, for liaison between the British and Indian Armies. In 1861 Sir Charles Wood sent Norman back to India as Deputy Adjutant-General of Bengal to contribute to the re-organisation of the armies, and in January 1862 he became Secretary to the Government of India in the Military Department. His flair for administration was widely recognised, and the flow of information and suggestions he sent back to London gained him further approval from Wood. 'The Duke of Cambridge and I agree that we have learnt more from your letter than from all other letters for three or four months past.'[3] As the man identified with implementing the staff corps and irregular systems, he was less popular with those of his brother officers in India who deplored these innovations, especially those who found themselves surplus as the number of officers required in the regiments was reduced. In 1868 he was involved in preparing the expedition to Abyssinia led by Sir Robert Napier, C-in-C, Bombay, and a future C-in-C, India.

In June 1870 he became Member for the Military Department and, after a two-year extension in that post, left India in 1877. A year later he was appointed a member of the Council of India, and was chairman of the Military Committee until his retirement in 1883 on appointment as Governor of Jamaica. 'With his usual accuracy of detail he recorded in his "log" or diary that he attended forty-one meetings of Council in the year, 137 meetings of committees, and spent 244 days in the office.'[4] One of the tasks allotted to him was to go to Egypt to investigate the contentious issue of what proportion of the costs of the Indian contingent sent there in 1882 should be borne by British and what by Indian revenues.

For over twenty years in these various posts Norman was in a position to influence the military affairs of British India. His official minutes, occasionally so long as to be divided into chapters, are a delight to read, cogently argued, elegantly expressed, beautifully cadenced and supported by a wealth of carefully compiled figures that overbore all counter-argument. In his later years he defended against other would-be reformers the system which he had implemented earlier, a system that served the British well in the creation of an Army which enabled them to hold their South Asian empire against any South Asian enemy.

In foreign affairs he was cautious. He always remembered arriving in India at the age of sixteen in 1842, and hearing of the retreat from Kabul from Dr Bryden, the sole British officer to return other than as a rescued hostage. He always remembered the Mutiny, in which his own regiment had been one of the few in Bengal to remain loyal to the government. He remained convinced that an insurrection in India was a more serious threat than an Afghan, or even a Russian invasion, and warned publicly (earning a rebuke from Cambridge) that a ministry locating British garrisons in Afghanistan might bitterly regret it, should the time come when they were needed in India.

As long as British politicians voted the Royal Navy enough ships to secure the Indian Ocean, the only external threat to British India from a major power was in the north west. Conscious that it was from this direction that every successful invasion of South Asia, except their own, had come, the British viewed with concern the gradual expansion south-eastwards of the Russian empire. Russian statesmen were baffled by this hostile attitude. Their view was that it was in everyone's interest for the corrupt, backward, and ill-governed khanates of Central Asia to come under the rule of a modern European and Christian state. If the two empires became co-terminous, each could help the other in suppressing disorders and conspiracies arising from irreconcilable Muslim or other local insurgents. In the event of another Indian Mutiny, something about which the British themselves remained concerned, Russian troops would thus be readily available to help the British restore European supremacy and maintain the values of Christian civilisation.

British Indian statesmen were not influenced by an appeal to Christian, or even European, solidarity. Scarred by the Mutiny experience, they were anxious to play down the identification of their rule over South Asia as an extension of Christendom. On the contrary, in order to conciliate the large and powerful Muslim element among their Indian subjects, the British were disposed to support the Ottoman Sultan (who in his role as *Khalifa* was, to the majority of Muslims, God's vice-gerent and His shadow upon earth) against the expansion of Holy Russia. How, they asked, could a Russian army from Central Asia come to the aid of its co-religionists in India if the green flag of an Islamic holy war were to be raised, at the Sultan's proclamation, against both simultaneously?

In British India, therefore, the question was not whether a Russian threat existed, but rather of how to deal with it. At one extreme, the 'forward' school advocated extending British influence as far into Central Asia as possible. This would ensure that, in the event of Anglo-Russian tension in Europe, Russian troops and Russian diplomats would still be remote from British India, and the less able to encourage any anti-British activities there (such as, for example, another Mutiny). The 'masterly inactivity' school argued that the best way of preventing such a disaster was to conciliate Indian opinion to British rule by good government, or at least by low taxation, which would not be achieved by costly remote garrisons or extravagant foreign policies. Their view was – let the Russians come, and be defeated on the Indus, at the end of extended lines of communication with a hostile Afghanistan in their rear. The forward school replied that Afghans with the prospect of looting Hindustan would be Russia's allies, and a British defeat (which the accidents of war, let alone the deficiencies of the Indian Army, made by no means impossible) might be followed by a rising in India. If the sepoy and the cossack were destined to cross swords, let it be on the banks of the Oxus, and meanwhile let the rupee try conclusions with the rouble there.

The election of the Conservative government in 1874 gave the forward school its chance. With Disraeli's support, Salisbury, the new Secretary of State for India, pressed for the installation of a British Resident at Kabul. The Amir of Afghanistan, Sher Ali, protested that he could not guarantee the personal safety of such an envoy, nor could he accept a British diplomat without also admitting a Russian one. Rather than implement Salisbury's policy of forcing a Resident upon the Afghans, the Governor-General, Lord Northbrook (a Liberal politician who had earlier been Cardwell's under-secretary of state at the War Office) resigned early in 1876.

His replacement, Lord Lytton, had no Indian background. His experience as a professional diplomat might have been supposed useful, but his main claim to notice was as a man of letters, with a talent for flamboyance and a gift for expression similar to that of Disraeli himself. All Lytton's correspondence suggests a man prey to violent emotions, especially in his judgement of others. The arrival of so colourful a figure, who lost no time in establishing his own collection of court favourites, produced an effect more akin to the succession of a new ruler at an Indian court than that of a simple change of a pro-consul. Indeed, the glamour and romance of oriental splendour appealed to him as it would do to no other Governor-General except Curzon, a generation later. He threw himself into plans for a great Durbar, 'the Imperial Assemblage' to announce the assumption by Queen Victoria of the title Empress of India, one of Disraeli's fanciful schemes, opposed by many in England because to them 'Imperial' sounded not merely foreign but tyrannical, being used by the Bonapartes, Habsburgs, Hohenzollerns and Romanovs of Europe. Opposition was strong enough to ensure that this adjective was confined to the Crown in India, and kept out of regimental titles, British or Indian. Even Disraeli, however, (by this time Lord Beaconsfield) was eventually to complain that some of Lytton's schemes sounded like tales from the *Arabian Nights*, and lived to regret his nominee's unauthorised declaration of war on Afghanistan in November 1878.

The principal military favourite at the new court was Colonel George Pomeroy Colley, a member of the group of self-consciously progressive military officers headed by the rising figure of Sir Garnet Wolseley. Wolseley himself, having made his name as a 'scientific' soldier in recent colonial campaigns, was appointed by Salisbury in November 1876 to the Council of India. Wolseley's Indian experience was limited to service as a junior officer during the Mutiny, but the addition of a 'modern major general' to this ultra-conservative body suggests the government's interest in overhauling the Indian military machine. His influence may be detected in the selection of Colley by Lytton to be his military secretary. This post had been created in 1868 primarily for liaison with the C-in-C, India, especially over appointments to units such as the Punjab Frontier Force and the Hyderabad Contingent, which were controlled not by the C-in-C but by the Foreign Department of which the Governor-General was the head. Colley had been a professor at the Staff College, and a staff officer in the Ashanti War. He had, however, never commanded a regiment and General Sir Frederick Haines, a British Army officer who had fought in the Sikh Wars and at Inkerman, and who became C-in-C, India, at the same time as Lytton became Governor-General, put a wealth of meaning into his description of Colley as 'the finest theoretical soldier' he ever met.[5]

Colley had no doubt that he had been sent to bring light into dark places. Treating officers in India, irrespective of their own experiences in peace or war, as though they were his students, he lost no opportunity of explaining that, fresh from his study of recent European wars, he appreciated, as they did not, the magnitude of the importance of the introduction of the breech-loading rifle. A single British regiment, thus armed and given enough ammunition, could, he declared, march at will the length of Afghanistan, once clear of the passes, and even the worst troops, armed with breech-loaders, could scarcely be dislodged from a defensive position.[6] When at last, as governor and C-in-C, Natal, he obtained a command of his own in 1881 he met his death and defeat on Majuba Hill at the hands of patriotic Boer farmers, who had never heard of the Staff College and did not know that his position was theoretically impregnable.

Lytton turned his attention to army reform shortly after assuming office as Governor-General. He admitted to Salisbury that the weight of opinion, led by 'the three Ns' (as he dubbed Northbrook, Norman and Napier) was opposed to change, though the staff corps system, with the 'inordinately wasteful cost of its provision for promotion and retirement' seemed on that account a bad one. The essential problem with the native Army seemed to be 'how to make it thoroughly efficient in the hands of British officers and comparatively useless without them', and if the system of relying on native officers was efficient then, if they revolted, it would be efficient against the British. Salisbury took much the same view: 'Mutiny is our one great danger, compared to which all other dangers are trivial: & therefore I should like to see the army built in mutiny-tight compartments. The more like the regiments are to each other ... the more likely to catch a mutinous contagion, when once started, from each other. Therefore I should like to see universal rules as to the number of officers in a regiment as much discouraged as possible.'

Soon after reaching India, Colley produced a note (described by Lytton as 'masterly') on Indian Army reform. Since the introduction of the breech-loader, he said, although the British Army itself, far less the Indian Army, had not so far appreciated it, the important level in combat was the company, not the battalion. Indian companies were commanded by native officers, yet if such officers were able to lead their companies in battle, not merely attend to their administration, then he, Colley, would recommend the immediate disbandment of the native army as a threat to British security. His solution was to re-muster the eight small companies of a battalion into four large ones, rather in the same way that, in the cavalry, troops which were commanded by Indian officers were paired to form squadrons, under a British commander and subaltern. His main proposal for economy was that the Indian Army should, like other modern armies, have a reserve, so enabling a reduction of 50,000 in the number of men serving with the Colours in normal times.[7]

Haines (as C-in-C, Madras, from May 1871–76) in December 1875 had expressed similar views on the officer problem only a few years earlier. He had pressed for a return to the old system of having European officers as company commanders. Indian officers only commanded on parade and did not exercise 'the most important of the functions of officers commanding companies, viz. the dealing with minor offences'. He was opposed to native officers of the Madras Army holding this disciplinary power, on account of their 'low social position, want of education, and great age', while 'the new tactics demand exceptional vigour, activity, and self-reliance' from company commanders. He therefore wished British officers to command companies both in the field and in barracks, rather than merely supervise.[8]

He was not, however, so much in accord with the reformers when the Government of India received an official memorandum by Sir Garnet Wolseley, as a member of the Council of India, recommending that the best way of achieving military savings would be to implement the reductions proposed in 1869. The Bombay Army, in Wolseley's view, faced no internal threat, and had more than enough men for the defence of its Sind frontier. Even more sweeping were his views on Madras, where he saw the only threat as coming from the Nizam's army which the 10,000 British troops in Madras alone should be able to deal with. He advocated therefore reduction of four Indian cavalry regiments (one each in Bengal and Bombay, and twenty battalions, out of the existing forty, in Madras). He argued that the British Army had been reduced in 1814, 1815, 1848, 1856, and 1870, with officers placed on the half-pay and their careers ruined, all accepted on the grounds of national interest, but in India there was such an outcry when reductions were proposed that 'one would think that India was made for the Army and not the Army for India'. It was wrong to make the Indian taxpayer support more troops than were needed or to 'keep up a larger number of possible enemies than can be avoided'.[9]

Salisbury was not so sure. 'I suppose there is no doubt that in hard logic he is right: but can you afford to disregard all sentiment in this matter? Again, if he is right generally – is this the time? You may be called upon to defend Herat – still more likely Bagdad: is it a moment for retrenchment?'[10] Lytton delayed an official reply. He later told the Permanent Under-Secretary at the India Office that 'I should have had to send home a budget of furious minutes' from Haines, and from the Military Member, Sir Edwin Johnson. He complained that the mistake had been to send Wolseley's proposals as those of an individual Council member without the views of the Secretary of State to support them 'for this only put up the backs of my Colleagues without practically advancing matters'.[11]

Financial embarrassments continued to crowd upon the Government of India. In the early 1870s there was a rapid fall in the value of the rupee, coined in silver, against sterling, valued in gold, though India still had to pay its charges to London (including the pay of British troops) in sterling. In 1876 famine struck in Madras, and during the next two years some 5 million people died of hunger. Lytton denounced all public expenditure on relief and argued that market forces would solve the problem. Asking Haines to prepare estimates for a force to be ready for operations in Central Asia, he referred to these difficulties and suggested that this force might be funded by reductions in the Army least able to contribute to it, that of Madras. Meanwhile 'we have no choice but to cut our coat according to our cloth ... the Nemesis of financial liability is an avenging deity whose scourge we cannot afford to provoke'.[12] To Wolseley he confided that the need for reductions in the native army to pay for war preparations had been represented to the C-in-C India and the Military Department, 'by both of which powers it is, of course, opposed with the usual *non-possumus*'.[13]

In April 1878 Cabinet changes brought Gathorne Hardy, newly raised to the peerage as Viscount Cranbrook, from the War Office to the India Office, replacing Salisbury who took over the Foreign Office. Taking up Cranbrook's interest in army reform, Lytton put forward a series of proposals. The Indian Army, he said, though the heaviest item of government expenditure, was the chief, if not the only, danger to the British in India, was of doubtful efficiency, and practically useless for most military purposes. With a peace establishment twice as large as that in the United Kingdom and nearly as large as that of Austria, it cost more than either. It was the only army in the world which had no reserves, and therefore kept up in peace all the men it wanted for war, or had to raise and train the extra men at additional cost. Reductions could be made, even without creating a reserve, but 'my Military Colleagues are at this moment engaged in savagely tearing to pieces a memorandum by Sir Garnet Wolseley containing similar suggestions'. He warned Cranbrook that there would be strong opposition to reform. 'The average military mind is more conservative than progressive in its tendencies: and the average Indian officer is the most narrow-minded and bigoted of his class. The sort of impenetrably self-satisfied contempt evinced by Indian officers for any military experience ... acquired out of India would often be amusing were it not always ... so detrimental to the interests of the Indian Army.' Pointing out that all reform at the War Office had been carried out by civilian ministers, with support from public opinion and a popular press in which progressive officers could express their views, he explained that none of these conditions existed in India. No civilian in or out of government was interested in the army, and with the C-in-C a member of Council, and the Military Member a serving soldier, 'the army rules itself ... saturated with purely military traditions and prejudices'. He asked, therefore, for Cranbrook's support in setting up an army commission, in which modern military science, India's military experience, local and financial interests, would all be represented to determine India's actual military needs in peace and war. He suggested that the president might be Wolseley or Sir Lintorn Simmons (an engineer officer thought to have modern views). 'Your Council at home – men like Norman especially – and a large part of my own Council out here will, if they can, oppose at every stage any rational reform.'[14]

Lytton continued to press for a commission as the only way of securing the adoption of a reserve system such as that which modern Western armies had adopted. Cranbrook suggested that a linked-battalion system, of the kind introduced into the British Army by Cardwell, might be worth considering, but was told by Lytton that having a large number of units only gave the impression that India could produce practically unlimited numbers of first-rate troops to serve in a European war. Although this could be the case, he said, in fact it was not, and 'our permanent military establishment in India is, for all war purposes, the most expensive and the most inadequate in the World'. With a reserve system, India could add to British imperial strength, but such a reform was possible, he thought, only under a Conservative ministry, as Liberals would dread the extra strength it would give to the spirit of British foreign policy.[15]

Further discussions of these questions were delayed by the beginning of the Second Afghan War in November 1878. One column, led by Major General Frederick Roberts, advanced up the Kurram Valley. A second led by Lieutenant General Sir Donald Stewart (another Bengal Army officer) marched from Quetta at the top of the Bolan Pass, and a third, led by Sir Samuel Browne, a Punjab Frontier Force officer, took the Khyber. After some fighting the Afghan army was defeated, the Amir fled and, in March 1879, his successor agreed to accept a British Resident. Sir Louis Cavagnari, one of Lytton's favourites, was appointed and the British began to demobilise – rather too rapidly as events would prove. There was, Haines later told Cambridge, 'an overwhelming desire to assume an aspect of perfect repose at as early a date as possible. In fact there is always a desire to do something either before Parliament rises or before it assembles, which sadly militates against the logical sequence of military plans'.[16]

With the coming of peace and the continuation of the financial crisis, Cranbrook called for cuts in public (and especially in military) expenditure. Lytton promised an immediate commission of inquiry into ways of achieving a leaner but fitter organisation. On 7 May 1879 he reported that 'after talking a great deal of nonsense and proclaiming a great many platitudes' his Council had given unanimous assent to setting up a reform commission, but three weeks later wrote that, after a renewed discussion 'got up by the Commander-in-Chief', three members had changed their minds. 'Haines and Johnson, who will listen to no arguments on the subject, passionately deny the possibility of the most infinitesimal reduction.'[17]

His aim was to ensure that the commission was composed as far as possible of those who would report in favour of reform. 'Stewart and MacGregor have, I know, long been fuming and fretting ... at the obstructive conservatism of

Major General Stringer Lawrence, 1697–1775. The first C-in-C, India, 1746–54. 'The father of the Indian Army'. Mezzotint by R. Houston after Sir Joshua Reynolds.

Major General Robert Clive, Lord Clive, 1725–74. C-in-C, India, and Governor of Bengal, 1756–60 and 1763–67. 'Clive of India', whose victories brought the beginning of British rule in India. Engraving after Nathaniel Dance.

The Storming of Seringapatam. Srirangapatnam, Mysore, 4 May 1799. Engraving by John Vendramini after Sir Robert Ker Porter.

General Charles Cornwallis, Marquess Cornwallis, 1738–1805. C-in-C, India, and Governor-General of Bengal, 1786–93 and July-October 1805. Reformed the East India Company's military and civil services and established the permanent settlement of the land revenue in Bengal. Engraving by Benjamin Smith after J.S. Copley.

Indian Infantry, c. 1856. At this period, regular sepoy regiments were clothed to resemble the European troops for whom they were a cheaper substitute. In the post-Mutiny reconstruction, Indian troops were given uniforms based on traditional local styles of dress.

The 1st Bengal European Fusiliers marching down from Dagshai, May 1857. Lithograph by W. Simpson after Lieutenant George Atkinson, Bengal Engineers.

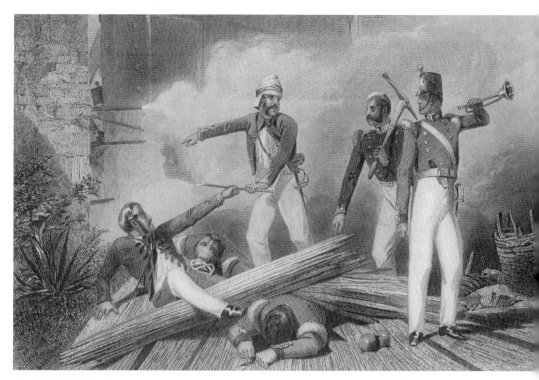

The blowing up of the Cashmere Gate.
Kashmir Gate, Siege of Delhi,
14 September 1857. Steel engraving by
Darley and Ridgeway.

Field Marshal Sir Henry Norman,
1826–1904. Military Member of the
Governor-General's Council, 1870–77,
and the Council of India, 1878–83.
Established the system by which all
Indian Army officers belonged to a Staff
Corps rather than individual regiments.
Engraving by Emery Walker after Carl
Vandyke.

(*Above left*) Field Marshal Sir Colin Campbell, Lord Clyde, 1792–1863. C-in-C, India, 1857–60. Commanded 'the thin red line' at Balaklava. Parsimonious with his soldiers' lives, he achieved lasting fame during the Indian Mutiny or Revolt of 1857 by his relief of Lucknow and subsequent victories in the field. Steel engraving.

(*Above right*) Field Marshal Sir Frederick Roberts, Earl Roberts of Kandahar, 1832–1914. Steel engraving by W. Roffe after Bourne and Shepherd.

(*Right*) Field Marshal Earl Kitchener of Khartoum, 1850–1916. C-in-C, India, 1902–09. Reconstructed the Indian Army as a unified force. His abolition of the Government of India's Military Department led to logistical failures in the First World War. Photograph, News Pictures.

The Road to the Takht-i-Suleiman. A defile leading to the Throne of Solomon massif, Waziristan, North-West Frontier, 1883. Photograph by Colonel Sir T.H. Holdich.

Shabash! Kuch Dar Nahin Hai. (Bravo! Fear is Nothing). The 40th Pathans at the Second Battle of Ypres, Flanders, 26 April 1915. Drawing by A.C. Michael.

Indian Officers from the Front visit the Royal Mews, Buckingham Palace, December 1915. An Indian Corps and Cavalry Division joined the British Expeditionary Force on the Western Front soon after the beginning of the First World War. The Indian Officers depicted here form a cross-section of the 'martial classes' from whom the British Indian Army was predominantly recruited.

A Sherman tank of the 9th Royal Deccan Horse, Burma, March 1945. By the end of the Second World War, Indian units were equipped to the same standard as their British counterparts. The Indian elephant, the equivalent of the tank in early Indian warfare, remained a valuable logistical asset.

Field Marshal Sir Claude Auchinleck, 1894–1991. C-in-C, India, January–July 1941 and June 1943–August 1947. After commands in Europe and the Middle East during the Second World War, was the last British C-in-C, India, prior to Partition and Independence in August 1947. Photograph by Elliott and Fry.

the Commander-in-Chief.'[18] For other members, he proposed Colonel T.D. Baker of the 18th Foot (his military secretary), Roberts, Bernard (a civil servant) and Major Oliver Newmarch, 'sensible and economical', of the Military Department. To Roberts he confided that, without a commission, the India Office would simply reduce the military vote and leave India only the option of how to spend what was available, without any question of reconstruction. He was sure that the members nominated by the Madras and Bombay Governments would be obstructive, as would be Sir Peter Lumsden, the former Adjutant General of Bengal (nominated by Haines), 'if from no other motive than personal jealousy of yourself'. The secretary was to be Captain E.E. Collen, of the Military Department, 'whose ability and sound judgement have I am sorry to say exposed him to the wrath of Lumsden and his chief'.[19]

As Haines seemed unlikely to agree to Roberts being president, and Lytton was opposed to Lumsden, and Stewart was still in the field, it was decided that the Army Reform Commission was to be chaired by the Hon. Sir Ashley Eden, Lieutenant-Governor of Bengal, an experienced Indian administrator, who would be neutral between the various armies, and have the civil servant's appreciation of the importance of achieving economies at their expense. As soon as he was appointed, however, he was told by Lytton that Cranbrook was looking for real reductions in the Madras Army,[20] a body whose men, in the Governor-General's view, were fit only for military police and too expensive for that. As for using it on the Afghan frontier 'you might as well employ Tuscans in the Caucasus'.[21] In addition to Lumsden, Roberts, Baker, Newmarch and Bernard, the Commission was made up of Colonel C.M. MacGregor of Bengal and Brigadier General Robert Phayre, Adjutant General of the Bombay Army (both of whom already had gained the approval of Colley) with Brigadier Generals H.T. Macpherson of Bengal and H.H. O'Connell of Madras. Cranbrook's response to those who objected to setting up the commission at all was to say that its deliberations should be as short as possible, to keep its costs down.

The official instructions to the commission began with a reference to India's parlous financial condition, requiring reductions in public spending as an imperative necessity. Eden was therefore to report on what share of these reductions could be borne by the Army without injury to its efficiency, and how savings could best be made.[22] Fifteen specific questions were posed. These were: how many troops were required for the internal security of India in normal times of peace; how should they be distributed; how many troops should the Government of India be able to field in war; what system should be established to provide an army reserve; how many troops should be permanently under arms; could the cost of the British element be reduced without also reducing the numbers; should there be a territorial organisation for ease of mobilisation; should the organisation of the mobilised army be combined with this territorial organisation, in the way that modern European armies were; were the presidential armies, with their separate headquarters and staff, essential for military efficiency; if the presidential armies remained, should they continue to serve, in peace time, only in their own presidential areas; should the Punjab Frontier Force continue as a separate body under the control of local civil authorities, or should it be brought under control of the C-in-C, India; who should command the Sind Frontier Force if Sind were to be united with the Punjab and a new frontier province formed from their trans-Indus districts (a plan of which Lytton was the originator and prime exponent); could the supply and transport organisation be improved; was the ordnance supply system satisfactory; and what new roads and railways were needed as lines of communication. The commissioners were invited to consider any other ways of improving the administration and reducing the cost of the army, with the proviso that 'any recommendation involving outlay should as far as possible be accompanied by proposals for savings in other directions'.[23]

On the sudden renewal of the Afghan War in September 1879 the four senior military commissioners hurried away to take up field commands. Haines tried to persuade Lytton to abandon the project but most recommendations had already been decided upon and the report was presented on 15 November 1878, a fortnight after the date originally set.

Its findings, set out in 180 pages of text plus a further sixty-six of appendices and annexures, identified a possible saving of 125 crores (1,250,000,000) of rupees per annum.[24] At the same time it recognised that no reductions in the number of native regiments could be implemented until any future commitment to garrison Afghanistan had been decided, and recommended that those which had given good service should, if possible, be spared. Beginning with the internal security problem, it recommended that encouragement be given to the local, part-time, volunteer force raised from the European and Eurasian communities. This force, which was patterned on the Volunteers of the British Army, had dwindled, since its origins at the time of the Indian Mutiny and the volunteering fashion of the 1860s, into a mere 7,000 effectives (of whom 2,500 were railway employees) organised into twenty-five corps of infantry, one of artillery, and one of mounted rifles. The Lieutenant-Governor of the North Western Provinces, where some of the hardest fighting of the Mutiny had occurred, wanted to make military training compulsory for all European civil servants but the commissioners declined to support his views. They recommended that plans be drawn up for the establishment of defensible posts or places of refuge for European civilians in case of rebellion, where they could hold out until rescued. The Gwalior army, recruited from Purabiyas, needed watching, they thought, as did that of the Nizam, which included many Afghan mercenaries. They urged that the armies of Indian princes should not be allowed to exercise together, that their field artillery should be kept strictly to within treaty limits, and that they should not be allowed to re-arm with modern rifles.

The report then turned to other questions. The number of troops should stay the same, but in fewer, larger, units, both for battle efficiency and to achieve economies of scale. Evidence had been given that about half the annual cost of a British unit in India was taken up by the pay of its officers (a cavalry regiment cost Rs 1,46,797 and Rs 1,14,061 and a battalion Rs 1,43,793 and Rs 1,76,126 for the officers and men respectively). They therefore proposed that the British contingent be made up of forty-three instead of fifty battalions of infantry, six instead of nine cavalry regiments, and seventy-seven instead of eighty-six batteries. The Indian element should be reduced from 166 to 126 units. Of those to be disbanded, seven cavalry and ten infantry were to come from Bengal, one cavalry and five infantry from Bombay, and two cavalry and fifteen infantry from Madras. The Madras Army was selected for a disproportionately high share of these proposed reductions on the basis of several arguments. It had suffered only a small number of officer casualties in the Mutiny and subsequent campaigns, but under the staff corps system many officers had been promoted by the passage of time to field rank, though still doing duties appropriate to captains and subalterns. This was not only bad for the morale and efficiency of the units, but meant that the average cost of a Madras regiment's salary bill, at least in respect of its officers, was higher than in the rest of the Indian Army. Moreover, Madras sepoys, unlike those of Bengal and Bombay, were accompanied by their families, and cost more to move. Therefore larger savings could be made by disbanding regiments in the Madras Army than in the other two. Few officers went to Madras out of preference. It was proving increasingly difficult to recruit sepoys from the Madras Presidency. Madras was a peaceful region and did not need so many troops.

The existing views of Lytton (following Colley) were reflected in proposals that the forces in India should be concentrated into a smaller number of large garrisons at points of strategic importance, and many of the smaller stations, which existed only as survivals from the campaigns of conquest, were to be abandoned. This meant savings in these areas, while making it easier to command and train the larger formations required in modern war, while the strategic railways and trunk roads would allow them to move in force rapidly to any threatened point. This was despite the views of witnesses who argued that the first insurgent action in a well-planned rising would be to cut the telegraph wires and destroy the railways. The creation of an Indian reserve along the same lines as that recently adopted in the British Army was recommended, and it was also proposed to group Indian regiments into threes, each group forming a separate corps.

This last step was linked with a proposal to abolish the staff corps system, primarily on the grounds of its expense. As promotion was by time rather than against vacancies on an establishment, most of its officers had reached high rank, and those in civil employment were being paid more than civil servants in the same duties. Out of 1,961 in the three Staff Corps only 201 were in Army staff posts. The rest were either at regimental or departmental duty or in non-military appointments. The creation of what were, in effect, large regiments of three battalions (though the battalions might still be called regiments), with promotion by regimental seniority to vacancies occurring against an establishment, would allow the twenty-one British officers in each of the new large regiments to have reasonable career prospects, but without the fluctuations in cost between units which arose from the staff corps system.

The report then turned to the question of the presidential armies. It pointed out that the areas allotted to them no longer coincided with the presidential boundaries. There were ten major local governments in British India. Some, with the largest amount of territory to administer, had no authority over the armies stationed in their areas of jurisdiction but others maintained a 'nominal connection' with them. There was no reason, the report argued, for the Bengal Army to be more directly connected with the Government of India than those of Madras and Bombay, while, if unity of civil and military administration was essential, then there should be ten armies. The C-in-C, India, since the Charter Act of 1833, had controlled all British Army troops in India irrespective of the presidency in which they were located. The presidential governors and Cs-in-C were appointed on the advice of the London authorities, and usually strangers to India, and therefore had no more expertise with regard to local troops than the Government of India itself, which, since 1864, had controlled all matters requiring expenditure. Moreover, the report added, from continued localisation in areas where no fighting was expected, the Bombay and Madras troops had lost their martial spirit.

Therefore it proposed to abolish the three presidential armies and replace them by four army corps. Two of these would be formed from the armies of Madras and Bombay respectively, and the other two by dividing the Bengal Army into its Hindustani and Punjabi elements, incorporating the Punjab Frontier Force in the latter. Each army corps would be commanded by a lieutenant general as GOC. The posts of C-in-C Madras and Bombay should be abolished (as had, indeed, been proposed by Peel twenty years earlier) and the C-in-C, India, would concentrate on the overall organisation of the army, training and planning for mobilisation and war. Copying the latest European model, each army corps in peace would be stationed in its own area, from which it would draw recruits, but each area would include a border district with the chance of active service against local tribesmen or a foreign invader. Thus the Madras army corps would garrison Burma, while Bombay, Bengal, and the Punjab would hold the frontiers of Baluchistan, Assam, and south-eastern Afghanistan respectively.

One more proposed change was of major constitutional significance. This was that the C-in-C, India, should cease to be a member of the Governor-General's Council. Instead, the Military Department should become the Government of India's War Department, and the Military Member of Council should perform in India all the functions which in the United Kingdom were carried out by the Secretary of State for War:

> It is the constant duty of the Commander-in-Chief to be ever urging on the government the expenditure of money for the improvement of the army and it is to him that the officers and men of the army must look to press their claims and state their requirements. It is the constant duty of the Government of India on the other hand, in the interests of the tax-payers of India, to refuse demands for expenditure which they consider unreasonable or unnecessary or beyond the power of the country to bear.

However, in India, the C-in-C: 'takes his seat on the bench with the judges, to decide in his own cause. If the application he has made is not accepted – and it very often happens that it is not – an acrimonious and bitter discussion too often takes place ... and a perpetual friction is maintained which permeates through the army'.[25] The proposal to make the Military Member head of a War Department was intended to overcome this. An experienced officer would be able to advise the Governor-General on military policy and exercise real financial control. It would be plainly seen that he was not commanding the Army, and it was anticipated that his relationship with the C-in-C would be one of co-operation, not rivalry.

Much weight was placed on the evidence submitted by Lord Sandhurst who, as Sir William Mansfield, had been C-in-C, India, from 1865 to 1870. If the C-in-C, he said, was

> a man of quick and powerful mind he finds his position difficult, at times almost intolerable. He has a great responsibility, is much appealed to ... while often feels and knows that around the head of Government are irresponsible and secret military advisers who regard him with hostility. Hence it is that many Commanders-in-Chief in India have been most anxious to live away from Government as much as possible, while others have been engaged in conflict leading to resignation. I conceive that the evil of divesting the head of the Government of India of his chief and *responsible* military adviser can hardly be exaggerated, yet if . .. (he) ... is

to be at the same time an executive Commander in Chief who is ever engaged in traversing the country on tours of inspection in times of peace, or at the head of the active army in time of war, it is utterly impossible for him to be in his place at the side of the Governor-General.[26]

The Commission considered the idea of abolishing the post of C-in-C altogether, leaving the Military Member to head the army, but, influenced by Lord Sandhurst, recommended that the post continue to exist as the chief military executive.

The Duke of Cambridge, although he had no powers of command in India, continued to have a strong influence over its military affairs. He had the right to nominate the three commanders-in-chief there, and corresponded regularly with them. Thus it was he heard from Haines both of Lytton's interference in army affairs, and of the questions being put to the C-in-C, India, by Eden and his reformers. Cranbrook warned Lytton several times that Cambridge supported Haines over both questions. The Duke, he said, 'dislikes Colley mainly because he is a friend of Wolseley, and he hates Wolseley because – he does not know why – but because he is able', and would never agree to Wolseley having an Indian command. Cranbrook considered that Cambridge was really basing his view of Indian affairs on information from Sir Edwin Johnson with Lytton being represented as under Colley's influence. He stressed the need to conciliate both Cambridge and Haines in order to ensure that the Eden report achieved acceptance.[27]

Lytton rejected the Duke's views. Colley, he said, was a first-rate soldier, with a remarkable genius for organisation and a keen intellect. But for his decision to go to Natal as High Commissioner in succession to Wolseley, he would have hoped to see him as Military Member in succession to Johnson. Wolseley would be an ideal C-in-C: 'India greatly needs an able and sensible Commander-in-Chief just now and she certainly has not got one at present.' He wrote that Cambridge's reservations as to Brackenbury's appointment to succeed Colley (on the grounds of his limited Indian experience) were equally unjustified. The real problem, he said, was that Haines and Johnson were rival courtiers of Cambridge. 'Their first and, as far as I can perceive, their sole, consideration in dealing with any military question is how to compete with each other in anticipating or carrying out the supposed wishes of His Royal Highness.' They were 'men who cling to everything that is old and bad as barnacles cling to rotten timber'.[28]

Johnson's likely opposition to abolition of the minor Cs-in-C was attributed by Lytton to motives of personal gain. He had suffered a paralytic stroke in 1878 but had after some months resumed his duties. His brother, Colonel Allen Johnson, secretary of the Military Department at the India Office, had been sent to India as the only one to whom he was prepared to delegate his work, and also as the only one thought likely to persuade him to resign before he had another stroke. Sir Edwin, however, was said to have found that his finances would not allow him to resign and was now looking forward to becoming C-in-C, Madras, and subsequently C-in-C, India. The slightest mention of the abolition of the Madras command, said Lytton 'now throws him into a paroxysm of nervous excitement, which if frequently renewed might I fear have a most fatal effect upon his brain'.[29] The problem was made worse because Sir Neville Chamberlain (by this time C-in-C, Madras) had given the impression that he intended to retire. Lytton, anxious to install Colley as Military Member, had asked Sir Edwin if he was interested in the post, and learned that, through Colonel Allen Johnson, Cambridge had already asked the same question. The scheme collapsed when Sir Edwin wrote to Chamberlain offering to buy his horses, etc., only to learn that Chamberlain had no intention of retiring before his time.

Haines strongly opposed the more sweeping of the Commission's proposals. If the armies were unified then their local arsenals and logistic services would disappear but these were insurances against possible disaster. It was only twenty years since all the installations in Hindustan were in the hands of an enemy, he said. A territorial army corps system might be suitable for homogeneous nations, such as Germany, where the population identified itself with the state, but not for India, occupied by alien rulers. To leave Hindustan and the Punjab garrisoned by its own population, though apparently scientific, would be a blunder of the first magnitude. The mixture and disposal of races throughout India, including the stationing of Madras troops in part of the Bengal Presidency, might be contrary to the latest theories, he argued, but was the sheet anchor of British security in India. As for the supposed loss of martial spirit in Madras, he pointed to the efficiency of Madras sappers, drawn from the same villages as the ordinary sepoys, during the recent Afghan campaign. Even in Madras, there were, he said, potential dangers, from the Moplas of Malabar, from the Nizam's army, and from irregular bands of Arabs, Sikhs and Rohillas in the pay of his nobles. Coorg had an army, and Mysore was about to be returned to princely rule after eighty years of British administration.[30]

Lytton, for his part, supported most of the Commission's proposals, and was in a hurry to have them implemented. For him, time had run out. The Conservative ministry, defeated in a general election in which the British invasion of Afghanistan had been one of many factors counted against it, resigned in April 1880. Lytton went with it, as the members of the new ministry had 'publicly proclaimed that I possess neither their confidence nor their esteem and ... omitted no opportunity of casting ridicule and discredit on my character'.[31] He handed over on 8 June to the Earl of Ripon, an experienced Liberal politician, who had been Secretary of State for India for a time in 1866. Rather than wait to have the Commission's report discussed in Council, as was the usual procedure, Lytton sent it to London, with his own views, a week before leaving office. After asserting that the only member of his Council in favour of the existing system of 'scattering the troops at small stations in peaceful parts of the country' was the Military Member, he recommended abolishing this appointment altogether. His plan was that, so far from giving up his seat in Council, as the Eden Commission recommended, the C-in-C should combine it with that of the Military Member. In his command function, the C-in-C would be assisted by a Chief of Staff who would be second in rank only to himself, and in administrative ones by a civil financial secretary.[32]

It was clear that a financial secretary might have been useful to the Military Department, which had just been found to have incurred £13,000,000 of expenditure, connected with the Afghan War, without warning the Finance Department. This arose from the practice of the Military Accounts branch taking note only of audited accounts (which as a result of the war, were greatly in arrears), not actual disbursements. In view of the political controversy over the justification of the war, and the constant demand for reductions rather than increases in defence expenditure, Lytton was suspected of wilful deception. He himself admitted that it was a public scandal, though claiming that he could not have questioned the estimates submitted without destroying the responsibility of those who prepared them:

> I cannot help feeling, with considerable bitterness, that the powers of military darkness, against whom I have been maintaining single-handed for four years such a fatiguing, and till now not unsuccessful, struggle, have in the last hours of my administration contrived to give me a *croc aux jambes* which no vigilance on my part could have prevented and which no explanations on their part or on mine can now solve.[33]

Johnson's special objection was to abandoning small stations. The number of troops, he said, was so small, and the area they had to garrison was so large, that there were few available for concentration even if that were something to be desired. He argued that the peaceful appearance of many districts was the result of troops being there, and their withdrawal to achieve economies would be followed by outbreaks that would cost more to put down than would have been saved. Indeed, he scarcely trusted the Indian troops themselves. 'To the impolicy of large concentrations of Native troops, unless absolutely necessary for strategical purposes, I have already drawn attention.' As for Lytton's remarks 'on my contention that we hold India by force, which he treats with scarcely disguised derision, I can only state that my conviction is shared by every man of long experience in this country who has ever given a thought to the subject'.[34] He opposed the formation of an Indian reserve on the grounds that, if efficient, its members would be a political danger.

He also opposed Lytton's scheme of replacing the Military Member by a more powerful C-in-C. 'The Commander in Chief, especially if he were a man of great force of character, would possess a power in his high professional rank, his military knowledge and great experience which would carry all before him and place the revenues of the country almost at his mercy.' Against this, a Governor-General and his civilian councillors 'would either be so deprived of resistance as could not fail to be dangerous to the State or would be driven to the mischievous alternative of relying on the irresponsible opinions of the military members of his personal staff' (meaning Colley). He warned of the dangers of 'placing military expenditure in the hands of a C-in-C whose interests might well easily lead him to undervalue the importance to India of a strictly economical administration.'[35]

Some months elapsed before the Government of India formed a collective opinion. Ripon had to take the measure of a Council whose members had been identified with Lytton's policies. Johnson, on the completion of his tenure as Military Member, was replaced in September 1880 by Lieutenant General Sir Donald Stewart, who had established good personal relations with Ripon during the final stages of the campaign and the withdrawal from Kabul. In February 1881 Ripon and his Council expressed general support for the proposals to abolish the armies and Cs-in-C of Madras and Bombay, and to replace them by four new army corps, though the latter were to be called 'armies' to conciliate local sentiment. The staff corps system, however, was to be retained, and the Bengal Staff Corps would provide officers for both the new Bengal and Punjab armies.[36]

In London these proposals were greeted without enthusiasm. Hartington, the new Secretary of State, found that the Council of India was against them and played for time. He told Ripon that to remove the armies of Madras and Bombay from their local governments would need parliamentary sanction, for which no time could be found in that session, so the whole subject could be considered over a further period.[37] Meanwhile the Government of India had decided to modify the Commission's plans for regimental reductions. Only eighteen native infantry battalions and four native cavalry regiments were to be disbanded. No reserve would be set up. The staff corps system would be retained.[38]

In October 1881 Ripon's government repeated many of the arguments of the Commission and again pressed for the four-army scheme to be accepted. To counter the objections made by Haines, it was argued that the Bengal Army had become too large and homogeneous and that the reasons for keeping the Madras and Bombay forces separate applied equally to dividing those of Bengal. Moreover, the composition of the existing Bengal Army was largely accidental, because in the Mutiny a new army had been raised from Punjabis and low-caste levies.

> With the restoration of peace this army had to be reduced and under financial pressure the reduction was as sudden and as little the result of deliberation as the first creation. The regiments selected for reduction were selected on no defined principle except that the high-class sepoy who had conquered India was generally discredited. A considerable number of new and untried levies were retained, which it may be observed have remained untried up to the present day, while contrary to expectation and against the advice of some of the most experienced authorities, the Punjabi troops were incorporated into the new Bengal army. That army as it now stands is therefore a mere fortuitous *congerie* of regiments raised in haste, brought together in haste, reduced in haste ... The present condition of the Indian Army is the result of circumstances quite unforeseen by its original founders. To assume that it works well in practice is equally to ignore experience.[39]

Ripon and his Council then turned to the British element of their army. They suggested a reduction of its composition by four infantry battalions and one cavalry regiment to forty-six and eight respectively, and of the artillery by five horse, five field and five garrison batteries, with an increase of four mountain batteries. The same total number of rank and file would be maintained by increasing unit strengths. They anticipated objections from the British Army that the number of its regiments had been fixed with reference to Indian demands, and that some would therefore have to be disbanded or transferred to the War Office vote. Against this, they complained that units sent to India, which ought to be at war strength because reserves could not arrive before mobilisation, were actually established at strengths below those in the UK, and therefore had a higher proportion of expensive field officers to bayonets. Moreover, while the British Army's contribution to the defence of India in terms of numbers and efficiency had remained unchanged, its cost had greatly increased because of changes in the British Army, especially the introduction of the short service system in order to create a reserve which was of no use to India. This, together with better pay and promotion prospects for all ranks, had been 'imposed with little or no reference to Indian wants and in most cases without the Indian Government having a voice in the matter'. They concluded by saying that they had not started this inquiry into military reform, but having inherited it from the previous administration and laboured on it for a year they were now unanimous (Sir Donald Stewart had succeeded Haines when the latter's tour expired in April 1881, and had been replaced as Military Member by Major General Wilson). They submitted their plan 'in the hope of obtaining the final and unqualified approval of Her Majesty's

Government and in the confident assurance that our recommendations will commend themselves to all persons who examine them in the same spirit of impartiality and freedom from prejudice as that in which they have been made'.[40]

None of this impressed the authorities in London. Norman wrote a long minute exposing various inconsistencies in the Government of India's proposals, and demonstrating that they would result, not in a reduction of expenditure, but an increase of two lakhs of rupees in the annual budget.[41] Old Madras and Bombay councillors rose to defend their presidencies. Sir Robert Montgomery, of the Punjab, expressed his agreement with Norman, and objected to the plan of placing the Punjab Frontier Force, with its expertise in mountain warfare and its ability to react rapidly to tribal incursions, into the new Punjab army corps, and under the C-in-C, India, instead of the Foreign Department.[42] The Duke of Cambridge noted that the idea of removing the C-in-C from the Governor-General's Council was so strange that it only proved the Commission's unfitness to deal with the subject at all, and the War Office refused to agree to any changes in the number of British units, except for the artillery. Harrington became Secretary of State for War in December 1882 and it was his successor at the India Office, the Earl of Kimberley, who told Ripon in July 1883 that the presidential army system must remain.[43]

Ripon and his Council expressed their 'deep regret' at this verdict, and once more urged the case for reform.[44] The existing system was 'cumbrous' they said, and when contingents from two armies went on operations together, the Military Department had to function as Chief of Staff, Commissary General, Inspector General of Ordnance, and so on, all detrimental to the prompt despatch of business. They denied any intention of altering the balance of the composition of the native army, and said that this was an issue quite unaffected by the abolition of local Cs-in-C. 'But', says a pencil note on their letter in the India Office files (probably from the other remarks and arguments in the same hand, written by Norman), 'they can't bind their successors'. The India Office replied briefly that the case had already been considered, and answered, and there was no point in replying again in detail[45] but Ripon insisted on the arguments being recorded for publication if Parliament called for them.

The Panjdeh incident of March 1885, when Afghan and Russian troops clashed over a border dispute, enabled Stewart to renew the demands, which Ripon had rejected, for extra troops. British civilians in India flocked to join the Volunteers which had previously been unpopular, as few had the time or inclination to drill in a hot climate. Indian princes placed their armies and purses at the disposal of the Government. At home, the Army Reserve was called out. The question of creating a reserve was re-opened by the Government of India in March 1885. With the Russians now on the northern (undefined) border of Afghanistan, there was a risk of some clash that might lead to an Anglo-Russian war in Central Asia. In such a campaign, the British element would need more Indian troops to support them than normally existed. Such troops could not be raised at short notice, nor could they be kept up in anticipation of a war because that would mean having a higher proportion of Indian to British troops than everyone considered safe. There-fore, it was proposed to create a reserve by increasing the establishment of battalions to a level higher than that actually required in peace and to grant long furloughs to those surplus to this requirement. Ex-regulars were offered reserve service.

The new Conservative ministry and Lord Dufferin, by whom Ripon had been succeeded in October 1884 were more ready to support military expen-diture. All Indian battalions were increased by 150 men, every Indian cavalry regiment was given a fourth squadron (just as the Eden Commission had recommended), and three new Bengal cavalry regiments, four new Sikh and five new Gurkha infantry battalions were raised. The Indian Army was thus enlarged by 16,540 men, or, counting 200 reservists per unit, 23,000.

Stewart used this figure to justify a bid for 16,000 extra British soldiers to maintain the ratio laid down by Peel.[46] These men would bring the British units up to their war establishment, necessary because there was no certainty that army reservists would arrive in time, or at all, especially if communi-cations with Europe were interrupted. The Government of India did not enlarge upon the circumstances in which the Royal Navy would be unable to escort its Indian troopships, or even lose control of the Indian Ocean, but clearly considered it possible, and by the same letter sought authority for expenditure on harbour defences. Stewart had long believed that the British Army in India was in practice always at war and should be manned accord-ingly. He was not, however, prepared to increase the Indian Army without the corresponding British element. Indeed he even took the view, when Indian troops were sent to the Red Sea campaign, that this did not weaken the British position in India, but merely allowed the corresponding number of British troops to be sent out of the country with them. On the other hand, to allow the strength of the British garrison to be run down without remon-strance would encourage Parliament to think its numbers too high, and so reduce them permanently.[47]

Dissenting minutes by two members of Dufferin's Council, Sir A. Colvin and Sir Courtenay Ilbert, objected to the increases. They denied any imme-diate danger of a further Russian advance and suggested that to keep a larger army than was needed for the defence of India would lead to military adventurism. The new Indian reserve, sending trained men into the civil com-munity, would be no more of a danger than the number of active sepoys who already took their discharge each year, and there was no need to increase either the British or native armies as a precaution against them joining a rebellion. If India had to maintain a larger force of British troops under arms because it could not depend upon the arrival of British reservists, the British Treasury should pay. Extra taxation in India would cause discontent at the very time a Russian advance would play on it. If no threat materialised, there would be pressure to reduce taxation and military expenditure to below what was prudent. 'We cannot admit that it is the business of the Government of India, under the apprehension that reliance cannot be placed on the Government in England, to assume more than its hitherto recognised share of the common obligation.'[48]

The India Office accepted the proposed increases. The British establishment was altered by the addition of 148 troopers for each of the nine cavalry regiments in India, and 100 rank and file for each of the fifty battalions. Eleven new batteries were formed, totalling thirty guns and 1,373 artillerymen, so that the overall increase was 196 officers and 10,567 men. Stewart pronounced himself satisfied. He had bid for a total British strength of 75,000 on the assumption that the War Office would only supply the 70,000 he really considered necessary and he had obtained agreement for 69,764. He also secured the incorporation of the Punjab Frontier Force into the Bengal Army (it actually took place in 1886 by which time he had handed over as C-in-C to Sir Frederick Roberts).

The offers of military assistance made by Indian princes at the time of the Penjdeh incident were taken up, both to encourage their support for the British Raj, and to add to the reserve of trained Indian soldiers. Trained and equipped on the same lines as the British sepoys, the troops of the Indian States Forces (as they were later called) amounted by 1907 to 7,100 cavalry, 421 artillerymen, 570 sappers, 9,384 infantry and 665 camel troopers, with four transport and two signals units. The greater princes produced contingents approaching brigade strength, the smaller ones, only troops or companies. Commanded and officered by subjects or servants of each prince, they cost the Government of India nothing apart from the extra twenty-one officers of the Indian Army attached to them for supervisory purposes. Indian princes continued to maintain their old armies, estimated to total 80,000 in 1907, but only these new contingents were considered suitable to serve in the British Indian order of battle. Some proved efficient. Others, with their training often disrupted by court ceremonial, and lacking fully trained officers, were less reliable but, if nothing else, they could be used on lines of communication to free the British sepoys for combat duties.[49]

In 1885 the Indian Government again raised the question of abolishing the presidential armies, suggesting that this might achieve savings that would be put towards the cost of the extra troops it had raised.[50] Again the proposal was rejected, with the old plea that parliamentary time could not be found for the necessary legislation.[51] There was, however, no objection to the achievement of economies by the centralisation of the logistic departments. In 1876 the three remount departments were amalgamated and brought into one under the Government of India in the Military Department. The ordnance and commissariat departments were similarly combined in 1884 and 1885 respectively, to be followed by the clothing, military works, education, and judge advocate departments. Another of the Eden proposals was implemented in 1886, with the grouping of regiments into threes or, in some cases, pairs, each group with a common regimental centre, and all new recruits accepting liability to be posted from one battalion to another within the group to allow reinforcement in time of war. Such postings were not intended to take place in peace, so the scheme had the double disadvantage that men, in war, would find themselves serving with strangers, while the mobilisation of one Indian unit would only be achieved by draining two others.

The amalgamation of the Armies was proposed again in 1888. In an attempt to placate the defenders of the established order, the Government of India suggested that the lieutenant generals who would be at the head of the Madras and Bombay army corps should continue as members of the respective Governor's Councils. The India Office thought this anomalous as the other two proposed corps commanders, who would have no functions in government, would therefore be unequal in status to their colleagues.[52] The Duke of Cambridge, asked for his views, said that he had on three previous occasions pointed out the disadvantages of the scheme, and had thought that he would hear no more of it. 'The composition and location of foreign legions have been delicate and difficult questions for all times. India has had her lesson on that head.' The idea of locally raised and based army corps was derived from Germany, he said, but the troops holding Alsace-Lorraine were certainly not recruited from those provinces. He saw no benefit in changing a system which for so long and with such success had achieved the desired result of securing the British position in India.[53]

Pressure for change nevertheless was growing stronger. Cambridge's final minute was forwarded by the War Office with a note that the Secretary of State for War, Edward Stanhope, was 'not disposed to express concurrence with the views put forward therein'. More importantly still, most of the senior posts in the Indian military were by this time held by former members of the Eden Commission. Roberts became C-in-C, India, in 1885 and, with a second term, would remain there until 1895. Newmarch, after a career spent in the Military Department of the Government of India, ending as its Secretary, became Military Secretary at the India Office in 1888 and remained there until 1899. Collen, the commission's secretary, had also risen in the same department and took Newmarch's place in India. Norman had left the Council of India in 1883 and been succeeded by Lumsden who would serve there for ten years. The Government of India was granted authority to draft the necessary orders for amalgamation though with the warning that parliamentary time was not yet available and that to introduce legislation was sure to attract opposition in the Lords that would only impede improvements.

Roberts, in all his forty-one years in India, never departed from the opinions he formed as a subaltern in the Bengal Army (and the son of a Bengal Army general with a Eurasian family) that men of the southern regions of India were inferior fighting material. Coupled with these ancient prejudices were the Darwinian theories shared by many of Roberts's contemporaries that lack of practice in fighting made men unfit to bear arms in the space, apparently, of two or three generations. When C-in-C, Madras, he introduced musketry competitions, arguing that modern technology ought to allow any keen Madrassi soldiers to overcome the combat disadvantage of their slighter physique. The failure of his scheme convinced him that the old martial spirit of the Coast Armies had died out and that the hardier races of the north, despite their lack of education, were better soldiers. That these were led by some of the best officers in the Indian Army, and the Madras sepoys by some of the worst, he did not dwell upon. Instead, he argued that the Indian Army must be ready to fight beyond the North West Frontier and that troops from the Deccan, from Madras, even from Hindustan, were physically and temperamentally unsuited to cope with either the terrain or the Russian enemy they were likely to meet.[54]

Under the influence of Roberts, and of its new Military Member (the reformist Sir Henry Brackenbury, once Lytton's private secretary), the Government of India revived the old proposals once more.[55] Four regional Army Corps should take the place of the three presidential Armies. The two minor C-in-Cs would be abolished and their local successors would not sit in Council. The C-in-C, India, would ensure that regional recruiting continued, if this was desired. There was hardly anything left of the presidential system, said the Government of India, but such as remained was harmful. It promised few savings, as these had already been made by the centralisation of the logistic departments, which had effectively destroyed the presidential system by administrative action.

This last argument proved decisive. Cambridge finally withdrew his opposition. Stewart, joining the Council of India in 1893, gave enthusiastic support. The Governments of Madras and Bombay gave reluctant acceptance. Bombay, faced with a rising nationalist movement led by Bal Gangadhar Tilak, who found his inspiration in the achievements of Sivaji, regretted any diminution in the number of officials in its Council. Madras said that the change was long foreseen and agreed that it had long lost any real control over military matters. Nevertheless, it thought that the local troops would soon see a difference once they came under command of a distant government whose officers would be predominantly men whose service had been in the north and who would have no knowledge of, interest in, or sympathy with the people of southern India.[56]

Accordingly, legislation was prepared and the Madras and Bombay Armies Act was passed in 1893.[57] New establishments were authorised and the four army corps scheme came into force in 1895. It had taken nearly twenty years for Eden's proposals to be fully carried through. Whatever improvements there were in efficiency, there were no reductions in expenditure. Estimates for ordinary military purposes (i.e. excluding operations and defence works), rose every year. From 12 crores of rupees in 1884–85 it reached 24 in 1904–5. Meanwhile the rupee continued to fall until 1891 when, at 20 to the pound, its value was half what it had been twenty years earlier. Only in 1895, after income tax had been revived and the tax on salt (an ancient government monopoly) increased, was the fall stopped and the rupee established at 15 to the pound, where it remained for the rest of the British period.

There was some difficulty in finding a Governor-General to replace the Marquis of Lansdowne under whom these charges took place. Lord Cromer, the Egyptian pro-consul, declined. Sir Henry Norman, in post as Governor of Queensland, first accepted and then, at the age of sixty-seven, decided that he could not face five years back in India. The second Earl of Elgin was appointed and in 1896 had to deal with an outbreak of bubonic plague in Bombay. When the inhabitants refused to co-operate with the health author-ities, British troops were sent into their houses, causing a great outcry, artic-ulated by Tilak, against military brutalism. Throughout British India the spirit of nationalism was rising and the same kind of modernisation that had led to the passing of the old armies would soon lead to the passing of the political system they had served to maintain.

Notes

1. *Cit.* in Keith Jeffery, *The British Army and the Crisis of Empire 1918–1922*, Manchester, 1984, p. 2.
2. Return of British troops sent out of India on Imperial Service 1864–1897, IOR L/MIL/7/5966.
3. Wood to Norman (pte) 12 March 1862, *cit.* in W. Lee-Warner, *Memoirs of Field Marshal Sir Henry Wylie Norman*, London, 1908, p. 241.
4. Lee-Warner, *op. cit.*, p. 259.
5. Robert S. Rait, *The Life of Field Marshal Sir Frederick Paul Haines*, London, 1911, p. 213.
6. *Ibid.*, p. 242.
7. Forwarded by Lytton to Salisbury with private letters dated 12 August 1876, IOR MSS/Eur/E/218/18.
8. *Cit.* in Rait, *op. cit.*, pp. 201–2.
9. Memo by Sir G. Wolseley forwarded by Sec. of State to Gov.-Gen., 12 April 1877, IOR L/MI177/5446.
10. Salisbury to Lytton (pte) 12 April 1877, IOR MSS/Eur/E/218/4.
11. Lytton to Sir Louis Mallet (pte) 15 July 1878, IOR MSS/Eur/E/218/20.

12. Lytton to Haines (pte) 19 July 1877 *ibid.*
13. Lytton to Wolseley (pte) 2 July 1877 *ibid.*
14. Lytton to Cranbrook (pte) 14 June 1878 *ibid.*
15. Lytton to Cranbrook (pte) 10 September 1878 *ibid.*
16. Rait, *op. cit.*, p. 274.
17. Lytton to Cranbrook (pte) 25 May 1879, IOR, MSS/Eur/E/218/21.
18. *Ibid.*
19. Lytton to Roberts (pte) 11 June 1879, *ibid.*
20. Lytton to Eden (pte) 14 July 1879, *ibid.*
21. Lytton to Cranbrook (pte) 14 July 1879, *ibid.*
22. Govt of India in the Military Dept to Lt.-Gov. of Bengal No. 202 (S) of 7 July 1879, IOR L/MIL/17/5/1687.
23. *Ibid.*
24. Report of the Army Organisation Commission 15 November 1878, IOR L/MIL/17/5/1687, L/MIL/7/5445.
25. *Ibid.*
26. *Ibid.*
27. Cranbrook to Lytton (pte) 21 September 1879, 29 September 1879, 17 December 1879, IOR MSS/Eur/E/218/6.
28. Lytton to Cranbrook (pte) 28 October 1879, 4 February 1880, 16 March 1880, 12 April 1880, IOR MSS/Eur/F7218/21–22.
29. Lytton to Cranbrook (pte) 10 August 1879 and 22 September 1879, *ibid.*
30. Rait, *op. cit.*, pp. 313–19; Minute by Haines (recirculated 26 February 1881), IOR L/MIL/7/15322.
31. Lytton to Cranbrook (pte) 20 April 1880, IOR MSS/Eur/E/218/22.
32. Minute by Gov.-Gen. 26 May 1880, enc with letter Gov.-Gen. in Council to Sec. of State in Council 1 June 1880, IOR L/MIL/7/15322.
33. Lytton to Harrison (PS to Cranbrook) 9 May 1880, IOR MSS/Eur/ E/218/22.
34. Minute by General Sir Edwin Johnson 7 July 1880, IOR L/MIL/ 7/7013.
35. *Ibid.*
36. Gov.-Gen. in Council to Sec. of State in Council No. 85 (Military) 28 February 1881, IOR L/MIL/7/15323.
37. Sec. of State in Council to Gov.-Gen. in Council No. 230 (Military) 16 June 1881, IOR L/MIL/7/15323.
38. Gov.-Gen. in Council to Sec. of State in Council No. 230 24 June 1881, IOR L/MIL/7/7013.
39. Gov.-Gen. in Council to Sec. of State in Council 29 October 1881, IOR L/MIL/7/15322.
40. *Ibid.*
41. Minute by Lt-Gen. Sir H.W. Norman 20 April 1882, IOR L/MIL/ 7/7013.
42. Minute by Sir Robert Montgomery 25 November 1881, IOR L/MIL/7/15322.
43. Sec. of State in Council to Gov.-Gen. in Council Despatch No. 243 (Military) 26 July 1883, IOR L/MIL/7/15323.
44. Gov.-Gen. in Council to Sec. of State in Council Letter No. 200 (Military) 15 October 1883, IOR L/MIL/7/15323.
45. Sec. of State in Council to Gov.-Gen. in Council Despatch No. 76 (Military) 13 March 1884, IOR L/MIL/7/15323.
46. Gov.-Gen. in Council to Sec. of State in Council Letter No. 135 14 August 1885, IOR L/MIL/7/5446.
47. Stewart's note book entries *cit.* in G.R. Elsmie, *Field Marshal Sir Donald Stewart*, London, 1903, pp. 410–12.
48. Enc in letter Gov.-Gen. in Council to Sec. of State in Council No. 135 14 August 1885, IOR L/MIL/7/5446.

49. *Imperial Gazetteer of India* Vol. 4. (Army) Calcutta 1907.
50. Sec. of State in Council to Gov.-Gen. in Council Despatch No. 275 29 October 1885, IOR L/MIL/7/5446.
51. Sec. of State in Council to Gov.-Gen. in Council Despatch No. 275 29 October 1885, IOR L/MIL/7/5446.
52. Gov.-Gen. in Council to Sec. of State in Council Letter No. 87 (Military) 1 June 1888, IOR L/MIL/7/15322–15332.
53. Minutes by the Duke of Cambridge 31 May 1881, 27 May 1882, 31 October 1882, 25 July 1888, IOR L/MIL/7/15322–15332.
54. F.S. Roberts, *Forty-One Years in India*, Vol. II, London, 1897, p. 383.
55. Gov.-Gen. in Council to Sec. of State in Council Letter No. 172 (Military) 2 November 1892, IOR L/MIL/7/15334.
56. Gov. of Madras in Council to Sec. of State in Council No. 24 19 May 1893, IOR L/MIL/7/15334.
57. 56 & 57 Vic, c. 62.

Chapter 7

The Staff and the Staff Corps, 1850–1902

It was not until the middle of the nineteenth century that much consideration was given to the requirement for officers, once commissioned, to obtain any further military qualifications before holding any post for which they might be selected. In this respect, the Indian Army followed the example of the British Army. In 1849 the Duke of Wellington, as Commander-in-Chief, ordered that none might be granted a first commission, either by purchase or any other method, unless able to show that he had received the education normally expected of a gentleman of the time. Thereafter, before promotion to the rank of lieutenant (and subsequently to captain), officers had not merely to be, as previously, the senior in their rank in their regiment able to produce the sum necessary for the purchase of the next one, but also to have passed a board of examination in their competence to perform its duties. In practice, little action was taken until early in 1854, when Sidney Herbert, the Secretary at War, and Lord Hardinge, the former Governor-General of India who had succeeded Wellington at the Horse Guards, secured Cabinet approval and Treasury funds for a system of 'garrison instructors' who would teach young officers the subjects in which they were to be examined. The outbreak of the Crimean War later that year initially delayed and subsequently hastened the implementation of these arrangements.[1] In the meanwhile the Indian authorities continued to address the problem in lengthy, unhurried and elegant correspondence among themselves.

The major difficulty about introducing promotion examinations into the Indian military service was that, to prevent corruption and nepotism, its entire system of promotion rested upon the principle of seniority of rank within each regiment. There was, any more than in the British Army, no way of ensuring that an officer was fit to perform any of the duties of the rank to which he had the right, under the existing rules, to be promoted when his turn came. In August 1854 the C-in-C of the Bombay Army, Lieutenant General Lord Frederick Fitzclarence, suggested that this problem could be overcome by the introduction of examinations to be passed prior to an officer being selected for 'staff duty'. This term in India covered a far greater range of appointments than in the British Army, and included all civil or military posts other than those held by field officers in a regiment, or captains and sub-alterns with companies or troops.[2] The C-in-C, India, General Sir William Gomm, pointed out a basic flaw in this plan. If the aim of introducing exam-inations was to ensure that officers were trained in their military duties, there was no point in setting the examination prior to them taking up staff employ-ment, because such employment could keep them away from regimental duty for fifteen years, so that on returning they would have forgotten whatever they had been examined in. Likewise there was no point in officers returning to their regiments to be examined on promotion because they would, imme-diately on passing, return to their staff employment. Thus, 'the means pro-posed would not, the Commander-in-Chief thinks, secure the result aimed at'.[3] Nevertheless he supported the concept that a suitable examination should be passed by anyone rejoining a regiment or company before he assumed command of it, or took up a position on its HQ staff. Such exam-inations, however, were not to demand a knowledge of arms other than their own, as 'the object should, he thinks, simply be to render the service as thoroughly efficient as possible, without imposing task work to such a degree as to render the Military Service irksome and distasteful to young men'.[4] He would not, however, countenance the idea of additional formal qualifications being demanded of formation commanders, on the grounds that it would be degrading to officers who had practised their profession for many years and often achieved distinction in it, if they were required to 'undergo ordeals of the nature proposed, which though they might result in proving the acquire-ment of a certain amount of theoretical knowledge, could do nothing towards securing the possession of sound judgement, discretion, habits of reflection, and the several other important qualifications so essential to the proper performance of the high and responsible situation referred to'.[5]

While the Indian Mutiny and the subsequent campaign in Central India raged on, the proposals regarding the qualifications to be demanded of officers pursued their steady course around the subordinate governments and headquarters. Lieutenant General Sir Patrick Grant, officiating as C-in-C, India (the first, and only, Company's officer to hold this post) reported in October 1857 that the Madras Army had adopted the promotion examin-ations prescribed for the British Army. He supported the Court of Directors' proposals for a mandatory Hindustani examination for promotion to captain. The Madras Government, in March 1858, added the recommendation that examinations should test officers' knowledge of local geography, of the history of their own Army and regiment, and the castes from which the men of their troops or companies were drawn. It also stressed that officers should first be given the means of obtaining the knowledge in which they were to be tested. The Bombay Government took a similar view, though recommending that separate examinations be held for promotion and for staff qualification, and that the word 'Indian' should be substituted for 'foreign' in the language requirement laid down for British staff officers in the Duke of Cambridge's regulations. It also stressed that these regulations were suitable only for army staff, but not for other Indian staff appointments, such as those in ordnance, commissariat, pay, judge-advocate, audit, public works and survey departments.

These questions had still not been resolved by the time that, as part of the reconstruction of the Indian Army after the Mutiny of 1857, a new system was introduced for the appointment of its officers. Previously, officers for the irregular regiments and for all other military and civil staff appointments were drawn from officers of the regular Indian regiments or from the British regiments serving in India, whose establishment in both cases was higher than it normally needed to be, thus allowing for a proportion being absent in this way. After the necessary legislation,[6] a Royal Warrant dated 18 January 1861 set up three Staff Corps, one each for the Bengal, Madras and Bombay Armies, to which all officers then serving in staff appointments, including those with irregular regiments (as which almost all Indian regular regiments were to be re-organised) were transferred, if they so wished and were appropriately qualified. The rest remained on the rolls of their old regular regiments (in the case of European regiments, having the option of transferring with them to the British Line), from which they could be employed on any duty at their government's discretion, and so provided a reserve for the Staff Corps until in the course of time they retired or became casualties from any other cause. Appointments to the army staff continued to have a tenure limited to five years. All other staff appointments were without time limit, so allowing members of the Staff Corps to make their career either with Indian troops or with a department of the Indian civil or military administration. Promotion in military rank within the Staff Corps was by time rather than vacancy. All below that rank entered as lieutenants. Captaincies were granted after a total of twelve (later reduced to eleven) years of commissioned service, majorities after twenty, lieutenant colonelcies after twenty-six, and colonelcies after thirty-one. The intention of this was to end the unfairness of the old system by which officers in one regiment might achieve promotion more quickly than those in another which had suffered fewer casualties. Appointment to any particular staff post, however, was to be by selection, without regard to seniority. Thus in some units captains became commanders of 'wings' (half battalions) or, in the cavalry, squadrons, while in others majors remained in posts which carried lower allowances and status. The salary of a Staff Corps officer was to be an amalgam of the pay of his rank and the allowances of his post.

In December 1861, in response to a hastening letter from the India Office, Lieutenant General Sir William Mansfield, C-in-C, Bombay, told the

Government of India that the language test for Bombay officers prior to staff employment was the same as that in the Bengal Army. For army staff appointments he would be content to rely upon the examinations of the new Staff College at Camberley. He pointed out that, whereas Fitzclarence's proposals of 1854 and 1855 for a system of examining officers had arisen from a system in which those on the staff could return to regimental duty, the establishment of the Staff Corps had brought about the reverse of this. Officers, once in a staff department, would spend their entire career there and never need to know another thing about military affairs. Even those remaining at regimental duty did not, he thought, need to be examined other than for appointment as adjutant, as a good adjutant would be qualified to become a good army staff officer, while the qualities required for the exercise of military command were moral as much as intellectual, and not ascertainable by examination.

The C-in-C, India, General Sir Hugh Rose, the victor of the hard-fought central India campaign of 1858–59, took a similar view. In support of the contention that those who could pass examinations were not necessarily the best staff officers, he said that he clearly remembered, from his service in the Crimea, an officer who had mastered all branches of science connected with his profession, but was practically useless in every one of the departments in which he had been employed. He did not see how it would be possible to prevent those officers of the old local armies who had not transferred to the Staff Corps from obtaining promotion by seniority rather than examination, because Parliament had guaranteed that their existing rights would be preserved, and their transfer from the service of the Company to that of the Crown had taken place before the Court of Directors' proposals for Hindustani examinations came into effect.

In principle, he considered that any promotion examinations in the Indian Army should be the same as those in force for the British Army, and thought it feasible, as staff appointments in the new system would be by selection, to make these conditional upon passing an examination. This, he thought, should be entirely practical, and appropriate to the arm or department, for although all officers would accept the justice of having some kind of test, it was not easy in Indian conditions to find either the teachers or books for scientific studies. Moreover, the prospect of a written examination several years after the cessation of their academic education would, in his view, deter many good officers from applying for transfer to the Staff Corps at all.[7] Details of the tests or examinations to be passed by officers joining the Staff Corps were not finally agreed and published until October 1871, more than twenty years after the proposal to examine officers in connection with their fitness for staff or regimental appointments had first been made.

Recruitment of officers for the Staff Corps from the Line was a constant problem. In May 1865 the C-in-C, India, (by this time Mansfield) argued that most officers only served with Indian units as a way of obtaining staff posts, and that recruits were not joining in sufficient numbers because such posts were being given to those who had not transferred to the Staff Corps. He made three major recommendations, intended to create a reserve which would ensure that regiments continued to have a viable complement of officers, and to encourage recruitment from the British Line against the time when the supply of locals for staff employment would be exhausted. He advocated the appointment of a seventh officer to each irregular regiment so that when anyone was on furlough, or became a casualty, the unit would remain fully officered without the need for a stranger to be brought in from another corps. This was accepted without objection, though in itself it would have made the manning problem worse, as it increased the numbers needed. It was therefore essential to improve recruitment. This he proposed to do by arranging for officers who had to surrender their commissions in the British Army (which, except in the Royal Artillery and Royal Engineers, they had in most cases obtained by purchase, both for their first appointment and any subsequent promotion) to have their purchase money refunded on entry to the Staff Corps. He also proposed allowing entry at any level by officers of any rank, without any test or period of service with Indian troops, as long as they were otherwise suitable for the department where they were needed.[8]

The latter scheme was strongly opposed by Colonel H.M. Durand, the Military Member of the Governor-General's Council. He argued that open appointment to staff employment in India would make officers even more reluctant to exchange a career in the British Army for one in the Indian Army because the prize of staff employment could always be given to a British Army officer over their heads. It would 'render the service with the Native Troops not the road to the Staff Departments of India, Civil, Political, and Military, but to a purely Military employment with black troops, which would be classed with service with African or West India Corps and would be held in much the same esteem in England. They would be regarded as a Local Indian Militia.'[9]

The Governor-General, Sir John Lawrence, concurred. There were, he said, far more applications from British Army officers for posts in civil or political employment than he could fill, and all had expressed their willingness to transfer to the Staff Corps. Against opening staff appointments to anyone, he argued that prior service with an Indian regiment allowed suitability for the exercise of authority over Indians to be assessed, while entry at an early age ensured adequate training for the more responsible positions in due course. Mansfield had also suggested that by allowing entry to the staff at any level, the Indian Staff Corps would be prevented from developing the corporate spirit of the Indian Civil Service, which he thought contrary to the public good, by achieving the reservation of particular government posts for its own members. He was referring to the civil servants' insistence that, in the older, or 'regulation' provinces, the principle laid down in successive India Acts that responsible positions should only be held by those who had made the civil service their career should be maintained. This served to prevent jobbery and denied such posts to military men. Lawrence, himself a former member of the Indian Civil Service, and one of the only four to become Governor-General, admitted that any special body of men would develop a feeling of exclusiveness and stand up for its privileges, but thought the overall advantages to the government of such a corporate spirit outweighed the disadvantages. Among the former should be a willingness to make short-term financial sacrifices, so he was opposed to refunding any commission money from Indian revenues.[10]

Mansfield did not accept this argument. He maintained that in India there was only a small number of educated Europeans from whom candidates for government posts could be drawn, and it was wrong to restrict it still further. He also claimed that no one in possession of the educational and other personal qualities which were demanded of entrants to the Staff Corps would join if he had any money or income of his own, or any prospects of investing in a respectable career in England. To require those without such means to surrender the commissions for which they had paid was to inflict a fine on those least able to afford it, which was not demanded in any other walk of life.[11] Lawrence replied that there was no more reason to refund the money paid to obtain a military commission than the fees paid for the university education necessary to qualify young men for entry as administrators in the civil service, or as barristers in the judicial service, or as clergymen for chaplaincies. He saw no reason to compensate individuals who were being appointed to offices with excellent prospects on the strength of academic qualifications far below those demanded for members of the civil service in the same department. He pointed out that cornets and ensigns joining the Staff Corps gained immediate promotion to the rank of lieutenant (without waiting for a vacancy and finding the purchase money that both would have been necessary for those remaining in the British Army), and an immediate increase in income of 25 per cent from the staff duty allowances. From his own personal career, he remained convinced of the benefits of Indian service beginning at an early age, and it was 'never more expedient than at the present time that officers who have belonged to British Regiments should be in the first instance attached to Native Corps ... to mitigate the contempt towards these people which is, I regret to say, more or less inherent in the Englishman, and which strikes me as being a good deal fostered in a British Regiment'.[12]

The continuing shortfall in the number of recruits attracted to the three Indian Staff Corps led to Lawrence being overruled by the India Office in May 1868. The problem was not in filling the departmental staff appointments to which Lawrence had referred. These were eagerly sought after at all times. They were indeed the prize for which many who had no intention of spending their career as soldiers, but who lacked the university education required for entry to the Indian Civil Service, joined the Indian military to obtain. It was in the regiments, from which appointments were kept filled, where the shortages were felt. Accordingly, it was ruled that officers transferring to the Staff Corps within four years of purchasing their first commission should have the cost of it refunded.[13]

The shortfall nevertheless continued, to the inconvenience of both the British and Indian Armies. In May 1869 the Duke of Cambridge, as C-in-C of the British Army, ordered all commanding officers of British regiments serving in India to give the fullest encouragement to their junior officers to prepare themselves for admission to the Staff Corps (he was referring to the language qualification, which, apart from a certificate of general efficiency, was the only one of the entrance tests actually in force by this time) and on no account to put any obstacle in the way of their doing so. Lieutenant Colonel Davis of the 37th Foot protested to Mansfield that this system of officering the Indian from the British Line sacrificed the latter to the former, as potential Staff Corps officers made their regiment 'a convenience and a stepping stone, caring little for its repute and doing nothing for its benefit'.[14] Whatever effect the refunding of commission money might have had in easing the recruitment problem ended in 1871 when the purchase system was abolished.

An immediate consequence of the abolition of purchase was the closure of the Royal Military College at Sandhurst.[15] The ranks of cornet and ensign were replaced by that of sub-lieutenant. This differed from the previous rank in that it was merely probationary. Whereas an ensign or cornet might remain in that rank for many years until a vacancy occurred for a lieutenant to which, by purchase or otherwise, he could be promoted, a sub-lieutenant, after the completion of two years' satisfactory regimental duty and passing the examination for elevation to lieutenant, was promoted automatically. There was thereafter no difference, for establishment purposes, between the two subaltern ranks. Appointment to sub-lieutenant was to be by open competitive examination in general academic subjects. The fear that such a method of entry would result in the Army being officered by a race of fragile intellectuals would prove unfounded as crammers (or 'army entrance tutors') rose to the challenge. Garrison instructors were appointed to provide tuition for the sub-lieutenants once appointed but by 1875 the weaknesses of this arrangement had become so apparent that the Royal Military College was re-opened, and gentlemen cadets (who had survived in the interim only at the Royal Military

Academy, Woolwich, where future officers of the non-purchase Royal Artillery and Royal Engineers were trained) were again appointed there.[16] One reason for the College's closure had been that no parent or guardian saw any benefit in paying its fees. Under the purchase system, gentlemen cadets successfully completing the Sandhurst course obtained their first commission as a free grant, thus effectively recovering the cost of their tuition fees. When commissions no longer had to be bought, it was cheaper for parents to keep their sons at their public schools for another year or send them to a crammer. The losers had been those who held the India cadetships which represented the last vestiges of the East India Company's patronage system and had provided a free, or at least subsidised, education at Sandhurst. After 1875 these were revived, and the holders entered the RMC by a limited competition among those nominated on the strength of their parent's service. All had to achieve a minimum pass mark in the open competitive examination which was now for entry to the College rather than for the award of a commission.

The War Office, when announcing that candidates for first commissions in the Line (whether joining regiments at home, in the colonies, or in India) would in future be required to attend the RMC as gentlemen cadets and pay fees accordingly, asked the India Office to bear a share of the costs of enlarging and maintaining the re-opened college. The estimates for the extra building amounted to £4,500 and the running costs were not yet certain. The India Office declined on principle to pay anything for an establishment over which it had no control, though agreeing to accept a charge, payable at the time he embarked, for the training of any officer actually joining a British regiment in India. This recognised the British Army's contribution to the defence of India, and the role of these regiments in producing officers for the Staff Corps.

In 1878 the requirement for a candidate for the Staff Corps to have served with a British regiment in India was abandoned, and any officer under the age of twenty-six, with not more than five and less than two years' service (or three years if with a West India regiment) could apply. Once in India, those who failed the language and other probationary tests were to be attached to a British regiment in India. No choice of presidency was allowed and officers on arrival were to go where needed. This scheme proved to be unsatisfactory to the British Army. The War Office pointed out that 'there is nothing to prevent a young Officer making a convenience of both Services and offering himself as a candidate for the Staff Corps, with a view to remaining in India as long as it suits him, or of seeing the country, travelling there and back at the public expense and escaping thereby a disagreeable quarter or an exacting Colonel'.[17] The Duke of Cambridge's view was that officers should volunteer for the Indian Staff Corps once and for all and be removed from the service if they were found unacceptable.[18] The Indian reply was that it seemed unjust to remove anyone without the court martial that would be necessary for this in the British Army and eventually a compromise was reached. Officers who failed probation but could produce a certificate that this was not on account of misconduct were allowed to return to their British regiments.[19]

At the end of the Second Afghan War a senior member of the Governor of Bombay's Council, L.R. Ashburner, an old Bombay civil servant, condemned the whole staff corps system. In a strongly worded minute, dated 4 October 1881, he said it had ruined the Bombay Army, and destroyed all *esprit de corps:* 'I have heard officers say openly that they have no confidence in their men and would be sorry to take them into action.' He forecast that the battle of Maiwand (where a brigade of Bombay troops had been routed by an Afghan army) would be followed by other such disasters unless the system was altered. It had led, he said, to a complete absence of sympathy between the British officers and their troops, made worse by the officers' growing taste for social amusements of the kind they could share with ladies, but deriving ultimately from the requirement for officers who wished to serve in the Indian Army having first to spend two years in a British regiment. 'There is no disguising the fact that officers of the British army look with contempt on the Native army. They speak of the officers as black officers, as Niggar regiments &c. I have known officers commanding British regiments discourage, if not prohibit all social intercourse with officers of Native regiments ... I am told the same feeling of contempt for the Native army exists very strongly at Sandhurst.' He compared this unfavourably with the atmosphere at Addiscombe, where the mutual devotion and achievements of officers and men of the Company's army had been a source of pride to the cadets. In the old days, he remembered, although many officers were in staff employment, they flocked back to their regiments at the mere rumour of a campaign, leaving their departments severely stretched. This he contrasted with the state of affairs in 1881, when officers did not scruple to appear at social events in Poona or importune for staff employment while their regiments were serving in the field. He recommended the revival of an Indian military college, a return to regimental promotion, and that, in the infantry, each company should have a British officer, who should fall in on foot with his men. He also recommended a liberal messing allowance and the construction of quarters, to be let by government to officers at modest charges, in all military stations. All this would involve expenditure, but nothing, he said, was a greater extravagance than to pay for an army which was inefficient.[20]

Ashburner's reference to company officers falling in, on foot, with their men, stemmed from the much derided practice of junior British officers in Indian infantry regiments riding chargers on parade. This, as they were actually, under the irregular system, regimental staff officers, was entirely in accordance with the military conventions of the time and derived from the requirement for such staff officers, in action, to see over the heads of those in the battle line, and, on the march, to move rapidly up and down the column. Although this practice emphasised that it was the Indian officers rather than the British officers who commanded the companies, it also meant that, while the former marched, the latter rode. Company officers in the British infantry marched, and looked with disapproval or envy at those of equal or junior rank in the Indian infantry who rode.

Rudyard Kipling summarised the British Army's view of this and the whole method of recruiting the Staff Corps in his short story 'Only a Subaltern'. Of an imaginary regiment, the Tyneside Tailtwisters, he wrote:

> the Colonel commanding had looked into the fourteen fearless eyes of seven plump and juicy subalterns who had all applied to enter the Staff Corps, and had asked them why the three stars should he, a Colonel of the Line, command a dashed nursery for double-dashed bottle-suckers who put on condemned tin spurs and rode qualified mokes at the head of forsaken Black Regiments. He was a rude man and a terrible. Wherefore the remnant took measures (with the half-butt as an engine of public opinion) till the rumour went abroad that young men who used the Tail-Twisters as a crutch to the Staff Corps had many and varied trials to endure.[21]

The 1879 Eden Commission recommended the abolition of the Staff Corps altogether. Instead, it proposed the introduction of General Lists, one for each of the three Armies, with direct recruitment from the Royal Military College, appointment against a fixed establishment (calculated to total 1,520 officers) and promotion to regimental vacancies as they occurred rather than by time. The aim was primarily to achieve economies, but also to ensure that the regiments were not drained of officers to fill staff posts. Sir Edwin Johnson, the Military Member, defended the existing system with vigour: 'What the Staff Corps organisation was intended to do it did thoroughly; it evoked order out of chaos, and from the debris of a revolted army created another whose efficiency, loyalty, and courage have never in past times been surpassed.'[22] The rest of the Government of India agreed that the Staff Corps should remain, though supporting the idea of direct recruitment from the RMC. When the Eden proposals reached the India Office, Norman produced statistics to prove that in normal times the regimental vacancies were all filled.[23]

The official view that officers of all the Armies readily identified with their men was belied by the reluctance of new entrants to join the Madras or Bombay Staff Corps, and their anxiety to obtain appointments in local units which, being under control of the Government of India in the Foreign Department, could be officered from any of the three Staff Corps. In practice, because the Bengal Staff Corps took the pick of the applicants and was closer to the Government of India, it secured most of such appointments, but the memoirs of one officer, who transferred to the Staff Corps from the Gloucestershire Regiment (then in Ireland) and found himself in the 9th Bombay Infantry (the word Native disappeared from unit titles in 1885, four years after the Bengal, Madras and Bombay regiments of the British Line were re-mustered as regular battalions of the new English or Irish territorial regiments)[24] reveal that influence could overcome this: 'Quite unexpectedly one night in mess a telegram arrived for me, posting me to the 1st Sikhs – a very fine regiment in the Punjab Frontier Force ... I owed this appointment to Lord Beresford, the Military Secretary to the Viceroy, who had heard from Lady Huntingdon who was a distant relation of mine.'[25]

Only four years after this, the Madras Army, when called on to provide the bulk of the troops committed by India to the Third Burma War, was so under-strength in officers that the Government of India called for eighty additional volunteers for the Madras Staff Corps. Any British officer under the age of twenty-five, even if he had not completed two years' efficient duty with his regiment or corps, was offered a place. These new officers joined their units strangers to their men and unqualified in southern, or indeed any other, Indian languages. The performance of the Madras Army in this, its first major campaign after the Staff Corps had been set up thirty-five years previously, highlighted the weaknesses in the staff corps system to which Eden had drawn attention.

A further weakness was that, if ever the British Army was engaged in a major war, in Europe or elsewhere, it would need all its officers, and therefore the flow of new recruits to the Staff Corps, even for the purpose of manning Indian regiments which might be needed to fight alongside the British, would come to an abrupt halt. As long as India was a military backwater, this was of little importance, but the Penjdeh incident of 1885 and the fear of a major war between Britain and Russia to be fought from India made this problem far more significant. It was first highlighted by Colonel Sir William Lockhart, an officer of the old Bengal Army who was, at this time, assistant military secretary for Indian affairs on the Duke of Cambridge's staff at the Horse Guards. He began by questioning the need for the Indian Staff Corps to be recruited from the British Army at all.[26] He wrote:

> I cannot pay much importance to the matter of social training and of the prestige which is claimed for officers who have once belonged to British regiments. What is wanted is a body of men capable of leading Asiatics in war and I believe that such a body existed in India before officers were filtered through the British Service into the Native Army and styled members of a 'Staff Corps' ... I think that the Indian officer of today

belongs to precisely the same class as his predecessor before the Mutiny, that is to say he is generally a man of gentle birth, and almost invariably a poor one. That his qualifications are higher than formerly is as true of him as it is of officers of the British service.

Lockhart therefore argued that there would be no deterioration in the quality of officers if they were to be recruited directly to the Indian Army, some from the RMC, some from selected universities and public schools, and some from the Militia, as well as by transfer from the Line. He pointed out the anomaly of the Indian soldier, often ill fed and poorly clothed, and armed with an inferior rifle, being expected to share the exposure and fatigue of campaign service alongside his British counterpart, with less than half the number of officers, and these more likely to be picked off by enemy sharpshooters. In addition to recommending a better recruitment system to ensure their replacement, because even the best regiment would become a mob when its British officers were placed *hors de combat*, he advocated the reorganisation of the most warlike material into regiments officered on the old regular scale, leaving the remaining irregulars as a kind of gendarmerie for use in minor wars and internal security duties, as it was better to have a moderate number of reliable troops than a large force of indifferent ones: 'The present plan of officering the Indian Army has been shown to collapse when tried by any serious test, but more serious tests than any hitherto experienced are possibly in store for it, under circumstances where failure may mean stupendous disaster.'[27]

The Duke of Cambridge was more concerned that the staff corps system was bad for the British Army. Endorsing Lockhart's memorandum, he complained that many officers joining the British Line, either from the RMC or from the Militia after taking the same final examinations as gentlemen cadets at the RMC, applied to join British battalions in India solely in order to transfer to the Staff Corps at the earliest opportunity. Failing that, they either joined a battalion at home for only as long as it took to go with a draft to a battalion of the same regiment serving in India, or went to one in the colonies just to complete the period of service necessary for applicants for the Staff Corps from outside India. The result was, he said, that British regiments were 'largely filled by a number of young officers who take but little interest in them, using them solely as stepping stones to another Service, and mutually also the permanent officers of the regiment, for their part, taking equally little interest in these migratory officers'. Conversely, officers destined for the Indian service sometimes grew so attached to their British regiments that they left only with 'such regret that their professional zeal is dampened in consequence'.[28]

In order to resolve this problem, it was decided to increase the establishment of the RMC by twenty gentlemen cadets in each batch, beginning in

1891, who would be guaranteed appointments with the Indian Army and thus committed to its service from the outset of their careers. The scheme nearly did not start at all, as the War Office initially refused to guarantee that the extra twenty cadets, in a grave emergency, would be available for India. The War Office's view was that this was the case already, so India would be no worse off.[29] It also urged that officers should be drawn directly from the Militia, as Lockhart had suggested, so giving the Indian Staff Corps the hundred new officers needed each year. The India Office agreed to offer one-quarter of the Staff Corps appointments to the Militia but insisted on a guarantee that the extra twenty gentlemen cadets at the RMC would always be available for the Indian service.[30] The British Army would be no worse off because it had not previously had them, and the fact that India had not previously had a guaranteed supply of officers in an emergency was the very reason why the twenty extra places were being created. The War Office, learning that Lord Crewe, the Secretary of State for India, would otherwise withdraw the Indian funds on which these places depended, decided that, after all, the guarantee could be given and that officers leaving the RMC or the Militia for the Staff Corps would be gazetted to the Indian Army.

The India Office pointed out that, by the Act of Parliament setting up the Staff Corps, no officer could join them except from the British Army, so that these new entrants should be commissioned into that while they did their probationary service, now fixed at one year with a British regiment and two with an Indian.[31] The Duke of Cambridge replied that officers could not be commissioned into 'the British Army' but only into a regiment or department, and so, reluctantly, he would create a new body, the Unattached List, with a uniform to which that worn at the RMC by gentlemen cadets could be converted at minimal expense.[32] This had the effect of distinguishing these officers from their fellow subalterns in the British regiments to which they were attached, and making it clear that, though in the British Army, they were destined for the Indian service. Those who failed their probation were to be given free passage back to England and then removed from the Army.

The Government of India used the introduction of this new system to propose the amalgamation of the three Staff Corps, of Bengal, Madras and Bombay, into one single Indian Staff Corps. It reported to Lord Crewe on 9 June 1890 that, in obedience to his instructions that some of each intake of direct entrants should go to each presidency, twenty of the first batch of thirty would be sent to Madras and Bombay, and ten to Bengal, even though there were already more candidates for the latter from British regiments in India than were needed. The result was that ten of the latter would now be disappointed, and as they would not volunteer for the Madras or Bombay Staff Corps, the Madras and Bombay Armies, which needed the whole new intake from England, would be left understrength. 'This disinclination on the part of young officers serving with British regiments in India to join the Madras and Bombay armies, but especially the former, is, as your Lordship knows, no new thing' ran the despatch, going on to explain that for the ten years or so after the introduction of the staff corps system (when there had been a large number of surplus officers from the old local armies), this had been of little account, but that since then almost the only candidates had come from British regiments outside India, who had to go where they were sent. It also regretted that the distribution of the new direct entrants between the Staff Corps was not made by the India Office before they sailed from England for, on arrival in India, 'The whole of the candidates invariably want to be posted to Bengal, and when a partial allotment is made to that army, all of them press to be chosen, and the Military Department of this Government is beset with applications by friends and relatives on their behalf, while it is difficult to discriminate between the relative claims of candidates.' Those not selected joined the service disappointed at the outset of their careers, but officers had to be provided for the Madras Army somehow. The Government of India therefore drew attention to the proposal, which had been made as early as 1870 by Sir Henry Norman, to meet this problem by the creation of a single Indian staff corps, with the prestige of an imperial rather than a local service and from which officers would go to staff employment anywhere in India. It then went further, by proposing the abolition of the title of 'Staff Corps' altogether, as a contradiction in terms when its members served in regimental appointments, and its replacement, when officers were gazetted, by the term 'Indian Army'.[33]

The amalgamation plan was accepted by the India Office as a matter of little significance, devised merely to solve the problem of officering the Madras and Bombay Armies. It was not intended as a step in the process of unifying the three presidential armies, which was at that time under discussion separately. The Royal Warrant of 28 January 1892 which created the new Indian Staff Corps used this title, rather than 'Indian Army' because the India Office, while admitting that its members were not staff officers in the sense in which the term was used in Europe, said they were in the sense in which it was used in India, and that even officers with regiments were regimental staff. Indeed, their whole system of pay continued to be based upon this. It was also the case that the old locals, still serving, held commissions in 'the Indian Army', on different terms from those of the officers in the Staff Corps.

Candidates for the Indian Staff Corps from the RMC or Militia were to go out to India in batches and, on arrival, be allotted to vacancies in any presidency according to local needs and posted to a British regiment stationed there. They, and officers already in the Staff Corps, would thereafter not be permitted to move from one of the three Indian Armies to another except by exchange and, although eligible for other staff employments outside their own presidencies, they could not move without the agreement of their local governments. This effectively ensured that officers reluctantly serving in Madras would remain there, as the prospects of anyone exchanging to a Madras regiment from the more prestigious Bengal Army were remote. Likewise, the need for the local government's agreement prevented Madras officers with friends in high places from using their influence to escape from Madras to staff employment with better prospects elsewhere in India. But for this, Madras would have ended with fewer officers rather than more, so worsening rather than solving the problem which had led to the amalgamation of the three Staff Corps in the first place.

The unified Indian Staff Corps only existed for ten years. Kitchener, who became C-in-C, India, at the end of November 1902, arrived with the intention of carrying out major reforms and began by ordering the abolition of the title 'Indian Staff Corps', effective from 1 January 1903. He repeated the longstanding argument that the majority of posts filled by the Staff Corps were, in practice, regimental duty. It was certainly the case that they were 'staff' only in the sense that those who filled them by this time all belonged to a corps which was not the same as their men's regiment (even though they wore its badges and uniform). Kitchener also felt that the abolition of the Staff Corps title would encourage officers to identify more fully with their regiments, as had been the case in the old regular system, rather than seeing them merely as an alternative to other staff appointments. Haines had said much the same thing to Napier thirty years before: 'I cannot but think it detrimental to military efficiency that a young officer, on joining his regiment, should have an object in view outside of his own profession, the attainment of which confers at once higher emolument and greater consideration.'[34] By 1902, moreover, the number of British officers in an Indian infantry battalion was twelve, twice as many as when the staff corps system had been set up, and large enough to permit them to establish their own *esprit de corps*, and indeed, to establish a viable officers' mess essential for the creation and continuance of such a spirit.

For practical purposes, however, the abolition of the term 'Staff Corps' was of little significance. Neither Kitchener nor the Government of India itself had the power to alter the terms and conditions of service of its officers. Regimental officers still continued to draw the pay appropriate to staff appointments and their income continued to be a combination of this and the pay of their rank. The only alteration Kitchener was able to make to the principle of promotion by time was by introducing an additional requirement in the form of a recommendation by an officer's seniors that he was fit for the duties of the higher rank.[35]

As the old Staff Corps disappeared, a new army staff was formed. Previously, in the British system, this had been divided between two major departments, that of the Adjutant General, which dealt with administration and discipline, and that of the Quartermaster General, which dealt with operations, intelligence, and logistics. In the ferment of military reform following British disasters in the South African War, where Kitchener, as Roberts's Chief of Staff, had been the architect of final victory, the idea of forming a General Staff (leaving the Quartermaster General to deal with logistics alone) had gained ground.[36] This concept, based on the German model, was not adopted by the British until after Kitchener had left India, but his creation of the Indian Staff College at Quetta, provided the Indian Army with a corps of trained army staff officers.[37]

Notes

1. B. Bond, *The Victorian Army and the Staff College*, London, 1972, pp. 56–7.
2. IOR L/MIL/7/2470–2472.
3. Adj.-Gen., Bengal to Sec. to Govt of India, Military Dept, 18 July 1855, IOR L/MIL/7/2470–2472.
4. *Ibid.*
5. *Ibid.*
6. 23 & 24 Vic, c. 100.
7. Adj.-Gen., Bengal to Sec. to Govt of India Military Dept, February 1862, IOR L/MIL/7/2470–2472.
8. IOR L/MIL/7/2470–2472.
9. Minute by Col. H.M. Durand to Gov.-Gen. in Council 24 July 1864, IOR L/MIL/7/2472.
10. Minute on above by Gov.-Gen. IOR L/MIL/7/2472.
11. IOR I7MII77/2472.
12. *Ibid.*
13. *Ibid.*
14. *Ibid.*
15. A.F. Mockler-Ferryman, *Annals of Sandhurst*, London, 1900, p. 38.
16. *Ibid.*, p. 39.
17. Correspondence relating to the Royal Military College, IOR L/MIL/ 7/2486–2600.
18. *Ibid.*
19. *Ibid.*
20. Minute by the Hon. L.R. Ashburner to Gov. of Bombay in Council 4 October 1881, IOR L/MIL/7/2486–2600.
21. Rudyard Kipling, *Wee Willie Winkie and Other Stories* (pocket edition), Macmillan, London, 1907, pp. 103–4.
22. Minute by Sir Edwin Johnson, IOR L/MIL/7/7013.
23. Minute by Sir Henry Norman, IOR L/MIL/7/7013.
24. F.G. Cardew, *A Sketch of the Services of the Bengal Native Infantry to the Year 1895*, Calcutta, 1903, p. 381.
25. R. Maxwell (ed.), *Jimmie Stewart: Frontiersman. The Edited Memoirs of Major General Sir J.M. Stewart*, Durham, 1992, p. 9; see also G. Arthur, *Life of Lord Kitchener*, Vol. 2, London, 1920, p. 125.
26. Minute by Sir William Lockhart 15 June 1889, IOR L/MIL/7/2511–2512.
27. *Ibid.*
28. Minute by the Duke of Cambridge on above, IOR L/MIL/7/2511–2512.
29. IOR L/MIL/7/2512.
30. *Ibid.*
31. *Ibid.*

32. *Ibid.*
33. Gov.-Gen. in Council to Sec. of State for India Dispatch of 9 June 1890 (Military), IOR L/MIL/7/2521.
34. *Cit.* in Rait, *op. cit.* p. 202.
35. Arthur, *op. cit.*, Vol. 2, p. 185.
36. Bond, *op. cit.*, Ch. 6.
37. T.A. Heathcote, *The Indian Army*, Newton Abbot, 1974, p. 140.

Chapter 8

Kitchener's Army, 1902–1914

At the door through which the Army in India enters the history of the twentieth century stands the figure of Lord Kitchener of Khartoum. It was he who gave it its formal title and ruled that the term 'Indian Army' previously used indiscriminately so as to signify, in some contexts, all the land forces at the disposal of the British in India, should mean only troops raised in South Asia and directly in the service of the Government of India. He had made his reputation as the man who, first as its Adjutant General, and then as its Commander-in-Chief, had reorganised the Egyptian Army and led it to victory at Omdurman in 1898. He had served thereafter in the South African War as Chief of Staff to Roberts, and succeeded him as Commander-in-Chief there in November 1900.[1] Roberts then succeeded Wolseley as Commander-in-Chief of the British Army, the only officer originally of the Indian service ever to hold this post, and as, as it turned out, the last officer to hold it before its abolition.[2] Despite their different ages (Roberts was sixty-seven and Kitchener forty-nine when they served together) and experience (Roberts's service was virtually confined to India and Kitchener's to Egypt and the Sudan) the two generals established cordial relations and many of the reforms later carried out by Kitchener in India reflected Roberts's own attitudes.

Roberts at this time was at the peak of his influence. He had been lucky, the first quality of any general, when at the end of the Second Afghan War Stewart sent him from Kabul to the relief of Kandahar. There, following the disastrous defeat of one of its brigades at Maiwand, a badly led division of the Bombay Army withstood a four-week siege until Roberts arrived and, on 1 September 1880, achieved an impressive victory to restore British military prestige. He held the post of C-in-C, India, for seven and a half years, the second longest tenure of that command. His friendship with Rudyard Kipling, who hymned him as 'Bobs Bahadur',[3] ensured his popularity with the British public and his genuine interest of the welfare of his British and Indian soldiers made him liked by the troops. As C-in-C of the British Army, he had an influential voice in the selection of the C-in-C, India, and gave his support to Kitchener's application, after failing to persuade the latter that his talents would be better employed at the War Office in reorganising the British Army.[4] There were, nevertheless, voices raised against Kitchener's being appointed. The Queen declared that she would never consent, because

Kitchener's brusque manner was such that he would alienate those with whom he would have to deal.[5] Lord Cromer, the proconsul under whom he had served in Egypt, took a similar view.[6] Others who knew him said that he would be disadvantaged by his lack of Indian experience and that he might provoke a mutiny, as he had during his administration of the Sudan, and that his reputation as a great organiser derived from an obsessive interest in detail, combined with an insistence on centralising everything in his own hands.[7] A further criticism was that he was excessively parsimonious in his approach to military expenditure but this, to the politicians, was a point in his favour. St John Brodrick, appointed Secretary of State for War in October 1900, was particularly keen to have Kitchener join him there as much for that reason as for the part he could play in achieving the reforms Brodrick wished to see in the British Army. None was more enthusiastic for Kitchener's appointment than the Governor-General of India, Lord Curzon. A rising member of the Conservative party, he had been briefly Under-Secretary of State at the India Office and had travelled widely in Asia, including Afghanistan and the Russian territories. Prior to becoming Governor-General in January 1899 (at thirty-nine the youngest since Dalhousie), he had been for three years Under-Secretary of State at the Foreign Office and so worked closely with Salisbury, who was both Prime Minister and Foreign Secretary. Actuated by a combination of natural ambition, a feeling of attraction to the romance of the Orient, a concern at the Russian threat and a desire to strengthen the British position in India by a policy of reform, he suggested himself as Governor-General in succession to Elgin.[8] At much the same time, though with less success, Kitchener, visiting London after his reconquest of the Sudan, proposed himself as the next Military Member in succession to Collen (once the secretary of the Eden Commission).[9]

Curzon's scathing criticisms of the conduct of business in India were felt as much by the military as by the civil branches. He complained at the exercise of their residual presidential powers by the Governments of Madras and Bombay, at the checks which the Council of India put on his freedom of action, and at the manner in which the Government of India conducted its business by careful correspondence.[10] He described it as a literary bedlam, with minutes circulating round and round like planets circling the sun, while every official through whose department they passed added or repeated their views. Collen, like others of long Indian experience, privately tried to persuade Curzon not to write comments on the system which would cause offence to his readers, but to no avail. The Military Department, Curzon told Brodrick, was a place where red tape and officialdom of the most rampant kind flourished and there was great jealousy and squabbling between it and Army HQ.[11]

He was equally critical of the military as individuals. He deplored their reluctance to read or study and their blatant practice of jobbery, often disguised by bogus claims of some need for special experience or services: 'They love a job as a German loves a shut railway carriage and a frowst.'[12] He made himself unpopular with the British troops in India by inflicting collective punishment on two units whose soldiers had committed serious assaults on their native fellow subjects (a fellowship which few British soldiers were ready to allow). Officers who had tried to hush up these incidents to protect their own men and the honour of their regiments were removed or reprimanded. In the first instance, in 1899, an infantry battalion was posted from Rangoon to Aden, the most unpleasant station which the Army in India had to fill. In the second, in 1902, the 9th Lancers had all leave stopped for six months. These actions were joint decisions, involving the Secretary of State, the C-in-C, India, and the Military Department, but Curzon took the credit, and, in the eyes of the Army and the European community, the blame. When the 9th Lancers rode past at the great Durbar held to celebrate the accession of Edward VII as King-Emperor, they were greeted in silence by the Indian spectators and with cheers by the Europeans, including even those among the Viceroy's own entourage. It was not surprising, therefore, that he sought Kitchener as C-in-C, India. The most notable soldier of the empire would not only add to Curzon's own prestige by his presence but would also be a potent ally in bringing about change: 'I see absurd and un-controlled expenditure. I observe a lack of method and system. I detect slack-ness and jobbery. And in some respects I lament a want of fibre and tone.'[13]

In terms of manpower and material however, he secured improvements well before Kitchener's arrival. In a formal despatch of November 1899[14] the Government of India pointed out that it was required to produce a field army for the defence of Afghanistan against Russia, or for operations elsewhere in India's area of interest, amounting to 20,000 men from an establishment of 222,000. The remainder were required to preserve order within India and suppress any outbreak of rebellion or mutiny. The basis of British power in India, this despatch declared unequivocally, was the Army, which was very small in proportion to the vast extent of the frontiers it had to defend and the large amount of territory it had to hold, especially in view of the increasingly independent spirit of large parts of the population. As great interests were at stake, and 'the old safeguards of separate interests can no longer be implicitly relied upon', improvements in the efficiency of the Army were essential. These consisted of re-arming the native troops with new bolt-action rifles in place of their worn-out Martini-Henrys (a controversial measure as, since the Mutiny, it had been the policy of the Government of India that Indian troops should be less well armed than their British comrades).

More serious was the effect of Brodrick's alteration in the terms of engage-ment in the British Army in 1902. Enlistment was henceforth to be for three years, followed by nine years on the reserve, or, for those who so wished, a further period with the Colours. Those who served overseas would receive extra pay, an incentive to re-engagement. The effect of this was to increase the cost to India of its British garrison by 50 per cent per annum. A claim by the India Office that half of this should be paid by the War Office was overruled by the Lord Chancellor, and Curzon's indignation was expressed in personal letters written in terms which began the strain in his old friendship with Brodrick.[15] His tendency to behave as though India was a separate country had already made him unpopular at the India Office, though he continued to enjoy support from Lord George Hamilton, the Secretary of State.

Even before landing in India, Kitchener had decided that he would form a single Indian Army, just as he had a single Egyptian Army.[16] The abolition of the presidential armies had not affected the organisation of their regiments, which all retained their old names and numbers. The Hyderabad Contingent still remained under the Foreign Department until April 1903 when one of Kitchener's first reforms was to order it liable for general service, and to place its cavalry in Bombay Command, and its infantry in Madras Command. On the voyage to India, his assistant military secretary (and a future C-in-C, India), Lieutenant Colonel W.R. Birdwood of the 11th Bengal Lancers (who had volunteered for service in South Africa, and been on Kitchener's staff there), worked on schemes for unification. He was then appointed secretary of a unification committee, made up of Indian Army officers, chaired by Major General D.J.S. Macleod. The other three members, including Brigadier General Beauchamp Duff, Deputy Adjutant General, ensured that each of the local interests was represented.[17]

The unification was achieved by numbering the units of each arm in a single sequence and discarding those titles which included the names of Bengal, Madras and Bombay. Despite the inevitable regrets of those serving at the time, the new titles were generally accepted as euphonious and logical and had a glamorous ring to them which went well with the imperial spirit of the time. Where they failed was in imparting a genuine spirit of unity. The 27th Madras Infantry for example, might become the 87th Punjabis (reflecting the extent to which Madrassis had for many years ceased to be recruited for it) but the 88th Carnatic Infantry was still easily recognisable as a 'down-country' regiment, the old 28th Madras Infantry, as were other regiments with high numbers but names not redolent of the north-western 'martial classes', which now made up 80 per cent of the army. Kitchener saw India as a single country and felt that, as it now had a single army, regiments should be posted anywhere in it, no matter how far from their homes, just like British units. He also decided that the field army should be organised in peace time in the same way as it would be in war, with the units allocated to permanent divisions and brigades, each with their staff and ancillary troops, instead of, as previously, these being put together only when actual operations were in preparation.[18] The four Army Corps were abolished.

Each of these new formations was to have a standard establishment. A division would consist of three brigades, each of one British and three Indian battalions, and divisional troops including an Indian cavalry regiment, a field artillery brigade of three batteries and a mountain artillery brigade of two, two companies of Indian sappers and miners, one Indian pioneer battalion and ancillary troops. Each cavalry brigade would consist of one British and two Indian regiments, and a battery of horse artillery. All artillery, except the mountain guns which posed no threat to British security, remained in British hands and most of it was concentrated as army troops, amounting to one horse artillery, nine field and six heavy batteries. For internal security he allotted one British and fourteen Indian cavalry regiments, seventeen batteries of horse, field or mountain guns, and twenty-one companies of garrison artillery, with twenty-five British and forty-seven Indian infantry battalions, including two of pioneers.[19] This left him enough units to form nine divisions and five cavalry brigades. Each division was also to provide the command structure for internal security troops located in its area. As in the British Army, units were not permanently allotted to formations, but moved around to ensure a variety of experience in different areas.

The most radical of all Kitchener's proposals was the abolition of the Military Department and its absorption by Army Headquarters, leaving the C-in-C as the sole military authority in the Government of India. With the centralisation of the army administration (beginning in 1864 with the three Departments of Military Accounts being merged into one under the control of the Government of India) and the abolition of the presidential C-in-Cs and military departments in 1895 the Military Department had grown in responsibilities, importance and power. As well as being British India's War Office, it controlled all the logistic units and services. Always a source of irritation and suspicion to successive C-in-Cs, the Military Member had since 1895 been a clear rival. Major General Sir Edmond Elles, who succeeded Collen in April 1901, signalled this by attending Council meetings in uniform, contrary to the long-standing custom of his predecessors. General Sir George Barrow, then a junior officer at Army HQ, commented on this in his autobiography and noted that he never once saw Sir Henry Brackenbury in uniform.[20] Elles, as an artilleryman, actually came from the British Army but had spent his entire career in India, commanding a division at Peshawar, and serving as Adjutant General to Kitchener's predecessor, Sir Power Palmer. As Military Member he inflicted various real or imagined slights on his old chief, who resented the authority which a former subordinate and visibly junior officer, had (and used) to criticise the C-in-C's proposals. When handing over to Kitchener, Palmer repeated his grievances against Elles and confirmed the suspicions which the new C-in-C already had of the Indian system of military administration.[21]

Within a few weeks of his arrival in India Kitchener formed the view that unless the C-in-C controlled the logistic services, as he had in the Sudan and South Africa but which, in India, belonged to the Military Department, the consequent division of responsibility would result in disaster when the Army went to war. 'No commander in the field can be expected to obtain decisive results unless he is perfectly sure that he can rely on these services; and no commander in the field can administer them with efficiency and economy unless they have been trained and administered under him in peace.'[22] He also argued that it was wrong for another military officer, junior in army rank to the C-in-C, to offer military opinions as a member of the Governor-General's Council or be in a position, as head of the Military Department, to decide on matters independently of the C-in-C.

This was a matter of special importance to Kitchener's self-esteem. No C-in-C relished a situation in which he might be told that he could not have additional logistic support in one area because the Military Department had decided that it was better to provide it in another. Nor indeed, would a senior general from the British Army like to know that a junior one (identified with the Indian Army) could speak in Council against his proposals on the grounds that his department considered them unsuitable for Indian conditions.

Several C-in-Cs had complained about the Military Department but none previously had considered the question of the Military Members' army rank a significant one. To some extent Kitchener's sensitivity on this subject may have arisen from his consciousness of his own achievements as a soldier. He was the first C-in-C, India, since Cornwallis to have commanded an army in the field against white men and, unlike Cornwallis, he had been victorious. He was the first since Campbell to have commanded an army other than in limited war. Rose, Mansfield, Stewart and Roberts had all led large numbers of troops to victory, but none were so proud of their laurels as to cavil at the military rank held by Norman, Chesney, Brackenbury or Collen. On the other hand, none of these stood forth as generals in uniform in the way that Elles did. Roberts, when C-in-C, India, had minuted that the Viceroy was 'apt only to see the Military Department's side in every case.'[23] On the other hand, when the C-in-C and the Military Member were in agreement, reforming governor-generals such as Lytton and Curzon complained of an unholy alliance. Elles, in accompanying Curzon on a frontier tour as a result of which they proposed military changes which were matters for the C-in-C India, alienated Kitchener from both of them.[24]

For the first two years, relations between Kitchener and Curzon were cordial enough. Neither was prepared to allow the other to encroach upon his own area of responsibility without registering an objection, but each credited the other with worthy motives. Kitchener supported Curzon in his efforts to suppress violence by British soldiers against Indians and Curzon supported Kitchener's reforms of the Indian Army. Curzon, however, was in a weakening position. He had made himself unpopular with the local European community, deriding the systems of administration of which they were so proud and, by his treatment of the British Army, supporting the brown man against the white, thereby weakening the prestige and, ultimately, fear, on which they believed British control of India to rest. He had alienated the prestigious Punjab school by, in 1904, creating a new North-West Frontier province (the old Afghan province of Peshawar) out of its trans-Indian districts, arguing that the rest of the Punjab was now settled, but that the frontier was so different in its ethnic composition, social development and strategic importance that it should have a separate status. He had irritated the princes by forbidding them to travel out of India without his leave. At first popular with the Western educated urban intelligentsia, he turned them into sworn enemies by his reorganisation of the Indian universities, seen as an attempt to reduce the numbers of arts graduates and lawyers they produced. Kitchener, meanwhile, considered Elles merely a major general of limited field experience whose obstinacy and opposition was an affront to the first soldier of the empire. Elles seems to have considered Kitchener as a megalomaniac. Lord Ampthill, Governor of Madras and acting Governor-General during Curzon's return to England between his two terms of Indian office, had to deal with a threat of resignation by Kitchener in his quarrel with Elles, arising initially from the appointment of an adjutant to a Volunteer Corps, but really from a dispute over the composition of brigades. Kitchener wanted these to be all British or all Indian, both for logistic convenience and because the British reinforcements he expected in the war with Russia that all thought imminent would arrive as complete brigades.[25] Elles pointed out the reasons for, and merits of, the long established Indian system of mixed brigades, irritating Kitchener still further. Ampthill complained of the C-in-C's disregard for the established constitutional machinery of the Indian government, and blamed the 'young lions' of Army HQ and his hero-worshipping personal staff for encouraging this attitude. Kitchener, in private correspondence to Brodrick (who succeeded Hamilton in September 1903), Roberts and Lady Salisbury (wife of the fifth Marquess whose cousin was Arthur Balfour the Prime Minister) condemned the senseless obstruction, useless delay, duplication, waste and inefficiency he saw as results of the existing system.

The Cabinet was disturbed by Kitchener's talk of resignation. He was not only popular with the British public but had a record of success in war. With war against Russia seeming imminent, this was not the time either to lose Kitchener or appoint an untried successor. It was therefore proposed to set up a commission, led by Hamilton, to visit India early in 1905 to review the systems of military administration. If he reported in favour of the existing arrangement, Kitchener's objections would seem less authoritative. The Government of India was asked for its views but, by the time that Kitchener had formally set out his proposals and every Member had minuted upon them and upon each other's minutes, the question was not considered in Council until 10 March, long after Hamilton had ceased to be available.

Kitchener recommended that the Military Member and his department be abolished, leaving the C-in-C as the sole military officer in the Governor-General's Council, heading both the Army and a new Army Department to which the administrative functions of the Military Department would be transferred, with the added benefits of Army HQ's experienced officers to help decide on them.[26]

The Military Department defended itself with all the statistical facility it had developed in Norman's time. It produced figures showing that, in Kitchener's time as C-in-C, 1,260 proposals had been accepted out of 1,559 made; that files had been retained by Army HQ rather than in the Military Department (in one case for three years); and that the staff of the Military Department was well qualified to form opinions on the subjects discussed as, of its five senior officers, all had passed out of the Staff College and had at least thirteen years' service in regiments, while four had previously served in Army HQ.[27] This was, however, exactly one cause of the trouble as previously the officers of this Department, even those like Norman and Johnson who had taken part in major conventional wars as young officers, had broken their connection with the field army on entering the Department and had neither the expertise nor the consequent inclination to comment on field matters. Elles argued that the C-in-C was not being subjected to checks by the Military Member as a soldier, but by the Government of India.[28] Constitutionally, every act of the Military Member was an act of the Governor-General in Council. The problem in Elles's view was that the C-in-C would not admit his subordination to the Government of India.

Curzon objected to Kitchener's scheme on several grounds. He thought that no one man could cope with the work which up to then had been done by two; that without another soldier in Council he would be left without military advice when the C-in-C took the field (as Kitchener intended to in the expected war with Russia, as Haines had wanted to, and as Roberts actually had in the war of 1885 which completed the British conquest of Burma) or even when on lengthy tours of inspection; and that the Military Department's special knowledge of Indian conditions was a valuable check on schemes which a C-in-C drawn from the British Army might put forward and which his own HQ staff were bound to support. He went further, arguing that it was necessary for the Government of India to have an alternative source of advice on military affairs so as not to be in the hands of a single expert. The effect of

Kitchener's proposals, he said, would be to establish a military despotism and take away from the Government of India its constitutional control over the Army.[29]

The India Office then set up its own committee. Each side complained that it was packed with supporters of the other and each felt defeated when a compromise solution was devised. This set up two new departments in place of the old Military Department. One, to be called the Army Department, with the C-in-C sitting as the Member of Council at its head, took over the Military Department's functions in respect of personnel, mobilisation plans and logistic services. The other, the Military Supply Department, took over the remainder and was thus responsible for the provision of ordnance, clothing, stores, etc., subjects in which the Military Department's origins had lain. The Military Supply Member could be a civilian or a soldier but, in practice, was to be the latter, as Indian Army experience would be required to supplement the views of the C-in-C from the British Army. Like the Military Members before Elles, he was to wear plain clothes.[30]

Curzon, however, made an issue of the personality of the new Member for Military Supply. He proposed that the appointment should go to Major General Sir Edmund Barrow, who was well known to be an able officer and who had both commanded the Peshawar Division and been Secretary to the Government of India in the Military Department. Kitchener, supported by the India Office, felt that Barrow was too closely associated with the old system (and with Elles) to be committed to the success of the new one. He thought him the one general in India who would be able to turn the Military Supply Department back into the Military Department and be able to challenge him in Council, and believed, with some justification, that Curzon had nominated him for that very reason. Curzon had indeed publicly implied that amendments made to the India Office proposals, with the agreement of the C-in-C, India, had preserved the status quo, provoking a telegram from Brodrick that 'no such public exhibition of disloyalty to the Home Government had ever yet been made by an Indian Viceroy'.[31] Curzon's view nevertheless had powerful supporters. Two previous C-in-Cs, Roberts and White, had both argued for the retention of the Military Department in something like its old form and Landsowne, a former Governor-General and at this time Foreign Secretary, stated in the House of Lords that the Cabinet had decided against Kitchener and that the position of the Military Member, on being renamed Military Supply Member, would otherwise be virtually unchanged.

Kitchener's choice was Major General Scott, an officer of the ordnance branch, whose specialist experience fitted him well to deal with the new Department's specialisation, but who was regarded by Curzon as a 'dear placid old dummy'[32] and believed by him to have been selected by Kitchener mostly on that account. Curzon also had formed the view that Kitchener was trying to make the Military Supply Department weaker than the compromise arrangements, just as he himself was thought by the India Office to be trying to make it stronger.[33] When Brodrick pointed out, quite accurately, that Members of Council were appointed by the Crown on the advice of the Secretary of State, not on that of the Governor-General, and that he did not think Barrow a suitable choice, Curzon made the question one of confidence, and his final offer of resignation, made on 12 August 1905, was this time accepted.[34] His final relations with Kitchener were sour. Several contemporaries referred to Kitchener as at best devious and at worst a bad liar. Curzon implicitly accused him of untruthfulness in denying that he had seen a particular set of figures on a file sent for his attention. Kitchener resented this and expressed regret that the old days of duelling were over.[35]

Within four months of Curzon's resignation there was not only a new Governor-General in India but a new Secretary of State at the India Office. The new Governor-General was Lord Minto, a Scottish aristocrat and a former Guards officer who had seen combat service during the Crimean War, the Second Afghan War, in the Sudan, and in the Riel rebellion in Canada, where he became a respected and successful Governor-General. He had held the rank of major general in the Canadian establishment and, before he left England for India, was told by Edward VII 'to make the most of his General's uniform, advice which Minto always followed, as his military interests were nearest his heart'.[36] He frequently wore it and was later commemorated in the uniform of a general in his statue at Calcutta. Kitchener welcomed him as a military man and each referred to the other in complimentary terms in their private correspondence to London. The new Secretary of State was John Morley, a Gladstonian Liberal, and a member of Campbell-Bannerman's Cabinet, which took over from the defeated Conservatives in December 1905.[37]

Morley's main interest in the military was as a source of financial savings. His policy of achieving full value for the taxpayer's money was expressed in actions which left the taxpayer less well defended against his potential enemies. The Cabinet, however, denied that there were any more major enemies, for (partly on account of Kitchener's estimates that for a war with Russia he would need an extra 160,000 British troops at once and another 300,000 in the second year of such a war) the British had in 1907 settled their differences with the Russians.[38] The result was not unlike what would occur eighty years later. The Russian bogey faded away, the politicians looked for their peace dividend and the soldiers, who for a generation had organised themselves to face one particular major enemy, had to face options for change. Kitchener, for lack of the necessary extra funds, had not completed his scheme of concentrating his troops from numerous small stations into their brigade and divisional locations, where new barracks would need to be built. Nor had he been able to form all the nine divisions for which he had planned. Despite protests from the Government of India, Morley ruled in 1908 that no further expenditure was to be incurred on such elements of the redistribution scheme as had not been carried out.

Morley's concentration on reducing defence expenditure had more far-reaching consequences. He declared to Minto that 'as the guardian of public money … I learned from Mill, and still more in my years of friendship with Mr Gladstone, to be a real dragon with fangs.'[39] As is the way with politicians in search of economies, eighteen months after deciding that the revised system of military administration should not be disturbed, and a matter of weeks after receiving a formal despatch sent in March 1907 by the Governor-General and a unanimous Council reporting their satisfaction with the new arrangements, he decided that Kitchener's original proposals should after all be adopted. This had nothing to do with Kitchener's argument that there should be only one military man in Council (which even Kitchener had ceased to press). It derived solely from the fact that the abolition of the Member for Military Supply meant a reduction of expenditure of one and a half lakhs of rupees per annum.[40] Scott lived down to Curzon's estimation of him by offering no real defence of his position. Such as there was came from Kitchener himself, with lukewarm support from Minto. Kitchener's view was that Morley's proposal was in line with his own original ones and that the absorption of the Military Supply Department into the Army Department would achieve greater efficiency. Nevertheless, he was in favour of leaving things alone for the time being. Minto and the rest of his Council felt that 'it would be very hard on us to expose us to criticism which would undoubtedly be stirred up if the Supply Department is done away with'.[41]

Faced with such weak opposition, Morley was able to carry the argument without difficulty. If the Military Supply Department was as superfluous as everyone seemed to agree, it ought to go, he told Minto, adding that 'in my creed, waste of public money is like the Sin against the Holy Ghost'.[42] He wrote again to Minto at the end of 1907 that public opinion in the United Kingdom had lost interest in the Curzon-Kitchener quarrel and that, even if controversy were again to be aroused, 'I could not for that reason consent to be a party to the retention of an arrangement which throws a heavy charge upon the revenues of India and which in your opinion had been shown by experience to be unnecessary and inconvenient'.[43] The official exchanges between the India Office and the Government of India which followed were mere formalities and in January 1909 orders were despatched to India abolishing the Military Supply Department and the offices associated with it.

All parties to the decision were, meanwhile, obliged to turn their attention to more pressing matters. Nationalist feeling had grown ever more intense during the Curzon period and in 1907 the approach of the fiftieth anniversary of the Indian Mutiny went unremarked by none. In England, Roberts, to Morley's strong disapproval, suggested some kind of jubilee award to all surviving veterans (of the British side).[44] In India, the British discovered to their alarm that there were attempts to spread disaffection in the Punjab, from which, as a result of their 'martial class' theory having been extended to its logical extreme, four-fifths of the native army by this time was recruited. Nationalist pamphlets were found in military lines. Soldiers in uniform were seen in the crowd at the political gatherings near their cantonments. The Intelligence branch reported that Russian staff officers and Irish-American agitators were attempting subversive contacts with Indian troops.[45] In May 1907 Minto wrote to his countess, then in London, that British infantrymen were sleeping with their rifles in their beds, and the artillerymen with gun-traces by their side.[46] Some commanding officers issued army weapons to British civilians, an act countermanded by Kitchener. Minto adopted a mixture of conciliation and firmness. He overruled the local Punjab government's Colonisation Bill, to which holders of lands granted as a reward for military service had objected. He deported Lajpat Rai and Ajit Singh, considered to be the most extreme of the Punjabi nationalists, but unrest continued, with outbreaks of bomb-throwing and attempts at political assassination, encouraged by articles in Indian newspapers. Morley refused to approve legislation aimed at the imposition of censorship around military cantonments, on the grounds that the existing regulations allowed the authorities adequate powers. Minto and Kitchener, supported by Roberts and by most conservative European opinion in India and in London, pressed for a firmer policy but in fact the crisis passed with only one sepoy, a Sikh, convicted of sedition.[47]

Nevertheless, both Minto and Morley agreed on the need to conciliate moderate opinion among the nationalists by measures of political reform. Early in 1907 Minto proposed the addition of an Indian Member to his Council. Morley supported the principle but could not obtain Cabinet approval and Kitchener and others objected that a Native Member would have access to secret military decisions.[48] The first reform was therefore the addition of two Indian members to the Council of India in September 1907 and only with the passage of the Indian Councils Act in 1909 was the appointment of an Indian Member of the Governor-General's Council secured.[49]

The same act enlarged the Governor-General's Legislative Council (the body composed of the ordinary and nominated local advisers who gave their opinion on new laws and regulations) from twenty-five to sixty, still with a small majority of officials, but with the remainder elected by various Indian constituencies (universities, landholders, municipalities, etc.), with separate representation from Muslims, who were otherwise under-represented in areas where a property qualification was demanded. Although the new Legislative

Council still had no real power, least of all over defence matters, its members could ask supplementary questions and table resolutions. These reforms served to calm much of the discontent among the Western-educated urban intelligentsia, and in 1912 the re-unification of Bengal (divided by Curzon) was equally well received. This last decision was announced at the same time as the transfer of the capital of British India from Calcutta to Delhi, the last step in the British assumption of the Mughal inheritance. Bengal, as a consolation, was given its own Governor.[50]

The Governor-General in office in 1912 was Lord Hardinge of Penshurst, appointed despite the strongest lobbying by Kitchener to secure his own selection. Edward VII (before his death in May 1910) and the Prime Minister, Asquith, both supported Kitchener but Morley, using Kitchener's own technique of threatening to resign if his view was not accepted, refused to accept him as Minto's successor.[51] The appointment of a known authoritarian, he insisted, would be fatal to the success of the political reforms and so he preferred Hardinge as a professional diplomat, with a useful knowledge of Russian and Iranian affairs. Kitchener had earlier failed, at least in the short term, to secure the appointment of his Adjutant General, Sir Beauchamp Duff (a trusted subordinate who would have remained suitably deferential had Kitchener become Governor-General) to succeed him as C-in-C, India.

The choice fell upon General Sir O'Moore Creagh who had played the role of extrovert, fighting, happy-go-lucky Irishman to perfection, complete with the broad Irish accent. Lady Minto noted in her diary that it was rumoured in London that his appointment was in some way due to her influence: 'I was not aware myself of having this subtle influence with Mr Haldane. I have never seen Sir O'Moore Creagh, and heard his name for the first time when Lord Morley mentioned him as Lord Kitchener's probable successor'.[52] Creagh's previous post had been Secretary of the Military Department at the India Office. Generally welcomed as a relief from Kitchener's astringent and energetic presence ('No More K'), he was content to implement the policies introduced by his more famous predecessor as far as the financiers would allow.

Although Morley himself left the India Office in November 1910 (at much the same time as Minto handed over to Hardinge), his approach to public expenditure remained and in 1912 a fresh investigation into Indian military organisation was ordered. This took the form of the Army in India Committee, with Field Marshal Sir William (later Lord) Nicholson of the British Army as its president and Sir William Meyer, the Member of Council for the Finance Department, as its most influential members. Their remit was to consider and report on the numbers and organisations of the military forces necessary to meet the Government of India's defence obligations in the circumstances of the time. As Russia had changed from being a threat into a friendly power, it appeared that a peace dividend could be declared and that there was no longer any need for India to maintain a force designed to engage in conventional operations against a Western-style modern army in the heartland of Asia. Setting aside the requirement for troops to hold India against the Indians (a role which Kitchener had played down in order to divert troops to his modernised permanent field army) the only conceivable major threat that could be found was that of aggression by the Pashtun tribesmen of the North-West Frontier, supported by the regular army of Afghanistan. The idea of these fierce mountain warriors swooping down upon the rich and prosperous plains of Hindustan to rob and pillage, in the tradition of Mahmud the Iconoclast and other invaders, was one with which the British made increasing play. Border chieftains were quoted declaring that if the British withdrew there would not be a rupee or a virgin left between the Himalayas and Cape Comorin. Others were said to be looking forward to the loot of India's cities 'if only they could get there in time'.[53] Despite this it was impossible to justify Kitchener's nine divisions as necessary to withstand a descent by an enemy which, however numerous and warlike, was armed mostly with rifles.

The implementation of such improvements as Nicholson and Meyer were prepared to recommend was made subject to financial restrictions. Their majority report recommended that the annual military budget for India should be fixed at £19,500,000 and none even of their own proposals should be carried into effect if the result would be to exceed that figure.[54] In March 1914 the Secretary of State for India, Lord Crewe, sent a formal despatch endorsing that approach and refusing to sanction any of the recommended changes unless the Government of India gave an assurance that no additional costs were involved. Creagh, as C-in-C and Army Member, complained at the effect of this parsimonious attitude on his Army's efficiency but, so far from 'having the revenues of India at his mercy' as Sir Edwin Johnson had warned might be the result if these two offices were combined, the alternative result which he had forecast came about and the C-in-C as Army Member assented to policies which denied the troops the supplies that they needed.[55] Creagh gave up office in April 1914, six months before his tenure expired, and later claimed this was because his professional advice was continually disregarded by Hardinge in favour of Meyer and the Finance Department. He did not make an issue of this, however, and his early departure following a mild stroke coincided with the onset of the hot weather.[56] He was later criticised by the Mesopotamia Commission on the grounds that he should have resigned earlier and more publicly, if he really thought that the imposition of these rigid economies was impairing the efficiency of the Army for which he was responsible.[57] His successor was Sir Beauchamp Duff.

It was an army organised and equipped primarily to deal with a single, identifiable, threat (which never materialised) that was in August 1914 sent to war against a completely different one, against which it proved less effective than would have been the case had it been organised to conduct the whole range of military operations. Although the financiers argue that it is wasteful to plan against the unforeseeable, this is exactly what armies must do. The threat which is foreseen, if it is properly guarded against, on that account rarely materialises. The threat which is most likely to materialise is the one which was not foreseen, and on that account was not guarded against. So it was that an army trained and equipped to fight a war against Pashtun tribesmen on the bare hills of the Indian North-West Frontier was sent to war in 1914 against conventional German and Ottoman troops in the mud of Flanders and the deserts of Iraq and against German colonial forces in the East African bush, while Kitchener, its old C-in-C, as Secretary of State for War, raised his new armies with all the energy he had brought to bear in his Indian command.

Notes

1. T. Royle, *The Kitchener Enigma*, London, 1985, pp. 174–5.
2. D. James, *Lord Roberts*, London, 1954, pp. 393–4.
3. W.H. Hannah, *'Bobs', Kipling's General*, London, 1972, pp. 191–2
4. P. Magnus, *Kitchener: Portrait of an Imperialist*, London, 1958, p. 175; D. Dilks, *Curzon in India*, Vol. 1, London, 1969–70, p. 205.
5. Dilks, *op. cit.*, Vol. 1, pp. 205–6.
6. *Ibid*, p. 204; Magnus, *op. cit.*, pp. 150–1.
7. Royle, *op. cit.*, p. 199.
8. Dilks, *op. cit.* Vol. 1, p. 63.
9. *Ibid*, pp. 203–4; Royle, *op. cit.*, p. 199.
10. *Ibid*, pp. 77–9, 81–2.
11. Curzon to Brodrick (pte) 27 June 1899 *cit.* in Dilks, *op. cit.*, Vol. 1, p. 197.
12. Curzon to Brodrick (pte) 16 March 1902, *op. cit.*
13. Curzon to Kitchener (pte) 31 March 1901, *cit.* in Magnus, *op. cit.*, p. 176.
14. Gov.-Gen. in Council to Sec. of State for India Despatch No. 192 (Mil) 2 November 1899, IOR L/MIL/7/5446.
15. Dilks, *op. cit.*, Vol. 1, p. 210.
16. W.R. Birdwood, *Khaki and Gown an Autobiography*, London, 1941, pp. 141–3.
17. *Ibid.*
18. *The Army in India and Its Evolution*, Calcutta, 1924, pp. 27–8, Appendix V.
19. *Ibid.*
20. G. de S. Barrow, *The Fire of Life*, London, 1942, p. 95.
21. Barrow, *op. cit.*, pp. 83–4; Dilks, *op. cit.*, Vol. 2, p. 19; Birdwood, *op. cit.*, p. 137.
22. *Cit.* in G. Arthur, *Life of Lord Kitchener*, London, 1920, Vol. II, p. 208.
23. *Ibid*, p. 204.
24. L. Mosley, *Curzon. The End of an Epoch*, London, 1961, pp. 105–6.
25. Dilks, *op. cit.*, Vol. 2, pp. 117–18; Arthur, *op. cit.*, Vol. II, pp. 166–7.
26. Dilks, *op. cit.*, Vol. 2, Chs 7–8, *passim*.
27. *Ibid*, p. 183.
28. Arthur, *op. cit.*, Vol. II, p. 215.
29. Magnus, *op. cit.*, p. 216; Arthur, *op. cit.*, Vol. II, p. 217; Dilks, *op. cit.*, Vol. 2, p. 188.
30. Sec. of State for India to Gov.-Gen. in Council (Military Dept) Despatch 31 May 1905, *cit.* in Dilks, *op. cit.*, Vol. 2, p. 189.

31. *Cit.* in Dilks, *op. cit.*, Vol. 2, p. 222.
32. *Ibid.*, p. 232.
33. *Ibid.*, p. 233.
34. *Ibid.*, pp. 235–8.
35. *Ibid.*, p. 239; Magnus, *op. cit.*, p. 223; Birdwood, *op. cit.*, pp. 162–3; Royle, *op. cit.*, p. 213.
36. Mary, Countess Minto, *India, Minto and Morley 1905–1910*, London, 1935, p. 422.
37. R.C.K. Ensor, *England 1870–1914*, Oxford, 1936, p. 384.
38. Keith Jeffrey, *The British Army and the Crisis of Empire 1918–1922*, Manchester, 1984, p. 33.
39. John, Viscount Morley, *Recollections*, London, 1917, Vol. 2, pp. 164–5.
40. *Ibid.*, p. 188.
41. Minto to Morley 29 August 1907, *cit.* in Arthur, *op. cit.*, p. 229.
42. Morley, *op. cit.*, pp. 230–1.
43. *Ibid.*
44. Morley, *op. cit.*, Vol. 2, p. 183.
45. Minto to Morley (pte) 27 June 1907, *cit.* in Minto, *op. cit.*, p. 148.
46. *Ibid.*, p. 136.
47. Arthur, *op. cit.*, Vol. II, pp. 253–9.
48. Morley, *op. cit.*, Vol. 2, pp. 210–11.
49. Dodwell, *op. cit.*, Vol. VI, p. 570.
50. V.A. Smith, *The Oxford History of India*, Oxford, 1958, p. 766.
51. Morley, *op. cit.*, Vol. 2, p. 333; Royle, *op. cit.*, p. 233; Magnus, *op. cit.*, p. 250.
52. Minto, *op. cit.*, p. 324.
53. *Ibid.* pp. 265–6.
54. Report of the Army in India Committee (7 Vols) 1912, IOR L/MIL/17/5/1751.
55. Mesopotamia Commission Report 1917 (Cd 8610), p. 104.
56. Birdwood, *op. cit.*, pp. 224–5.
57. Mesopotamia Commission Report 1917 (Cd 8610), p. 105.

Chapter 9

The Officer Problem, 1902–1947

Kitchener's reform of the Indian Army in 1902 abolished the title Indian Staff Corps, but the system by which officers were paid and promoted remained essentially the same and the change did little to solve the problem of officer recruitment. In fact, by modernising the Army, Kitchener increased its requirement for officers by 938. In 1906 an inter-departmental committee, chaired by General Sir John Gordon of the British Army, with the India Office represented by its Military Secretary, General Stedman, reported on 6 July that India would need a substantial increase in its intake from Sandhurst and the universities, and suggested that recruiting from the Militia and from the British Army outside India should be resumed, with a reduction in the number drawn from the British Army in India.[1] The Government of India decided against taking officers from the Militia but approved the idea of taking more university candidates. It agreed to take applicants from battalions outside India, but only if the C-in-C, India, saw detailed reports on them beforehand and if they were made to pay their passage back from India should they fail to qualify in Hindustani. While admitting that in war the British regiments in India would fail as a source of officers, it wanted to go on using them in peace because new entrants came out from England only in March-April or October-November each year, and vacancies occurring at other times could only be filled by officers already serving there. A further point was that many of the best officers in the Indian Army came from the Royal Artillery in India, but officers of this regiment (who were trained at the Royal Military Academy, Woolwich, rather than at the Royal Military College, Sandhurst) were ineligible to join it by any other route. While the Government of India did not agree with the committee's highest estimate of the numbers required, it accepted that at least 150 new officer recruits would be needed each year.[2]

On the outbreak of war in August 1914 a 15,700-strong Indian Corps of two infantry divisions sailed for France.[3] On 8 October 1914, before their troops had seen any serious fighting, but after the likely scale of casualties had been appreciated, the India Office telegraphed to the Government of India for a 50 per cent reinforcement for the officers. The total establishment of officers in the Indian Army then amounted to about 2,500, of whom, by the beginning of November, nearly 600 would be in or en route to France, and just over 400 with the expedition against German East Africa. A total of 250, who had been on furlough in the United Kingdom on the outbreak of war had been lent to the War Office to help fill out the British Army's order of battle, especially in Kitchener's new armies; another 250 were employed in army staff and departments in India; and the remaining 1,000 were with their units in India. Of these, the frontier units had to have at least ten officers each, as two would have to be withdrawn in order to form depots or staff the lines of communications if operations against the border tribes became necessary, leaving the eight officers by this time considered the minimum for efficient performance in action. That left a rough average for the rest of India of eight officers in each cavalry regiment and seven in each battalion. On 23 October 1914 the Government of India warned the India Office that each of these units would be reduced by one officer a month, on the assumption that the units out of India would need reinforcements at a rate of 10 per cent per month, unless urgent action was taken to recruit replacements. It therefore asked for 800 to 900 cadets to be sent to India to be trained there, using the buildings of the staff college at Quetta (which like that at Camberley had been closed on the outbreak of war, apparently on the assumption that staff officers were either invulnerable or unnecessary in the very kind of major war for which they were trained) and of the cavalry school at Saugor.[4]

It had already become clear that, as Lockhart had forecast a quarter of a century earlier, the British Army could not be relied upon to produce even the number of officers normally required by India, still less the reserves needed to replace war casualties. On the outbreak of hostilities the War Office reduced the length of the RMC course to three months (or six months for gentlemen cadets who had not reached the required standard at the end of their first three months), with a competition for entrance every three months. An extra competition held in September 1914 had no Indian Army places provided on it, so that one successful candidate, who wanted to make his career in India, had to resign and re-apply at the next one. In November 1914 the War Office announced that all fees would be waived for the duration of hostilities, apart from £35 to pay for uniforms, books and instruments, and that, while fees were suspended, no more vacancies for the Indian Army would be available at the RMC. In response to protests from the India Office and a broad hint that it would set up its own system of cadet training in competition with that of the British Army, the War Office agreed to offer the 'usual' number of RMC cadets for India each year, but not the 15 per cent of the enlarged RMC intake for which the India Office asked. Even those who were posted to the Unattached List were not permitted to sail for India if they were needed by British units. Major General Robbe, the Military Secretary, privately warned his opposite number in the India Office that the attitude of the new Secretary of State, Lord Kitchener, was that India would have to rely entirely on its own devices.[5]

Various devices were tried. These included the offer of temporary commissions in the Indian Army Reserve of Officers to businessmen and planters from India who happened to be in Britain and others who had retired from military, official or commercial employment in India, on the promise that after training with the new armies they would join Indian units in France. The 240 officers still serving with the new armies were returned. In India, 100 in civil employ returned to their regiments, but all those who had been away from them for more than ten years were no longer on the Army's effective strength and could not be spared from their normal duties in the machinery of Indian government. Businessmen and planters, especially those who were in the Indian Volunteer Force, were offered IARO commissions. By mid-January 1915 some 900 such commissions had been granted. Thirty officers on the Unattached List had reached India and forty had been found from elsewhere. Nevertheless, the officer casualties in the Indian Army at the same time, less than three months after first becoming seriously engaged on 24 October 1914, amounted to 334 (103 killed, 133 wounded, seventy-four invalided sick, and twenty-four missing). At that rate, the Government of India considered it would need another 1,200 officers to meet the wastage.[6]

This gave added impetus to the idea of training cadets in India. The India Office in October 1914 had considered the Government of India's forecast of casualties to be too high and had shied away from the prospect of adding 800 or 900 regular officers to the strength of the Indian Army. It had instead preferred to consider the number of cadets which the Government of India offered to train as including those who would hold temporary commissions in the British Army and recommended that they be attached, in special troops or platoons of fifty, to the three cavalry regiments and nine infantry battalions which were the only units of the regular British Army then left in India. After six months' training, cadets surplus to Indian requirements should go, it suggested, to reinforce those British units which had been sent out of India to serve in France or elsewhere.

In January 1915 the India Office dropped this scheme in favour of setting up two Indian Cadet Colleges, with cadets to be recruited and trained in exactly the same way as those at the RMC, except that Hindustani would be a compulsory subject. Quetta could take 100 on each course and Saugor eighty. This would produce 180 every six months (at Sandhurst it had been found that many cadets could not reach the required standard in three months, even without studying a language) and India offered to increase this to 300 if sufficient applicants were forthcoming. On 4 February 1915 the War Office agreed to offer 100 vacancies at Quetta in the next quarterly RMC examination, though warning applicants for Quetta that they would be superseded by those gentlemen cadets who, passing in to the RMC at the same time, would be commissioned three months earlier. This was a matter of significance not merely for any promotion that arose during the war but subsequently, because all these cadets were future regular officers, joining the Unattached List of the British Army prior to transfer to the Indian Army, just as had been the case before the outbreak of war.

Indeed a number of places at the RMC continued to be offered to those who wanted to make their career in the Indian Army. Those joining from Quetta were sent to a British unit in India for 'such training as circumstances permit' and then to an Indian unit. The Indian Cadet Colleges, because they were training British cadets who had not yet entered the Indian Army, were funded and controlled by the War Office. The Quetta Cadet College opened at the end of May 1915. Financial arrangements for its cadets were the same as those at Sandhurst, with free passage to India (and back for those who failed). The scheme attracted a large field of applicants. At the first entrance examination for the RMC which gave Quetta as an option, 168 expressed a willingness to train there and 141 achieved enough marks to be selected. The first commandant at Quetta, Colonel Austen, was promoted to Brigadier General rather reluctantly by the War Office which argued that although commandants at Sandhurst held this rank, they commanded a much larger number of cadets. The Governor-General, who had already promised promotion to Austen, successfully claimed that the problems of setting up a new establishment merited the higher rank.

The first reports by Austen on his new college and its cadets were taken by the Government of India as evidence that their experiment was a success and in June 1915 the quarterly competition for candidates to the RMC offered eighty places at a second Indian College. This was at Wellington, a station in the Nilgiri Hills, rather than Saugor as originally planned, since the latter was a plains station. As such it was vacated by European troops for six months in the year, so that a college located there could not have continued its courses during the hot weather. Of the RMC candidates, 287 indicated their willingness to go to a college in India (the title cadet college was chosen in preference to cadet school) and of these, 226 qualified, from whom the eighty vacancies were easily filled.[7]

These cadets, unlike the 'temporary gentlemen' granted commissions in Kitchener's new armies or in the Indian Army Reserve of officers, would, if they survived the war, be the next generation of the Indian Army's regular officers. There was accordingly some concern that the social origins of the first intake at Quetta Cadet College were in many cases very different from that of those joining the Unattached List from the pre-war RMC. The cause was at once perceived to be the abolition of fees. Sons of military and naval officers, who had always paid lower fees than those in other professions, no longer had an advantage in this respect and were joined by the sons of those who previously would not have been able to afford any fees at all. As it was still the case that those less affluent cadets, whether from the old or new back-grounds, could not afford the life-style of a British line regiment in peacetime, but could afford, as their predecessors had done, to live on Indian pay and conditions, the effects of abolishing fees was more noticeable by the Indian than by the British Army.

Six courses were held at each of the two Indian colleges. Despite the hope-ful opinions of their commandants that cadets from the new backgrounds would prove just as much a credit to themselves and the Army as those from the old ones, a more jaundiced view was formed at the India Office. Barely a fortnight after the Armistice, it telegraphed to India 'Owing to war conditions some candidates selected here for Indian Army and now in India are not up to desirable educational, professional, and social standard. Those still on proba-tion should not be admitted unless reported thoroughly suitable.'[8]

Less concern was felt about the social origin of those in the Indian Army Reserve of Officers. Like those of Kitchener's army, IARO commissions were effective for the duration of hostilities only and so had no impact on the composition of the regular cadre. The IARO was only forty-three strong in August 1914 but had expanded to 2,600 by the end of 1916 and was sub-sequently increased to 4,500. Many of the extra officers were old soldiers drawn from the ranks of the regular British Army, or from the territorials sent to replace the regulars withdrawn from India for active operations elsewhere.

The stresses of the First World War, which led the Government of India to recruit officers from previously unthought-of British classes, also led it to accept the previously inadmissible idea of recruiting them from the popula-tion of India. Indian nationalist opinion had long pressed for this. Since at least the Russo-Japanese war of 1905 it had not been possible for anyone to deny that Asian officers were fit to lead men and command armies in European-style warfare and to defeat a major European army and navy while they were about it. The question had been considered at least as far back as 1836, when Lieutenant Colonel John Briggs, a Madras officer, had submitted a scheme to the President of the Board of Control for setting up military colleges in India to which the sons of Indian officers could be sent to receive the sort of cadet training that would fit them to be regimental officers in the Indian Line. This scheme, which would have had the merits of allowing the traditional ruling classes of India to hold the same level of appointment under British rule as they had under Indian rule, as well as of allowing savings to be made in expensive British expatriate manpower, came to nothing.[9] At first the irregular system went some way towards providing a legitimate outlet for the military ambition of Indians who came from leading families in their community. Eventually, however, the reverse effect occurred, so that most Indian officers were promoted from the ranks, just as they had been in the old regular regiments. There were some young jemadars, who had been given accelerated or even direct appointment to that rank, but even these had no formal military or other Western-style education.

The objection to granting commissions to Indians rested as much on political as military grounds. In 1885 Sir George Chesney, as Military Member, said that it was a waste of potential ability to restrict Indian officers to the command of companies.[10] Roberts, as C-in-C, replied that British officers would not accept Indians as their equals, nor would British soldiers as their superiors 'however well-educated or clever a native may be, and however brave he may have proved himself'.[11] In 1887 Chesney re-opened the question, pointing out that it was only in the military that Indians were barred from the higher levels of public service. Roberts's answer was that he did not consider Indians incompetent to become officers, but rather the reverse. Having in his youth seen what mutinous sepoys could do without officers, he thought it safer to keep all commissioned appointments in British hands, just in case there was another mutiny or national rising of any sort.

There was equal determination to exclude Western-educated Indians from joining the military, regardless of the fact that these were by definition the only ones who could pass the same examinations as British candidates for commissions. In 1890, when Chesney proposed offering professional educational opportunities to suitable Indian officers, Roberts objected that his favoured martial classes would be disadvantaged, as 'in India the least warlike races possess the highest intellectual capacities, the Gurkhas and Pathans and to a lesser extent the Sikhs, are as notoriously averse to mental exertion as they are fond of manly sports'.[12] Curzon, in his *Memorandum on Commissions for Indians* of June 1900, took the same line. The sons of the intellectual Westernised classes were, to him, 'the very last type of young officer that we should desire to procure'.[13] Nevertheless, four years later, a Westernised Asian army showed itself able to defeat the same European power that the Indian Army itself had for the previous thirty years been preparing to fight. If Japanese soldiers actually had done as well as Indian sepoys were expected to, why could not Indian officers be expected to do as well as Japanese officers actually had done?

The answer which could no longer be openly given was that they could, but the British authorities did not want them to. The reasons in the last resort were political. Enlightened correspondents to the Anglo-Indian press pointed out that Kitchener's army at Khartoum had included regiments commanded by Egyptian officers who had performed creditably; and that the history of Indian wars showed that Indian soldiers had followed Indian officers against the British no less readily than they had followed British officers against Indians. Against this, others argued that those Indians who passed the examination for entry to the civil services chose to enter the sedentary branches rather than outdoor, manly, branches such as the forestry service, and said that soldiers drawn from the traditional martial classes would never follow officers drawn from the emergent Westernised middle class. Much the same arguments had been advanced when British officers had all been obliged to take examination. Why the race of weedy bookworms who in both instances it was feared would take over the army actually would have wanted to enter an arduous profession, allegedly so alien to their background and life-style, was not explained, nor was it mentioned that in most civil services administration carries more prestige than sylviculture.

By 1908, with constitutional reform approaching, the question was no longer whether Indians should hold military commissions, but rather of the terms on which these should eventually be granted.[14] A special conference was convened at the time of the Imperial Durbar of George V, newly crowned King-Emperor. General Smith-Dorrien, representing the War Office, raised no objection to Indians being granted their King's commission, but insisted that all such officers, if they were to be allowed powers of command over British troops, must be trained alongside British cadets in England. A separate college in India, even with the same examinations and syllabus, was not acceptable.[15] The eventual decision to turn to Indian as well as British sources for officers was a political rather than a military one. The colleges at Sandhurst, Quetta and Wellington were able to produce over 300 British cadets each year for permanent commissions alone (compared with seventy normally required in peace-time) and the shortfall for war-time needs was being made up by the enlarged Indian Army Reserve of Officers. The number of commissions initially offered to Indians was, in terms of military manpower, quite insignificant. The only military value was the incentive to flagging recruitment among the traditional martial classes of a promise that their members might be at last eligible for full commissions.

The political imperative for granting commissions to Indians derived from the Montagu-Chelmsford Reforms of 1917.[16] These had the avowed aim of leading India to the achievement of self-government, following the pattern set by Canada, Australia, New Zealand and South Africa. The citizens of these dominions, including French Canadians and Dutch South Africans, provided the officers for their armies. The differences, however, were twofold. One was that the self-governing dominions, unlike India, were not centres of British military power. Indeed, a strong argument in favour of their self-government had been that they would take the burden of their defence upon their own shoulders and lift it from those of the British taxpayer. In India the reverse was the case and a third of the British Army was stationed there at the expense of the Indian taxpayer. The other difference was that Dominion officers were of European descent. The few British Army personnel who served with them were less reluctant to accept their authority than the many who served in India were to accept that of Asians.

The sensitivity of the subject was indicated by the opening paragraphs of the despatch which proposed granting commissions to Indians.[17] The importance was stressed of maintaining the popularity of the Indian service among those British families which had traditionally sent their sons to it. Every change was to be very gradual to prevent a break in the hereditary connection 'which experience has shown to be of the highest benefit to the State'. Without dwelling on what this experience or this benefit had been, the despatch went on to say that the performance during the war of 'the fighting classes of India' had established claims by them on the Government of India which could no longer be deferred. Therefore, Indians from these classes should be given, 'gradually' and 'as far as circumstances permit', opportunities in the Indian Army equal to those of the 'non-fighting classes' in the civil administration. It was admitted that 'legitimate aspirations' had not been satisfied by the grant of commissions in the Native Indian Land Forces, a reference to the ill-fated Imperial Cadet Corps scheme founded by Curzon for the military education of the scions of princely houses.[18]

What was called 'British commissioned rank' was to be obtainable by Indians by three different methods. One would be by the extension of the grant of honorary commissions to a wider field of senior Indian officers than the holders of the Indian Order of Merit (an award for valour) who until then had been the only eligible candidates. Although honorary commissions carried no powers of command over British troops, such grants would be seen as awards for loyal service. The second would be by attendance at a school, modelled on the French *École de Sous-Officiers* at St Maxent, by young jemadars, many of whom it was expected would have attended one of the colleges set up by Lord Kitchener for the sons of Indian officers. This route was intended to avoid alienating the martial classes, whose traditional disdain for Western education seemed certain to put them at a disadvantage in competition for entry to a cadet college. These jemadars were to be trained to function as sub-unit commanders. The majority would go on to become subadars but some would be selected for the grant of full commissions and 'Indian officers of this class would probably command the confidence of their men in a higher degree than those recruited from Sandhurst'.[19] This last remark indicated the paradox of the proposal since, if Indian officers from Sandhurst were to be less esteemed by Indian soldiers than those from the jemadars' school, there was no military point in sending them to Sandhurst at all. Moreover, the same despatch argued that the sepoy was 'a shrewd judge of character', which was why nothing should be done that would result in his British officers becoming anything other than 'representative of the best class of English gentleman'.[20] Unofficially, most British traditionalists held the views they attributed to the sepoys. At the same time, however, the British Army maintained its view that only Indians trained as cadets on the British model, indeed, in Britain itself, could be allowed command over British troops.

So it was that the most important proposal in the despatch was that ten places be allotted each year on the British Army's Unattached List for the Indian Army to Indians who had qualified for admission in the same way as British candidates, that is, by attendance at either a military college or at a major British university which had a recognised course of military studies. It was agreed that, for the sake of establishing comradeship between Indian and British cadets and of countering the racial prejudices of British officers and men, the military college they attended should be the same for both. The only question was where it should be. The Government of India's view was that it must be in England, as British parents would not send their sons to India, far from parental influence and at an impressionable age, younger than that at which British Army recruits could be sent overseas. The evidence that parents, many from the class that sent its sons to boarding schools at a tender age, were sending them just as happily to Quetta or Wellington was disregarded. The argument that Indian parents might have the same objections to sending their sons to England was admitted, but countered by the view that they already sent sons to the United Kingdom to receive legal, medical, engineering or other professional education and that the RMC course was significantly shorter. This view seemed also to concede that the parents of Indian cadets would be from the same 'non-martial' classes whose sons were presumed to be the sole aspirants to a Western education.

The closing paragraph of the despatch summed up its constitutional and political implications:

> Our object in formulating these proposals has been to place Indians of the fighting classes on a footing of equality with other subjects of ... [the Crown] ... in the spirit and letter of the Queen's Proclamation of 1858. The ideal we have placed before us is the evolution of an Imperial Army which will include all the elements of the Empire in one great comradeship of arms. These elements must be moulded together on the basis of mutual regard for each other's traditions, customs, prejudices. Some may regard these proposals as conceding too much, others as not going far enough. The Commander-in-Chief is of opinion, however, that they mark the extreme limit to which we can with safety proceed. In this opinion we entirely concur.[21]

Little had been done to implement these proposals by the time the war ended in November the following year. Their acceptance in principle had achieved the immediate political aim of making concessions to the nationalist as well as the traditional martial pressure groups in India without unduly alarming vested interests on the British side. A college for Indian cadets was set up at

Daly College, Indore, with the student body drawn from the martial classes and selected by a series of non-academic tests, including personal interview with the Governor-General. Like the defunct Imperial Cadet Corps, set up by Curzon to train a few scions of princely families, and unlike the cadet colleges at Quetta and Wellington, it was not a British Army establishment. Its thirty-nine graduates were commissioned in December 1919 and granted full commissions in the Indian Land Forces. When the India Office asked the Government of India for its views on retaining Wellington as a college for training Indian cadets together with British cadets in India, the reply was that the objections to an Indian College stated the previous year still stood and 'Our experience with the Training School for Indian Cadets at Indore confirms these views'.[22]

The training of cadets at Quetta and Wellington was thereupon discontinued. The course at Wellington, programmed to begin in January 1919, could not be stopped, as its cadets had been appointed and some were already en route to India. The last course at Quetta finished in April 1919 and the Indian Staff College re-opened in its pre-war home. The destination of cadets who had entered the competition held in November 1918 for admission to Quetta the following year seemed a problem. Consideration was given to the War Office's proposal to train them on premises previously used by one of its officer cadet battalions, which had been closed after the Armistice. Finally it was decided to fit them in at the RMC and train them with the cadets who had passed in there at the same entrance examinations.[23]

Despite Montagu's own preference for the concept that Indian cadets should be trained in their own country, the view prevailed at the India Office that they should go to Sandhurst. It was held that it would be disastrous for the Indian Army if it drew its British officers other than from Sandhurst and that, in any case, the few Indians suitable for training at the RMC could be fitted in there without difficulty. Even if the required number of British cadets could be found willing to train in India, there would be little merit in disadvantaging seventy British for the sake of ten or fifteen Indians. Although the first five Indian gentlemen cadets arrived at Sandhurst at the end of 1919, the India Office remained primarily concerned with the recruitment of British cadets. One difficulty was that the Indian Army was reducing from its greatly expanded war strength to its new peace-time establishment, which pressure from the financiers and politicians alike soon set at lower than its pre-war one. There were therefore far too many regular officers, especially among those recruited between 1914 and 1919, notwithstanding the heavy casualties (668 former cadets of the RMC alone were killed or died of wounds or disease)[24] suffered in the war. Redundancies were minimised by increasing, on grounds of military efficiency, the establishment of commissioned officers, but India's financial position made this impossible to sustain. Enough funds

Table 1.   British and Indian gentlemen cadets at the Royal Military College, 1925–1928.

Date	British cadets	Indian cadets	Total	Vacancies offered
Summer 1925	12	6	18	25
Winter 1925	18	4	22	25
Summer 1926	29	3	32	35
Winter 1926	9	5	14	35
Summer 1927	27	1	28	35
Winter 1927	22	7	29	35
Summer 1928	32	7	39	35

were found for a variety of resettlement schemes but until 1926, by which time the last of the surplus officers were discharged, the number of Indian Army vacancies offered to RMC cadets each year was reduced to fifty. The numbers of cadets for the Indian Army from the half-yearly batches passing out from the RMC between 1925 and 1928 were as shown in Table 1.[25]

A suggestion by the War Office in October 1928 that, in the light of these figures, the thirty-five vacancies allotted to the Unattached List should include the ten Indian cadets then in each batch was successfully resisted by the India Office. It was argued that the Indian cadets (who were being grouped into eight 'Indianised' units where they were doing the duties of the old-style Indian officers, to whom the title Viceroy's Commissioned Officer had by this time been given) were going to experimental units, whose value was not yet proven. The clear implication of this was that, whatever the British Army thought, the Indian Army did not accept that RMC-trained Indians were the same as RMC-trained British cadets. The rest of the Indian Army, described as its 'effective strength' would therefore need to recruit at the same rate as before the war to maintain its efficiency. This was because although none of the thirty-five British cadets from Sandhurst would be required by the eight units to which, but for Indianisation, some of them would have gone, the annual wastage rate of British officers was at this time 120. To replace them the Indian Army wanted, every half year, thirty-five cadets from Sandhurst, six from the universities, and twenty transferees from the British Army – and from none of these sources were enough coming forward. Another objection raised was that as Indian cadets generally passed out lower than British cadets, but had to go to India, it would be unfair to any British cadet who passed out higher but was excluded from the thirty-five vacancies on their account. Both these arguments were weak, in that ordinary cadets passing out high in order of merit already could be excluded by British holders of Indian Army cadetships ('King's India Cadets') passing out lower than them, and that the Indian Army was, in effect, seeking the same number of RMC cadets for a smaller number of units. The deciding factor was reference to a Cabinet decision of 22 December 1927, supporting a sub-committee of the Committee of Imperial Defence recommendation that Indianisation of the eight units was acceptable only if British officer recruitment to the Indian Army was maintained, and if possible restored, to its previous level.[26]

Nevertheless, the War Office, faced with serious shortages of subalterns in the British Army, maintained its insistence that British needs must take priority. In August 1930 it agreed only with reluctance to allow the six lowest candidates for the Unattached List to join it, and in January 1931 one candidate was not permitted to join, in consequence of the British Army being 151 subalterns under-strength. It responded to complaints from the India Office by pointing out that thirteen Army cadets at the RMC had applied for the Unattached List and that the India Office had rejected ten of them so that the British Army had to 'find room' for them. Army cadets were bright young regular NCOs considered by their commanding officers to be suitable as officer material. They were nominated without the need to pass the entrance examination and were not required to pay fees. The scheme was introduced in 1922 as a way of filling up the Royal Military College, for which there were not enough candidates forthcoming from the traditional sources. Although the military performance of Army cadets at the college compared well enough with that of ordinary cadets, it is clear that in some instances at least there was prejudice against them.

The recruitment of British officers continued to be a problem for the Indian Army until the outbreak of the Second World War in September 1939, when the last regular commissions in the British Indian Army were granted. The figures for the intake in summer 1936 were typical of those throughout the 1930s. The sixty subalterns then required, to meet an annual wastage rate of 120, were made up of thirty ordinary cadets, nine King's India Cadets and thirteen Army cadets from the RMC, five from the universities, one from the Supplementary Reserve, and two from the Territorial Army.

Indian cadets were trained at the RMC between 1919 and 1934 (see Table 2).[27] They were required to pass an examination held in India, corresponding to the RMC entrance examination, to ensure that they would be able to cope with the work at Sandhurst. Those who passed were then interviewed by a selection board and the final nomination was made by the Governor-General on the Commander-in-Chief's recommendation. This allowed the British authorities to ensure that, irrespective of their position in the order of marks, at least half of the cadets appointed each year were drawn from the traditional martial communities who might otherwise have been excluded by the Westernised urban intelligentsia. The 'martials' were thought of as being both better officer material and more politically reliable, or at least inert, which they made clear they would not be if their past contribution to the Indian Army was not recognised by this share of cadetships.

Table 2.   Summary of Indian gentlemen cadets joining the Royal Military College between January 1919 and September 1932.

Date of joining	No. of cadets joined	No. of cadets commissioned	Resigned, failed etc.	Remarks
Jan./Feb. 1919	5	2	1	2 died: dates coincide with influenza epidemic.
Sep. 1919	5	4	1	–
Jan./Feb. 1920	4	1	3	–
Sep. 1920	4	2	2	–
Jan./Feb. 1921	3	2	1	–
Sep. 1921	3	3	–	–
Jan./Feb. 1922	3	2	1	–
Sep. 1922	3	3	–	–
Jan./Feb. 1923	5	2	3	–
Aug. 1923	6	5	1	–
Jan./Feb. 1924	6	6	–	–
Aug. 1924	5	4	1	–
Jan. 1925	4	4	–	–
Sep. 1925	5	3	2	–
Feb. 1926	2	1	1	–
Sep. 1926	9	7	2	–
Jan./Feb. 1927	6	6	–	–
Sep. 1927	7	7	–	–
Feb. 1928	2	2	–	–
Aug. 1928	3	3	–	–
Feb. 1929	1	1	–	–
Aug. 1929	8	8	–	–
Jan. 1930	13	13	–	–
Aug. 1930	9	9	–	–
Jan. 1931	11	11	–	–
Aug. 1931	9	9	–	–
Jan. 1932	13	13	–	–
Sep. 1932	8	8	–	–
Total	162	141	19	2 died

Note: The figures do not tally exactly with those of Table 1, which shows the figure for cadets passing out. Although the standard duration of the course at this time was eighteen months, in some cases cadets (British and Indian alike) who had not made sufficient progress in their studies completed an extra term.

The figures in Table 2 show that the number of those in the first batches of Indian cadets who failed to complete the RMC course, though small, was disproportionately high. In financial terms alone, the wasted costs of their passages to and from India and their fees at the college, which were all borne by the Indian government, were a matter for concern. To remedy this, the Prince of Wales's Royal Indian Military College was established in March

1922 at Dehra Dun, in the old home of the Imperial Cadet Corps. This was a boarding school, initially for seventy boys, conforming to the pattern of an English public school of the time. Fees were charged, but a number of scholarships were available for the sons of Viceroy's Commissioned Officers. The cost of the college was charged to the Army budget, and the staff included a number of military instructors, including a sergeant major for the school cadet corps. In effect, this became a preparatory school for Indians wishing to join the RMC, and those who subsequently arrived at Sandhurst from Dehra Dun were better prepared for the culture shock of cadet life. No Indian cadet joining the RMC after January 1927 failed the course, even though at the same time the number of cadetships available on each half-yearly intake was increased from ten to twenty.

Proposals from the Government of India for an increase in the number of Indian officers were greeted with horror when they reached the India Office in September 1921. Lieutenant General Cobbe, Secretary of the Military Department, argued that to commission Indian officers in any significant numbers would have a detrimental effect on the Indian Army's efficiency: 'few, if any, Indians having the natural aptitude for leadership possessed by the average Englishman'. He repeated the old argument that the martial classes were not educated and the educated classes were not martial, and, challenging the whole policy of Indianisation, suggested that Indians should not be given commissions equal to those held by British officers. Instead, they should be concentrated into a few units, or employed only in a new dominion force which he proposed should be established with the same status as those of Canada, Australia, New Zealand and South Africa. This force, initially officered by British volunteers from the Indian Army would, in his plan, gradually replace the latter, at least for the defence of India, in much the same way that, under the system of 'dyarchy' then being introduced at the same time, the civil government of India was to consist of two parallel hierarchies, with areas being progressively transferred from British to Indian-controlled authorities. The Cobbe scheme also avoided the difficulty of British officers serving under Indians. It received the support of the Secretary of State for India, Viscount Peel, and was sent to the Governor-General, Lord Reading, for consideration.[28]

There was a crucial difference between Cobbes's proposal and the precedent set by colonial forces in their approach to self-government. In no other dependency had the local forces not simply become the armies of the new dominions. There had been no attempt to create new separate armies, nor to deny to colonial officers commissions that would confer command over all troops in their own country. Indian officers under Cobbes's scheme would have stood in much the same relationship to British officers as had the Company's officers to those of the British Army before Cornwallis's reforms.

The whole tone of his thinking, in common with that at the War Office at the time, was to separate the Indian Army from the Government of India, so that even if the British yielded the latter to Indian hands, they might somehow retain the former in their own.

Most of this plan was rejected by Reading out of hand. He telegraphed to London that Indian nationalist opinion would not accept a change of policy over Indianisation of the existing army, which had already been declared. It would, he said, be considered a test of the sincerity of British declarations that they really intended India to become fitted for self-government.[29] Nevertheless, although the idea of a dominion force was dropped, that of concentrating the Indian cadets, who were by this time passing out of the RMC, into particular units, was adopted. Eight units, drawn from both the cavalry and the infantry, were selected by the C-in-C (India) and from 1922 onwards every vacancy created in them by the promotion or transfer of a British officer was filled by an Indian.[30]

It is clear that this 'eight-unit' scheme was welcomed by British officers of the Indian Army (at least outside the units concerned) because it meant they did not have to serve under Indian officers. An article in the *RMC Magazine* quoted the statement made in the House of Lords on 20 February 1923 by the Under-Secretary of State for India, Earl Winterton, that 'There will never be a case in which British officers will be serving under senior Indian officers because the scheme will begin at the bottom and work upwards'. The problem was, according to the *RMC Magazine*, not that Indians were unfit to command, but 'the inherent dislike of the Englishman of any rank or class to being commanded by a man of another race ... [even] such a General as the French were able to provide in the person of Marshal Foch'. It added that Englishmen, whether from public schools or Board schools, had an inborn capacity for leadership, 'especially as regards Orientals' and, in evidence, pointed to the way in which a few officers and NCOs could be found administering areas the size of English counties in the Arab territories recently captured from the Turks. Now that the eight-unit scheme had been set up, the article urged 'English boys ... to work on parallel lines with those others who, though men of a different race, yet are citizens of the same Empire, and have been granted the right of showing what they can do in its service'.[31]

A later article, while repeating the assertion that Englishmen were natural leaders, calculated the remote chances of Indians ever commanding them. It was based on a lecture given to the cadets by an Indian Army officer, Colonel W.E. Wilson-Johnstone, which was considered important enough to print, on the grounds that because of the acoustics in the gymnasium, where it had been given, 'many of those present heard with difficulty' (a condition to which cadets attending lectures were often prone). Wilson-Johnstone held the conventional views of the British Indian military establishment. India was a sub-continent inhabited by a great diversity of peoples, most of whom were unfitted to be soldiers from the effects of an enervating climate or generations of oppression, but were, in their ignorance, prey to political agitators.[32] British cadets considering a future in the Indian Army, however, need have no fear of being asked to serve under Indians, as of the army's 132 battalions of infantry and twenty-one regiments of cavalry, only six and two respectively were being Indianised. The government, he told the cadets, was saying to the Indians 'Now prove to us that you can produce Indian Officers who can administer these units in peace and lead them in war. We will give you every assistance but until you prove your case we will not further extend Indian-isation as to do so might jeopardise India.'[33] Meanwhile, as there were at the time only seven Indian captains in the army, of whom two were about to leave and two were in Indianised units, few of the 1,563 British captains were likely to find themselves under one of the remaining three, none of whom, he thought, would, by virtue of their age, reach the rank of lieutenant colonel. Of the 480 subalterns, fifty-three were Indians, and of these six were more than forty years of age, and a further twenty-two were aged between thirty and forty. Most of these, he predicted, would see that their age limited their prospects of promotion to senior rank, while it would be logical to expect the remainder to be promoted in the Indianised units. Thus, he argued, in twenty years' time very few would be found in the 131 units to which British cadets were restricted. Although Wilson-Johnstone expressed his good wishes to the few Indian gentlemen cadets present at the college, it appears that he had little confidence in their ability to 'prove their case' as he envisaged that even after twenty years there would not be a single extra unit in which they might serve. In fact, by 1945 there would not be a single unit, except those recruited from Gurkhas, in which they would not.

The eight-unit scheme, however satisfactory to the British, was unac-ceptable to Indian public opinion. Indianisation was again discussed in the Legislative Assembly in February-March 1924. The government, against a background of increasing terrorism, needed to conciliate Indian moderates and agreed to set up a committee to consider the best ways of attracting and employing Indian officers. This, chaired by Lieutenant General Sir Andrew Skeen, Chief of the Indian Army's General Staff, and including the leading Indian politicians Motilal Nehru and Muhammad Ali Jinnah, assembled in August 1925 and reported in November 1926. It recommended abolishing the eight-unit scheme and permitting Indian officers to serve in all arms, including armour, artillery, engineers and signals, and the Royal Air Force in India (four Indians had held RAF commissions during the First World War). It also recommended the establishment of an Indian Military Academy by 1933 and that in the meanwhile the number of Indian gentlemen cadets at the RMC be doubled, with six Indians being admitted as gentlemen cadets on each half yearly intake to the Royal Military Academy (for the technical arms) and six on each intake of flight cadets at the RAF College, Cranwell.

In March 1928 the Government of India announced that it accepted the proposals relating to the RMA, RMC and RAFC, but rejected the remainder. The eight units were to be re-organised with the same establishment of officers as in British Army units. This meant that the duties of platoon or troop commander, previously performed by VCOs, would be done by sub-alterns, whose numbers were increased in consequence. The chances of Indian subalterns eventually reaching the rank of lieutenant colonel were thereby reduced to one in eight (the same as that for British Army officers before the introduction of promotion by time a few years later increased it to 60 per cent) instead of one in three as it had previously been in the Indian Army, for British and Indian officers alike. It also reduced the promotion prospects of the sepoys, as VCOs in these units were abolished, leaving warrant officer rank as the highest to which they could reasonably aspire, as in the British Army at this period. The British could argue that Indian officers now conformed to officers of the British and dominion armies.[34] Indian public opinion, however, saw that Indian officers were at a disadvantage com-pared with British officers of the Indian Army, financed by Indian taxpayers. Their personal status was inevitably diminished in that the duties they per-formed in the eight units were still performed by VCOs in the rest of the Army and they were inevitably therefore seen as more like a VCO and less like an officer, despite the fact that they had gone through exactly the same training at the RMC as British officers joining the Indian Army at the same time.

This, indeed, was the root of the problem for, as the RMC was producing more Indian cadets than the eight units needed under the existing organ-isation, there was nowhere to send them except to the other units which were exclusively British officered. If they went to those regiments, they would automatically become senior to officers, British or Indian, joining from sub-sequent batches and the promises that no British officer would ever serve under an Indian would have to be broken. Some Indian politicians suspected a deliberate policy of keeping Indian officers in as small a number of units as possible, in case the Army became politically affected by the Babbar Akali movement, which many Sikh ex-soldiers had joined, or by the Naujawan Bharat Subha (Indian Youth Organisation), though in fact the first genera-tions of Indian officers, despite the prejudice which they were liable to encounter, were the least revolutionary group in all India almost by instinct. In the Legislative Assembly, it was pointed out that replacing VCOs with officers, who were more expensive to train and maintain, the government was adding to the cost of the Army in general and of the Indianised units in particular.

After the Round Table Conference between British and Indian politicians (November 1930–January 1931) the military made further concessions in order to placate moderate opinion. A defence sub-committee was appointed, chaired by J.H. Thomas MP, with six Indian members, including Muhammad Ali Jinnah, drawn from a cross-section of the religious and ethnic spectrum. As a result of its recommendations, it was agreed to grant sixty commissions each year to Indians and to double the number of Indianised units to form an infantry division and a cavalry brigade, approximately one-eighth of the army's front-line order of battle. A committee was formed in May 1931 under the C-in-C, General Sir Philip Chetwode, to implement the establishment of the long-awaited Indian Military Academy.[35]

This academy was opened at Dehra Dun on 10 October 1932. It had an establishment for 240 gentlemen cadets, with a three–year course, producing each year the sixty needed for the Indian Army and a further twenty for the Indian States Forces. Of the sixty regular vacancies available each year, six were reserved to be filled by the C-in-C's nomination from those who had qualified by examination, but had not passed in high enough to gain one of the competitive places. Graduates of the IMA were granted commissions as 'Indian Commissioned Officers in His Majesty's Land Forces'. Their powers of command were the same as those of British officers but could be exercised only in India or, like those of dominion armies, when serving with their own army elsewhere. Their rates of pay were lower than those of British officers on the grounds that, serving in their own country, Indians did not need the additional incentive required to compensate expatriates, though the British still enjoyed the better promotion prospects. Indian officers commissioned from the RMA and RMC continued to be paid at the same rates as British officers, but the latter gained more rapid promotion. As a result of the resentment felt by Indian politicians and officers at this position, another Indianisation committee was set up in 1939. Its Indian members felt frustrated by the continued British opposition to progress on the issue and, with the return of the military members to active duty on mobilisation in September, the committee was dissolved.

On the outbreak of the Second World War, trained regular officers of any kind were a precious resource. The policy of segregation was abandoned and officers, British or Indian, were posted wherever they were most needed. Officer Cadet Training Units were established to produce 'Emergency Commissioned Officers' and British and Indian cadets trained together, as they would fight together. During the war, the number of Indian officers increased from 1,500 to 15,000, of whom 8,000 were in combatant units. The proportion of Indian to British officers in these units rose from ten per cent to twenty-five per cent.

A post-war study revealed very little difference between the performance of British and Indian commissioned officers. Pre-war regulars were thought to be better than the emergency-commissioned officers, irrespective of their country of origin. All British personnel joining the Army after September 1939 were conscripts, as voluntary engagements were not permitted during the emergency. Indian personnel were all volunteers, and a number joined as much for government employment as for glory. Moreover, the troubled political environment deterred many from coming forward to fight for their British rulers. A disturbingly high number of Indian officers captured in Japan's early successes joined the Indian National Army, for political as much as for personal reasons, though they were shunned by the vast majority of regular officers after the war for having broken their freely given oath. The advantages of officers who could identify fully with the culture and languages of their men were universally acknowledged.[36]

Notes

1. Report of War Office/India Office Interdepartmental Committee, 6 July 1906, IOR L/MIIV7/2600.
2. War Office/India Office Correspondence November 1906–January 1907, IOR L/MIL/7/2600.
3. J.W. Merewether and F. Smith, *The Indian Corps in France*, London, 1919; C. Lucas, *The Empire at War*, Vol. 5, Oxford 1926, pp. 202–16.
4. IOR L/MIL/7/2635–2647.
5. *Ibid.*
6. *Ibid.*
7. *Ibid.*
8. Telegram Indian Office to Govt of India in the Military Department, 17 November 1918, IOR L/MIL/7/2694.
9. Briggs, *Letter to Sir John Hobhouse* (1836), and Lawrence, *Essays, Military and Civil*, London, 1859, *cit.* in S.P. Cohen, *The Indian Army. Its Contribution to the Development of a Nation*, Berkeley, Cal. 1971, p. 63.
10. *Cit.* in G. Arthur, *Life of Lord Kitchener*, London, 1920, Vol. II, pp. 177–8.
11. *Ibid.*
12. *Ibid.*
13. *Cit.* in S.P. Cohen, *op. cit.*, p. 64.
14. Mary, Countess of Minto, *India, Minto and Morley 1905–10*, London, 1935, pp. 262–70.
15. IOR L/MIL/7/2694.
16. W.A.J. Archbold, *Outlines of Indian Constitutional History*, London, 1926, pp. 167–206.
17. Gov.-Gen. in Council to Sec. of State for India Despatch No. 57 (Army) 3 August 1917, IOR L/MIL/7/2694.
18. Minto, *op. cit.*, p. 268; Arthur, *op. cit.*, Vol. II, pp. 180–1.
19. Gov.-Gen. in Council to Sec. of State for India Despatch No. 57 (Army) 3 August 1917, IOR L/MIL/7/2694.
20. *Ibid.*
21. *Ibid.*
22. Gov.-Gen. in Council to Sec. of State for India 27 November 1918.
23. IOR L/MIL/7/2694.
24. Indian Army Panels, Royal Memorial Chapel, Royal Military Academy, Sandhurst.
25. Registers of Gentlemen Cadets at the Royal Military College, PRO WO 151.

26. Public Record Office Cabinet Papers 326/27; *also* IOR L/MIL/ 7/2760–2761.
27. Registers of Gentlemen Cadets at the Royal Military College, PRO WO 151.
28. Indianisation Minute by Lt-Gen. A.S. Cobbe, dated 14 September 1921, IOR L/MIL/17/ 5/1774.
29. Gov.-Gen. to Sec. of State Telegram dated 18 February 1922 *cit.* in Cohen, *op. cit.*, pp. 83–4.
30. IOR L/MIL/17/5/1778–1779, L/MIL/7/2708–2788.
31. *RMC Magazine and Record*, Easter 1923, pp. 29–33.
32. RMC *Magazine and Record*, Easter 1925, p. 47.
33. *Ibid.*
34. P. Mason, *A Matter of Honour. An Account of the Indian Army, its Officers and Men*, London, 1974, p. 455.
35. IOR L/MIL/5/885, L/MIL/17/5/1783–1790.
36. S.P. Cohen, *op. cit.*, p. 145.

Chapter 10

The Army of India, 1914–1947

On the outbreak of the First World War the British Indian empire changed from being, in military terms, a debtor into a creditor. Previously the assumption had been that, if involved in a major war at all, the military in India would be reinforced by troops from the United Kingdom, at least as soon as the Army Reserve had been called out and units on the home establishment had been mobilised and brought up to war strength. It was appreciated that some time would elapse before their arrival and therefore, contrary to the normal principles of modern European military science, British units in India had a peace establishment larger than their war one, by 25 per cent in the case of the infantry and 33 per cent in the cavalry, to allow for the replacement of battle casualties, etc., during the two months before reinforcements could reach India. In the autumn of 1914, however, large numbers of troops, Indian as well as British, were sent out of India to support the British war effort in France and Flanders, in Egypt, East Africa and Mesopotamia (Iraq). Although all costs in excess of those which would have been incurred had these troops stayed in India were met by the British, not the Indian, exchequer, India still had to pay their ordinary charges as though they were still in India. Although mostly withdrawn from France when Kitchener's armies arrived to replace them, Indian troops also served in Salonica, Russia, Iran and elsewhere, while Gurkhas and the majority of the pre-war regular British garrison of India took part in the ill-fated Dardanelles campaign. By the end of the war the number of Indian personnel under arms had risen from 155,423 to 573,484. Between 700,000 and 800,000 had actually passed through the Army during the war, a figure which rises to 12 lakhs of men if the non-combatant followers, without whom no Indian army could take the field, is included.[1]

None of this was greatly welcomed by the Government of India. As noticed in the previous chapter, the War Office's reluctance to provide the Indian Army with its due share of gentlemen cadets and Kitchener's appropriation of Indian Army officers on furlough in the United Kingdom for service with his new armies both caused irritation to the Indian military authorities. The Government of India's view was that it was responsible for the defence of India and that this was imperilled by the demands made upon Indian military resources by the War Office in general and Kitchener in particular, who as a former C-in-C should have known how limited these resources were. As

Haines had forecast, the abolition of the presidential armies had been followed by the abolition of their separate war-making resources and by 1914
there was, in the name of economy, only one modern rifle factory in all India.
Even this had been targeted for closure by the Nicholson Committee on the
grounds that better value for money could be obtained by having rifles manufactured in England. Duff's objections to Kitchener's demands received what
the Governor-General described as 'an angry message in reply'.[2]

Nevertheless, the pressure to subordinate India to imperial military requirements continued. Kitchener went so far as to argue that the loss of the war in
Europe would be a more serious matter than the loss of India. The Indian
government did not see matters in that light and took an equally extreme
position, arguing that it could not spare men for other theatres because, having
given up all its new rifles to arm Kitchener's new armies, it had nothing left
with which to equip the units it would have to raise to replace those sent out
of India. It had, moreover, used Kitchener's own prejudice against the Territorial Force to argue that territorials (the successors of the old Volunteer
Force) were unacceptable substitutes for the regulars who had been recalled to
Europe.

We could not send Territorial Infantry and Artillery against Turks.
Territorials are, of course, quite unfit for frontier work.

We cannot regard Territorials as fit to cope with Pathans in hill warfare.

It would be madness to send Territorial troops to the North-West
Frontier.[3]

In March 1915 Hardinge, supported by his C-in-C, refused to send any
more troops out of India unless directly ordered to do so. The risks of a
descent by the tribes on a weakened frontier, and of a rising by anti-British
elements in India were, they said, simply too great. Duff said he would like to
see every European woman out of India, and in April 1915 Hardinge cabled
to the India Office that the demands made by the United Kingdom government upon the military resources of India placed the lives of loyal subjects,
Indian and British, in peril.[4] Nevertheless, the Secretary of State, Lord
Crewe, gave in to the Army Council, which declared that the maintenance of
British rule in India should not be paramount over all other military questions. He ordered the immediate despatch of reinforcements to Mesopotamia
and relieved Hardinge and Duff of responsibility for the consequences.
Neither of them resigned.

The scale of casualties sustained from the impact of modern weapons
demonstrated that the policy of drawing recruits from only a small number of
selected communities was suitable only for small campaigns of limited
duration. Troops highly trained to function as marksmen in the hills of the
North-West Frontier were used as mere cannon fodder on the Western Front

and were mown down in swathes in offensive after offensive against the German lines. Equally disastrous tactics were employed by the generals in Mesopotamia and Palestine until better officers took their place and began a war of movement that led to the defeat of the Turks in October 1918. Indian Army losses, however, were not easy to replace. The class company system meant that losses in a company drawn from one community could not be made good by posting across men from another, in the same unit, but from a different ethnic group. Subedars and jemadars from companies of one class were not easily accepted by those of another and it took time for British officers joining new units to gain the trust of their sepoys.

The system of reserves which the scientific school of reformers had pressed upon the Indian Army for the previous thirty years proved a failure. As Norman had pointed out, it was a system unsuited to Indian conditions. It worked well enough in a Western industrialised society, but India was an oriental agricultural one. Soldiers who had served their time with the Colours settled down with their families and grew old, mentally if not physically. Most of the reservists recalled in August 1914 were unfit for active duty, and out of date in their recollection of their duties and skill at arms.

The alternative reserve system, the old pattern favoured by Norman and Haines (of using those battalions which were not on active service as a source of drafts for those in their linked group which were) also failed. Under the pressure of demands for the various fronts, every unit was mobilised and although drafts were indeed sent from one to another to replace casualties, the problems encountered were much the same as those of posting men from one company to another, but to a more marked degree.

Recruiting new replacements became difficult. The Punjab, the reservoir of British Indian military manpower, was drained dry, contributing 136,000 Muslims and 88,000 Sikhs, but only in response to immense pressure from the authorities. Sir Michael O'Dwyer, the Lieutenant-Governor, toured his province, offering praise and honours for those districts (and their local magnates) who produced recruits, and putting shame on those who failed to meet the demands made on them. Political leaders were reminded that, if the Punjab could not produce soldiers, other provinces would, and thereby deserve a better claim on the British when constitutional reforms were in the air. Despite this, many farmers preferred to keep their sons on the land when the price of produce rose during the war. Others, especially in Western India, saw in the booming war-time industries a more lucrative and less hazardous, if less heroic, form of employment. Recruiting in the traditional areas went on much as it did in the United Kingdom before conscription was enforced there, with black looks from the squire and parson and moral pressure on the families of young men who did not volunteer, cheers, praise, and a clap on the back from those same worthies for those who did, and the local worthies themselves gaining recognition for their recruitment efforts by honours and awards from a grateful government.

A later Secretary of State for India, Edwin Montagu, writing in 1920, told the Cabinet that Indian young men had been 'persuaded, and to face the matter quite frankly, persuaded with great vigour, in certain places, particularly in the Punjab, to join His Majesty's forces during the war'.[5]

Seventy-five groups not considered martial in 1914 were found to be so during the following four years. Most were groups very similar in origin and background to those already enlisted and others had previously been recruited and still had a tradition of military service on which to build.[6] Generally speaking, most performed at much the same level, reflecting the training, leadership and morale factors which can make any unit good or bad regardless of its racial composition.

Public opinion in England only became concerned with the weakness of Indian military administration when the Mesopotamian campaign produced not only military defeat but logistic collapse. At first all had gone well. War between the Entente powers and the Ottoman empire began on 31 October 1914. Troops from Bombay landed at the north of the Persian Gulf and captured Basra without difficulty on 22 November. In the spring of 1915 the British advanced along both the Euphrates and the Tigris, and the collapse of local resistance led the Government of India to sanction a further offensive with the aim of capturing Baghdad. With hindsight it became clear that, even if Baghdad had been captured, it could not have been held. At Ctesiphon, ten miles short of the city, the British were stopped. They fell back to Kut-el-Amara, where the Turks surrounded them. Attempts at relief were made by forces hastily assembled, inadequately staffed, poorly commanded, and badly equipped. Kut surrendered on 29 April 1916 after a siege of 146 days, the longest in the history of the British Indian Army. Outrage at these defeats and at the stories reaching home of the collapse of the medical service, led to the establishment of a Parliamentary Commission of Inquiry in August 1916.

Sir Edmund Barrow, by this time Military Secretary at the India Office and the senior general of the Indian Army, had never been reconciled to Kitchener's combination of the appointments of C-in-C and Military Member. Indeed even Kitchener seems to have conceded that his scheme failed to allow for the consequences that would follow if these combined posts were held by someone incapable of filling them efficiently, such as Sir O'Moore Creagh, whom he had considered unworthy to succeed him.[7] Barrow, preparing for the Commission, minuted that the evil consequences of the change did not become immediately evident because there were still three Commands, each with a lieutenant general and staff, who administered and inspected the troops in their areas. Thus, in the conduct of the Mesopotamian campaign, the GOC

Western Command would have inspected troopships, seen the returning wounded and been able to report personally to the C-in-C. 'All this personal touch is lost by the present one-man system.'[8] He claimed that excessive concentration of work resulting from the abolition of these Commands in 1912 had led to congestion at Army HQ, so that the C-in-C could not leave the seat of government and therefore lost touch with the army, while the Governor-General and the rest of the Council had to depend, in military affairs, on the view of this sole adviser. Barrow admitted that it was impossible in the middle of a war to revive the Military Department, or the Department of Military Supply or even the three Commands, and that 'none of these measures, even if possible, would be accepted by as confirmed an opponent of them as the present Commander-in-Chief'.[9]

He offered two improvements. One was to give the C-in-C a Chief of Staff to carry out inspections on his behalf or to represent him in Council, though not sitting as a member, in his absence on tours of inspection. Kitchener himself had offered Curzon a similar proposal. The second was to revive the two subordinate army HQs which had been replaced by the Commands in 1908. 'I had the honour and misfortune to fill one of these thankless posts for four years,' he wrote, but suggested they might be useful as an intermediate level of command to take some of the pressure of work off Army HQ at Simla. 'The only difficulty is the crucial one of whether Simla will consent to relax its present feeble grip on a highly centralised system ... something must be done, and short of recalling the Commander in Chief I see no other way.'

The Mesopotamia Commission, headed by Curzon's old friend Lord George Hamilton, adopted Barrow's views. It reported that 'the duties of Commander-in-Chief in India and Military Member of Council cannot adequately be performed by any one man in time of war, and that the existing organisation is at once over-centralised at its head and cumbrous in its duality below'.[10] Duff, in evidence, had disagreed with Barrow's opinion that, under the Kitchener system, the C-in-C was trying and failing to do the work which, before the unification of the presidential armies, had been done by six men, but had admitted that in time of war the task was too much for one man. His attempt to avoid blame for the failures in Mesopotamia was supported by over forty Blue Books and other documents produced by the Army Department, a true successor to the old Military Department at least in respect of its attention to detail. Nothing, however, could excuse his neglect of his command duties in favour of his administrative ones, nor such a response to urgent requests for logistic support in Mesopotamia as that given to Major General Cowper, the expedition's Assistant Quartermaster General: 'Please warn General Cowper that if anything of this sort again occurs, or I receive any more querulous or petulant demands for shipping, I shall at once remove him from the force and will refuse him any further employment of any kind.'[11]

Publication of the Mesopotamia Commission's report only increased general indignation. There was outrage at the details of the way in which the sick and wounded were left literally to rot without even basic sanitary arrangements being available, of the parsimony practised at the soldiers' expense by Sir William Meyer and the Finance Department, of Duff's denial that any shortcomings existed, of Hardinge's reluctance to make Duff correct them, and of the failure of Austen Chamberlain, who had become Secretary of State for India in May 1915, to make Hardinge act. Hardinge, with all the skill of his experience as a diplomat, argued that as the constitution of India only gave him one source of military advice, he could not be blamed for accepting it. Chamberlain resigned, as at this period ministers considered themselves responsible for the acts of their subordinates. Kitchener, who had been lost at sea with HMS *Hampshire* in June 1916, was not mentioned in the report, but provided a convenient scapegoat. No one thought of Lord Morley as the true guilty figure, the politician who in his hunt for retrenchments in public spending had, for the sake of a few lakhs of rupees, abolished the Military Supply Department which even Kitchener had been prepared to leave in place.

The First World War had as profound an impact upon India as upon all other countries which it touched. Initially Indian public opinion in general supported the war effort. By 1916, however, the mood had changed. The fall of Kut-el-Amara and the associated disasters in Mesopotamia, following failures in the Western front, in the Dardanelles, and East Africa weakened British prestige. Even the Royal Navy, on whom the defence of India's long coastline rested, had for a time seemed unable to prevent German cruisers from threatening Indian ports. In the face of increasing discontent the British were obliged to make political concessions to the Indian nationalist movement. On 20 August 1917 Chamberlain's successor, Edwin Montagu, declared in the Commons that the policy of the British government was 'the progressive realisation of responsible government in India as an integral part of the Empire'.[12] From then on, the end of British rule in India was merely a question of time.

In the short term, steps were taken to improve the domestic military situation. Duff, who had failed even in his field of expertise, military administration, was succeeded by Sir Charles Monro in October 1916. Monro began by ordering his staff to wear khaki like the fighting soldiers instead of the blue uniforms discontinued elsewhere on the outbreak of war. His task was eased by the transfer of the Mesopotamian Campaign to the War Office, and by the filling of the vacant Southern Army Command in April 1917. The Northern Army Command had been filled in May 1916. The introduction of conscription in Great Britain in 1916 was followed by a general demand for compulsory military training for Europeans in India. The Indian Volunteer Force had been liable for embodied service since August 1914 but, except for individuals who had joined the IARO and a small number of men who enlisted for embodied service overseas, they were essentially a home guard for local emergencies only. In 1917 the passage of the Indian Defence Force Act revived the old principle of a compulsory militia. All British European males of military age were required to undertake part-time military training in a local corps (either the old Volunteers or newly-formed bodies) which could be called out to relieve the regulars of garrison duty or for internal security tasks. Indians and Eurasians were not subject to conscription but could join voluntarily, and a number of public-spirited members of the Western-educated urban middle class took the opportunity to bear arms and practise warlike activities. This force continued in being until 1920, when it was replaced by the Auxiliary Force (India), patterned on the former Volunteer Force.

The Armistice of November 1918 brought little immediate relief to the British Indian empire. The German, Russian, Austro-Hungarian and Ottoman empires had fallen, and extremists saw no reason why this example could not be followed in India. The world influenza epidemic killed 5 million Indians and left millions more depressed, debilitated and distressed financially as well as emotionally. Thousands of demobilised men returned to their villages to find much the same difficulties as the ex-soldiers of Western nations at the same time. Meanwhile, the Government of India, which had sent 182 battalions and 131 squadrons of Indian troops overseas during the war, was still maintaining many of them in the territories conquered from the Ottomans. Even so, each of these units had its depot in India, to deal with recruits, men returning from overseas, etc., so that India was full of soldiers, but most of them were in the depots. Of the 491,000 troops actually in India only one in seven belonged to the British Army, and of these only one cavalry regiment and eight battalions were regulars who had been kept in India throughout the war. A mutiny in the 1st Connaught Rangers, a regular battalion sent out in 1919 to help restore the pre-war ratio of British to Indian troops, was attributed by the military authorities to Irish nationalist agitation. Monro insisted on the death penalty for the alleged ringleader to remind Indian troops of the consequences of such acts, even though the only deaths in the mutiny had been caused by the battalion's own officers.

In 1919 there were fears that the second Indian Mutiny which the British had guarded against for fifty years was about to break out. The delay in implementing the constitutional reforms agreed by Montagu and Chelmsford (Hardinge's successor as Governor-General) caused widespread discontent. By contrast, the Rowlatt Bill, which was intended to counter subversion by extending the wartime defence regulations so as to allow judges to dispense with juries when trying political prisoners and to permit provincial authorities to intern political suspects without trial, was speedily implemented. Mahatma Gandhi, a leading figure in the Indian nationalist movement, organised protests which in several northern cities turned into riots. The threat of a breakdown in British control was especially serious in the Punjab, with so many ex-soldiers in its population. Several attacks were made upon Europeans. At Amritsar, Brigadier General Dyer ordered his troops to fire on an unauthorised assembly which contained many innocent people, but which he feared would turn into a mob such as those which had arisen in 1857. Official estimates were that 379 were killed and 1,200 wounded before his ammunition ran out. This certainly stopped another Mutiny, but went far beyond the doctrine of minimum force. The extent to which Dyer was lionized by the European community alienated Indian public opinion still further from the British, even though (with the noted exception of Sir Michael O'Dwyer) the authorities did not approve of his Cromwellian behaviour.

Disturbances continued. The Third Afghan War (May–August 1919) was sparked off by the threat of the new Amir of Afghanistan, Amanulla, making common cause with Muslim nationalists in the North-West Frontier province. British arms proved successful, with the dashing relief of Thai by Brigadier General Dyer a notable feature of the campaign, as was the bombing of Kabul by the new Royal Air Force. Many Muslims were shocked at the dismemberment of the Ottoman empire by the victorious Western powers, and the Khilafat movement developed in protest. Communist groups were active in the North West, while in the South the Mopla (Mapila) rising of 1921 gave the lie to those who asserted that years of peace under the British had bred all warlike characteristics out of the men of Madras. A combination of repression (including the arrest of Gandhi in 1922) and conciliation (the introduction of the Montagu-Chelmsford reforms) brought an end to the post-war crisis, during which the Indian military had been radically reorganised.

As soon as the world war ended, the India Office proposed setting up a committee to review the Indian military system.[13] It suggested that the chairman might be Sir William Birdwood, Kitchener's old protegé, who had had a good war including successful command of the Australian and New Zealand Army Corps and the British Fifth Army in France. The Government of India favoured the idea, though with the proviso that the committee should be appointed by and report to the C-in-C, India, and concern itself primarily with the terms and conditions of service in India. The suggestions being made of closer relations between the Army in India and the War Office, it considered, should be a matter for the Cabinet.[14]

At the War Office, the Chief of the Imperial General Staff, Field Marshal Sir Henry Wilson, desperate to find manpower with which to meet his many commitments, took a different view. He considered that for the membership of the committee to be drawn entirely from the Indian service, as the India Office envisaged, was inappropriate for a subject which affected the British empire as a whole. 'The military forces of the Empire can no longer be adequately considered departmentally or even territorially. Their case is now in some respects parallel to that of the British Fleet which though organised and administered by the Admiralty in London is not concerned purely with the defence of the United Kingdom ... the Imperial General Staff alone can fix India's responsibilities to the Empire and co-ordinate the whole question of Imperial defence in one comprehensive scheme.'[15] He suggested a different set of names with British Army officers forming the majority.

Montagu decided to adopt a policy midway between these two extremes. He told the Government of India that the committee must have a wider focus than merely internal affairs, and that therefore he, not the C-in-C, India, would appoint it.[16] At the same time, he replied to the War Office that he disagreed with the CIGS and that the primary object for which the Army in India was maintained and paid for out of Indian revenues was the defence and internal security of India. Imperial defence could be taken into account only after these needs had been met.[17]

Montagu decided in June 1919 that the badly needed reorganisation of the Army in India could not wait indefinitely for a massive paper on imperial defence and proceeded with his own committee. Neither Birdwood nor his suggested replacement, Haig, was available and the committee was presided over by Viscount Esher. This influential nobleman had, in the earlier part of the century, played an important part in reforming the British Army and War Office and in establishing the Committee of Imperial Defence, a body enabling the Prime Minster to co-ordinate all departments of state in the preparation and conduct of war. He was a friend of Haig and had been a member of the Indian Reform Committee from which the Montagu-Chelmsford reforms had proceeded. Although by inclination a reformer (he was a keen supporter of the proposal which eventually, in 1935, replaced the Council of India by an advisory body without any real power), he was not a political progressive. His committee was made up of British officers, with the Indian civil administration represented by Sir Michael O'Dwyer, a provocation to nationalist opinion. A sign of the changing times came with Montagu's decision to enlarge Esher's committee by the addition of three Indian members, Sir Krishna Gupta and Sir Dinshaw Wacha, representing the Westernised professional and commercial classes, and Umar Hayar Khan, representing the traditional martial aristocracy of the Punjab.

Esher had no interest in the Indian Army as a separate force. He made his attitude quite clear in his invitation to Field Marshal Sir William Robertson (CIGS 1915–1918) to 'come and talk to my Indian Committee ... There would be great resistance by the Government of India to the principle that the

General Staff is one and indivisible ... I refuse to go to India, I am too old' (he was, indeed, sixty-seven years of age). 'There are also other reasons.'[18] These reasons were, as he told the new CIGS, Field Marshal Sir Henry Wilson, 'If I go with my Committee *en bloc* to Delhi we shall most of us be captured by the hospitality of the Viceroy ... I shall send only a small delegation to get local information on subsidiary questions.'[19] To Curzon, who complained at not being invited to give evidence, he replied that only soldiers were being consulted.[20]

The committee submitted the first part of its report on 2 November 1919. It began by reprising the idea of some kind of unified imperial defence organisation. 'We cannot consider the administration of the Army in India otherwise than as part of the total armed forces of the Empire, yet we have no indication of the form of organisation which may be set up in the future for the control of other parts of those forces, or the whole.' It argued that during the world war an 'Imperial Cabinet' performing 'real functions of Imperial Government' had come into being, 'accepted apparently without demur by the united peoples'. From this rather questionable statement, Esher and his colleagues went on to envisage a truly Imperial General Staff, with a new Imperial Naval Staff and Imperial Air Staff and even an Imperial Foreign Office, under the leadership of the British Prime Minister of the day, but (unlike the War Office, Admiralty and Foreign Office which before the war had effectively functioned as Imperial bodies) as agents of a body not exclusively responsible to the Westminster Parliament. He therefore recommended close connections between the War Office and the Army in India. The practice of the C-in-C, India, corresponding directly with the CIGS should be recognised as a permanent right, he said, only copies going to the Secretary of State for India. The military secretary at the India Office should be a deputy CIGS, a high-ranking officer of 'Indian experience' (i.e. not necessarily of the Indian Army) and have the right to attend the Army Council when Indian matters were discussed. He should be appointed by the Secretary of State for India on the recommendation of the CIGS.

In accordance with his earlier preferences, Esher recommended that the Council of India should cease to have members of high military rank. 'It is undesirable that the Secretary of State for India should be left in any doubt as to the quarter from which military advice should be offered him ... The sole responsible military adviser of the Secretary of State should be the Chief of the Imperial General Staff.' The CIGS would act either through his DCIGS at the India Office or in person, and have the right to attend meetings of the Council of India when military matters were discussed. The C-in-C, India, would look to the CIGS for directions in imperial military matters affecting India, and the Governor-General would look to the C-in-C, India, for advice on Indian military matters. Thus 'unity of military policy will at last be established between Great Britain and India.'[21]

Further steps in the direction of unity were recommended. The Committee of Defence set up in India during the war was to be given a permanent secretariat just as the Committee of Imperial Defence had been in 1905 and the two committees should deal directly with each other. The idea of appointing a civilian member of the Governor-General's Council for the Army Department was firmly rejected and instead it was proposed to merge that department with Army HQ, leaving the C-in-C, India, the sole Military Member of council as before, but no longer filling two separate offices. The post of Secretary to the Government of India in the Army Department would be abolished because, like those of other departments, he was constitutionally secretary to the Government of India as a whole and therefore had the right of access to the Governor-General, 'thus rendering possible an interference with the sole right of the Commander in Chief to offer advice'. The C-in-C was instead to have a military council of his principal staff officers, though these would have no collective responsibility such as that held by the Army Council in London. He was to have a Chief of General Staff, appointed on the advice of the CIGS, to undertake his office duties while the C-in-C was absent on inspection tours. The C-in-C was never to take command in the field in war. 'We are too well aware of the inconvenience and danger created in 1914 by stripping the War Office of its most experienced advisers.' Finally, though remaining an extra-ordinary member of the Governor-General's Council, he was to be excused attendance except when military business was discussed.

Montagu's reaction was far from favourable. He agreed to relax India Office control over Indian Army matters and to forego it completely in respect of the British Army in India, but was not prepared to see any extension of the direct communication between the C-in-C, India, and CIGS. He would not allow it to extend to domestic administrative matters. 'Nor should War Office and Commander in Chief initiate measures of military policy over our heads.'[22] He would not accept Indian military posts being filled at the CIGS's nomination, nor was he keen on the amalgamation of Army HQ and the Army Department. If there was an objection to its secretary being a soldier, then why not, he asked, let him be a civil servant? It would be 'intolerable and disastrous' for the CIGS to give orders to the Army in India before consulting the India Office and the Government of India. 'Projects for making the Indian Army more efficient for Imperial purposes might easily destroy its indigenous character, its popularity, and its domestic usefulness. I am averse to giving War Office greater control in India than it could obtain in a self-governing dominion.'[23]

Chelmsford took a broadly similar view. He was happy to see the end of the Military Members of the Council of India, agreeing that the idea of a second adviser was bad in principle and adding that advice from the Council of India was liable to be out of date. He saw advantages in the Secretary of the India Office's military department being a DCIGS, as ill-feeling occurred when he (technically on behalf of the Secretary of State) overruled the C-in-C, which would be less marked if he were seen to be acting for the CIGS. The CIGS, however, must instruct the C-in-C as the representative of the War Cabinet or Committee of Imperial Defence, not of the War Office. He pointed out that the Indian Defence Committee set up during the war was a less formal body than the CID in London. To make the secretary a permanent member rather than an ordinary staff appointment would be to revive the second military adviser in India. He was prepared, unlike Montagu, to see the Army Department merged with Army HQ, but insisted on retaining a Secretary to government in the new organisation.[24] The Secretary should, however, no longer be a soldier but a civil servant, a change he felt long overdue. 'You know how difficult it is for a military officer of inferior rank to stand up against his superiors, but it is quite a different case where a civilian can point out a different point of view.'[25]

There matters rested until Esher's committee met Chelmsford in India in February 1920. Without Esher at their head the members of his committee were in a weak position and had to listen while Chelmsford complained that there were still 180,000 Indian troops serving in areas controlled by the CIGS and that India had no say in their retention or return and that protests had proved of no avail. He warned that the new Indian Legislative Assembly would take an interest in military matters and would object to Indian soldiers serving overseas in some imperial force. At the same time he feared that a forceful Secretary of State for War might attempt to make India pay for a greater share of such a force than India needed, or station it in India at Indian expense. He stressed that the Military Secretary at the India Office must be from the Indian Army (the committee said they had not discussed this point). He said that it was not the case that the C-in-C had swallowed up the Army Department but vice versa. The work of the Army Member was so onerous that he could not get through it, and Chelmsford therefore welcomed the idea of setting up a new Department for Supply (the committee said this was only one of their options). He repeated that the new Army Secretary must be a civil servant, as no military man considered that a junior officer had the right to express an opinion in the presence of a senior one. He added that it was a matter of regret that military rank had been given to businessmen and others who had been brought into Army HQ in the war on account of their special expertise, as this had led to their opinion being discounted by officers of higher military rank. 'His Excellency held very strong views with regard to the chaos prevailing at Army Headquarters,' but considered that, because of the seniority question, no military man could remedy them as a departmental

Secretary unless he held the rank of field marshal, so it was therefore essential for this post to be held by a civil servant.[26]

When his committee returned from India, Esher pressed for a Cabinet decision on Part One of its report before it went on to write the rest. His influence in the post-war world was, however, on the wane, and he was told that his idea of a CIGS who would be to the self-governing dominions what Marshal Foch had been to the Allies at the end of the war was premature, and he must base his findings on the existing constitution. The essence of the matter was, as Montagu told the Committee of Imperial Defence, that 'The Indian Army, in so far as it is paid for out of Indian revenues, is as much the property of India as the armies of Australia and Canada are the property of those dominions.'[27] The War Office, however, continued to take the view that 'the only sound and economical method of imperial defence is to regard the forces of any portion of the Empire as being available for use in any other',[28] a view which, while militarily reasonable, entirely disregarded the constitutional position of the military in British India, past, present and, with the introduction of the Montagu-Chelmsford reforms, certainly the future.

Most of Esher's findings were accepted by the Government of India. The majority of the committee (seven against four, including Esher himself) reported in favour of a new civil Member of the Governor-General's Council, with responsibility for a Department of Supply. This was implemented despite the opinion of the minority that this would mean a revival of the old Military (or, at least, Military Supply) Member. The critical difference was the new Member would not be a soldier and therefore could not be seen as a rival source of military opinion. The Army Department, however, remained separate from Army HQ, and the Secretary of the Department remained a secretary to the Government of India as a whole, though still a senior serving soldier.

These decisions brought a strong dissenting minute signed by Cox, the Military Secretary at the India Office, and Sir G. Fell, both of whom had been members of the Esher Committee. In response to the objections to their proposal to increase the influence of the CIGS over the C-in-C India, they wrote: 'Unless all idea of uniformity of Military Policy between Great Britain and India is to be given up it is difficult to see what other method of securing this object could be found which would be less likely to prove irksome to the Government of India.' As for the refusal to abolish the Army Department and downgrade the position of its Secretary: 'There was no subject on which there was so strong a consensus of military opinion on the Committee as that relating to the Secretary. So long as the Army Department in any shape or form continues to exist, it cannot be said that the dual attributes of the Commander-in-Chief have been abolished ... The idea that the views of the Commander-in-Chief and his Principal Staff Officers can be better communicated and explained to the Viceroy through the medium of an officer, whether military or civil, of lower rank and status, is one which is peculiarly obnoxious to the military mind.'[29]

The objections to the combination of the duties of Army Member and C-in-C in the same person which had been said to underlie the disasters of the Mesopotamian campaign were ignored. Despite increasing pressure of business in Council arising from constitutional progress, the two posts were held in conjunction until almost the end of the British period. In fact, the monopoly of military influence held by the C-in-C was enhanced by the decision in 1921 that the Army Department Secretary should be, after all, a civil servant and not a soldier.[30] This change at least had the merit of meeting the military argument (which even Kitchener had never raised) that a serving officer could not act as secretary to the Government of India because he would thereby have access to the Governor-General independently of the C-in-C. It also accepted Chelmsford's view of the Army Department, that military's obsession with deference to those of higher rank meant that only a civil servant could carry out the duties of the post satisfactorily.

The Montagu-Chelmsford reforms, expressed in the Government of India Act of 1921, gave India a new constitution. The Governor-General was still responsible to the Secretary of State for India, but his executive council, appointed by the Secretary of State, would in future contain at least three Indian members of its total of seven (inclusive of the C-in-C). The old Legislative Council was replaced by a Legislative Assembly to which the members were elected on the basis of a property qualification from a variety of general or communal constituencies. In some subjects, derided by nationalists as 'parish-pump issues', the Assembly had much the same powers as had the House of Commons to vote or withhold supplies and thus a measure of democratic control was achievable. In all the important ones, such as defence, the British retained power in official hands and the Assembly had no powers other than to pass resolutions. Nevertheless, the skill of Indian politicians, many of them lawyers, enabled them to ensure that, even though they might in the last resort be overruled, they could exert a strong political influence and have their views taken into account. As defence spending made up 32 per cent of the Indian budget, compared with a pre-war 25.7 per cent, their voice could not be lightly disregarded.

In its first session, in March 1921, the Assembly passed a series of fifteen resolutions on defence proposed by Sir P.S. Sivaswamy Aiyer, a moderate with an interest in military matters. In essence, these stated that the purposes of the Army in India should be to defend India against external aggression and to maintain internal peace, and that its organisation and equipment should be the same as, and no less efficient than, that of the British Army. The old principle of keeping the Indian Army inferior to the British in case of another

Mutiny was thus implicitly rejected. These resolutions also spelt the end of the War Office's dreams of using Indian troops other than for the defence of India itself, to the disgust of the CIGS, Sir Henry Wilson.

The major reason for the high cost of the Indian Army at this time was the military and political pressure to bring it up to modern standards. After the scandals arising from the Mesopotamia campaign, public opinion expected Indian soldiers to be given conditions of service, medical treatment, etc., up to the level of those in Western armies. The Government of India itself pointed out that an army well-equipped, well-paid, well-clothed, and well-housed, would be both more efficient and more contented.[31] The most immediate effect of this was the abolition of the silladari system (whereby horses etc. were obtained regimentally), and the re-mustering of all cavalry regiments on the regular pattern, which had survived only in the last three former Madras cavalry units.

The post-war re-organisation of the Army took place in 1922. The main aim was to improve the system of reserves and reinforcements. The Indian infantry was re-organised into twenty regiments, each with an average of five combat battalions and a training battalion (numbered the 10th), each the successor of a previous single-battalion regiment. The Gurkha Rifles remained in a separate line of ten regiments each of two battalions and a depot. The total combat strength, including pioneers, thus amounted to 107 battalions. At the same time the Indian cavalry was reduced, by amalgamations, from thirty-six to twenty-one regiments, an early recognition of the diminished importance of this arm in the changed pattern of warfare. These reductions allowed comparable cuts in the number of British units (in the cavalry from nine to six, and in the infantry from fifty-one to forty-five), without disturbing the ratio of British to Indian troops. Artillery, apart from the mountain batteries, remained exclusively in British hands.

In the same year a Retrenchment Committee headed by the Earl of Inchcape ordered savings regardless of the army's commitments. They were dictated solely by the amount of money (50 crores of rupees) that the financiers were prepared to make available. Further reductions in strengths were the inevitable result, and when in 1923 it was decided to achieve this by disbanding an entire regiment rather than single battalions from several regiments, it came as no surprise that the choice fell upon that of Madras. (The British remained obsessed by the martial class theory, and now used it to justify their resistance to claims by nationalist politicians for greater association with the conduct of military affairs.) Other defence cuts included a ten per cent reduction in artillery, savings on expenditure on hospitals, transport, training establishments, the consumption or sale of reserves of equipment, and reductions in messing. The result of Inchcape's short-sighted policy was that by 1927 the Army in India was declared by its C-in-C to be ineffective for war and an extra ten crores of rupees had to be voted with a view to its being re-equipped within the following four years.

Demands by Indian nationalists for further constitutional progress continued unabated. The Simon Commission, appointed to examine this question, alienated Indian opinion by omitting to include any Indians in its membership. When touring India in 1928–29 it was greeted with boycotts and anti-British demonstrations. In 1929 the British declared that the goal of their policy in India was the achievement of dominion status there, but refused to accept Mahatma Gandhi's call for this to be granted immediately. A civil disobedience campaign followed, which in many places turned into rioting. The Governor-General, Lord Irwin, achieved a truce with the nationalists and organised a Round-Table conference in January 1931. The Prime Minister, Ramsay MacDonald, agreed to recognise the principle of the executive becoming responsible to the Indian Legislature, but clashes between Hindu and Muslim organisations, disputes within the Indian National Congress itself, and the election of the Conservative National government in the United Kingdom all worked to prevent agreement. The second session of the Round-table conference achieved nothing. Gandhi was arrested, and by April 1932 there were nearly 35,000 other political prisoners in Indian gaols. Most of these were released in the following July, after the third session of the Round-table conference, where further reforms were agreed, leading to the Government of India Act of 1935.

The Government of India's inability to pay for its army without reductions in other government services, or additional taxation, both of which were politically unacceptable, forced the British government to admit that a proportion of the troops really were kept up for British rather than local Indian purposes. In 1933 it accepted the findings of a tribunal under Lord Garran that the British Treasury should pay to India £1,500,000 annually as a military subsidy, the first time a part of the cost of the military in British India was shouldered by the British themselves.

Although the Act was a significant step in the achievement of Indian self-government, the British still retained control of defence, law and order, and foreign policy. The electorate was enlarged from 1,000,000 to 30,000,000, with women enfranchised equally with men. The eleven provinces each had legislatures elected by popular vote, but governors could still exercise reserved powers over them. At the centre, the Governor-General could still overrule the Legislative Assembly if the necessity arose, and the Secretary of State for India, answerable to the Westminster Parliament, remained supreme. A vital part of the new constitution, the establishment of a federal system with central government made up of representatives from the provinces of British India, and from the princely states, came to nothing when the princes could not agree upon the terms by which they would join. The main military changes at this time were that the Army Department became the Defence Department, though still headed by the C-in-C, India, and that Burma ceased to be part of the Indian empire. The 20th Burma Rifles ceased to be part of the Indian Army and the Government of India saw no more reason to accept responsibility for the defence of Burma than it had for Ceylon, a British dependency under the Colonial Office.

Demands for military reforms were no less pressing than those for political ones. A modernisation committee chaired by Major General Auchinleck of the Indian Army reported in October 1938 that 'since the year 1934 when the process of modernisation may be said to have begun in earnest in other armies, the value of the Army in India ... has decreased to an alarming extent in comparison with the armies of first class powers, and is also showing a tendency to fall behind the forces of such minor states as Egypt, Iraq, and Afghanistan'.[32] It was, said Auchinleck, 'unfit to take the field against land or air forces equipped with up-to-date weapons'. Mechanisation had proceeded only to the extent that four British cavalry regiments were being re-equipped with light tanks and two Indian ones with armoured cars. Every other combat unit still relied upon animals for its transport. While the British Army else-where had begun to modernise, in India it had not, so that drafts reaching the units there had to be retrained with obsolete weapons and tactics, while units leaving India had to be re-armed and retrained on joining a British formation. At the same time, it would be inefficient to have modernised British and unmodernised Indian units in the same brigades, and although homogeneous brigades were possible in theory (as Kitchener had advocated) they were not in practice (as he had found) because their barracks were in the wrong place. Nor would Indian politicians agree to India paying for the expensive modern-isation of the British contingent in India while Indian units were left un-modernised. The relegation of the Indian Army to the role of a 'glorified constabulary' (which it had in effect been for fifty years after the Mutiny) would, he said, destroy its morale and make it useless for wider imperial purposes.

Auchinleck identified five different functions which the Army in India was required to undertake. These were: frontier defence, coastal defence, internal security, the provision of a general reserve, and the conduct of operations beyond India's borders. He considered the idea of maintaining separate, specialist forces for each of these, only to reject them in favour of the existing unified army which had evolved over the years by the amalgamation of just such bodies. Separate forces cost more, he said, and would develop their own tactics and organisation so that interchanging units or personnel would become difficult. The advantage lay with troops that could perform any role. Although insisting that air forces could only supplement, not replace, land forces for frontier defence, he was in favour of replacing most of the coastal artillery by aircraft and thought that two squadrons, which could if necessary also be used for frontier defence, would be enough for this, leaving the other six then in India for service on the frontier or elsewhere. The possibility of attack by Afghan airmen flying German or Italian aircraft, or even from German or Italian airmen operating from bases in Afghanistan, was considered to represent more of a threat to civilian morale and British prestige than to military operations, but he nevertheless asked for three anti-aircraft batteries instead of the half-battery then stationed in India.

His proposals were for a scheme of modernisation and mechanisation to be completed within five years. This was for an army with six light tank regiments (two British and four Indian), four armoured car regiments and seven 'motor regiments' (all Indian) from which cavalrymen would fight on foot. The artillery, replacing their horses with tractors and cars, would consist of six British and two Indian field regiments plus one anti-tank and three anti-aircraft batteries (all British) and five regiments of mountain artillery (all Indian with pack mules). The infantry would consist of thirty-four British and seventy-five Indian battalions with mechanical instead of animal transport. This force was intended solely to meet the needs of the defence of India and internal security, and made no allowances for a surplus to be available for overseas expeditions. The report envisaged that two horsed cavalry regiments, two field artillery regiments and five battalions, all from the British Army, together with five Indian battalions, might be stationed in India for such purposes, as long as the British government rather than the Indian government paid for them. This left a surplus of three horsed cavalry regiments and sixteen battalions of the Indian Army, who would be disbanded, and, from the British Army, one horsed cavalry regiment, three horse batteries, five field artillery regiments, four battalions of infantry, and five companies of the Royal Tank Corps, all to be sent out of India and disposed of by the War Office.

Faced with the deteriorating international situation, the British government set up a committee headed by Admiral of the Fleet Lord Chatfield, to examine the best way of rearming and reorganising the forces in India. His terms of reference drew attention to the increased cost of modern weapons and to the limited resources available in India for defence purposes.[33] The committee met in London in October 1938 and proceeded to India where it toured for three months during the cold weather before submitting its report in February 1939. Its tour was boycotted by the Congress Party and by the Muslim League. Both argued that the cost of the British contingent in India was an unfair burden on Indians, as it was an army of occupation used to subjugate India, that it was not needed for India's protection, and its presence was inconsistent with British declarations of progress towards self-government. Chatfield dismissed this as 'a striking ignorance of the true facts or a refusal to admit them', and said that not only was India dependent on a British naval and military presence for her defence against foreign attack, but that British units should remain to maintain law and order in view of the rising communal tension between Hindus and Muslims.

Chatfield reported that the political outlook for defence questions was gloomy. The elected legislature, with no control over the executive in defence matters, could only criticise. If federation were to be achieved, federal ministers might restrain their followers even though defence was still to be reserved for the Governor-General. In fact, Congress was insisting that this subject should not be reserved but instead come under an elected federal minister. Congress wanted a national army open to all classes, as a way of reducing the disproportionate percentage of Muslim soldiers, or else a militia force which would, reflecting the balance of population, be predominantly Hindu and under the control of Congress ministers. If the British gave up control of defence, said Chatfield, the result would be 'a sectional oligarchy in unlimited power'.

Chatfield also had to admit the consequence of British politicians having for twenty years paid more regard to the Treasury than to the Admiralty. 'It is by no means impossible', he reported, 'that owing to the circumstances of war a considerable period might elapse before the Navy could establish command of the Indian Ocean; and that during this period India's coasts and her trade might be exposed to attacks. The fact must be faced that Great Britain may not now be in a position to guarantee India's external security.'[34] No more damning indictment could be found of the decline of the British hegemony of South Asia. It was naval power alone, by the exclusion of other Europeans, that had allowed the British to build up their empire in India, to concentrate their army on the only practicable inland invasion routes, and to move that army wherever else it was wanted in furtherance of British policies. India had been told for generations that the benefits of British rule and the compensation for funding British investments included a sure defence at sea by the Royal Navy. If the British could no longer perform that function of government which they most doggedly reserved for themselves, defence, there was no longer any justification, moral or practical, for their retention of it.

Chatfield introduced a new term, 'external defence', for the use of troops, on the Indian establishment, in overseas campaigns. The troops maintained for this purpose (conforming to those suggested by Auchinleck, almost all of whose proposals were adopted by Chatfield) were to form an imperial reserve division, though this title was not to be used as it implied a distinction between Indian and Imperial needs. It was to have the most modern equipment, but units might rotate through it, to achieve the widest benefit. In recognition of its 'imperial' purpose, however, the British subsidy for the cost of this division would be increased from £1,500,000 to £2,000,000 per annum.

Indian politicians had demanded that if units were to be disbanded those selected should be the 'foreign' ones (British and Gurkhas) rather than Indian, but the only concession made by Chatfield to the nationalist opinion was to recommend none of the Indianised units be considered for disbandment. They were now judged efficient as long as all their field officers were British, an arrangement expected to last until 1945: 'When that stage is reached the whole experiment will have to be reviewed.' Chatfield also recommended against any actual reductions for at least a year, in view of the international situation. The cost of mechanisation, etc., was estimated at Rs 45 crores (£34,000,000) payable by the United Kingdom over a five-year period – 75 per cent as a gift, 25 per cent as an interest-free loan. In return for rearming at British expense, India allotted one-tenth of her army to external defence anywhere between Suez and Singapore.

On 3 September 1939 Lord Linlithgow, the Governor-General, issued a proclamation that India was at war with Germany. He alienated Indian political leaders by failing even to make a gesture of prior consultation which might well have achieved their full co-operation. Anxious to achieve democracy for themselves, few had any sympathy for the cause of fascism. Both Congress and the Muslim League asked for a definition of war aims, but when Linlithgow was unable to provide one, the ministers of all seven provinces where Congress held the majority resigned and their British governors assumed full control of the administration. In March 1940 Congress resolved to give no support to the war unless the British promised to grant independence without delay, and the Muslim League riposted with a call for the partition of an independent India into separate states, allowing Muslims to avoid living under Hindu rule. The British authorities were still not ready to concede that full independence, with or without partition, was near enough to be considered, at least while they were at war.

The shock of British defeats in Malaya and Burma in 1942 was profound. Extreme nationalists felt that the whole edifice of India might fall, just as had that of the Dutch in the East Indies and the French in Indo-China. The 'Quit India' riots of August-September 1942 caused widespread disruption of communications in Bengal, Bihar, and the United Provinces, requiring the use of fifty-seven battalions in internal security duties before order was restored. More serious was the defection of 20,000 Indian prisoners of war to join the Indian National Army, which the Japanese promised would lead the march on Delhi. Many of these men, especially the officers, felt they had been betrayed by the British, who sent them to war without modern weapons, under the leadership of poor generals. As in the Mutiny of 1857, some were genuine patriots, some were opportunists, some were anti-British, some just went along with their comrades. The majority defied their Japanese captors and suffered the same brutal treatment afforded to their British fellow prisoners.

Political and strategic considerations again combined to bring changes in the Indian military machine. In the summer of 1941 the Governor-General's Council was enlarged to twelve, of whom one was the C-in-C and eight were Indians, who thus for the first time outnumbered the British in council. In March 1942 a Cabinet mission led by Sir Stafford Cripps offered to give every seat in the Council to Indians except that of the C-in-C, and to divide responsibility for the Defence Department between the C-in-C as 'War Member', and an Indian 'Defence Member'. Although the Cripps Mission failed in its main aim, this last proposal was implemented by July, with the addition to Council of three more Indian members, of whom one, Sir Firoz Khan Noon, became member for the Defence Department. The C-in-C (now Sir Archibald Wavell) sat as Member for War, with the division of responsibilities between the two similar to that which had obtained in the period before the Curzon-Kitchener controversy.

In 1943 it was decided that a new Allied South East Asia Command (SEAC) should be set up to conduct operations against Japan, and that the C-in-C, India, (India Command) should concentrate on the training and organisation of the expanded army of India. Wavell was judged unsuitable for SEAC, having been defeated in the Middle East and in his most recent offensive in Arakan. He was instead nominated as Governor-General in succession to Linlithgow. Auchinleck, who had succeeded him as C-in-C, Middle East, returned as C-in-C, India, the post he had previously held from January to June 1941. Among Wavell's first problems was the famine in Bengal. The loss of Burma caused a shortage of rice, the staple grain. Reliance on market forces failed, because much coastal shipping which could have brought supplies from elsewhere in India had been sunk by Japanese attacks, and many smaller vessels had been impounded in case they fell into Japanese hands in an invasion which never materialised. Railways had largely been given over to military traffic and earlier economies had taken their toll of rolling stock and installations. Wavell intervened to institute a system of rationing, and used the Army to distribute food stocks and provide aid for refugees. Still, over a million people died of starvation and associated diseases and the consequences were still being felt by the time that the war ended with victory over Japan in August 1945.

Among the unfinished business was the question of the men who had joined the INA. Some were considered to have been misled and were reinstated. The majority were given their back-pay and discharged. A few, mostly officers, were deemed to be collaborators and were court-martialled in the Red Fort at Delhi for bearing arms against the King-Emperor. The first batch, consisting of one Sikh, one Muslim, and one Hindu, allowed nationalist opinion to unite in defence of those who claimed to have been fighting for independence. Riots in Calcutta left thirty dead and hundreds injured. The defence, led by

Pandit Nehru and Bhulabhai Desai, displayed great forensic skill and the prosecution was visibly shaken. The accused were sentenced to life imprisonment, commuted by Auchinleck to cashiering with forfeiture of pay arrears. In the Indian Army, opinion was ambivalent, with the conservatives arguing that these men had broken their oath and that political views, in whatever cause, might be held but not acted upon by professional soldiers. Progressives, however, felt that patriotism came first. There was less sympathy, however, for Captain Burhanuddin, accused of having had a fellow officer beaten to death. A sensation was caused when the defence claimed that, as the brother of the Mehtar of Chitral, he was not a British Indian subject, and could not be tried by a British Indian court for offences committed outside British India. He was sentenced to seven years, actually spent in house arrest in his brother's palace. Auchinleck withstood political pressure for leniency in this and similar cases, arguing that, without punishment of the guilty, discipline would collapse and that faithful men would be aggrieved. The general amnesty of August 1947 allowed them to be released unnoticed. They were subsequently offered reinstatement with loss of seniority for the period of their INA service.

To the British government, the question was no longer one of if, but of how soon and to whom, sovereignty in India was to be handed over. On 2 September 1946 an interim government took the place of the Governor-General's Council, with Pandit Jawarhalal Nehru as Vice-President and Member for External Affairs, a portfolio previously held by the Governor-General alone. A leading Sikh minister, Sardar Baldev Singh, became Member for Defence, and the post of War Member previously held by the C-in-C was abolished. In October, the Muslim League agreed to join the government but refused to accept that any of the seats reserved for Muslims could be filled by Muslim members of Congress, whom it regarded as stooges of the Hindus. These events took place against a background of inter-communal disorders. Demonstrations called for by Mahatma Gandhi in accordance with the doctrine of non-violence generally became violent riots. The 'Calcutta killing' of August 1946 left thousands dead in the streets of the second city of the British empire. In October and November thousands more died as Hindus and Muslims attacked each other in Bengal, Bihar and the United Provinces, in what Nehru condemned as a competition in murder and brutality. In December Wavell told the Prime Minister, Clement Attlee, that the British must either re-establish direct rule and stay in India for at least another fifteen years, or withdraw their officials and garrisons from each province in turn, falling back to northern India before leaving the subcontinent altogether.[35]

Neither of these alternatives were acceptable. The Labour government, elected in 1945, had no mandate for the reconquest of India. The British

Army in India was composed mostly of men called up for the defence of their own country against fascist dictators. They now wanted to return to their interrupted lives at home, not to soldier on in a strange land where the continuation of British rule was as unpopular with them as, apparently, with the Indians themselves. Men of the Royal Air Force in India drawn, to much the same extent as the old Company's European troops had been, from the most intelligent and articulate sectors of the working class, followed their example by going on strike, in this case at the delay in their repatriation. The Indian Army too had become more politically aware than at any time since 1857. Auchinleck himself had publicly stated that every Indian officer ought to be a nationalist, at least in outlook. Indian soldiers, drawn from every kind of background during the war, had been exposed to modern political views and had been able to buy and read political articles on every railway station bookstall as they moved between their postings. At the same time, the idea of a retreat to the sea would both have injured British national pride and soured relations with whoever took over rule in the subcontinent, to the detriment of the hoped-for continuance of political, military, and commercial links. On 20 February 1947 Wavell's earlier offer to place his office at Attlee's disposal was taken up (at what he considered short notice) and the charismatic figure of Lord Louis Mountbatten, the King's cousin and the victorious Allied Supreme Commander in South East Asia, was appointed in his stead.

Mountbatten's appointment was accompanied by a declaration that the British would withdraw from India in June 1948. Nevertheless, deadlock continued between the Congress, which stood for the continued political unity of the subcontinent, and the League, which insisted that Muslims must have their own state, free from the fear of Hindu domination. Many Sikhs also held out for a state of their own, a successor to the Kingdom of Lahore annexed by the British a hundred years earlier. Each party by this time had large private armies, containing many ex-servicemen, used to discipline and practised in skill at arms. The Hindu Rashtriya Swayam Sewak Singh, or national self-defence squads, mustered 150,000 men, mostly in northern India. The Muslim National Guards, fighting for their own state, to be called Pakistan (the land of the pure in religion) consisted of 91,500 and the Sikhs of the Shiromani Akali Dal, 'the party of the disciples', amounted to 90,000. Mountbatten formed the view that partition of the Indian empire into two successor states, one with a mainly Muslim population, the other with a Hindu majority, was the only solution, and on 3 June 1947 announced that the Cabinet had decided to bring forward the date on which the British would hand over to the governments of these states to 14 August 1947. Treaties with Indian princes were abrogated as the British could no longer provide the protection which was stipulated in them, and the princes were advised to join one or other of the two new dominions. This plan was carried into effect on the appointed day, with scenes of general rejoicing and public ceremonial. At Lucknow the last British sappers cut down the flagstaff on which the Union flag had flown by day and night since 1858 and cemented over the base.

Partition of the Indian empire implied partition of its army. Auchinleck was slow to accept this, though he was well disposed towards the achievement of dominion status, perhaps more so than a C-in-C from the British Army might have been. He replaced British by Indian units on the North-West Frontier, and reorganised the Army to set up all-Indian formations. In November 1946 he decided to give Indian regular officers, none of whom had so far progressed beyond the rank of brigadier, accelerated promotion over the heads of British officers of the Indian Army, recognising that, with independence approaching, the British officers would have to leave. At the same time he ordered that any talk of partitioning the Indian Army was to be kept secret, because of the unsettling effect this would have on Muslim officers and sepoys.

Even when partition became probable, he still hoped to keep the army as some kind of supra-national organisation, at least for the period, which he at first estimated would take several years, while its assets, personnel, and responsibilities were equitably divided among those of its two successors. These, he believed, would be unable to provide an adequate defence capability until this was done. As the various installations and arsenals of British India were no longer divided evenly throughout the country (a result of the unification of the armies half a century earlier), an amicable division of these assets was essential if each side were to have its fair share. Auchinleck envisaged some kind of joint defence treaty, whereby some facilities might be pooled and remain for use of both sides, rather than be divided between them. Field Marshal Montgomery, the CIGS, visiting British troops in India in the autumn of 1946, afterwards said that he found Auchinleck concerned primarily with the future of the Indian Army and neglectful of the British troops in India at this time. This charge, rebutted by Auchinleck's admirers, may owe something to the superiority complex that the British Army always had in its approach to the Indian Army, even, as it seems, from one field marshal to another.

If the announcement of February 1947 came as a shock to Auchinleck and his officers, that of 3 June came as a bombshell. He was left with seventy-two days to 'reconstitute' the Indian Army, a term he chose in preference to 'divide', on the grounds (not entirely accurate) that its officers and men had long considered themselves a unified body, regardless of their creed or class. On 5 July he set up an Armed Forces Reconstitution Committee, whose terms of reference set out the principles on which partition would take place. Existing terms and conditions of service would be retained by those transferred to each new Army. If such terms were changed later, those who did not wish to accept them might resign with whatever benefits they had earned under British rule. Liability for pensions, etc. for Indian personnel would be accepted by the new states. No changes in nomenclature or the organisation of units would take place before the completion of reconstitution. British officers might stay longer than had been expected, in order to carry out this reconstitution. Auchinleck considered it essential to retain their goodwill and loyalty if the process were to go smoothly. Units with a majority of Muslims in the ranks were to be moved to stations in the future Pakistan (Sind, Baluchistan, North-West Frontier Province, Muslim areas of the Punjab, and East Bengal), and change places with those non-Muslim units serving there. Muslim companies, etc., of units leaving the future Pakistan, would change places with non-Muslim companies of units arriving there. Individual Muslims domiciled in areas outside Pakistan were not allowed to transfer to units which were not (or not about to be) stationed there. No non-Muslims were offered service in the future Army of Pakistan, which would be by definition an Islamic state where only believers might bear arms.

The Indian Independence Act received the royal assent on 18 July 1947. At the beginning of August new Commanders-in-Chief designate were appointed to the Armies of Pakistan (General Sir Frank Messervy) and of the Republic of India (General Sir Rob Lockhart). Mountbatten was designated the first Governor-General of the new Indian dominion. All British personnel of the old Indian Army were transferred to the British Army. The post of C-in-C, India, was abolished on the achievement of independence. Auchinleck remained in India as Supreme Commander to complete the reconstruction of the Army, but his powers of command were limited to British personnel, including British Army and RAF units, prior to their repatriation from India or Pakistan, and to units of the old Indian Army in transit between the two new dominions.[36] He also had ultimate responsibility for the Punjab Boundary Force, composed of Indian Army units, formed in a futile attempt to prevent the massacres and other horrors which resulted from the partition of the Punjab between the two new dominions.

British India ended on 15 August 1947. The military, British, Indian, Pakistani, and, later, Bangladeshi, all had greater or lesser parts to play in the various conflicts in South Asia that followed either immediately or at a later date. The British Army, after leaving the Indian subcontinent, was gradually driven from its other imperial garrisons by the same forces of nationalism that had ended the Indian empire. It unexpectedly found a new commitment in the form of a permanent peace-time garrison in the Federal Republic of Germany. For the following half-century, until the fear of the Russian invasion of North-West Germany diminished as quickly as had that of a Russian invasion of North-West India, the British Army of the Rhine followed the way of life of the British Army in India, with its separate camps, cantonments, and married quarters, its domestic and supporting civilian staff drawn from the local population, and many of the opportunities for recreation, travel, and financial rewards for spending long periods in a foreign land that had been associated with its Indian experience. During the same time span the Indian Army undertook campaigns from the Himalayas to Sri Lanka and from the Punjab to East Bengal. With an approximate strength of ten lakhs of men, it became the largest all-volunteer army in the world.

Notes

1. The Army in India and Its Evolution', p. 31 Percival Spear, *Oxford History of Modern India*, 1965, p. 335; S.P. Cohen, *The Indian Army. Its Contribution to the Development of a Nation*, Berkeley, Cal., 1971, p. 69.
2. Telegram from Viceroy to Secretary of State, 1 October 1914, *cit.* in Parliamentary Report of Mesopotamia Commission, Cd 8610 of 1917, p. 124.
3. Various telegrams, Gov. Gen. and C-in-C to India Office and War Office September 1914–January 1915, *cit.* in Mesopotamia Commission Report p. 124.
4. *Ibid.*, p. 125.
5. Of. in K. Jeffery, *The British Army and the Crisis of Empire 1918–22*, Manchester, 1984, p. 99.
6. 'Recruiting in India before and during the War of 1914–1918', Army HQ India 1919, *cit.* in Cohen, *op. cit.*, p. 69.
7. D. Dilks, *Curzon in India*, London, 1969–70, Vol. II, p. 252.
8. Minute by Barrow, August 1916, IOR L/MIL/17/5/1757.
9. *Ibid.*
10. Mesopotamia Commission Report Cd 8610, p. 116.
11. *Ibid.*, p. 107.
12. *Cit.* in Spear, *op cit.*, p. 336.
13. Sec. of State in Council to Gov.-Gen. in Council 2 December 1918, IOR L/MIL/7/5510.
14. Gov.-Gen. in Council to Sec. of State in Council 26 December 1918, IOR L/MIL/7/5510.
15. Secret Memo by CIGS, enc. in War Office letter to India Office, 11 February 1919, IOR L/MIL/7/5510.
16. Telegram to government of India in the Military Dept No. 773 dated 18 February 1919, IOR L/MIL/7/5510.
17. Secret Memo India Office to War Office 18 February 1919, IOR L/MIL/7/5510.
18. Esher to Robertson 14 August 1919, *cit.* in *Journals and Letters of Reginald Viscount Esher*, London, 1938, Vol. 4, pp. 241–2.
19. Esher to Wilson 16 August 1919, *ibid.* p. 242.
20. Esher to Curzon 9 November 1919, *ibid.* pp. 260–1.
21. Report of the Esher Committee Part 1, IOR 1VMIL/7/5510.
22. Telegram Sec. of State to Gov.-Gen. 10 December 1919, IOR L/MIL/7/5510.
23. *Ibid.*
24. Telegram Gov.-Gen. to Sec. of State of 6 January 1920, IOR L/MIL/7/5510.
25. Chelmsford to Montagu (pte) 18 December 1919, IOR L/MIL/ 7/5510.
26. Minutes of meeting held at Viceregal Lodge, Simla 7 February 1920, IOR L/MIL/7/5510.
27. Secret minute from Montagu to CID, 115–D 23 April 1920, IOR L/MIL/7/5510.
28. War Office to India Office 2 June 1920, IOR L/MIL/7/5510.
29. Minute by Gen. Sir H.V. Cox and Sir G. Fell, India Office 25 September 1920, IOR L/MIL/7/5510.
30. Government of India, *The Army in India and Its Evolution*, Calcutta, 1924, p. 54.
31. Gov. Gen. in Council to Sec. of State in Council Despatch 22 March 1920, IOR L/MIL/ 17/5/1793.

32. Report of Modernisation Committee, IOR L/MIL/17/5/1802.
33. Report of the Chatfield Cabinet Committee and associated correspondence, IOR L/MIL/17/5/1802.
34. *Ibid.*
35. Penderell Moon, *The British Conquest and Dominion of India*, London, 1989.
36. Margaret M. Wright, ed., *The Military Papers 1940–1948 of Field Marshal Sir Claude Auchinleck*, Bulletin of the John Rylands University Library, Manchester, 1988, pp. 339–40.

Presidents of the Board of Control for India, 1784–1858, and Secretaries of State for India, 1858–1947

	Ministry	*Appointed*
Henry Dundas (1st Viscount Melville)	Tory	1784
Viscount Castlereagh	Tory	1802
T. Grenville	All Talents	1806
2nd Viscount Melville	Tory	1807
Earl of Harrowby	Tory	1809
2nd Viscount Melville	Tory	1809
Earl of Buckingham	Tory	1812
George Canning	Tory	1816
C.B. Bathurst	Tory	1821
C.W.W. Wynn	Tory	1822
2nd Viscount Melville	Tory	1828
Lord Ellenborough	Tory	1828
Charles Grant	Whig	1830
Lord Ellenborough	Con.	1834
Sir J.C. Hobhouse	Whig	1835
Lord Ellenborough	Con.	1841
Lord Fitzgerald	Con.	1841
Earl of Ripon	Con.	1843
Sir J.C. Hobhouse	Whig	1846
Fox Maule	Whig	1852
J.C. Herries	Con.	1852
Sir Charles Wood	Lib.	1852
Lord Ellenborough	Con.	1858
Lord Stanley	Con.	1858
Sir Charles Wood (Lord Halifax)	Lib.	1859
Earl de Grey and Ripon	Con.	1866
Viscount Cranborne	Con.	1866

Sir Stafford Northcote	Con.	1867
Duke of Argyll	Lib.	1868
Marquess of Salisbury	Con.	1874
Gathorne Hardy (Lord Cranbrook)	Con.	1878
Marquess of Hartington	Lib.	1880
Earl of Kimberley	Lib.	1882
Lord Randolph Churchill	Con.	1885
Earl of Kimberley	Lib.	1886
Sir Richard (later Viscount) Cross	Con.	1886
Earl of Kimberley	Lib.	1892
H.H. Fowler	Lib.	1894
Lord George Hamilton	Con.	1895
St John Brodrick	Con.	1903
John (later Viscount) Morley	Lib.	1905
Earl of Crewe	Lib.	1910
Viscount Morley	Lib.	1910
Earl of Crewe	Lib.	1910
Austin Chamberlain	Coalition	1915
Edwin Montagu	Coalition	1917
Viscount Peel	Con.	1923
Sir S. (later Lord) Olivier	Labour	1924
Earl of Birkenhead	Con.	1924
Viscount Peel	Con.	1928
W. Wedgwood Benn	Labour	1929
Sir Samuel Hoare	National	1931
Marquis of Zetland	National	1935
L.S. Amery	Coalition	1940
F.W. (later Lord) Pethick-Lawrence	Labour	1945
Earl of Listowel	Labour	1946
	Office abolished, August 1947	

Governor-Generals in British India, 1774–1947

	Date of appointment
Warren Hastings, Esquire	October 1774
Sir John Macpherson	February 1785
Lieutenant General the Earl (Marquess) Cornwallis	September 1786 also C-in-C
Sir John Shore	1793
Sir A. Clarke	March 1798
Earl of Mornington (Marquess Wellesley)	May 1798
General the Marquess Cornwallis (second appt)	July 1805 (also C-in-C)
Sir George Barlow	October 1805
Baron (Earl of) Minto I	July 1807
General the Earl of Moira (Marquess of Hastings)	October 1813
John Adam, Esquire	January 1823
Baron (Earl) Amherst	August 1823
W.B. Bailey, Esquire	March 1828
General Lord William Bentinck	July 1828 (also C-in-C from October 1833)
Sir Charles Metcalfe	March 1835
Baron (Earl of) Auckland	March 1836
Baron (Earl of) Ellenborough	February 1842
W.W. Bird, Esquire	June 1844
Sir Henry (Viscount) Hardinge	July 1844
Earl (Marquess) of Dalhousie	January 1848
Viscount (Earl) Canning	February 1856
Earl of Elgin I	March 1862
General Sir Robert Napier	1863
Sir William Denison	1863
Sir John (Lord) Lawrence	January 1864
Earl of Mayo	January 1869
Sir John Strachey	1872

Note: Acting appointments are *in italics*.

Lord Napier of Merchistoun	1872
Baron (Earl of) Northbrook	May 1872
Baron (Earl of) Lytton I	April 1876
Marquess of Ripon	June 1880
Earl of Dufferin (Marquess of Dufferin and Ava)	December 1884
Marquess of Lansdowne	December 1888
Earl of Elgin II	January 1894
Baron (Marquess) Curzon	January 1899
Lord Ampthill	April 1904
Marquess Curzon (second appt)	December 1904
Major General the Earl of Minto II	November 1905
Baron Hardinge of Penshurst	November 1910
Baron Chelmsford	April 1916
Earl of Reading	April 1921
Lord Lytton II	1925
Lord Irwin	April 1926
Earl of Willingdon	April 1931
Sir George Stanley	1934
Marquess of Linlithgow	April 1936
Baron Brabourne	1938
Marquess of Linlithgow	1938
General Viscount (Earl) Wavell	1943
Sir John Colville	1945
Rear Admiral Viscount (Earl) Mountbatten	March–August 1947

Note: Acting appointments are *in italics*.

Commanders-in-Chief in the East Indies, 1748–1947

Rank and title on appointment	Assumed command
Major Stringer Lawrence	January 1748
Colonel John Adlercron	1754
Colonel Robert Clive (also Governor)	December 1756
Major John Cailland	February 1760
Major John Carnac	December 1760
Lieutenant Colonel Eyre Coote	April 1761
Major Thomas Adams	1763
Major John Carnac	January 1764
Major Hector Munro	July 1764
Brigadier General John Carnac	January 1765
Major General Lord Clive (also Governor)	April 1765
Colonel Richard Smith	January 1767
Brigadier General Sir Robert Barker	March 1770
Colonel Alexander Chapman	January 1774
Lieutenant General Sir John Clavering	November 1774
Lieutenant General Sir Eyre Coote	March 1779
Lieutenant General Robert Sloper	July 1785
Lieutenant General Earl Cornwallis (also Governor-General)	September 1786
Major General Sir Robert Abercromby	October 1793
Lieutenant General Sir Alured Clarke	March 1797
Lieutenant General Gerard Lake, later Lord Lake	March 1801
General Marquess Cornwallis (also Governor-General)	July 1805
General Lord Lake	October 1805
Lieutenant General George Hewitt	October 1807
Lieutenant General Sir George Nugent	January 1812
General Earl of Moira, later Marquess Hastings (also Governor-General)	October 1813
Lieutenant General the Honourable Sir Edward Paget	January 1823
General Lord Combermere	October 1825
General Earl of Dalhousie	January 1830

General Sir Edward Barnes	January 1832
General Lord William Bentinck	October 1833
(also Governor-General)	
Lieutenant General the Honourable Sir Henry Fane	September 1835
Major General Sir Jasper Nicolls	December 1839
General Sir Hugh Gough	August 1843
General Sir Charles Napier	May 1849
General Sir William Gomm	December 1850
General the Honourable George Anson	January 1856
Lieutenant General Sir Patrick Grant (officiating)	June 1857
General Sir Colin Campbell	August 1857
General Sir Hugh Rose	June 1860
General Sir William Mansfield	March 1865
General Lord Napier	April 1870
General Sir Frederick Haines	April 1876
General Sir Donald Stewart	April 1881
General Sir Frederick Roberts	November 1885
General Sir George White	April 1893
Lieutenant General Sir Charles Nairne (provisional)	March 1898
General Sir William Lockhart	November 1898
General Sir Arthur Palmer	March 1900
General Viscount Kitchener	November 1902
General Sir O'Moore Creagh	September 1909
General Sir Beauchamp Duff	March 1914
General Sir Charles Monro	October 1916
General Lord Rawlinson	November 1920
General Sir Claude Jacob (officiating)	April 1925
Field Marshal Sir William Birdwood	August 1925
General Sir Philip Chetwode	May 1930
General Sir Robert Cassels	May 1933
Lieutenant General Sir Claude Auchinleck	January 1941
General Sir Archibald Wavell	July 1941,
(re-appointed)	February 1942
General Sir Alan Hartley	January 1942
General Sir Claude Auchinleck	June 1943
(promoted to Field Marshal, June 1946)	
Office abolished 15 August 1947	

Appendix IV

Military Members of the Council of India, 1858–1929

Captain W.J. Eastwick	1858–61
Lieutenant Colonel H.C. Rawlinson	1858–59
Major General Sir R. Vivian	1858–74
Colonel Sir P. Cautley	1858–68
Colonel Sir H.M. Durand	1859–62
Colonel W.E. Baker	1861–76
Major General Sir H.C. Rawlinson	1868–95
Major-General E.B. Johnson	1874–77
Lieutenant-General Sir R. Strachey	1875–78
Colonel H. Yule	1876–89
Major-General Sir A. Wilde	1876–78
Major-General Sir G. Wolseley	1876–78
Colonel Sir W.L. Merewether	1877–80
Lieutenant General Sir H.W. Norman	1878–83
Lieutenant General Sir R. Strachey	1879–89
Lieutenant General C.J. Foster	1880–88
Major General Sir P. Lumsden	1883–93
Colonel Sir O.T. Burne	1887–96
Lieutenant General Sir A. Alison	1889–98
General Sir D.M. Stewart	1895–1900
General Sir J.J. Gordon	1897–1906
Lieutenant General A.R. Badcock	1901–07
Lieutenant Colonel Sir D. Barr	1905–15
General Sir C. Egerton	1907–17
General Sir E.G. Barrow	1917–24
General Sir Havelock Hudson	1924–29

Appendix V

Secretaries of the Military Departments of the Court of Directors, 1809–1858, and at the India Office, 1858–1947

Military ranks as at date of first appointment

Major James Salmond	1809–37
Philip Melville	1837–58
Colonel W.E. Baker	1859–61
Major General T.T. Pears	1861–77
Colonel A.B. Johnson	1877–89
Major General O. Newmarch	1889–99
Major General E. Stedman	1899–1907
Lieutenant General Sir O'Moore Creagh	1907–09
Lieutenant General Sir Beauchamp Duff	1909–14
General Sir Edmund Barrow	1914–17
Lieutenant General Sir Herbert Cox	1917–20
Lieutenant General Sir Alexander Cobbe	1920–25
Field Marshal Sir Claude Jacob	1926–30
General Sir Alexander Cobbe	1930–31
Major General S. Muspratt	1931–33
Lieutenant General Sir John Coleridge	1933–36
Major General R.C. Wilson	1937–38
Lieutenant General Sir Sydney Muspratt	1938–41
Brigadier R.M. Lockhart	1941–43
Lieutenant General G.N. Molesworth	1943–44
General Sir G.O. Mayne	1945–47
General Sir G.A. Scoones	1947

Military Members of the Governor-General's Council, 1834–1947

Ranks at date of appointment

Lieutenant Colonel W. Morison	1834–39
Major General W. Casement	1839–44
Major General Sir G. Pollock	1844–48
Major General J. Littler	1848–52
Major General J. Low	1853–58
Major General Sir J. Outram	1858–60
Major General Sir R. Napier	1861–65
Colonel H.M. Durand	1865–70
Major General H.W. Norman	1870–77
Major General Sir E.B. Johnson	1877–80
Major General Sir Samuel Browne	1877–78
General Sir Neville Chamberlain	1878–79
Lieutenant General Sir D.M. Stewart	1880–81
Major General T.F. Wilson	1881–86
Major General G.T. Chesney	1886–91
Lieutenant General Sir H. Brackenbury	1891–96
Major General Sir E.H. Collen	1896–1901
Major General Sir E.R. Elles	1901–05

Member for the Military Supply Dept

Major General C.H. Scott	1905–09

Members for the Defence Dept

Sir Firoz Khan Noon	1942–6
Sardar Balder Singh	1946–47

Note: Acting appointments are *in italics*.

Appendix VII

Secretaries to the Governments of India and Bengal in the Military Department, 1800–1906

Military ranks as on first appointment

Captain Lionel Hook	c. 1800–1807
John Richardson	1807–09
John Thornhill	1809–11
John Adam	1811–13
C.W. Gardiner	1813–17
Major J. Young	1817–19
Lieutenant Colonel W. Casement	1819–39
Lieutenant Colonel J. Stuart	1839–54
Colonel R. Birch	1854–61
Lieutenant Colonel H. Norman	1861–70
Colonel H. Burne	1870–80
Colonel G. Chesney	1880–86
Major General O. Newmarch	1886–88
Lieutenant Colonel E. Collen	1888–96
Major General P. Maitland	1896–1901
Major General E. Barrow	1901–03
Major General E. de Brath	1903–06

Secretaries to the Government of India in the Departments of Military Supply, the Army, Defence and War, 1907–1947

Military Supply Department
Colonel E. Maconchy   1906–09

Army Department
Major General A.W.L. Bayley   1906–09
Major General R.I. Scallon   1909–11
Major General M. Grover   1911–12
Major General W.R. Birdwood   1913–14
Brigadier General B. Holloway   1914–16
Major General A.H. Bingley   1916–21
Sir G. Fell   1921–23
E. Burdon   1923–26
G.M. Young   1926–32
G.R.F. Tottenham   1932–35

Defence Department
G.R.F. Tottenham   1935–36
Sir Charles Ogilvie   1936–45
A.D.F. Dundas   1945–47

War Department
C.M. Trivedi   1942–46

Bibliography

The writer of any history which seeks to cover events in an entire sub-continent over a period of three and a half centuries has so wide a field of sources upon which to draw as to make it impossible in a limited number of pages to do more than list those upon which the greatest reliance has been placed. These are, in order:

Official papers
India Office Records (IOR) in the India Office Library, part of the Oriental Collections of the British Library. These include dispatches and letters to and from the East India Company and its servants in India; between the Secretary of State for India in Council and the governments of India, Bengal, Madras and Bombay in their several departments; the Proceedings in those departments (minutes, reports, etc.) on which policies were formed, and Previous Communications ('pre-coms') between the Court of Directors of the East India Company and the Board of Control for the affairs of India. Those most consulted in the preparation of this work are the Military Department's series 5, 7 and 17, and, for the period 1939–47, the War Staff series. In the National Archives, formerly the Public Record Office (PRO), the War Office series WO 149 and 151 have been those most used.

Parliamentary papers
Command Papers, 'Blue Books', compiled from these official papers and laid before the Houses of Parliament each session in response to addresses or as a routine. These were frequently edited to excise sensitive material, but nevertheless generally form a convenient and detailed record of actual events as they were reported.

Private papers
The National Army Museum (NAM) contains the military papers of Field Marshals Lord Roberts, Sir Paul Haines, and Lord Rawlinson, all of whom were C-in-Cs, India. Manchester University holds the papers of Field Marshal Sir Claude Auchinleck, the last C-in-C India, and Supreme Commander, India and Pakistan. Of the Governor-Generals of India, those whose papers were consulted include the Marquess of Dalhousie (Scottish Record Office), and Lords Northbrook, Lytton, and Lawrence (India Office Library).

Doctoral theses on the Indian military
Bourne, J.M., 'The Civil and Military Patronage of the East India Company 1784–1858', Unpub. Ph.D., Leicester, 1978.
Bryant, G.J., 'The East India Company and its Army 1600–1778', Unpub. Ph.D., London, 1975.
Cameron, A.D., 'The Vellore Mutiny', Unpub. Ph.D., Edinburgh, 1984.
Crowell, L.M., 'The Madras Army in the Northern Circars 1832–33: Pacification and Professionalism', Unpub. Ph.D., Duke, 1982.
Davis, P.K., 'British and Indian Strategy and Policy in Mesopotamia 1914–1916', Unpub. Ph.D., London, 1981.

Greenhunt, J., 'Imperial Reserve: the Indian Infantry on the Western Front 1914–18', Unpub. Ph.D., Kansas, 1978.

Howlett, D.J., 'An End to Expansion: Influences on British Policy in India c. 1830–1860', Unpub. Ph.D., Cambridge, 1981.

Jackman, L., 'Afghanistan in British Imperial Strategy and Diplomacy 1919–1941', Unpub. Ph.D., Cambridge, 1980.

Jacobsen, M.H., 'The Modernisation of the Indian Army 1925–39', Unpub. Ph.D., California, 1979.

Leask, I.D., 'The Expansion of the Indian Army during the Great War', Unpub. Ph.D., London, 1989.

Peers, D.M., 'Between Mars and Mammon: the Military and Political Economy of British India at the time of the First Burma War 1824–6', Unpub. Ph.D., London, 1988.

Rawson, J.O., 'The Role of India in Imperial Defence Beyond Her Frontiers and Home Waters 1919–1939', Unpub. Ph.D., Oxford, 1976.

Sen, Amiya, 'The Structure and Organisation of the Bengal Native Infantry with Special Reference to Problems of Discipline', Ph.D., London, 1961 (pub. later).

Stanley, P., 'White Mutiny: the Bengal Europeans 1825–75', Australian National University, 1993.

Published books and articles

Ali, Imran, *The Punjab under Imperialism 1885–1947*, Princeton, NJ, 1988.

Allen, C. (ed.), *Plain Tales from the Raj*, London, 1977.

Archbold, W.A.J., *Outlines of Indian Constitutional History (British Period)*, London, 1926.

Arthur, G., *Life of Lord Kitchener*, 3 Vols, London, 1920.

Babington, A., *The Devil to Pay. The Mutiny of the Connaught Rangers in India–July 1920*, London, 1991.

Balfour, B. (Lady), *The History of Lord Lytton's Indian Administration 1876–80*, London, 1899.

Ball, C, *The History of the Indian Mutiny*, 2 Vols, London, 1858–59.

Ballhatchet, K.A., *Race, Sex and Class under the Raj. Imperial Attitudes and Policies and Their Critics 1793–1905*, London, 1980.

Barber, N., *The Black Hole of Calcutta. A Reconstruction*, London, 1965.

Barnes, J., and Nicholson, D. (eds), *The Empire at Bay. The Leo Amery Diaries 1929–45*, London, 1988.

Barrow, G. de S. (Lt.-Gen. Sir), *The Fire of Life. An Autobiography*, London, 1941.

Basham, A.L., *The Wonder That Was India. A Survey of the Culture of the Indian Subcontinent before the Coming of the Muslims*, London, 1954.

Bayly, C.A., *Rulers, Townsmen and Bazaars. North Indian Society in the Age of British Expansion, 1770–1870*, Cambridge, 1983.

Bayly, C.A., *The New Cambridge History of India, Vol. II.1, Indian Society and the Making of the British Empire*, Cambridge, 1988.

Bayly, C.A., *The Raj. India and the British 1600–1947*, London, 1990.

Beckett, I.F.W., *Riflemen Form. A Study of the Rifle Volunteer Movement, 1859–1908*, Aldershot, 1982.

Beckett, I.F.W., *The Amateur Military Tradition, 1558–1945*, Manchester, 1991.

Bence-Jones, M., *Clive of India*, London, 1974. Beveridge, H., *A Comprehensive History of India*, 3 Vols, London, 1865.

Birdwood, F.T., *The Sikh Regiment in the Second World War*, Norwich, 1953.

Birdwood, W. (Field Marshal Lord), *Khaki and Gown. An Autobiography*, London, 1941.

Blacker, V., *Memoir of the Operations of the British Army in India during the Mahratta War of 1817, 1818 and 1819*, London, 1821.

Blomfield, D. (ed.), *Lahore to Lucknow. The Indian Mutiny Journal of Arthur Moffat Lang*, London, 1992.

Bond, B., *The Victorian Army and the Staff College*, London, 1972.

Bosworth Smith, R., *Life of Lord Lawrence*, 2 Vols, London, 1885.

Branson, C, *British Soldier in India. The Letters of Clive Branson*, London, 1944.

Brock, W., *A Biographical Sketch of Sir Henry Havelock KCB*, London, 1858.

Broehe, W.G., Jr., *Crisis of the Raj. The Revolt of 1857 through British Lieutenants' Eyes*, Hanover, New Hampshire, 1986.

Broome, A., *History of the Rise and Progress of the Bengal Army*, Calcutta, 1850.

Bruce, F., *The Burma Wars 1824–1886*, London, 1973.

Burn, R. (ed.), *The Cambridge History of India, Vol. 4, The Mughal Period*, Cambridge, 1937.

Burton, R.G., *The Revolt in Central India*, Simla, 1908.

Burton, R.G., *The Mahratta and Pindari War*, Simla, 1910.

Burton, R.G., *The First and Second Sikh Wars*, Simla, 1911.

Butler, W.F., *The Life of Sir George Pomeroy-Colley 1835–81*, London, 1899.

Cadell, P., *History of the Bombay Army*, London, 1938.

Callahan, R., *The East India Company and Army Reform 1783–98*, Cambridge, Mass., 1972.

Candler, E., *The Sepoy*, London, 1919.

Cardew, A., *The White Mutiny*, London, 1929.

Cardew, F.G., *A Sketch of the Services of the Bengal Native Army to the Year 1895*, Calcutta, 1903.

Cassar, G.H., *Kitchener. Architect of Victory*, London, 1977.

Chaudhuri, K.N., *The Trading World of Asia and the English East India Company 1660–1760*, Cambridge, 1978.

Chaudhuri, N.C., *Clive of India. A Political and Psychological Essay*, London, 1975.

Cohen, S.P., *The Pakistan Army*, Berkeley, Cal., 1984.

Cohen, S.P., *The Indian Army. Its Contribution to the Development of a Nation*, Berkeley, Cal., 1971, reprinted as 2nd edn 1990.

Collen, E., *The Indian Army. A Sketch of Its History and Organisation*, Oxford, 1907.

Collier, R., *The Sound of Fury. An Account of the Indian Mutiny*, London, 1963.

Connell, J., *Auchinleck*, London, 1959.

Connell, J., *Wavell, Supreme Commander, 1941–43*, London, 1969.

Corr, G.H., *The War of the Springing Tigers*, London, 1975.

Das, M.N., *India under Morley and Minto*, London, 1964.

Datta, V.N., *Jallianwala Bagh*, Ludhiana, 1969.

Davies, A.M., *Warren Hastings. Maker of British India*, London, 1935.

Denholm, A., *Lord Ripon 1827–1909*, London, 1982.

Dilks, D., *Curzon in India*, 2 Vols, London, 1969–70.

Dodwell, H.H., (ed.), *The Cambridge History of India, Vol. 5, British India 1497–1858*, Cambridge, 1929.

Dodwell, H.H., (ed.), *The Cambridge History of India, Vol. 6, The Indian Empire 1858–1918*, Cambridge, 1932.

Duff, J.G., *A History of the Mahrattas*, 3 Vols, London, 1826.

Duffy, C.J., *The Military Experience in the Age of Reason*, London, 1987.

Dutton, D., *Austen Chamberlain. Gentleman in Politics*, Bolton, 1985.

East India Registers, published annually, London, 1807–57.

Edwardes, M., *A History of India*, London, 1961.

Edwardes, M., *Battles of the Indian Mutiny*, London, 1963.

Edwardes, M., *High Noon of Empire. India under Curzon*, London, 1965.

Edwardes, M., *Red Year. The Indian Rebellion of 1857*, London, 1973.

Edwardes, M., *Warren Hastings. King of the Nabobs*, London, 1976.

Elliot, H.M. and Dawson, J., *The History of India as Told by Its Own Historians*, 8 Vols, London, 1867–77.

Elsmie, G.R., *Field Marshal Sir Donald Stewart. An Account of His Life, Mainly in his Own Words*, London, 1903.

Ensor, R., *England 1870–1914*, Oxford, 1936.

Esher, O. (3rd Viscount) (ed.), *Journals and Letters of Reginald, Viscount Esher*, 4 Vols, London, 1938.

Farrington, A., *Guide to the Records of the India Office Military Department*, London, 1982.

Feiling, K., *Warren Hastings*, London, 1954.

Forbes, A., *Havelock*, London, 1890.

Forbes, A., *Colin Campbell, Lord Clyde*, London, 1895.

Forrest, G.W. (ed.), *Selections from the Letters, Despatches, and other State Papers Preserved in the Military Department of the Government of India 1857–58*, 3 Vols, Calcutta 1983–1902.

Forrest, G.W., *A History of the Indian Mutiny Reviewed and Illustrated from Original Documents*, 3 Vols, Edinburgh and London, 1904–12.

Forrest, G.W., *Life of Field Marshal Sir Neville Chamberlain*, Edinburgh, 1909.

Forrest, G.W., *Life of Lord Clive*, 2 Vols, London, 1918.

Foster, W., *A Guide to the India Office Records 1600–1858*, London, 1919.

Fox, R.G., *Lions of the Punjab. Culture in the Making*, Berkeley, Cal., 1985.

Furneaux, R., *Massacre at Amritsar*, London, 1963.

Gopal, S., *The Viceroyalty of Lord Ripon 1880–84*, London, 1953.

Goradia, N., *Lord Curzon. The Last of the British Moghuls*, Oxford, 1993.

Government of India, *The Army in India and Its Evolution*, Calcutta, 1924.

Government of India, *The Third Afghan War 1919. Official Account*, Calcutta, 1926.

Gough, C. and Innes, A.D., *The Sikhs and the Sikh Wars*, London, 1897.

Greenwood, A., *Field Marshal Auchinleck*, Durham, 1991.

Grimshaw, R., *Indian Cavalry Officer 1914–1915*, Tunbridge Wells, 1986.

Gubbins, M.R., *An Account of the Mutinies in Oudh*, 3rd edn, London, 1859.

Gupta, P.C., *Nana Sahib and the Rising at Cawnpore*, Oxford, 1963.

Hamid, S., *So They Fought and Rode*, Tunbridge Wells, 1983.

Hamid, S., *Disastrous Twilight. A Personal Record of the Partition of India*, London, 1986.

Haig, W., *The Cambridge History of India, Vol. 3, Turks and Afghans*, Cambridge, 1928.

Hannah, W.H., *'Bobs', Kipling's General. The Life of Field Marshal Earl Roberts of Kandahar VC*, London, 1972.

Hardinge, C. (2nd Viscount), *Viscount Hardinge and the Advance of British Dominion into the Punjab*, Oxford, 1900.

Hardy, P., *The Muslims of British India*, Cambridge, 1972.

Harrison, J.B., 'A Temporary Officer in a Temporary Battalion', *Indo-British Review*, Vol. 16, No. 1, 1989.

Heathcote, T.A., *The Indian Army. The Garrison of British Imperial India 1822–1922*, Newton Abbot, 1974.

Heathcote, T.A., *The Afghan Wars 1839–1919*, London, 1980.

Hewitt, J. (ed.), *Eye Witnesses to the Indian Mutiny*, Reading, 1972.

Holmes, T.R., *A History of the Indian Mutiny*, London, 1904.

Hunter, W.W., *The Indian Empire. Its Peoples, History and Products*, London, 1892.

Hutchinson, D. (ed.), *Chick's Annals of the Indian Rebellion 1857–58*, London, 1974.

Imperial Gazetteer of India, 25 Vols, Calcutta, 1909.

India Office Lists (Army and Civil) published annually, London, 1858– 1947.

Irvine, W., *The Army of the Indian Moghuls. Its Organisation and Administration*, London, 1903.

Jackson, D., *India's Army*, London, 1940.

James, D., *Lord Roberts*, London, 1954.

Jeffery, K., 'An English Barrack in the Oriental Seas?', *Modern Asian Studies*, 15:3 (1981).

Jeffery, K., *The British Army and the Crisis of Empire 1918–22*, Manchester, 1984.

Jocelyn, J.R.J., *The History of the Royal and Indian Artilleries in the Mutiny of 1857*, London, 1915.

Kadian, R., *India and Its Army*, New Delhi, 1990.

Kaye, J.W., *The Life and Correspondence of Major General Sir John Malcolm*, 2 Vols, London, 1856.

Kaye, J.W., *A History of the Sepoy War in India*, 3 Vols, London, 1877–80.

Keay, J., *The Honourable Company. A History of the English East India Company*, London, 1991.

Killingley, D.M., *Farewell the Plumed Troop. A Memoir of the Indian Cavalry 1919–45*, Newcastle upon Tyne, 1990.

King, L. (ed.), *Memoirs of Babur*, trans. Leyden and Erskine, 2 Vols, Oxford, 1921.

King, P., *The Viceroy's Fall. How Kitchener Destroyed Curzon*, London, 1986.

Kolff, D.H.A., *Naukar, Rajput and Sepoy. The Ethno-history of the Military Labour Market in Hindustan 1480–1850*, Cambridge, 1990.

Lambrick, H.T., *Sir Charles Napier and Sind*, Oxford, 1952.

Lawford, J.P. and Catto, W.E. (eds), *Solah Punjab. The History of the 16th Punjab Regiment*, Aldershot, 1967.

Lee-Warner, W., *Memoirs of Field Marshal Sir Henry Wylie Norman*, London, 1908.

Lees-Milne, J., *The Enigmatic Edwardian. The Life of Reginald, 2nd Viscount Esher*, London, 1986.

Lewis, R., *The Chief. Field Marshal Lord Wavell, Commander in Chief and Viceroy 1939–47*, London, 1980.

Llewellyn-Jones, R., *A Fatal Friendship. The Nawabs, the British and the City of Lucknow*, Delhi, 1985.

Lucas, C., *The Empire at War*, Vol. 5, Oxford, 1926.

Lyall, A., *Warren Hastings*, London, 1920.

MacLagan, M., *'Clemency' Canning. Charles John, 1st Earl Canning. Governor General and Viceroy of India 1856–1862*, Oxford, 1962.

MacMunn, G.F., *The Martial Races of India*, London, 1932.

MacMunn, G.F., *The Armies of India*, London, 1911.

Magnus, P., *Kitchener. Portrait of an Imperialist*, London, 1958.

Mainwaring, A., *Crown and Company. Historical Records of the 2nd Battalion Royal Dublin Fusiliers*, Aldershot, 1911.

Malleson, G.B., *The Indian Mutiny of 1857*, London, 1891.

Marshall, P.J., *The New Cambridge History of India, Vol. II.2, Bengal. The British Bridgehead 1740–1828*, Cambridge, 1987.

Martin, M. (ed.), *The Despatches, Minutes and Correspondence of the Marquess Wellesley KG During His Administration in India*, 5 Vols, London, 1837.

Mason, P., *A Matter of Honour. An Account of the Indian Army, Its Officers and Men*, London, 1974.

Masters, J., *Bugles and a Tiger*, London, 1956.

Masters, J., *The Road Past Mandalay*, London, 1961.

Maurice, F., *The Life of General Lord Rawlinson of Trent. From His Journals and Letters*, London, 1925.

Maxwell, R.M. (ed.), *Jimmie Stewart – Frontiersman. The Edited Memoirs of Major General Sir J.M. Stewart*, Durham, 1992.

Menon, V.P., *The Transfer of Power in India*, London, 1957.

Merewether, J.W.B. and Smith, F., *The Indian Corps in France*, London, 1919.

Metcalf, T.R., *The Aftermath of Revolt 1857–70*, Princeton, 1965.

Misra, B.B., *The Central Administration of the East India Company 1773–1834*, Manchester, 1959.

Minto, Mary (Countess of), *India, Minto and Morley 1905–10*, London, 1935.

Mockler-Ferryman, A.F., *Annals of Sandhurst. A Chronicle of the Royal Military College from its Foundation to the Present Day*, London, 1900.

Montgomery, B., *The Memoirs of Field Marshal the Viscount Montgomery of Alamein*, London, 1958.

Montgomery Martin, R., *The Indian Empire*, 3 Vols, London, 1858.

Moon, P., *Warren Hastings and British India*, London, 1947.

Moon, P., *The British Conquest and Dominion of India*, London, 1989.

Morley, J. (Lord), *Recollections*, 2 Vols, London, 1917.

Mosley, L., *Curzon. The End of an Epoch*, London, 1961.

Mukherjee, R., *Awadh in Revolt 1857–1858*, Delhi, 1984.

Napier, C.J., *The Defects, Civil and Military, of the Government of India*, London, 1857.

Napier, H.D., *Field Marshal Lord Napier of Magdala*, London, 1927

Napier, W., *The History of General Sir Charles Napier's Conquest of Scinde*, London, 1857.

Napier, W., *The Life and Opinions of General Sir Charles James Napier*, 4 Vols, London, 1857.

Norman, H.W. (ed.), *Delhi- 1857. Correspondence of the late Col Keith Young CB Judge Advocate General, Bengal*, London, 1902.

O'Dwyer, M. (Sir Michael), *India As I Knew It 1885–1925*, London, 1925.

Orme, R., *A History of the Military Transactions of the British Nation in Indostan from 1745*, London, 1763.

Palit, D.K. (ed.), *History of the Regiment of Artillery*, New Delhi, 1972.

Palmer, J.A.B., *The Mutiny Outbreak at Meerut in 1857*, Cambridge, 1966.

Pemble, J., *The Invasion of Nepal. John Company at War*, Oxford, 1971.

Philips, C.H., *The Evolution of India and Pakistan, 1858–1947, Select Documents*, London, 1962.

Philips, C.H., *The East India Company 1784–1834*, Manchester, 1961.

Pollock, J.C., *Way to Glory. The Life of Havelock of Lucknow*, London, 1957.

Prasad, S.N., *Expansion of the Armed Forces and Defence Organisation. Official History of the Indian Armed Forces in the Second World War 1939–1945*, Calcutta, 1956.

Praval, K.C., *India's Paratroopers. A History of the Parachute Regiment of India*, Delhi, 1974.

Qureshi, M.I., *The First Punjabis. History of the First Punjab Regiment 1759–1956*, Aldershot, 1958.

Rait, R.S., *The Life and Campaigns of Hugh, First Viscount Gough, Field Marshal*, 2 Vols, London, 1903.

Rait, R.S., *The Life of Field Marshal Sir Frederick Paul Haines*, London, 1911.

Rapson, E.J., *Cambridge History of India, Vol. 1, Ancient India*, Cambridge, 1935.

Rawlinson, H.G., *India. A Short Cultural History*, London, 1937.

Richards, F., *Old Soldier Sahib*, London, 1936.

Ridley, J., *Lord Palmerston*, London, 1970.

Roberts, F.S. (Field Marshal Lord), *Forty One Years in India*, 2 Vols, London, 1897.

Robson, B., *The Road to Kabul. The Second Afghan War 1878–1881*, London, 1986.

Robson, B. (ed.), *Roberts in India. The Military Papers of Field Marshal Lord Roberts 1876–93*, Stroud, 1993.

Ronaldshay (Earl of), *The Life of Lord Curzon. The Authorised Biography*, 3 Vols, London, 1928.

Rose, K., *Superior Person. A Portrait of Curzon and His Circle*, London, 1969.

Ross, C. (ed.), *The Correspondence of Charles, First Marquess Cornwallis*, 3 Vols, London, 1859.

Ross, D., *Cambridge History of India Vol. IV The Mughal Period*, Cambridge, 1937.

Royal Military College *Magazine and Record*, 57 Vols, Sandhurst, 1912–39.

Royle, T., *The Kitchener Enigma*, London, 1985.

Russell, W.H., *My Indian Mutiny Diary*, London, 1860, repub. London, 1956, ed. M. Edwards.

Sandes, E.W.C., *The Military Engineer in India*, 2 Vols, Chatham, 1933–34.

Sandes, E.W.C., *The Indian Sappers and Miners*, Chatham, 1948.

Sandhu, G.S., *The Indian Cavalry*, Delhi, 1982.

Sarkar, J., *Mughal Administration*, Calcutta, 1924.

Sarkar, J., *Fall of the Mughul Empire*, Calcutta, 1950.

Sen, S.N., *Eighteen Fifty-Seven*, Delhi, 1957.

Sen, S.N., *The Military System of the Marathas*, Calcutta, 1958.

Seton-Kerr, W.S., *The Marquess Cornwallis*, Oxford, 1890.

Singh, K., *A History of the Sikhs*, 2 Vols, Princeton, 1963–66.

Singh, R., *History of the Indian Army*, Delhi, 1963.

Sheppard, E.W., *Coote Bahadur. A Life of Lieutenant General Sir Eyre Coote KB*, London, 1956.

Skinner, M.A.R., *Sworn to Die* (History of Skinner's Horse), Delhi, 1984.

Smith-Dorrien, H., *Memories of Forty-Eight Years Service*, London, 1925.

Smith, V.A., *The Oxford History of India*, Oxford 1923, revised edn, 1958.

Spear, P., *The Twilight of the Mughals*, Cambridge, 1951.

Spear, P., *India. A Modern History*, Ann Arbor, 1961.

Spear, P., *The Oxford History of Modern India 1740–1947*, Oxford, 1965.

Spear, P., *Master of Bengal. Clive and His India*, London, 1975.

Spencer, A. (ed.), *Memoirs of William Hickey (1749–1775)*, 4 Vols, London, 1913–25.

Spiers, E.M., *The Late Victorian Army, 1868–1902*, Manchester, 1992.

Stokes, E., *The Peasant Armed. The Indian Revolt of 1857*, Oxford, 1986.

Stubbs, F.W., *History of the Organisation, Equipment and War Services of the Regiment of Bengal Artillery*, London, 1877.

Sutherland, L.S., *The English East India Company in Eighteenth Century Politics*, Oxford, 1952.

Taylor, A.J.P., *English History 1914–45*, Oxford, 1966.

Thompson, E. and Garratt, G.T., *The Rise and Fulfilment of British Rule in India*, London, 1934.

Tod, J., *The Annals and Antiquities of Rajasthan*, 3 Vols, reprint Oxford 1920.

Tuker, F. (Lt.-Gen. Sir), *While Memory Serves*, London, 1950.

Verner, W., *The Military Life of HRH George Duke of Cambridge*, 2 Vols, London, 1905.

Verney, G.L., *The Devil's Wind. The Story of the Naval Brigade at Lucknow from the Letters of Edmund Hope Verney*, London, 1956.

Vibart, E., *The Sepoy Mutiny as Seen by a Subaltern*, London, 1898.

Watson, J.S., *The Reign of George III 1760–1815*, Oxford, 1960.

Wellington (2nd Duke) (ed.), *The Despatches, Correspondence and Memorials of Field Marshal Arthur, Duke of Wellington*, 13 Vols, London, 1856–58.

Willmott, H.P., *Empires in the Balance. Japanese and Allied Pacific Strategies to April 1942*, Annapolis, 1982.

Wilson, W.J., *History of the Madras Army*, 3 Vols, Madras, 1882.

Woodward, E.L., *The Age of Reform 1815–70*, Oxford, 1954.

Wright, M.M., *The Military Papers 1940–48 of Field Marshal Sir Claude Auchinleck*, Bulletin of the John Rylands University Library, Summer 1988.

Wylly, H.C., *A Life of Lieutenant General Sir Eyre Coote KB*, Oxford, 1922.

Wylly, H.C., *Neill's 'Blue Caps'*, 3 Vols, Aldershot, 1923.

Ziegler, P., *Mountbatten. The Official Biography*, London, 1985.

Index

KENT AND ITS CRICKETERS
AT ODDS WITH AUTHORITY

First published in the United Kingdom in 2016 by Derby Books Publishing an imprint of JMD Media Ltd.

British Library Cataloguing in Publication Data

A catalogue record for this book is available from the British Library

ISBN 978-1-78091-544-9

Printed and bound in Great Britain by Marston Book Services Ltd, Oxfordshire

KENT AND ITS CRICKETERS
AT ODDS WITH
AUTHORITY

IAN LAMBERT

David Sayer

Right-arm Fast Bowler.
Lower Order right-hand
batsman.

*In action against
Middlesex at Lord's*

First Class Career Statistics

Batting:	I	NO	R	HS	Av	Bowling:	R	W	Av
Kent:	173	64	835	39	7.66		10,587	441	24.00
Others:	64	22	417	62	9.93		3721	171	21.12
Total:	237	86	1252	62	8.29		14,308	612	23.37

- England Schoolboys, 1955.

- 204 1st-class matches. B/B 7–37. 5 wkts in inns 19. 10 wkts in match 2.

- Kent, 1955–76. Debut while still at School. No 1st-class matches 1956–57 due to National Service. Retired 1970–75. Recalled 1976 for one John Player League game V Glamorgan at Canterbury due to Test calls and injuries, analysis 8-1-19-1.

- Oxford University, 1958–60 (3 Blues).

- Played for Gentlemen V Players at Lord's in 1959 taking 6-69 in 1st inns.

- Toured Brazil and Argentina in 1958/59 with MCC (not 1st class).

- Toured New Zealand in 1960/61 with MCC 'A' Team, playing in three 'Unofficial Tests'.

- Played for his home club, the Mote, and was captain when the team reached the Lord's Final of the National Club Knockout Cup in 1973.

FOREWORD

By David Sayer

I have known Ian Lambert as a friend since we were in the same Maidstone Under-19 Yorkshire Cup team, and I was delighted to be asked to write a foreword to his book and to be mentioned in it.

Few students of the game would disagree that there is something special about cricket and cricketers. Whether played at the highest level or on the village green, few sports can provide hours of entertainment for players and spectators alike, camaraderie with team mates and opposition, instant recall of events long past, statistics studied on every aspect of the game and of course the occasional 'half-a-pint'.

I am proud and privileged to have played with so many great players and characters, including Colin Cowdrey, Brian Luckhurst, Mike Denness, Peter Richardson, Alan Brown, John Shepherd, Derek Underwood and Alan Knott for Kent - as well as future captains of their countries, The Nawab of Pataudi (India) and Javed Burki (Pakistan) at Oxford. All Test players and many, many more.

Where better to play as a professional than a full house at Canterbury, a personal soft spot for the Mote, and the home of cricket at Lord's. That is not to forget all the grounds in Kent that give so much pleasure throughout the season.

Ian's book is full of interesting and personal memories for me and will, I am sure, make a welcome addition to any Kent cricket lover's collection.

David Sayer

ACKNOWLEDGEMENTS

As a schoolboy my summer holidays were spent at Whitstable at the home of my grandparents, with one week spent on the beach and the other with my father watching cricket at Canterbury, with Middlesex and Hampshire the then regular opponents. Large crowds would witness Kent household names such as Leslie Ames, Godfrey Evans and Doug Wright pitting their skills against the likes of Denis Compton, Bill Edrich and Derek Shackleton. This book, therefore, could not have been written without the Kent County Cricket Club and its players and includes actions which have both delighted, fascinated and frustrated its many supporters over countless years.

My love of cricket and sport in general has continued but my involvement in the literary world is comparatively recent. A chance remark resulted in a draft of this book being produced but it has developed to this stage with the help of Jamie Reid, a past editor of the Kent Annual, who is an experienced broadcaster/journalist. His advice and support has been invaluable.

I would also like to thank the staff at the Centre for Kentish Studies, Maidstone, for their willing help while conducting research and to David Sayer for kindly agreeing to write a foreword. Included in the bibliography are the books which were consulted and thanks are given to the photographers, both named and anonymous, for their contribution to the book. Specifically, I would like to thank the past and present editors, statisticians, curators, contributors, photographers etc. of the Kent Annual for making research such a pleasure (long may it continue); the *Kent Messenger*, David Frith for his help relating to the Rev J C Crawford, and to Anthony Roberts and Tom Morris for the use of their photographs. Apologies are given if there has been any unintentional use of copyright material.

I admit that the interpretation of *At Odds With Authority* is sometimes a little flexible, for which I trust I will be forgiven, along with the omission of any of your favourite stories.

Finally to JMD Media for their guidance and expertise in helping me to fulfil an ambition.

Ian Lambert

CONTENTS

INTRODUCTION

It is widely acknowledged that cricket was born and first nurtured in Kent. There are early references to games in the 1600s with teams playing under the banner of Kent in the following century. The 1800s saw Kent firmly established as a cricketing force, with five great players in the first half of the century, who were immortalised in the lines:

'And with five such mighty cricketers, t'was but natural to win

As Felix, Wenman, Hillyer, Pilch and Alfred Mynn.'

The County Club as we know it today was formed on 6 December 1870. It is not surprising, therefore, that with this pedigree the County, its players and administrators have been involved in the development of the game and have continued to do so until the present day.

The highs, lows and controversies over the centuries have invariably involved the actions of players whose individual strengths, weaknesses and aspirations have influenced the outcome and decisions of 'those in charge'.

This book therefore looks at a wide range of circumstances involving Kent cricket: players who at some stage have played for Kent, the County's officials and its facilities, and where some differences of opinion or expectations have taken place. It can be a range of emotions, but generally would reflect the 'ups and downs' of a community.

Kent cricket has its long traditions and during the research for this book it was pleasing to note the number of former players who may have had differences with the County during their playing days but have maintained interest and in some cases taken up important roles in the running of the Club.

CHAPTER ONE

INVOLVEMENT WITH THE LAW

During the early development of the game, gambling was rife. In 1719, a match was arranged to be played at Lamb's Conduit Fields between sides representing Kent and London but was not completed. Kent's reason was 'the violence of the rain,' while the opposition's view was that several of the Kent players had anticipated losing the game and had left the ground, thereby hoping to save their money. This led to a lawsuit at Guildhall, London, before the Lord Chief Justice Pratt who ordered the match to be replayed which resulted in the Kentish men being bowled out for 9 and losing the match. This proved to be an expensive fixture for the losers, with legal costs amounting to £200 plus the match fees of a guinea per man, each side.

This was not the first time that Lord Chief Justice Pratt had been involved in a cricketing dispute or indeed reached the same conclusion. In 1724, Edwin Stead, a landowner who was a noted patron of cricket in the County and a compulsive gambler, had gathered together a Kent team to play Chingford who refused to play to a finish when Kent had the advantage. This led to a court case and his Lordship ruled that the match must be played out so that all wagers could be fulfilled. It was 1726 before the match was completed.

Lord John Sackville (1713–65) was a keen cricketer who was closely connected with sport in Kent. He was also a notorious rake and a coward. He refused to join the Guards when they were sent abroad and was eventually committed to a private lunatic asylum, from which he was sent abroad in exile.

Robert Colchin was a highly influential Kent cricketer in the mid-1700s and was associated with Bromley Cricket Club. He was known as 'Long Robin' because he was so tall and was born and bred a gentleman. His chosen lifestyle was different from his early upbringing and he became an underworld figure, choosing his companions from the blackguards of the day. His favourite amusement was attending the executions at Tyburn.

Montague Druitt was a member and former secretary of the Blackheath Club and an accomplished all-rounder who, based upon his on-field performances, should perhaps have played County cricket. In some quarters, those who were familiar with the murky underworld had suspicions that he was Jack the Ripper but there was no hard evidence.

Thomas Bell came from Dartford and his brother John also played for Kent. In July 1762 he was condemned to death at Maidstone Assizes for robbing Thomas Bradshaw on the highway but was later reprieved.

In his early days, William Ayling (Kent, 1806) was a bit of a poacher. On this account he moved from Sussex where he was born. When batting he stood square to the bowler and held the bat in his right hand only, grasping it with his left immediately before receiving the ball.

Alfred Mynn is a cricketing legend and was known as 'The Lion of Kent'. However, the state of his finances did not reflect his status in the game. Although variously described as a farmer and hop merchant it is unlikely that he derived much income, if any, from these occupations. He played all of his matches as an amateur but would have been paid to play. This income was insufficient to fully fund his lifestyle and family commitments. He was declared bankrupt in 1845

14

and was imprisoned for debt on several occasions, twice in Maidstone Jail. Often he was saved from his creditors by wealthy patrons who wanted him free to play in a match in which they had an interest.

George Bennett played for Kent from 1853 to 1873 and has been described as one of the best all-rounders of his day, taking part in the first English tour of Australia as a member of HH Stephenson's XI in 1861/62.

How different things might have been, since at the age of 19 he appeared at the Maidstone Assizes in 1848, charged, alongside six other accomplices, with burglary and stealing five sovereigns, five half sovereigns, one half-crown, one shilling and one sixpence, one pistol, one gun and other articles to the value of £7. *3s. 6d.* from Joseph Thorpe. As well as one ladle, one mug and other articles to the value of £2. *4s.* from Ann Boorman. And at the same time feloniously beating the said Joseph Thorpe at Meopham.

On the night of 12 April, most of the gang had been drinking at the White Horse, Luddesdown since 5 p.m. and were joined by Bennett at about 10 p.m. They left after a further pot of beer. Around midnight access was gained to a house in Meopham via an upper window using a five-barred gate as a ladder.

Three men entered the room of 84-year-old Mr Thorpe, all of whom had their faces covered with crepe and were carrying candles. He was threatened by the men, one of whom had a pistol and another a hammer, and his hands and feet were tied before the men left. Later, Bennett was identified as the man with the pistol.

Previously, 86-year-old Mrs Boorman and her niece Catharine Simmons, a widow, were in bed when they were disturbed by three men entering the bedroom seeking money and drink.

Mr Thorpe was untied by his sister and niece and the matter was reported in the early hours of the 13 April. Following various leads the gang were identified and apprehended. The constable at Shorne went to Bennett's house the same day and found nothing but during a visit the following day, 14 April, he found the pistol and two half sovereigns.

Bennett pleaded guilty and was sentenced to two years imprisonment. A certificate of good character in his favour was put in from the Minister of his Parish.

Having paid his debt to society he was able to make the most of his cricketing ability but it is interesting that four of the gang were transported to a penal colony and had Bennett received this punishment, he may well have shown his cricketing prowess in Australia.

Towards the end of his cricketing career he was to have one further brush with authority when he was reprimanded by the County in 1870 for getting drunk.

Sir Lyttleton Holyoake Bayley played first-class cricket from 1846 to 1848. He was called to the Bar in 1850 and later emigrated to Australia where he was Attorney General of New South Wales from March to October 1859. The appointment offended the legal fraternity as he had only been resident for a short time but he survived a resolution censuring his nomination. He later held appointments in India.

Charles Hoare played one match for Kent in 1872. The family of an underage girl with whom he was having a relationship sought a court order restricting Hoare from continuing the affair and seeking his imprisonment. The judge did not approve the application to send Hoare to prison.

From 1890 to 1895 Lord Harris served as Governor of the Presidency of Bombay in British India. His governorship was notable mainly for his enthusiastic pursuit of the sport of cricket amongst his fellow

Europeans in the colony, at the expense of connecting with the local population. When the Bombay riots of 1893 broke out, Harris was out of the city at Ganeshkhind enjoying cricket matches. He returned to Bombay only on the ninth day of rioting and then primarily to attend a cricket match there.

Many later writers credited Harris with almost single-handedly introducing and developing the sport in India. The game however was well established locally before his arrival.

When Harris left India, having virtually ignored famine, riots and sectarian unrest, a publisher circulated a collection of newspaper extracts from his time as Governor. The introduction stated: 'Never during the last hundred years has a Governor of Bombay been so sternly criticised and never has he met with such widespread unpopularity on account of his administration as Lord Harris.'

James Mason made a single first-class appearance for Kent against Yorkshire at Headingley in 1900. He made his living from the law, working as a solicitor. He had been in partnership with a William Weed but the partnership was dissolved in 1912. He was later a legal partner at Amery-Parkes & Co. with four other people. This partnership was also dissolved in 1914 following the retirement of a partner, although the firm continued under a different structure. His brother Jack played Test cricket for England and captained Kent.

In 1920, James Seymour was awarded a benefit but the ramifications of this decision could not have been foreseen. He was to receive a demand for income tax on that part of his benefit money which accrued from entry fees paid at the gate but his appeal to the Income Tax Commissioners decided in his favour. The Crown appealed to the High Court and lost but they won their further appeal to the Court of Appeal. Seymour then appealed to the House of Lords and won his case. Throughout this long drawn-out process he had the support of Lord Harris. Other

current recipients of tax-free benefits (soon to change) owe much to the events early in the twentieth century.

The report to KCCC members on the 1948 season contained the following statement from the President about an important source of income for beneficiaries, 'While having every sympathy with professionals who wish to increase their Benefit Funds, the Committee has reluctantly decided to limit the number of local matches played for this purpose. First-class cricket is hard work and County matches must come first. Rest days should not be interfered with.'

Arthur Fagg was awarded a benefit in 1951 and arranged the majority of his matches before and after the County season as illustrated by the list of fixtures (Opposite). One interesting match was against the West Indian Wanderers played at the Riverside Sports Club ground at Rochester in front of a crowd of 2,000. Batting first, the visitors scored 213-3dec with the main contributions coming from Test players, KR Rickards (89) and AF Rae (45). Fagg's XI included Kent players Arthur Phebey, Stuart Leary, Peter Hearn, Colin Page and Claude Lewis and won by three wickets with

Arthur Fagg

FAGG'S BENEFIT MATCHES

1951			Venue
Sat., April 21st	The Mote C.C.		Maidstone
Sun., ,, 22nd	Tonbridge C.C.		Tonbridge School
Sat., ,, 28th	Sevenoaks Vine C.C.		Sevenoaks
Sun., ,, 29th	Harrietsham C.C.		Harrietsham
Sun., May 6th	Sheerness		Sheerness
Sun., ,, 27th	Catford Wanderers C.C.		Catford
Sun., June 24th	West Indians		Rochester
Sun., July 8th	Crayford C.C.		Crayford
Sun., ,, 29th	Charlton Ath. F.C.		Maidstone
Sun., Aug. 5th	Canterbury		Canterbury
Sat., Sept. 1st	Snodland C.C.		Snodland
Sun., ,, 2nd	Ashford C.C.		Ashford
Wed., ,, 5th	Gore Court C.C.		Sittingbourne
Sat., ,, 8th	Hawkhurst C.C.		Hawkhurst
Sun., ,, 9th	Margate C.C.		Margate
Wed., ,, 12th	Westerham C.C.		Westerham
Sat., ,, 15th	Rochester (Kings School)		Rochester
Sun., ,, 16th	Bexley Heath C.C.		Bexley Heath
Sat., ,, 22nd	Herne Bay C.C.		Herne Bay
Sun., ,, 23rd	East Peckham C.C.		East Peckham
Sat., ,, 29th	Gravesend		Gravesend
Sun., ,, 30th	Smallhythe		Tenterden

All Matches are arranged to start at 12 noon and draw stumps at 6 p.m.

Fagg scoring 114 with shots 'that schoolboys dream of'. The winning runs were scored by Ron Beaumont who, with Dennis Franks, was a well-known Chatham footballer. The success of the benefit games were down to local organisers. In this case special mention for WG Clements (Hon. General Sec. of the Sports Club) and HA Sharman (Hon Sec. of the cricket section) and their committees.

The situation had not changed as Dave Halfyard found out when he was awarded a testimonial in 1965. He was only allowed three Sunday games owing to the strain imposed upon members of the team playing seven days a week.

Hartley Alleyne was born in the West Indies and played for Kent in 1988 and 1989. After a spell in Lancashire League cricket he coached schoolboys, initially on the Wirral, before moving to St Edmunds School, Canterbury in 2006. The following year he was refused a work permit by the Home Office and threatened with deportation, despite having obtained the necessary qualification in sports coaching. With the support of the local MP he was granted leave to remain in the United Kingdom for three years.

His profession as a banker limited the appearances of Albert Lubbock to four matches for Kent between 1863 and 1875. A run on Lubbock's Bank cost £80,000 due to unusual circumstances. An old lady slipped outside the main entrance to the bank and fractured a leg. A large crowd assembled around her and people passing assumed a 'run on the bank'. Word travelled and anxious depositors rushed to withdraw before it was too late.

Charles Henry Bull made his Kent debut in 1929 and moved to Worcestershire at the end of the following season after having played only four games. Bull was one of the top table tennis players in England and represented his country several times in the World Table Tennis Championships. At Stockholm in 1928 he was in the English team which included Fred Perry, who went on to win three Wimbledon tennis singles titles in the 1930s.

Some countries objected to a professional sportsman taking part in World Championships, even though Bull paid his own expenses to take part. The response of the International Table Tennis Federation was to be one of the first sports federations to remove the distinction between amateurs and professionals.

Charles Bull was tragically killed in a car accident in 1939 on the Sunday rest day of a match between Worcestershire and Essex at Chelmsford. He had been playing golf and was a passenger, when the car he was travelling in collided with a stationary lorry. Team mate Syd Buller, who went on to become a much respected umpire, was also injured.

AC 'Charlie' Wright played 225 matches for Kent (1921–31) and was a fast-medium bowler who shared the seam bowling with George Collins, at a time when Tich Freeman was the dominant spinner.

Wright did not gain a regular place until 1923 and the year before he had signed for the Lancashire League club Oswaldtwistle but Kent had refused to release him from a five year commitment to the County.

Makhaya Ntini was a South African bowling legend taking 390 Test match wickets and only played briefly for Kent in 2010 as an overseas player. He was the first ethnically black cricketer to play for the South African team.

His career looked like it was coming to an early end in 1999 when he was charged and then convicted of rape. He was finally acquitted on appeal having maintained his innocence throughout. The case caused widespread controversy in South Africa with his conviction causing negative publicity in view of his status as the first black player to represent his country. Afterwards, he successfully returned to the international game.

Ryan McLaren was born in South Africa and played for Kent (2007–09) on a Kolpak deal, having earlier represented South Africa Under-19s. The Kolpak ruling is a European Court of Justice ruling handed down on 8 May 2003 in favour of Maros Kolpak, a Slovak handball player. It declared that citizens of countries which have signed European Association Agreements have the same right of freedom of work and movement within the EU as EU citizens. Thus, any restrictions placed on their right to work (such as quotas setting maximum numbers of such foreign players in sports teams) are deemed illegal under EU law.

County Cricket Clubs could already employ EU residents under the Bosman ruling but the doors were now open under the Kolpak ruling to cricketers from countries such as South Africa, with an association agreement with the EU. Previously, under ECB, ruling Counties were limited to one overseas player. Various measures have since been tried in order to reduce the input of Kolpak players on the County scene.

McLaren excels in all forms of the game, batting left handed, bowling right-arm, medium-fast and athletic in the field. He made a significant contribution to Kent winning the 2007 Twenty20 Cup Final against Gloucestershire by taking a hat trick.

Two limited-over finals were reached, and lost the following year but McLaren the philosopher, summed up the season as follows, 'To be beaten in two finals, you have to get to two finals.'

During his stay with Kent he was called up for the South African one-day side but had to withdraw as Kent would not release him from his Kolpak contract. After renouncing his Kolpak status McLaren has since represented South Africa in all formats of the game at international level. He has also played in the IPL and for both Middlesex and Hampshire.

Bearsted Cricket Club can trace its history back to 1749 and Lord Harris has written that it can be considered a nursery of the noble game. Famous players such as Alfred Mynn, Fuller Pilch, Felix and Edgar Willsher have played on the village green and much later Tich Freeman, Godfrey Evans and Leslie Ames, all lived in the village at the

same time. The village sign is shown and reflects the cricketing tradition associated with the village.

In 2011, a bank holiday annual charity match was being played between the village team and the local Mens' Club when the pitch was invaded by a female resident complaining about balls being hit into her garden. The strong arm of the law came into play, in the form of two members of the home team who were off-duty policemen. She was arrested and taken to the Maidstone police station in handcuffs, where she was held in a cell for six hours, had her DNA and fingerprints taken and issued with an £80 penalty notice for public disorder and being verbally abusive. The incident was subject to a complaint about her treatment and an appeal against the fine. The family had lived in the property for about five years and solicitors had been involved in issues with the club.

CHAPTER TWO

MEN OF THE CLOTH

The involvement of the Church in cricket, has provided records and dates going back centuries due to its opposition to cricket being played in churchyards and on Sundays. For example, Romney Marsh appeared in 1629 when parishioners of Ruckinge were in fact prosecuted for playing cricket in a churchyard on a Sunday. Seven players were fined two shillings each by the churchwardens for playing on the Sabbath in 1654 at Eltham and in 1668 similar charges were made against four parishioners of Hunton.

In an account of his life printed in 1672, it was recorded that Rev Thomas Wilson, Minister in the County of Kent had seen in Maidstone 'morrice dancing, cudgel playing, stoolball, crickets and many other sports openly and publickly on the Lord's Day.'

An essay in The Gentleman's Magazine of 1743 under the title of 'Cricket matches, public, the folly of,' complains of the 'exhibition of the game taking apprentices and others from their work. Lords and gentlemen, clergymen, and lawyers, associating themselves with butchers and cobblers. It is a most notorious breach of the laws'.

It was not until 1969 that professional cricket on a Sunday was introduced in the form of a Sunday League, which Kent were to win three times in the 1970s. A relaxation of the laws preventing certain activities on the Sabbath led to its introduction. Today, it might be considered surprising that the first League sponsor was John Player, an international cigarette company, and that there was opposition to playing professional cricket on a Sunday. The desire of Churches and Religious groups to maintain Sunday as a day of rest had considerable support and campaigns on sport and other activities were led by the Lord's Day Observance Society to keep Sunday sacred.

Sunday cricket was also an issue with many local clubs who were playing on grounds which were subject to external controls. Southborough Cricket Club was an example where cricket had been played on the common since 1794 but a by-law prohibited Sunday cricket close to the adjacent church. It was not until 1973 that the first Sunday match was played and a full Sunday fixture list established.

Several first-class cricketers have been associated with Southborough cricket, including John Willes, Frank Woolley, the three Hutchings brothers and Peter Hearn. Kenneth Hutchings played 163 matches for Kent (1902–12) and seven Test matches for England. He was tragically killed during World War I in France in 1916 and a plaque dedicated to him has been erected in Southborough.

Lord Frederick Beauclerk was an outstanding but controversial English first-class cricketer for 35 years from 1791 to 1825 (Kent 1806). He was the great- grandson of King Charles II and Nell Gwynne. He

served as President of the MCC in 1826. Thereafter he regularly attended matches at Lord's and he was invariably accompanied by a nasty yapping dog when the rule for everyone else was, 'No dogs allowed'.

He was vicar of St Michaels Church at St Albans and a Doctor of Divinity although he was variously described as 'completely devoid of Christian charity', 'a cleric without it would seem, the faintest interest in being a clergyman or any kind of Christian' and 'never allowing his clerical duties to interfere materially with the claims of cricket'.

Other descriptions of his character were little better, including 'an unmitigated scoundrel', 'a foul-mouthed dishonest man who was one of the most hated figures in society', 'he bought and sold matches as though they were lots in an auction' and 'cruel, unforgiving, cantankerous and bitter'.

A verse written by a contemporary concluded,

> 'My Lord he comes next, and will make you all stare
> With his little tricks, a long way from fair.'

He could be a vindictive man and in 1810 he was due to partner Thomas Howard against George Osbaldeston and William Lambert. Osbaldeston was taken ill but Beauclerk refused to postpone the match, which was lost, together with his temper, due to Lambert deliberately bowling wide.

Beauclerk was to gain his revenge, initially using his influence to secure a change in the Laws of Cricket so that wide balls were banned for the first time in 1811. Some years later he produced witnesses to implicate Lambert in match fixing, who was then banned by the MCC from ever playing again at Lord's. Osbaldeston relinquished his MCC membership in 1818 following his anger at being beaten at single wicket by George Brown of Sussex. Later he asked to be reinstated by Beauclerk who refused his application. When Beauclerk died in 1850 his unpopularity was such that *The Times* did not give him an obituary.

George Louch played for Kent on six occasions between 1773 and 1792 and the following newspaper article appeared in August 1789.

'We are happy to hear that the report of Mr. Louch being killed last week at Bourne Paddock by a ball from the point of the bat struck with such force that it lodged in his body is devoid of foundation. Yet the melancholy tale occasioned some debates in the Club whether the striker was fairly out: and a violent altercation ensued after the news arrived in the country, between the Clerk, the Cobler and the Curate who each contended for the honour of perpetuating his memory in the following epitaths.'

Clerk:

He lies the cricketer, poor Louch
We hope his bones do well-he
His zeal for catching balls was such
He caught them in his belly.

Cobler:

Deth minds a krikketter no more
Than he does cracking nuts
Louch could not stop the ball before
He cocht hur in

Curate:

Good Master Louch, down here doth crouch,
A cricketer so staunch
That vexed his hands should miss the ball
He caught it in his paunch.

The above lines, although they can boast neither merit nor refinement are interesting on account of their antiquity.

Richard (Dick) May, whose brother Tom also played for Kent, was known to have been a gamekeeper on Sir Horatio Mann's estate at Bourne. He died in a drunken fit about 1796 when he was middle-aged. His dying request to his friend George Ring was that Ring should kill his favourite dog and bury it with him. Apparently this was done,

despite the remonstrance of the officiating clergyman who said it was sacrilege.

In 1837, Kent played Sussex at Town Malling. In the course of a sermon on the day before the match the vicar Mr GF Bates declared from his pulpit that even to attend a match was sinful even if no bets were placed. Undeterred, there was a large crowd including many neighbouring clergymen.

Playing in that game was Fuller Pilch who contributed to Kent's two wicket win with a top score of 44 in the first innings. Originally from Norfolk, he was lured to Kent and moved to Malling in 1835 where he took over The Cricketers Arms, adjacent to the cricket ground. It is now a private house and a nearby plaque records his occupation. Accompanying Pilch to Kent at that time was another leading Norfolk player called William Stearman.

The Rev John Henry Fagge was born at Chartham in 1814 and died there in 1884. He was described as a most energetic cricketer and owing to his profession he sometimes played under the name of Fredericks. In a match between The Gentlemen of England and The Gentlemen of Kent, the Hon Robert Grimston was bowled by a slow ball from Fagge, an outcome that was not unusual, and upon his return to the pavilion he exclaimed 'I wish that Fred Fagge was dead.' 'What a bloodthirsty expression!' said one of his friends. 'Well,' replied Grimston, 'I don't wish him DEAD, but I wish that they would make him a Bishop, so that we should see him no more'.

The Hon and Rev Edward Vesey Bligh once took part in a curious single-wicket match. During a meeting between Kent and Sussex at which he was not present, some gentlemen offered to back Edwin Napper, who was the second Sussex club captain from 1847 to 1862, against any gentleman of Kent. The challenge was accepted by Captain Henry Brenchley, and it was arranged that the match should take place at Gravesend three weeks later. Napper won the toss, and was given out lbw by the substitute for his umpire, whose train was late, to the second ball sent down. Napper made so much fuss that, the match being for a considerable bet as between Captain Brenchley and the others, it was determined that the match should be off. The decision naturally gave much disappointment to the very considerable field which had assembled, including the Mayor of Gravesend.

Bligh stated that 'The first ball of the only two bowled was precisely similar [to the second] and I appealed for that also ('not out'). I bowled with hand over the wicket, and was always of the opinion that both balls were undoubtably lbw according to the most rigid construction of the law.'

The Rev JC Crawford played 10 matches for Kent in the 1800s and his three sons all played first-class cricket, with JN (Jack) representing England. In 1883, he became the first chaplain of the Cane Hill Asylum at Coulsdon during which time as a MCC Member he was the only

objector to a motion to increase the bowling crease. In a match at Mote Park in 1866 when bowling fast, he hit a swallow, which was carried on to the batsman, who struck unsuccessfully at both bird and ball.

He was often referred to as 'Parson' or simply 'Pa' and the caption 'Asking pa's consent' was a familiar phrase. The drawing is by Roland Pretty Hill (1866–1949) who was a cricket cartoon artist, known as RIP and spent much of his life in London. It appeared in the April 2013 edition of the Parish Magazine of St Mary's Church, Merton where several family members are buried and shows 'Parson' with his son Jack who is asking to go on Tour to Australia.

The services of a vicar are required for many different reasons. Sadly this was doubly true for John Boys, a musician in the band of the Royal Artillery stationed at Woolwich who only played occasionally for Kent due to the difficulty in obtaining leave. His end was a melancholy one, for he died age 26, just 16 days from his 27th birthday and on the day on which he was to have been married, in 1883.

Asking pa's consent

The Rev Richard Thornton captained Kent in his first appearance and went on to play 45 games (1881–88). The match was against Somerset at Bath and was not ranked as first class. Born in Folkestone but playing his cricket in Devonshire, Thornton made it known that he would be available for the Kent game if required. Lord Harris instigated his selection and Thornton was the only amateur in the side. Thornton was known as 'Parson' and tactically he used to advance down the wicket as the bowler ran in and also stand out of his ground, picking up overthrows from frustrated fielders.

In 1885, he was captain of a short tour to North America arranged by EJ Saunders, which included two other Kent players, his brother AJ Thornton and the Rev Trevitt Reginald Hine-Haycock. The most important opposition was Philadelphia, who recorded a historic victory over the tourists. Whilst in Philadelphia, Thornton preached at St Paul's Church, Chestnut Hill.

Charles Absolom died in tragic circumstances aged 43 in 1889. After 13 years of first-class cricket, playing for Cambridge University, Kent and England, he became a ship's purser, but he was accidently buried by a misplaced load of sugar, whilst loading at Port of Spain in Trinidad.

Bishop Cecil Wilson played 28 matches for Kent (1882–90) with the highlight being a partnership of 215 with George Hearne against Yorkshire at Canterbury. He was educated at Tonbridge school and Cambridge University before becoming Bishop of Melanesia (1894–1911) where his residence was on Norfolk Island and his Diocese being the Solomon and New Hebrides Islands. There was some concern over his consecration in view of his age and lack of experience, but his work in the Islands justified the appointment and he was actively involved in raising funds to replace the mission ship Southern Cross. The new ship was a steel three-masted schooner with an auxiliary steam engine and built in Newcastle upon Tyne by Armstrong Whitworth &

Co. Bishop Wilson officially launched the ship. After retiring in 1911 he went to Australia where he was Archdeacon of Adelaide until 1917 before serving the next 20 years as Bishop of Bunbury, and then living in retirement in Perth. He died at the age of 80 in 1941.

The life of the Rev William Benton can be described as eventful. A talented cricketer he played two matches for Middlesex in 1913 at the age of 39, against Cambridge University and Hampshire with a top score of 19 not out. While he was curate at Bearsted before the first world war, he played for the local village side, scoring at least one century and for the Mote Cricket Club with a top score of 84 against Eton Ramblers in 1913.

Benton was born into a privileged family which he rebelled against and joined the army under an assumed name. Following a fight with a corporal he deserted and went to Australia, where he served in the Australian Artillery as a gunner in the South African (Boer) war. After the war he obtained work in Cape Town on Robben Island which had a profound effect upon him.

He gave himself up to the authorities, was court martialled and went to prison. He was ordained as a priest in 1909 following a King's Pardon and two years at a Theological College. He arrived at Bearsted three years later following appointments at Walsall and a return to Robben Island.

When war broke out, he initially went to the Front as an army chaplain. However he resigned his chaplaincy and took a commission in the Manchester Regiment. He was a born leader and was a specialist Officer in scouting and sniping. He died on 17 August 1916 from injuries sustained in action on the Somme while attempting to rescue a wounded soldier.

William Temple was Archbishop of Canterbury (1942–44) and a renowned teacher and preacher. His view of cricket was expressed

33

thusly, 'Personally, I have always looked on cricket as organised loafing'.

Claude Lewis was a great servant to Kent cricket for over half a century as a player, coach and scorer. He played from 1933–53 as a slow left-arm bowler taking 301 wickets and was in competition with the likes of Tich Freeman, Doug Wright, Frank Woolley and Charles Marriott.

On one occasion when undertaking 12th man duties, a 'gentleman of the cloth' asked to see Bryan Valentine, the Kent captain but was told that the skipper always had a massage after lunch. The clergyman then told Lewis to tell his skipper that he was his headmaster at school and Lewis was suitably embarrassed when he realised that he had been talking to the Archbishop of Canterbury.

The Kent second XI that beat Wiltshire at Trowbridge in the Minor Counties Championship in 1948 included AF Woollett, AH Phebey, GH Ward, DG Ufton, JAC Bentall, MD Fenner, BJK Pryer, RE Meredew, JCT Page, C Lewis and GA Simpson of whom, only two did not play for the first XI.

Allan Rutter, a 19 year old born in Bromley, and making his debut for Wiltshire, was stumped by Ufton, off the bowling of Lewis for seven in Wiltshire's first innings total of 59. In the second innings, it looked like a repeat when he was out of his ground with the wicket broken by the keeper. As he made his way to the pavilion it was realised that Ufton had removed the bails without the ball in his gloves and he had not been given out. He returned to the wicket to resume his innings but making sure that he was at all times behind the popping crease, to avoid being stumped or run out. The comment from the umpire was, 'Did you enjoy your walk?' He was soon bowled for 14.

Rutter went to Cambridge University, where he made two first-class appearances against Sussex and Surrey, and later played for Norfolk where he made his only List A appearance against Hampshire in the Gillette Cup. The Norfolk side included Bill Edrich and Henry Blofeld. Rutter had a further Kent connection when he spent three years as a Scientific Liaison Officer at East Malling Research Station. He studied theology at Durham and was ordained as a Church of England deacon in 1959 and priest in 1960. He served various parishes in England and South Africa, and was a vicar and RAF chaplain on Ascension Island.

In the 1995 Annual, it was reported that Graham Cowdrey wrote to the *Daily Telegraph* after England selectors chairman Ray Illingworth had 'sacked' cricketing parson Andrew Wingfield Digby from his duties in the dressing room.

'Having toured India twice with Christians in Sport, my life has been strengthened by the considerable support and guidance of Wingfield Digby and others', said Cowdrey. 'He is the most sensitive of cricket watchers, quietly seeking the confidence of the players; he has an extraordinary gift of understanding the pressures of professional sport, on and off the field.'

In more recent times, the Harris Room steward was enforcing the rule requiring gentlemen guests to wear ties, before being allowed entry. He explained the situation to one man, regretting that there were positively no exceptions. Unfortunately the next guest was a vicar!

CHAPTER THREE

ABSENTEEISM

Generally the full complement of players will only be absent from the field of play due to inclement weather. Rain stopped play is an occupational hazard for cricketers, but combined with snow is unusual, particularly in May, which is what happened in 1967 when Kent played Nottinghamshire at Trent Bridge on a pitch behaving awkwardly. Requiring 178 to win, which would have been the highest innings total of the match, the latter stages of the game were reported as follows, 'An interesting finish was spoilt by a snowstorm, followed by rain, in mid-afternoon and more rain caused the match to be abandoned as a draw 70 minutes from time with Kent 36-4 and caught on a drying wicket.'

The following games were played during a four week period from 14 June 1980 when rain caused frustration to both players and spectators alike, and a lack of success when play was possible.

At Tunbridge Wells V Hampshire, 14, 16 and 17 June

After the loss of two and a half hours to the weather, Hampshire reached 153-6 by close of play. The innings was quickly over for a total of 179. Early in the Kent innings, rain stopped play until 5 p.m. and they finished day two on 63-4. After one over and four runs, no further play was possible on day three, with the match drawn and Kent with 4 bowling points.

At Tunbridge Wells V Sussex, 18, 19 and 20 June

Play was possible on the first two days, with fluctuating fortunes, seam movement, low bounce and occasional sun. An aggressive 83 from Chris Cowdrey saw Kent gain a first innings advantage but a century from Paul Parker allowed Sussex to declare, asking Kent to score 225 in 150 minutes, but rain intervened at 75-2. Match Drawn. Kent 6 points. (2 batting, 4 bowling.)

At Old Trafford V Lancashire, 21, 23 and 24 June

Only 32 overs were possible, spread over the last two days, with Kent scoring 40-0. The not-out batsmen were Rowe (26) and Taylor (13). The match was abandoned. Kent 0 points.

At Old Trafford V Lancashire, 22 June

The John Player League Match was restricted to 12 overs a side, which Lancashire won by 7 wickets. Kent 79-2. Lancs. 80-3.

At Canterbury V Derbyshire, 28 and 30 June, 1 July

No play was possible on the first day and on day two Kent struggled to 175-8 off 75 overs, before rain arrived at the tea interval. With rain overnight and most of the final day, any further play was impossible. Match drawn. Kent 1 batting point.

At Canterbury V Derbyshire, 29 June

Despite a blank first day in the Schweppes County Championship, a normal 40 over John Player League match was completed with Derbyshire winning by 8 wickets. Kent 133-8. Derbyshire 136-2. Future Kent coach John Wright scoring 88 not out.

At Maidstone V Leicestershire, 5, 7 and 8 July

Play was only possible on the first day of this match when Leicestershire scored 254 (Jarvis 5-63) and in an hours batting, the Kent reply was 16-2, with only 10 runs coming from the bat. Match drawn. Kent 4 bowling points.

At Maidstone V Leicestershire, 6 July

The weather was a factor in this John Player League Match with Kent scoring 121 in a reduced number of 34 overs, but Leicestershire scored 56-1 in 11.4 overs to win by 9 wickets on a faster scoring rate.

At Maidstone V Surrey, 9, 10 and 11 July

When the rains stopped, a one innings match was started on the second day. Batting first, Kent were 88-6 but were rescued by John Shepherd (100) and Stuart Waterton (40) and declared at 222-8. Surrey started at a good rate and required 132 from the final 20 overs with all wickets standing. Wickets then fell at regular intervals and the visitors fell 14 runs short with 3 wickets left. Former Kent batsman Graham Clinton top scored for Surrey with 70.

Some of the players who appeared for the County during the season, L to R: Chris Tavare, Alan Ealham, Kevin Jarvis, Alan Knott, Asif Iqbal, Derek Underwood, Chris Cowdrey, Graham Johnson, Bob Woolmer.

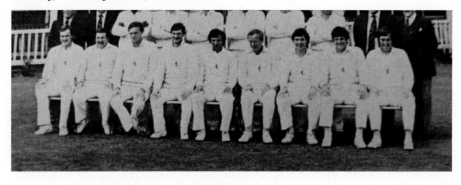

With 'normal service' resumed, Kent went to Trent Bridge, where Nottinghamshire won by an innings and 1 run, after Kent were bowled out for 67 in their first innings. Maidstone unfortunately suffered another blank day on 20 July when the John Player League Match against Sussex was abandoned without a ball being bowled.

The opposite was the case in 1999 when bright sun caused the abandonment of play half an hour early on the third day of Kent's match against Lancashire at Old Trafford. Jim Cumbes, Lancashire's Chief Executive reported, 'I've been out there to look and you can't see a thing. As well as with the sun's reflection on the slanted roof of the media centre, the low angle of the sun at this time of year is an insurmountable problem.' The alignment of the wickets has since changed.

Similar conditions have also been a problem at Canterbury when Colin Blythe liked to bowl out of the setting sun. During a Canterbury Week he was bowling to CB Fry and tossing the ball high. The batsmen were dazzled. Fry was not amused and demanded that stumps were drawn. The crowd did not think much of the batsman appealing against the light on a warm evening with the St Lawrence ground bathed in sunshine. Accompanied by boos, Fry eventually lost patience and left the square to tell the crowd what he thought of them. A slanging match ensued before calm prevailed and play was completed in silence.

This was not the first time that Fry had been involved in controversy at St Lawrence. In 1907, he was the next scheduled batsman waiting with his pads on. A wicket fell with 20 minutes remaining on the second day but Fry decreed that Robert Relf should go in despite the fact that he was changed and ready. Relf survived having prepared in haste and suffered the Kentish jokes about the two minute rule.

Sun was a problem in the T20 Blast match in 2016 against Sussex Sharks at Canterbury when the umpires stopped play due to the visitors' batsmen having difficulty with the evening setting sun over the Woolley stand. A further delay occurred with the sun reflecting from a temporary broadcasting structure behind the bowlers arm at the Nackington Road end. Kent went on to win the game.

One of the reasons for play being suspended was the pace bowling of Kagiso Rabada, the South African Test player who was making his debut, as his deliveries were reaching 90 mph. Still only 21 years old, the Kent Annual described Rabada as one of the hottest fast bowling talents on the international scene who made a huge impression since breaking into the South African side. He topped the bowling averages against England with 22 wickets at an average of 21.90 in the 2015/16 tour of South Africa.

Matches due to be played under floodlights have not been without problems either and before the erection of permanent pylons, portable lights were hired from the ECB. There were safety issues in high winds and in such conditions at Canterbury in 2008, Kent batted first against Leicestershire, scoring 226, but the opposition only managed six overs before the match was abandoned due to bad light, as the floodlights could not be raised to their normal operating height. This was the first Kent limited over match not to be completed because of floodlighting problems.

Further difficulties arose the following year in the Pro40 game against Surrey at St Lawrence when again the floodlights could not be fully extended and the umpires decided to reduce the game to 27 overs per side. Batting in good light, Kent posted 167. In fading light the Surrey innings finished at 110 after 19.4 overs when the umpires decided that no further play was possible and Surrey lost by 8 runs (D/L).

In a Twenty20 Cup match against Sussex at Hove the same year, a faulty generator left both floodlights at one end of the ground out of action. Having been advised that the match was likely to finish prematurely, stand-in captain Martin van Jaarsveld chose to field first.

Chasing a total of 131 the game was abandoned after 11 overs of the Kent innings when fast bowler Robin Martin-Jenkins was recalled with one end of the ground in near darkness. Sussex won by 2 runs (D/L).

There were problems at the Yorkshire Bank 40 match in 2013 against Warwickshire at Canterbury. Scheduled to be completed under floodlights, the match was abandoned following the failure of one of the pylons and the inability of the two teams to agree to continue with the reduced output. An unnamed umpire's comment about bad light as an evening drew in was, 'You can see the moon, how far do you want to see?'

The St Lawrence Ground, Canterbury

Benjamin Aislabie played only once for Kent, against MCC at Lord's in 1823, when he went in last and scored 1 and 0. He was no cricketer but possessed a very sound knowledge of the game and from 1822 until his death in 1842 was Hon Secretary to the Marylebone Club. He was a great lover of the game and during the latter part of his career, when he weighed about 19 or 20 stone, he always had someone to run as well as field for him.

'He doats on the game, has played many a year,

Weighs at least seventeen stone, on his pins rather queer;

But he still takes the bat, and there's no better fun

Than to see him when batting attempting a run.'

In 1862 the St Lawrence ground was to witness a Kent side refusing to play against an opposing side during the Festival Week. The manager of the week William de Chair Baker agreed to EM Grace appearing for the Gentlemen of the MCC, to replace a player injured in the previous match, despite not being a MCC member. There had been no consultation with the Kent captain W South Norton who, with the support of the Kent side, declined to play the match on the basis that there were competent cricketers on the ground who were MCC members.

With reluctance the Kent side agreed to play to prevent the entrance money being returned to spectators which would have caused the Club to suffer. The mood of the players could not have been improved by the performance of Grace who carried his bat for 192 and took 15 wickets in the 12-a-side match which the MCC won by an innings and 104 runs.

Kent played two first-class games at Preston Hall, Aylesford and in 1846 the game against Surrey ended in somewhat unusual circumstances. Requiring only 57 runs to win the match with W and E Banks at the wicket, the brothers left the ground during an interruption for rain and declined to play any longer, pleading another engagement. This changed the balance of the game and a drawn result occasioned great disappointment and no little dissatisfaction.

Charles Fox was a useful all-rounder who scored large numbers of runs for the Crystal Palace Club. The avuncular-looking luxuriantly moustached Fox was a genuine amateur who played the game for

pleasure. Playing for Kent against Sussex at Hove in 1891 he was 0 not out at lunch but left the ground and arrived back too late to resume his innings excusing himself with the immortal words 'I was lunching with a widow'.

Frank Marchant was Kent captain from 1890 to 1897 and is pictured here with his successor, JR Mason in 1902. He admitted that 'as responsibility increased, pleasure declined'. An early difficulty for him, was to ensure that he had a full team for consecutive games. At York, against Yorkshire, he found himself in the position of

Frank Marchant was Kent captain from 1890–1897 and is pictured below to the right of his successor, J.R. Mason (no cap) in 1902

knowing that on the first day, he would be at least three short until about 4 p.m. Winning the toss he decided to bat in the hope that the late arrivals would rescue the situation, but to no avail, as Kent were dismissed for 46 at lunchtime, with the absentees being listed as 'absent hurt'. They managed 167 in the second innings with a full complement but could not prevent Yorkshire winning by 8 wickets.

No fault could be attributed to the three players concerned but rather an unfortunate set of circumstances. A telegram sent to Stanley Christopherson had been changed by a clerk from 'Can't do without you' to 'Can do without you', and one sent to Walter Hearne arrived too late for him to catch the train from London. Hugh Spottiswoode was delighted to respond at short notice to make his debut. As a result of this experience, Marchant opted to confirm his teams in advance, rather than rely on telegrams.

Injuries were plentiful at Maidstone in 1979 when Lancashire's team contained several players who were not fully fit and during the game both David Lloyd and Barry Wood were both forced to retire hurt, although they were later able to resume. The opening bowler, Robinson, sustained a hamstring injury at the start of Kent's second innings and could not bowl and Derek Underwood was unable to bowl in Lancashire's first innings. Despite the invalids, the match went to the final over, with Lancashire failing to score 6 off the final ball and the match was drawn.

Two Warwickshire players were listed as 'absent hurt' and did not bat in either innings, in a match at Edgbaston in 1988 when Kent won by an innings and 46 runs. Both players, Kallicharran and Reeve, had sustained broken fingers. Kent were denied the chance of a fourth bowling point in an otherwise maximum-points win. The top three positions in the final Championship Table are shown below and it is interesting to speculate on the possibilities for Kent had the full XI batted for Warwickshire.

	P	W	L	D	Bonus Points Btg	Bwl	Pts
Worcestershire	22	10	3	9	55	75	290
Kent	22	10	5	7	57	72	289
Essex	22	9	5	8	61	69	282

History was to repeat itself in 1995 when two players were 'absent hurt' when Kent played Warwickshire at Canterbury. Replying to the visitors first innings score of 468-6dec (NV Knight 174, RG Twose 109) Kent scored 239, but both Graham Cowdrey, with a robust 147 ball century, and Alan Igglesden broke fingers. The nine men in the second innings could only muster 124 and Kent lost by an innings and 105 runs.

This team photo is of the 1906 County Champions and is, L to R, Back Row: FE Woolley, FH Huish, W Hearne (scorer), A Fielder, C Blythe; Middle Row: CJ Burnup, RNR Blaker, CHB Marsham (captain), KL Hutchings, JR Mason; Front Row: WJ Fairservice, E Humphreys, A Hearne, J Seymour. The middle row comprises amateurs who collectively played a total of 880 matches for Kent.

Early in the 1900s amateurs tended to be selected around the time of Canterbury Week to the exclusion of professionals, when the atmosphere, crowds and festivities were a considerable attraction.

George Marsham (Kent captain 1904–08) confirmed that 'there is a tradition that Canterbury Week is also a social event and we make it a practice to play at least six amateurs,' he added, 'but it's not cricket'.

After Kent beat the Australians in 1884 each amateur who played in that match, received a cap from Lord Harris showing the White Horse of Kent, which had been embroidered by Lady Harris. This recognition continued, embracing those amateurs who played in the Canterbury Week but a supply problem arose when Lady Harris went to India. An alternative supplier was found in Eton, but by this time other Counties had adopted the idea, so Kent's professionals were allowed to wear the cap which enhanced the identity of the team on the field.

At Maidstone in 1936, APF Chapman made no objection to Middlesex playing Gray instead of GO Allen who stood down after the start of the match.

John Dudlow was born and died in West Malling. He made one first-class appearance for Kent in 1841 against Nottinghamshire. Despite being on the winning side he neither batted nor bowled in the game and was in fact absent.

John Cocker (pictured right), was born in 1815 at Thurnham, Kent, the village where Alfred Mynn was later buried. He played one first-class game for Kent in 1842 and four years later he emigrated to Adelaide, Australia, with his family. He formed the Kent and Sussex Cricket Club which was among the first generation of South Australian cricket and scored the first recorded century in the state. In 1865 he was asked to prepare a pitch on land where the Adelaide Oval now stands.

Although the Australians retained the Ashes in 1899 Kent were victorious by 2 wickets at Canterbury with AH du Boulay having an eventful match. He gained the prize wicket of Victor Trumper with his very occasional medium pacers followed by the second highest score of 33 batting at number 7. He went one better in the second innings with a top score of 27 but batting at number 3 because for unspecified reasons he 'had to leave early'.

When Kent played the 1948 Australian tourists, Leslie Todd faced the first ball of the match against Ray Lindwall and was hit on the toe. On being given not out lbw despite his protestations that he was plumb, he left the next ball and was bowled. In the safety of the pavilion he claimed that he could take no further part in the match. No damage was detected by the medical staff but Todd still refused to take further part in the match. He was suspended for the remainder of the season.

Having returned from an arduous first tour of Australia (1954/55) played on hard wickets, Colin Cowdrey became eligible for National Service having decided not to complete his final planned year at Oxford University. The possible interruption to his Test career did not materialise, as he was discharged on medical grounds from the RAF, after two weeks service instead of the normal two years, because of a long history of foot trouble.

The problem was hereditary with stiff and rigid toes, which had necessitated an operation and missing two months of school. The medical history, plus the prospect of permanent damage being caused by the rigours of service life in regulation footwear, made the decision inevitable. As expected, the press had a field day, questions were asked in the House of Commons and aggrieved parents of other servicemen made their feelings known. It is perhaps unfortunate that a 'purple patch' of run scoring followed, but the decision making was out of Cowdrey's hands.

Terry Alderman was a fine fast medium bowler who took 170 Test wickets for Australia including 42 in the series in England in 1981. He was Kent's overseas player for 1984–86. He was prevented from playing for over a year by a shoulder injury sustained in 1982 when he rashly

tackled an English-supporting ground invader at the WACA Ground in Perth.

For the first time in 36 years there were no scorecards available at the start of play in the game against Nottinghamshire at Dartford in 1988. The printer had arrived late through no fault of his own, but the matter was soon rectified some half an hour after the first ball had been bowled. The game

itself swung backwards and forwards, with Kent eventually requiring 111 off 24 overs and winning by 2 wickets with Chris Cowdrey steering them home with 35 not out.

Niall O'Brian played for Kent (2004–06) and is regarded as one of Ireland's best wicket-keepers. On his own admission he has a fiery temperament and in 2006 he was banned for one ICC Intercontinental Cup match after an outburst criticising the groundsman at a cup game with Scotland because of the condition of the pitch.

Transport has caused many a problem and late appointments, and cricket is no exception. As early as 1906 the Lancashire team was delayed on its journey from Manchester to Canterbury, and having lost the toss, it was not until 12.25 p.m. that they took the field in front of a record Ladies Day crowd in excess of 13,000.

When looking at a team photograph one assumes that there are a minimum of 11 players, at least this 1926 photo recorded that the captain, WS Cornwallis, was absent, although one has to speculate on the reason.

Standing (left to right) C. Wright, G. P. Bolce, W. H. Ashdown, H. T. W. Hardinge, S. G. Hearn.
Seated: J. C. Hubble, A. L. Hilder, J. A. Deed, J. Seymour, A. P. Freeman. (Absent) W. S. Cornwallis).

Similarly, in a benefit match for Doug Wright against Whitstable, it appears that a player has gone missing, although who and for which team is not known. However, a young Colin Cowdrey can be identified standing far right.

In 1943, Kent and Surrey beat Middlesex and Essex by 9 wickets in a one-day game at Lord's. Arthur Fagg was in the team but did not bat, as he spent the day looking for his bag which had been mislaid on the railway and a substitute fielder was required. Other Kent players were Sq Ldr Ames, Sgt Evans, Sgt Todd, L Cpl Mallet and Lt Wright.

At Tunbridge Wells in 1963, Middlesex were 29 runs behind Kent with 7 wickets left at the close of the first days play on a Saturday. The visitors went home that evening but at the scheduled starting time for the second day's play on the Monday, only three Middlesex players were present including one already out and the 12th man. The umpires declared the innings closed after a generous time allowance. After three hours a full Middlesex side was present but not before five Kent Players had taken the field as substitutes. John Prodger took a spectacular catch to dismiss Luckhurst for 4 but the weather had the last word.

At The Oval in June 2002, Surrey were 111-5 at the end of the first day in reply to the Kent score of 153. On the second morning the pitch was still damp but any chance of the Kent bowlers using the favourable conditions were undone when the majority of the team were stuck in traffic, taking four hours to travel seven miles from their hotel in Bayswater. Play started at 12.30 p.m. with the pitch rapidly drying out. Surrey went on to eventually win by 9 wickets after scoring 381 in their first innings.

Traffic was not the problem for Charles Payne and Edgar Willsher who were staying at Peterborough in advance of the first day of the Kent game against Cambridgeshire in 1868. Due to an oversight, they were not called at the hotel and 8 wickets were already down when they arrived at the ground at lunchtime, which had been taken half-an-hour early to give the pair the opportunity to arrive.

Syd O'Linn played football for Charlton Athletic, cricket for Kent and represented South Africa in seven Test matches. He was a member of the South African tour of England in 1960, which was the first to be confronted by anti-apartheid demonstrations. Imagine his disappointment as he left the field of play at Trent Bridge having made his highest Test score of 98 but controversially given out caught in the slips by his Kent colleague Colin Cowdrey.

Kent second XI's victory by 150 runs over Glamorgan second XI in 1994 was achieved without a full complement of players in a first innings total of 257 due to the absence of Graham Cowdrey who was performing 12th man duties for the first XI. He opened the batting in the second innings, scoring 24 in a total of 225-2dec.

In 1967, when Oxford University played Northamptonshire at the Parks, the opposing captains both had Kent connections – GNS Ridley (1 game in 1965) and former player Roger Prideaux. Batting first, Northants scored 254 and Oxford were dismissed for 137 on the last day, after rain had prevented any play on the second day. The situation then became confused when the umpires wrongly applied the two-day ruling and Oxford were asked to follow on. Oxford believed that Northants had forfeited their second innings and chased the target. Victory was in sight when telephone calls were made to Lord's to clarify the position. In light of the information received, Ridley called the batsmen in with 20 minutes remaining and 40 runs required. The match was drawn.

Carl Hooper endured a controversial period in the mid-90s when he was fined as a disciplinary measure following the 1995 West Indies tour of England. The charge was that he was absent without leave during the latter stages of the tour. He was left out the international one-day Sharjah Cup in the United Arab Emirates and also made himself unavailable for the home Test series against New Zealand in 1996.

Hooper blamed health reasons and personal problems but soon returned to the fold and finally played his last Test match in 2002 against India.

Duncan Spencer, who played for Kent as a fast bowler in 1993 and 1994 was banned for 18 months by the Australian Cricket Board after testing positive for the banned anabolic steroid nadrolone. He was randomly tested after an interstate one day final between Western Australia and New South Wales. Spencer claimed that it was taken to relieve the pain caused by a chronic back injury.

Kent were deprived of the services of Andrew Symonds for the last three games of the 1999 season, following his call-up to the Australian team for matches arranged at the last minute in Los Angeles. Skipper Matthew Fleming described the visit as, 'Disneyland cricket' and Chief Executive Paul Millman was of the view that 'this was no way to run international cricket and had to be a factor when signing overseas players'.

The following is an article which appeared in the *Kent Messenger* on the 22 February 2013.

Coles sent home early from tour

By Steve Tervet

KENT bowler Matt Coles has been sent home from the England Lions tour of Australia for unprofessional conduct.

The Maidstone-born 22-year-old is one of two England players flying back from Down Under, the other being Durham all-rounder Ben Stokes.

A statement on the ECB website said the pair "had contravened their conduct obligations previously during the tour and had been issued with written warnings."

ECB performance director David Parsons said: "On a very challenging tour to Australia, both Matt and Ben have ignored the instructions given to them around their match preparation and recovery and, following previous warnings, it is regrettable that it has been necessary to terminate their involvement in the tour."

Coles said: "I am sorry about what has happened in Australia and I believe I have learnt my lesson.

"I have apologised to the players and coaches involved, so would now like to move forward from this by looking ahead to the start of the county season at Kent."

England Lions trail 2-0 in their five-match series with Australia A.

Coles finished the first one-day international in Hobart with bowling figures of 0-53 and did not play in the second game.

His rise to prominence last season thrust him into the international reckoning.

In September, he was named in the England Performance Programme squad for their tour of India.

Having made his Kent debut in 2009, aged 18, Coles started to impress with both bat and ball.

In four seasons of county cricket, he has 120 first-class wickets at an average of 29.42. Last summer he took 59 wickets at an average of 22.35 and scored his maiden County Championship century, against Yorkshire at Headingley.

Kent County Cricket Club refused to comment.

Coles played for Hampshire in 2014 but returned to Kent for the following season. During his spell with Hampshire he had had further disciplinary problems but Kent's Cricket Chairman, Graham Johnson explained, 'Since his return to Kent, Matt has demonstrated that he has learned from things in the past. He has applied himself to his role on the field and represented Kent cricket to good effect in off-field activities.'

These words were expressed after umpires Nick Cook and Rob Bailey had reported Matt for throwing the ball near an opposition batsman during the Championship match at Canterbury on 1–4 May 2016, thereby incurring a level two breach of the ECB Discipline Code.

The code is administered by the Cricket Discipline Commission (CDC) and operates at arm's length from the ECB. Breaches in the Laws of Cricket and/or the Spirit of Cricket have been categorised into four levels which incur fixed penalties and remain on a player's record for two years.

While at Hampshire, Matt had previously received a reprimand following three penalty points for a level one breach in August 2014 and six penalty points for a level two breach in September 2014. The latest incident carried a penalty of six points for a further breach at level two within a 24-month period, resulting in an automatic ban and Matt missing two Kent Championship games.

Kent made representations to the CDC but the Chairman's nominee, Chris Tickle, did not consider that the consequences of this penalty might produce a result that was manifestly unfair. Under the process relating to cricket discipline, there is no opportunity to appeal the outcome of the CDC's decision.

Graham Johnson was frustrated by the decision and in his view was that, 'The outcome in this set of circumstances I believe is disproportionate. It does not reflect the seriousness of the recent incident and does nothing to help a cricketer who has made big strides since rejoining Kent.'

It is worth taking a closer look at how the custodians (umpires) of the Laws on the field of play can be directly affected by some of those Laws.

BREACHES

LEVEL 1

(c) Showing dissent at an umpire's decision by word or action.

(d) Using language that is obscene, offensive or insulting and/or making an obscene gesture.

(e) Excessive appealing.

LEVEL 2

(a) Showing serious dissent at an umpire's decision by word or action.

(c) Charging or advancing towards an umpire in an aggressive manner when appealing.

(e) Throwing the ball at or near a player, umpire or official in an inappropriate and dangerous manner.

(f) Using language or gesture that is obscene or of a serious insulting nature to another player, umpire, referee, team official or spectator.

LEVEL 3

(a) Intimidating an umpire or referee.

(b) Threatening to assault another player, team official or spectator.

(c) Using language or gesture that offends, insults, humiliates, intimidates, threatens, disparages or vilifies another person on the basis of that person's race, religion or belief, colour, descent, national or ethnic origin, age, disability, gender, sexual orientation or background.

LEVEL 4

(a) Threatening an umpire or referee.

(b) Physical assault of another player, umpire, referee, official or spectator.

(d) As for Level 3 (c) but using language or gesture that SERIOUSLY offends.

There are other breaches that involve the umpires such as time wasting, 'beamers', pitch damage and physical contact but are potentially less confrontational. There is a comprehensive system of penalty points and any resultant punishment.

Darren Stevens joined Kent from Leicestershire in 2005 and has become an integral part of the team. He is considered by many to have been unlucky not to have been selected by England for limited-over internationals, with his explosive batting and accurate bowling.

While playing in the Bangladesh Premier League in 2013 he was charged by the ICC on two counts of failing to report a corrupt approach, which carried a global ban of one to five years. Playing for the eventual champions, the then named Dhaka Gladiators, who had already qualified for the semi-finals. It is understood that Stevens was asked to undertake the duties of off-field captain against the then named Chittagong Kings, which included tossing the coin but not to skipper the team on the field. Having turned down this role, Stevens was run out by the eventual captain and Bangladesh star batsman, Mohammed Ashraful who later admitted fixing the game. He batted unusually slowly for 33 runs off 48 balls and his side scored 88-8 chasing a total of 142 in a 20 over match.

'STEVENS CLEARED'

These were the headlines in the local and national press in February 2014 following a tribunal in Dhaka. Having pleaded not guilty and endured a long period of uncertainty Stevens reacted as follows:

'I would officially like to thank the tribunal for their verdict today and in particular their determination of not guilty findings in charges brought against me by the Bangladesh Cricket Board.

This has been a long journey and I would like to express my gratitude to my partner Katie, my family, friends, Kent County Cricket Club, my fellow peers, legal team and all those who have supported me.

I can assure all the fans of the Dhaka Gladiators, the people of Bangladesh and all cricket followers, that I have always played the game of cricket honestly, with integrity and to the best of my ability.

I have loved playing cricket in Bangladesh, as well as everywhere else in the world and I hope that I will be allowed to continue playing cricket globally.

Thank you for all your support, and *assalamu alaykum*.'

Kent Chief Executive Jamie Clifford said, 'I am delighted for Darren that this verdict was reached. This has been a stressful time and he will be hugely relieved that this cloud has been lifted.'

In 1995, Kent played Somerset at Canterbury in the semi-final of the Benson and Hedges Cup and Sarah Benson, who was awaiting an operation, discharged herself from the adjacent Kent and Canterbury hospital in order to watch her husband Mark bat. Benson was run out for 29 and the match went into a second day due to bad light and rain, by which time Sarah was back in hospital, failing to witness a home win and Benson fracturing a finger holding a skied catch.

Kent started well against Yorkshire at Scarborough in 1999, scoring 302 on the first day. On day two, they were without the services of leading bowler Julian Thompson who answered a call from his expectant wife. It was a false alarm and the anticipated birth did not take place. In his absence Yorkshire posted a first innings lead of 289,

and although he returned to bowl in their second innings, Yorkshire went on to win by 5 wickets. His wife Tanya later gave birth to a son Jack.

Julian Thompson was born in South Africa but educated in England. He was a qualified doctor who took 'time off' from a medical career to play cricket. He was Kent's Player of the Season in 1999 but despite two knee operations, he was forced to retire through injury without playing a match in 2000.

Needing 343 to avoid the follow-on away to Derbyshire in 2016, Joe Denly was 34 not out at the close of play on the second day (23 May). He did not resume the next morning, in order to be with his wife Stacey, as she went into labour. The baby had not been due until June. It was congratulations all round as the Denlys were the proud parents of a 7 lb 2 oz baby boy and Kent went on to beat Derbyshire by 7 wickets after they had bowled them out for 94 in their second innings. Denly did not feature in Kent's second innings because they scored the required 176.

CHAPTER FOUR

GROUNDS

S ince 1806, 34 grounds have hosted Kent fixtures but now just over half no longer exist or have little or no cricket played on them. Only two first-class matches were ever played by Kent at Hawkhurst one in 1825 and another in 1826 and the lowest match aggregate still stands against Sussex from 1826. Kent (62 and 6-1) Sussex (23 and 43).

Hawkhurst was listed as one of the early cricketing sites in Kent but rather unkindly is better remembered for its smugglers rather than its cricketers. Its history is dominated by the Hawkhurst Gang who between 1735 and 1749 were the most notorious of the Kent gangs and were based at the Oak and Ivy Inn, Hawkhurst. They operated along the full length of the South Coast and were totally ruthless with anyone who interfered or crossed their path.

In 1873, an annual County Championship Cup to be played at Lord's, was put forward by the MCC to increase the popularity of County Cricket. Despite initial promises to compete, several Counties withdrew and the competition was not played. However, Kent and Sussex agreed to play their game and Kent won by 52 runs on a dangerously bad wicket. Much of the damage, literally, was done by Kent's new and very fast bowler, George Edward Coles, with a match analysis of 41.2 O 13 M 70 R 10 W and the second innings of the Sussex batsman, George Humphreys, was described as 'not out (retired, hurt by Mr Cole's bowling) 32'.

Kent should have played Surrey at The Oval in August 1914 but the match was transferred to Lord's, because The Oval was in the occupation of the military Authorities. The match was for Jack Hobbs' Benefit but did not produce the expected income, as it was over in two days.

The weather caused Kent to play their Benson and Hedges Cup quarter-final against Warwickshire in 1981 outside the County, when it was transferred to The Oval to be completed on the third day in overcast conditions. Only a few hardy supporters were present but at least Kent had the consolation of reaching the semi-final, if not the healthy gate receipts that they might have expected. Kent scored 193-8 in their 50 overs with Chris Tavaré being the backbone of the innings with 76, which earned him the Gold Award. In reply Warwickshire only scored 37 in the first 20 overs but victory looked likely as the run rate increased. However, wickets were lost at crucial times and Kent won by 14 runs.

The semi-final was played at Taunton with Somerset winning by 5 wickets with 6.3 overs to spare. Kent 154, Somerset 157-5. Derek Underwood was at his miserly best with an analysis of 11-4-15-2.

Kent did in fact play a scheduled 'home' fixture against Essex at The Oval in 2010 when, in an innovative move, they hired the ground for a Twenty20 Cup match which attracted a bumper crowd of 7,620, which had been marketed to include commuters on their way home to Kent. The downsides were that Kent lost a close game, and many loyal supporters were not happy with the travelling involved to watch a local derby. Kent scored 171-6 (Darren Stevens 50 not out) with 91 runs coming in the last 7 overs. The Essex side, included former Kent players Matt Walker and David Masters, and won by 4 wickets with two balls to spare.

A look at the fixture list in the 1950s showed that Kent played at Blackheath, Canterbury, Dartford, Dover, Folkestone, Gillingham, Gravesend, Maidstone and Tunbridge Wells. A combination of poor facilities for both players and spectators, sub-standard wickets and a need to channel resources into a central ground means that virtually all cricket is now played at Canterbury, with a nominal week at Tunbridge Wells and occasional visits to Beckenham. Kent are no different from other Counties who also concentrate fixtures at the main headquarters.

Nowadays, a groundsman has the impossible task of satisfying many differing interests and often being in the hands of extreme weather conditions. The paying customers and accountants wish to see an exciting match running its full course. On the pitch, batsmen and each of the bowling disciplines have different expectations of how the wicket should perform.

In 1992, Kent had to supplement their own 3,000-gallon water tank by buying water from outside sources when a total hosepipe ban was imposed by Water Authorities during the summer drought. They were denied the right to be treated as a special case. In the previous two seasons they had been severely restricted as to the amount of water they could use from the ordinary supplies.

The County were in fact reprimanded during that year for producing a below par pitch for the Championship match against Somerset. Kent groundsman Brian Fitch explained, 'Everything went wrong for me in that match. The weather had been very dry beforehand but we had one hell of an overnight storm on the eve of the match that made one half of the pitch damp while the other stayed tinder dry.'

Fitch admitted he was worried about the condition of the square at St Lawrence. 'We are in a business and if you don't get the water to prepare your wickets properly they become at best unpredictable and

at worst downright dangerous' he said. Brian Fitch was Head Groundsman at St Lawrence for 28 seasons, winning many awards and commendations.

In 1994, a relaid pitch proved unpredictable in a Canterbury Week fixture against Hampshire which resulted in umpires Sharp and White reporting it as unfit for first-class cricket. Kent escaped censure and moved to a different part of the square for the next game against Durham.

In the same year the pitches at St Lawrence were rated 18th in a merit table of 18 counties and 2 major universities based on marks by first-class umpires. The following year saw an improved position of 11th and 6th in the one day markings.

On day one, in the match against Surrey in 1997, 19 wickets fell. The visitors only managed 124 with Kent replying at 217-9. Umpires Jesty and Whitehead reported the pitch as poor with ECB pitch inspector Harry Brind penalising the Club 10 points, suspended for 12 months.

Popular overseas player, Aravinda de Silva, took over the captaincy in 1995 against Nottinghamshire at Trent Bridge when Benson sprained an ankle, in a game that realised a Kent record match aggregate of 1,642 runs. He scored 225 in the first innings and his 'agreement' declaration in the second innings left the unlucky Neil Taylor one short of a well-deserved century. Notts won by 3 wickets in the final over

having scored 331. In this image he is shown receiving his Man of the Match award for scoring a century in a John Player League match.

He was captain of the Sri Lanka team that played against Kent in a limited over challenge match. The match was abandoned after 25 deliveries as umpires Jesty and Holder deemed the pitch too dangerous and a new game was started on a used pitch within 30 minutes and with the loss of 5 overs a side. At the time there were obvious concerns with Kent already on a suspended 10-point penalty from the previous year and with St Lawrence chosen as England's World Cup preparation headquarters for 1999.

An interesting match took place in 1999 against Northamptonshire, although in this case no action was considered necessary. The following match report was included in the KCCC Annual 2000:

KENT V NORTHAMPTONSHIRE, Canterbury, 24–26 August 1999

Kent won the toss

Kent won by an innings and 12 runs

Points:	Kent	16	(0 batting, 4 bowling)
	Northants	4	(0 batting, 4 bowling)

Scores: Northants (1) 69 (Bailey 22, Davies 15*, Thompson 11-4-27-6)

Kent 167 (Willis 67, Thompson 22*, Taylor 18.2- 5-55-4)

Northants (2) 86 (Swann 23, Penberthy 20, Ealham 11.2- 1- 35- 6)

'Kent won an incredible game despite being 35-6 in chasing a feeble Northamptonshire total of 69. There was no play on the first day because of persistent drizzle and bad light. Then 17 wickets fell on the second in sultry conditions on a pitch that had some moisture but was exonerated from blame by umpires Nigel Cowley and Bob White. The visitors reached 32 before losing a wicket, only for 8 more to crash for

13 runs. Thompson got dangerous swing and movement off the pitch from the Nackington Road end and claimed 6 wickets for 2 runs in the space of 23 balls with splendid support from Ealham. Smith and Wells reached double figures, but Kent's reply was no better against accurate pace bowling by Devon Malcolm and Paul Taylor and after a hold-up for rain, they were 53-7 at the close, which meant that 17 wickets had fallen in the day for 122 runs in 45 overs. The game turned on the third morning, thanks to brave and determined batting by the Kent tail, led by Willis, who was in the side as deputy for the injured wicket-keeper Marsh. He had come in at 35-6 and was 7 not out overnight, but with stoic support from McCague, Patel and Thompson – who shared successive stands of 32, 50 and 44 – he went on to his highest Championship score in what proved to be his final first-class innings, hitting 67 off 113 balls before being last out. Willis gave two chances, but he rode his luck and played some bold shots especially against the still-dangerous Malcolm. With conditions by now much improved Kent could have expected sturdy resistance from a side anxious to avoid being dropped to Division Two. Instead Northamptonshire surrendered in the most dismal fashion after the experienced Rob Bailey, their top scorer in the first innings, departed to the third ball. This time it was Ealham who did most damage. Skipper Tony Penberthy and Graeme Swann offered a hint of resistance before 5 wickets fell for 10. The game was all over before tea, the visitors having been put out twice for a total of 155 in 56.3 overs.'

Players often express their opinions although not always in public as Bob Woolmer did when he was coach of Warwickshire, 'We played on some terrible pitches in 1993, not least at Edgbaston and my old County at Canterbury which produced the slowest, lowest wicket I've ever seen. We need hard, fast wickets which mean the groundsmen have got to leave grass on, roll it in while it's wet and get the surface true, fast and bouncy.'

Steve Marsh, shown in action above, also complained at the lack of bounce and pace in the St Lawrence pitch after Kent's defeat by Leicestershire. 'Why sign a world-class leg-spinner like Paul Strang and give him a wicket like that to bowl on? All over the country other Counties are producing wickets that seem to deteriorate naturally and turn by the third day, but we can't seem to do that here.' Head groundsman Brian Fitch said in response, 'The day before the match, the players all seemed rather pleased with the pitch, but unfortunately the weather intervened. Because of the rain there were only three days of cricket over the four days. Sure enough the wicket was low and slow, but it was turning towards the end. Had it been a proper four day game it would have turned for Paul Strang on the last day'.

In 1998, the St Lawrence ground suffered at the hands of students. Firstly the University of Kent's hockey teams were banned from holding functions at the ground following bad behaviour at a dinner and this was followed by slight damage to the square after an end-of-term party organised by students of Christ Church College, Canterbury.

First-class cricket has been played at the St Lawrence Ground, Canterbury, since 1847 and from the outset a lime tree has stood within

the playing area. Whether the ball hits the trunk or the highest branch, the score will only count as four runs. The question often asked, is how many times has the tree been cleared, and the answer is three for certain.

Col AC Watson achieved the feat off Tich Freeman's bowling when playing for Sussex in 1925, as did the famous West Indies batsman Learie Constantine in the 1928 Tourist match. Some 64 years later another West Indian, popular Kent overseas player Carl Hooper, cleared the tree while scoring a century in his debut match against Durham.

Robert Relf for Sussex in 1907 and Jim Smith for Middlesex in 1939 are two other players who may have a claim to have achieved this feat, but the evidence is inconclusive.

In 1998, a report from experts diagnosed tree fungus with a maximum life expectancy of ten years. The following year, a replacement was planted by EW Swanton outside the playing area in readiness for the demise of the diseased tree. This happened earlier than expected, in 2005, when high winds caused permanent damage and the replacement was moved to its permanent place within the boundary and close to the original.

To mark this occasion, a ceremony was held which included a Blessing by the late Supporters Club President, the Rev Canon Chris Byers and the following poem entitled 'Farewell St Lawrence Lime' written by broadcaster and writer Irving Rosewater, was read by Chris Cowdrey.

Not merely just for Kentish men,
Nor just for Men of Kent,
For all who saw its noble boughs,
Knew proudly what they meant.

Not just a tree,
Not just a lime,
But Kent's own icon
Set in time.

Here Felix, Pilch and Alfred Mynn,
Wenman, Willsher too,
Adorned the Ground with majesty
As this mighty icon grew.

Then Harris (Lord) and Ivo Bligh,
And Woolley, Blythe and Ames,
Chapman, Fagg, Cowdrey, Knott
An immortality of names.

The regal lime, it saw them all
At third man or at deep long on:
Nature now has made her claim,
Some Kentish grandeur gone.

Former Australian fast bowler, David Gilbert who has played for the Mote put the Australian perspective, 'It's typical of English cricket. A tree gets in the way for 200 years and when it falls down, instead of cheering, they plant a new one.'

The first reference to Leeds & Broomfield Cricket Club was in 1762. It has played in the grounds of the historic Leeds Castle, outside

Maidstone, and enjoyed the patronage and financial support of the castle owners. The original ground was by the lake and is shown in the photograph with horse-drawn maintenance being undertaken. The Club moved to its present ground in the late 1940s and many changes have taken place over the years to the ground, pavilion and facilities.

This photograph shows the ground as it is today, sharing with the St Lawrence ground, a tree within the field of play. The tree in question is the large one to the left and the castle can be seen in the distance on the right.

On the first day at Canterbury against Essex in 1905, while players were practising, a ball was hit onto the match wicket and driven over by the roller on a good length which necessitated cutting a new strip.

The year 1906 was a golden year for Kent cricket when they won the County Championship for the first time since its formation. A crucial game was at Blackheath in early August against Surrey who were above Kent in the Table at that stage. Surrey were favourites for most of the match but were bowled out for 80 in their second innings leaving Kent as the unlikely winners. This unexpected collapse caused surprise in cricketing circles but Lord Harris explained events with the following letter to *The Times*.

In his letter it should be clarified that JR Mason was captaining Kent in the absence of CHB Marsham. The relative of Hayward was his Uncle, Tom Hayward Snr who played for Cambridgeshire and the bowler for the Australians was CE McLeod in 1899.

Sir,

We who sit on the benches like to theorize about remarkable events at cricket; so I venture to send my theory as to one cause which influenced the collapse of the Surrey eleven yesterday. I believe it was due to a factor of which sufficient consideration is not taken – viz the wind.

I inquired about the wicket directly I got to the ground yesterday morning, and was assured that it was as good as the previous evening when Kent could make 300, and certainly the first 45 minutes play bore out that description; although the first two batsmen scored but slowly, and had to play very carefully, they did not appear to be in difficulties, and I certainly anticipated that, when we got to the best batsmen, and the bowlers were getting tired, runs would come more easily.

I was sitting nearly opposite the pavilion, and noticed that the wind was blowing at first almost directly in my face, but that during that 45 minutes it was constantly freshening and backing against the sun, so that by the end of that time it was blowing almost directly against the sweep of Blythe's arm.

All credit belongs to Mr. Mason for his admirable management of the bowling, and his personal success, but I am sure he would admit that it was Blythe who won the match so far as the Surrey second innings was concerned.

My theory is that the wind caused Blythe's ball to hang in its flight and break back from the pitch, and that this was the important influence in making Blythe as unplayable as he was. He is, of course one of the best bowlers of his type that we have seen, but none of them – Jimmy Shaw, the Woottons, George and Jim, Rhodes, or any, however good they be – have ever met with such remarkable success on a good fast wicket unless there was some other influence assisting them; to entirely beat Hayward twice in a quarter of an hour is a remarkable performance, for we can say, as truly of him as was written 50 years ago of his relative:-

"You may bowl your best at Hayward, and whatever style you try
Will be vanquished by the master's steady hand and certain eye."

Some years ago at Canterbury, in a match against the Australians Mr. Burnup and an Australian bowler met with very remarkable success when bowling from the pavilion end against the wind, which was coming directly against the sweep of their arms; an extraordinary number of catches in the slips were made on that occasion; this was again, I think, largely due to the ball hanging in the wind and then going away; at any rate these two very similar incidents seem to me to give some justification for the theory I venture to propound.

Yours faithfully

HARRIS
3 Old Jewry, EC
August 2, 1906

Lord Harris was again involved during the South African tour in 1924 when their early season preparation was hampered by bad weather and there was talk of wickets being covered to enable some cricket to take place. Technically this was against the Laws and he was believed to be opposed to the suggestions. Percy Fender, the Surrey captain, went public with a story of Lord Harris seeking his advice on covering the square at Scarborough to save a festival match. Harris was not amused and his response was, 'Don't you ever write anything about me, my views or MCC in print again, young man'. Fender was forever convinced that this incident had deprived him of the England captaincy.

England may have won the football World Cup in 1966 but cricket in Kent did not prosper, mainly due to the weather. Cars were bogged down during Canterbury Week and only one day during Maidstone Week was not affected by rain. The annual report noted that pitches were deteriorating with Dartford and Blackheath not up to standard. Dover had however improved but due to over-watering the County game only lasted two days.

The following year the Club made it clear that it hoped that its policy of playing in various parts of the County would be permanent but it was vital that wickets were of first-class standard.

Rectory Field, Blackheath.

In May 1970, Warwickshire beat Kent by 93 runs at the Bat and Ball ground, Gravesend, with Rohan Kanhai scoring 107 out of Warwickshire's first innings total of 204. He batted for 190 minutes, giving a masterly display on a sub-standard pitch. Derek Underwood took 14 wickets in the match.

By 1972 Gillingham, Gravesend and Blackheath had disappeared from the fixture list and 25 years later only Canterbury, Maidstone and Tunbridge Wells remained.

Equally, problems were experienced at Folkestone as long ago as 1931 when the two festival games both finished in two days. The first game of the following year against Lancashire provided Tich Freeman with a match return of 13 for 144 and Kent with a further two-day victory which resulted in doubts being expressed about the suitability of the wicket. During the week the wicket had been described as both 'like powdered chalk' and 'badly crumbled'.

In spite of the criticisms there had been some excellent batting performances during the 1930s and 40s and no other spinners had matched Freeman's figures. Nevertheless, after World War II the wicket was dug up and relayed with more durable clay.

In 1979, Kent achieved their only home win of the season against

Notts on what was described as 'a suspect Folkestone wicket'. Spinners dominated the game with Derek Underwood having a match analysis of 13-71. At one stage the Notts batsmen also had to contend with mist.

Little did David Nicholls think that his benefit match against Essex at Folkestone in 1980 would be over in two days and played on a wicket that the Kent Annual described as 'dreadful' and was the subject of a report to Lord's by the umpires as being unfit for first-class cricket. In all, 40 wickets fell for 362 runs in just over nine hours of play.

Requiring just 119 runs to win, Kent could only manage 68, with Essex winning by 50 runs. The highest individual match score was by Essex batsman, Stuart Turner with 35. Graham Gooch 'bagged' a pair and Derek Underwood had a match analysis of 12-99.

In 1985, Folkestone hosted Derbyshire in weather that was described as 'wretched' and 'dark, dreary and wet'. The cricket was no less inspiring on the last day as Derbyshire battled through 84 overs to an excruciating draw, reaching 70-7 with Kent bowling 57 maidens. The main bowlers and their statistics are seen below:

	O	M	R	W
Eldine Baptiste	10	6	10	1
Derek Underwood	37	28	23	3
Laurie Potter	30.4	22	13	3

The following year at Folkestone Kent beat Warwickshire by an innings and 30 runs. Warwickshire 267 and 65. Kent 362. Derek Underwood exploited a worn last day pitch and with Richard Davis, making his Championship debut, the pair took all 10 wickets in the visitor's second innings, bowling a combined total of 47 maidens.

	O	M	R	W
Underwood	35.5	29	11	7
Davis	31	18	38	3

Chris Cowdrey had a fine match, scoring a century and taking five catches in Underwood's 7 wickets.

Davis was to feature with fellow left arm spinner, Min Patel, when they shared the 20 Leicestershire wickets that fell at Dartford in 1990, with 10 apiece. The ball turned from the start and Kent won by 7 wickets, with Mark Benson scoring a century in the first innings. Dartford was the subject of a report by the TCCB inspector of pitches, Harry Brind, after he had been called in by the umpires on the second day, effectively ending Dartford as a first-class venue.

Richard 'Dickie' Davis was raised in East Kent and was a talented slow left arm bowler who played 125 first-class matches for Kent between 1981 and 1993 taking 320 wickets and scoring 1,795 runs. Derek Underwood and later Min Patel were also left arm bowlers on the staff so Davis moved to Warwickshire for two years where he was part of the team that won the treble, i.e. The Championship, Benson and Hedges Cup, and AXA League. He was now in competition with Ashley Giles for the spinning role and in 1996 he moved to Gloucestershire. He

joined Sussex in 1998, playing just four List-A matches and at the end of the season he retired to concentrate on coaching.

A surprising finale came to his first-class career in 2001, when he helped Leicestershire out of an injury crisis when he appeared in one match against Nottinghamshire. He scored a half-century and took 6 for 73 and became the first cricketer to have represented five different first-class Counties. Sadly Richard Davis died in 2003 at the age of 37, having been diagnosed with a brain tumour shortly after his last game.

David Masters, born in Chatham, is another bowler who has found success by moving to other Counties. Making his debut for Kent in 2000, he achieved his best bowling performance of 6-27 for the County in only his fourth senior game against Durham at Tunbridge Wells. Kent won by 190 runs and two features of the game were, Matt Walker's maiden first-class victim when he caught and bowled Paul Collingwood and 16 leg-before decisions that were given by the umpires. Masters moved initially to Leicestershire and then to Essex and his accurate fast medium bowling has benefitted each County, both in Championship and one day cricket.

Kent finished runners up in the Championship in 1967, which was the highest position since 1928. Leicestershire finished third and with Kent earned the lowest marks for home pitches. The wickets at Gillingham and Dover were said to be causing grave concern to the MCC's Special Committee.

Kent defeated Worcestershire by an innings and 101 runs at Tunbridge Wells in 1960 with the game completed in a single day. The match was preceded by unsettled weather, heavy thunderstorms and overnight rains, and played on a wicket described as grassless and damp, which broke up as it dried out. Colin Cowdrey described the wicket as a travesty and apologised to the Worcestershire team.

The complete scorecard is reproduced below:

KENT V WORCESTERSHIRE, Tunbridge Wells, 15 June 1960

Kent won the toss and elected to bat

Kent won by an innings and 101 runs

Kent won the toss and elected to bat   Umpires: T.J. Bartley and J.S. Buller

KENT	1ST INNINGS	
A.H. Phebey	b Gifford	16
P.E. Richardson	b Flavell	23
*M.C. Cowdrey	c Broadbent b Pearson	17
R.C. Wilson	c Headley b Flavell	0
S.E. Leary	st Booth b Slade	23
P.H. Jones	c Broadbent b Slade	73
A.L. Dixon	c Dews b Pearson	17
†A.W. Catt	st Booth b Gifford	0
D.J. Halfyard	st Booth b Gifford	0
A. Brown	b Gifford	1
P.A. Shenton	not out	7
Extras	(B 7, LB 2, NB 1)	10
TOTAL	(all out)	187

FOW: 1-41, 2-43, 3-43, 4-68, 5-104, 6-151, 7-154, 8-161, 9-179

Bowling	O	M	R	W
Flavell	18	8	25	2
Pearson	16	7	35	2
Slade	18	5	54	2
Gifford	17	5	63	4

WORCESTERSHIRE	1ST INNINGS		2ND INNINGS	
J.B. Sedgley	c Leary b Brown	7	(2) c Richardson b Brown	2
R.G.A. Headley	b Halfyard	0	(1) c Wilson b Halfyard	0
A.H. Spencer	b Brown	0	c Leary b Brown	4
D.W. Richardson	b Brown	0	b Halfyard	2
R.G. Broadbent	b Halfyard	0	c Catt b Halfyard	22
*G. Dews	lbw b Brown	0	b Brown	0
†R. Booth	b Brown	2	c Wilson b Halfyard	7
D.N.F. Slade	b Halfyard	9	c Leary b Shenton	11
N. Gifford	not out	0	c Brown b Shenton	4
D.B. Pearson	b Halfyard	0	c Cowdrey b Halfyard	2
J.B. Flavell	b Brown	1	not out	0
Extras	(B 1, LB 5)	6	(B 5, LB 1, W 1)	7
TOTAL	(all out)	25	(all out)	61

FOW: 1-6, 2-7, 3-8, 4-9, 5-9, 6-9, 7-24, 8-24, 9-24

1-0, 2-6, 3-7, 4-17, 5-18, 6-40, 7-51, 8-51, 9-61

Bowling	O	M	R	W
Halfyard	9	4	7	4
Brown	8.1	5	12	6

	O	M	R	W
Halfyard	13	2	20	5
Brown	8	2	22	3
Shenton	4.5	0	12	2

Kent won by an innings and 101 runs

Due to the lack of support and the poor accommodation, 1890 was the season that saw the end of County cricket at West Malling. More than a century later the Maidstone public were again to be deprived of County cricket when the Mote venue was withdrawn.

On the 11 April 1913 the Tunbridge Wells cricket pavilion was burnt down by militant suffragettes. An arson campaign was being conducted to attract attention to their cause and the targets tended to be buildings which represented male privilege. An unknown Kent official may have provoked the attack with the comment, 'It is not true that women are banned from the pavilion. Who do you think makes the teas?' The mayor denounced the action, declaring that 'Tunbridge Wells is a hotbed of militants' and a public meeting was convened at the Great Hall to protest against the atrocity.

Baroness Orczy, the famous author of the Scarlet Pimpernel, moved into Snowfield, a large property next to Bearsted Green, around 1908 and was a friend of Pelham Warner. She is known to have been interested in cricket and a match on the Green was also a target of suffragettes. Local residents awoke to find slogans had been placed all over the pitch. The main perpetrator was later discovered to be an employee of the Baroness.

In June 2005, Kent played the last game at the Mote ground, Maidstone. The decision remains contentious within the Kent cricketing public who have been deprived of a popular and well-supported venue in the centre of the County.

Earlier, heavy rain resulted in the match against Gloucestershire being played on a seamer-friendly surface which Kent won by 7 wickets in just over two-and-a-half days.

An extract from the Season Review of 2005 reported in the 2006 Club Annual is reproduced below:

The next County Championship match – against Gloucestershire at The Mote, Maidstone – will be remembered for all the wrong reasons. The decision of the ECB to relieve the County of eight points as a punishnent for a sub-standard pitch left the bitter taste of injustice in the mouths of all those connected with Kent cricket. The damp pitch was exploited by Kent's bowlers after David Fulton won the toss and invited the visitors to bat. A number of bad strokes did not help Gloucestershire's cause and lunch was reached at 92 for 7; however, thanks to 27, 39, and 25 by numbers 7, 9, and 10 the score – on a rain affected day – was almost doubled to 183 all out. By now the ECB pitch inspectors were on their way, and the Kent cause was not helped when 18 wickets fell on the second day for a total of 288 runs – exactly 16 runs per wicket. Eventually Kent scored the 78 runs required for victory for the loss of three wickets and the match ended early on the third day.

Kent's main gripe appeared to be that even if the pitch was a bit on the dodgy side it was the same for both sides. Secondly, if this was worthy of a deduction of eight points then Surrey's similar punishment for deliberate ball tampering earlier in the season must surely be worthy of a much greater 'fine'. To equate the two 'crimes' was nonsense. An appeal against the loss of points was dismissed.

The fact that Derbyshire knocked up over 300 off 50 overs on the same square two days later in a one-day game simply rubbed salt into the wounds and Kent's plans to return to Maidstone had been put on hold for the foreseeable future.

Taking the team to all parts of the county now seems to be dead and buried as a concept with only Tunbridge Wells and the recently reinstated Beckenham surviving alongside Canterbury. In 1955, over 60 years ago, long before covered pitches and pitch inspectors, Kent played two three-day Championship matches at Gravesend, Tunbridge Wells, Blackheath, Maidstone, and Dover, as well as Canterbury, and one three-day game at Gillingham and at Folkestone. A total of eight different venues!

Maidstone had hosted County Cricket since 1859 with very few problems. Indeed, Carl Hooper was quoted as saying, 'This must be one of the flattest tracks in the country and I do love the short straight boundaries. During the four years I've played here the ball doesn't seem to have swung or seamed, so once you're in good nick and you can apply yourself, you should do well.'

In 2000, Mote groundsman, Malcolm Bristow had prepared wickets for the Maidstone festival for 38 years, earning awards and a reputation

for excellence. This photograph shows him receiving a silver salver from the Kent chairman, Carl Openshaw, on behalf of the County for his outstanding contribution to Kent cricket.

In 1862, Kent were due to play Yorkshire at Maidstone for the benefit of Richard Mills but was switched to Cranbrook following a financial disagreement between the County and the Mote Park Club.

Lord Harris was forced to add his apologies for a match against Sussex in 1929 when the wicket had been watered too late or too well, with Tich Freeman taking 13-105, resulting in Sussex losing by an innings.

Kent scored 296 on day one against Hampshire at Mote Park in 1967 but the following day the opposition were bowled out for 96 and 32 with Derek Underwood having match figures of 12-50 with the wicket crumbling at one end. There was a great furore at the time but it is open to question as to whether the outcome would have been the same against bowlers of lesser ability in such conditions.

However, the writing had been on the wall for the long-term future of County Cricket at the Mote since 1990, when the Maidstone Borough Council and the Mote Cricket Club agreed to subsidise the continuation of the Festival week. In 1995, the Council withdrew its subsidy on the basis that it was not the intention to provide funding for profit-making commercial concerns. The Mote Cricket Club agreed to increase its contribution in order to maintain cricket in Maidstone. In 1990, Kent were playing a Festival week at Maidstone with a limited overs game played between two Championship matches. By 1995 this had been reduced to one Championship and one limited-over match, a format which continued until County Cricket ceased at the Mote.

County Cricket was last played at Tonbridge in 1939. On one occasion the umpire decided that the ground was too wet and abandoned play for the day. The spectators were outraged by the decision and invaded the pitch which was deliberately vandalised. The police were called and persuaded the crowd to disperse, despite being threatened. The match resumed on the following day on a new pitch.

Kent played a total of 107 first-class matches at the Angel ground, Tonbridge between 1869 and 1939 and at one stage a canvas screen

was erected to prevent people from using the back gardens of High Street shops to obtain a free view. When some of the more enterprising brought in scaffolding there was a race to see whether it would finish higher than the screen.

Other Counties have ground problems and in 1904 the match at Harrogate against Yorkshire was declared non first-class after the pitch had been rolled, watered and doctored by persons unknown between the end of play on the first day and the start of the second day's play. For the benefit of spectators, play took place on the second day but not on the third.

The afternoon session of the final day of Lancashire's County Championship Match against Kent at Old Trafford in June 2007 was delayed due to burning gravy. A pan containing gravy caught fire in the Old Trafford kitchen and with smoke billowing, the pavilion had to be evacuated and the fire brigade called.

At Blackpool, acting captain DM Green faced a dilemma when winning the toss in 1966. Deciding to bat on a pitch of doubtful lasting qualities, Lancashire were bowled out for 62 with Underwood taking 6-9 off 10.1 overs. Facing a Kent total of 251 Lancashire could only manage 159 and lost by an innings and 30 runs in two days.

In the AXA league game at Northants, Kent won by 7 wickets on a suspect pitch that had previously been used for a four day Championship match. The reason given was that the black sightscreen sheets draped over the new indoor cricket school on an alternative wicket would have partially obscured the view of dignitaries attending the official opening, performed by Earl Spencer, the County's patron.

In a match winning innings of 65 in 61 balls, Carl Hooper celebrated the event by smashing one of his five sixes onto the balcony of the school, shortly after the ceremony. This was not the end of a Kent connection as surprisingly Northants played their next home match against Sussex on the same pitch, which they won by 136 runs but were given a 25-point penalty after an investigation by the ECB, chaired by Mike Denness.

A cricket match was played on the frozen water of the great lake at Eridge Castle in February 1879, the seat of the Marquis of Abergavenny. Some 2,000 visitors witnessed hockey being played at one end of the lake and cricket between Lord Henry Neville's side and ES Williams' side at the other. The captains led the way, both scoring half centuries, and displaying skill with both skates and bat. Bad light prevented a result with the scores, Lord Neville's side 228. Williams' side 176-8, with five of the side being run out.

Gerald de Lisle Hough played 14 matches for Kent in 1919/20 with a top score of 77 and was appointed manager of Kent in 1936. In 1916, he had appeared at an unlikely venue for the Officers against the Sergeants in a cricket match behind the lines and organised by the Royal West Kent Regiment. The Sergeants  were dismissed for 9 (6 byes). In reply, Hough dispatched the first ball into the mule lines and taking advantage of no boundaries and a reluctance of the fielding side to take issue with aggressive mules, the opening batsmen passed the total, all ran, and the match was won with a single shot.

Another unusual venue for cricket is the Goodwin Sands, which are located off the coast of Ramsgate, Deal and St Margaret's. This is a treacherous ten mile sandbank and has accounted for countless shipwrecks and loss of life. Tides, together with weather conditions and those forecast, should be taken into account, which was not the case in 2006 with the making of a TV programme recreating cricket on the Sands, resulted in the involvement of lifeboats and a rescue helicopter.

There were no such problems in 1985 when a fundraising match was played between a Kent XI and a Select XI. Numerous fishing boats from Deal and Walmer conveyed the players and spectators, to supplement the resident seals, with excellent TV, radio and press coverage. A cricket match on the Sands was first recorded in 1813 and others have been played periodically ever since.

CHAPTER FIVE

OBJECTIONS

By the 1870s Counties were beginning to take proper qualifications seriously. On Kent's first visit to the present Hove ground in 1872, Sussex objected to George Shaw, a left arm fast bowler from Notts, employed on the ground staff at St Lawrence. Shaw umpired instead of William Fryer who was drafted in to play. Fryer was a useful batsman, bowler and wicket-keeper who played for Kent until 1870 despite losing an eye in 1862 when he gave up keeping. Attitudes varied regarding qualifications and Shaw made subsequent appearances for Kent in that season.

After the World War I reformists were looking to change cricket and fortunately 'extreme' proposals such as penalising the batting side for playing a maiden, a maximum of four professionals per side and a ban on left handed batsmen (no Woolley or Chapman?) were rejected. Only one change was approved: play ending at 7.30 p.m. and this only lasted for the 1919 season with both players and spectators preferring an earlier finish.

Over the years there have been many changes introduced into the game, with the usual 'fors and againsts' and it is important that these voices are heard, regardless of the eventual outcome. It is interesting therefore to record some of the various views expressed by John Evans, former editor of the Kent County Cricket Club Annual in the Editorial of the 1992 and 1996 editions:

'I have not met one regular follower who is not appalled at the way that Tuesday and Friday starts were suddenly introduced last season without approval or apparently even consultation. Do cricket's rulers realise, for instance, that people still take week's holidays to coincide with cricket weeks – or at least, they used to?'

'One competition that nearly everyone agrees is in need of drastic overhaul, if not abandonment, is the Sunday League. Here again, suggestions that coloured clothing, black sightscreens, white balls and whatever would somehow persuade a new category of cricket-watcher through the gates were unrealistic. All that would have done is deter the dwindling band of Sunday followers even more.'

'Perhaps by next season someone will have won over the logical idea of having two divisions of nine teams playing 50-over matches and each of the top two qualifying for semi-finals.'

'As for logos painted on outfields...the mind is already boggling.'

'The longer four-day game may prove to be one way of producing more effective players for England in the long run (at least according to those who administer the game), but it leads to much cricket that even the most dedicated can find predictable, not to say tedious.' (1996)

'Whether this in itself is a key factor in the decline of crowds at County games is open to conjecture. Certainly the followers are becoming more and more polarised; a completely different group on Sundays from the traditionalists in the week.' (1996)

Some interesting comments from around 20 years ago, coupled with the statement that the views of contributors do not necessarily reflect the official views of Kent CCC!

When Peter Richardson decided in 1958 to leave Worcestershire and join Kent, his new County were acquiring a proven Test player with a sense of humour. He would keep his team-mates entertained with his off-field banter and was not above involving the 'establishment'. On one occasion, Richardson was batting and EW Swanton was commentating when Kent played Hampshire. Involving other parties in the practical joke, Richardson protested that a 'booming' noise was affecting his concentration and the game was held up. Swanton was not amused to be told that his voice was the source of the problem and informed Richardson that he would be a better player if he concentrated more on his batting rather than silly jokes.

Brian Johnston also 'suffered' at the hands of Peter Richardson when he was advised that the father of Mike Denness was a sheep farmer from Banff and Mike used to travel hundreds of miles each weekend to play cricket in Inverness. This information was conveyed over the radio and Brian Johnston spoke to Mike Denness at tea, hoping that his father had been listening to the broadcast on his sheep station. A surprised Mike Denness explained that he had never played cricket in Inverness and his father was a sales manager living in Ayrshire.

After his retirement Richardson wrote outrageous letters to the *Daily Telegraph* from fictitious Colonel Blimps.

The year 1970, saw Kent finish runners-up to Lancashire in the Players County League with an interesting 10-over match between the two sides, which Kent won by reaching the Lancashire total after 9 overs. Lancashire challenged the result on the basis that the competition regulations required the Kent innings to last a minimum of 10 overs. The result was upheld by Lord's.

The result of Kent's match against Sussex at Eastbourne in the John Player League on 9 August 1981 proved to be contentious. Batting first, Kent scored 164-4 from 39 overs (Chris Tavare 44) but rain reduced the

Sussex target to 148 from 35 overs. From 47-1 they collapsed to 79-6 but recovered, requiring just 4 runs from 10 balls with 4 wickets in hand. In a dramatic finale, Woolmer and Jarvis each took 2 wickets, to bowl Sussex all out for 147. One short of the winning total.

However, the revised Kent total was marginally over 147 and they were declared winners on the basis of the faster scoring rate. Sussex maintained that the result was a tie and were unhappy with the interpretation of the rules. Their objection was referred to Lord's by the umpires and Kent's win was confirmed. Sussex then appealed to the TCCB and after a few weeks' delay, the result was again confirmed in Kent's favour. In the event, Sussex finished fifth in the League and points for a tie would not have changed that position.

In May 1994 Kent were due to play Warwickshire in the quarter-finals of the Benson and Hedges Cup. On arrival they found variable ground conditions, making it impossible for the game to proceed. In the absence of an agreement to transfer the game to Derby, there was no alternative but to take part in a bowl out, which Kent lost after Nigel Llong missed

with his two attempts. Kent could not understand how a Test ground could have failed to produce conditions that were playable, but despite an exchange of angry letters between the Clubs and a formal complaint to the TCCB, the result stood.

Many supporters had made a fruitless journey to Birmingham and matters were not helped when Warwickshire went on to win the trophy.

Alan Igglesden, after the bowl out defeat, remarked 'We came to play cricket but lost at skittles'.

The cricket correspondent for *The Times*, Alan Lee, writing in The Cricketer Magazine said that Warwickshire had let themselves and their public down very badly by failing to use the Brumbella to dry the pitch, 'Kent were rightly resentful even before they lost'. In the same magazine, Matthew Fleming was reprimanded by the TCCB for criticism of Warwickshire's arrangements.

Fleming was always prepared to voice his opinions on matters which he felt strongly such as his condemnation of the England selectors in their selection of the party for the limited-overs tour to Zimbabwe. He pointed out that, 'We have none, yet Essex – third from bottom in Division Two – have three players. It is pretty clear that the selectors don't think much of their domestic competitions.'

Another player who shared his strong views was Graham Cowdrey in the 1997 edition of Cricketers' Who's Who, 'I feel an underlying depression is quietly destroying the game. If we all enjoy it, success will come.' He later added, 'I suppose I'm a bit of a traditionalist and hopefully I won't be around when people start hacking the Championship into two leagues. I've seen a lot of hogwash written by people who clearly don't watch Championship cricket and couldn't name half the Kent or Yorkshire sides. They think that because England aren't performing well at Test level there is something wrong with the County set-up. Other people blame the Sunday League, saying the 40-over game has ruined our Test team, but where's the evidence?'

His father, Lord Cowdrey was quoted in the 1998 Kent Annual as saying, 'When I see the expressions on the faces of so many players today I find it difficult to comprehend. They're being well paid to play cricket, yet they look like they're slogging through a bad nine-to-five day at the office. I loved every minute of my career and I'd like to see that kind of enjoyment among today's players. In my day we used to practise and practise playing cricket. If I'd had to do as much work in fitness rooms as they do today I probably wouldn't have survived very long.'

In the 1997 Championship match against Derbyshire at Canterbury it was realised when Kevin Dean came on to bowl for the visitors, that he was not on the team sheet submitted by the Derbyshire captain and therefore was an ineligible player. Kent captain Steve Marsh and the secretary Stuart Anderson consulted with umpires Ken Palmer and Peter Willey and the game continued after it was accepted that a genuine mistake had been made.

In 2006, Kent retained the Second Eleven Championship with it being decided on average points, rather than total points, as the number of games played by each County varies. Kent played six games, which was the minimum requirement and the

Academy Director, Paul Farbrace, was of the view that winning is not the be all and end all of second team cricket and producing and developing players is the main aim. He favoured the new structure of second team cricket and in particular the combined games. Sam Northeast, a future Kent captain, made an impressive debut as a 15 year old. There were counter views and some concern, from County coaches who felt that learning to win was an important part of young players' development and that the minimum number of games should be raised to ten in order that teams of similar strengths were pitted against each other.

In a second XI competition match against Sussex, Kent had to play with only nine men due to a misunderstanding over the rules. Kent believed that they could play three capped players, as well as three over 25s. Sussex appealed and the ECB ruled that only three capped players over 25 could play. Coach Alan Ealham was not impressed when Sussex refused to allow substitute fielders and rejected the offer to play the game with 11 men with Kent conceding the points.

Kent also lost another second XI competition match to MCC Young Professionals in controversial circumstances. Following overnight rain the overs were reduced from 55 to 33 a side. The visitors made 160-8 before rain ended play with Kent 128-4 after 26.5 overs. Kent thought that they had won on faster scoring rate based on completed overs but it was ruled that the calculation should be based on balls faced and Kent lost by 0.08 of a run.

In 2005, Hampshire might have won the Championship if Kent had held Nottinghamshire to a draw. Hants captain Shane Warne accused David Fulton of gifting the Championship to Notts in what he described as, 'one of the dumbest things I've seen in my life'.

David Fulton for injured Steve Marsh

The report of the match which caused his consternation is shown below:

KENT V NOTTINGHAMSHIRE, Canterbury, 14–17 September 2005

Nottinghamshire won the toss

Nottinghamshire won by 214 runs

Score at 130 overs: Nottinghamshire 478-8

Points:	Notts	20	(5 batting, 1 bowling)
	Kent	3	(1 batting, 2 bowling)

Scores at close of play:

First Day: Nottinghamshire (1) 397-5; Gallian 191, Ealham 24

Second Day: Nottinghamshire (1) 455-6; Ealham 61, Swann 13

Third Day: Kent (1) 237-5; Dexter 79, O'Brien 56

Nottinghamshire were crowned County Champions for the first time since 1987 by clinching a 214-run win after Kent's run-chase gamble petered out on a somewhat farcical last day at Canterbury.

Just when it appeared this rain-affected match that lost 100 overs to inclement weather would peter out into a draw, the captains David Fulton and Stephen Fleming came up with a rather ludicrous run chase deal.

Home captain Dave Fulton ended his side's innings in arrears after agreeing that Notts would not enforce the follow-on and declare once they had a decent total. But his counterpart Stephen Fleming was in a better negotiating position because Notts could still have taken the title with a draw here and a win next week whereas Kent needed victory.

So Kent declared 249 runs behind on first innings on their overnight score of 237 for 7. Nottinghamshire then tucked into some very friendly part-time bowling from Kent to add 170 for 3 inside 23 overs as former skipper Jason Gallian followed his first innings of 199 with a brisk, unbeaten 74. It all left Kent with 70 overs in which to chase 420 runs for a victory that would just about keep their outside title chances alive. It was a desperate gamble that Fulton afterwards described as his only chance of remaining in the title race.

Andrew Harris took 6-76 in an impressive display of reverse swing to bowl the home side out for 205. The Championship trophy, Nott's first in 14 years, was presented by former Nott's chief executive David Collier, later in the same role at the England and Wales Cricket Board.

Subsequently, Test star Shane Warne hit out at Kent's run-chase deal with Kiwi Stephen Fleming which the Australian bowling wizard believed gifted the Frizzell Championship title to Nottinghamshire.

For the 2016 season, only one team from Division Two of the County Championship would be promoted and from the outset Kent had set their sights on this achievement, with winning performances a necessity. They must have wondered why the first two matches were both scheduled away, on the 10 April at Worcester, with its susceptibility to flooding and two weeks later at Leicester.

The inevitable happened, with the ground obviously unplayable and dubbed 'Waterlogged Worcester' no play was possible on any of the four days despite two days of sun. Kent were obviously aggrieved at the inactivity and went into the next game, having not bowled a ball, with some other Counties having played two games.

The CDC under the Chairmanship of Gerard Elias QC, subsequently investigated the circumstances prior to and during the match, and concluded that there were no grounds for any further action. Nevertheless, Elias recognised that significant financial losses and inconvenience, as well as disappointment, will have been experienced by both Counties and their supporters, as well as other members of the public as a result of the abandonment.

Accordingly he invited the ECB to consider whether any further actions and/or safeguards were possible to seek to ensure that County grounds staging matches in April were more likely to be able to do so satisfactorily. No further comment was to be forthcoming from the CDC. In the event Kent finished in second place, 23 points behind Essex.

This however was not the end of the story as the ECB decided that Durham should be relegated due to financial problems, with Hampshire who finished next to bottom being reprieved from the drop. Kent were aggrieved at this decision and felt that they should have been promoted to replace Durham. The ECB's stance was that the decision was in line with the season's rules for two down and one up. Kent decided to appeal and a decision is awaited.

This was not the first time that the option to make alternative arrangements had not been taken. Relegation was a possibility in 2007 and the fact that the game against Worcestershire at New Road was abandoned without a ball being bowled did not help in this respect. The Worcestershire

Chief Executive was adamant that play would be possible, despite reservations from the umpires. Various options were considered, including relocating the game to Kidderminster, rescheduling the match and a compromise of additional points for an abandonment. The ECB commented that Worcestershire had acted 'in good faith but highly optimistically'. None of the options were implemented but fortunately it was not a relegation issue.

The same year Kent beat Gloucestershire in the final of the Twenty20 competition at Edgbaston. Kent chose to field first and restricted Gloucestershire to 146-8. With 32 on the board Rob Key was controversially caught by Marshall at mid-wicket and was later censured by the ECB for his expression of dissent.

Rob Key was also in trouble with the ECB in the following year and 2008 saw the end of Kent's record of being the only County to have played all of its cricket in Division One of the Championship. No doubt the frustration of being early Championship contenders and late relegation candidates came to the surface when they lost in two-and-a-half days to Durham at Chester-le-Street. The Kent captain said that the playing surface was 'absolutely ridiculous' and dubbed the pitch panel as 'a bit of a Muppet Show' for taking no action. He was later fined £1,250 by the ECB and went on to admit that his remarks were 'inappropriate'.

Playing against Sussex in the South Group of the Twenty20 Cup in 2007 at Canterbury, Rob Key failed to see the funny side of being run out by Joe Denley, acting as his runner, after he himself had been run out.

The Royal London Women's One-Day Cup match in 2015 between Kent and Sussex ended in a controversial tie. With Sussex requiring two to win off the last ball, Charlotte Edwards beat the bat and the keeper, Lauren Griffiths, removed the bails believing that Kent had achieved a narrow victory. As the celebrations started, Sussex ran a single believing that they had levelled the scores. After discussions between the umpires and both sides, the match was declared a tie. Kent appealed to the ECB who found that there was no reason to overturn the decision of the umpires on the day and the match was therefore a tie.

CHAPTER SIX

UMPIRES AND OFFICIALS

Those in charge do not have an easy time. They can land in hot water but the game could not continue without them. The scorebook of the match between Benenden and Penshurst in 1892 contains the note 'umpire ducked in pond for giving unsatisfactory decision'. Fortunately the Laws and Spirit of the game usually prevail.

In the early days however, discipline could be lax and two examples in the 1700s illustrate the point. In a game between Kent and England at the Artillery ground it was reported that the match came to an abrupt conclusion owing to a dispute concerning the dismissal of one of the players on the England side. A similar outcome occurred at Carshalton involving a Surrey batsman, but this escalated from words to blows, which resulted in several broken heads.

Thomas 'Daddy' White was a noted English cricketer during the 1760s and 70s. His main club was Surrey but he also appeared for Kent during 1774 and 1776. In 1771 White was playing for Chertsey against Hambledon when he tried to use a bat which was as wide as the wicket. Not unreasonably, there was an objection and a formal protest to the MCC with the result that the Laws were formally changed in 1774 to restrict the width of a bat to four-and-a-quarter inches.

In the late 1800s a list of 20 umpires and their addresses were published, and were described as reliable men, with a thorough practical knowledge of the game and a large majority of them with extended experience in umpiring. The Dickie Bird of the day was Robert Thoms, from London, who is known to have officiated at Kent matches and in one 18-year period he umpired in more than 1,000 matches. Of the 20 named umpires, three lived in Kent. WH Luck and

G Martin, both from Tunbridge Wells, and WH Fryer from Coxheath, who played 75 matches for Kent (1852–72). In 1862 he was thrown out of a trap and lost the sight of one eye as a result of the accident. He continued to appear in County Cricket, though he gave up keeping wicket.

During the Eton V Harrow match at Lord's in 1870 the future Lord Harris ran out CA Wallroth on the grounds that he had been stealing runs by backing up before the ball was bowled. Such action is considered as 'not done' and the Harrow supporters showed their displeasure. Years later one of Wallroth's sisters was still saying, 'That George Harris! I shall never forgive him!'

Lord Harris was touring Australia nine years later and in the second match against New South Wales the umpire for the tourists, George Coulthard, from rival state Victoria gave a close run out decision in favour of the visitors. This resulted in a pitch invasion and, while defending the umpire, Lord Harris was struck by a stick. Armed with stumps and directed by Harris, the team defended its position and refused to leave the ground. Apologies from the Authorities were accepted and the game was later resumed.

George Ulyett of Yorkshire was known to have placed bets during this tour of Australia and his on-field performances were described by Lord Harris as, 'something of a failure, missing catches and playing some childish innings'. In a match against Victoria in December 1881 on a private tour of Australia, Ulyett was implicated with John Selby of Notts to be in collusion with local bookmakers to ensure that the home side won. Despite both performing poorly in the field, the tourists eventually won.

The events were widely reported in the British press, attracting a wide range of correspondence including a letter from Lord Harris which included the statement, 'I know George Ulyett as well as any professional in England, and I would willingly stake my honour on his'. Lord Harris was known as a champion of the professional cricketer but one can only doubt the wisdom of his involvement in this issue.

In his report of a match against Philadelphia on the Kent tour to America, CJ Burnup commented, 'A curious incident occurred during my innings, when I had scored about 50 a bumping ball from King hit me on the thumb and bounced up towards third man. All eyes were fixed on the ball which fell short of the fieldsman. I looked round and saw the bail off and then realised that the rubber had come off my glove and fallen on the wicket. The wicket-keeper had picked up the bail and replaced it and the game proceeded. They never realised I was out until the next ball had been bowled. Should I have walked or not?'

Lord Harris in his cricketing biography *A Few Short Runs* (1921) stated, 'I was caught in the Kent V Derbyshire match twice in one season by the same wicket-keeper, off the same bowler, off exactly the same spot – viz the extreme point of the rubber thumb, and given on each occasion "not out" by the same umpire: no doubt he could not see the very slight impact, and would not trust to the sound…'

Surely if there were a case for an honest departure, this was it. But Harris continues 'now this is a case where

the umpire on appeal, has decided that the batsman is not out and therefore the batsman, though he knows he was out, has no business to retire from the wicket'.

Tony Pawson's view as to whether or not to 'walk' was governed by his experience in one of his early appearances for the County at the hands of Frank Chester, the leading umpire of the day. Given out twice in single figures when no contact had been made with the ball, his philosophy during his career was to leave decisions to the umpire. Alan Knott however drew the distinction that he would walk in County Cricket but not in Test cricket.

Colin Cowdrey, former president of the International Cricket Council and President of the Umpires Association, on a poll which revealed an increase in sledging, aggression towards umpires, cheating and dissent said, 'I see this as the most important issue in sport. Fortunately in cricket we have it written in the Laws that the captain is responsible for the behaviour of his players: in the next few months there will be moves to see that they are made more responsible'.

According to Mike Selvey in his obituary of Colin Cowdrey in the *Guardian* it was mooted that he was given to walking for obvious decisions and then not doing so for the less obvious, in the hope that his reputation would fool the umpire.

Colin Cowdrey captained the England team to the West Indies in 1967/68. He took over from Brian Close who lost his place in controversial circumstances when he was accused and found guilty of time wasting in Yorkshire's match with Warwickshire at Edgbaston in August 1967.

In the second Test, a bottle throwing riot in the afternoon of the third day disrupted play and affected the England players who had been in the field at the time. At one stage England looked to be comfortable winners, only requiring 91 to win, but they ended up fighting for survival and finishing on 68-8. The atmosphere was electric which seemed to unsettle the umpires, including an lbw decision against Cowdrey for a duck off his bat.

There was victory in the 1957 Test series at home to West Indies but how things may have been different had 'Hawk-Eye' been available in that era. Set 289 to avoid an innings defeat in the first Test, England were saved by a stand of 411 between Colin Cowdrey and Peter May who employed a strategy of bat/pad forward play to combat the spinning skills of Sonny Ramadhin who was completely disillusioned. Regular appeals were rejected by the umpires, as was the practice in England at that time, for balls striking the pad some way down the wicket. Ramadhin may have had a point as it was quoted from an England source that 'Colin kicked him to death. He never tried to play with the bat'.

This does not mean to say that front foot decisions are never given, as Kent found out to their cost in the Benson and Hedges final against Lancashire at Lord's in 1995. Needing 275 to win, Kent were 81-3 before

a partnership between Aravinda de Silva and Graham Cowdrey gave Kent a glimmer of hope, when Cowdrey was given out lbw by umpire David Shepherd, sweeping at full stretch, as shown in the picture.

Cricketers everywhere will be familiar with the comments of Steve Marsh, 'It wouldn't have hit another set' and Graham Cowdrey, 'an atrocious decision'. Lancashire went on to win the game.

Kent coach Daryl Foster was perhaps a little more tactful after a Benson and Hedges quarter-final against Northamptonshire when Trevor Ward was given out lbw on 98 by umpire Jack Bond. He felt that Ward was unlucky and a long way down the wicket. He further added that the sweep shot gets us into trouble at times.

Mark Ealham was noted for his 'wicket to wicket' bowling and against Sussex at Tunbridge Wells he had three leg-before victims in ten balls. One of his victims was Sussex skipper Alan Wells, later to join Kent,

who showed his displeasure at umpire Graham Burgess's decision by standing his ground and then hitting the ball to the edge of the square. He later admitted that it was a mistake and out of frustration due to a combination of things.

Middlesex and England spinner Philip Tufnell, who carved himself a career in the media, found himself in trouble against Kent when he was reprimanded by umpire Nigel Plews for having a

Mark Ealham

tantrum and throwing his cap on the ground, when an appeal from fellow spinner Paul Weeks for a bat-pad catch against Mark Ealham was turned down.

Doug Wright was reprimanded by an umpire on the MCC tour to South Africa in 1948/49 for licking his fingers.

Shortly afterwards the following verse appeared in *The Times*:

> As finger – bowls would be denied
>
> To cricketers (fastidious souls)
>
> So Wright claims right upon his side
>
> And having licked his fingers, bowls.

Several Kent players have umpired at the highest international level but even they have encountered problems. In 1973 Arthur Fagg became the first Test umpire to refuse to continue standing, following an altercation with the West Indies captain, Rohan Kanhai, over his rejection of an appeal against Geoffrey Boycott. Kanhai continued to make his feelings known, as did Fagg with his refusal to officiate on the following day, with an explanation in the following press statement. 'If they will not accept decisions, there is no point in carrying on. Why should I? I am nearly 60. I don't have to live with this kind of pressure. I've had to live with it for over two hours out there. People don't realise how bad it has become. I don't enjoy umpiring in Tests any more.'

Play resumed on the next day with a replacement umpire but following persuasion from fellow umpire Dickie Bird and an apology from the West Indies, Fagg resumed at the end of the first over. Although ,this was not the end of the story as the session was played in a hostile atmosphere and the use of dubious bowling tactics. Matters improved after lunch following a warning to both captains by the umpires that the match was in danger of being called off.

David Constant was a very experienced umpire, having been appointed a first-class umpire at the age of 27 in 1969 and a Test umpire in 1971 after a

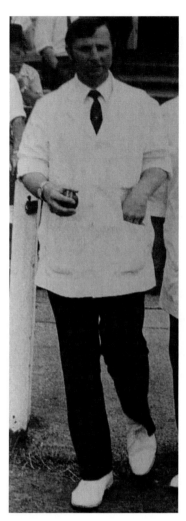
David Constant

playing career of eight matches for Kent and 53 for Leicestershire. Members of the MCC disgraced themselves during the Centenary Test at Lord's in 1980 when they mobbed umpires David Constant and Dickie Bird for their decision that the ground was unplayable after rain.

In 1982, Pakistan claimed that one of the decisions by Constant caused the loss of the Headingley Test and with it, the rubber. On a return visit in 1987, a Pakistan request that Constant did not officiate in that series was refused and he stood in the first two matches. The Pakistanis took it as a sign that they were treated as an inferior touring team.

It is difficult to please everyone as illustrated on the 1987/88 tour of New Zealand when Graham Dilley was fined £250 for an outburst in the first Test at Christchurch. On a frustrating final day as New Zealand blocked out for a draw, Dilley felt he had dismissed Martin Crowe, caught off his boot. The umpire disagreed and Dilley responded with a frustrated bellow of 'Jesus, s***, b*******!'

Mark Benson was a great servant of Kent cricket for 15 seasons, scoring over 18,000 runs at an average of 40.27. He captained the County and played one Test and one ODI for England against India in 1986. Forced to retire with a knee injury at the end of the 1995 season, he made his first-class umpiring debut in1997 and stood in international matches for the first time in 2004.

During the second Test between South Africa and India in December 2006, Benson was forced to leave the field suffering from heart palpitations. Just over a year later, India narrowly lost the second Test in Australia when a number of umpiring decisions went against them and India's team manager was highly critical of the umpires' performance. Much of the criticism was aimed at Steve Buckner who was officially replaced for the

next Test. Mark Benson was not due to umpire in the third Test and had a good match in the first Test, although there were some errors in the second.

He made history against Sri Lanka when he gave Tillakaratne Dilshan out caught behind and he was the first umpire to be asked to refer a decision, which was reversed. There was speculation that he was upset with the referral system when he withdrew in the middle of the second Test between West Indies and Australia in November 2009. This was denied by the ICC, saying that Benson was ill. In February 2010 it was announced that he was retiring from international umpiring but would continue to umpire in English domestic cricket. He stood down in 2016 due to a back injury requiring surgery.

Bob Woolmer had a distinguished career as a coach after the end of his playing career, both at County and International level. He was no stranger to controversy and during the 1999 World Cup he attracted attention, when as the South African coach he communicated during matches with his captain Hansie Cronje using an earpiece. A practice that was later banned.

Moving on to the 2006 Test series in England against Pakistan, he was actively involved as the visitors' coach, in the infamous ball tampering incident. Initially the England team were awarded five penalty runs and a replacement ball was selected after the umpires, Hair and Doctrove, had ruled that the ball had been tampered with. In what was obviously a volatile situation, the Pakistanis initially refused to take the field of play after tea, which resulted in the umpires taking the premature action of declaring England the winners by forfeiture.

Subsequently the captain of Pakistan, Inzamam-ul-Haq was found guilty of 'bringing the game into disrepute' but cleared of 'changing the condition of the ball'. Eventually the result of the match stood but only after the ICC had reversed its original decision, which it had no authority to make, to declare the result a draw.

Bob Woolmer was forced to defend his reputation in 2006, when it was claimed by a former ICC match official that Pakistani players lifted the seam of the ball during 1997 when he was in charge of the team. Woolmer could not recall any such incident and indicated that he had contacted the match officials of one match referred to, and they had no recollection of any such incident either.

Paul Farbrace was a wicket-keeper for Kent (1987–89) before moving to Middlesex (1990–95). On his retirement, he became a coach and in 2007 he was appointed Assistant Coach for Sri Lanka. The team bus was attacked by terrorists in 2009 and he sustained a minor injury.

The motives of the thieves who broke into the car of umpire Barrie Leadbeater at Canterbury and stole his white coat and coloured Sunday jacket may never be known. It is unlikely that they were after cricketing memorabilia as the items were later recovered. In the meantime it was business as usual for Leadbeater, using borrowed clothing from a local umpire.

The umpire in the Sunday League match against Surrey, had a busy over, which lasted for 14 balls. The bowler Duncan Spencer commented, 'After the first two balls, a no-ball and a wide, the lads told me to relax. I was so nervous, I was scared to let go of the ball. I couldn't get the length right but then Monte Lynch pulled one from outside the off stump straight to Matthew Fleming and after that I had my confidence.'

Eddie Crush played as an amateur for Kent from 1946 to 1949 and in 1948 he failed to appeal for a catch behind the wicket which would have dismissed the great Don Bradman, playing for the Australian touring team against Kent. Both Godfrey Evans and Bradman later confirmed that the ball had touched the bat. Asked why he had not appealed Crush said, 'He was my hero, thousands of people, including me, wanted to see him bat – the words just would not come out'. The happy ending was that Bradman was eventually caught by Valentine off the bowling of Crush for 65.

Cricket was in David Halfyard's blood and he enjoyed a remarkable career starting with Surrey second XI before making his first-class debut for Kent in 1956. The picture shows him taking the field at Maidstone. L to R: A. Fagg, A, Phebey, D. Halfyard, D. Ufton, S. Leary, A. Dixon.

Known affectionately as 'the Machine' because of his accurate and consistent right-arm fast-medium bowling, he took over 100 wickets in five consecutive seasons from 1957 to 1961 and was on course for a sixth season, when in 1962 he was seriously injured in a head-on collision in his car on his way to Weston-Super-Mare for a match against Somerset.

It was thought that his career was at an end and although he appeared in two games for Kent in 1964, he gave up first-class cricket to become an umpire. Somewhat surprisingly he was offered a three-year contract by Nottinghamshire and despite questions about his fitness, he gave full value to his new County, with 77 first-class appearances and 38 List A matches.

Following his second retirement from first-class cricket, he played Minor County Cricket for Durham (1971/72), Northumberland (1973) and Cornwall (1974–1982). He also returned to stand as an umpire in first class, List A and Minor Counties Cricket until 1996. In that year, he suddenly died at the age of 65 when weeks before he had been playing in the Devon County League. Following a game for Tiverton the previous year Halfyard said, 'I've got a bit of a bad back and my running between the wickets isn't quite what it was, but I bowled 20 overs unchanged so that can't be bad'.

During a match against Essex at Canterbury, Ronnie Irani was the victim of a leg side 'stumping' when keeper Steve Marsh, originally standing back to Mark Ealham, advanced to the stumps. Square-leg umpire Michael 'Pasty' Harris turned down the appeal on the grounds of unfair play but later conceded that he should have declared the ball dead.

Recent times have seen the introduction of match referees and off field umpires to assist in the control and decision making in important matches. From 1996, Mike Denness (right), served as an occasional Test match referee and in November 2001 he created a furore over his actions in a Test between South Africa and India at Port Elizabeth. He had imposed penalties on four Indian players, reported by the umpires for over-aggressive appealing. He also applied suspended bans on Captain Sourav Ganguly for failing to control his team and Sachin Tendulkar for ball tampering, which was explained that he had not asked the umpires to supervise the removal of mud from the ball.

Denness was unfairly branded as a racist and despite support from the ICC, he was replaced for the next Test by the two competing boards after India had refused to play if he officiated. The dispute only disappeared on humanitarian grounds after Denness underwent heart surgery. He was to officiate in two more Tests in Pakistan in 2002 but in 2003 he was not elected to the newly formed Elite Panel of Referees, despite being put forward by the ECB.

Ed Smith

Ed Smith was four day vice-captain in 2004 and will remember taking over the reins from the injured captain David Fulton in the match against Worcestershire for all the wrong reasons. Smith had, early in the season, published a frank diary of the 2003 season entitled *On and Off the Field*, which had not endeared himself to his team mates.

As Worcester piled on the runs, the attitude of players, led by overseas player Andrew Symonds, left much to be desired and David Fulton, who had travelled with the team, decided to assist by taking the field as 12th man. This was not a success, particularly as he was advised by the umpire that he could not move fielders as 12th man.

In an attempt to placate matters, the chairman of cricket, Mike Denness, journeyed to Worcester but frustrated by the slowness of the County's disciplinary procedures, he tendered his resignation from the post. It is a shame that Ed Smith left Kent at the end of the season with his close friend Alex Loudon. Both had so much to offer Kent cricket but were critical of how the County was being run.

Amjad Khan

In 2009 Amjad Khan joined the England Test squad on their tour of the West Indies as cover for Andrew Flintoff who was struggling with a hip injury. He played his only Test in the fifth Test, taking one wicket and was reprimanded by the match referee for excessive appealing.

An unusual incident was described in a report in the *Kent Messenger* of a game played in 1930 at Thurnham against Maidstone Corporation Transport. During the match a swarm of bees invaded the pitch. An umpire and several of the players were stung, and the game had to be suspended until the bees dispersed.

Kent drew an exciting match with Glamorgan at Tunbridge Wells in 1995 with the help of an umpire in an unusual role. Requiring 271 to win the visitors were on target at 242-5 when umpire Allan Jones was hit by the ball while taking evasive action from a straight drive by Hamesh Anthony. Instead of disappearing towards the boundary, the ball was by the umpire, and was thrown by bowler Martin McCague to wicket-keeper Steve Marsh who ran out the batsman who was stranded having anticipated a run. The fall of this wicket slowed progress and with 7 wickets down Glamorgan required 2 runs to win off the last ball. They failed to score with wicket-keeper Colin Metson being run out.

It was a difficult time for umpires in the National League match against Hampshire at Canterbury in 1999. Initially Neil Mallender was hit on the back of his head from a throw by a Hampshire fielder. Matthew Fleming and Steve Marsh showed Kent's sporting instinct when they refused a third run, which was available as a result of the incident. During the interval, Tony Clarkson was taken ill and unable to continue. Mallender had to stand permanently at the bowler's end, while the square-leg duties were undertaken by Hampshire's dressing room attendant, who was a qualified umpire.

Gordon Littlewood, who was 70 at the time, was in the wars when umpiring for the Mote second XI against Blackheath in 2015 as he required a partial hip replacement following contact with a Mote batsman taking a quick single.

Accidents have also happened to spectators over the years and fortunately are relatively few, even in more recent years, with abortive attempts at catching huge sixes with heavy bats in limited-over cricket. As long ago as 1906 when Kent played Lancashire at Canterbury it was reported in the visitor's second innings that AC MacLaren made a big off drive, and the ball clearing the ring, struck the forehead of an elderly gentleman with so much force as to necessitate his removal to hospital.

Players also suffer injuries. Two of the more unusual incidents are shown below.

While playing for the Gentlemen of Kent against the Undergraduates of Cambridge at Canterbury in 1848, the ball was thrown to CG Whittaker from long leg who sustained a serious injury to his thumb. An operation was necessary to remove the bone between the first and second joints. The bone was mounted in silver and made into a tobacco stop.

The services of a clergyman were not required at Cardiff in 2007 when a rib belonging to Glamorgan batsman Michael Powell that had been removed during an operation, was buried under the Sophia Gardens outfield. Powell who was born in Wales and finished his career at Kent (2012/13) said, 'I am glad that part of me will be at Sophia Gardens for ever.'

Cricket also features unusual dismissals. South African born Sean Dickson earned a contract with Kent for the 2016 season thanks to the runs he scored for the second XI the previous summer. He could not have imagined that before the end of May he would have carried his bat for 207 not out against Derbyshire, missed a game following a freak domestic accident requiring stitches in his hand and been only the second Kent batsman since George Bennett in 1872 to have been given out handled ball, thereby joining a select band of only 60 first-class cricketers to have been dismissed in this fashion.

This latter incident occurred against Leicestershire, and seeing the ball roll back towards the wicket, he reached down to deflect the ball with his hand rather than using his bat or boot. The appeal was led by former Kent wicket-keeper Niall O'Brien and despite checking with his square-leg colleague, Dickson was given out by umpire Russell Evans in contravention of Law 33.

There will be mixed emotions from those players who have 'caught the eyes' of the Selectors to represent their country, only to discover at a later date that there will not be another opportunity. Kent have 14 players who have made a single Test appearance for England, namely CA Absolom, MR Benson, DW Carr, S Christopherson, AJ Evans, HTW Hardinge, A Hearne, GG Hearne, A Khan, WHV Levett, FA MacKinnon, CS Marriott, JW Martin and F Penn.

VA Barton (Hampshire) and J Shuter (Surrey) both played one Test after leaving Kent and AP Wells (Sussex) played one before joining Kent. CJ Tavare played 30 Tests while with Kent, but only one further appearance after joining Somerset.

Charles Marriott (1895–1966) was a leg break bowler and made 12 appearances for Lancashire (1919–1921), the County of his birth, and gained a Blue at Cambridge University in both 1920 and 1921. In 1921 he was included in the squad against Australia at Old Trafford but did not make the final XI.

He became a master at Dulwich College and played for Kent in the summer holidays, making his debut in 1924. In 1924/25 he went on tour to South Africa, under the captaincy of Lord Tennyson. It was dubbed as England's 'Second Team' as there was a parallel tour to

Australia, and the matches between the two countries were 'Unofficial Tests'.

It was not until 1933 that Charles Marriott received international recognition and would consider himself unlucky not to have had an extended Test career after an outstanding debut against the West Indies, taking 5-37 in the first innings and 6-59 in the second, as England won by an innings and 17 runs. He was however selected for Douglas Jardine's MCC team to India in 1933/34 but did not feature in any of the three Test matches, although he twice took 5 wickets in an innings and a hat trick against Madras.

Known as 'Father', he was described as a man of great charm. His batting and fielding were not of the highest quality and the number of wickets exceeded the runs scored during a career lasting from 1919 to 1938.

Kent cricketers have also made single appearances in the international arena at both football and rugby union. Of the footballers, Wally Hardinge can consider himself unlucky to have only one cap at each of the sports. Other Kent players to have played once for England at football are Morton Betts, Derek Ufton, Cuthbert Burnap and Herbert Rawson.

Herbert Rawson played on the losing side in the 1874 cup final for the Royal Engineers with his brother William on the opposing side, Oxford University. The following year, both brothers played for England against Scotland which was the first time that two brothers had played for England in the same match.

Henry Renny-Tailyour was an officer in the British Army and uniquely represented Scotland just once, at both football and rugby. John Le Fleming was also a single rugby cap against Wales in 1887.

CHAPTER SEVEN

WELL BOWLED?

From the early days of underarm bowling to the present day, the development of the bowler's art has caused its fair share of controversies. Kent cricketers played a significant part in legitimising overarm bowling which came in two stages.

The origins of round arm bowling have been attributed to various people, including John Willes who is credited with realising the potential of the new action when his sister, Christina, was bowling to him in a wide arc to avoid contact with her hooped skirts. What is not in dispute is that Willes took a Kent team to play MCC in 1822 and was no-balled for bowling round arm. He reacted angrily and departed on his horse. The battle may have been won, but not the war.

In 1827 Fuller Pilch was picked to play for England V Sussex for three 'experimental' games staged to evaluate the controversial round-arm, so called 'Sussex bowling'. By this stage much of the prevailing under-arm bowling was delivered from hip level or from under the armpit with a jerk or what reads very much like an out and out throw, but after the second match, Pilch was among those who signed a declaration refusing to play in the third unless the 'Sussex players play fair: that is abstain from throwing'. Despite an agreement to bowl underarm, the new style was used, but Pilch did play and subsequently coped with round-arm bowling better than anyone. Later in life, when asked about facing the old under-arm bowling, he asserted 'Gentlemen, I think you might put me in on Monday morning and get me out by about Saturday night'. The traditionalists were not pleased and William Denison, described as the Swanton of his day, wrote that the new style bowlers had 'destroyed all hopes of ever seeing good taste adorn cricket society again'.

Round-arm was not actually legalised until 1835. Although efforts were made to appease the traditionalists, it took another Kent player, Edgar Willsher who was playing for England V Surrey, to force the MCC into accepting the inevitable when in 1862 he was no-balled six times in succession for over-arm bowling. Two years later, the Law was revised by MCC members to read, 'The ball must be bowled: if thrown or jerked, the umpire must call no-ball'. All reference to height no longer existed and bowling is what we understand today.

Edgar Willsher

Willsher's throwing style was featured in the following poem:

Jackson's pace is very fearful, Willsher's hand is very high;
William Caffyn has good judgement, and an admirable eye;

Jemmy Grundy's cool and clever, almost always on the spot;
Tinsley's slows are often telling, though they sometimes catch it hot.
But however good their trundling, pitch or pace, or break or spin,
Still the monarch of all bowlers, to my mind, was Alfred Mynn.
William Jeffrey Prowse (1836-70)

Although the revised Law gave greater freedom, it also created many bowlers with dubious actions and Lord Harris was in the forefront of recognising that the problem needed resolution. In 1884, Kent should have played two matches at Tonbridge but the first against Lancashire was cancelled due to Kent objections to the bowling actions of Watson, Nash and Crosland. The latter being the most successful fast bowler in England, but his quicker deliveries were considered to be blatant throws.

Kent also had problems with Christopher Collins, a right arm fast-medium bowler, who played eight times between 1881 and 1885. Owing to his action being suspect his County career was of short duration.

In 1888 Kent lost the services of Walter Hedley, who after three games had taken 17 wickets but his action brought complaints, although not previously when playing for the Royal Engineers. As Kent had taken a positive stand over doubtful actions, Lord Harris was obliged to withdraw the services of Hedley, after being watched by independent observers who could not confirm that his action was above suspicion.

EB Shine (23 matches, 1896–99) was another Kent player who had an influence on the Laws of the Game. He was a fast bowler, forceful bat and

Col Sir Walter Coote Hedley KBE, CB, CMG

fine field. While playing for Cambridge against Oxford, he caused a change in the follow-on rule, from compulsory to optional. Acting on his captain's orders, he bowled two no-balls, thus preventing Oxford from following-on. The reaction to this was such, that the rule was changed before the start of the following season.

Edward 'Punter' Humphreys made his debut for Kent in 1899 at the age of 17 as a slow left-arm bowler, but he soon developed into a right-hand opening batsman. In a trial match the previous year he thought his chances had gone when he bowled a no-ball and was sent from the field by Lord Harris. He learnt a valuable lesson when Lord Harris explained that a fast bowler can be excused the occasional no-ball but with a slow bowler it is carelessness.

The competitive nature of the Ashes did not start with the bodyline tour as Frank Woolley found on his England debut at The Oval in 1909. His introduction to facing his first ball lasted for 18 minutes while Warwick Armstrong bowled trial balls which were allowed to reach the sightscreen. Fielders did not fetch the balls and it was left to spectators or policemen to act on their behalf. This piece of cynical gamesmanship led to the abolition of trial balls the following year.

Frank Groves had a trial for Kent in 1904 at the age of 20 and he was described as 'medium left arm, quite plain- no bat'. In that season he played with Frank Wooley for Kent Club & Ground against Canterbury & District but he was to become a professional with various Club sides, although he later represented Kent second XI on three occasions (1910/11).

In 1910 he was employed by the Mote Cricket Club and proved to be a fine acquisition, taking 88 wickets in his first season. The following year saw the start of a remarkable sequence of 100 wickets in three consecutive seasons for the Mote and the final figures were:

Mote vs Harlequins 21 and 22 August 1912. F.S Groves, back row, far right.

	O	M	R	W	Ave
1911	505.3	124	1449	100	14.49
1912	589.3	135	1686	111	15.13
1913	453	88	1556	117	13.21

In 1913 there was an interesting exchange of views, starting with the following report in the local press:

'It is not often that a bowler has the galling experience of being taken off because he is bowling too well, but this is just what happened to Groves on Saturday in the match against London Hospital. He had secured the dismissal of all the first time batsmen of a cost of but 29 runs. His last over was a maiden and a wicket with his final ball. It was at this point that his Captain (the Rev. H.R. Ellison) informed him that he was bowling too well. He was taken off and with a less troublesome attack, the batsmen scored more freely...'

The following week there was correspondence from an unnamed Mote player, the gist of which was that Groves was unlikely to hold a grievance in order that other club members might have a bowl. Such members being under the delusion that they can bowl and do not necessarily play to field at deep-mid on at both ends.

This prompted the editor to put the view that Groves was a professional and upon his success depends his living. It is only fair that he should be given every opportunity to take wickets. A report of the Mote season included the following, 'Groves has exceeded all his previous performances with the ball.'

There can be a light-hearted side to contraventions of the Laws of the Game as illustrated when Kent played the Australians at Canterbury in 1938. The Australians only needed 7 runs to win after Kent had saved the innings defeat, when Howard Levett opened the bowling using a bread roll for the first ball, which was no-balled. Three further legitimate deliveries were sufficient. The picture shows him in his normal wicket keeping role, with Frank Woolley at slip, watching a successful stumping.

The actions of Kent and Nottinghamshire in the first County Championship match in 1946 caused some debate when the captains agreed to play an extra half-hour when a draw at the scheduled close of play on the third day looked certain. Notts won on the penultimate ball of the last over of the added time. The issue was that this was not an isolated match, but part of a competition involving other Counties and the possibility of the eventual winner of the Championship being decided on the whim of individual captains to extend or curtail the hours of play, and this should not be allowed. In the event, neither County was in contention for the Championship, with Yorkshire easily taking the title with 216 points against Kent with 144 and Notts 96.

Asif Iqbal played for Pakistan in the second Test match at Lord's in 1974 when England were captained by Mike Denness and included Knott and Underwood. The match was drawn but rain and leaking covers spoilt the match, with Underwood taking full advantage of damp patches. His figures were:

	O	M	R	W
First Inn:	14	8	20	5
Second Inn:	34.5	17	51	8

The Pakistan Manager accused the MCC in an official protest, 'an appalling show of negligence and incompetence in not covering the wicket adequately'. The MCC secretary issued a comprehensive reply which included an expression of regret.

Wishing to maintain a Championship challenge in 1977, Kent were required to score 244 in the fourth innings in two-and-a-half hours following a declaration by Surrey at The Oval. The game ended in a draw but their efforts were not helped by a slow over rate which saw the umpires speak to the Surrey captain, John Edrich, under the Law relating to Unfair Play, when only 8 overs had been bowled in the first 40 minutes.

Slow over rates were still a problem in 1994 when on several occasions, play had to continue for an hour or more past the scheduled finish time in order to meet the quota. At Northampton, with Kent batting, there were still 15 overs remaining when bad light ended play at the expected 6.30 p.m. close of play.

A match at Somerset in 2001 was heading for a draw on the last day when another 'part time' bowler, Rob Key, imitated the Pakistan pace man Shoaib Akhtar which resulted in him being no-balled for throwing by the square-leg umpire.

Golfers are known for an attack of the 'yips' when putting, but this can also happen to bowlers, as Martin McCague can testify. In 1997 against Somerset at Taunton he lost his rhythm and confidence, with the result that he sent down a series of wides, bumpers and beamers before he was withdrawn by umpire Alan Whitehead in his third over. This was not the end of his problems as a back injury prevented him bowling in the second innings.

However, the game had a dramatic finale with Kent needing 7 runs to win at the start of the final over to take them clear at the top of the table. After 4 singles Fleming was out on the fifth ball, and needing 3, captain Marsh could only manage 2. The match was drawn with the scores level, and Kent remained in second place.

Ball tampering has been an issue but in his capacity as chairman of the ICC (1989–93), Sir Colin Cowdrey quoted, 'All Countries have been guilty of tampering with the ball. When a new trick appears, everyone is trying to see what advantages they can get from it. The sudden furore is about the scale on which it has been done over the last year or so.'

In January 2004, Rahul Dravid, who was a Kent overseas player in 2000, was found guilty of ball tampering during an ODI with Zimbabwe. Match referee Clive Lloyd adjudged the application of an energy sweet to the ball as a deliberate offence although Dravid himself denied that this was his intent. Lloyd emphasised that TV footage caught Dravid putting a lozenge on the ball during the Zimbabwean innings on Tuesday night at the Gabba.

According to the ICC's Code of Conduct, players are not allowed to apply substances to the ball other than sweat and saliva. Dravid was fined half his match fee.

The Indian and former Kent coach, John Wright, came out in defence of Dravid, stating 'it was an innocent mistake'. Wright argued that Dravid had been trying to apply saliva to the ball when parts of the lozenge he had been chewing stuck to the ball. Dravid then tried to wipe it off.

Another controversial issue has been that of throwing and for a limited period during 2003, Kent had the services of Muttiah Muralitharan who has been at the centre of that controversy. Muralitharan has been rated as the greatest Test match bowler ever and his haul of 800 wickets in 133 Tests would support this assertion. However, his bowling action has been queried on a number of occasions by umpires and all sections of the cricketing community. He has been called for throwing during three matches in Australia but biomechanical testing on several different occasions has allowed him to continue bowling.

Former Kent favourite Aravinda de Silva, who was acting Sri Lankan captain during the controversy surrounding the no-balling for throwing during the Test match series in Australia said, 'Muralitharan has not changed his action. He's bowled the same way for so long he can't change. The turmoil he has been going through has been difficult to handle, but the way he has kept his spirits up, is great'.

The Indian bowler Vinoo Mankad twice ran out batsman Bill Brown during their 1947 tour of Australia for backing up. A batsman dismissed in this fashion is said to be 'Mankaded' and the first in an ODI was Brian Luckhurst by Greg Chappell at Melbourne in 1974/75.

Geraint Jones arrived at Kent in 2000 having played for Glamorgan second XI the previous year, via Papua New Guinea where he was born of Welsh parents and Queensland, Australia where he grew up. Having

established himself in the Kent side he played the first of his 34 Tests for England in 2004 against the West Indies.

He was a key member of the 2005 Test team that regained the Ashes after an interval of 18 years. Not only did he make valuable contributions with the bat, notably a stand of 177 with Andrew Flintoff at Trent Bridge, but he will be remembered for his leg-side catch off the bowling of Steve Harmison to dismiss Michael Kasprowicz at Edgbaston that ensured the narrowest of victories by 2 runs, and prevented Australia from taking a 2-0 lead in the series. The ball came off the batsman's glove but it appeared from TV replays that Kasprowicz had taken his hand off the bat before the ball hit the glove and therefore should not have been given out.

In a County Championship match in 2012, Durham beat Notts by 16 runs and Mitch Claydon, later to join Kent, scored 17 runs in Durham's first innings total of 194. That was his only and important contribution, as he was replaced by Graham Onions, who had been on England duty but was not included in the final XI against South Africa. Onions had a hand in all Notts first innings wickets, taking 9-67 and effecting a run out.

Gloucestershire defeated Kent in June 2016 by 7 wickets with four balls to spare in the T20 Blast in near darkness at Beckenham. The general feeling was that the umpires should have seen common sense, and taken the players off for bad light, particularly as fast bowler Matt Coles was not allowed to bowl after a Gloucestershire batsman was hit on the head.

The same year Mitch Claydon was in the headlines in a T20 Blast match against Gloucestershire at Bristol, and with the home side requiring 13 runs to win from the final over, he was withdrawn from the attack by the umpires after bowling a second no-ball full toss above waist height. The over was finished by David Griffiths but the drama continued as Barry Howell was caught off another no-ball for height, only to be run out as he went for a second run. Gloucestershire fell three runs short and Kent captain Sam Northeast was full of praise for Griffiths, 'He has been a death bowler for us, so he was a good guy to have up our sleeves'.

Wahab Riaz, a left arm fast medium bowler, was an overseas player for Kent in 2011. He was successful during his brief spell with the County, including a hat trick in figures of 5-17 in a T20 game against Gloucestershire at Beckenham.

However he came close to achieving an unwanted record with an analysis of 0-110 in his allotted 10 overs when playing in an ODI for Pakistan against England at Trent Bridge in 2016. These were the second most expensive figures after 0-113 by Australian Mick Lewis.

CHAPTER EIGHT

MISCELLANEOUS MATCHES

In 1875, Kent played Derbyshire at Catford at a time when the venue was new and the quality of pitches variable. It was decided that each innings would be played on a newly prepared wicket which was not the normal practice. Lord Harris won the toss and may have regretted his decision not to bat, as the visitors scored 213 and Kent could only reply with 70 and 83, to lose by an innings.

The Tunbridge Wells Week in 1960 saw Worcestershire and Sussex as the visitors and there was some concern about the second match when Worcestershire were beaten in a single day. Ted Dexter, the Sussex captain, was offered the choice of two newly prepared wickets and he must have regretted his decision to bat first when Sussex were bowled out for 69 (E Dexter b Brown 0). Normality returned when Kent won by an innings after scoring 391-8dec with both Colin Cowdrey and Stuart Leary scoring centuries, the match lasted three days.

In a drawn match against Sussex at Brighton in 1884 a total of 1,083 runs were scored for the loss of 37 wickets. When Kent batted for the second time they faced a deficit of 515 runs with only 2 hours and 20 minutes of play remaining. At the scheduled end of the match, Kent were 130-7. The Kent captain, Lord Harris (40 not out), offered to continue the game for another 15 minutes but this sportsmanlike offer was not accepted. In the Sussex innings of 464 all 11 of the Kent team bowled.

Another high-scoring draw was played at Southampton against Hampshire in 1912 with the combined total of the two first innings in excess of 1,000. The only players who did not bowl in the match were the two wicket-keepers.

A match with Surrey at The Oval in 1887 was drawn and a report of the match recorded a most unusual incident in Kent's second innings, 'Mr WH Patterson having played a ball to point made no attempt to run, but stepped out of his ground under the idea that the fieldsman would return the ball to the bowler. But instead of doing so, Mr Read, the cricketer in question, threw the ball to the wicket-keeper, who removed the bails. Mr Patterson was fairly out, but it was very unsatisfactory to see so good a batsman got rid of in such a way.'

Frederick Henry Huish was the first of a long line of outstanding Kent wicket-keepers claiming 1,328 victims in a career lasting from 1895 to 1914. Playing against the Australians at Canterbury in 1902, an Australian batsman went for a short run from a ball played just behind the wicket. Huish attempted to run out the non-striker by kicking the ball, but although his attempt missed, it was of sufficient strength to break the wicket at the bowler's end and achieve an unlikely run out.

When Leicestershire played Kent in 1912 they were concerned that it would be impossible to hit Colin Blythe off his length. Arthur 'Pecker' Mounteney, a well-known footballer for Birmingham City, Preston North End and Grimsby Town, decided that with an element of luck, it would be possible to target Blythe himself, which he did, striking

Blythe on the thigh, only to be caught at mid-off. Blythe finished with a match analysis of 15-45.

At Dover in 1937, Kent beat Gloucestershire by 8 wickets, scoring 219 in 71 minutes. The main contributors were Woolley making 44 out of 68 in 25 minutes. Ames hit 70 out of 100 in 36 minutes and then Watt gave such an amazing display that the last 51 runs came in 10 minutes. The win was achieved in 23.2 overs at a run rate of 9.4 runs per over which today's cricketing public, brought up on a diet of limited-over cricket, would not consider unusual.

Northamptonshire were lucky to escape defeat at Northampton against Kent in 1955, the were 79 behind with only 1 wicket left at the close of play. The top scorer in their first innings was 'Extras' with a total of 73 (48 B 23 LB 2 W). The unfortunate wicket-keeper was Tony Catt with sunburn seriously impeding his movements and Doug Wright spinning the ball sharply. The picture shows him displaying his normal skills.

The events of the final session of the opening day of a match against Oxford University in the Parks in 1958 could not have been anticipated after Kent had crawled to 167-6 by tea. They crashed to an all-out total of 172 with David Sayer taking a hat trick against his own County. The University reached 23 without loss, when Fred Ridgway decided to get in on the act by also taking a hat trick.

A remarkable day's play ended with two hat tricks and although Oxford eventually lost by 164 runs, the match was a personal triumph for Sayer, ending with a match analysis of 11-91. In 1964 he was to take a hat trick in his home town of Maidstone, but this time for Kent against Glamorgan.

Scintillating stroke-play was not the order of the day at Canterbury against Middlesex in 1965 when the visitors were beaten by 76 runs. No innings exceeded 3 runs per over and Middlesex could only manage one and a half in their first innings. The feelings of the spectators were summed up with the following 'offering' penned during the match.

> *When Middlesex play Kent*
> *It feels just like Lent*
> *At tea they eat buns*
> *But deny themselves runs*
> *I don't wish to be a bully*
> *But I long to recall the great Frank Woolley*
> *I had rather live in Persia*
> *Than witness such crass inertia*

The pulses were not racing either, according to the following details and report of a drawn match between Kent and Essex at Tunbridge Wells in 1983.

KENT V ESSEX

Kent: 287 and 289-5dec (NR Taylor 116 not out).

Essex: 285 (KS McEwan 142, EA Baptiste 5-104) and 54-2.

Whilst a much improved Kent had many moments to be proud of

in 1983 this fixture did not count among them as spectators were forced to endure one of the dullest encounters imaginable. A lifeless wicket and slow outfield, the result of the recent rains, made Kent bat cautiously and doggedly to reach 287 in 103 overs, only Aslett (47) providing genuine entertainment.

Essex in reply were little quicker, falling two runs behind the Kent total, and were indebted to McEwan, reaching a century in three hours. Potter and Taylor, both playing for their place in the side, put on 47 in 75 minutes before the close and on the final morning Kent plodded along at a run-rate similar to that of Saturday. With Taylor taking his total time at the crease to nine hours. Johnson declined to declare until after tea, when Essex were set an impossible 292 in 95 minutes, which Fletcher, possibly mindful of his own more generous captaincy at Chelmsford a few weeks earlier, described as 'a disgrace to the game'.

Note: At Chelmsford in a rain affected match, two innings were forfeited and Kent won by 6 wickets scoring 321-4 off 74.3 overs.

Kent beat Gloucestershire, (a side which included Brian Broad, father of Stuart Broad; David Graveney, nephew of Tom Graveney; and David Shepherd who was to become a respected Test umpire,) by an innings and 158 runs at Gloucester in 1979. Gloucestershire 154 and 77. Kent 389 (C Rowe 102, A Ealham 87, A Knott 63).

The match was a personal triumph for Derek Underwood with the following bowling figures, which included a spell of 5wickets in 7 overs in the second innings.

	O	M	R	W
First Inn:	31.4	19	39	4
Second Inn:	23.1	14	24	6
Match Figures:	54.5	33	63	10

In 1979, Derek Underwood played 23 first-class matches for Kent, took 5 wickets in an innings on 10 occasions, 10 wickets in a match on 4 occasions, with a best performance of 8-28. Figures for the season were 799.2 O 335 M 1575 R 105 W 14.85 Av. In all for Kent, he took 100 wickets in a season seven times (144 in 1966), 9 wickets in an innings three times and 10 wickets in a match 38 times.

Needing 234 to beat the West Indies in the second Test at Lord's in 1963, the English batsmen had to withstand some hostile bowling from Wes Hall, resulting in Colin Cowdrey having to retire with a broken bone just above his left wrist.

When Hall started the last over of the match, England required 8 runs with 2 wickets left. A run-out off the 4th ball meant that Cowdrey came to the crease with 2 balls left and 6 runs needed. He did not have to face a ball and the match ended in a draw. If required, Cowdrey would have batted left handed to protect his left arm.

On a perfect batting wicket at Gravesend in 1966, Kent faced a formidable Middlesex total of 337 but slumped to 163-9. The last

wicket pair of Alan Brown (pictured) and David Sayer showed how things should be done with a whirlwind partnership of 94 in an hour. Secretary/Manager Leslie Ames did not think that it had been bettered for Kent by batsmen 10 and 11.

England beat Pakistan by 8 wickets at The Oval in the third Test match in 1967. The match however was dominated by a magnificent innings of 146 from Asif Iqbal, who was to join Kent as an overseas cricketer the following year and become a firm favourite with the Kent fans. His century was greeted by a pitch invasion from hundreds of Pakistan supporters as they lifted Iqbal shoulder-high in celebration. Play was held up for five minutes, Iqbal was revived and he continued on his merry way until stumped by Alan Knott. Colin Cowdrey and Derek Underwood were also in the England side.

Ian Botham was rightly named as Man of the Match in the third Test match against Australia at Leeds in 1981, but the input of Kent's Graham Dilley tends to be forgotten.

Australia batted first and declared at 401-9 (Botham 6-95). England scored 174 (Botham 50) and were invited to follow on. At 135-7 they looked in trouble and the decision of the England players to check out of their hotel looked like a good move. However, Botham and Dilley had other ideas and put on 117 in 80 minutes before Dilley was out for 56. Botham ended up with 149 not out and Australia, as clear favourites, requiring 130 to win. England however achieved a magnificent victory by 18 runs with Bob Willis taking 8-43.

Best forgotten is the abuse which the umpires received at the end of the third day when cushions were thrown at them by spectators. This followed their decision to abandon play for the day in circumstances where the TCCB subsequently clarified the ruling so that play in future Tests could restart at any stage in the extra hour.

Brighter cricket was not the order of the day in the match against

Surrey at The Oval in 1979 when reports indicated that it petered out into the dullest of dull draws. Both sides contributed to the lack of entertainment, with Surrey declaring with a lead of 67 which left Kent with a deficit of 35 going into the final day, with little room to manoeuvre. Surrey used eight bowlers as Kent plodded for most of the day, before a late declaration, with Rowe taking 40 minutes to score and Downton hitting one boundary in a two hour stay. The match will be remembered for a maiden first-class century against his former County by Surrey's Graham Clinton and a last wicket stand of 47 for Kent involving Kevin Jarvis (4*) whose batting only contributed 38 runs for the season in 16 innings.

In the same year at Northampton, bowlers Graham Dilley and Derek Underwood showed how it should be done when they put on a 9th wicket stand of 129 after coming together at 152-8, with the previous 5 wickets falling for only 12 runs. Dilley scored 81 in 115 minutes, with 60 in boundaries, eclipsing his previous best for Kent of 23 in 115 minutes. Underwood's contribution to the overall total was 45 and together they

avoided the follow-on. Requiring 262 to win, Kent finished on 127-5.

For generations, Oxford and Cambridge Universities have been nurseries for cricketing talent that has graced the Test and County scene. Kent has benefitted and one only has to see the list of post-war captains, which includes: BH Valentine, W Murray-Wood, MC Cowdrey and CJ Tavare who have gained 'Blues'. Sadly the influence of University cricket has declined and the significance of the match against Oxford University at Oxford in 1983 can be queried.

After a poor start, Oxford were rescued by a 7th wicket stand of 127 between RS Cowan and SJ Halliday, both of whom recorded maiden first-class centuries, allowing Oxford to declare at 306-8. In reply Kent scored 616-6dec with four players scoring centuries Woolmer made 126, Taylor 127, and with what was described as the easiest batting practice they were likely to encounter all season, Tavaré followed with 125 and Benson 120. Statistics showed that it was the highest score by any County since 1949, Kent's largest total since 1934, only the tenth instance of four County batsmen scoring centuries in one innings and the first such occurrence for Kent since 1908. The match was rained off at tea on the last day when Oxford were 55-5 and facing defeat by an innings.

A report of the game between Essex and Kent at Southend in 1991 described it as 'One of the bizarre Championship matches' and posed the question 'was it either a product of three-day cricket at its worst, with a points system which only substantially rewards the winners or a triumph for positive cricket thanks to the imagination and willingness of the captains?'

Essex declared at 251-2, in reply to Kent's 380 who were 24-0 in their second innings at the end of day two. Following heavy rain on the third morning, Gooch and Pritchard 'donated' 159 runs in 10.1 overs, leaving Essex to score 314 runs in 52 overs, which they never looked likely to achieve, eventually losing by 112 runs.

The same year, in a four-day match at Canterbury against Middlesex, the visitors also required just over 300 for victory on the last day. Expectations of an exciting finish were high after major innings from Mike Gatting (174), Mark Ramprakash (87), Trevor Ward (235 not out) and Neil Taylor (101) during the first three days. In the event Middlesex collapsed to 96 all out and lost by 208 runs. The Middlesex wicket-keeper, Paul Farbrace, returning to his former County collected a pair and Mike Gatting had a pot of hot tea spilled over him during an interval.

In 1995, Kent beat Staffordshire in the National Westminster Bank Trophy by 91 runs having scored 349-8 in the allotted 60 overs, with

Trevor Ward, Neil Taylor and Graham Cowdrey all scoring half centuries. Former Kent man Laurie Potter, (right), took 1-79 in his 12 overs and thoroughly earned his Man of the Match award for his 105 not out in Staffordshire's reply of 258-6, reaching his century with his third six in the final over.

Potter was born in England but brought up in Australia. He is the only person to have captained both the Australian and England national teams which he achieved at Under-19 level.

He made his debut for Kent in 1981 scoring 2,413 runs at an average of 29.42 with a highest score of 165* and taking 43 wickets with his left arm spin. He played first-class cricket in South Africa and after leaving Kent he moved to Leicestershire. After his retirement from first-class cricket he was the captain of a teenage Kevin Pietersen during a period with Cannock Cricket Club in the Birmingham League.

In the same season as his success against Kent, Potter also took the Gold Award in Minor Counties' surprise defeat of Leicestershire in a preliminary round of the Benson and Hedges Cup, scoring 32 and taking 4-13, including South African Hansie Cronje, for a duck. He had therefore won match medals against both his former first-class Counties in limited-overs competitions.

It may come as some surprise that cricket is recorded as being played in Scotland at Schawpark, near Alloa in the year 1785. Two years later in England, the first match was played on the original Lord's cricket ground and the father of Thomas Lord was Scottish.

Over 200 years later Kent were to lose to Scotland, for the first time in 44 limited-over matches against non-first-class opposition. They have played nine such matches in a variety of competitions against Scotland with the only loss being at Edinburgh in 2009 in the 50 over Friends Provident Trophy. Rain overnight and during the day restricted play with Kent batting first only scoring 65-4 from 19.5 overs. The Scotland target under the D/L method was 77 in 18 overs which they easily achieved with 13 balls to spare and only 1 wicket down.

CHAPTER NINE

CAREER CHANGES

Cricket, and indeed all sports, can be unforgiving as participants' aspirations can be dashed, whether released at the start or end of one's career, relieved of or denied responsibility, or clashes of personality.

Following the death of both parents in 1823, Nicholas Wanostrocht, at the age of 19, was obliged to take over the running of the school where his father had been headmaster. He was beginning to take an increased interest in cricket with the result that when playing, he began using the name Felix. It appears that this was to avoid offending the pupils' parents who might object to a Headmaster involving himself in an ungentlemanly pursuit.

From 1842 The Old Stagers provided a varied programme of drama and entertainment as part of the Canterbury Cricket Week. Many of the amateur players on the field also trod the boards. However, thespian activities were not considered appropriate for young professional men to appear in public and it became the custom for them to assume stage names to hide their true identities.

Three of the founders of I.Z. and O.S.: the Rt. Hon. Sir Spencer Pensonby Fane, Mr. John Loraine Balldwin and the Earl of Bessborough.

140

This practice continued for nearly 60 years.

John Shuter was born in Surrey but living in Bexley, he played club cricket in Kent in his early days. In 1874 he played for Kent against Lancashire at Maidstone but his potential was not appreciated by Kent and in 1877 he moved to Surrey. Shuter played 274 matches for Surrey as a stylish right-hand opening batsman from 1880 to 1893 and represented England in one Test in 1888.

In 1893 a Young Players Committee was set up to encourage local talent and the following year an Imported Players Committee was asked to find talent from outside Kent. Five young players were selected from around 50 applicants. Unfortunately none were up to standard and were not retained after a year. Apparently they had not been seen in action before their engagement.

In 1895 Kent took on Claude Buckenham, a 19 year old fast bowler who was born at Herne Hill and educated at Alleyns. The following year the Young Players Committee reported that he had moved to Essex. Buckenham went on to play 258 games for Essex (1899–1914), taking 1,150 wickets and representing England in four Tests on the 1909/10 tour of South Africa. He was described as one of the deadliest bowlers of his time but his record suffered because of poor slip catching.

George Thompson was a public schoolboy who became a professional and was capped six times for England. Unfortunately, it was not while playing for Kent as he had returned to Nottinghamshire following allegations of poaching, despite having signed an agreement and taken up residence in Kent to achieve qualification.

Arthur Wellard was born at Southfleet, Kent, in 1902 and had played well against Kent Club and Ground sides, captained by the then coach, Gerald Weigall, for his club Bexley. He had been heard to say that instead of a trial, he was advised that his future was as a policeman and Kent rued the day that he was allowed to go to Somerset, where he became a renowned striker of the ball and went on to represent England on two occasions.

Douglas Carr made his debut for Kent in 1909 at the age of 37 having achieved outstanding success with his leg breaks and googlies in Kent club cricket. In that same year, he played for the Gentlemen against the Players and made his only Test appearance for England against Australia at The Oval, where his captain, Archie MacLaren, was criticised in some quarters for bowling him into the ground.

As a schoolmaster, Carr played for Kent in the holidays but his short yet successful cricketing career was to end in 1914 at the age of 42, when his analysis against Surrey was 0-134 in 28 overs and the match

report concluded that, 'Carr bowled with so little of his customary skill that he did not assist Kent again'.

Sadly for Kent supporters, 1936 was the last season for Tich Freeman, (left), who retired at the age of 47, having taken over 3,000 wickets for the County. His tally of 108 wickets for that season was poor by his standards and was attributed by some to the excessive demands upon his body.

He declined an offer to play on a match basis in 1937 and the Club announced with great regret that his contract had been terminated, with recognition of his services to the County. There were some who felt that his criticism of short pitched bowling in the match against Essex, that he had written in a local newspaper, could have been a factor in his departure, as both County Committees were unhappy with the comments.

William Murray-Wood was an amateur who captained Kent for two years from 1952 but left in controversial circumstances. Having lost the support of the team it was announced by the Committee that he was being relieved of his post and replaced by Doug Wright.

Before and after World War II, it was possible for hundreds of players to earn a living from both cricket and soccer. These days, however, with the high degree of overlap between seasons, preseason training and Clubs wishing to protect players from injury, it is now impossible to combine the two sports.

In the post war period, Kent had many players playing semi-professional football in the Kent League and a strong connection with

Charlton Athletic who were in the top tier of the Football League. Charlton players included Derek Ufton, who was to win one football cap for England, Syd O'Lynn who was capped by South Africa at cricket and Stuart Leary who undertook National Service in the RAF and received an Under-23 England football cap, but was deprived of a full cap on the basis that his father was born in South Africa.

Stuart Leary

143

An uneasy alliance was formed regarding representation, with Charlton taking the view that the players were footballers who also played cricket, whereas Kent took the opposite view.

In a report about the Kent second XI by the Cricket Sub Committee for season 1967, the following paragraph related to fast bowler John Dye.

'Dye, who never appeared to be quite 100% fit at times bowled really well and at other times very moderately. Considering his unquestioned ability and experience in First-Class Cricket he could and should do far better in this class of cricket. It is not suggested that he does not try, but it appears that he shows a certain lack of interest if he is not playing in the first XI. If he is keen to get a permanent place in the Eleven the one sure way of doing it is to be really successful in the second XI, thus  forcing his way in. There is a wonderful opportunity for Dye, if he would only appreciate it. He is very much younger in years than both Brown and Sayer, and the latter will be unable to play full time in 1968, and he has the additional advantage of being different in that he is left handed. With a different approach to the game he could be 50% more effective.'

A change of air when he joined Northamptonshire in 1972 was obviously beneficial, as he took 79 wickets at 18 apiece in his first season.

After six trophies in five years, Mike Denness had every reason to be pleased with his reign as captain and would assume that his employers would be equally pleased. Looking to the future he broached the

144

Alan Ealham

subject of his standing down and a successor who he felt should be Graham Johnson. He believed that this was accepted by the Club but the timing was to be resolved. He was shocked to subsequently learn that the Cricket Sub Committee had already made the decision to accept his resignation and appoint Asif Iqbal as captain for 1977 with Graham Johnson as vice-captain.

It was to emerge that senior players had complained about him and the Sub Committee vote was 11-1 against Denness continuing as captain. Apparently the Chairman had informed him that he was, 'aloof, stand-offish, non- communicative and not good with young players'. Denness deserved far better treatment than he received, before he transferred his allegiance to Essex.

The 1970s was a vintage period for Kent cricket and under the captaincy of Alan Ealham, the Championship title was won in 1978. The following years saw drops to 5th and 16th positions and Ealham was sacked as captain. He had not sought the captaincy but had willingly accepted when asked by the Committee. A popular figure, he had every reason to feel aggrieved at the manner in which the matter had been handled, a view which was held by many throughout the County.

In 1985, Graham Johnson was shocked to be advised at Chelmsford during the game against Essex, that after 21 years he was not being retained for the following season. His subsequent refusal to play against the Australians led to his contract being cancelled and disciplinary action being taken. An unfortunate end to a fine career with both sides feeling aggrieved.

John Shepherd was a firm favourite with the Kent supporters during his 16-year stay and he had hoped to be involved with the County for many years after. This was not to be and despite the disappointment that he was not being retained at the end of the 1981 season, he would have been prepared to continue playing on a non-contract match basis, but this was not pursued. Instead he  moved to Gloucestershire where he enjoyed three successful seasons, including a century against Kent.

Chris Cowdrey was selected for England's 1984/85 tour of India and played in all five Test matches of the series. He was not selected again until 1988 when he was asked to lead the side against the West Indies, already 2-0 up after three matches in a five match series.

Under Cowdrey's leadership, Kent were top of the Championship table and Peter May, Chairman of Selectors, and Cowdrey's godfather, claimed amongst charges of favouritism that, 'Cowdrey's style of leadership is what is now required'. England lost heavily by 10 wickets and injury prevented Cowdrey from being given his chance to prove his credentials in the final Test and he was never to captain or play for England again.

Chris Tavare left at the start of the 1989 season to join Somerset where he was to remain for five years, four as captain before retiring. He was captain of Kent in 1983 and 1984, leading them to two losing Lord's finals but Chris Cowdrey was appointed to be the new captain for 1985 in his place. Tavare (below) was unhappy at the way the change had been made and requested to leave. The County would not agree and he was required to see out his contract which he honoured before departing to the West Country.

Former England fast bowler, Ed Giddens was suspended from first-

class cricket until the 1998 season after testing positive for cocaine at the Kent V Sussex match at Tunbridge Wells in 1996. He was unsuccessful in his appeal against the TCCB decision and was sacked by Sussex. During the ban he turned out for Bromley in the Kent League and later appeared for Warwickshire.

A rift between Alan Wells and Sussex was

concluded when he accepted an offer to become a vice-president at the start of the 1997 season, the year he joined Kent after 18 years with Sussex. The departure of several first team players from Sussex, including Alan Wells, led to a complete reorganisation of the Sussex Club structure which included the loss of Nigel Bett, the former Kent marketing manager.

Support for Steve Marsh, when he was sacked as Kent captain, came from his father-in-law and former Kent player Bob Wilson, who resigned from the Kent Committee. The *Kent Messenger* recorded that, 'Marsh has been made to pay for the under-achievement of fellow senior players at the Club. It is they, as well as the Committee who should be hanging their heads in shame, following this latest public relations disaster.'

At the end of each season there is a review by the County to decide who is to be retained and who is to be released. There is sometimes a 'big name' involved but invariably it is those who have not quite 'made it' who are the majority.

One such season was 1999 when six players left as part of a major rebuilding programme. The most senior was Trevor Ward who signed a three year contract to join

148

Leicestershire who were captained by ex-Kent player Vince Wells. He was unhappy in the years before he left and following his release he said, 'At 31, I've still got six or seven good years ahead of me. I just want to get rid of all the excess baggage from Kent, put a smile on my face and enjoy my cricket again, playing around people I can trust and people who will encourage me and want me around.'

Ward claimed that it had been made clear to him on a few occasions during the summer that team selection wasn't just down to cricket and that things had become personal. He conceded that he had under-achieved in the last two seasons but said that losing his place in the one-day side was the last straw.

Nigel Llong also went after a 20 year association when his attempts to negotiate a contract to play in limited matches only failed, and he was not retained. He felt that he had not been given a fair chance and was disappointed not to have been selected for the one-day matches in the first half of the season. When selected he was pleased to have made some major contributions. He is one of the most respected umpires in the country and regularly officiates at international level.

Also not retained were Simon Willis, who was disappointed not to gain a first team place but accepted the post of cricket administration manager at St Lawrence; Will House, who left for Sussex after successfully appealing against an ECB ruling that he should remain a list one player, thus preventing other Counties from approaching him without Kent's permission. Chris Walsh and Jamie Ford both left to take up careers outside cricket, having appeared in only four and one first-class matches respectively.

Azhar Mahmood represented Pakistan at both Test and ODI levels and made his debut for Kent in 2008. In 2000 the then Chairman of the Pakistan Cricket Board told him, in front of senior players, that Mahmood would be the next captain of his country. How would this appointment have changed his life, if this had come about?

The end of the 2002 season saw more changes when Paul Nixon, Martin McCague, David Masters, James Hockley, Matt Banes and James Golding were not retained and Matthew Fleming retired. Paul Nixon had been signed three years earlier to replace Steve Marsh and the 2003 Annual announced in a bland statement that the County had been unable to reach agreement with him over a new contract and that as a result he would be replaced by second XI wicket-keeper Geraint Jones.

Azhar Mahmood

Nixon returned to his previous County, Leicestershire. Nixon was angry at the way the matter had been dealt with and that the offer of a new contract involved a substantial wage cut which would always be unacceptable with the prospects of his replacement having a much longer tenure.

Martin McCague was not happy at the manner of his own departure either. He was sacked after 12 years with the Club and did not make a first team appearance during the whole season. McCague played three Test matches for England. He was born in Northern Ireland but had been raised in Western Australia from the age of two and had played for that State between 1990 and 1992, having attended the Australia Cricket Academy in Adelaide.

There was a certain irony that his Test debut was against Australia at

Trent Bridge in 1993 at a time when the England team had been likened to a foreign legion. The indignation of the Australian hierarchy had been aroused and they wanted stricter application of the qualification rules for Test cricket. It was also pointed out that Australia had invested time and money in McCague to benefit Australian rather than English cricket.

In 18 first-class matches in 2001, David Fulton scored 1,892 runs at an average of 75.68. His form was noted by the national selectors, who according to Nasser Hussain, originally selected him in place of Mark Butcher for the fourth Test V Australia before having a change of heart and reinstating Butcher.

Mark Ealham left at the end of 2003 and terminated a 40-year association with the County that he and his father Alan had enjoyed.

Andrew Symonds

He found the offer of a one year contract did not provide the security he was looking for. Instead he opted for a three year contract with Notts, which culminated in winning the Championship after six seasons.

The loan system in 2014 allowed James Tredwell to play for Sussex in four day matches and for Kent in one-day games.

Andrew Symonds was very much a 'Jekyll & Hyde' character during his stay as

Kent's overseas player between 1999 and 2004. He played 26 Tests and 198 ODIs for Australia and was twice a World Cup winner. An outstanding all-rounder and fielder, he was unfortunately not always easy to control and from mid-2008 he spent most of his time out of the Australian team due to disciplinary reasons, including alcohol. In 2009 he was sent home from the Twenty20 World Cup and his central contract withdrawn. In 2012 he announced his retirement from all forms of cricket, having appeared for Surrey in 2010 and the IPL from 2008 to 2011.

Charlotte Edwards CBE announced her retirement from international cricket in May 2016, having made her England debut as a 16 year old in 1996. Some 20 years later she was the all-time leading run scorer in women's ODI cricket and the scorer of more T20 runs than any other player (man or woman). She made more international appearances than any other female cricketer with a total of 23 Test match caps, 191 ODI caps and 95 T20 caps. She is shown holding the coveted Woman's Player of the Year Award in 2008.

Her ambition was to carry on playing until after the 2017 World Cup to be held in England. However, one disappointment among a long career, would have been the unexpected defeat to Australia in the 2016 World

Twenty20 semi-final and hardly made easier by the pronouncement by new coach Mark Robinson that the players needed to 'get fitter'.

Subsequent events showed that Edwards was not part of the future direction as envisaged by the new coach and the reluctant retirement from someone acknowledged to have done more for women's cricket than anyone else in its history, was a sad end to a glittering career.

She will not be lost to cricket and will continue to captain and play for Kent.

CHAPTER TEN

PROBLEM TOURS

John Sackville, 3rd Duke of Dorset, had a love of sports which included cricket (he was a good player and important patron), billiards and tennis. He liked to gamble and had a reputation as a womaniser. In 1773 he presented the Vine Cricket Ground at Sevenoaks to the Town.

A move to Paris in 1784 as Ambassador to France, saw Dorset take the opportunity to promote cricket amongst the locals and expatriates. To further this objective he arranged for a team to play in France. Unfortunately the French Revolution intervened and caused the cancellation of the first international cricket tour for political reasons.

Kent were the first County side to undertake a major overseas tour when they toured North America in 1903. The team was JR Mason (capt), CJ Burnup, EW Dillon, J Seymour, WM Bradley, HZ Baker, A Hearne, HC Stewart, KL Hutchings, FH Huish, C Blythe and CJV Weigall with T Pawley as manager. Sailing from Liverpool on the SS Oceanic they travelled from Jersey City to Philadelphia for the first game but were not happy with the hotel. The waiters were mostly Irishmen and were not friendly towards the English contingent. The tour however was a complete success with all four games being won, three in Philadelphia, and one in New York. The party were unaware that there had been a hurricane on the day of their arrival in New York, until after they had landed.

The 1932/33 tour to Australia was dubbed the 'bodyline tour' and the England tactic, of Larwood bowling fast and short to a packed leg side field, caused the Australian Board of Control to send a cable which read: 'Bodyline bowling has assumed such proportions as to

menace the best interests of the game, making protection of the body by the batsmen, the main consideration. This is causing intensely bitter feeling between the players as well as injury. In our opinion it is unsportsmanlike. Unless stopped at once it is likely to upset the friendly relations existing between Australia and England.'

Larwood maintained that his conscience was clear. That he had never bowled at batsmen and his bowling was leg-theory and not bodyline.

Although the series was won with Australia's leading batsman Don Bradman's contribution reduced, the tour will not be remembered as a triumph but rather as an embarrassing campaign.

Leslie Ames was the only Kent cricketer to take part in the bodyline series and was chosen for all five Test matches.

The scheduled 1968/69 tour to South Africa was cancelled in circumstances known as the D'Oliveira Affair in which a Kent player was to play a significant part. Basil D'Oliveira had established himself on the County scene with Worcestershire and had already represented England on 15 occasions. Not selected for the final Test against Australia, the withdrawal of a member of the original XI allowed him to play. A first innings score of 158 and a contribution with the ball seemed to have guaranteed him a place in the party to be announced for the South African tour. He was in fact left out, but owing to the withdrawal by Tom Cartwright he was subsequently included. Due to the country's racial laws the MCC were informed that he was not an acceptable member of the touring party, whereupon the tour was cancelled.

The player whose withdrawal due to pleurisy allowing D'Oliveira to play against Australia and forcibly make a case for his inclusion in the

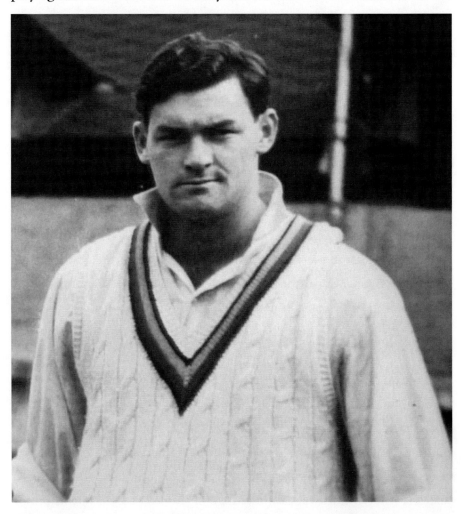

touring squad was Roger Prideaux, who was educated at Tonbridge and Cambridge University (Blue 1958 and 1960). He played for Kent (1960/61) before moving to Northamptonshire (1962 and 1970) when he played three Tests for England and was selected for the ill-fated tour to South Africa. He finished his career at Sussex (1971 and 1973).

In 1896 KS Ranjitsinhji was omitted from the side to play Australia at Lord's because Lord Harris disapproved of overseas players representing England. Lord Harris, captain of England in 1878–79, was born in Trinidad.

A Rest of the World team was assembled to play five-day cricket matches against the full England team in 1970 after cancellation of the scheduled tour by the South African cricket team. At the time the matches were deemed to be Test matches with the award of England caps, but this was later revoked.

In his book *Boot Boy to President*, Brian Luckhurst wrote, 'The first Test against the Rest of the World began on June 17 and was played at Lord's. I still regard it as my Test debut in fact, as in my eyes I played 26 Tests for England and not 21…despite what the record books now show. The Rest of the World team was incredibly strong and it is to that

England side's credit that we could easily have forced a drawn series.'

The 1970/71 England Team to Australia regained the Ashes and the major pre-tour issue was who should be captain. Of the two contenders, the appointment went to Ray Illingworth with Colin Cowdrey as his vice-captain, with other Kent players Brian Luckhurst, Alan Knott and Derek Underwood also in the party. David Clark (left) the former Kent captain was the manager.

The tour emphasised the difference between the 'old and the new' with Illingworth describing Clark as, 'an amiable but somewhat ineffectual man'. After several clashes, the captain effectively took over the running of the tour with the support of the players. Clark's only ally was Colin Cowdrey who became isolated in this modern style touring party with combative leadership. He was a shadow of his former self, with the loss of leadership originally due to injury, seemingly too much for him.

In 1973/74 John Shepherd became the first black cricketer to tour South Africa with DH Robin's side which was managed by Leslie Ames and included Kent colleagues Bob Woolmer and Graham Johnson. The following is an extract from an article by Bill Day which appeared in the 1999 Kent Annual:

'He regrets nothing of that trip that left him in the international wilderness. "I didn't go to be a martyr. I was never going to influence the political thinking. When the boys went off to play golf on that trip, I'd go to the non-white cricket grounds. I spent a lot of time in hotel kitchens where black staff were slaving over the pots and pans. I learned a lot down there.

'Batting at the Wanderers, I was applauded all the way to the wicket and all the way back after scoring a half century. Les Ames, the tour manager, said my reception in Johannesburg that day was equal to the applause given to Don Bradman on his last appearance at The Oval."'

In May 1977 the cricketing world woke up to the announcement that Kerry Packer had signed 35 of the world's best cricketers on lucrative contracts, between one and three years, to play a series of one-day games during the Australian summer of that year. Packer, the son of an Australian media tycoon, had tried to negotiate the exclusive rights to televise matches on his commercial Channel 9 but following refusal by the Australian Board of Control, he decided to organise his own World

Series, which was to be labelled by the establishment as a circus.

The final 'rebel' list included Kent players, Alan Knott, Derek Underwood, Bob Woolmer, Asif Iqbal who was relieved of the Kent captaincy but retained as a player, and Bernard Julian who was not retained by Kent at the end of the 1977 season. The Cricketers Association was in a dilemma as to whether Packer would benefit all cricketers or only the 'star' players.

The whole of the 1977 season was played with the spectre of World Series Cricket. Knott and Underwood both played against Australia in the summer Tests but at the end of July the ICC banned World Series players from Test cricket. The TCCB extended the ban to include County games. The Kent Committee took a strong line, in that the contracts of Packer players would not be renewed after the 1978 season.

In November 1977 it was ruled that a professional cricketer needs to make a living and should not be prevented from playing for a private promoter in the winter, when no winter employment was offered by

Alan Knott

the employer.

Midway through the 1978 season, the Kent Committee reversed its decision on players' contracts which resulted in David Clark resigning from the County Committee, due to a conflict of interest with his other roles as President of the MCC and Chairman of the ICC.

In April 1979 the Australian Board of Control did a deal over TV rights and much of the opposition disappeared. Packer is still blamed to this day for the direction that cricket has taken. Most traditionalists remember 'the good old days' with affection, but accept that Packer only hastened an inevitable change in cricket, as in society.

In the post-Packer era, various rebel tours to South Africa were undertaken during the apartheid years. The recruitment for the first rebel tour was undertaken by Geoffrey Boycott and captained by Graham Gooch. It included Kent players Alan Knott and Derek Underwood, with Bob Woolmer, who was playing and coaching in South Africa, later joining the party. All players were banned from playing for England for three years.

Richard Ellison was a member of a rebel England team that toured South Africa in defiance of the international cricket boycott of the country, which was still under apartheid rule. The tour was cut short after just nine matches because of protests from anti-apartheid demonstrators. In 1990 Chris Cowdrey joined another rebel tour to South Africa.

Other Countries also made unofficial tours to South Africa and Terry Alderman was banned from Test cricket for three years by Australia which meant that he missed the 1985 Ashes series.

OFF THE FIELD OF PLAY

Individual and team performances on the field, generally attract the headlines, as matches ebb and flow, records are broken and match changing performances are recorded. But, as all cricketers know, the intrigue of the game is not confined to the hours of play and this chapter captures some interesting off-field events that have occurred over the years.

Richard Fielder played a dozen times for Kent between 1791 and 1796. He was a horse-breaker and trainer, and was a member of R Leigh's XI at Dartford. In 1792 he eloped with Miss Cage, of Milgate, nr Maidstone, who he was teaching to ride and afterwards they kept the Woolpack Inn at Tenterden.

Betting played a big part in the early days of cricket and allegations of match fixing were rife. A lot of money was lost, when in 1842 Kent were beaten by 9 wickets by an England

Alfred Mynn

team after scoring 278 in their first innings. Kent were dismissed for 44 in their second innings and despite his popularity, Alfred Mynn was hissed at Maidstone market. The only person to score double figures was Sir Emilius Bayley, who stated after the match, 'The Kent people thought we had sold the match, which of course was nonsense'.

There was some debate as to whether Mynn or Sam Redgate was the premier fast bowler of the day. Sadly, Redgate died in 1851 at the early age of 40, which was attributed to his liking for brandy, whereas Mynn, although three years older played until 1859 on a diet of English beef and beer.

Playing for the South V North at Leicester in 1836, when Mynn scored his only century before the use of pads, his legs were so badly bruised by Redgate that his captain, Lord Frederick Beauclerk, sent him to London stretched out on the top of a stagecoach. Doctors examining him at the Angel Tavern considered amputating his leg, but decided not to operate. After convalescing for two years, he fully recovered.

Tom Adams played for Kent from 1834 to 1858 and was a prominent member of the Kent XI of that era. In 1845 he formed The Bat and Ball Ground at his home town of Gravesend. Adams once agreed to a contest with a prize-fighter involving boxing, shooting and cricket with the boxing match to take place first and the winner of two events to take the stakes. His opponent intended to so injure Adams that he would be unable to take part in the remaining two events, but was baffled when Tom lay down before receiving a blow and was counted out. He went on to make a profit by easily winning both the shooting and cricket.

In 1864 four Sussex players observed a man drawing a water cart onto the ground at the end of the first day of their game against Kent at Margate. He admitted that he was going to water the wicket as he had bet a sovereign that Kent would not get 50 on the next day. The wager was lost as they scored 104.

The following year at Hove, small holes were found on a good length before the start of the Kent innings. Whether vandalism or something more sinister, it was of no avail as Kent won the game.

Allegations of match fixing have surfaced from time to time up to the present day, Kent were involved in the 1970s when an article in the *Mail on Sunday* included claims by former player John Shepherd that there was an arrangement to lose the Sunday League match against Hampshire in return for winning the Championship game which was due to be concluded on the following day.

The outcome did not seem to support the claim as Hampshire won both games but it did not prevent Kent from securing the Championship title under the leadership of Alan Ealham who denied any collusion with the Hampshire captain.

Charles Thornton played over 200 first-class games for 22 different teams, including Kent and his own team CI Thornton's XI. He was a great character but any opposing captain had to be wary if Thornton was tossing the coin, as he used to call 'woman' which could be either heads (Queen Victoria) or tails (Britannia). He would then decide to bat before the opposition realised what was happening.

Paintings of Kent cricket

Charles Thornton

are legion, whether depicting the County games or traditional venues showing country houses and village greens. The scene shown is a painting described as the First Australian Team to visit England to play a single-innings cricket match against Willsher's gentlemen at Chilham Castle, Kent in August 1878 and the original is in the National Gallery of Australia in Canberra. A copy is at the St Lawrence Ground, Canterbury.

The Australians were on tour to England in 1878 but the only problem with the painting is that despite extensive research there is no evidence that this match was ever played. Indeed the team were elsewhere in England during this period. Manufactured matches depicted on canvas are not unknown, but in the meantime the picture and its mystery can be enjoyed.

Cricketers have occupied themselves during the close season and in retirement, in a variety of ways and some of the more extreme follow here.

Charlie Absolom was nicknamed the 'Cambridge Navvy' because of his physique. He was quite tireless and was known to arrive at a match after walking 12 miles, carrying his bag, having breakfasted on a quart

Charlie Absolom

of beer and a pint of gooseberries. It is told that he once hired himself to a farmer at haymaking time for five shillings a day and his beer. He did the work of two men, but the next day the farmer came to him with tears in his eyes and besought him to accept ten shillings a day and find his own beer.

Edward Martin kept a cricketers shop at Oxford. In 1851, his last season playing for Kent, he sold his stock and moved to a farm at Leominster. It was not until 1869 that he was heard of again, having been thrown from his horse and killed. His papers disclosed the addresses of relatives, who were astounded to find that he had lived unknown for so many years and had assumed that he had probably been robbed and murdered.

John 'Foghorn' Jackson was an outstanding fast bowler of the 1850s. Mainly associated with Nottinghamshire he represented Kent in 1858.

He took part in the first ever overseas cricket tour when he was a member of the England team visiting North America. He lived his later life in extreme poverty and he died in 1901 at Brownlow Hill, a Liverpool workhouse.

MP Betts played two matches for Kent (1872 and 1881). In 1872 he played for Wanderers in the first FA Cup Final when he scored the only goal but he played under the pseudonym of AH Chequer as he had played for Harrow Chequers in an earlier round. He was normally a full back but his one appearance for England against Scotland in 1877 was as a goalkeeper.

MP Betts

Tonbridge was an early location for nuturing Kent talent and it was acknowledged that there is an element of luck in finding talented youngsters. How Colin Blythe came to join the Nursery was unusual in that he was in the crowd when Kent was playing at Blackheath and he bowled a few balls to Walter Wright. On the basis of this introduction he joined the Nursery. However Blythe was born and lived at Deptford and at that time it would not be considered as a source of cricketing talent with only the roughest parts of Blackheath to develop their skills.

Colin Blythe went on to play 381 games for Kent and represent England in 19 Tests and together with Wilfred Rhodes from Yorkshire, they were considered the main left-arm spinners of the Edwardian era. He was sadly killed in action near Passchendaele, Belgium in 1917.

During the latter part of his career and due to increasing weight and lack of physical fitness, Percy Chapman found batting more difficult. Team mates and observers noticed that he frequently left the field during matches and they suspected that he was drinking in the pavilion.

KENT TEAM . 1932.

Left to Right.—H. T. W. Hardinge, T. A. Pearce, A. P. Freeman, A. E. Watt, C. S. Marriott, B. H. Valentine
A. P. F. Chapman, W. H. Ashdown, L. E. G. Ames, A. M. Crawley, F. E. Woolley.

He was divorced in 1942 and after the war he was frequently seen drunk in public, although his appearance and manners were impeccable. The cricket establishment ignored him, regarding him as an embarrassment, particularly the occasions he watched matches at Lord's.

Towards the end of his life he suffered from alcoholism, arthritis, loneliness and depression. He died on 16 September 1961 following a knee fracture, resulting from a fall at his home.

Colin Cowdrey was born into a family with a love for cricket. His initials were MCC and soon after his birth, his father had put the wheels in motion for his son to be a member of that famous club. It should therefore have been no surprise that that he was destined for an illustrious cricketing career.

Rob Key has been criticised for his weight and at one stage early in his career weighed 16 stone, before Alec Stewart told him to 'buck his ideas up'. Key himself said of the matter 'I'll never be the most athletic bloke but I'm a hell of a lot fitter than I was at 19 or 20'. An anagram of Robert Key is – **OK try beer!**

Kent Team 1922

H. T. W. Hardinge, A. P. Freeman, J. C. Hubble, G. C. Collins, J. Seymour, W. H. Ashdown,
H. J. Taylor, A. J. Evans, L. H. W. Troughton, W. S. Cornwallis, F. E. Woolley.

Alfred John Evans was captain of Kent in 1922 and played in one Test for England. During World War I he was a pilot with the Royal Flying Corps and his exploits in escaping from prisoner of war camps led to a book, *The Escaping Club*.

Another prisoner of war was Harold Lawrence Hever, left handed at both batting and bowling, played six matches (1921–25) for Kent. He was born at Southborough in 1895 and turned out for the local club.

Aiden Crawley was a journalist, TV Editor and politician. He was an RAF pilot and a prisoner of war after being shot down. He was a member of both major political parties being Labour MP (1945–51) and Conservative MP (1962–67) for Buckingham and West Derbyshire respectively. He made 33 appearances for Kent and was President of the MCC in 1972.

The following paragraph appeared in the Annual Report of the 1962 season, 'A glance at the bowling averages immediately reveals our main weakness. Brown, who through injury missed nine matches, topped the averages with 55 wickets at an average of 22.07, but this was mainly due to excellent bowling during Maidstone Week when he took 17 wickets against Leicestershire and Lancashire. Brown, who has a fearful long drag in his delivery stride, often appears to lose his rhythm and with it pace and direction. There are occasions when he looks an England prospect but all too often he is very mediocre.'

This was an interesting summary of Alan Brown, as prior to the start of the season he had toured India, Pakistan and Ceylon with the MCC and played two Test matches for England.

Several players have been involved with journalism, but Chris Cowdrey could not have been happy with his fine of £500 by the TCCB disciplinary committee for his criticism of the England team management in an article in the *Sun* newspaper.

Alan Brown

As long ago as 1892 there were complaints from the press about the facilities in Kent where tents were provided for the reporters. The facilities at the Canterbury festival were considered too crowded and uncomfortable.

Despite opposition on religious grounds and ancient legislation that restricted a starting time of 2 p.m., Sunday Championship cricket was popular with increases in attendance. This move laid the foundation for the John Player Sunday League in 1969.

A spectator's life is not always a happy one and Kent Secretary Stuart Anderson said, 'For some time standards of behaviour relating to increased consumption of alcohol at cricket matches have been on the decline. We are taking this measure now so that the minority will no longer spoil the enjoyment of a day's cricket for the vast majority.

'Sundays are for the enjoyment of our members, supporters and for families in particular. The short matches are the vehicle for introducing young people to the game. We don't want foul-mouthed people driven by drink harassing players and supporters alike.'

Kent introduced alcohol restrictions on their Sunday League games, following trouble between rival fans outside the ground after a Benson and Hedges Cup semi-final against Northamptonshire when a policeman was injured and an offensive weapon seized.

The restrictions meant that supporters were liable to have containers and cool boxes searched and were limited to two normal-sized cans of beer or lager or a standard bottle of wine. No additional alcohol was allowed to be taken into the ground on re-admission after lunch or tea intervals.

CHANGES to GROUND REGULATIONS FOR 2007

The implications of the 2006 Health Act were the catalyst for a full review of the Club's ground regulations this winter and the following changes were implemented with effect from 1 April.

Alcohol

Regretfully there were three incidents of crowd disorder during 2006 and a common denominator was that those involved had been consuming alcohol they had brought into the ground.

Therefore, in line with a significant number of other County cricket clubs, Kent County Cricket Club is banning the import of alcohol into the ground for all Twenty20 Cup and Pro40 League matches.

At all other matches, spectators may continue to bring in small amounts of alcohol as in previous years.

Smoking

The dangers of smoking, such as increased risk of heart disease, bronchitis and lung cancer have been well documented and there is now an increasing concern about passive smoking – the effects of breathing in other people's tobacco smoke.

The Independent Scientific Committee on Smoking and Health found that passive smoking could increase the risk of lung cancer in non-smokers. In addition, tobacco smoke is a cause of discomfort and irritation to many people, particularly those suffering from respiratory illnesses, such as asthma and bronchitis and may lead to an exaggeration of these problems.

The overwhelming research has now been translated into law and The Health Act, passed in July 2006, prohibits smoking in almost all enclosed public spaces, as well as other designated public places.

Therefore from 1 April 2007 smoking will be prohibited in all buildings at both the St Lawrence Ground and the Kent County Cricket Club Ground at Beckenham. This ban includes the dressing rooms , the stands, seats and hospitality areas during cricket matches.

Smoking, however will be permitted in areas behind behind the stands, behind the seats and in car parks.

Barbeques

Because of health and safety concerns and the impact they have on other spectators, portable and disposable barbeques may not be brought into the grounds at anytime.

Dogs on Leads

Dogs may continue to be brought into grounds on match days as long as they are under the control of their owners at all times; however, the leads used by owners must be of the traditional short chain variety. Dogs on telescopic/extendable leads will not be permitted on the grounds as these are a potential trip hazard – we had several near misses last year!

At the end of the 1948 Annual is a section covering the Club Rules, and the following bye-law section is reproduced. The stipulation on autograph collection seems a little draconian.

BYE-LAWS

The Charges (including tax) for admission of the public shall be as follows:- s d

Each Person (all matches) 2 0

After 4 p.m.	.....	.....	1 0
School Boys and Girls (all day)	.....	.....	1 0

CAR PARKING

Cars or Carriages constructed to contain not more than 10 passengers
with driver.....   ....   10 0

Cars or Carriages constructed to contain not more than 20 passengers
with driver.....   ....   20 0

Cars or carriages constructed to contain not more than 30 passengers
with driver.....   ....   25 0

5/- extra per day is charged for each vehicle which is parked in a position whence the game may be viewed.

Each person during second eleven matches to Ground and Enclosure
.....   1-0

Autograph collection will not be allowed. Offenders against this bye-law are liable to be turned off the ground.

It should not be expected that Lord Harris should pay an admission fee to watch his own County, yet this happened in 1929 at Hastings against Sussex. The previous year Kent had beaten Sussex by an innings at Maidstone, on a wicket that had been watered. Despite apologies from Lord Harris, the Sussex captain, Duleep, was not impressed, demanding that Harris attend the return match at Hastings. This he duly did, but to add insult to injury the gateman insisted that he pay admission. Sussex won by 167 runs.

The same thing nearly happened to David Sayer when making his debut for Kent in 1955 against Sussex at Tunbridge Wells while still at Maidstone Grammar School . Sayer, who was at times the quickest bowler in the country, arrived at the ground by public transport from Maidstone and walked from the bus station. The gateman was not convinced that this youngster was in fact a player and initially refused him entry. After a stern warning to stay where he was, checks were made, and he was allowed in.

Samuel Hulme Day was also at school, Malvern, when he made his debut for Kent at the age of 17 against Gloucestershire at Cheltenham in 1897 and scored 101 not out. He was at the wicket for three hours without giving a chance and hit eleven fours. He went on to play 128 matches for Kent (1897–

David Sayer

1919) and gained a Cambridge Blue in the four years, 1899–1902. His two brothers both played for Kent, Arthur Percival (143 matches, 1905–25) and Sydney Ernest (11 matches, 1922–25). Day was a noted soccer player, playing for Corinthians and three times for England in the 1905/06 British Home Championships.

The preparatory school that Colin Cowdrey attended was Homefield at Sutton in Surrey. Had the advice of the Headmaster been followed, he would have gone to Uppingham or Marlborough, but neither had a vacancy before his father returned from leave in September 1945. A young Cowdrey therefore went to Tonbridge because they did have such a vacancy and the rest is history.

David Sayer played in glasses as did Henry Wyche Andrews who was a wicket-keeper in the mid-1800s

174

and had designed a cricketing outfit with the jacket and trousers joined using buttons, thereby not requiring either belt or braces. The end result was odd looking and the outfit was only worn on one occasion. Andrews had a large family and it was a great disappointment that none of his 11 sons were to represent Kent but one turned out for Sussex!

Travel to and from the grounds has changed over the years but the inherent problems of long journeys, delays and accidents remain.

At the start of the 1977 season, Bernard Julian failed to let the County know that he had been injured in a car accident in Trinidad. A friend had apparently failed to inform the County, who were not amused and Julian was fined a week's wages.

On his Test debut in India, Chris Cowdrey bowled Kapil Dev with the 4th ball of his first over, becoming the 19th England bowler to take a wicket in an introductory over. His father, Colin Cowdrey, was listening to Test Match Special on his car radio and was so delighted that he inadvertently drove the wrong way down a one-way street.

With Aravinda de Silva as a passenger, Min Patel survived a high-speed car-crash on the M6. Having to avoid a traffic cone in the carriageway,

his car collided with an articulated lorry. The car was badly damaged but fortunately neither player was hurt. On another occasion, Patel's car was virtually wrecked in a hotel car park where it had been left before travelling to Southampton for a preseason friendly against Hampshire.

Southampton also proved a problem for Matthew Fleming,

Rob Key, Steve Marsh and coach John Wright who had credit cards stolen from the dressing room during a Championship match against Hampshire. The thief then had the temerity to phone the Hampshire office, purporting to be the police, and asking for the card pin numbers so that the cards could be recovered. Matthew Fleming had lost £200 before the theft was discovered, but felt that he had probably saved money as he had immediately cancelled the joint account while his wife was on a shopping spree in Canterbury.

In order to play professional cricket, Matthew Fleming had brought himself out of a Royal Green Jackets commission that involved active service on the streets of Belfast. He put matters in perspective with the following comments, 'It certainly made you grow up pretty quickly, but thankfully we all came home virtually unscathed. If I make a mistake playing for England the worst thing that could happen is that someone can hit me out of the park and we lose the game. If I make a mistake in Belfast someone would have lost their life. There is no comparison.'

During his playing career, Matthew Fleming was appointed vice-chairman of the Cricketers' Association and he was actively involved in seeking improved conditions for County players. He commented, 'There is too much dead wood in English County Cricket. Staffs are too big and we need to cut them down and pay bigger wages to encourage the elite. Perhaps that's a difficult thing to justify to people who will be affected by the cuts — and it could easily turn out to be me – but I think everyone would accept that there are too many people vying for a too small a slice of the pie.'

After the Benson and Hedges final defeat against Hampshire, it was discovered that a bat belonging to Neil Taylor had been stolen. A year later the police informed him that the bat had been found undamaged, to which Taylor replied, 'Obviously the guy who took it couldn't get any runs with it either'.

Neil Taylor

Clothing, both on and off the field has changed over the years. The formality of players wearing jackets and ties has largely disappeared but Jim Swanton expressed his views in the *Daily Telegraph* following

Kent's Sunday League success in 1995, on coloured clothing by referring to 'the team in the horrible clothes they are obliged to wear, squirting champagne at one another with strictly modified rapture'.

Matthew Fleming's comments on the subject in The Cricketer International were, 'Jim Swanton, that doyen of Kent cricket, had telephoned me that morning to remind me that Kent cricketers "drink champagne and don't spray it like those motor racing drivers." Sorry Jim!'

A few years later Jim Swanton expressed further views on the game in the *Daily Telegraph*, 'Bad behaviour at a club and school level stems, I am afraid, from the parrot-talk about English cricket needing to be more aggressive: Tough competition and good manners have gone together on the cricket field ever since the days of Hambledon'.

Tony Pawson was a character and an all-round sportsman. However he was not popular when, after having been awarded his County cap by captain Bryan Valentine, he was informed that he was now a regular in the side but his reply was, 'Thanks skipper but amateur's privilege, I'm afraid I am just off on a three week fishing holiday in Scotland'. He was a prominent fly fisherman and was world individual champion in 1984. In 1988 he was awarded the OBE for 'services to angling'.

Pawson also had the experience of sleeping overnight in a deckchair outside the Canterbury pavilion when the County forgot to book his hotel and he was shut out of the YMCA.

The first game of the season in the Britannic Assurance Championship at Chelmsford in April 1988 saw a run feast with five centuries as shown in the following match summary.

Kent 400-7dec (M Benson 110) and 384 (G Cowdrey 145, S Marsh 120)

Essex 616 (G Gooch 275, D Pringle 128) and 170-2

Essex won by 8 wickets, scoring 170 in only 21.2 overs. That they required this target was largely due to the batting of Graham Cowdrey and Steve Marsh after Kent were facing an innings defeat.

It was understandable that the two Kent centurions had cause for celebration and after their arrival at Hove in advance of a Benson and Hedges match, they went for a 'nightcap' before returning to their hotel where they shared a room, which was the custom on away games. In the early hours, Marsh drank a much needed glass of water but had not realised that he had drunk Cowdrey's contact lenses which were in the glass. A round-trip to Canterbury was required to pick up spare lenses but no harm was done, as Kent beat Sussex by 7 wickets with Cowdrey taking 1-6 in 4 overs and scoring 40 not out.

GM Kelson played 69 matches for Kent and was a well-known writer on fishing. During a crowded Canterbury Week in the 1860s he had to share a bedroom with another amateur from the opposition. Kelson was having his bath when the other occupant asked, 'Whatever are ye at?' 'Having a cold bath,' was the reply. 'A cold bath? Ye make me shudder.

Towards the end of the 1800s FA MacKinnon introduced the idea of the amateurs getting together to hire a house during Canterbury Week rather than finding their own accommodation. This arrangement worked well with Frank Marchant commenting 'MacKinnon was an ideal house-keeper, and we all deplored his entrance into the bonds of matrimony, which caused him to relinquish his post. He was succeeded by George Marsham, who has now completed his 20th year of management, and the amount of time and trouble he has taken cannot be estimated'.

BIBLIOGRAPHY

KENT COUNTY CRICKET CLUB ANNUALS, 1947 Onwards.

KENT COUNTY CRICKET CLUB: FIFTY OF THE FINEST FIRST-CLASS
MATCHES
by David Robertson, Howard Milton & Derek Carlaw

IMAGES OF KENT CRICKET
by John Evans with Derek Carlaw & Howard Milton

THE HISTORY OF KENT COUNTY CRICKET CLUB
by Dudley Moore

TROPHIES AND TRIBULATIONS
by Clive Ellis & Mark Pennell

HISTORY OF KENT CRICKET
by Lord Harris

KENT CRICKETING GREATS
by Dean Hayes

WHO'S WHO OF CRICKETERS (1864–1983)
by Phillip Bailey, Philip Thorn & Peter Wynne-Thomas.

NO-BALLS and GOOGLIES
by George Tibballs

BATS BALLS & BAILS
by Les Scott

IT'S NOT CRICKET
by Simon Rae

CRICKET-WIT, WICKETS & WISDOM
by Richard Knott

THE GOLDEN AGE OF CRICKET, 1890–1914
by David Frith

250 YEARS OF CRICKET IN BEARSTED, 1749–1999

SOUTHBOROUGH CRICKET, 1794–1994

66 YEAR'S MEMORIES OF KENT CRICKET
by Sir Charles Igglesden

WISDEN ANTHOLOGIES, 1864–1982.
Edited by Benny Green

IAN LAMBERT

Ian was born and educated in Kent where he has spent most of his life, apart from a few years in Hertfordshire. A lifelong supporter and current member of Kent County Cricket Club, he played the game into his 60s, before switching to golf, a move determined by the rigours of fielding! He is a regular contributor to the Kent County Annual and has been involved with books about Sport and Local History in the village of Bearsted where he lives.